ENCYCLOPEDIA
OF LIBRARY
AND INFORMATION
SCIENCE

VOLUME 4

ADVISORY BOARD

ENCYCLOPEDIA OF LIBRARY AND INFORMATION SCIENCE

Editors

ALLEN KENT AND **HAROLD LANCOUR**

Assistant Editor

WILLIAM Z. NASRI

GRADUATE SCHOOL OF LIBRARY AND INFORMATION SCIENCES
AND THE KNOWLEDGE AVAILABILITY SYSTEMS CENTER
UNIVERSITY OF PITTSBURGH
PITTSBURGH, PENNSYLVANIA

VOLUME 4
Calligraphy to Church

MARCEL DEKKER New York

LIBRARY OF CONGRESS CATALOG CARD NUMBER 68-31232

ISBN No. 4-0-8247-2004-0

PRINTED IN THE UNITED STATES OF AMERICA

CONTRIBUTORS TO VOLUME 4

DONALD M. ANDERSON, B.F.A., M.A., Professor, Department of Art, University of Wisconsin, Madison: *Calligraphy*

FLORENCE ANDERSON, Secretary, Carnegie Corporation of New York: *Carnegie Corporation of New York*

EDWARD M. ARNETT, Ph.D., Pittsburgh Chemical Information Center; Professor, Department of Chemistry, University of Pittsburgh: *Chemical Information Centers*

DALE B. BAKER, B.Ch.E., M.S., Director, Chemical Abstracts Service, Ohio State University, Columbus: *Chemical Abstracts Service*

C. DAVID BATTY, Head, Department of Information Retrieval Studies, College of Librarianship Wales, Llanbadarn Fawr, Wales: *Chain Indexing*

STANTON BELFOUR (dec.), Director and Secretary, The Pittsburgh Foundation, Rockwell-Standard Building, Pittsburgh: *Carnegie, Andrew*

MARTHA BOAZ, Dean and Professor, School of Library Science, University of Southern California, University Park, Los Angeles: *Censorship*

FLORENCE W. BUTLER, B.S.Ed., B.L.S., Director of Work with Children, Sioux City Public Library, Sioux City, Iowa: *Children's Libraries and Librarianship*

LEON CARNOVSKY, Professor, Graduate Library School, University of Chicago: *Chicago. University of Chicago, Graduate Library School*

ELAINE CARUSO, M.L.S., Ph.D., Assistant Professor, Interdisciplinary Doctoral Program in Information Science, University of Pittsburgh: *CARUSO*

JAY E. DAILY, B.A., M.L.S., D.L.S., Professor, Graduate School of Library and Information Sciences, University of Pittsburgh: *Catalogs and Cataloging; Censorship, Contemporary and Controversial Aspects of*

FRANCES deCORDOVA, B.A., M.L.S., Assistant Professor, Texas Woman's University, School of Library Science, Denton: *Children's Literature*

HERMAN DE JAEGER, Advisor, Centre National de Documentation Scientifique et Technique, Bibliothèque Royale de Belgique, Brussels: *Centre National de Documentation Scientifique et Technique*

BETTY JOHNSON DE VODANOVIĆ, Assistant Director (CENID), Santiago, Chile: *Centro Nacional de Información y Documentación (CENID)*

PETER M. DOIRON, Editor, CHOICE, Middletown, Connecticut: *CHOICE*

J. H. D'OLIER, Deputy Director, Centre de Documentation du C.N.R.S., Paris: *Centre National de la Recherche Scientifique (CNRS)*

iii

THOMAS J. GALVIN, Director of Students and Associate Professor of Library Science, School of Library Science, Simmons College, Boston: *Case Studies and Case Method*

ALAN GELBERG, Director, Management and Scientific Information Systems Design Division, Bureau of Drugs (BD-36), Food and Drug Administration, Department of Health, Education, and Welfare, Rockville, Maryland: *Chemical Notations*

JOSEPH A. GENOVESE, B.A.E., LL.B., Patent Counsel and Assistant Secretary, Control Data Corporation, Minneapolis, Minnesota: *Character Recognition*

STANLEY E. GWYNN, Associate Director, University of Chicago Library: *Chicago. University of Chicago Library*

EUGENE R. HANSON, Associate Professor, Department of Library Science, Shippensburg State College, Pennsylvania: *Catalogs and Cataloging*

SIDNEY L. JACKSON, Ph.D., Professor, School of Library Science, Kent State University, Ohio: *Chained Libraries*

ALLEN KENT, Director, Office of Communications Programs, and Professor, University of Pittsburgh: *Centralization, Decentralization, and Specialization*

ANTHONY K. KENT, Director, The Chemical Society Research Unit in Information Dissemination and Retrieval, The University, Nottingham: *Chemical Society Retrieval Unit in Information Dissemination and Retrieval*

JAMES J. KORTENDICK (Rev.), S.S., Ph.D., Chairman, Department of Library Science, The Catholic University of America, Washington, D.C.: *Catholic University of America, Graduate Department of Library Science*

ALEX LADENSON, Chief Librarian, Chicago Public Library: *Chicago Public Library*

WILLIAM KAYE LAMB, M.A., Ph.D., LL.D., F.R.S.C., Ottawa, Ontario, Canada: *Canada National Library*

JOHN LOTZ, Ph.D., Director, Center for Applied Linguistics, Washington, D.C.: *Center for Applied Linguistics*

MARGARET MASTERMAN, Director of Research, Cambridge Language Research Unit, Cambridge, England: *Cambridge Language Research Unit (CLRU)*

NICOLAS MATIJEVIC, Professor, Director de la Biblioteca Central de la Universidad Nacional del sur, Argentina: *Centro de Documentación Bibliotecologica (CDB)*

ELIZABETH HOMER MORTON, M.A., LL.D., Library Consultant; Former Executive Director, Canadian Library Association: *Canada, Libraries in; Canadian Library Association*

RALPH MUNN, Director Emeritus, Carnegie Library of Pittsburgh: *Carnegie Library of Pittsburgh*

WILLIAM Z. NASRI, B.A., LL.B., M.L.S., Research Associate, Graduate School of Library and Information Sciences and the Knowledge Availability Systems Center, University of Pittsburgh: *Central Asia, Libraries in*

J. C. T. OATES, Under-Librarian, University Library, Cambridge, England: *Cambridge University Library*

IGNATIUS T. P. PAO (dec.), Director, National Central Library, Taipei, Taiwan, China: *China, Libraries in the Republic of*

RALPH H. PARKER, Ph.D., Dean, School of Library and Information Science, University of Missouri, Columbia: *Charging Systems*

THOMAS C. PEARS III, Pittsburgh: *Caxton, William*

ABRAHAM PIMSTEIN-LAMAS, Professor, Director, Escuela de Bibliotecologia, Universidad de Chile, Santiago: *Chile. University of Chile, School of Library Science*

ELSPETH POPE, B.A., B.L.S., M.A., Instructor, Graduate School of Library and Information Sciences, University of Pittsburgh: *Cataloging-in-Source*

MARY JANE PUGH, Pittsburgh Chemical Information Center, University of Pittsburgh: *Chemical Information Centers*

SAVINA A. ROXAS, Ph.D., Professor, Clarion State College, Clarion, Pennsylvania: *Translator: Centro de Documentación Bibliotecologica (CDB); Centro de Investigaciones Bibliotecologicas de la Universidad de Buenos Aires; Chile, Libraries in; Chile. University of Chile, School of Library Science*

JOSEFA E. SABOR, Directora, Centro de Investigaciones Bibliotecológicas, Universidad de Buenos Aires: *Centro de Investigaciones Bibliotecológicas de la Universidad de Buenos Aires*

MARIA TERESA SANZ B-M., Directora de Bibliotecas de la Universidad Catolica de Chile, Santiago, Chile: *Chile, Libraries in*

JESSE H. SHERA, Ph.D., Dean Emeritus, School of Library Science, Case Western Reserve University, Cleveland; Visiting Professor, Graduate School of Library Science, University of Texas, Austin: *Case Western Reserve University, School of Library Science*

GEORGE M. SINKANKAS, Graduate School of Library and Information Sciences, University of Pittsburgh: *Centralized Cataloging*

RUTH S. SMITH, Head Librarian, Institute for Defense Analyses, Arlington, Virginia: *Church and Synagogue Library Association*

ERIK J. SPICER, Parliamentary Librarian, Library of Parliament, Ottawa: *Canada. Library of Parliament, Ottawa*

ROY B. STOKES, Director, School of Librarianship, University of British Columbia, Vancouver: *Chapbooks*

DON R. SWANSON, Ph.D., Dean, Graduate Library School, University of Chicago: *Chicago. University of Chicago, Graduate Library School*

R. S. THAMBIAH, Librarian, Jaffna College, Vaddukoddai, Ceylon: *Ceylon, Libraries in*

TSUEN-HSUIN TSIEN, Ph.D., Professor of Chinese Literature and Curator, Far Eastern Library, University of Chicago: *China, Library Association of*

IRVING A. VERSCHOOR, Ph.D., Dean, College of General Studies, State University of New York at Albany: *Certification of Librarians*

ALBERTO VILLALÓN-GALDAMES, Director, Escuela de Bibliotecologia, Universidad de Chile, Santiago: *Chile. University of Chile, School of Library Science*

ROBERT WALL, Ph.D., Department of Linguistics, University of Texas, Austin: *Categorial Grammars*

JAMES M. WELLS, Associate Director, The Newberry Library, Chicago: *Caxton Club*

JOYCE L. WHITE, Librarian, The Maria Hosmer Penniman Memorial Library, University of Pennsylvania: *Church Libraries*

B. ROSE WILLIAMS, Librarian, Chamber of Commerce of The United States of America, Washington, D.C.: *Chamber of Commerce of the United States of America Library*

MATTHEW R. WILT, Executive Director, The Catholic Library Association, Haverford, Pennsylvania: *Catholic Library Association; Catholic Periodical and Literature Index*

HOWARD W. WINGER, Ph.D., Professor, Graduate Library School, University of Chicago: *Chronicles*

FRANCIS J. WITTY, M.S. in L.S., Ph.D., Associate Professor, Department of Library Science, Catholic University of America, Washington, D.C.: *Cassiodorus, Flavius Magnus Aurelius; Catholic Libraries and Collections*

K. T. WU, Ph.D., Head, Chinese and Korean Section, Orientalia Division, Library of Congress, Washington, D.C.: *China, Libraries in the People's Republic of*

ENCYCLOPEDIA
OF LIBRARY
AND INFORMATION
SCIENCE

VOLUME 4

CALLIGRAPHY

As the paintings in the caves of Altamira and Lascaux demonstrate, man possessed the ability to communicate elegantly long before he discovered the art of writing. With this talent various peoples throughout the world created pictographs which enabled them to record events, myths, and limited narratives. This precursor to the art of writing is seen in many differing styles and on many different materials. The Mayan culture produced impressive records in stone, while the Aztec people recorded tribal history in embroidery and the Plains Indians of North America commemorated the lives of chieftains with pigment on buffalo skins. Thus, it is clear that early systems of writing employed different graphic means and were similar only in the phonetic principles governing the art of writing.

The earliest act of writing is credited to the Sumerian people, who settled the Tigris-Euphrates Valley before 3000 B.C. These inventive people equated signs with words in their system of speech and recorded the signs on clay tablets with various tools which they pressed into the plastic material. These units of writing in clay, hardened by fire, recorded simple transactions in trade, and the word-sign for a cow could be executed with extreme economy of means. Thus, the early tablets from Uruk, an important site in this early civilization, show a crude power which is important to the aesthetic record but which has been neglected except for those facsimiles published by scholars of paleography interested in decipherment and word content.

As the principles of writing became more sophisticated, passing from a logographic system of signs and words to signs and syllables, the Sumerian method became more precise. By the use of a few shaped forms made from the ends of reed plants as stamps, all the written signs came to be executed in a typically stylized form. The Sumerian writing in clay is called *cuneiform* from the Latin *cuneus* (wedge) and *forma* (form). With Hammurabi's expansion of power in 1720 B.C. Semitic peoples, first the Babylonians and then the Assyrians, held control of the Tigris-Euphrates Valley. These peoples adopted the cuneiform method of writing which thus dominated the area until alphabetic writing, promoted by energetic Aramaic traders, became important around 500 B.C.

Several more ancient systems of writing were developed at the eastern end of the Mediterranean. The Hittites, of Biblical note, were an important people in Turkey and Syria between 1500 and 700 B.C. Passing through the pictographic, logographic, and syllabic systems of writing, the Hittites produced some fine records in stone. On Crete Sir Arthur Evans was impressed by pictographic elements carved on semiprecious stones. Evans also discovered writing of Linear Class A impressed on clay tablets, and these too are interesting in form. Many of these clay tablets and those carrying the signs of the celebrated Linear Class B are of lesser interest visually, however. The signs were cryptic in nature and were scratched into wet clay without particular regard for elegance of appearance.

The visual qualities of Egyptian writing are better known from their appearance

1

on important architectural monuments. In ancient Egypt purely pictographic elements were executed on a large scale. Incised in stone, these monumental sculptures are rightfully included in an article on written forms because they recorded historical events, albeit with bias. Word-signs, which constitute the phonetic part of Egyptian writing, were executed similarly, intaglio in stone, and accompanied the larger figures. These word-signs—animals, parts of human anatomy, and objects—were carved with precision. The forms, relying on profile features, became strictly codified in the static Egyptian society, in which the earliest phonetic elements appeared ca. 3000 B.C.

However impressive, Egyptian inscriptions were supplemented by another method of writing which was to outlast the arc of power founded on the Nile River. The medium was papyrus, a flat, thin, organic material developed from a reed plant *Cyperus papyrus* which grew in the swamps of the Nile Delta. Strips from the core of this plant were laid together and overlaid with other strips placed at right angles to the first layer. This manner of manufacture permitted the use of long continuous rolls. The Harris Papyrus (Egyptian) in the British Museum measures 133 feet by 17 inches, but most rolls were of more modest dimensions. Papyrus was of the greatest importance in Western writing. Greek penmen used papyrus, as did the Romans, and even after the use of skins for recorded literature became prevalent ca. A.D. 400, papyrus was used in royal edicts and church documents until A.D. 1100. The manufacture of papyrus continued in Egypt long after Egypt's decline as an area power, and other sites in the Mediterranean area supplemented the supply.

The tool developed for writing on papyrus was made from a solid-stem rush plant. Roughly pointed, it could be called either a pen or a brush. Around 600 B.C. professional Egyptian scribes began to use pens made from the hollow reed *Phragmites aegyptia*. The tip of the Egyptian pen was cut to produce thick and thin strokes and was quite similar to modern pens made from bamboo and other reed plants. There were two forms of pen-written letters. The first to be developed was called *hieratic,* and the word and syllable signs were derived from *hieroglyphic,* the inscription form. Another pen-written form called *demotic* was a later development and was a kind of shorthand version of the hieratic shapes. Egyptian writing proceeds from right to left. Many Egyptian manuscripts were written with elegance, and some can be compared to the fine manuscripts produced in the Middle Ages in Europe.

The Alphabet

Alphabetic writing was developed out of experiments that took place at the eastern end of the Mediterranean during the first 500 years of the second millenium B.C. Inscribed on stone and metal or roughly painted on clay, these scattered pieces of Semitic writing lack aesthetic appeal for most people. After the establishment of alphabetic writing ca. 1000 B.C., two related Semitic peoples produced writing of genuine quality. The Phoenicians, sea travelers with headquarters on a 20-mile-wide strip of land at the eastern end of the Mediterranean, created some fine inscriptions. One notable inscription, the Baal of Lebanon, was executed on a bronze cup found on Cyprus and dated ca. 800 B.C. Phoenician inscriptions have been found at many sites throughout the Mediterranean area and beyond, and the people of Carthage left their mark in remnant alphabets used in North Africa today.

Speakers of Aramaic were resourceful land traders, and spread alphabetic writing east from Asia Minor. When the Israelites returned from their enforced stay in the Mesopotamian Valley, they learned Aramaic, and Jesus and his contemporaries spoke this language. Scribes who wrote Aramaic developed an emphatic and visually compelling style of pen letters executed on ceramics, skins, and papyrus. Impressive Aramaic pen-written documents exist from the fifth century B.C. The cut of the reed pen employed produced a definitive thick-and-thin content, and in execution the pen was pointed more west than north in reference to map direction. An example of Aramaic writing is seen in Figure 1.

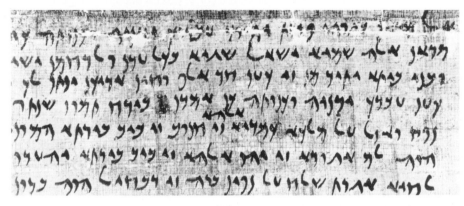

FIGURE 1. *Aramaic pen writing, fifth century* B.C. *British Museum, London.*

Syriac, an important derivation of Aramaic, came to be spoken over large areas north and east of Palestine. The most important script is called *Estrangela,* and the signs employed were the 22 Semitic consonants with names changed. Similar to other Semitic scripts, Syriac was written from right to left. After A.D. 431 the Syriac language and script followed a religious split and developed an eastern and a western form. The western branch was called *Serta* and developed into two varieties named *Jacobite* and *Melkite.* The eastern Syriac language and script was called *Nestorian* after Nestorius, who led a secession movement out of the Orthodox Church of Byzantium. Many of the professional scribes who wrote these related scripts were very skilled, and many manuscripts exhibit elegant writing. While Aramaic and Hebrew scripts featured strong horizontal elements at the top of the letter forms, Syriac writing came to depend on a strong horizontal base line. In some Jacobite writing, this base line is continuous throughout several words, which means that ligatures were frequent and became a means of displaying calligraphic artistry, as distinct from Aramaic and Hebrew scripts which form signs one by one. The Jacobite Christians survived, as did the Syriac script. Contemporary type characters are directly based on the fine Syriac pen-letter forms.

The Nestorian Church penetrated deeply into Asia, spreading its word and script. Semitic-Aramaic pen-written forms were also adopted by the Sogdians, a highly influential people in central Asia between A.D. 500 and 1000. Although the language was Indo-European, the Sogdian scribes used the Semitic signs beautifully.

Aramaic influence is also seen in the scripts of Uigher, used by a powerful Turkic people who created an empire in central Asia in the eighth century, and in the Mongol era. Mongol manuscripts are written in a vertical line, and numerous ligatures are present. The Aramaic influence is also seen in the manuscripts associated with the Mandaean sect of the Mesopotamian Valley and in Manichaean manuscripts. Manichaean writing was named for Mani or Manichaeus, who founded a religion in A.D. 247. The doctrine of this cult was a peculiar blending of Christian and Zoroastrian beliefs, together with mystic elements of Gnostic sects. In southern Europe this religion was a principal rival of Christianity until banned by Justinian in the sixth century. The followers of Manichaeus were good scribes.

Thus, through trade and religion, Aramaic, known as the mother of languages, penetrated well into Asia and provided the basis for all of the languages in the area—Chinese, of course, excepted. Tibetan scribes are particularly good.

Writing in India goes back to the third century B.C. during the reign of Asoka (272–231 B.C.). Many of Asoka's writings were committed to stone and were stiff and angular in form. Many fine inscriptions date from the European medieval period and were executed in stone and in copper. The fourteen principal languages of India are inter-related through Sanskrit, the ancient scholarly language of the sacred Vedas. *Devanagari* is the script most closely associated with Sanskrit, and there are many fine pen-written documents in this alphabetic form. Most signs have a strong horizontal stroke at the top and are frequently ligatured. The Devanagari script may be observed in Figure 2.

While some Asian writing exists on gold or ivory surfaces, a traditional method of book production in southern areas involves the use of rectangular pieces of palm leaves. Each leaf of a book is perforated twice, and then a series of leaves is tied with a thong. A good-sized book might contain 400 leaves and, with stiff wooden covers protecting the top and bottom, be 6 or 7 inches thick.

Arabic is one of the important modern languages derived from Aramaic. As is its mother language, Arabic is composed of the 22 consonant signs, expanded now to 28, and similar to Aramaic it is written from right to left. The *qualam* or reed pen is cut not square at the tip but with the right corner forward of the left.

In the first millenium B.C. Arab settlers inhabited the Fertile Crescent, the arc extending up the Mediterranean coast, around to the headwaters of the Tigris, and down to the Persian Gulf. They were a wandering people, driven by the seasons, and practiced barbarous customs. Although the Arabs told stories and admired poetry, there were few early signs of their later success. Syriac was the language and script of the church in this area, and Arabic, being a language neither of ruling peoples nor of a powerful church, remained in the background as the language of common people until well after the birth of Mohammed ca. A.D. 570. One of

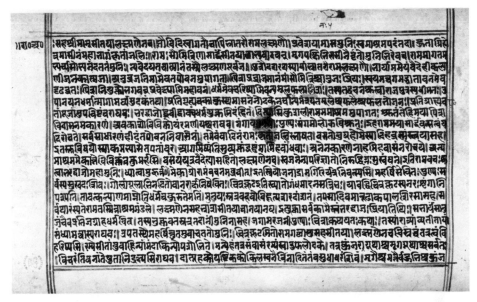

FIGURE 2. *Pen-written Sanskrit from the seventeenth century. British Museum, London.*

the finest accounts of the origins of the Arabic script is found in *The Rise of the North Arabic Script* by Nabia Abbot writing in *Oriental Institute Publications,* Vol. L (University of Chicago Press, 1939).

Mohammed transformed the religious, political, and social organization of his people. In 622, having received revelations, he fled his native city of Mecca and went north to Medina. Moslems consider this date the year 1, and the appropriate number of years must be added to dated Arabic manuscripts to bring them into our frame of reference. By conquest and persuasion, Islam spread to Spain, through North Africa, and east to India, with shafts of the faith penetrating China, Africa, and southeast Asia. In Europe Charles Martel stopped an army of Moors at Tours in 732, and for this reason European remnants of Islamic culture exist principally in Spain.

Arabic writing is the calligrapher's delight. The act of writing for its own sake was highly developed and greatly admired; it was an art form of high status, not merely accepted but assumed to be a part of civilized life.

The earliest Arabic pen form, Kufic, was a highly mannered imitation of inscription letters and most early manuscripts were devoted to the Koran, the sacred writings of Mohammed. During the eighth, ninth, and tenth centuries, the common Arabic scripts became more cursive and flowing. Several recognizable styles grew out of this cursive tradition, with Naskh the most common and most legible style. Thuluth, which has tall risers and elegant curves, was used for special occasions and for the Koran. Nastaliq (now commonly called Farsi), which has a unique slant, is usually associated with Persian manuscripts.

Scribes writing Arabic delight in decoration, visual puns, and unusually shaped messages with the letters carefully designed within. Many of the manuscripts were written on paper, for knowledge of papermaking had been acquired by the Arabs long before they took it to Europe.

Another contemporary language and script derived from Aramaic is Hebrew, termed *ivrit*. The earliest Semitic form used by the Hebrews is called Old Hebrew and was derived from the Phoenician-Canaanite variety of early Semitic ca. 1100 B.C. This language was lost, except as practiced by a rare sect of Samaritans, and after their return from exile the Hebrews learned Aramaic. Before 1947 Hebrew manuscripts predating the Christian Era were very few. In that year, however, the first of the Dead Sea Scrolls were discovered by an Arab shepherd named Muhammad the Wolf. This amazing tale is too lengthy to relate here, but since 1947 some 300 caves have been explored northwest of the Dead Sea and 11 of them have yielded fragments from every book in the Old Testament except the Book of Esther. Some of the copies, the manuscript of Daniel for example, are thought to follow the original writing (ca. 165 B.C.) by only 50 years. For an understandable book on the significance of the Dead Sea Scrolls, the reader should consult *The Dead Sea Scrolls* by Menahem Mansoor (available from Wm. B. Eerdmans).

These early Hebrew manuscripts, written on skins, reveal a square letter with *lamed* the sole character with a riser; in some manuscripts this riser is very tall and instantly recognized. The letters in the Dead Sea manuscripts also reveal a horizontal stroke at the top of most letters. Thus, the Square Hebrew of that day became the Square Hebrew of the present day with comparatively little change. Hebrew basically still has 22 consonant letters, a few slightly changed in form depending upon their position in a word. Additional signs indicate vowels.

After these early views of Hebrew writing there is nothing to be seen in manuscripts until A.D. 900. In the late Middle Ages the Square Hebrew form was given local interpretations, but it is unlikely that a trained paleographer would have any trouble in discerning individual letter forms. In the late Middle Ages a more cursive form of Hebrew letters emerged called Rabbinical. Informal letters written in Hebrew do not use the Square Hebrew form but rather a different set of cursive forms. Perhaps because Jews have been scattered and isolated this form never seems to have become standardized, and no doubt the preservation of Square Hebrew is in large measure the result of its usage in religious documents.

Chinese Writing

Before turning to the Greek and Roman tradition of letter forms, we must consider Chinese writing. These forms emerged from a primitive Chinese culture in the middle part of the second millenium B.C. during the Shang dynasty (1765–1123 B.C.). The earliest records were incised on bones of animals, such as the scapulas of cattle, deer skulls, or the breastplates of tortoises. These "oracle bones," of which about 100 thousand have been discovered, are identified with any number of subjects such as births, deaths, hunting expeditions, and ancestor worship. The vocabulary of the Shang writers has been estimated to include 2,500 words The principles governing Chinese writing emerged at this time. Signs exhibited abstractions of parts of the human body, animals, and objects in the environment. These were word-signs just as $ is a word-sign in Western lands. The essential nature of the Chinese system has not changed, and Chinese writing never went through the change most usual in ancient systems of writing, namely, that from word-signs to syllable signs to an alphabet.

Succeeding the Shang dynasty, the Chou dynasties, Eastern and Western, date from 1122 B.C. to 256 B.C., and a number of fine bronze utensils with inscribed characters stem from this period. Brush writing is probably quite ancient. A grave dating from the Period of the Warring States (468–221 B.C.) has produced a brush and it is now believed, contrary to Chinese tradition, that the brush as a writing tool goes back to the Shang dynasty.

Brush writing came into eminence during the Han dynasty—Western Han or Former Han, 206 B.C. to A.D. 23 and Eastern Han or Later Han, A.D. 25–220. One of the monuments of this period is an inscription of Confucian classics of which a few fragments remain to show the brush character of the period. One of these appears in Figure 3. The formal *li shu* script of Later Han is deliberate and elegant, but bold experimentation laid the basis for the creative brush scripts to follow.

The most revered genius of Chinese writing is Wang Hsi-chih (A.D. 307–365). His stature has been compared to that of Michelangelo, Beethoven, and Shakespeare. Two of his uncles had been calligraphers, and the young Wang Hsi-chih had been tutored by a lady named Wei Fu-jen who came from a long line of calligraphers. The young master learned all the older, stiffer styles, along with the contemporary *li shu,* and went on to create models of writing emulated to the present day. The best account of these developments appears in *Chinese Calligraphers and Their Arts* by Ch'en Chih-mai (Melbourne University Press, 1966). Another fine piece of writing on Chinese scripts can be found in *Chinese Art* (Universe Books, New York, 1964); this masterful article is by Roger Goepper.

The principal tool of Chinese writing was and is a pointed brush made of animal hairs. Many animals have lent their fur to this great art, including mice. The instrument is held vertically so that it can move unhindered in several directions. This freedom of movement is not quite the perfect license it might seem to be, since the various characters must be composed well within an imaginary square, sometimes in manuals broken down into nine squares. Brush strokes must not be weak but must possess "bones," and some of the strokes are more strictly codified than Western observers might suspect. Skills in brush writing parallel skills in brush drawing of animals, landscapes, and vegetation, since the same tool is used in both painting and calligraphy.

It should be noted that Chinese writing proceeds from top to bottom and from right to left. Most documents are signed in the lower left with a printed seal using older inscription characters. Certainly Chinese writing is aesthetically among the great triumphs of man as an artist.

Japanese writing stems from Chinese, and the borrowing of signs may have occurred as early as the fourth century A.D. Many early Japanese scribes were trained

FIGURE 3. *Chinese writing, Confucian classics from the Han Dynasty. A rubbing from brush-written calligraphy inscribed in stone from* Ta-lu tsa-chih, *Vol. X, No. 5.*

to write Chinese, and the marvelous calligraphic content of Chinese writing came to be a part of Japanese writing. Phonetically Japanese is in no way related to Chinese, so some Chinese characters were used for the basic set of 50 characters needed for the Japanese syllable system. Invented characters provided the remaining signs needed. The tradition of brush writing in Japan is very impressive but the basic rules are not the same.

Greek Writing

With the brilliant decipherment of Linear Class B documents by Michael Ventris and John Chadwick in 1952, it was learned that there was a Greek language 700 years before Homer. A successful invasion by illiterate Dorian Greeks ca.

1100 B.C., however, destroyed the earlier civilization and the Aegean area was without the art of writing for hundreds of years. The art of writing was reintroduced to Greek speakers by Phoenicians at some mutual trading center at the eastern end of the Mediterranean. The date of this exchange has long been debated, and for lack of records much of the evidence is circumstantial. To some scholars the eighth century B.C. seems to be the likeliest time for the Greeks in Asia Minor to have received the alphabet from their neighbors.

The Phoenician language was Semitic in character, using 22 consonant signs. Greek speakers, using an Indo-European language, were able to use many of the Semitic consonant signs and converted others, such as *aleph* and *he* to the vowels *a* and *e*. Several new signs were invented and placed at the end of the Phoenician alphabet before *omega*. Slightly differing versions of the new Greek alphabet were used in different areas of Greece, but a standard version was achieved through the acceptance of the Ionic order of letters in 403 B.C.

The first important Greek document, the Dipylon vase, was executed in the eighth century B.C. and the letters on it were written from right to left, with *A* lying on its side in the Phoenician manner. On the beautiful Lemnos Stela of the sixth century B.C., the stone-inscribed letters were written in the *boustrophedon* manner, that is, as the ox plows. Alternate lines were written right to left and then left to right. The arms of *K*, facing right here, faced left in a line of letters arranged from right to left. Thus, alphabets deriving from this period show alternate forms for certain letters.

Inscriptions deriving from the fifth century B.C. are seen in greater quantity. Incised in stone, these documents exhibit a typical form that marked Greek writing for many centuries. The letter signs, now arranged from left to right, are stiff, angular, and geometric. Often they are arranged in the manner called *stocheidon,* that is, in vertical alignment. This form of Greek writing is shown in Figure 4.

Pen-written Greek documents deriving from the fourth and third centuries B.C. are exceedingly rare, but the sureness of execution suggests an earlier start. A reed pen was used on papyrus. The letters are deliberately spaced, as in inscriptions, but many of them exhibit curved members. For example, a penman could exercise his prerogative in executing the vertical stems of an *eta* and make them curved instead of stiff and vertical. Through the centuries pen-written Greek demonstrates a cursive freedom which, straying from the inscription letter form, eventually leads to a minuscule Greek alphabet.

The most celebrated Greek manuscripts are bibles executed in the fourth and fifth centuries of the Christian Era. Three of these are *Codex Vaticanus, Codex Sinaiticus,* and *Codex Alexandrinus.* The last-mentioned two are in the British Museum. In its original state *Codex Sinaiticus* consisted of 730 leaves (1460 pages). Each of these pages was 14 inches wide and 16 inches high, and they were written on skins. Four columns of writing appeared on each page. *Codex Sinaiticus* was uncovered by Constantine Tischendorf at the monastery of St. Catherine on Mount Sinai in 1844. A part of the manuscript had been burned as rubbish but a large part of 390 leaves eventually came to the library at St. Petersburg and was purchased for the British Museum in 1932 for a price of £100,000.

The pen letters used in *Codex Sinaiticus* and other bibles of this period are

FIGURE 4. *Greek inscription, stocheidon composition, fifth century* B.C. *Otto Kern,* Inscriptiones Grecae.

called Greek Uncial. Pens used were held vertically, and a geometric play of round and vertical strokes, profound in simplicity, give the Greek Uncial bibles a most impressive appearance. A reduced-size facsimile of *Codex Alexandrinus* was published by the British Museum in 1957.

The Greek alphabet was used by other peoples employing other languages. Augmented by some Egyptian characters, it appears in a number of pen-lettered documents left by the Copts. Greek letters were also used in a short-lived version of the Gothic language by Bishop Ulfilas in the fourth century. Ulfilas translated the Bible into Gothic, and fragments of this translation, executed in the fifth and sixth centuries, exist in the *Codex Argenteus,* now at the University of Uppsala, Sweden. Written in silver and gold on parchment tinted purple, *Codex Argenteus* is visually most impressive. A facsimile of this document was published by the University in 1928.

With a split in the Roman empire in 395, the Greek language and culture became important in the Byzantine Empire in the Middle Ages. Peoples of the Balkan area came to use the Greek alphabet, largely through the efforts of Cyril, a brilliant Greek missionary who worked among the Slavs in the ninth century. Cyril devised an alphabet called Glagolitic (*glagol* means "word"), which conveyed Slavic speech into written form. Through a conversion of the Russians ca. 988, this alphabet spread in usage and eventually served many peoples in Europe and Asia.

Manutius initiated a Greek type font in 1495, a difficult task because of the numerous ligatures found in manuscript writing. Claude Garamond, working in France about 50 years later, designed the first elegant Greek font, the Grec du Roi.

One of the finer Greek fonts in use today is the Porson Greek produced by Mono-type, London.

Contemporary calligraphers occasionally have need to try Greek letters. Edward Johnston's examples are among the best to be found.

Roman Writing

It is assumed that a Greek colony at Cumae near Naples introduced alphabetic forms to the Etruscans, then the dominant people of the peninsula, around 675 B.C. The Marsiliana Abecedarium, a writing tablet inscribed with the Etruscan alphabet, is an important find. This and other Etruscan inscriptions are written from right to left, and the forms are stiff and angular. Etruscan writing has not been deciphered and the origins of the Etruscan people are still a subject of specu-lation. Through the North Etruscans, alphabetic forms were introduced to the peoples in northern Europe before the Christian Era, resulting in the celebrated Runic writing. Most of the 4000 Runic inscriptions, executed on stone, wood, and a variety of other materials, feature rigid alphabetic forms. Some are distinguished. The Franks Casket in the British Museum is one of these. This Anglo-Saxon casket, dated ca. 700, was carved in whalebone and features fine relief work on the theme of Romulus and Remus.

Other peoples of the Italian peninsula who received the alphabet were the Oscans, Umbrians, and Latins. In 509 B.C. the Latins drove the Etruscans out and began the era of power that made Western history. Not the least among the accomplishments of the Latins was the spread of alphabetic writing throughout Europe and thence to the Western hemisphere. The first Latin inscription known appears on a gold brooch, the Praeneste Fibula, dated ca. 600 B.C. In this short inscription the letters are arranged in right-to-left order. In subsequent centuries Latin writings appeared in this Semitic order and in boustrophedon, becoming fixed in a right-to-left order in the third century B.C. In the first 500 years of its exist-ence, the Latin inscription form offers no visual feast. Some inscriptions show crude power and some examples from the third century B.C. show something of the art of subtle spacing. The serif, that terminal appendage to main strokes which remains intact in the capital letters of the present day, first appeared in the second century B.C. Concurrent with the appearance of the serif, certain letters in inscrip-tions exhibited thick-and-thin content. Thus, the stiff and angular qualities of the inscription letter came to be relieved by certain calligraphic graces derived from a pen, or brush, wide at the point of contact. The mystery of this development re-mained for many centuries, in fact until the latter half of the nineteenth century. Perhaps a partial explanation of the calligraphic inscription form can be found on the walls of Pompeii, interred by lava flow in A.D. 79. Revealed here is evidence of a professional sign-writing trade capable of producing election notices. The brush used may have resembled a small house-painting brush or the square-tipped brush used in oil painting today.

After the introduction of this instrument, Roman inscription forms can be considered a subject apart from other forms carrying the Latin language. The wall signs showed that the instrument of execution was pointed in a more westerly direction than the 45° angle described as northwest. Vertical strokes were thinner than horizontal strokes. Many inscriptions exhibited this same characteristic, and it is clear that before the carver began his work the letter image was traced on stone with a brush charged with pigment. The inscription letter received its most subtle and noble interpretation in the centuries following A.D. 1. In these years certain fine inscriptions came to be executed with a stronger vertical stroke, and the serif structure became more difficult to explain. As shown by Edward M. Catich in his *Origin of the Serif* (The Catfish Press, Davenport, Iowa, 1968), the skilled Roman brush writer was able to rotate or twist the hand of execution in midstroke, and Catich presents the most convincing theory concerning the compound strokes found in the Roman inscription letters.

One of the most admired of Roman inscriptions is the one at the base of the Trajan Column in Rome. Executed ca. A.D. 113, the inscription outlined Emperor Trajan's accomplishments on the frontier in about 30 words. Full of fine slow curves, strong verticals, and occasional diagonal strokes, the Trajan letters communicate a sense of dignity and elegance which remains valid on any scale. The letters of the Trajan inscription measure only about 4½ inches in height. Another fine Roman inscription is devoted to a eulogy to Emperor Hadrian, the able successor to Trajan. This was found, in pieces, at Wroxeter, Shropshire, England, and had been erected over the gateway to the forum of the Roman town Uriconium in A.D. 130. In this stately carving, 12 feet wide, the letters in each of five lines were designed larger as the distance from the eye increased. This was not the only practice that enhanced the visual quality of Roman stone letters. The V-cut letters were painted with a red lead pigment. Letters appearing over the entrance to the Pantheon, erected in Rome in A.D. 120, were filled with bronze late in the nineteenth century.

If the walls of Pompeii accurately represent the usage of letters, writing was widespread in Roman towns. In one early method, letters were drawn on a wax-covered wooden tablet with a metal stylus. This was the method of the illegible hand discussed in *Pseudolus* by the Roman playwright Plautus (ca. 254–184 B.C.). A number of tablets could be hinged together through drilled holes, and this constituted an early form of *caudex,* later *codex,* or book with leaves, which eventually replaced the papyrus roll. The wax-and-stylus method rather encouraged a free interpretation of the Latin alphabet. Instruments used in writing *graffiti* on the walls of Roman towns were equally free of the restraints felt by those who carved letters in stone. Narrow-tipped reed pens used on papyrus constituted a third Roman writing medium which permitted free play in alphabetic form. These several methods encouraged cursive writing and different forms of many of the letters. In this development informal or street writing became allied with legal writing, and there was no standard alphabet. The present forms of *a* and *b* and other minuscule letters were combed out of this flux of experimental writing. Excellent Roman cursive examples were produced in the fourth century A.D., and the style seems to have reached a high point in legal documents from Ravenna in the sixth century.

The Romans also developed pen styles to record literature. A foundation hand for these efforts is the style called Rustic. Reed pens used produced a thick-and-thin graphic content and were pointed west of northwest. Vertical strokes were thinner than horizontal strokes, and thus this form of Roman pen writing was allied to inscription forms and brush writing. Although there are large gaps in the record, the Rustic style was written on papyrus documents dating from the early years of the Christian Era. A characteristic that distinguishes Rustic manuscripts from Roman cursive documents is that the letters in Rustic, as in inscriptions, are presented one by one, clearly, without entangling alliances with other letters, and this influence is of prime importance in the development of letter forms. This feature is illustrated in *Codex Vaticanus 3225,* Figure 5.

FIGURE 5. *Roman Rustic capital book hand, fourth or fifth century. From* Codex Vaticanus 3225, *Vatican Library, Rome.*

Writing in the Middle Ages

Book hands descending from the era of Roman power reached maturity at the time of political decay in the fourth and fifth century. In these times the use of animal skins as carriers for pen writing superseded papyrus. Animal skins were used at the eastern end of the Mediterranean in the first millenium B.C., and the sophisticated processing of skins for writing appears to have originated in Pergamum in Asia Minor ca. 200 B.C. Vellum, processed from the skins of young animals, was the material used in the great books of the Middle Ages. Four pieces of vellum might be placed on top of one another and then folded in the middle. This would give eight leaves called a *quaternio,* four sheets folded. Three- and five-sheet folds were also known, and the generic term for such gatherings is *quire.* This development is of central importance to the modern book.

Existing codices executed in the Rustic capital style are not numerous, and the most important of these are two manuscripts in the Vatican Library dating from the fourth or fifth century. *Codex Vaticanus 3225* is an illustrated edition of the *Aeneid. Codex Palatinus 1631,* a Virgil text, features an extremely polished version of the Rustic hand. Rustic was never again used as a book hand but was used as a title script at various times and places into the late Middle Ages.

Another famous book hand is the Square Capital or *quadrata,* in which the scribe used the pen in imitation of inscription letters, turning the hand in execution to achieve difficult serifs. Square Capital is something of an anomaly in the history of manuscript styles, since there is little precedent for its existence and no subsequent usage. Its fame resides in two manuscripts devoted to the works of Virgil. Most frequently reproduced is the *Codex Vaticanus 3256.*

One unique and influential style of book hand descending from the Roman Era is the Uncial. This is in every way a classic among pen hands, because the pen was given its own way in the formation of the letters and there was no attempt, in the earliest phase of the hand, to imitate the serif endings of inscription letter forms. Some of the essential forms in the Uncial style stemmed from older inscription capitals, while some letters derived from cursive writing. The letters *d*, *h*, and *l* were given an element ascending above the top line, and *g*, *p*, and *q* possessed descending parts. Essential to fine visual qualities in this script is a constant repetition of curved and vertical elements and a generous white space inside most of the letters. Uncial retained its importance as a book hand from the fourth to the ninth century. The style was taken to England by missionaries around 600, and a revision of it was developed in scriptoria in England between 700 and 800. The twin abbeys of Wearmouth-Jarrow produced great manuscripts in the late Uncial style, among them the magnificent *Codex Amiatinus,* now in the Biblioteca Laurenziana in Florence, which was written in the years prior to 716. Pages of this Bible are over 13 inches in width and almost 21 inches high. The pen of execution was held in a vertical position and serif endings were reintroduced in a number of letters. Late Uncial manuscripts reveal the influence of Celtic writing. In some writing centers in England, Anglo-Saxon scribes sat next to Irish scribes.

Uncial forms were also enlarged and decorated in the Middle Ages, and along with inscription forms served as a basis for what would now be termed capital letters. Used to begin verses and to furnish adornment, the Uncial in this guise lasted into the Renaissance period.

Another influential book hand emerged from scriptoria in Italy in the sixth century. This style, sometimes referred to as half-Uncial or semi-Uncial, is the ancestor minuscule of Western writing. The letters *b*, *d*, *h*, and *l* possessed the ascender permanently, and *g*, *p*, and *q* acquired permanent descending appendages. Ascenders, derived from cursive writing, were executed with a stroke up and then down, and the resultant club-shaped ascender became a sign of identification in central European manuscripts.

Early writing in the French-German areas under the domination of Clovis and the Merovingian line of rulers seems to have been influenced by cursive writing. Each scriptorium, at Luxeuil, at Corbie, and at other locations, developed individual styles during the sixth and seventh centuries but many manuscripts exhibit typically long descenders and ascenders.

In the century following the death of St. Patrick, ca. 461, numerous monasteries were founded in Ireland. These formed the base for Celtic culture and writing which were profoundly influential in the next three centuries. European manuscripts that influenced the earliest alphabetic writing produced in Irish scriptoria are an unknown quantity, but they appear to have been of the half-Uncial type, with a defined pattern of ascenders and descenders. Many Irish manuscripts of the period are impressive in the manner of the writing and notably in the illumination, which is wildly imaginative. A priceless diamond among these is the magnficent *Book of Kells* or *Codex Cenannensis,* now at Trinity College, Dublin. A facsimile of the *Book of Kells* was published by Urs-Graf-Verlag (Berne, 1951).

The *Book of Kells* was executed in Latin, ca. 800, and contains the lives of Mathew, Mark, Luke, and John, together with other material. In direction, the pens used pointed toward the top edge of the page. Ascenders and descenders were short, and initial strokes attached to *b*, *h*, *l*, *m*, *n*, *r*, and *u* were wedge-shaped and double-stroked. Ligatures were very frequent and in some words all the letters were joined at the shoulder line or the base line or both. Resulting enclosures or voids were randomly tinted with color. Decorated initial letters are seen frequently, and these two features together make a visual feast. The style of the *Book of Kells* is termed Irish majuscule, and the Celtic scribes also developed another style called Irish minuscule, using letter forms much closer to our own lower-case alphabet. Featuring spiky initial strokes, this minuscule style remained in usage for many centuries.

With a zeal for missionary work, Irish monks founded monasteries in Scotland, northern England, and several European areas, including Italy. Through the monastery at Iona, founded ca. 635, Celtic learning spread to centers in northern England. A strong pillar of Irish learning was established at Lindisfarne (now Holy Island) off the east coast of northern England. Here and at other centers, Irish writers taught their majuscule letters to Anglo-Saxon speakers. The high point of this exchange is revealed in the *Lindisfarne Gospels,* a large New Testament manuscript written by Bishop Eadfrith between the years 698 and 721. Written forms are similar to those of the *Book of Kells,* but this is a monumental document in the art of written forms. The original manuscript is now in the British Museum, and a facsimile was issued by Urs-Graf-Verlag in 1956.

This notable manuscript exhibits a gloss or Anglo-Saxon translation between the lines of Latin. During these years Roman letters were used to express Anglo-Saxon speech, except for several sounds expressed by Runic signs. Thus, the Anglo-Saxon minuscule style as seen in such manuscripts as Bede's *History of the English People,* which carries this chronicle to the year 731, exhibits an exceedingly fine semi-cursive style with a pen slant well to the left of vertical. Used for both Latin and Anglo-Saxon, or in effect for both religious and secular needs, the Anglo-Saxon minuscule lasted well beyond the invasion of French speakers in 1066. A tenth century version of this hand may be seen in Figure 6.

A brief renaissance in scholarship took place under Charlemagne, who unified western Europe during the period of his power between 771 and 814. One of the important scholars in Charlemagne's court was an Anglo-Saxon called Alcuin of York. Alcuin, born in 735, had been head of the scriptorium at York and under Charlemagne he became advisor in matters of book production. In this connection he and his staff developed a new book hand called the Carolingian minuscule or Caroline. The book hands existing in Europe before Alcuin's time varied considerably and few were models of legibility, but Carolingian minuscule, developed in the years prior to 800, was remarkable in this respect. For the most part each letter was presented in isolated fashion, with ample space inside and outside the forms. The excessive length of ascenders and descenders was sensibly moderated and the relationship of these appendages to the main body of the minuscule letter was 1:1:1. Relaxed and agreeably cursive, the Carolingian minuscule became through decree the official hand of the Carolingian Renaissance.

Under Alcuin there was a considerable effort to codify the function and style of other letter usage. Important titles were pen-drawn versions of classic Latin inscription capitals; Uncial forms were often used for title material of lesser importance, and the ancient Rustic capitals were also employed for subheadings. Larger letters used in the text were drawn from Uncial or inscription capital forms.

The Carolingian minuscule reform book hand became an international hand in the three centuries after 800. Charlemagne's domination of the Italian peninsula ended below Rome, and south of this line a somewhat separated culture existed in Benevento. There, in Monte Cassino and other monasteries, another book hand was developed in which the pen of execution was pointed more west than north. This distinctive hand seems to have disappeared entirely by the thirteenth century.

Elsewhere in Europe the Carolingian style was executed with changes initiated by local scribes. Distinctive hands are seen in manuscripts emanating from England and Spain where writers used long ascenders in the minuscule. In the eleventh century the style became slightly more cramped, with less space inside the counters and an increasingly stiff interpretation of vertical strokes. This tendency continued in the twelfth century and legibility suffered. At the same time minuscule letters became more vertical, with a pronounced angularity in initial and foot strokes.

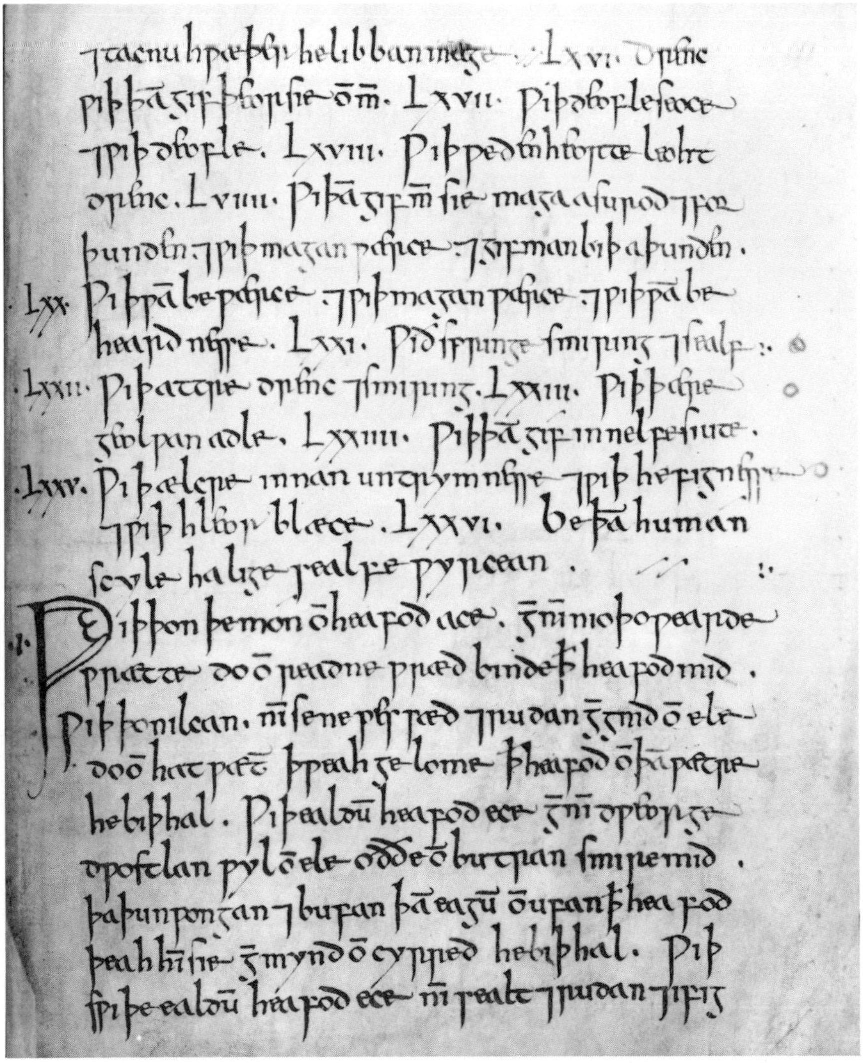

FIGURE 6. *Anglo-Saxon writing, tenth century. British Museum, London.*

These tendencies finally resulted in two new styles in book hands. In northern Europe and in England, this new form became the well-known Black Letter, also termed Old English, and so on. A different version developed by Italian scribes is called Rotunda. Strict dating is impossible in this gradual development, but the styles seem to be distinguishable by 1200. In the Black Letter style of northern Europe, the minuscule letters were executed with a pen cut wide at the nib, giving strong verticals and thin diagonals, and the letters of the minuscule came to lose their distinguishing features. In some manuscripts the letters look like a picket fence. Two principal variations of Black Letter are recognized. One, *textus prescissus,* featured flat feet; and in the other, *textus quadratus,* most letters were given an angular foot. In terms of unity of structural components, Black Letter is a style to be studied, and its visual qualities were most appropriate for the prose of the Old Testament. The Achilles heel of illegibility is, however, an undeniable feature of Black Letter pages. Descendant type designs have limited usage in most countries but were dominant in Germany until 1930, when Roman types gained the advantage.

Rotunda, although vertical and cramped, avoided the excesses of the northern letter because Italian scriptors retained curved parts for letters *b*, *c*, *e*, *d*, *g*, *h*, *o*, *p*, *q*, *r*, *s*, and *z*. In certain manuscripts ascenders and descenders were drastically shortened, permitting many lines per page and, with a lateral condensation, many

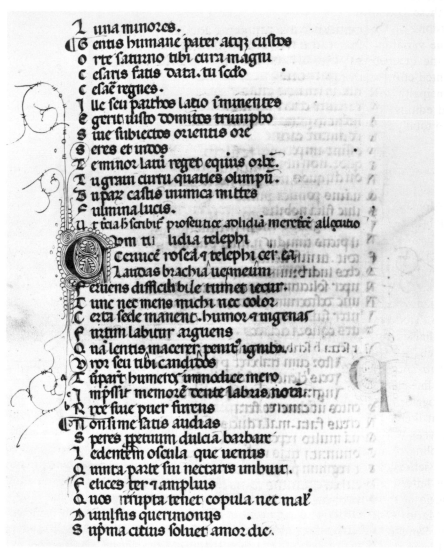

FIGURE 7. *A Horace manuscript in the Rotunda style written in Italy in 1391. British Museum, London.*

characters in a line, but a fundamental play of vertical and curved elements remained inherent in the structure of Rotunda. It survived the distaste of Renaissance humanists mainly through Church usage and was converted to types ca. 1480 in Italy, where its survival was mainly confined to a 100-year period. A few contemporary type designs derive from Rotunda. Termed Round Gothic, its usage is very limited at the present time. A fine example of the Rotunda style, executed in Italy in 1391, is seen in Figure 7.

The pure style of Black Letter was seen in various crosses with cursive writing in the later Middle Ages and well into the Renaissance period. Many fine examples of these Bastarda styles were executed in France, and all of the many manuscript versions of Chaucer's *Canterbury Tales* executed in the fifteenth century feature some variation of this illegible book hand, perpetuated temporarily in type designs of the incunabula period all over Europe and in England through Caxton's first printed efforts on English soil in 1477. Caxton's notable contribution to printing is principally based on about 75 editions printed in English and on his translations and editing. Perhaps in imitating prevailing manuscript forms Caxton is not to be held totally responsible for his ugly and illegible type pages.

The Renaissance and Reform

Alphabetic reform in the Renaissance period is attributable to Humanistic scholars beginning with Petrarch (1304–1374). The great poet wrote a distinctive hand which reflected qualities seen in older manuscripts. In fact it was this quest for original Latin manuscripts that led to the new handwriting. Petrarch possessed a library of 46 manuscripts, of which one-third were written between A.D. 900 and 1100. Coluccio Salutati (1330–1406), a chancellor of Florence and the leader of Humanist scholarship, acquired a library of 800 manuscripts. Of these, one-third were dated between A.D. 800 and 1100. It can be concluded that Coluccio was very familiar with the graceful Carolingian hand in several of its aspects and tried to model his own writing on these older models. These admired letters were called *lettera antica* and it is probable that the Renaissance scholars did not know their true lineage.

Poggio Bracciolini (1380–1459) was the first scholar to transcribe classical Latin literature using the new hand *lettera humanistica* or Humanistic minuscule; the year was most probably 1400. The form of the letters was very much like the Carolingian antecedent and very much like our present Roman minuscule or lower-case letters. Poggio used the ancient Roman inscription form for his capital and title letters, and this was important too. Other trained scholars began to emulate Poggio at the prolific book production centers in Italy. Among these were Antonio di Mario, Giacomo Curlo, Gherardo del Ciriago, Antonio Sinibaldi, and Bartolomeo Sanvito, who was still alive in 1518. Poggio's pen hand of 1406 is reproduced in Figure 8.

In 1465 the Humanistic manuscript hand was converted to types in a rather crude effort by Sweynheym and Pannartz at Subiaco near Rome. A Frenchman,

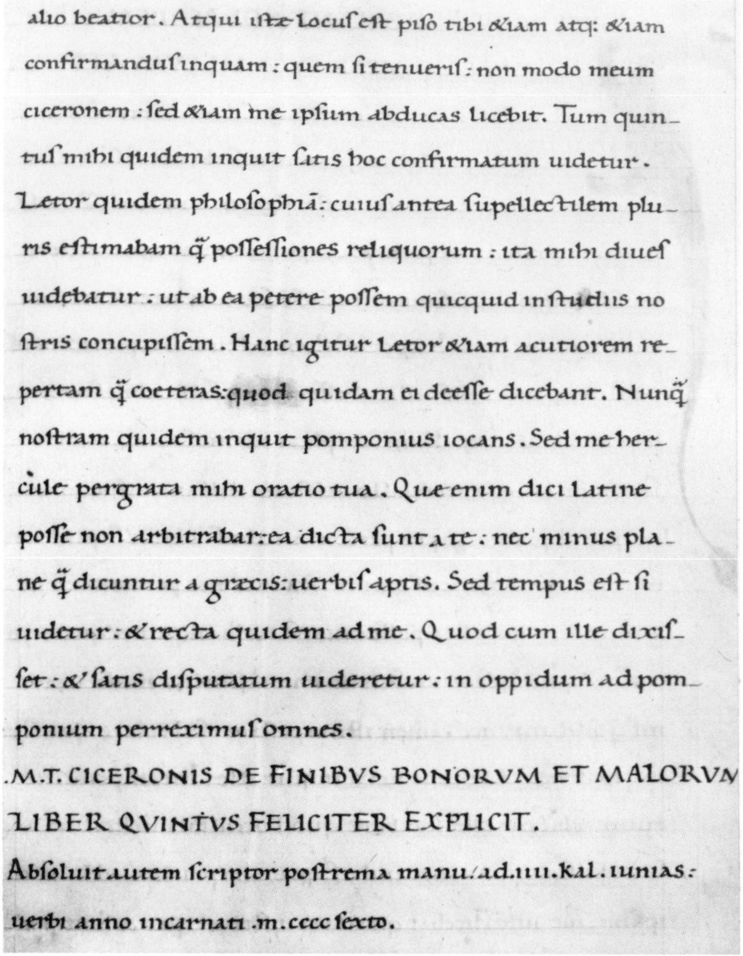

alio beatior. Atqui iste Locus est piso tibi etiam atq: etiam
confirmandus inquam : quem si tenueris: non modo meum
ciceronem : sed etiam me ipsum abducas licebit. Tum quin-
tus mihi quidem inquit satis hoc confirmatum uidetur.
Letor quidem philosophia: cuius antea supellectilem plu-
ris estimabam q possessiones reliquorum : ita mihi dives
uidebatur : ut ab ea petere possem quicquid institutis no
stris concupissem. Hanc igitur Letor etiam acutiorem re-
pertam q coeteras: quod quidam ei deesse dicebant. Nunq
nostram quidem inquit pomponius iocans. Sed me her-
cule pergrata mihi oratio tua. Que enim dici Latine
posse non arbitrabar: ea dicta sunt a te : nec minus plane q dicuntur a graecis: uerbis aptis. Sed tempus est si
uidetur: et recta quidem ad me. Quod cum ille dixis-
set : et satis disputatum uideretur: in oppidum ad pom-
ponium perreximus omnes.
.M.T. CICERONIS DE FINIBVS BONORVM ET MALORVA
LIBER QVINTVS FELICITER EXPLICIT.
Absoluit autem scriptor postrema manu./ad.iiii.kal.iunias:
uerbi anno incarnati .m.cccc sexto.

FIGURE 8. *Humanistic minuscule by Poggio Bracciolini dated 1406. Biblioteca Laurenziana. Florence.*

Nicolas Jenson, understood the manuscript hand better than the two German pioneers of printing in Italy. In 1470 Jenson created the first genuinely beautiful type version of the contemporary scholarly letter forms. Many critics believe that Jenson's pages are unsurpassed to the present day. Jenson followed the scribal practice and used the ancient Latin capital form for printed capitals. The style originated by Jenson and other fine printers in Venice is termed Venetian. The Venetian type designs have been influential in more recent times. Jenson's model was the basic influence in Centaur, designed by the distinguished American book designer Bruce Rogers. Rogers began work on Centaur around 1914 and the design was used in the Oxford Lectern Bible, one of the finest books of the century.

While Nicolas Jenson printed about 150 books, the books and types initiated by Aldus Manutius, a genuine Renaissance prototype, were more influential. Manutius set up a printing establishment in Venice in 1495. He initiated a Greek font and with the aid of Francesco Griffo, designer and punch cutter, created a new Roman minuscule and capital font. This type was used to print the famous *Hypneroto-machia Poliphili* by Francesco Colonna which Manutius published in 1499. Artistically, Griffo's design was the first to bring small and capital letters into an integrated relationship. Through sales in Europe, Griffo's designs became well known, influencing Claude Garamond and generations of capable type designers in France. Most contemporary book faces owe much to the Manutius–Griffo types. A most distinguished design based directly on these early types is Bembo, developed by the Monotype Corporation Ltd., London, in 1929.

Italic, the sloped version of *lettera antica,* grew out of the personal writing of Humanistic scholars. Individual cursive pen styles had existed in Roman times and this personal identity in written forms pervaded the *lettera antica* of Carolingian forms early in the fifteenth century. Noted writing in this style was executed by Niccolo Niccoli (1363–1437), a Florentine scholar of inherited wealth who collected some 800 manuscript volumes. His hand of 1427 shows that some letters were executed separately, as in Poggio's hand, but others were joined in the natural

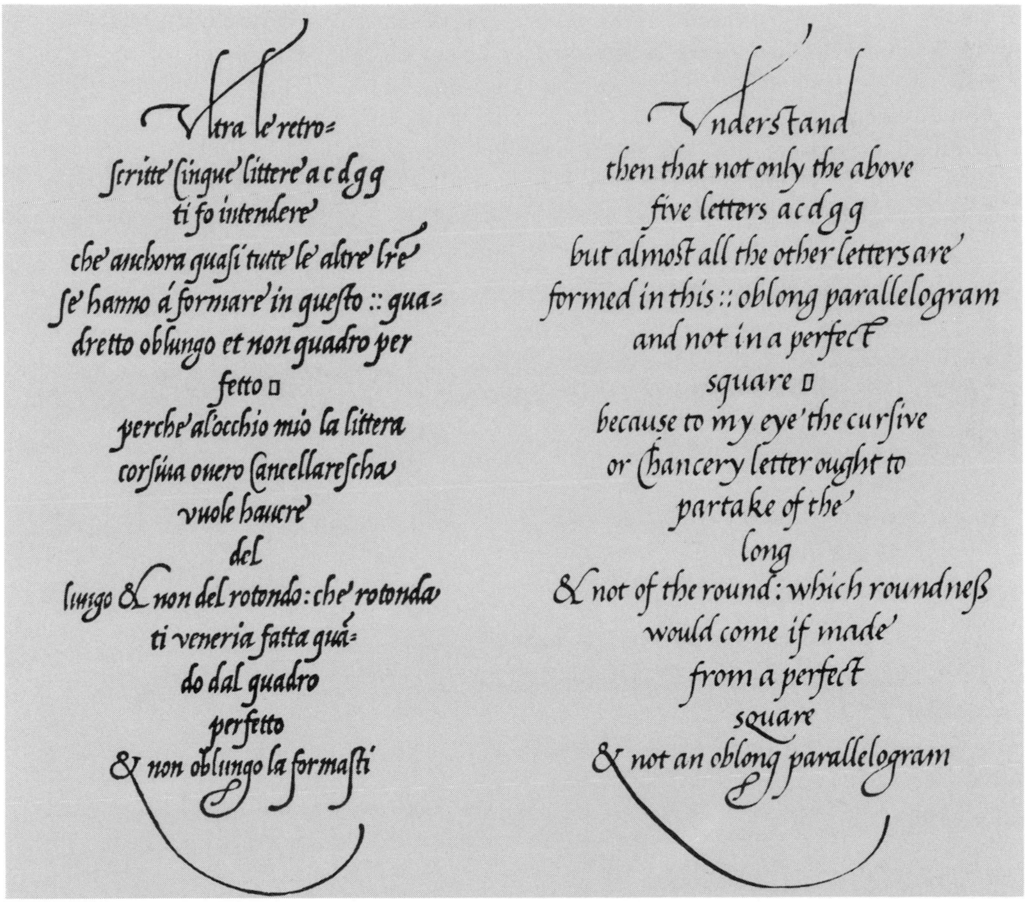

FIGURE 9. *Original writing by Arrighi (left) and John Howard Benson's transcription (right) from* The First Writing Book: Arrighi's Operina, *Yale University Press, 1954.*

consequence of swift hand movements. Niccoli's verticals slant in the natural manner of right-handed penmen.

Slow to become an established hand, the Renaissance formal cursive is seen in development in the styles of Pietro Cennini between 1462 and 1474, the remarkable Marcus de Cribellarus, a Venetian whose colophon read *calamo volanti,* the superb Bartolomeo Sanvito, Antonio Sinibaldi, and anonymous scribes. By 1480 this Humanistic cursive could be designated a unique form of Renaissance writing separate from the upright form because several scribes could do either at will.

The first version cut in types was designed by the Manutius–Griffo team in 1500. Manutius needed a smaller book and the first Italic font by Griffo was on the order of a 12-point type, very small in comparison to the upright Roman types of that era. The first semicursive types by Griffo bear a remarkable resemblance to the personal handwriting of Pompaneo Leto, an important scholar in Rome.

The Italic hand was perfected by a succession of scribes in the Papal office— whence the name, Chancery, in current usage. This script was the principal form of writing to be observed in the first writing manual, published by Arrighi (Vicentino) in 1522. This manual, *La Operina,* was a sensitive interpretation of the author's hand-written models cut in relief on wood blocks. Subsequent writing manuals by Giovanbattista Palatino and Giovanantonio Tagliente, famed scribes, contained many pages devoted to the Chancery cursive form, and it was then featured in writing manuals issued in other European centers. It was, however, never popular in Germany. Arrighi's italic, with John Howard Benson's transcription, is seen in Figure 9.

Undeniably talented, sixteenth century writing masters made something of a

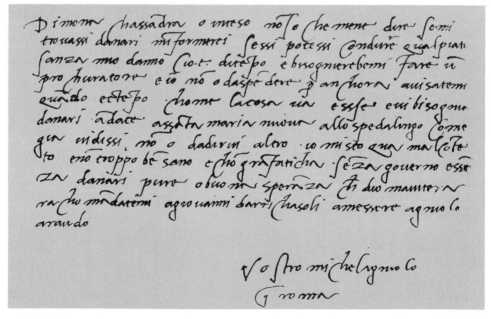

FIGURE 10. *The cursive hand of Michelangelo, dated 1508. British Museum, London.*

formula of the Chancery hand, but gifted "amateurs" such as Raphael, Cellini, and notably Michelangelo gave it a refreshing rendering. Michelangelo's hand appears in a letter dated 1509, Figure 10.

The Chancery script became popular in England among the scholars, secretaries, and teachers around Henry VIII after 1508. Some royal offspring learned the hand at a very early age. Roger Ascham, a Greek scholar who wrote elegant letters for Cambridge, became tutor to Princess Elizabeth in 1548 and she wrote a good cursive hand after becoming Queen. Bartholomew Dodington (1536–1595), a professor of Greek at Cambridge, was a particularly fine writer, the equal of Italy's best.

After Griffo cut the first Italic types in 1500, Arrighi followed with a version in 1523 which was no artistic success. Arrighi's second design, with punch cutting by Lautitio di Meo de Rotelli, a skilled metal worker, was much more successful and still retained something of Arrighi's now famous pen hand. Italic types used by Antonio Blado, who was appointed printer to the Holy See, were also influential in the middle decades of the sixteenth century. These designs were largely the work of Arrighi. In the first 100 years of its existence, Italic in types was not an auxiliary face. Whole books were printed in Italic types. Modern designs based on these early calligraphic type designs are Arrighi, Bembo Condensed Italic, Blado, Lutetia, and Spectrum.

Writing Masters

The publication of *La Operina* in 1522 ushered in the age of the writing master and his writing manual. Tagliente published his *Lo presente libro insegna* etc. in 1524 and, according to Alfred Fairbank, this manual went through 30 editions. Palatino published *Libro nuovo d'imparare a scrivere* in 1540. Other famous manuals were published by Vespasiano Amphiareo (1548), Ferdinando Ruano (1554), and Giovan Francesco Cresci, a Vatican scribe. Cresci's first manual was *Essemplare di più sorti lettere,* published in Rome in 1560. This manual was printed by the famous house of Blado. A second manual, *Il perfetto scrittore,* was published in Cresci's own printing house in 1570. A remarkable engraver named Francesco Aureri cut the wood blocks for both manuals. Each manual contained a fine set of Roman capitals. Cresci was one of the few masters of the century who studied ancient inscription forms as seen at the base of Trajan's Column (not arch) in Rome.

These manuals, along with those produced in Spain by Juan de Yciar (1550), Francisco Lucas (1577), and the German Johann Neudorffer (1538), were among the art manuals of the century. They not only pioneered the new humanistic hands, upright and Italic, but preserved national remnants of hands descending from the late Middle Ages, obscure clerical hands, and initiated decorative alphabets. These fascinating manuals were produced by carving letters in relief or intaglio on end-grain wood blocks. The method, difficult enough, did not encourage virtuosity. There was a gradual change to intaglio metal production of images for writing manuals, however, and this development encouraged brilliant and hollow burin virtuosity. The first manual printed from metal plates was *Lo scrittore utile* by Giulantonio Hercolani, which appeared in 1574.

Perhaps the only genuinely new writing form to emerge from the burin technology was the continuous cursive, a formal application of the unbroken flow of forms seen in ordinary handwriting. This form was termed Ronde in France, Round Hand in England, and Spencerian in the United States after Platt R. Spencer, a successful nineteenth century publisher of business writing methods.

In the seventeenth and eighteenth centuries writing styles were increasingly designed to meet the needs of a rising commercial class. Writing masters often ran schools to train youth in writing, arithmetic, and commercial forms. Many writing masters in England became prosperous, vain, and pompous figures, quarreling with rivals in the public press and demonstrating the temperament of opera singers. Benjamin D'Israeli took note of these outrageous capers and was moved to dissect the "maniacal vanity" of England's writing masters in a choice essay.

William Morris

Although the art of writing was bent to meet the demands of commercial necessity, there was a serious decline in taste, and in the nineteenth century old values were lost. It was this trend that led to the modern revival of pen calligraphy and the emergence of the private press as an art form. Both of these related movements can be traced back to William Morris (1835–1896). Morris, the great thinker on social reform, began penning his own manuscripts about 1870. Believing that writing was important, he studied manuscripts of the Middle Ages and the Renaissance. His *Odes of Horace,* now in the Bodleian Library of Oxford University, is executed in a Renaissance cursive form and generously illuminated. A notable effort by Morris was his rendition of *Beowulf.* Figure 11 reproduces two facing pages of the Horace written by Morris.

There were, of course, private presses before Morris established the Kelmscott Press in 1891, but the Kelmscott Press initiated an important movement in private printing which was widely influential. Printing skill at the Kelmscott Press was furnished by Emery Walker. First efforts of the press used existing type, but Morris, Walker, and their fellow workers designed three new type faces to carry texts selected or written by Morris. Golden Type, an upright Roman, was influenced by the types of Jacques de Rouge, a printer in Venice in the years 1472–1478. The other two designs were based on Rotunda, a manuscript style of the late Middle Ages. The larger of these Round Gothic designs was named Troy and was 17 points in height. A smaller version was called Chaucer.

Five other influential presses were established in England in or before 1900: the Vale Press, the Ashendene Press, the Doves Press, the Essex House Press, and the Eragny Press. The Doves Press, founded by Emery Walker and Thomas James Cobden-Sanderson, was especially distinguished. Dublin's Cuala Press was established in 1902 and published the works of William Butler Yeats and his circle. In

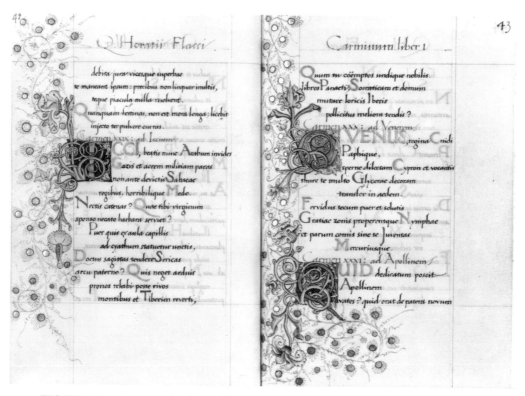

FIGURE 11. *A manuscript by William Morris. Bodleian Library, Oxford University.*

Sweden the printing of Waldemar Zachrisson was important, and in Germany the Janus Press and the Ernst Ludwig Press were influential in the first decade of the century. In the United States the Merrymount Press was established in Boston by Daniel Berkeley Updike in 1893. Architect Bertram Grosvenor Goodhue designed a large Roman type called Merrymount for certain texts published by this important press. Frederic W. Goudy started the Village Press in Park Ridge, Illinois, in 1903. His first book was an essay, *Printing,* by Emery Walker and William Morris. Goudy enjoyed a long and successful career as a printer and designed many distinguished type faces. These efforts inspired others to set up presses and engage in fine printing.

Calligraphy and the London Circle

In calligraphy, people in England began writing personal correspondence in historical hands on the inspiration of William Morris. Poet Robert Bridges and his wife were among these and worked for reform in hand scripts. Easily the most important figure in this calligraphic revival was Edward Johnston (1872–1944), who made a careful study of ancient manuscript styles in the collections of the

British Museum and other important libraries in England. Johnston extracted the meaning in these manuscripts and found out how they had been written. He began teaching classes based on his researches at the suggestion of a sympathetic school man, W. R. Lethaby. The first class was held at London's Central School of Arts and Crafts in 1899. One of Johnston's finest students, Graily Hewitt, stayed on at the Central School when Lethaby and Johnston moved their operation to the Royal College of Art in South Kensington in 1901.

Johnston's brilliant students were to have a profound effect upon manuscript writing, inscription writing, and type design in the following decades, not only in England but also in Europe and the United States. In addition to Hewitt, the early classes included the great Eric Gill and Percy Smith. In 1906 Johnston issued *Writing & Illuminating & Lettering,* perhaps the most influential book on writing to be published in this century. It contained in about 500 small-format pages the essentials of Johnston's knowledge of earlier writing styles, and the volume is still in print.

Johnston's foundation hand (Figure 12) was based on late Carolingian manuscripts from British collections. His Roman or Renaissance writing was heavily influenced by book hands of the Middle Ages.

New Efforts in Europe

In Europe a somewhat parallel revival was initiated in Vienna by Rudolf von Larisch, who published a manual in 1906. The movement in central Europe was not confined to calligraphy, inscription writing, and type design but included many craft areas. Anna Simons, a native of Prussia, studied with Johnston and in 1905 began teaching courses in calligraphy in Dusseldorf. These courses were quite suc-

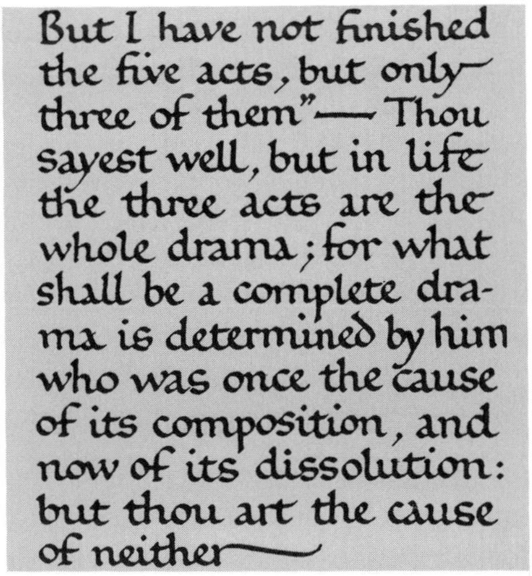

But I have not finished the five acts, but only three of them"— Thou sayest well, but in life the three acts are the whole drama; for what shall be a complete drama is determined by him who was once the cause of its composition, and now of its dissolution: but thou art the cause of neither—

FIGURE 12. *Edward Johnston's foundation hand. From* Writing & Illuminating & Lettering, *Sir Isaac Pitman and Sons.*

cessful, and in 1910 Simons effected a translation of Johnston's text into German. Other important figures in Germany include Ernst Schneidler of the Stuttgart Akademie, whose *Der Wassermann* in four portfolio volumes was published in 1933, and Rudolph Koch, who established an important workshop in Offenbach. Like Johnston, Koch trained a number of students who became well-known calligraphers, type designers, and graphic artists: Berthold Wolpe in England, Fritz Kredel and Warren Chappell in the United States, and Henri Friedlaender, now Director of the Hadassah Apprentice School of Printing in Jerusalem. Friedlaender is also an expert on modern Hebrew calligraphic styles.

Continuing a great German tradition in calligraphy and type design were Otto Echmann, Walter Tieman, Fritz Helmuth Ehmcke, and Emil Weiss. Jan Tschichold, involved in Bauhaus typography in the third decade of the century, later became interested in the more traditional aspects of typography. A prolific author and careful scholar, Tschichold, still active in 1969, has recently designed an elegant type font called Sabon Antiqua.

Continuing this early line of excellence is the incomparable Hermann Zapf of Frankfurt. A superb calligrapher, self-taught with the help of Johnston's book and Koch's work, Zapf has produced many type designs for the Stempel type foundry. Among these are a modified sans serif, Optima, and a fine Roman called Palatino.

Regarding German efforts, special mention should be made of *Aventur und Kunst* (Frankfurt, 1940), the finest survey book on the history of printing ever assembled. This remarkable example of printing on the subject of printing was compiled under the direction of Dr. Konrad F. Bauer, a veteran art director at Bauersche Giesseri, the distinguished type house in Frankfurt.

In Czechoslovakia the great man of letter design was Oldrich Menhart (1897–1961). Menhart was not only a fine calligrapher, engraver, and illustrator but also designed books and type faces. Akke Kumlien and Waldemar Zachrisson were among the leaders in printing and book design in Sweden. Karl-Eric Forsberg, Bror Zachrisson, and Erik Lindegren, a most talented calligrapher, carry on this earlier tradition. In Denmark, Bent Rohde is a well-known calligrapher and author on writing.

Jan van Krimpen (1892–1958) is one of the grand men of letter design in Holland. In association with the famous type house of Enschedé en Zonen, van Krimpen designed many beautiful type faces. S. H. de Roos (1877–1962) was another distinguished Dutch designer of letters. His type designs are too numerous to mention, but Erasmus, Egmont, and Libra received wide acclaim and distribution. Chris Brand, a talented calligrapher, was born in Utrecht in 1921. In association with Ben Englehart, Brand has produced a fine series for primary schools called Ritmisch Schrijven.

Walter Kaech, a graphic designer in Zurich, is a fine calligrapher and has published a number of books, among which is *Rhythm and Proportion in Lettering*.

In Italy Alessandro Butti (1893–1959) was a prominent figure in type design. Aldo Novarese continues this fine work for the house of Nebiolo. Hans Mardersteig, founder of the famous Officina Bodoni, deserves special mention. In addition to directing one of the finest printing houses in the world, Mardersteig has pro-

duced many fine facsimile editions of such writing masters as Arrighi, Brun, Cele-
brino, Feliciano, Mercator, and Pacioli, using the finest types available. Mardersteig's contributions to scholarship and printing are indeed remarkable.

Scholarship in England

Britain's leadership in calligraphy was based on very sound investigations into
the history of past endeavors in calligraphy, wood engraving, type design, and
bookmaking. Morris, Johnston, Eric Gill, Graily Hewitt, Percy Smith, and Sir Sydney Cockerell were all motivated by a sense of the past and all of them wrote on
the subject of writing. These investigations continued under the brilliant leadership
of the late Stanley Morison, who died in 1967. Morison's contribution to the
understanding of calligraphy and type design is beyond present evaluation. A tireless worker, Morison put his penetrating intellect to many ventures, not the least of
which was a new program in type design for the Monotype firm. Although many
participated in advancing this program, Morison was its spiritual leader and personally designed the famous Times Roman font.

Frederic Warde was also an outstanding figure in Britain's history of calligraphy
and scholarship. Warde supervised an edition of Arrighi's manual of 1522 in facsimile in 1926. He designed the elegant Arrighi Italic font for the Monotype Corporation in England, still much admired among fine printers. Unfortunately
Warde's career was cut short midway in the 1940s.

Alfred Forbes Johnson and the late James Wardrop also contributed zealous
efforts in scholarship. Among other works, Johnson produced a bibliography of
sixteenth century writing master manuals, and Wardrop's most notable effort centered on *The Script of Humanism,* published by the Oxford University Press in
1963. Wardrop's notes are significant, and special stress is placed on the gifted
Renaissance scribe Bartolomeo Sanvito.

The editing of Oliver Simon in *The Fleuron* and *Signature* was also very noteworthy in the continuing reevaluation following the Johnston impact. Mervyn C.
Oliver, a famous teacher, also contributed writing, as did Nicolette Gray and the
late Beatrice Ward, who used the pseudonym Paul Beaujon. John Ryder, C. M.
Lamb, A. S. Osley, Berthold Wolpe, John C. Tarr, James Moran, James Mosley,
and Alfred Fairbank are others contributing to scholarship emanating from
England.

Fairbank's special interest was the Italic form in calligraphy. After some years
of studying Renaissance hands, Fairbank in 1926 began to make individual copy
books for friends in the Society of Scribes and Illuminators. His early Italic letters
were largely his own, although he was impressed by the diagonal joins of Tagliente
and the curvature of Lucas. Fairbank's work was accepted widely and his volume
A Book of Scripts was enormously popular. His research led to the successful type
font Condensed Bembo Italic, designed for the Monotype Corporation, and to the
discovery of several important Renaissance scribes, among them Antonio Torphio,
Ludovicus Regius, and Bartholomew Dodington.

Johnston and the early contributors to the revival of calligraphy were succeeded by other accomplished calligraphers and teachers of this and allied subjects. It is interesting to note that in Britain teaching has produced many talented women. Among those connected with the Johnston-Hewitt era were, in addition to Oliver, Irene Wellington, Dorothy Mahoney, Thomas W. Swindlehurst, Rosemary Ratcliffe, Reynolds Stone (a fine engraver), Margery Raisbeck, Irene Base, Will Carter (a carver and printer), Madelyn Walker, Louise Powell, William Gardner, John Woodcock, Pamela Wrightson, Dorothy Hutton, Florence Kingsford (Lady Sydney Cockerell), Margaret Alexander, C. Harry Adams, and Margaret Adams.

Continuing this line were Freda Hands, Joan Pillsbury, Heather Child, Ann Camp, Stuart Barrie, Sheila Waters, and Marie Angel, all very talented individuals.

Calligraphy and Design in the United States

In the United States the response to Johnston's work was a generation late, and reform in areas of printing, book design, and type design had appeared earlier and was rather based on the work of Morris and the resultant effort in printing and bookmaking. No figure in the United States in individual enterprise cast a shadow as large as Morris did, but active efforts were made. Daniel Berkeley Updike, founder of the Merrymount Press in 1893, published his memorable *Printing Types* in 1922. The original manuscript was read by Rudolph Ruzicka and parts of it were read by William A. Dwiggens. Both continued to apply their distinguished talents to the fresh American enterprise. Dwiggens (1880–1956) was a man of many talents and interests. He became a fine calligrapher, and designed many excellent type fonts for Mergenthaler Linotype Company. Dwiggens also designed books and jackets for Alfred A. Knopf for over 30 years. His excellent skills were augmented by helpful contacts with a great number of workers in the field.

Ruzicka is also blessed with many talents. An engraver of great skill, his impressive reputation resides chiefly in the many type designs he has executed for the Mergenthaler Linotype Company. His Fairfield series of Roman types is considered something of a classic.

Frederic Goudy (1865–1945) and Bruce Rogers (1870–1957) were also strongly influential in the first half of the twentieth century. Goudy, as mentioned, initiated his Village Press in 1903 and printed books for most of the remainder of his career. Goudy was also an author; his *The Alphabet and Elements of Lettering* dates back to 1918 and more recently appeared in a fine edition produced by the University of California Press. Goudy designed well over 100 type faces, and a great number of them are produced by the Monotype Corporation of America. After some years of struggle, Goudy became successful with types named Kennerly Old Style in 1911. He drew the capitals and lower-case letters for this font in 1 week.

Rogers' chief contribution was in the area of book design, the careful control of all the elements that go to make up a beautiful and legible book. He was a superb artist with type, and coined the word "typistry" to describe his work in that area of production. During his long career Rogers directed presswork for both Cambridge and Oxford Universities in England.

Although a few calligraphers from the United States studied in England in the early decades of this century, real progress in the area of calligraphy seems to have been marked by two books. The first of these, *The Technique of Manuscript Writing* by Marjorie Wise, appeared in 1924. This volume sold about 1000 copies a year for at least 20 years. Frances M. Moore produced the second book in 1926, *Handwriting for the Broad-Edged Pen,* which was a manual with copy books. Miss Moore, a teacher, had studied with Graily Hewitt in 1923. Later she turned to more scholarly work and has been influential among calligraphers for many years.

Since 1926 Paul Standard has been busy promoting calligraphy in various ways, first through his superb artistic accomplishments and also through his inspiring teaching in the New York area and through his writings. In 1947 Standard's article *Our Handwriting,* published in *Women's Day,* reached millions of readers, but the jewel among Standard's works is the brilliantly illustrated essay, *Calligraphy's Flowering, Decay and Restoration,* published by the Society of Typographic Arts (Chicago, 1947). Now a senior critic in the United States, Standard writes penetrating reviews for *Publishers Weekly* and other journals.

The late George Salter was also an important teacher in New York. Salter was trained in Germany and arrived in New York in 1934. While he executed many designs for publication, including many book jackets, he is principally remembered for his disciplined teaching of letter forms at Cooper Union over a period of 30 years. A most elegant part of Salter's work is seen in *Am Wegesrand* (*On the Roadside*), a collaboration with his distinguished countryman Fritz Kredel published in Frankfurt in 1962 by Bauerische Giesserei, the type house.

Alexander Nesbitt is another important eastern teacher of calligraphy. Born in 1901, Nesbitt studied at the Art Students League in New York and traveled and studied in Germany. His career as a designer and teacher is notable and among his published works is the excellent review *The History and Technique of Lettering,* available currently in a reprint.

Oscar Ogg, another honored veteran in the field of letter usage, founded the calligraphic work at Columbia University in 1946. His book designs and jacket designs have won numerous awards, and in 1948 he published *The 26 Letters.* Later Ogg arranged a facsimile of three important writing masters, Arrighi, Tagliente, and Palatino in a 1953 production titled *Three Classics of Italian Calligraphy.* This was a most valuable contribution to the field.

The untimely death of John Howard Benson in 1956 cut short a distinguished career as calligrapher, author, teacher, and stone carver. Benson taught at the Rhode Island School of Design and revived the John Stevens shop of inscription writing in Newport, Rhode Island. With Arthur G. Carey, he wrote *Elements of Lettering,* a fine text of wide influence. One of Benson's finest projects was a transcription of Arrighi's *La Operina,* and one of his students, Crimilda Pontes, produced *Instruments of Writing,* a translation of Palatino's treatise by the Rev. Henry K. Pierce to which Benson contributed technical notes. Philip Hofer, the eminent collector, librarian, and scholar at Harvard, wrote of Benson's work in *Typophile* in 1957.

Another fine eastern artist is Warren Chappell of Norwalk, Connecticut. Chappell studied at the Art Students League and in Germany with Koch, by whom he was strongly influenced. Strong in calligraphy, illustration, and design, he is the author of the series of type faces named Lydian. In 1935 he wrote *The Anatomy of Lettering,* motivated by the demise of Koch a year earlier.

Edward Karr, an outstanding calligrapher and designer in Boston, has exhibited widely. He has had a long career as a teacher at the Museum of Fine Arts School in Boston. Fred Eager of Grand Island, New York, has long been an expert advocate of the Italic hand and produces an interesting newsletter featuring articles on various calligraphers. Eager's company furnishes information and materials for scribal practice.

Freeman Craw is another accomplished designer and calligrapher associated with the New York area. Craw's name is connected with several successful type faces. Enid Eder Perkins, a native New Yorker, studied with Arnold Bank and in England with Irene Base. Thus, for many years she has been one of the calligraphers in the United States with special talents in the art of illumination, an art strongly pursued in England but not in the United States. Other noted calligraphers and designers having past or present connections with the New York area are Hollis Holland, Philip Grushkin, Jeanyee Wong, Martin D. Oberstein, Fridolf Johnson, Catherine Fournier, and Reynard Biemiller.

Arnold Bank, a genuine veteran of calligraphic practice and instruction in the United States, now teaches at the Carnegie-Mellon Institute in Pittsburgh. Bank, a colorful and inspiring teacher, spent his early teaching career in the New York area and a part of the 1950s in England as a Fulbright scholar. Bank's experimental work has been exhibited widely.

Chicago and the Newberry Circle

Calligraphic enterprise in the Chicago area centered on the Newberry circle and Ernst Detterer (1888–1947). Detterer studied with Johnston in 1913 and taught at the Art Institute of Chicago from 1921 to 1931. He was known as a strict and persistent teacher. In 1931 Detterer became curator of the distinguished John M. Wing Foundation of the Newberry Library in Chicago, which now houses a brilliant collection of manuscripts and printing specimens. Many of Detterer's unpublished studies in the history of letter formation are now in the Newberry Library where Detterer started a study group in calligraphy in 1941. At one time or another this group included such members as Ray Da Boll, R. Hunter Middleton, Rodney Chirpe, James Hayes, and Joseph Carter. Detterer's own calligraphy was strongly influenced by Johnston, and some of his students felt this emphasis.

Ray Da Boll, born in 1892, had considerable experience in graphic enterprises before becoming interested in calligraphy at an exhibition of Johnston's work in 1937. He became a superb calligrapher, initiating a number of fine projects. Now residing in Arkansas, Da Boll is still quite active.

R. Hunter Middleton became an accomplished calligrapher but is best known for his work in type design for the Ludlow Typograph Company in Chicago. Middleton's reputation in this connection is quite secure for this century. It is interesting to note that Detterer developed a Venetian type named Eusebius in 1928 and that Middleton completed its development later.

After Detterer's departure in 1947, the study group at the Newberry Library was led by James Hayes and James M. Wells until 1960. Wells, a former Fellow of the American Council of Learned Societies in London, is currently Associate Director of the Newberry Library and a distinguished authority on the history of printing and calligraphy. Hayes has enjoyed a reputation as the finest professional calligrapher in the midwest area for many years. He also produced an excellent study, *The Roman Letter,* for the R. R. Donnelley printing firm in Chicago in 1951.

At midwestern universities the study of calligraphy and fine printing is by no means a major activity within art departments. Programs at the University of Indiana, Michigan State University, and the University of Wisconsin are respectable, and the University of Iowa employs resident printers, currently Harry Duncan and Kim Merker.

Father Edward Catich, a teacher at St. Ambrose College in Davenport, Iowa, is in a separate class. Catich, a native of Montana, became an expert sign writer in Chicago before becoming interested in Roman inscription forms during the 1930s. He is now one of the finest inscription writers alive and has executed many important commissions in the United States. His recent theory on the origin of serif structure in ancient Roman inscriptions can be found in *The Origin of the Serif,* published in 1969. This is undoubtedly the most serious paleographic study now available on this subject, which is unaccountably shrouded in the speculations of amateurs in all countries.

West Coast Calligraphy

West coast activities in calligraphy and teaching are led by Lloyd Reynolds at Reed College, Portland, Oregon. Similar to many other veteran teachers in the United States, Reynolds was mainly self-taught, with help from Johnston's book and from Arnold Bank and other friends. An important exhibition of calligraphy at the Portland Art Museum in 1958 was largely the result of Reynolds' efforts. A number of professionals in the area attest to Reynolds' influence among resident scribes, such as Norman Paasche, Shirley Orbeck, Clyde Van Cleve, and Jacqueline Svaron. The influence of important teaching methods in calligraphy is evident in the work of students from Marylhurst College, Marylhurst, Oregon. This work is under the direction of Sister Loyola Mary, whose personal writing hand is simply unexcelled.

The California group of calligraphers is headed by men of wide experience. Byron Mac Donald of San Francisco, like Edward Catich, learned the trade of showcard writing before he became interested in fine pen writing. He is master of many styles and in particular can produce impressive works with strong and heavy letters. MacDonald's range can be observed in part in his book *The Art of Lettering: The Broad Pen,* published in 1966.

Maury Nemoy of Los Angeles is an outstanding and original calligrapher. A designer of broad talents, he has executed hundreds of commissions for motion pictures, television, and record albums. Nemoy's teaching is generally associated with the University of California at Los Angeles, and he has, with the help of Henri Friedlaender of Jerusalem, done original work in the Hebrew scripts.

Egdon Margo, born in Boston, is another superb calligrapher working in Los Angeles. Margo studied at the Art Students League in New York and was well underway in a career in Washington, D.C. when he enlisted in the Air Force and was sent to England. While there, his interest in calligraphy was sparked by a student of Johnston. Margo has for some years augmented his efforts by becoming a printer, in part using neglected fonts.

The late Warren W. Ferris, artist, typographer, and calligrapher, spent the last 15 years of his full career in Los Altos, California. Ferris, born in 1890, enlisted in World War I and stayed on to sketch in France after the armistice. Later, in Washington, D.C., he designed for printing or wrote in handscript many important documents. In the era of Franklin D. Roosevelt, Ferris came close to playing the role of court scribe, although this contribution has been overlooked in recent years. Even in retirement in California, he executed many important commissions in an intimate connection with Stanford University, which provided him with working space near its rare book collection where he continued to pursue the great writing of the past.

Certainly calligraphic enterprise in the United States is marked by unique individuals, strong in personal conviction, many of whom are self-taught and "loners" so to speak. The genius of Catich, a native of Montana, should occasionally be expected in the history of this country, even as Goudy came out of prairie life to achieve an international reputation with his types. Yet it should be said that calligraphers in the United States still remain in the penumbra of Johnston and Fairbank, unable to shake Arrighi and achieve new forms of expression. In this sense, Britain's new discovery of old writing in 1900 declines in value as the years progress.

DONALD M. ANDERSON

CAMBRIDGE LANGUAGE RESEARCH UNIT (CLRU)
See also *Clumps, Theory of*

The CLRU came into formal existence in 1956 to deal with basic problems of the working of language and the application to machine translation of any progress that could be made on them. Since then CLRU's interests have broadened considerably, so it is appropriate to look afresh at the field with which CLRU concerns itself.

CLRU has had six main fields of corporate interest, though individual members of it have from time to time pursued further lines of research:

1. Semantic thesauri interpreted as a product of lattices that could be operated upon with Peek-a-Boo techniques.
2. Construction and operation of a machine-handleable Interlingua with about 50 primitive semantic elements, which could also be interpreted as a set of information retrieval descriptors.
3. Automatic multiple classification (Clumps).
4. Automatic segmentation of written text into "phrasings," thus permitting phrasing-by-phrasing syntactic analyses and also phrasing-by-phrasing machine translation.
5. Studies of algebraic hierarchies within Brouwer free choice systems, including digital and analog simulations (partly in collaboration with Gordon Pask).
6. Computer science; in particular the development of multiaccess systems, especially on small machines; and the development of on-line systems useful for the understanding of natural language.

As can be seen from the above, almost everything CLRU does is concerned with information processing in a very broad sense (for example, there is little work done that could not appropriately be reported at the periodic Congress of the International Federation for Information Processing), though this itself is far too wide a statement. Work has extended from syntax and semantics of natural languages into the cognate area of information retrieval, which in its turn has led to comparatively abstract work on classification theory, without any of the original lines being lost. Concurrently the necessity to have convenient means of carrying out the computations of language data-processing has led to research programming languages and notations, and further development in the field of on-line computer operating systems. The emphasis here is on special-purpose multiaccess on-line systems using small machines with large disks, with a view to making dictionary and thesaurus information readily accessible to those who want it in an economical manner.

Over the years, then, CLRU has developed skills in a wide range of subjects, all of which are of considerable difficulty, and which are of continuing interest to a great many other research workers. The most general statement that can be made is that all the work has taken its stimulus from the desire to perform definite (i.e., mechanizable) operations on material derived from systems that have some or all of the properties of natural language. The relevant problems are those of scale, complexity, and variability. The need to handle large quantities of text led directly to the interest in computing.

The complexity and variability of natural language material has led to the interest in developing a simplified basic picture of language rather than to detailed forays into examining diversified languages, and to finding ways of describing and encoding the syntactic and semantic classification, both by human and automatice means. The need to be able to perform operation on texts economically has led to studies of simplified methods of text segmentation, to avoid the complexities inherent in textual analysis programs as previously conceived.

Accordingly, the field of action of the CLRU is different both from academic linguistics, to which questions of practical feasibility are largely irrelevant, and from computer science, which is concerned with advancing the art of computation without particular reference to any special class of computer usage. In spite of its evident centrality and importance to all mechanized data processing that requires analysis of natural language, there is as yet no convenient word or phrase in general currency that satisfactorily sums up the field in question; the intention of this contribution is to delineate it discursively.

Workpaper List

The CLRU workpaper list provides a naturally developing, informal, but also authentic record of what might be called the "flow of ideas" characteristic of CLRU.

For this reason, it has been printed in its entirety, without emendations (other than the substitution of full names for initials); and without "tidying up." Where two authors writing two papers in collaboration have reversed the order of their two names, for example, we have left the reversal, since it probably means that the author whose name is placed first wrote most of the paper. Where, for inscrutable reasons, there are gaps in the numbering, we have left these gaps also; so that the numbers opposite to the titles in this list physically correspond to sets of artifacts stored in CLRU boxes.

On the whole the workpapers—contrasting in this respect with the lists of formal publications that follow them—deal with work actually developed in CLRU; they do not comment on authors or theories. They are thus valuable as a record of the thinking that occurred, even when their expository style or critical standard leaves something to be desired.

Author	Title of Paper	Number
Margaret Masterman	The Potentialities of a Mechanical Thesaurus.	1
A. F. Parker-Rhodes	Appendix to No. 1. Application of the Lattice Syntax-Programme to the Translation of the Italian Paragraph, Showing in Detail Its Transformation from Output I to Output II.	2
M. A. K. Halliday	The Linguistic Basis of the Thesaurus-Type Mechanical Dictionary and Its Application to English Preposition Classification.	3
CLRU	Annexe 5. An Account of the Pilot Project of the CLRU (Chinese Sentence).	4
R. H. Richens	A General Programme for Mechanical Translation between Any Two Languages via an Algebraic Interlingua.	5

Author	Title of Paper	Number
CLRU	Broadcast: "Programming the Inexactness of Language."	6
CLRU	Meeting at King's College.	7
A. F. Parker-Rhodes	An Algebraic Thesaurus.	8
A. F. Parker-Rhodes	Computer Operations Required for Mechanical Translation (not issued as a Workpaper).	9
CLRU	The Mechanical Study of Context: The Mechanical Composition of Lecture-Style Discourse.	10
R. H. Thouless	The Mechanical Study of Context (Paragraph Using the Roget Head "Wonder").	11
R. H. Thouless	Note on Works Similar in Type to Roget's Thesaurus.	12
	Notes on the Structure of Roget's Thesaurus.	13
M. A. K. Halliday	Linguistic Problems of Machine Translation: Research Report.	14
R. H. Richens	The Thirteen Steps.	15
A. R. Penny	Work on the Mechanical Study of Context.	16
R. H. Thouless and A. F. Parker-Rhodes	Mechanism of Parody (not duplicated).	17
R. M. Needham and K. I. B. Sparck-Jones	A Note on Some Further Work on Parody, Progression of Thought and Similar Topics.	18
Flynn Woolner-Bird and A. R. Penny	Comparative Analysis of a Passage from White's "Natural History of Selborne."	19
E. W. Bastin	The Pask Machine. Physical Description of The Pask Machine.	20
Margaret Masterman	Fans and Heads.	21
Margaret Masterman	The Use in Brouwer of the Terms "Fan," "Spread," "Spread-Law," "Complementary-Law."	22
Margaret Masterman	Note on the Properties of the Successor-Relation.	22a
Timothy Joyce	The Problems of Information Retrieval.	23
Margaret Masterman	Outline of a Theory of Language.	24
CLRU	Progress Report: January–August, 1957 (NSF).	25
F. Woolner-Bird and J. K. Pulling	Further Experiments in Constructing Paragraphs from Thesaurus Heads.	26
CLRU	Description of Current Work in Syntax at the CLRU.	27
R. M. Needham	Description of the Thesaurus Approach to Retrieval Problems and the Pilot Project.	28

Author	Title of Paper	Number
Timothy Joyce and R. M. Needham	Information Retrieval.	29
R. M. Needham	Note on Proposed Work on Mechanical Preparation of Retrieval Lattices.	30
R. H. Richens	"Magnum Multitudinem Vidit": An Application of the XIII Steps.	31
CLRU	"Magnum Multitudinem Vidit": Bench Test.	32
CLRU	"Agricola Incurvo Terram Dimovit Aratro" (first version).	33
A. H. J. Miller	Notes on the Testing of the CLRU Library Retrieval System (200 items).	34
R. M. Needham	Note on Methods of Encoding Non-Boolean Lattices for Computing.	35
Margaret Masterman	The Effect of the Use of Electronic Techniques for Examining Language.	36
A. F. Parker-Rhodes	Project for an Optical Peek-a-Boolean Computer to Perform Operations Mechanically on a Roget-Like Thesaurus.	37
A. F. Parker-Rhodes	Procedure for Encoding an Arbitrary Lattice.	38
A. F. Parker-Rhodes	Practical Guide to Boolean Calculation for Members of the C.L.R.U.	39
R. H. Richens	"Agricola Incurvo Terram Dimovit Aratro."	40
Brian Mayoh	Two Approximate Methods of Translation Using Roget's Thesaurus and a Strictly Determinate Procedure.	41
K. I. B. Sparck-Jones	Test 2: (Ad Ludum Ambulamus).	42
A. F. Parker-Rhodes and R. M. Needham	Non-Boolean Lattice Algebra. Extract.	43
Margaret Masterman and K. I. B. Sparck-Jones	First Thoughts on How to Translate Syntax Mechanically with a Thesaurus.	43a
R. M. Needham, Margaret Masterman, and K. I. B. Sparck-Jones	The Analogy Between Mechanical Translation and Library Retrieval.	44
Timothy Joyce and R. M. Needham	Information Retrieval and the Thesaurus.	45
Timothy Joyce and R. M. Needham	The Thesaurus Approach to Information Retrieval.	45a
A. F. Parker-Rhodes	Appendix to 45a. The Mathematical Relationships Between the Thesauri Used for Information Retrieval and for Machine Translation.	46

Author	Title of Paper	Number
Stephen Wheeler	An Analysis of the Structures of Language-Communication Using a Thesaurus (Lattice).	47
Matthew Shaw	Can Some Thesaurus Heads be Superimposed on Others?	48
CLRU	Report to National Science Foundation for Half-Year Period Ending December 1957.	49
J. M. Staniforth	General Schema of a Thesauric Translation Programme Using a Punched-Card Technique (first version).	50
A. F. Parker-Rhodes and R. M. Needham	Encoding Roget's Thesaurus.	51
Colin Wordley	A Mechanical Procedure for Finding the Number of Occurrences of the Thesaurus Head Holes in the Thesaurus Pack, over a Pre-Judged Section of Input Text, thus Enabling Sentence Structure Lattices to Be Constructed.	52
A. F. Parker-Rhodes	The Use of Statistics in Language Research.	53
R. M. Needham	Digital Machinery and M. T. Experiments.	54
A. H. J. Miller	Note on the Extension and Testing of the CLRU Library Retrieval System (400 items).	55
CLRU	Research Report, February, 1958.	56
A. F. Parker-Rhodes	Encoding Problems Arising in the Design of a Thesaurus-Type M. T. Programme.	57
J. M. Staniforth	General Schema of a Thesauric Translation Programme Using a Punched-Card Technique (second version).	58
K. I. B. Sparck-Jones	Brief Description of the Staniforth Punched-Card Programme Showing Specimens of the Cards Used at Each Stage.	59
K. I. B. Sparck-Jones and R. M. Needham	A System of Two-level Access to a Translation Output Using a Thesaurus.	60
Matthew Shaw	The Compacting of Roget's Thesaurus.	61
K. I. B. Sparck-Jones	Arrangement Information, Lists, Syntax Factors, Alphabetical Dictionary Entries.	62, L1, L2, L3
K. I. B. Sparck-Jones	Method of Coding on Hollerith Card.	63
K. I. B. Sparck-Jones	A Specimen Punched-card.	64
K. I. B. Sparck-Jones, R. M. Needham, and Colin Wordley	Library for Mechanical Translation.	65
R. M. Needham	Research Note on a Property of Finite Lattices.	66

Author	*Title of Paper*	*Number*
Colin Wordley	A Test to Compare Lattices Constructed with Semantic Heads Chosen over Different Lengths of Input Text (Appendix by K. I. B. Sparck-Jones).	67
A. F. Parker-Rhodes and Colin Wordley	Mechanical Translation by the Thesaurus Method Using Existing Machinery.	68
Robert Dutch	Roget New Edition.	69
R. M. Needham and K. I. B. Sparck-Jones	Schema of Two-level Access to the CLRU Information Retrieval System.	70
R. H. Richens	Preliminary Note on Word Decomposition by Exhaustive Extraction (also Flow Chart).	71
Margaret Masterman	Syntax (Monolingual and Interlingual).	72
A. F. Parker-Rhodes and R. M. Needham	A Reduction Method for Non-Arithmetic Data and Its Application to Thesauric Translation.	73
A. F. Parker-Rhodes and Colin Wordley	The Status of Lattice Theory in the Library Retrieval System of the CLRU.	74
R. M. Needham	The Problems of Chunking.	75
R. H. Richens	Principal Nude Elements (1).	76, L4
A. F. Parker-Rhodes	The AFP-R Translation Procedure.	77
E. W. Bastin	The Use of a Self-Organizing Machine in Investigating the Logical Structure of Fundamental Physics.	78
CLRU	Principal Nude French Standard Formula in Nude Ia.	79, L5
R. M. Needham	Simulation of a "Self-Organizing System" (CASPAR) on a Digital Computer (EDSAC).	80
Martin Kay	Marcode.	81, L10
CLRU	"Agricola Incurvo Terram Dimovit Aratro" (2nd version).	82
E. W. Bastin	A "Self-Organizing Machine" (CASPAR) Having A Hierarchical Structure of Algebraic Levels.	83
E. W. Bastin	Abstracts of ML 83.	83a
CLRU	Essays on and in Machine Translation.	84
E. B. May	Preliminary Memorandum from an Administrative Point of View on the Report by Y. Bar-Hillel on the State of Machine Translation in the U.S. and in Great Britain.	85
R. H. Richens	Logical Looseness About Interlinguas.	86
K. I. B. Sparck-Jones	Note on the Inappropriateness of Division made by Bar-Hillel Between FAHQMT and MMPT.	86a

Author	Title of Paper	Number
K. I. B. Sparck-Jones	The Use of Decision Procedure in Machine Translation.	87
Martin Kay	The Relevance of Linguistics to Machine translation.	88
R. M. Needham and A. F. Parker-Rhodes	This Question of Lattice Theory.	89
Margaret Masterman	What is a Thesaurus?	90
Margaret Masterman	Fictitious Sentences in Language.	91
E. W. Bastin and R. M. Needham	A New Research Technique for Analysing Language.	92
CLRU	R. See's Letter re Lattice Theory.	93
CLRU	Specimen Translation: Italian Interlingua English.	94
Margaret Masterman	Classification, Concept-Formation and Language.	95
CLRU	Nude Ia (3).	96, L6
CLRU	Elements of Nue-France.	97, L7
CLRU	Key to Italian Monolingual Symbols in Italian. Interlingual Dictionary.	98, L8
CLRU	Monolingual Grammatical Symbols in Italian.	99, L9
E. W. Bastin	Proposal to OSR-USAF for Research on Information Structures, June 1959.	100, P1
M. B. Hesse	Analogy Structure in a Thesaurus.	101
CLRU	Draft Report for the NSF.	102
CLRU	Work of the CLRU, Sept. 1959 (Rome Report).	103, L16, L18
A. F. Parker-Rhodes	A Survey on Current Research in Machine Translation, Documentation and Related Fields, etc.	104
M. B. Hesse	On Defining Analogy.	105
R. H. Richens	Interlingual Machine Translation.	106
R. H. Richens	Sample Outputs.	107
CLRU	Stages of Tranformations of Richens' Output into a More Sophisticated Pidgin.	108
R. M. Needham, K. I. B. Sparck-Jones and A. H. J. Miller	The Information Retrieval System of the Cambridge Language Research Unit.	109
Martin Kay and R. McKinnon Wood	A Flexible Punched-Card Procedure for Word Decomposition.	119

Author	*Title of Paper*	*Number*
A. F. Parker-Rhodes	Some Recent Work on Methods in Machine Translation.	125
A. F. Parker-Rhodes and R. M. Needham	The Theory of Clumps.	126
A. F. Parker-Rhodes	Comments on a Document by Harris.	127
Margaret Masterman and R. F. Needham	Specifications and Sample Operations of a Model Thesaurus.	128
A. F. Parker-Rhodes	Comments on the Idalyzer.	129
A. F. Parker-Rhodes	Method of Contracting Dictionary-Entries.	130
CLRU	Information Retrieval Term List.	131
A. F. Parker-Rhodes	Bracketing Program Dictionary.	132
Margaret Masterman and Martin Kay	Mechanical Pidgin Translation.	133
A. F. Parker-Rhodes	A Commentary on Rand.	134
A. F. Parker-Rhodes, R. M. Needham, Martin Kay, and P. Bratley	CLRU Computer Program for Syntactic Analysis.	136
K. I. B. Sparck-Jones	Mechanised Semantic Classification I.	137
A. F. Parker-Rhodes	Contribution to the Theory of Clumps.	138
Margaret Masterman	The Theory of Clumps II.	139
K. I. B. Sparck-Jones	Mechanised Semantic Classification II.	140
Margaret Masterman	Semantic Message Detection for Machine Translation Using an Interlingua.	141
A. F. Parker-Rhodes and Margaret Masterman	A New Model of Syntactic Description.	142
A. F. Parker-Rhodes	A General Procedure for Syntactic Description (Formerly A New Model . . .) (Paradigms).	143
R. M. Needham	Description of the GR-Clump Program and of Tests Now in Progress.	144
K. I. B. Sparck-Jones (ed.)	The Application of the Cambridge Language Research Unit Model of Syntactic Analysis.	145
A. F. Parker-Rhodes	A New Model of Syntactic Description (combination of ML 142-143), Teddington paper.	146
A. F. Parker-Rhodes et al.	A Lattice Model of Syntactic Description (ed. Sparck-Jones, K. I. B.), four-part report.	147
Margaret Masterman	Commentary on the Guberina Hypothesis.	148
R. M. Needham	Research on Information Retrieval Classification and Grouping, 1957–61 Report.	149

Author	Title of Paper	Number
R. M. Needham	Memorandum on the Possibility of Using Simpler Apparatus for Machine Translation Research and for Information Retrieval Research.	150
Prof. N. Andreev	Paper, Correspondence, Commentaries.	151
R. M. Needham	A Method for Using Computers in Information Classification.	152
R. M. Needham	How to Construct a Syntactic Dictionary Entry.	153
R. M. Needham	Supplement I to ML 147.	154
Margaret Masterman	A Theory of the Semantic Basis of Human Communication, Applied to the Phonetics of Intonational Form.	155
Margaret Masterman	The Semantic Basis of Human Communication (Leeds Lecture).	156
A. F. Parker-Rhodes	Synopsis of Lecture Course.	157
Margaret Masterman	Semantic Message Detection Research for M. T. (short note).	158
A. F. Parker-Rhodes	CLRU Syntax Dictionary for English Vocabulary, No. 1.	159
Eloise Rigby	A Preliminary Investigation of the Consistency and Objectivity of the Parker-Rhodes Dictionary.	160
Eloise Rigby	Interim Status Report.	161
Eloise Rigby and Yorick Wilks	A System for Producing English Syntactic Dictionary Entries.	162
Eloise Rigby and Yorick Wilks	Colloquium Report.	163
K. I. B. Sparck-Jones	A Note on "NUDE."	164
D. S. Linney, R. A. McKinnon-Wood, and Yorick Wilks	Inter-Lingual Syntax Bracketing Programs.	165
R. M. Needham	Abstracts of Venice Lectures.	166
CLRU, Margaret Masterman, and Yorick Wilks	Annual Summary Report for USAAF. The SEMANTIC BASIS OF COMMUNICATON Including Report of the Florence Colloquium.	167
K. I. B. Sparck-Jones	May's Thesaurus.	168
Yorick Wilks	Nucode.	169
K. I. B. Sparck-Jones	Synonymy and Semantic Classification.	170
Margaret Masterman, Yorick Wilks, David Shillan, John Dobson, and K. I. B. Sparck-Jones	Semantic Basis of Communication.	171
A. F. Parker-Rhodes	Computer Testing of Interlingual Bracketing Program.	172

Author	*Title of Paper*	*Number*
Yorick Wilks	Application of CLRU Semantic Analysis to Information Retrieval.	173
K. I. B. Sparck-Jones	The Use of the Theory of Clumps for Information Retrieval Report on SRC-Supported Project at the CLRU, June, 1965.	174
R. A. McKinnon Wood	Implementation of Reactive Keyboard Input System on CLRU 1202 Computer.	175
Yorick Wilks	Computable Semantic Derivations.	176
K. I. B. Sparck-Jones	A Note on Current Research on the Theory of Clumps at the CLRU.	177
K. I. B. Sparck-Jones	Semantic Classes and Semantic Message Forms.	178
David Shillan	A Method and a Reason for Tune Analysis.	179
Margaret Masterman	A Picture of Language.	180
K. I. B. Sparck-Jones	Semantic Markers.	181
David Shillan	A Linguistic Unit Adaptable to Economical Concordance-Making.	182
David Jackson	Notes on a Procedure for Finding Clumps.	183
J. E. Dobson	Report of an Experiment to Find Semantic Square in an Interlingually Coded Text Taken from a Travellers Handbook.	184
J. E. Dobson	A Note on Finding Phrasings in Raw Natural Language Text by Algorithm.	185
F. Woolner-Bird	Further Notes on Thesaurus Heads.	185a
David Shillan	Anomalous Finites (May 1965).	186
Margaret Masterman	The Mechanical Study of Context I.	186a
A. F. Parker-Rhodes	An Interlingual Procedure for Description and Extraction of Syntactic Structure.	187
Margaret Masterman	A. F. P.-R.'s Syntax Program: Its Pros and Cons.	188
R. M. Needham, D. M. Jackson, and K. I. B. Sparck-Jones	Notes on the Extension of Clump Finding Techniques.	189
K. I. B. Sparck-Jones and D. M. Jackson	The Use of the Theory of Clumps for Information Retrieval. Report to the SRC 1966.	190
A. F. Parker-Rhodes	On the Making of Dictionary Entries for the CLRU Syntax Program.	191
D. M. Jackson	A Note on an Experiment with 16 Requests on the CLRU Library of Abstracts, Using the Theory of Clumps.	192
Yorick Wilks	Semantic Interlingua in Information Retrieval— OSTI Report 1966.	193

Author	*Title of Paper*	*Number*
D. M. Jackson	A Note on a Procedure for Calculating Matrices for Use in Automatic Classification.	194
CLRU	A Description of TRAC (Text Reckoning and Compiler).	195
A. F. Parker-Rhodes	MURIEL.	195a
K. I. B. Sparck-Jones	A Small Semantic Classification Experiment Using Co-occurrence Data.	196
David Shillan	Segmenting Natural Language by Articulatory Features.	197
Margaret Masterman	Main-Aided Computer Translation from English to French Using an On-Line System to Manipulate a Bi-Lingual Conceptual Dictionary or Thesaurus.	198
K. I. B. Sparck-Jones and D. M. Jackson	Interim Report with First Results, on Results of Experiments in the Use of Clumps for Information Retrieval.	198a
H. C. Rutherford	Preliminary Syntactic Coding Based on Word Order.	199
H. C. Rutherford	Syntactic Coding, Comparison of work done by H. C. Rutherford with that of Kathleen H. V. Booth.	199a
K. I. B. Sparck-Jones and D. M. Jackson	The Use of the Theory of Clumps for Information Retrieval. Report to OSTI 1967.	200
David Shillan and E. W. Bastin	The Application of Instrumental Methods for Determining the Role of Rhythmic and Intonational Factors in Continuous Prose.	201
A. F. Parker-Rhodes and J. E. Dobson	An Experiment with Structured Coding for Information Retrieval.	202
Yorick Wilks	Research on Computable Semantic Derivations 1967.	203
D. M. Jackson	Notes on the Stability of Automatically-Generated Classifications.	204
H. C. Rutherford	LINKS. An Examination of Structure Words in the English Language with Reference to a Computerised Method of Syntactic Coding Based on Word Order (ML 199). (Revised June 1969).	205
D. M. Jackson	Comparison of Classifications.	206
D. M. Jackson and A. F. Parker-Rhodes	Automatic Classification in the Ecology of the Higher Fungi.	207
D. M. Jackson	A Note on a Set of Functions for Information Retrieval.	208

Author	Title of Paper	Number
David Shillan	A Set of Semantic Markers for a Machine Translation System.	209
Margaret Masterman	Semantic Language Games or Philosophy by Computer.	210
K. I. B. Sparck-Jones	The Use of Automatically-Obtained Keyword Classifications for Information Retrieval. (Final Report).	211
D. Shillan and H. Rutherford	A Calculus of Phrasing Patterns and Its Application to Determining Syntactic Possibilities.	213

BIBLIOGRAPHY OF PUBLICATIONS BY PRESENT AND PAST MEMBERS OF CLRU

(Where authors have been with CLRU for a limited period, publications from that period alone are listed)

Anderson, Robin:

Fellowship Dissertation, Churchill College, Cambridge, "Meaning Memory and Non-Unitary Theory," 1970.

"Conclusive Analogical Argument," *Revue Internationale de Philosophie, Brussels,* In press.

Bastin, Edward W.:

M.Sc. Thesis, London, "An Application of the Theory of Eddington to the Problem of Liquid Helium," 1949.

Ph.D. Thesis, London, "Eddington's Theory and Its Significance for the Theory of Scientific Knowledge," 1952.

"Some Experiments in Precognition" (with J. M. Green), *J. Parapsych.,* 17(2), 137 (1953).

"The Analysis of Observations" (with C. W. Kilmister), *Proc. Roy. Soc.* (London), A212, 559 (1952).

"The Concept of Order I. The Space-Time Structure" (with C. W. Kilmister), *Proc. Cambridge Phil. Soc.,* 50, 278 (1954).

"The Concept of Order II. Measurements" (with C. W. Kilmister), *Proc. Cambridge Phil. Soc.,* 51, 8, 454 (1955).

"The Concept of Order III. General Relativity as a Technique for Extrapolating over Very Long Distances" (with C. W. Kilmister), *Proc. Cambridge Phil. Soc.,* 53, 462 (1957).

"The Concept of Order IV. Quantum Mechanics" (with C. W. Kilmister), *Proc. Cambridge Phil. Soc.,* 55, 66 (1959).

"Eddington's Theory in Terms of the Concept of Order" (with C. W. Kilmister), *Proc. Cambridge Phil. Soc.,* 50, 439 (1954).

"Eddington's Statistical Theory" (with C. W. Kilmister), *Rend. Circ. Matematico, Palermo,* 2, V (1956).

Fellowship Dissertation, King's College, Cambridge, "The Limits Imposed on Measurement, in Quantum Theory and in Cosmology and to Connexions between Them," 1956.

"Self-Organisation and the Notion of Level" (with others), USAF Office of Scientific Research Tech. Note (printed).

"Self-Organizing Mechanisms as Models for Scientific Theories" (with Karen Sparck-Jones), USAF Office of Scientific Research Tech. Note (printed).

"A Theory of the Origin of Mass within a Control Model of the Elementary Particles" (with Ann Woodside), USAF Office of Scientific Research Tech. Note (printed).

"Limitations on the Use of Metrical Concepts in Very Large Scale and in Very Small Scale Physics," *Proc. Cambridge Phil. Soc.,* **57**, 848 (1961).

"A Cybernetic Approach to a Theory of Physical Measurement, Part I. Eddington's E-frame Re-envisaged as a Level in a Cybernetic Model," CLRU Workpaper (cyclostyled).

"Applications of a Control System Model in Quantum Electro-Dynamics and Elementary Particle Theory" (with C. W. Kilmister and A. F. Parker-Rhodes), CLRU Workpaper (cyclostyled).

"A Preliminary Interpretation of Mass" (with C. W. Kilmister), CLRU Workpaper (cyclostyled).

"The Interaction between Levels in a Hierarchy," CLRU Workpaper (cyclostyled).

"On the Origin of the Scale-Constants of Physics" *Stud. Phil. Gandensia,* **4**, 77 (1966).

"What the Vitalist Means is Right," review of *Of Molecules and Men,* by Francis Crick, *Theoria to Theory,* **2**, 1 (1967).

"A General Property of Hierarchies," contribution to *Towards a Theoretical Biology,* I.U.B.S. Symposium, Vol. 2 (C. H. Waddington, ed.), Edinburgh Univ. Press, Edinburgh, 1968, p. 252.

"Colloquium on the Quantum Theory and Beyond: A Report," *Theoria to Theory,* 3(2), 69 (1968).

"An Unconscionable Time A-Dying," review of *Science and E.S.P.* (J. R. Smythies, ed.), *Theoria to Theory,* **2**, 3 (1968).

"The Continuity Problem: A Way Out?," symposium contribution in *Trieste International Conference on Theoretical Physics,* Vienna, 1969, Vol. II, p. 451.

"A Discrete Theory of Physical Space and of Spin," symposium contribution in *Quantum Theory and Beyond* (E. W. Bastin, ed.), Cambridge Univ. Press, 1970, In press.

Jackson, David:

"Current Approaches to Classification and Clump-finding at the Cambridge Language Research Unit" (with K. Sparck-Jones), *Computer J.,* 10(1) (May 1967).

"Some Experiments in the Use of Automatically Obtained Term Clusters for Retrieval" (with K. Sparck-Jones, *Proceedings of the FID/IFIP Conference on Mechanised Information Storage Retrieval and Dissemination, Rome, 1967.*

"A Note on a Set of Functions for Information Retrieval," *Inform. Storage Retrieval,* **5**, 27–41 (1969).

"Comparison of Classifications," Colloquium in Numerical Taxonomy, held at the University of St. Andrews, September 1968, p. 75.

"Automatic Classification in the Ecology of the Higher Fungi" (with A. F. Parker-Rhodes), Colloquium in Numerical Taxonomy, held at the University of St. Andrews, September 1968, p. 149.

Linney, Duncan Stuart.

"The Missing Wittgenstein," *Cambridge Rev.*, (October 1965).

"Wittgenstein's Late Philosophy," *Theoria to Theory* (1969).

Discussion contribution with C. F. von Weizsäcker on epistemology of quantum theory in *Quantum Theory and Beyond* (E. W. Bastin, ed.), Cambridge, In press.

Masterman, Margaret (Mrs. R. B. Braithwaite):

"Linguistic Philosophy: the Study of Framework," *Theology*, (March 1951).

"The Possibility of Applying a 'Combinatory' Logical System to the Analysis of Classical Chinese Sentences," submitted to the Universities China Committee in London, Awarded Research Grant.

"The Pictorial Principle in Language," Proceedings of the XI International Congress of Philosophy, Brussels, 1953.

"Words," *Proc. Aristotelian Soc.* (1954).

"Metaphysical and Ideographic Language," in *British Philosophy in Mid-Century* (C. A. Mace, ed.), Allen and Unwin, London, 1953.

"The Thesaurus in Syntax and Semantics," *Mech. Trans.*, 4(2), (November 1957).

"The Analogy between Mechanical Translation and Library Retrieval" (with R. M. Needham and K. Sparck-Jones), Proceedings of the International Conference on Scientific Information, Washington, November 1958.

"Classification, Concept-Formation and Language," (read at 4th Annual Symposium of the British Society for the Philosophy of Science, Cambridge, September 1959.

"Translation" (with Mr. W. Haas), *Proc. Aristotelian Soc.*, (1961).

"Semantic Message Detection for Machine Translation, Using an Interlingua," Proceedings of the First International Conference on Machine Translation of Languages and Applied Language Analysis, Teddington, September 1961, Paper 36.

"Freeing the Mind," *The Times Literary Supplement*, p. 60, June 1962.

"Commentary on the Guberina Hypothesis," *Estratto Rivista Methodos*, 15(57–58), 139 (1963).

"The Semantic Basis of Human Communication," *ARENA*, 19, 18 (April 1964).

"The Nature of a Paradigm," in *Proceedings of the International Conference on Logic and Philosophy of Science, London, 1965*, Vol. 4, In press.

"Semantic Algorithms," Proceedings of the Conference on Computer-related Semantics, Las Vegas, December 1965, No. 4.

"Mechanical Pidgin Translation," in *Machine Translation* (A. D. Booth, ed.), 1967, pp. 197–226.

"Man-aided computer translation from English into French using an on-line system to manipulate a bilingual conceptual dictionary or thesaurus," Rapport de la 2ème Conference Internationale sur le Traitement Automatique des Langues, Grenoble, August 1967.

"Computer Poems" (with poems by Alan Trist), *UNIT* (University of Keele magazine), (December 1968).

"Computerized Japanese Haiku" and "Computer Poetry from CLRU" (with R. McKinnon Wood), *Cybernetic Serendipity* (special issue), (1968).

"Private Poets" (with poem by Alan Trist), *Queen Magazine,* (August 1969).

"Bible Translating by 'Kernel'," *The Times Literary Supplement,* March 19, 1970.

Dialogue (with George Steiner and others): "Translating the Bible," *Theoria to Theory,* 4(2) (April 1970).

Needham, Roger Michael: M.A., Ph.D.

"The Thesaurus Approach to Information Retrieval" (with T. Joyce), *Amer. Doc.,* 9, 192–197 (1958).

"The Analogy between Mechanical Translation and Library Retrieval" (with Margaret Masterman and K. Sparck-Jones), in *Proceedings of the International Conference on Scientific Information, 1958,* Vol. 2, National Academy of Sciences-National Research Council, Washington, D.C., 1959, pp. 917–935.

"A Reduction Method for Non-Arithmetic Data" (with A. F. Parker-Rhodes), in *Information Processing: Proceedings of the International Conference on Information Processing,* Paris, 1960, pp. 321–327.

"The Information Retrieval System of the Cambridge Language Research Unit" (with A. H. J. Miller and K. Sparck-Jones), CLRU, 1960.

"The Theory of Clumps" (with A. F. Parker-Rhodes), CLRU, 1960, mimeo.

"The Theory of Clumps II," CLRU, 1961, mimeo.

"Research on Information Retrieval, Classification and Grouping," CLRU, 1961, mimeo. Ph.D. Thesis, University of Cambridge, 1961.

"A Method for Using Computer in Information Classification," in *Information Processing 62: Proceedings of IFIP Congress 1962* (Popplewell, ed.), Amsterdam, 1963, pp. 284–287.

"Automatic Classification for Information Retrieval," in *Information Retrieval* (Serbanesou, ed.), IBM European Education Centre, Blaricum, Holland, 1963.

"Automatic Classification for Information Retrieval," lectures given at the NATO Advanced Study Institute on Automatic Document Analysis, Venice, 1963. Abstracts, CLRU, 1963, mimeo.

"Keywords and Clumps," with K. Sparck-Jones, *J. Doc.,* 20, 5–15 (1964).

"Automatic Classification—Models and Problems," in *Mathematics and Computer Science in Biology and Medicine,* The Medical Research Council, London, 1965, pp. 111–114.

"Review of Ellegard, Karlgren and Spang-Hanssen," *Structures and Quanta, Journal of Linguistics,* 1 (1965).

"Computer Methods for Classification and Grouping," in *The Use of Computers in Anthropology* (Hymes, ed.), The Hague, 1965, pp. 345–356.

"Applications of the Theory of Clumps," *Mech. Translation,* 8, 113–127 (1965).

"Semantic Problems of Machine Translation," in *Information Processing 65: Proceedings of the IFIP Congress 1965,* Vol. 1 (Kalenich, ed.), Washington, D.C., 1965, pp. 65–69.

"Information Retrieval and Some Cognate Computing Problems," in *Advances in Programming and Non-Numerical Computation* (Fox, ed.), London, 1966, pp. 201–218.

"Automatic Term Classifications and Retrieval" (with K. Sparck-Jones), in *Information Storage and Retrieval,* Vol. 4, 1968, pp. 91–100.

Parker-Rhodes, Arthur Frederick:

"A Theory of Word-Frequency Distribution," *Nature, 178,* 1308 (Dec. 8, 1956).

"Computer Operations required for Mechanical Translation," *Proc. Inst. Elec. Engr.* (London), *Part B, 103,* Suppl. 3 (1956).

"The Use of Statistics in Language Research," *Mech. Translation,* 5(2), 67 (November 1958).

"Some Recent Work on Thesauric and Interlingual Methods in Machine Translation," in *Advan. Doc. Lib. Sci., 3,* Part 2, 923–934 (1959).

"A Reduction Method for Non-Arithmetic Data" (with R. M. Needham), *Information Processing: Proceedings of the International Conference on Information Processing,* Paris, 1960, pp. 321–327.

"A New Model of Syntactic Description," presented at the First International Conference on Machine Translation of Languages and Applied Language Analysis, Teddington, September 1961.

"Is There an Interlingual Element in Syntax?," in *Proceedings of the Ninth International Congress of Linguists,* Cambridge, Mass., 1962, p. 176.

"On Talking to Computers," *Proc. Amer. Doc. Inst.* 1, 477 (October 1964).

"The Communication of Algorithms," *Computer J., 7,* 28 (1964).

"Automatic Classification in the Ecology of the Higher Fungi" (with D. M. Jackson), Colloquium in Numerical Taxonomy at the University of St. Andrews, September 1968, p. 149.

"The Theory of Clumps" (with R. M. Needham), CLRU 1960, mimeo.

"Contributions to the Theory of Clumps," CLRU 1961, mimeo.

Shillan, David:

Spoken English, Longmans Green, London, 1954; with teaching tapes, 1966.

"Detecting Meaning through Speech," *META* XI, 3 (Montreal) (1966).

"Metodo e Ragione per l'Analise melodica del Linguaggio," *DELTA, 6,* (La Spezia) (1967).

"Phrasings in Teaching and in Translation," in *Report of International Language Conference of Institute of Army Education, Eltham Palace, London,* 1967.

"An Articulatory Unit for Speech and Text," *English Language Teaching, 21,* 2 (1967).

"Segmenting Natural Language by Articulatory Features," 2nd International Conference on Computational Linguistics, Grenoble, 1967.

"Phrasing and Meaning," *META* XII, 2 (Montreal) 1968.

Rutherford, H.C.:
(See list of workpapers for publication.)

Needham, Karen (publishing as Karen Sparck-Jones):
"The Information Retrieval System of the Cambridge Language Research Unit" (with R. M. Needham), CLRU, 1960, mimeo.

"Mechanised Semantic Classification," in *Proceedings of the 1961 International Conference on Machine Translation and Applied Analysis,* London, 1962.

Ph.D. Thesis, Cambridge, "Synonymy and Semantic Classification," 1964; CLRU, 1964, mimeo.

"Keywords and Clumps" (with R. M. Needham). *J. Doc.* **20,** 5–15 1967.

"Experiments in Semantic Classification," *Mech. Translation,* **8,** 97–112 (1965).

"Semantic Classes and Semantic Message Forms," in *Proceedings of the Conference on Computer-Related Semantic Analysis (1965),* Wayne State Univ. Press, Detroit, Mich., 1966, pp. X1–X17.

"Current Approaches to Classification and Clump-Finding at the Cambridge Language Research Unit" (with D. M. Jackson), *Computer J.,* **10,** 29–37 (1967).

"Some Experiments in the Use of Automatically-Obtained Term Clusters for Retrieval" (with D. M. Jackson), in *Mechanised Information Storage, Retrieval and Dissemination* (Samuelson, ed.), Amsterdam, 1969.

"Automatic Term Classifications and Retrieval" (with R. M. Needham), *Information Storage and Retrieval,* **4,** 91–100 (1968).

"Automatic Term Classification and Information Retrieval," in *Proceedings of IFIP Congress 68.*

Wilks, Yorick:

"Semantic Consistency in Text," SDC SP-2738, March 1967.

"Transformational Grammars Again," SDC SP-2961, October 1967.

"Computable Semantic Derivations," SDC SP-3017, March 1968.

Review article on Chomsky's "Current Issues on Linguistic Theory," *Linguistics,* (1967).

McKinnon Wood, T. R.:

"Computer Programming for Literary Laymen," *Theoria to Theory,* 1 (1967).

"A Multi-Access Implementation of an Interpretive Text Processing Language," in *Proceedings of IFIP Congress 68.*

"Computerized Japanese Haiku" and "Computer Poetry from CLRU" (with Margaret Masterman), *Cybernetic Serendipity* (special issue), (1968).

MARGARET MASTERMAN

CAMBRIDGE UNIVERSITY LIBRARY

The earliest specific references to a library of the University at Cambridge are to be found in the wills (both proved in March 1416) of William Hunden and William Loring, the former bequeathing to it three volumes "to remain forever in the new library at Cambridge for the use of graduates and scholars in residence," and the latter all his books of civil law "to remain forever in the common library of the scholars of the University." There are, of course, earlier references to books in the possession of the university. Richard de Lyng, three times Chancellor of the University, who died in 1355, is included as the donor of a chest of books in an early service in commemoration of the university's benefactors; and an inventory made in 1363 of the contents of the university's common chest includes a small number of books as well as money, vestments, charters, etc. Thus, although the earliest surviving collection of the university's statutes, believed to have been compiled about 1250, and the collection of statutes written at the end of the fourteenth century to replace originals destroyed in 1381 make no mention either of a library or of a librarian, the available evidence suggests that from the middle of the fourteenth century at least, the university owned and kept in chests in its treasury a small collection of books which began to be expanded and was formally established as the Common Library of the University during the second decade of the fifteenth century.

This expansion was made possible because at this period the university began to develop the site known as the Old Schools which housed its first regular lecture rooms and other essential offices and institutions, comprising four ranges of two-storied buildings facing the four points of the compass so as to enclose a central courtyard (see Figure 1). The northern range, containing a school of theology below and a chapel above, was completed around the year 1400 and was followed by the ranges on the west (a school of canon law below and a library above, in course of erection in 1420), south (philosophy and civil law below and a library above, 1457–ca. 1470), and east (offices below and a library above, 1470–1475). For the building of the upper story of the eastern range the university was indebted to the generosity of its Chancellor Thomas Rotherham (1423–1500), Archbishop of York. The other buildings were financed, slowly and painfully, by the university itself, the surviving accounts providing ample evidence of its impoverished condition.

It was thus on the upper story of the western range that the University Library found its first home, and it is the library as it was there established that its earliest surviving catalog (preserved in the University Archives) portrays. This catalog, entitled *A register of the books given by various benefactors to the Common Library of the University of Cambridge,* lists 122 volumes in nine subject divisions; sets out the contents of each volume, with their authors, at length; identifies each volume by quoting the first word of its second leaf and the first word of its last leaf but one; and names the donors (31 in all) of 99 of the books. Analysis of this catalog shows that it is the work of seven successive hands and also shows the library first as it was in 1424 and then as it developed down to about 1440. More than half of its contents were works of theology and religion, and there were 23 volumes of canon law. The writers of ancient Rome were represented by Lucan alone, and the early Christian poets and the English Chroniclers were entirely absent. Of the recorded donors the most eminent in affairs of church and state were William Loring (a benefactor of Merton College, Oxford, also), Richard Holme (Warden of the King's Hall at Cambridge and councillor to Richard II, Henry IV, and Henry V), John Aylemer (Warden of New College, Oxford, and a friend of

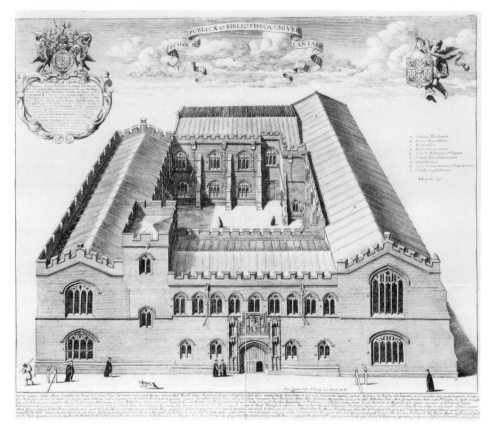

FIGURE 1. *Cambridge University: The Old Schools and the library, from the east.* (*From David Loggan's* Cantabrigia illustrata, *1690.*)

William of Wykeham), and Thomas Langley (Bishop of Durham, a cardinal, and twice Chancellor of England). Of the remainder two were successive Masters of Peterhouse (Thomas de Castro Bernardi and John Holbroke) and nine were Fellows of Cambridge Colleges. Eleven others were described as *magistri* and may be presumed to have been Cambridge graduates, though no trace of them can be found in the surviving records of the university and colleges.

By the time the library's second earliest catalog was drawn up in 1473 the collection had been moved into the room on the upper story of the newly completed south range. This catalog (also preserved in the University Archives) shows 330 volumes disposed on seventeen lectern cases, each of which had hanging at its end a written "table" of the books it contained. Religion and theology still accounted for more than half the collection; but there were some significant newcomers among the authors now represented, including Ovid, the younger Seneca, Cicero, Josephus, and Petrarch. The most "contemporary" authors were William Lyndwode (1375?–1446) and the first Provost of King's College, William Millington; and since Millington (who had been one of the overseers of the building accounts) lived probably until 1466, it may be that we must accord him the distinction of having been the first author ever to see his own works on the library's shelves. This catalog of 1473 is less informative than its predecessor, but some of the additional books listed in it can be associated with known benefactors. By far the most important of them was Walter Crome, a Fellow of Gonville and Caius College, who died as Rector of St. Benet's Sherehog, London, in 1453, bequeathing 93 volumes to the university and 7 to his college.

The library room that Thomas Rotherham built and furnished with books ran the whole length of the eastern range of the schools and was entered at its south end by way of a turret stair that also gave access to the other library room in the southern range. These two rooms, which for more than 200 years proved sufficient (and for a time more than sufficient) to hold the university's entire library, provided also a natural division to its contents, the south room holding the "common library" of the university while the east room, to which there was only restricted access, held the "new library" or "library of our Lord the Chancellor," as it was first known. Unfortunately no contemporary list of Rotherham's donations survives, though references to gifts of unspecified books received from him are not infrequent in the university's records during the last quarter of the fifteenth century. It is certain, however, that among them were the first printed books which the university ever possessed, and there is reason to conjecture that by 1500, when Rotherham died, the number of volumes in both library rooms together had risen to perhaps 600. They were, however, still primarily medieval in content, for the fresh air of the Renaissance came late to Cambridge, where there was no dominant figure to establish by influence and example a school of modern learning. It was not until 1511 that John Fisher brought Erasmus to Cambridge and not until 1518 that the University established a lectureship in Greek. Although soon afterward Roger Ascham could write of the enthusiasm with which Greek studies were being pursued at Cambridge, the holdings of the University Library did not reflect that enthusiasm until in 1529, shortly before his translation to Durham, Cuthbert Tunstal, Bishop of London, gave the university a number of Greek texts, both manuscript and printed, each with a gift inscription in his own fine hand. To these books, which included the *editio princeps* of Homer and the first volume of the Aldine Aristotle, Tunstal added a copy of the Complutensian Bible and a very fine copy, printed on vellum, of the first English arithmetic book, his own *De arte supputandi*.

Of the library's administration during these early years little is known for certain. Its general superintendence lay, as at Oxford, with the University Chaplain, to whom also were entrusted the vestments, plate, and books of religion pertaining to the University Chapel in the northern range of the schools, the jeweled cross which he carried on processional occasions, and the general security of the schools themselves. There were, however, no statutes or regulations which defined in detail his duties in the library. The framing of general decisions concerning the use of the library lay with the body of Regent Masters, whose earliest recorded regulation is of 1471–1472, when they took the right of admission to the library away from undergraduates, unless accompanied by a graduate, because they had abused its contents, and ordained that nonresident graduates might only enter the library in their proper academical dress. In 1500 they permitted the use of the library to members of religious houses who had been sent to study at the university, and several "graces" of the Regents are recorded during the early years of the sixteenth century granting this permission to named individuals. Of the same period also are several graces permitting the borrowing by specified persons of specified books for specified periods, though the earliest recorded grace of this kind (it permitted Rotherham's servant to borrow a book which in all probability Rotherham himself had given) is of 1487.

Although the University Library suffered, as did all other English libraries, terrible destruction and neglect during the Reformation and the years that followed it, some volumes from its earliest years still survived. Thus the library still possesses one of the books bequeathed by Loring in 1416, 3 other books listed in the catalog of 1424–1440 (including an illuminated Boethius, *De consolatione,* with Chaucer's translation), 15 others that had entered the Library by 1473, 4 manuscripts and 35 printed books certainly or probably given by Rotherham, and 3 manuscripts and 12 printed books given by Tunstal, including his Homer (though this volume was alienated from the library at an unknown date and returned to it through the generosity of a benefactor in 1918). Although, therefore, a catalog of the library drawn up for Cardinal Pole's commissioners in 1557 lists fewer than 200 volumes, all of them gathered together into the east room, the survival of so many is emphatically more remarkable than the loss of the remainder; and it may be added that the wind of change, if it took many books from Cambridge, also brought to it four manuscripts that had belonged to Balliol College, Oxford, including a Thucydides in Latin bequeathed to it by one of the most distinguished early English collectors, William Grey.

There is, however, no evidence that the Cambridge Library was deliberately and spectacularly purged of its contents. Rather it would seem that it was eroded meanly and by degrees because its books were thought to be irrelevant to the times and no longer useful; and most illuminating of all is the bleak fact that for forty-five years after Tunstal's benefaction there is no official record of any donation or bequest to the library or of any expenditure on the maintenance of its furniture and fittings. Books were, in fact, safer in private than in public hands. We need not doubt that some books were stolen from the library by men who wished to destroy them because they thought their doctrine dangerous or evil; but it is equally certain that others were taken away—sometimes even officially borrowed—by men who wished to preserve them. Thus Roger Ascham borrowed from the library in 1539–1540 but never returned to it a manuscript that soon after 1600 found its way into the Library of Trinity College, and Sir John Cheke similarly borrowed between 1540 and 1543 three manuscripts that never came back, one of them passing eventually into the possession of Queen Christina of Sweden and so into the Library of the Vatican. In the same way we certainly owe the preservation of Crome's surviving manuscripts to Andrew Perne, who removed them from the library and kept them privately for thirty years or more until it was once again a place to which he might safely restore them.

Andrew Perne, Master of Peterhouse from 1554 until his death in 1589, was a man who preferred continuity to controversy, and though he excited derision by successfully accommodating his principles to those which it was politic to hold under the successive reigns of Edward VI, Mary, and Elizabeth I, he was for more than forty years a central and influential figure in the university. It is to him that we owe the restoration of the University Library in 1574. He saw that, if such a thing were to be done and the necessary books procured, he must first engage the support of an impressive patron who might give the lead to others. To that end he turned to Matthew Parker, Archbishop of Canterbury and the most eminent and influential bookman in all England, and then, through Parker, to Sir Nicholas Bacon (Lord Keeper of the Great Seal), Robert Horne (Bishop of Winchester), and James Pilkington (Bishop of Durham). These four benefactors agreed to furnish between them, subject by subject, a representative collection of the most recent works of scholarship put out by the great publishing houses of Europe. Thus Horne gave 50 volumes of the Fathers; Pilkington 20 volumes of histories; Bacon 94 volumes (in each of which was placed an armorial gift plate, believed to be the earliest English specimen of its kind—see Figure 2) of philosophy, grammar, rhetoric, astronomy, geography, music, and mathematics; and Parker himself 75 volumes of

FIGURE 2. *Sir Nicholas Bacon's gift plate.*

Protestant theology and 25 manuscripts, including several of the old English chroniclers and 6 in Anglo-Saxon. Of his manuscripts the most important and celebrated are perhaps MS. Ii.2.4 (Gregory's *Pastoral Care* in King Alfred's translation, written ca. 1050–1075, almost certainly at Exeter), MS. Ii.2.11 (the Gospels in West Saxon, of about the same date, presented to Exeter by Bishop Leofric), MS. Ii.4.6 (Aelfric's *Homilies*, ca. 1050), and MS. Ff.1.27 (a mixed manuscript, part twelfth and part fourteenth century, of miscellaneous histories including Gildas and Nennius). All these books, and what remained from the pre-Reformation library, were set up in Rotherham's east room (the south room having been evacuated of books in 1547), all the new printed books except some of Parker's being chained to their lecterns in the fashion then still prevailing from earlier times. A catalog drawn up in 1583 shows that the volumes numbered about 450 and enables their arrangement to be ascertained with detailed exactitude.

This fair beginning soon stimulated other benefactions. In 1581 the French reformer Theodore Beza sent to the library from Geneva the fifth-century manuscript of the Gospels and Acts in Greek and Latin which is still its most treasured possession, the *Codex Bezae Cantabrigiensis* (MS. Nn.2.41)—a manuscript so deviant from the normal that Beza himself thought it "a book to keep rather than to publish" lest its eccentricities should give offense to the faithful (see Figure 3). Perne himself gave in 1585 (or bequeathed in 1589) well over a hundred manuscripts, about half of which had once belonged to the Library of Norwich Cathedral Priory. Before the end of the century there were also added about 140 books of medicine bequeathed by Thomas Lorkyn, Regius Professor of Physic, in 1594; and 87 volumes, mostly of theology and history, which were duplicates from his own shelves (many of them had once belonged to Thomas Cranmer), were given by John, Lord

FIGURE 3. *The* Codex Bezae Cantabrigiensis.

Lumley, in 1598 in fulfillment of a promise he had made to Perne ten years earlier. Thus, with the library's holdings at last approaching 1000 volumes, the south room was again taken into use as a library.

Meanwhile, the chaplaincy of the university having been abolished as a relic of popery in 1570, the office of University Librarian with a yearly stipend of £10 was created in 1577. In the beginning it was not an office of any great repute since, a financial crisis almost immediately supervening, the university was compelled to appoint to it such persons (including, during 1587–1593, an honest but illiterate tradesman of the town) as might be satisfied with a reduced salary of £3 6s. 8d.; and when in 1601 the university drew up a memorandum of the university's chain of command for the guidance of its new chancellor Sir Robert Cecil, it listed its librarian among the "Ministers for the necessary Use of the University" and placed him lower in that section than the auditors, printers, appraisers, and vintners. At the same time, in 1582, the university agreed the first set of regulations governing the conduct of the library and the duties of the librarian. There was to be a triple inventory of the library's contents, of which the vice-chancellor was to hold one copy, the University Chest another, and the librarian the third. All manuscripts and books with colored pictures, all globes and mathematical instruments, and all valuable books of mathematics and history were to be locked up under two keys, of which the vice-chancellor was to hold one and the librarian the other. The librarian himself was to attend in the library during term, except on Sundays and holidays, 8–10 A.M. and 1–3 P.M.; he was to see that all necessary repairs were promptly carried out and that all books were closed and in their right places when he went off duty; he was to give a bond of £200 against the proper performance of his duties and was to replace lost or mutilated books "or else lose his office and pay the triple value." Admission to the library was confined to masters of arts, bachelors of law or physic, and doctors, but only ten persons (excluding sight-seers) might use it at one time, and no reader might study the same book for more than an hour if it was wanted by another.

At the beginning of the seventeenth century, then, hopes were high though funds were low. Plans to build a new library to rival Sir Thomas Bodley's at Oxford were actively canvassed, but when at last the university found in the Duke of Buckingham, whom it elected to be its chancellor in 1626, a man who it might reasonably hope would forward and finance the project, political assassination removed him before he could be persuaded to the point of opening his coffers. Thus for the first quarter of the century the library's history is one of frustration and trivial incident, the only accessions of consequence being presentation copies from their authors of King James's *Works* in their Latin translation (1620) and Bacon's *Instauratio Magna* (1620) and *De dignitate et augmentis scientiarum* (1623). In 1629, however, things took a turn for the better with the appointment as University Librarian of Abraham Whelock, a man of modest and nervous disposition but a good scholar whose abilities won him a reputation in the learned world beyond Cambridge and the friendship especially of Sir Henry Spelman and Sir Thomas Adams, on whom he prevailed to establish in the university its first lectureships (to which he was himself appointed) in Anglo-Saxon and the Oriental languages. He enjoyed too in the library the intermittent assistance of young men who had been his pupils, and the last year of his regime (he died in 1653) saw the official appointment of an Under Library-Keeper, Jonathan Pindar by name, of quite remarkable competence and industry.

Whelock's talents and personality and his obvious devotion to the library over which he presided thus began not only to give it a certain respectable status in the world of scholarship but also to attract to it donations of books which it was itself too impoverished to buy. As the friend and correspondent of public men he knew how and where to drop a hint or proffer a suggestion, and though excessively shy and timorous he pursued potential donors—or set other men pursuing them—with resolution and tenacity. He procured many small gifts from his contemporaries at Cambridge and from members of the learned booktrade there and in London, and presentation copies of books from their authors—they included Herbert of Cherbury, Caleb Dalechamp, Pierre Delaune, Johannes Hevelius, Christoph Arnold, and G. J. Vossius—witness the respect in which he and his library were held at home and abroad. But it was, of course, to the procuring of Oriental books that he first addressed himself: he obtained from William Bedwell a Koran, having cleverly informed him that his old College Trinity already possessed one, and from his heirs the Arabic-Latin Lexicon in nine volumes which he had spent much of his life compiling; and he set Richard Holdsworth, himself a future benefactor of the library, extracting from the widowed Duchess of Buckingham in London the library of Oriental manuscripts which her husband had bought in conditions of great secrecy from the widow of Thomas Erpenius in Leiden in 1626. It had, to be sure, always been the dilatory Duke's intention to give them to Cambridge, though it was not until 1632 that the Duchess was finally persuaded. They numbered eighty-seven volumes (one of them being not a manuscript, but a Chinese printed book, the first to come into the library's possession) and included some of the oldest surviving manuscripts in Malay, an important commentary in old Persian on the Koran (MS. Mm.4.15), and a short but unique chronicle of events in Sicily, A.D. 827–965, appended to a text of Eutychius. Several of Erpenius's manuscripts were sent from Cambridge to help Brian Walton (and the other editors of his Polyglot Bible) and Edmund Castell in the compilation of his *Lexicon heptaglotton*.

The middle years of the century saw larger events in the library's history as well as the nation's. In 1647 Parliament, instigated by John Selden, voted to buy for the library at a cost of £500 a collection of Hebrew Books, including a few manuscripts, which the London bookseller George Thomason had imported from Italy. The number of volumes was 167 and they contained more than 400 items covering a wide range of subjects from liturgies, codes of the law, and biblical commentaries to history, medicine, and poetry. Nor was this the only occasion at this time on which Selden earned the university's gratitude. In 1610 Richard Bancroft, Archbishop of Canterbury, had bequeathed the library which he had formed in his palace at Lambeth to his successor in the See provided he gave assurance that he would continue the inheritance to successive archbishops forever; otherwise the library was to pass to the projected College of Divinity at Chelsea, if it should be built within six years, or, if it should not, to the Public Library of the University of

Cambridge. Thus the Lambeth Library passed from Bancroft to Abbot and from Abbot to Laud. In 1640, however, Laud was impeached and his possessions appropriated by the State, and with the abolition of episcopacy in 1643, the projected college at Chelsea still being no more than a project, the university had a good title, which the Commons were persuaded by Selden to admit early in 1647; and so, the Lords having concurred, the Lambeth Library of some 10,000 volumes—about eight times the number held by the University Library—was delivered to Cambridge sometime during the academical year 1648–1649. Nineteen bookcases to receive them were quickly supplied, the work of a local joiner but the gift of Sir John Wollaston (an Alderman of the City of London), and were set up in the south room, and a scheme of college contributions was inaugurated to provide the University Librarian and his newly acquired Under Library-Keeper with stipends suitable to their new responsibilities.

Whelock himself died before work on the collection was begun, but his two immediate successors were both men of energy and distinction and under their direction the admirable Pindar arranged and cataloged the books with all the efficiency the opportunity demanded. The rare books and manuscripts from Lambeth were set up in the east room, which was so arranged that Lambeth books stood on one side of it and Cambridge books on the other, while in the south room the books of the old Common Library were sorted in with the other newcomers on Wollaston's bookcases. In both rooms each bookcase was denoted by a letter of the alphabet, those in the south room being additionally distinguished by a sign like a musical sharp placed before the letter; the shelves in each bookcase were given a Greek letter, and each book was given a number on its shelf. Its complete class mark—B.α.12, for example—was written inside the front cover of each book, and since the books stood in the fashion of the time, front edge outward, a small label bearing the book's running number on the shelf was affixed to one of its covers at the front edge. All this was the work of Jonathan Pindar, who also wrote the necessary shelf lists and compiled an author catalog (and other indexes) which he clearly modeled upon Thomas James's published Bodleian catalog of 1620. At last, it appeared, Cambridge could claim without fear of ridicule that its library rivaled those at Oxford and the Vatican.

All this work was to be undone almost immediately. With the restoration of the monarchy in 1660 came the restoration of episcopacy also, and the new Archbishop William Juxon, heir and successor of Bancroft, Abbot, and Laud, claimed the return of his library, proposing that the university should receive in its stead the library of Richard Holdsworth, who had died as Master of Emmanuel in 1649, leaving his executors a complicated set of "Directions" in which he tried to foresee all possible eventualities: his library was to go to the university if it pleased God to make a resettlement of the Church within five years and if the university returned the Lambeth Library; otherwise it was to go to Emmanuel College, provided they built a library room to receive it; otherwise it was to go to Trinity College, Dublin; and if his executors chose not to bestow his library on any of these places, then they were to sell it and employ the money so raised on pious uses. Juxon's suggestion thus ignored the fact that, God having failed to resettle the Church by 1654, the college had an arguable claim, which it now advanced. The subsequent proceedings are very copiously documented; but eventually in December 1664, Holdsworth's Library was adjudged to the university, the Lambeth Library having been returned to the Archbishop the previous February.

Holdsworth's Library contained 10,095 printed volumes and 186 manuscripts and must have been numerically the largest private collection in England of its time, though Selden's surpassed it in quality. It was the library of an academic, its great strength lying in its books of divinity, which accounted for more than half of it. It contained more than 200 incunabula, including four Caxtons (the first to come into the library's possession), and of course many hundreds of English books of the period which we now call *S.T.C.* (*Short Title Catalogue of English Books 1475–1640*). Its manuscripts included a fine twelfth century Boethius, *De arithmetica* and *De musica* (MS. Ii.3.12), a thirteenth-century Bestiary of great artistic interest (MS. Kk.4.25), a Latin Josephus written ca. 1125 and containing some of the most accomplished illuminations of its period (MS. Dd.1.4), an important manuscript of Chaucer written ca. 1430 (MS. Gg.4.27), a number of other early literary texts in English including the manuscript from which William Bedwell had published in 1631 *The Tournament of Tottenham,* and (textually perhaps the most important of Holdsworth's manuscripts) the famous ninth-century Juvencus with near-contemporary glosses and added versus which are reputed to be the oldest written remains of the Welsh language (MS. Ff.4.42).

Simultaneously with the acquisition of Holdsworth's books the library was further augmented by the bequest of nearly 4000 volumes (all of them printed) from Henry Lucas, the University's Member of Parliament. The collection proved an excellent supplement to Holdsworth's, containing many books of contemporary history, political memoirs, travel, genealogy, archaeology, and antiquities, a few books of genuine scientific importance (including Galileo's *Dialogo* of 1632), and many more of near-scientific curiosity, and (for the first time in the library's history) some hundreds of books in French and Italian. Other benefactions followed in quick succession. In 1666–1667 Tobias Rustat, Yeoman of the Robes to Charles II, whom he had followed devotedly throughout his exile, gave the University £1000 to endow its first fund for the purchase of books, thus removing what had so far been its greatest disability, the lack of an annual income to be spent exclusively on the library. In 1670 John Hacket, Bishop of Coventry, bequeathed 1000 volumes, manuscript and printed, with the sensible provision that duplicated works already in the library might be sold and others bought with the proceeds. Several other not inconsiderable gifts of money, to be spent outright on books, came in before the end of the century, and many hundreds of books were also received into the library under the provisions of the Licensing Acts of 1662–1679 and 1685–1695.

Thus all seemed set fair for a period of expansion and greater usefulness; but the university, alas, proved grievously unequal to the challenge. The Regent House, to be sure, passed solemn resolutions that certain things were to be done by certain dates, issued from time to time minatory notices, and appointed committees of learned men to draw up orders and regulations for the better government of the library. But its staff still consisted of one University Librarian and one Under Library-Keeper, and even though local booksellers were called in to help them, they could hardly be expected to deal effectively with so vast a problem. One librarian proved so idle that he was persuaded in 1668 to retire, and his successor after fifteen years' toil announced that he did "most thankfully and willingly" recede from his place. Eventually the books were sorted and set up, after a fashion. Holdsworth's printed books and the printed books of the pre-Holdsworth collection were shelved in the south room, where the bookcases continued to be denoted by letters as in the "Lambeth" period, though the shelves in each case were now given numbers instead of Greek letters. The manuscripts, Rustat's books and Hacket's, and certain books in small formats were placed in the east room, where the bookcases were given numbers instead of letters. Shelf lists were eventually written and, one must hope, an author catalog, though none survives. And so, with ever-increasing pressure on staff and space, the library fell into a confusion that persisted for more than a century.

Early in the eighteenth century during the librarianship (1684–1712) of John Laughton—by no means negligible as a scholar, and as a librarian a considerable improvement on his immediate predecessors—the library began to assume a modern appearance. In 1706 it adopted for the first time a general bookplate (engraved by William Jackson, who made bookplates for some of the Cambridge Colleges also and for Eton) and in the same year the books were reversed on the shelf so that they stood spine outward and could now be labeled with their full class marks visible to readers as they scanned the shelves. In 1709 (in which year the learned German Zacharias Conrad von Uffenbach visited the library and found little to please him) the library was included among the privileged libraries of copyright deposit under the first Copyright Act, and in 1715 it received by gift from King George I the magnificent library collected by John Moore, Bishop of Ely, who had died in the previous year. These last two events are the outstanding events, not of the century only, but of the library's whole history.

The Copyright Act of Queen Anne—"An Act for the Encouragement of Learning, by Vesting the Copies of Printed Books in the Authors or Purchasers of such Copies, During the Times Therein Mentioned"—gave publishers copyright protection (though not the perpetual copyright they wanted) provided they entered their titles before publication in the Stationers' Register and sent nine copies of each book, also before publication, to Stationers' Hall to be forwarded to the nine privileged libraries. Unfortunately, the operation of the Act soon proved uncertain, for though it specified penalties for failure to deliver or forward the required copies, it specified no penalty if a publisher failed to enter a title; and so the trade argued that entry of each and every title was not obligatory and that they need enter (and so deposit) only those books for which they wished to obtain copyright protection. Hence it became the common complaint of the privileged libraries that the Act brought them not the large, learned, and expensive works that they required but the popular best sellers and cheap pamphlets that their publishers feared might be pirated if they did not register them as their copyrights. In addition the publishers, who understandably resented having to give so many copies away, devised ingenious methods of evading their obligation of deposit even in the case of books they registered; and against these tactics the libraries found themselves powerless since it proved impossible to take legal action against a delinquent publisher within the limits of three months after publication as the Act required. And this unsatisfactory situation persisted for just over a century.

Nor did the library take active steps to improve it. It did not, for example, as did some of the privileged libraries, appoint persons with powers of attorney to act as its official collecting agents, but was content simply to receive from Stationers' Hall such books (they were usually delivered at Lady Day and Michaelmas) as the clerk of the Hall chose to garner in return for a small quarterly fee. Moreover, the library thought many of the books which were sent, especially fiction, unsuitable for admission to a learned library, and from 1751 sold such books and bought with the proceeds noncopyright books which it thought more useful. Soon afterward it delegated to one of the Cambridge booksellers the duty of receiving the Stationers' parcels and settling the university's expenses in carriage of the books and fees to the Stationers' clerk, allowing him to retain books which appeared "unsuitable" in return for appropriate credits on the library's book bills. This deplorable situation (which, however, was neither unique nor in its contemporary context so disgraceful as it now appears) was radically changed early in the following century.

The result of this policy of noncooperation on the one side and shortsighted lethargy on the other is that the library is conspicuously lacking in copyright copies of many major works of fiction, poetry, and drama published during the eighteenth century (though very many of them have, of course, been acquired since). Exactly what proportion of registered titles the Stationers delivered and the library kept is impossible to determine since there survive no accessions lists of Stationers' books before 1758 and no complete file of correspondence with Stationers' Hall before 1814; but it is likely that of the 17,000 or so titles registered between those dates the library possesses in original copies of deposit no more than one-sixth.

The library of John Moore, which from the circumstances of its donation became known as the King's or Royal Library of the University Library, was renowned throughout Europe and contained some 30,000 volumes, of which 1790 were manuscripts; and it is understandable that a gift of such magnitude (it trebled the size of the existing collections), though rapturously received, should prove something of an embarrassment to its recipients. The immediate requirement, of course, was for shelf space, and with commendable promptitude the university at once made over to the library the upper floor of the western range of the schools (then used as a Law School) and built at their southwest corner a room that connected the southern and western ranges (see Figure 4). This structural work and the furnishing of the west room with bookcases (made by John Austin) were completed in 1718–1719.

Once the books were unpacked, however, it immediately became clear that yet more space was needed. The only room left for expansion was the upper room of the northern range, and since this room, formerly the University Chapel, was the official meeting place of the Regent Masters, an entirely new building for the conduct of university business had to be provided. The building of the present Senate

INSIDE VIEW OF THE PUBLIC LIBRARY, CAMBRIDGE.

FIGURE 4. *The Cambridge University Library's west room looking south. (From a caricature by Rowlandson, 1809.)*

House, completed in 1730, therefore followed, the task of fitting up the north room (with bookcases made by James Essex) being undertaken in 1731 and finished in 1734. At this point, however, things began to go wrong. The Senate House had been conceived as one wing of a grand new building, over the design of which protracted controversy now ensued. Eventually the scheme was abandoned and a new one, involving the demolition of the eastern range of the schools so that it might be rebuilt in a politer style of architecture to match the Senate House, was taken up instead and carried out in 1754–1758. Thus nearly twenty years elapsed between the reception of Moore's books and the provision of space for them in the west and north rooms, and nearly twice that time before all the changes consequent upon their arrival were completed. During those years quantities of Moore's books lay about unsorted in heaps, and shameful depredations were committed upon them, the largest by Henry Justice, Fellow-Commoner of Trinity (whose library he also abused), convicted felon, and in the last stage of his career publisher at The Hague of an engraved edition of Virgil in imitation of Pine's *Horace*.

The university's answer to the problems posed by the arrangement of so large a collection had been to create in 1721 a new office grandly entitled *Protobibliothecarius* and to appoint to it Conyers Middleton, principally with the object of annoying his old enemy Richard Bentley. Middleton produced in 1723 a pamphlet *Bibliothecae Cantabrigiensis ordinandae methodus,* in which he made some sensible recommendations as to the classification and shelving of the books, and thereupon (it would seem) retired from all further effort. The practical work of setting up the books in the west and north rooms appears to have been carried out, with the help of young Bachelors of Arts, in 1732–1734 during the librarianship of John Taylor, editor of Lysias and Demosthenes and later Headmaster of Shrewsbury School. The arrangement and shelving of the manuscripts and of certain of the rarest printed books that were locked up with them was the work of Francis Sawyer Parris, *Proto-bibliothecarius* in succession to Middleton, soon after 1752. Parris's elegant shelf lists contained an author index of their own; the rest of the Royal collection was cataloged in four massive folio volumes, the non-Royal collection being served by a copy (bought in 1752) of the Bodleian printed catalog of 1738 interleaved and annotated. The new bookcases were again distinguished by letters, the printed books running from A to Cc and the manuscripts (those of the old collections were sorted in with the newcomers) from Dd to Mm; and since most of the printed-book class

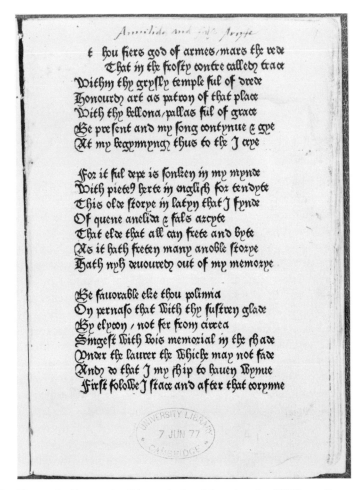

FIGURE 5. *Chaucer's* Queen Anelida and the false Arcyte (*William Caxton, ca. 1477*), *the only known copy.*

marks duplicated those in the old collections in the south room, books soon began to get into the wrong places, even though the Royal books were distinguished by a bookplate engraved for them by John Pine. To overcome this difficulty the University Press was commissioned to print some thousands of asterisks, one of which was solemnly pasted onto the spine of each of the pre-Royal books.

This munificent benefaction brought to the library a comprehensive collection of books of all periods (there were about 470 incunabula) in all departments of literature and learning, including many of the library's most valuable rarities. To particularize among so many is difficult, and not very useful: but mention may be made, among printed books, of Moore's unique copies of quartos printed by Caxton (see Figure 5) and Wynkyn de Worde and, among manuscripts, of his Bede's *Ecclesiastical History* with the *Hymn of Caedmon* at the end (MS. Kk.5.16, written ca. A.D. 737), *Book of Cerne* (narrative of the Passion, with prayers, hymns, and monastic charters; MS. Ll.1.10, of the ninth century), *Book of Deer* (a gospel book, with Gaelic charters, etc.: MS. Ii.6.32, of the ninth/tenth centuries—see Figure 6), *Winchester Pontifical* (MS. Ee.2.3, early twelfth century), and the copiously illustrated *Life of King Edward the Confessor* (M.S. Ee.3.59, ca. 1250—see Figure 7).

All other events of the library's history during the eighteenth century are relatively insignificant or altogether trivial. In 1726 George Lewis presented a cabinet containing a small but valuable collection of Persian manuscripts and a number of

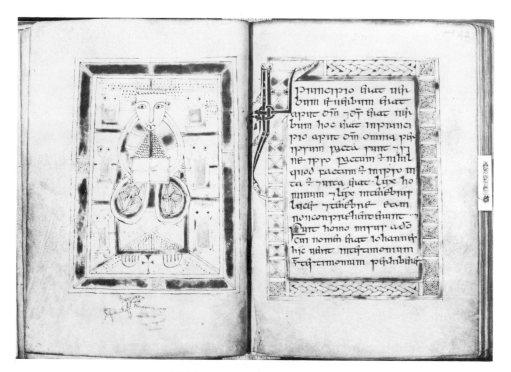

FIGURE 6. Book of Deer.

FIGURE 7. Life of King Edward the Confessor.

Oriental curiosities which proved a great attraction to tourists; Thomas Baker, non-juror and ejected Fellow of St. John's College (where, nonetheless, he happily resided until his death) bequeathed in 1740 a large portion of his multivolume manuscript transcriptions of historical documents, invaluable especially for matters pertaining to the University; in 1785 the library bought a number of Greek manuscripts at Anthony Askew's sale, prompted no doubt by the *Protobibliothecarius* Richard Farmer (black-letter collector and author of the *Essay on the Learning of Shakespeare*), who himself in the same year bought and gave to the library a number of books from the working library of the former librarian, John Taylor; and in the last years of the century James Nasmith completed, but did not publish, a descriptive catalog of the library's manuscripts.

The two principal events of the eighteenth century had increased the status of the library to a point where it could no longer remain, as it had in effect hitherto been, a private library for such senior members of the university as cared to use it. Its story in the nineteenth century is of its gradual emergence (and the process was a painful one) as a central and vital institution in the university and as a place of scholarly repute and usefulness beyond it.

The process began in 1812, when the university sued under the Copyright Act a publisher who had not delivered a book which he had not registered, and somewhat to its own embarrassment won its case. It could now no longer dispose of such Stationers' books as it thought unworthy and so (though squabbles with the Stationers continued for some time) began at last to assume its responsibilities as a repository of national literature. An immediate effect, of course, was a modest in crease in the library's establishment, which rose to five by 1823, though it dropped to four five years later when by grace of the university the *Protobibliothecarius* and the University Librarian became one flesh enjoying two stipends, the office of *Protobibliothecarius* lapsing and being finally abolished in 1845. One of the new-comers was John Bowtell, nephew of a well-known Cambridge bookbinder, who was appointed in 1819 and remained (in his latter years a pillar of irascible reaction) until persuaded into an honorable retirement in 1852 at the age of seventy-five. During his long years at the library he was effectively responsible for all its practical work and in particular between 1819 and 1826 compiled in forty-two volumes a manuscript author catalog that superseded those inaugurated in 1752. The same period also saw a considerable enlargement of the library's premises with the construction in 1842 of the opulent Cockerell's Building, running parallel with the old northern range of the schools but extending beyond it on the west to form one side of what (with additional ranges put up in 1864–1868 and 1890–1891) was to become another quadrilateral of buildings eventually wholly devoted to the library. The most conspicuous feature of the first half of the century was, however, the failure of the authorities to attract and procure any really notable and sizable additions of the library's holdings. For this the library's antiquated system of administration—a syndicate (to use the Cambridge word) of all the officials of the university, established in 1751—was responsible; and when in 1853 the syndicate was reconstituted on a rational basis and reduced to a membership of seventeen, the immediate effect was to stimulate a good deal of confused and argumentative activity since no steps were taken at the same time to strengthen the library's executive staff. One immediate and lasting piece of work dates, however, from this period in the institution of a new form of catalog in which manuscript entries produced with the aid of a manifold writer were pasted into large volumes of blank paper in their proper sequence but leaving spaces for additions. The present system using printed catalog entries was a logical development and was introduced in 1861. These years also saw the compilation, by several learned hands, and publication of a catalog of the library's western manuscripts (five volumes and index, 1856–1867).

What the times required was a strong librarian who could prepare the way for the reforms that were needed and being increasingly demanded. Such a man came forward in 1864 in the person of John Eyton Bickersteth Mayor (1825–1910), University Librarian from the date until 1867 and afterward Professor of Latin, a man whom some members of the library's staff could remember, when the present writer joined it in 1936, as a reader in his old age in the place over which he had once presided. Not everything he attempted was practicable or even sensible, but he was combative when combat was called for, expressed his opinions unequivocally in speech and print, gave a great deal of pain to persons who well deserved it, and in four short years shook off from the Library the dust which two centuries of indifference had allowed to accumulate upon it.

He was succeeded by Henry Bradshaw, one of the most distinguished scholar-librarians of his time, who held the librarianship until his death in 1886. Administration was not his forte (nor did he enjoy it), but he began the establishment

within the library of an efficient departmental organization and instituted procedures and routines some of which have survived effective to this day. A man of
great learning in many fields—especially palaeography, bibliography, and liturgiol-
ogy—he set about restoring to order the library's collections of manuscripts and
rare books, in particular its incunabula, which he gathered together from all over
the library into what he called his *museum typographicum,* there arranging them,
after minute analysis of their typography, into groups by countries, towns, and
presses in their correct chronological order—a practical application of the "natural
history" method of study (as he called it) which Robert Proctor and other in-
cunabulists have since adopted and developed. At the same time Bradshaw greatly
added to the collection by wise (and sometimes spectacular) purchases, especially
in the field of early Netherlandish printing.

Bradshaw's work was continued by his pupil and successor at one remove
Francis Jenkinson, librarian from 1889 to 1923, and by Jenkinson's successor
Alwyn Faber Scholfield, 1923–1949. Jenkinson frankly detested administrative
work, but he tolerated it and with the help of the library's first secretary, H. G.
Aldis (bibliographer of Scottish printing and author of the handbook, still in its
revised editions current and useful, entitled *The Printed Book*), performed it efficiently. His great contribution to the library was the result of the charm and gentle
goodness of his character ("Jenkinson was a saint," men who served under him
would say), producing within the library an atmosphere where a still inadequate
staff worked happily and well and attracting to it men of scholarly capacity such as
A. T. Bartholomew, bibliographer of Bentley and editor of Samuel (*Erewhon*)
Butler, and Charles Edward Sayle, author of *Early English Printed Books in the
University Library, Cambridge* (four volumes, 1900–1907) and of *Annals of
Cambridge University Library, 1278–1900* (1916). Jenkinson's personal friend-
ships also brought to the library a constant stream of donations and benefactions,
especially those of Samuel Sandars (founder of the University's annual Reader-
ship in Bibliography), donor of many fine incunabula and illuminated manuscripts,
and John Charrington, whose principal interest lay in early Florentine books with
wood-cut illustration.

A. F. Scholfield, an accomplished classical scholar, deliberately subordinated his
own interests to the organizational needs of the library, establishing an efficient
departmental structure and devoting his energies to problems of classification and
cataloging. The outstanding event of his librarianship was the removal of the
library from its Old Schools site to its present building, built with the generous
aid of the Rockefeller Foundation and opened in 1934 (see Figure 8); here, with
a depleted and in large part temporary staff, he guided the library's fortunes successfully through the difficult years of World War II.

These three men, then, transformed the University Library into a place where
scholarship might be pursued and its needs adequately served. The results of their
labors may be seen in the great accessions that have come to the library during
the last century in all departments of its collections, beginning with Bradshaw's gift
of Irish books in 1868. Of major benefactions received since then mention may be
made of the Ritschl collection of foreign dissertations (1878); Sir T. F. Wade's

FIGURE 8. *The Cambridge University Library, 1934.*

Far Eastern Library (1886); John Venn's collection of books on logic (1888); the early printed books of John Couch Adams (1892); the Near Eastern libraries of R. L. Bensly (1895), E. J. W. Gibb (1901), E. B. Cowell and Frank Chance (both 1903), E. G. Browne (1936), A. J. Arberry (1948–1952), and C. H. Armbruster (1957); the Japanese collection of W. G. Aston (1911); the library of historian Lord Acton (60,000 volumes, 1902); the J. W. Clark collection of books, pamphlets, and ephemera relating to the University (1910); the notebooks, etc., of bibliographer Edward Gordon Duff (1924); the early printed books of Francis Jenkinson (1908, 1917, 1923), F. W. Seebohm (1925; Erasmiana), J. W. L. Glaisher (1928; books of arithmetic), A. W. Young (1933, 1936; included the Gutenberg Bible), Karl Pearson (1936; Reformation pamphlets), Sir Stephen Gaselee (1934, incunabula; 1940, sixteenth-century books; 1943, Petroniana), R. E. Hart (1946; five blockbooks and a Caxton), and L. C. G. Clarke (1960; Restif de la Bretonne); the working library of typographer Stanley Morison (1968); in music the collections of F. T. Arnold (1944; largely eighteenth century) and Marion Margaret Scott (1953; Haydn); portions of the very extensive Crawford collection of broadsides (proclamations, church briefs, miscellaneous broadsides; deposited 1945); and, among collections of papers (some on deposit only) the nineteenth century archive of Jardine Matheson & Co., merchants in the Far East, Sir Robert Walpole's archive from Houghton (handlist by G. A. Chinnery, 1953), the papers of Charles Hardinge, 1st Baron Hardinge of Penshurst, Viceroy of India from 1910 to 1916 (handlist by N. J. Hancock, 1968), papers and correspondence of Charles Darwin (handlist of the papers, 1960) as well as books and pamphlets from his library, with his manuscript notes, the Ely Diocesan Records, and the papers of Stanley Baldwin (d. 1947) and of Samuel Hoare, 1st Lord Temple-wood (d. 1959). A recent event of outstanding importance is the deposit on long-term loan of the pre-1800 printed books of the Peterborough Cathedral Library (March 1970).

The library's present holdings are estimated at 2,500,000 printed volumes and 15,000 volumes of manuscripts, excluding its large collections of correspondence and of political and other papers; it also possesses 600,000 maps, 250,000 music scores, and 4700 microfilms. Its staff (including clerical, technical, and maintenance staff) numbers 170. A large proportion of its books are on open-access and are borrowable (as, under certain safeguards, are some of the books on closed shelves) under various entitlements by senior members of the university, resident Bachelors, and third-year undergraduates. It is, however, open to all members of the university, whatever their status, and to visiting bona fide scholars. Its subject coverage is comprehensive, except that it deposits in the university's law library (the Squire Law Library) most of the current British law books and periodicals received under the Copyright Act. The acquisition of current foreign periodicals in the sciences is to some extent left to other libraries in the Cambridge system (and especially to the Scientific Periodicals Library, formerly called the Philosophical Library), and the University Library also refrains from claiming under the Copyright Act certain minor periodicals which are not of academic interest, and some newspapers.

The University Library's primary function is as a research library in arts subjects, and it does not make any special provision for undergraduates or stock multiple copies of the textbooks which they need, these needs being left to the appropriate faculty and departmental libraries, of which there are sixty-one, and to the twenty-nine colleges, most of which have undergraduate libraries as well as rich historic collections of rare books and manuscripts.

The colleges are, of course, independent self-governing foundations, though the university has in recent years made a substantial contribution to their purchase of books for undergraduate use through its College Libraries Fund. The faculty and departmental libraries are each administered by the faculty or department concerned under the over-all supervision of the General Board of the Faculties, to which the University Library's Administrative Committee (the University Library Syndicate) is also responsible. The system and its possibilities and implications for future development have recently been very fully described and discussed in the First Report of the General Board's Committee on Libraries, published in the *Cambridge University Reporter* (Vol. 99, pp. 1190–1315, March 28, 1969). The Fitzwilliam Museum, whose library has rich collections of illuminated manuscripts, literary and other autographs, music, early printed books, illustrated books, and fine bindings, occupies a position somewhat apart from the main system.

The Library has a small bindery and a photographic laboratory.

An extension to the Library is now in the course of being built.

J. C. T. OATES

CANADA, LIBRARIES IN

The earliest libraries in Canada belonged to individuals, the religious orders, the government, the military, and the fur traders. The first private library belonged to Marc Lescarbot, Parisian scholar and advocate, who sailed into Annapolis Basin, then Acadie and now Nova Scotia, in the summer of 1606 on the *Jonas*. In his *Histoire de la Nouvelle France* Lescarbot describes his evenings of reading and writing.

Volumes bearing the *ex libris* of La Bibliothèque de la Mission Canadienne de Jésuites, 1632, are still in existence as are also titles from the Collège des Jésuites de Québec, 1635, the first college library in North America. The fur traders were in the main men of education sent by their companies in Europe to explore the country and to trade with the Indians. By 1700 there were books in the Hudson's Bay post, York Factory on Hudson's Bay. The first library in British Columbia belonged to John McKay, who in 1786 arrived in Vancouver Island on a fur trading exploration. Two years later at Fort Chipewyn, now in Alberta, Roderick MacKenzie's collection of books began to circulate.

Of the military-political leaders, John Graves Simcoe made the greatest contribution when he donated his private library to the Province of Upper Canada of which he was the first lieutenant governor, 1792–1796. In 1779 Sir Frederick Haldimand inaugurated a bilingual library in the city of Quebec on the basis of fees adequate to keep the collection current which resulted in only the more wealthy belonging. The first subscription library in Upper Canada (now Ontario) was opened in Niagara in 1800 through townspeople interested in the education of the community and especially of the young. In the last decade of the eighteenth century the professional or special libraries appeared; for example, in 1797 the Law Library was established in Halifax. Lord Dalhousie established the Garrison Library, Halifax, in 1816, a library still giving service as the Cambridge Library. The Royal Engineers brought with them a subscription library, the titles chosen by Sir Edward Bulwer-Lytton in 1858. When the Engineers completed their assignment in British Columbia most of the collection became the New Westminster Public Library.

With an increasing population in the nineteenth century more subscription and social libraries appeared as did also school district libraries. The government, college, and university libraries, the libraries of the professions, those of the mechanics institutes, and the free public libraries multiplied.

The first Mechanics' Institute was in St. John's, Newfoundland, in 1827. Others followed quickly in Montreal in 1828, in Toronto in 1830, in Halifax in 1831, in Kingston in 1834, and in many other centers. They were financed by membership fees and by government grants as early as 1835. As education improved the classes of the Mechanics' Institutes were no longer needed and most of the institutes devoted their funds to the improvement of their libraries which later provided the nucleus collections for many public libraries. The Mechanics' Institute of Montreal with its Atwater Library is the only one remaining. It still provides popular lectures and has contributed greatly to the intellectual life of Montreal. In 1851 the first Public Libraries and Mechanics' Institute Act was passed by the Baldwin-Lafontaine government of the United Canadas, followed soon after by the first School Libraries' Act.

Nova Scotia and Upper Canada (Ontario) led in efforts to serve the rural population through school district libraries—libraries for public use administered by the local school organization. Joseph Howe in Nova Scotia and Egerton Ryerson in Upper Canada were the prime movers. In both provinces legal provision was made in 1850 through the Nova Scotia Education Act, and the Province of Canada Common School Act. In Lower Canada (Quebec) the parish library managed by parishioners under the local curé was instituted by Bishop Ignace Bourget of Montreal in 1843, the Library and Reading Room of L'Institut Canadien of Montreal in 1844. New Brunswick in 1858 and Prince Edward Island in 1877 introduced school district legislation, as did the Northwest Territories at the turn of the century. Research is needed to estimate the influence of these measures prior to the passage of legislation authorizing the tax-supported free public library.

In 1867 agreement was reached regarding confederation by the Canadas (Lower and Upper Canada), New Brunswick, and Nova Scotia under the name of the Dominion of Canada with Lower Canada to be Quebec and Upper Canada, Ontario. The divided powers of government were legislative jurisdiction over all subjects of general or common interest to the federal government of Canada and legislative jurisdiction over all local interests including education to the provincial governments. Three years later Manitoba and the Northwest Territories were added to Canada and in the years following, British Columbia in 1871 and Prince Edward Island in 1873. Reorganization of the Northwest Territories created the Yukon as a separate territory in 1898, and the provinces of Saskatchewan and Alberta in 1905. With the addition of Newfoundland in 1949 Canada became the second largest country in the world with an area of 3,851,809 square miles. It achieved independence in 1931 under the Statute of Westminster but elected to remain a part of the Commonwealth of Nations. The single limitation on Canada is imposed by the federal nature of its union for the Statute of Westminster did not enlarge the power of the federal government at the expense of the provinces. In 1947 the Canadian Citizenship Act created the distinct nationality of the Canadian citizen. In 1960 "An Act for the Recognition and Protection of Human Rights and Fundamental Freedoms" was passed by the Canadian Parliament. In 1964 a national flag was adopted.

Government of Canada and Libraries

With education the prerogative of the provinces, there is no national office of education. The national education services have to be arranged through federal-provincial action, by nongovernmental associations such as the Association of Universities and Colleges of Canada, the Canadian Library Association, etc., by advisory councils, and by the federal departments in subject fields. Special concessions are allowed libraries; for example, the library postal rate for interlibrary loans, government document depository collections, free customs entry of library books, exhibitions of library work at international fairs, e.g., Brussels and Expo 67, exhibits of housing and of urban renewal problems by the Central Mortgage and Housing Corporation, documentary film deposits by the National Film Board, and library statistical services by the Dominion Bureau of Statistics. Technical libraries have been assisted by the Technical and Vocational Training Agreement. A system of scholarships for students training for the federal government library services assists recruitment of staff.

The Royal Commissions of the Federal Government of Canada have accepted briefs on library needs. Thus the Royal Commission on National Development in the Arts, Letters and Sciences reported in favor "that a national library be established without delay," "that a body be created to be known as the Canada Council for the encouragement of the arts, letters, humanities and social sciences to stimulate and help voluntary organizations within these fields." The Royal Commission on Publications recommended financial support of periodical indexing. The Canadian Centennial Commission made funds available to assist in building over one hundred new libraries varying in size from the National Library covering thirteen acres to small community libraries.

The Federal Government of Canada is responsible for the financial support of The Library of Parliament, the National Library, the National Science Library, the libraries of the government departments, the Royal Commissions, the crown corporations, the Public Library Service of the Northwest Territories, the Yukon Regional Library system, and the development of library service to the 558 Indian bands.

The territorial libraries that come under the Department of Indian Affairs and Northwest Development are discussed separately. The public library service to Indian bands is a joint effort of the provinces and the Federal Government of Canada and is part of a program to encourage total participation in the social and economic life of Canada. The bands operate on the same basis as local municipalities and a library grant of one dollar per capita is made from the federal Grants to Bands Funds. The bands take the initiative to establish library service, contribute annually to qualify for the grant, and establish a working arrangement with a larger library system. Band contributions and federal grants take the place of local tax funds. To obtain Indian field staff, positions in regional and provincial library systems were found for Indian university students wishing to work in the summer with the federal government paying toward salary and travel. A fully qualified Indian librarian is employed by the Saskatchewan Provincial Library as liaison between the bands, the regional library of their area, and the department. This arrangement brings a knowledge of the Indian cultures, languages, and points of view quickly into the system. Federal scholarship funds are available for Indian graduates to train as librarians. A special library consultant charged with Indian public library development is in the Department of Indian Affairs and Northern Development. Discussions with the provinces have arranged for the necessary cooperation. In some instances a change in the provincial library act has been necessary.

The only libraries to receive federal financial aid are the university libraries which benefit from the university grants policy developed on a per capita formula, the money paid to each province to distribute at its discretion, and from the University Capital Grants Fund administered by the Canada Council. This fund has aided the erection of new library buildings or in renovations or extensions.

Since research is of national importance financial aid was arranged through some federal agency for national university library studies following the *Resources of Canadian University Libraries for Research in the Humanities and Social Sciences* by Edwin E. Williams. This survey, published in 1962, was made on behalf of the National Conference of Canadian Universities and Colleges and was financed by a grant from the Council on Library Resources, Washington. The report was widely reviewed and pointed up the statement of the national librarian, Dr. W. Kaye Lamb, in the Preface that "library resources in Canadian universities in the field of the humanities and social sciences are clearly grossly inadequate, and very substantial expenditure will be necessary to raise them to a proper standard."

On behalf of the Association of Canadian Medical Colleges the *Library Support of Medical Education and Research in Canada; Report of a Survey of the Medical College Libraries With Suggestions for Improving and Extending Medical Library Service to Local, Regional and National Levels* by Beatrice V. Simon was issued in 1964. This survey and the one by Williams became the point of departure for *Science-Technology Literature Resources in Canada; Report of a Survey for the Associate Committee on Scientific Information [of the National Research Council of Canada]* by George S. Bonn, who omitted medical literature as this had received attention from Miss Simon. Bonn called for a strong central science library and a science service library network across Canada. In 1966 the National Research Council Act was amended to allow the Council "to establish, operate and maintain a national science library."

It became apparent that a general study of academic libraries was needed next. Through the action of the Canadian Association of Colleges and University Libraries (a section of the Canadian Library Association), the sponsorship of the Association of Universities and Colleges of Canada, formerly the National Conference of Canadian Universities and Colleges, was obtained. With funds supplied by the Canada Council and the Council on Library Resources, this study, *Resources of Canadian Academic and Research Libraries* by Robert B. Downs, was issued in 1967. Many of the forty-one recommendations designed for the academic and research libraries are applicable to the public libraries. This report was presented at a workshop called for the purpose in Montreal. A complete estimate of costs to implement the recommendations and to correct the situations shown as substandard was entrusted to Dr. Robert H. Blackburn, whose paper on "Financial Implications of the Downs Report on Canadian Academic and Research Libraries has been published by the Association of Universities and Colleges of Canada. Further research on the collections is being conducted by the Office of

Library Resources, National Library of Canada, established in January 1968—an office recommended by Williams and confirmed in the Downs Report.

Provincial and Territorial Governments and Libraries

The provinces of Newfoundland, Prince Edward Island, Nova Scotia, New Brunswick, Quebec, Ontario, Manitoba, Saskatchewan, Alberta, and British Columbia are responsible for their public, school, and university libraries, the libraries of the provincial legislature, and those of the provincial government departments, commissions, etc. The school libraries are under the Education Act; the universities and colleges with the exception of Queen's University are incorporated under provincial acts. Ontario alone has a Minister of University Affairs. The public library acts are administered in Alberta and British Columbia by the Provincial Secretary, in Manitoba by the Minister member of the Executive Council designated as the minister responsible for the administration of the Public Libraries Act, in New Brunswick, Newfoundland, Nova Scotia, Ontario, and Saskatchewan by the Minister of Education, and in Quebec by the Minister of Cultural Affairs. In Prince Edward Island, where there is no act, the responsibility for libraries is assigned to the Department of Education.

The special libraries belonging to industry, business, the professional associations, learned societies, and private foundations are incorporated under private charters or the Companies Acts of provincial or federal governments.

Each province has it own characteristics which bespeak its geography, its ethnic pattern, and its history. The "Canadian mosaic" or "a multicultured society" are the terms used to describe the peoples of Canada and their languages. According to the *Canada Year Book, 1967,* some 67.4% speak English only, 19.1% speak French only, 12.2% speak both English and French, and 1.3% speak neither language. The ethnic population is roughly 8 million British, 5½ million French, over 1 million German, nearly half a million Ukranian with nearly as many of Italian or Dutch origin, a somewhat smaller number of Scandinavians and Poles, about a quarter million Indians and Eskimos, over 100,000 each of Jewish, Asiatic, and Russian descent, and approximately 1 million of other nationalities. Books, periodicals, and newspapers are published in more than thirty languages, as exhibited in the Canadiana Library at Expo 67. The major languages are English and French. Canada's philosophy of nationhood imposes on libraries the responsibility of preserving, promoting, and distributing by print, manuscript, and mass media the heritage of the nations who are now a part of the Canadian people. This task, primarily a provincial one, is also a responsibility of the Federal Government of Canada's National Library, National Film Board and National Gallery, and the Canadian Broadcasting Commission.

Between all varieties of libraries there is close cooperation, including interlibrary lending, generally telecommunication service, some joint bibliographical undertakings, and the exchange of accession and duplicate lists, local library periodicals, and publications.

The territories administer territorial library systems and are more akin to the provincial library systems, so they are treated with the provinces. The territories, as noted earlier, are financed from the Federal Treasury.

The provinces and territories are arranged according to their major library development and/or influence—Quebec, Ontario, British Columbia, Prince Edward Island, Nova Scotia, New Brunswick, Newfoundland, Manitoba, Saskatchewan, Alberta, the Yukon, and Northwest Territories.

QUEBEC

(Area, 594,860 square miles, largest province)

It is a matter of pride to Quebec that the library of the Collège des Jésuites de Québec established in 1635 predates Harvard. There are 736 volumes with the *ex libris* of this library in the Laval University library, some bearing the *ex libris* of La Bibliothèque de la Mission Canadienne de Jésuites, 1632. The titles deal with agriculture, geography, general history, ecclesiastical history, history of America, philosophy, literature, architecture, botany, navigation, astronomy, military art, mathematics, chemistry, physics, medicine, civil law, dogma, pathology, Councils, lithurgy, and sacred writings. Periodicals are included. The Quebec reading tradition comes not only from the ecclesiastical leaders, the military and government officials, and the explorers, but from ordinary citizens like Marie Rolland Hébert, who is shown reading to her children in the 1620s in the bas relief of the monument to her husband, Louis, Canada's first farmer and Champlain's apothecary.

Public library history of this province has been the subject of studies by Phyllis Gale in *The development of public libraries in Canada,* an unpublished M.A. dissertation, 1965; by Mary Duncan Carter, *A survey of Montreal library facilities and a proposed plan for a library system,* an unpublished Ph.D. thesis, 1942; and by Violet Coughlin in the historical chapters of her *Larger units of public library service in Canada.* Aegidius Fauteux and Antonio Drolet have written on the private collections of New France and Marie Tremaine in *Canadian imprints to 1800* identifies the early Canadiana.

The social library appeared in Quebec City in 1779. Referred to as the Quebec Library, it was founded by Sir Frederick Haldimand, was bilingual and supported by subscriptions until 1886 when it was sold to the Literary and Historical Society of Quebec. The second was the Montreal Public Library, established in 1796; the third the Craig Library, Montreal, organized around 1810; the fourth the Literary and Historical Society of Quebec Library, formed in 1824. The Mechanics Institute of Montreal was established in 1828, and its library still gives service under the name of the Atwater Library. The Quebec City Mechanics Institute was established around 1845.

The Baldwin-Lafontaine government of United Canada passed the 1851 Library Association and Mechanics Institute Act, which was followed in 1887 by Province of Quebec legislation regulating mechanics' institutes and library associations.

The introduction of the school district library in the Common School Act of United Canada caused controversy and led in part to the establishment of parish libraries in 1843 by Bishop Ignace Bourget of Montreal. The Institut Canadien of Montreal was founded in 1844 as an intellectual center for graduates of the classical colleges in the absence of a university.

> The Institut maintained a library and a reading room; held debates and lectures; and provided a free forum for that fervent discussion of general ideas so dear to young French-Canadian intellectuals. Despite the foundation of two rival institutions, L'Oeuvre de bon livres, and the Sulpician Cabinet de Lecture, whose establishment under clerical auspices, was inspired by Bishop Bourget, the Montreal Institut and others modeled on it throughout the province grew rapidly until 1858, when the bishop took formal steps against it.

Mason Wade in his study of *The French Canadians, 1760–1967* chronicles the stages of this struggle which resulted in 1868 on the Institut's yearbook, which contained a eulogy of free thought and annexation speeches by Dr. Louis-Antoine Dessaulles and Horace Greeley of *The New York Tribune,* being put on the *Index.* The Provincial Council of the hierarchy denounced impious and immoral books, libraries which contained both good and bad books, and certain newspapers. The controversy became political, waged for years, gradually subsiding around the midseventies.

The Commission of Enquiry into Library Conditions and Needs of Canada (sponsored by the American Library Association and financed by a Carnegie Corporation grant) after its 1930 visitation of Quebec concluded:

> The library problem of Quebec . . . is by no means an easy problem to solve. It needs wise, sympathetic, intensive, expert study to design a system adequately meeting the needs of elements so diverse—sometimes so conflicting. Such a study must be the first important step toward the realization of a provincial library policy. All interests—French and English, Roman Catholic and Protestant, urban and rural, social and educational—will have to combine to create a strong and united public opinion in its support ere such a policy can be adopted.

The commission suggested the passing of a library act embodying modern features, and the appointment of a library field agent to study local aspects.

Kathleen Jenkins twenty-five years later pointed out that the two languages and two religious groupings of Quebec indicate the necessity of deviation from the library development pattern established elsewhere in Canada. Legislation is permissive, enabling "any municipality to aid in the establishment and maintenance of a free public library." Libraries may be incorporated under private acts or under the Companies Act of the province.

In 1932 the Quebec Library Association was incorporated. It was composed of French and English members chiefly from the Montreal area. After a number of attempts to interest the provincial legislature in both a library act and improved library service, it joined forces in 1950 with L'Association Canadienne des Bibliothécaires de Langue français, the former L'Association Canadienne des Bibliothécaires catholiques, established in 1943, to present a formal submission to the provincial government which eventually resulted in the passage of "An Act Respecting Public Libraries" in December 1959.

This act, initially under the Secretary of the Province, was placed on April 1, 1961, under the authority of the Minister of Cultural Affairs. It created two interdependent bodies: The Quebec Public Library Commission of seven members and the Quebec Public Library Service, an administrative body comprising the Public Library Director, Mr. Gérard Martin, and the necessary supporting staff. The first action of the service was a careful survey of the 1672 large or small, urban or rural, municipalities of Quebec; population, income, per capita expense for recreation, education, and libraries. This survey allowed the service to estimate the achievements, goodwill, interest, apathy, and even opposition toward reading and culture. A second survey was conducted in every municipal, association, and parochial library, to ascertain its quality and the community's interest in it as an institution, to see what role it might play in a well organized and structured library network.

The three existing types of libraries—municipal, association, and parish—were dealt with by the service according to their performance. Municipal libraries receive $0.20 per capita, plus 20% of the municipal contribution, plus $1000 for each full-time professional librarian, plus $5000 for the chief librarian who holds a B.L.S. or M.L.S. degree. No more association libraries are to be established and existing ones are encouraged to become municipal libraries or parts of municipal libraries with special establishment grants for the reorganization. In 1966 to 1967, grants of $852,981 were made to public libraries not including the three regional libraries. Inactive libraries received no assistance.

The Quebec Public Library Service decided on three pilot regional library projects after advice received from officers of the staff and surveyors from Ontario and Saskatchewan. In 1962 Le Service des Bibliothèques de la Mauricie was organized, centered in Trois Rivières (see Figure 1), a city with a public library system established for sixteen years, a collection of 44,000 volumes, a budget of $55,000, and a staff of thirteen of which six held library diplomas. The service is now called La Bibliothèque regionale de la Mauricie and is separate from the city library although there is close cooperation. By 1967 the regional library served forty rural municipalities in four counties and expected to expand. Its collection was 60,000 volumes and holdings of films and records, with service to unorganized rural areas by bookmobile and deposits of books and nonbook materials.

While La Mauricie was being organized Claude Aubry, chief librarian, Ottawa Public Library, made an intensive survey of the Western Quebec area, east of the Ottawa River. His study revealed very different conditions from La Mauricie. The City of Hull, of this area, was organizing its own public library and could give no assistance. Therefore the assistant director of La Mauricie was appointed director of La Bibliothèque regionale du Nord de l'Outaouais in August 1964. The 1967–1968 "Rapport Annuel" gives a vivid picture both of the progress made since establishment and the diversified program as a unit of the Cultural Affairs Ministry. Its film loans between 1965 and 1967 increased from 2500 to 7819, its

FIGURE 1. *Trois Rivières Public Library.* (*Courtesy La Bibliothèque municipale cité des Trois Rivières. Photograph by Le Nouvelliste.*)

audience attendance from 204,425 to 573,742. Art shows, a traveling theatrical troupe, and special events have been successful and are illustrated with photographs. While in 1965 a population of 31,000 living in eight municipalities was served; in 1967 the number had been increased to 85,105 in fifty municipalities. There were thirty-one branches and twenty bookmobile stops, and the book collection had tripled from 20,000 volumes to 60,036.

Meanwhile a third survey was undertaken of the western part of Montreal Island by Marion Gilroy, director of regional libraries for Saskatchewan. Here too were very different circumstances from La Mauricie and Outaouais. The West Island Regional Library Service—le Service régionale des bibliothèques de West Island, with headquarters at Pointe Claire—was established in 1965.

Regional libraries have been incorporated under the Quebec Companies Act under the name Central Public Library of ——— [name of region] rather than under Regional library. Special grants have been made. In 1966 and 1967 La Mauricie received $110,000 Outaouais, $165,000; West Island, $35,000, a total of $310,000.

Découpage du territoire Québécois en Régions de Bibliothèques by Gilbert Gagnon was released in 1967. This divides the province into 23 regions, with five factors considered: (1) the greatest economic and social homogeneity possible; (2) the general sentiment of the population; (3) the highway network and other communications; (4) the maximum area of each region; and (5) the ideal number to be served, ranging from 50,000 to 250,000. This scheme is more advantageous than an earlier one which recommended 35 regions.

The Quebec Public Library Service proposes the early establishment of a Bibliothèque Centrale du Québec to compensate for the slow development of a network of regional libraries, and to facilitate making loans individually and collectively to Quebec citizens who are without free access to books and culture outside the cities and the existing regional libraries.

A complete outline of the legislation, work of the Service and the accomplishment of the years 1960–1967 by the director concludes:

> The present legislation certainly has its weaknesses and flaws, but its deficiencies stem from the fact that it does not find its corollary and support in a municipal and fiscal legislation coordinated towards its aims.
>
> As it is, however, without any coercive measure in this particular field, but by using the sole power of persuasion and the ability to take advantage of competitive situations, it succeeded within a period of seven years, in obtaining the following results:
>
> a) *in the professional field,* the enrolement at the university of Montreal School of Library Science has increased by 553 per cent, since 1961:
>
> b) *at the municipal level,* the municipal financial support to the libraries has increased 137 per cent;
>
> c) *at the governmental level,* the grants to the public libraries have been raised 1,075 per cent;
>
> d) *as to the libraries themselves,* the number of the communities served has increased by 220 per cent; the number of library users, by 78 per cent, thus giving the proof of a better service; the number of books, by 72 per cent due to the increase of 262 per cent in the purchasing budgets, and, at last, the salaries paid as a whole in the libraries have increased by 1,218 per cent.
>
> It now remains to be hoped that this upward thrust that started very late never stops.

To the usual purpose of the public library there is added in Quebec the safeguarding of the heritage of the French language and culture in Canada and the making available to the minority population the finest examples of the writing and culture of the English speaking and other linguistic groups.

On August 10, 1967, the Bibliothèque Nationale du Québec Act was passed transforming the former La Bibliothèque Saint Sulpice, the province's reference library, into a national library to give important services to the libraries of the province. As time allows these services will include a current bibliography of Quebeciana, an index to Quebec periodicals, a union catalog of Quebec libraries, the maintenance of a central exchange office for documents, etc.

Because of the lack of public libraries in Quebec for so many years, a climate of benevolence toward library service flourished at McGill University, in privately founded libraries, and in the special libraries. For example, through the generosity of the McLennan family and with the encouragement of the librarian of McGill, Dr. Charles Gould, an endowment was established in 1901 to provide a traveling library service for rural Canada. On application and the payment of a fee of $4.00 per box for four months, boxes of thirty to fifty books selected according to the needs of the borrowers were sent from the McGill University Library to schools, small libraries, and reading groups. For many years these were the only books available to rural Quebec and the Maritime Provinces. In 1947 the service was named the McLennan Traveling Libraries, attached to MacDonald College, and instituted bookmobile as well as mail and rail service. This library received a government grant of $50,000 in 1966–1967.

Another example is the Fraser-Hickson Library, which supplied a reading room and circulation and reference services for many years in downtown Montreal and now is housed in a fine new building in Notre Dame de Grâce, where it gives complete book and audiovisual services for adults and children. Examples of citizen efforts working in collaboration toward establishing libraries for children are the Montreal Children's Library and La Bibliothèque des Enfants.

Free municipal public libraries are the Civic Library of Montreal (see Figure 2),

FIGURE 2. *Montreal Public Library.* (*Courtesy La Bibliothèque de la Ville de Montréal. Photograph by Albert J. Giroux.*)

with a growing system of branches and the valuable Gagnon Collection of Canadiana, which complements the unique holdings of La Bibliothèque Saint Sulpice, now the National Library of Quebec. The Westmount Public Library, which for many years was under Miss Mary Saxe and Dr. Kathleen Jenkins, has presented a consistent pattern of excellence in public library community service which has been most helpful to the group of recently organized libraries throughout the province.

For many years the Legislative Library of Quebec has opened its rich collections to all research workers and as noted by its librarian, Mr. Jean-Charles Bonenfant, in "Progrès des bibliothèques au Canada français," a chapter of *Librarianship in Canada, 1946 to 1967,* edited by Bruce B. Peel, served as a public library for Quebec City pending the organization of a municipal library.

School Libraries. Since 88% of Quebec is of the Roman Catholic faith, its educational system has differed from that of the other provinces. In 1856 the Council of Public Instruction was created and, composed of a Roman Catholic Committee and a Protestant Committee, acted as the agent of the provincial government, and reported to the provincial secretary. In 1964 the council was replaced by a Department of Education under a cabinet minister who is advised by the Superior

Council of Education. The department has a deputy minister and two associate deputy ministers (one Roman Catholic, one Protestant), each of whom is assisted by an advisory denominational committee. The Cité des Jeunes is a new trend in Quebec education whereby on a single campus there are all types of schools attended by students in their teens—French, English, Roman Catholic, Protestant, classical, and technical and trade schools, with school library service provided.

Quebec school libraries do not publish consolidated reports. A short review of developments from 1936 to 1967 is given by Mary Mustard and Doris P. Fennell in their report of libraries in Canadian schools. Statistics and information about elementary and secondary schools are given by the Research and Information Division of the Canadian Education Association in its 1962–1963 information report. This report noted that the Roman Catholic School Board maintained a model library and a reference collection to serve all teachers in the Province. Statistics were given for a sampling of schools under the Roman Catholic and Protestant School Boards jurisdiction, noting that lists of reading are prepared by both boards, that the training of school librarians is by summer sessions of both the University of Montreal and McGill (MacDonald College) as well as by the graduate library schools at McGill and the University of Montreal. Provincial grants not to exceed $1.00 per elementary student and $2.00 per secondary student are given. A report issued by the Bureau des Bibliothèques Scolaires of the Department of Education in 1966 reports on personnel, books, periodicals, quarters, and budgets as of January 31, 1966, for a much larger sampling.

The development of the Technical Institutes and provincial trade school libraries shows Quebec with 42 schools, a full-time enrollment of 16,409 students, collections amounting to 136,548 volumes, and expenditures of $15.17 per full-time student. Nine professional librarians and 17 nonprofessional staff man these libraries. The total expenditure amounted to $190,665 for 1965–1966. During the years 1961–1967 the Technical and Vocational Training Agreement has provided shared costs between the federal and the provincial governments and consequently has aided the libraries.

College and University Libraries and Education for Librarianship. Included in the Profiles of Colleges and Universities of the Downs Report are Bishop's University (Lennoxville); Centre des Études Universitaires (Trois Rivières); Collège de l'Immaculée-Conception (Montreal); Collège Sainte-Anne-de-la-Pocatière; Collège Saint-Laurent (Quebec); Collège Sainte-Marie (Montreal); Ecole des Hautes Etudes Commerciales (Montreal); Ecole Polytechnique (Montreal); Université Laval (Quebec); Loyola College (Montreal); MacDonald College (Ste-Anne-de-Bellevue); McGill University (Montreal); Marianopolis College (Montreal); Université de Montréal; Séminaire de Québec (Quebec); Séminaire Saint-Augustin (Cap Rouge); Université de Sherbrooke (Quebec); and the Sir George Williams University (Montreal). The distinguished collections of Laval and McGill tower above all others. Excellent new buildings mark the libraries of Bishop's, Laval, Loyola, McGill, and Sir George Williams. Laval University library has pioneered in experimentation in bibliography, indexing, and listing by machine methods under the direction of Mr. Guy Forget.

Library education is carried on by McGill University, Graduate School of Library Science and Montreal University, Ecole de Bibliothéconomie.

Special Libraries. The special libraries are numerous, due to the concentration of business and industry in Montreal, which city is the headquarters for many firms, banks, insurance companies, and professions.

Library Associations. Library associations are active and include the Quebec Library Association, the Montreal Branch of the Special Libraries Association, and the Association Canadienne des Bibliothècaires de la Langue française. All have been organized as inclusive associations and the need for a purely professional association to speak for professional librarians has been accelerated by the recent union strike of the University of Montreal library staff and by the growing influence of the two library schools and their graduates. This Association was established after much discussion during 1968–1969 and is named La Corporation des Bibliothécaires professionels.

Publications. The library associations all issue bulletins, membership lists, conference reports, and miscellaneous publications. The University of Montreal Library School issues valuable bibliographies. Laval University produces by automation *Index Analytique,* which indexes both European and Canadian periodicals mainly in the French language. The National Library of Quebec issues a newsletter and its publication plans for the future have been noted elsewhere. The Public Library Service of Quebec publishes surveys, reports, and statistics. The regional, municipal, university, and college libraries issue annual reports, lists, and miscellaneous brochures.

The Future. Monseigneur Lussier, former rector of the University of Montreal, in discussing educational finance in Quebec in 1958 closed his remarks with a quotation from William of Orange: "In the absence of hope it is still necessary to strive." The library situation in Quebec which for so many years showed an absence of hope, now through the striving of its leaders, has entered into a period which justifies the words of C. P. Snow: "It is a time of hope."

ONTARIO

(Area 412,582 square miles; second largest province)

At Confederation the Ontario public libraries and mechanics institutes were under "An Act for the Incorporation and Better Management of Library Associations and Mechanics Institutes," passed on August 30, 1851, by the government of Canada. By 1867 the program of the institutes had been reduced in most centers to a library with a reading room and discussion groups with members paying a small fee: "mechanics institutes" came to mean "libraries." As the population grew they became unsatisfactory as a substitute for a public library. Dr. Egerton Ryerson's attempt to organize school district libraries had introduced the principle of local support and responsibility for public libraries. School district libraries functioned until 1880 when the Ontario Department of Education ceased reporting them but continued reporting the mechanics institutes. In this year the government was paying grants to some seventy-four institutes. On January 21, 1868, the Association of Mechanics Institutes of Ontario was organized in Toronto to provide liaison between the institutes, to assist them to compile a catalog of suitable books for institute purchase, to procure such books at the lowest possible price, and to receive and impart information on evening class instruction, lectures, libraries, reading rooms, exhibitions, etc. In 1881 the government undertook an investigation of the mechanics institutes. The result was that the maximum government grant of $400 was reduced.

The period 1851–1881 was one of city growth. The *Canada Statistical Abstract and Record for the Year 1886* reports the population of Toronto, the provincial capital, as 77,034, that of Hamilton as 33,359, and that of Ottawa as 25,600. In 1882 an act was passed that established free libraries and is the foundation of the Ontario public library system. Article 8, Paragraph 1 of the act established the Free Library Rate of one-half mill upon the assessed value of all ratable real and personal property, while Paragraph 2 allowed the raising of free library debentures for purchasing and erecting buildings and in the first instance for obtaining books and other things required. Article 10 laid down the procedure whereby mechanics institutes could become free public libraries. An amendment to the act in 1883 permitted the institutes to transfer to the public libraries in the same localities their property and grants. In the 1886 act other imperfections in the legislation were corrected. In 1895 an act passed by which public libraries became "free public libraries" and mechanics institutes "association public libraries." The former were tax supported and anyone could borrow; the latter continued to require membership fees and had a list of borrowers. All were supervised by the inspector of public libraries, the former superintendent of mechanics institutes up to 1882, Dr. S. P. May, who among other duties controlled the government's system of grants to both types of libraries.

Eight cities used the 1883 legislation as soon as it became law to establish public libraries and to transfer the property of the local mechanics institute. The largest and most prosperous was the Toronto Public Library, which opened on March 6, 1884, with books first issued on April 2. In the period before opening a careful survey had been made by visitation of the services of various public libraries in the United States. The chairman of the board, Alderman John Hallam, and the chief librarian, James Bain, Jr., traveled to England on a book purchasing trip. Both were outstanding collectors, particularly Dr. Bain who in the following years built up an exceedingly fine Canadiana collection for Toronto and was one of the founders of the Champlain Society. The city had authorized debentures of $50,000 for the gradual purchase of 150,000 volumes. The Toronto library expanded rapidly, mastered the recommended techniques, and soon became an example to other centers. Ontario librarians and board members attended the conferences of the American Library Association, established in 1876, and at the 1900 conference, in Montreal, were among the group to propose and set up a Canadian Library Association. Implementation of a national organization proved difficult and resulted in the decision in October 1900 to set up provincial library associations first. The Ontario Library Association was organized and held its first conference in the spring of 1901. The Ontario Library Association was fortunate in having for twenty-five years a devoted and progressive educator as its secretary-treasurer, Dr. E. A. Hardy, originally a member of the Simcoe Public Library Board. The association was active in presenting new ideas and at its open forum discussions at its annual conference, generally held on Easter Monday, urged that these ideas be put into practice. It developed a healthy sense of rivalry between libraries. It urged reforms at the government level. It aided librarians to become an organized group. It interested itself in education for librarianship. In 1907, at the request of the Ontario Library Association, the inspector of libraries organized an experimental two-day institute at Brantford at which library problems were discussed. The next year there were three institutes. Their success made them an annual event with all travel and out-of-pocket expenses paid by the government and pointed up the need for library training in the province.

In 1901 Andrew Carnegie set up his scheme to give away 300 million dollars to libraries. More than 2½ million was spent in Canada with 125 buildings between 1903 and 1919. Of these nearly 100 were built in Ontario at a cost of 2 million dollars. Localities received not only modern buildings but also maintenance pledges from the recipient locality amounting to $200,000, i.e., 10% of the gift. This thrust forward of library service called for better trained librarians and was supported by succeeding library inspectors—Dr. S. P. May, Mr. T. W. H. Leavitt, Mr. W. R. Nursey, and, from 1916 to 1929, Mr. W. O. Carson.

McGill had pioneered with a short course in 1904 under Dr. Charles Henry Gould and in 1911 the Ontario Department of Education organized a short-term (three-week) course in Toronto under Miss Mabel Dunham, chief librarian of the Kitchener Public Library. This experiment was so successful that the time was increased to two months by 1917 and to three months in 1921. In 1928 it became a joint school with the University of Toronto School of Library Science under the direction of Miss Winifred G. Barnstead; later it was accredited by the American Library Association.

The Department of Education concerned itself with provision of books to readers in isolated areas by setting up a traveling library service. It was continued until 1967.

In 1916, W. O. Carson, chief librarian of the London Public Library, became inspector of libraries. With the Ontario Library Association cooperating, a complete revision of the Public Libraries Act was prepared; it became law in 1920 and changed the basis of support from the mill rate on property to a service per capita rate with compulsory support provided if the library board demanded it of the municipality, the minimum being fifty cents per capita and the maximum one dollar. This was the legislation in force in the summer of 1930 when the Commission of Enquiry into Library Conditions and Needs of Canada, sponsored by the American Library Association and financed by the Carnegie Corporation of New York, visited Ontario. The commissioners were Mr. John Ridington, chairman, an English journalist who emigrated to Canada and became librarian of the University of British Columbia, a member of the British Columbia Public Library Commission, and president of the Canadian Library Association proposed again in 1927; Dr. George H. Locke, a Canadian of Irish extraction, born in Ontario, with a career both as an educator at the universities of Toronto, Harvard, Chicago, and McGill, and in publishing, chief librarian since 1908 of the Toronto Public Library, a past president of the Ontario Library Association, and in 1926–1927 president of the American Library Association; and Miss Mary J. L. Black, a Canadian born in Ontario, chief librarian of the Fort William Public Library, a member of the Library Extension Board of the American Library Association, and a past president of the Ontario Library Association.

The commissioners visited Ontario separately, calling on high government officials, libraries, librarians, and trustees. Their study, *Libraries in Canada; a Study of Library Conditions and Needs,* published in 1933, reported on Ontario's position of "leadership and opportunity," and acknowledged that:

> The Province of Ontario has, in the past, given to the library movement in the Dominion of Canada nearly all it has received in leadership and in example. Other provinces, endeavouring to express a library consciousness have, for the most part, been content to tread the trails it blazed.

Although the report on the city libraries was favorable, the Toronto Public Library (cited as a model by Mr. Ridington and Miss Black) and the state of the multitudinous small libraries, both public and association—all ill-supported with few books of distinction on their shelves—caused the commissioners to recommend:

> The immediate need is for a thorough study of the situation in its social and economic relations by an interested, enthusiastic and practical person, who will conduct the social experiment with the same care and interest as would a man a problem in a laboratory.

Further recommendations included the need for library service to rural Ontario, standards of professional qualification for all public librarians appointed in municipalities of a certain population size, the organization of the county library, a diminution in the services of the traveling libraries and the library institutes, and the need for greater cooperation between the school and the public library, concluding:

> The Commission is convinced that an important part of the solution of these problems lies in this direction: there should cease to be additions to the number of small libraries, and more of the amalgamation and combination of these efforts around a convenient and accessible centre.

Unfortunately, the report appeared during the economic depression of the 1930s and little action followed. Miss Dorothy Carlisle, chief librarian, Sarnia Public Library, gave leadership to county library cooperation in Lambton County and inspired similar experimentation elsewhere. Mr. F. C. Jennings, bibliophile and teacher of English literature, who succeeded W. O. Carson as inspector of public libraries, supported library cooperation within the counties and advocated some system of certification for librarians. He was succeeded by Angus Mowat, formerly chief librarian of the libraries of Trenton, Belleville, and Windsor (in Ontario) and of the Saskatoon Public Library in Saskatchewan. Under Mr. Mowat a certification system with government grants according to qualifications was inaugurated. County library cooperatives were established for which the county councils passed bylaws permitting their establishment and recognizing in the cooperative "the only solution that has yet been found to the problem of book services for rural areas in Ontario." The Ontario government made substantial grants-in-aid to the cooperatives, which increased from one in 1933 to twelve in 1947 to eighteen in 1964. The number of public libraries in 1947 was 214 and of association libraries 252, making a total of 466. Public and association libraries with receipts of less than $5000 numbered 400. Finding an alternative to the small library as a public library center was slow, but the county cooperatives with their bookmobiles, the autonomy of the member libraries, and the various services they offered were exciting public imagination. The Ontario Library Association, trustee groups, school authorities, and interested citizens stressed the need for improvement at all levels, urging a provincial library, increased provincial grants, augmentation of the services and staff of the director of provincial library service (the former public library inspector), and the need for a survey of the province to examine the relative responsibility of the province and the local community. In 1957 the province published the *Report on Provincial Library Service in Ontario* by Dr. William Stewart Wallace, a past president of the Ontario Library Association and formerly librarian of the University of Toronto. Mr. Mowat was succeeded by William Roedde, librarian of the Northwestern Regional Library Cooperative, to whose credit goes the 1966 revision of the Public Libraries Act and the division of the province into fourteen regional library systems.

In the meanwhile great changes were taking place in urban Ontario and affecting library service provincially. Only Ontario and Quebec have cities with metropolitan populations of over 1 million. Both have cities with organized metropolitan services. In Toronto the number of services affected and the planning have been more far-reaching than in Montreal. In 1951 the City of Toronto applied for an order amalgamating the thirteen neighboring municipalities. This was refused. Instead it was recommended that the constituent municipalities federate for the provision of certain metropolitan services. As a result the Municipality of Metropolitan Toronto (generally referred to as Metro) was incorporated on April 2, 1953, and began operations January 1, 1954. Metro is responsible for the planning, financing, construction, administration, and operation of certain specified services, and through a Metropolitan School Board for the over-all planning of school services and the construction of school buildings.

In 1958 the Ontario Legislature gave the Council of the Municipality of Metropolitan Toronto power to make grants to any library system within its domain which was rendering service to citizens of other Metro municipalities. The Council of Metro requested a survey to provide the information on which these grants should be based. The Library Trustees Council of Toronto and District, composed of the trustees of the thirteen library boards within Metro, requested that the survey be enlarged to study existing library facilities and to make recommendations for future development. The Council of Metro agreed and supplied the necessary funds. Dr. Ralph Shaw of Rutgers University, New Brunswick, N.J., took charge.

Libraries of Metropolitan Toronto, by Ralph Shaw, was released in 1960 and received national attention, not only because of its recommendations for Metro but because of its application throughout Ontario and elsewhere. The recommendations were intended to bring library services in Metro up to at least minimum standards within 10 years or so. The first recommendation was the establishment of a Metropolitan Library Board constituted to provide adequate representation of the communities, to advise the Metropolitan Council on steps to be taken to effect equalization of library services to the people of Metro, and to provide research and development facilities to help the library boards of the constituent municipalities to develop better, more economical, and more effective service outlets and services. It might also advise on centralized cataloging and oversee such services.

The Metropolitan Library Board assumed office January 1, 1967. Its territory, the former thirteen municipalities, had been reorganized into six boroughs (North York, East York, York, Scarborough, Etobicoke, and the City of Toronto). Provincially it is one of the fourteen library regions of Ontario—the smallest, the most populous, the wealthiest, and the only completely urban one. The board, deeply conscious of the difficult task of any superimposed level of government to work out its role, spent much time concluding a program for the concerted action of the city and the boroughs. In the first year it established its relationship to the Metro council and the libraries of Metro. It appointed Mr. John Parkhill, formerly with the Toronto Public Library, the Metropolitan librarian as of January 1, 1968. After considerable discussion and negotiation between the Toronto and Metro boards, an agreement was signed on December 21, 1967, whereby the Toronto Public Library transferred to the Metro board its Central Library Collections, the Music, Business and Municipal Reference, and the Languages and Literature Centre libraries—and in return the Metro board undertook to pay the Toronto board "for the maintenance, operation and expansion of the central collections and of the service of them to the Metropolitan area, the sum of $500,000 for the year 1967 and not less than the sum of $500,000 for the year 1968." The Metro board reserved the right to return any of these collections, in the event of its decision not to retain them. Spirited discussions followed over the nature of the central collections, their relation to the borough collections, the advisability of keeping this collection and that, and the question of "circulating" versus "reference" books. Finally, it was agreed that these all constituted central collections, a unique public library asset for Metro and therefore one that ought to be retained.

Mr. Parkhill has pointed out that neither the Metro nor the Toronto board has underestimated how drastic and delicate the surgery must be to excise from a library system so major and integral a part as the Central Library forms in the Toronto Public Library system. Considerable time and thought were devoted to preparing for the transfer, which eventually took place earlier than originally planned, on October 1, 1968. Leases of space had to be prepared and approved; arrangements for purchase of service in both directions had to be made. The Metro Library Board has taken over most of the former Toronto Public Library Technical Services, with the exception of Registration and Book Binding, which Toronto is retaining, and Finishing and Display, which have been divided between the boards.

The Metropolitan board has undertaken to provide cataloging service at cost to Toronto and so on. The Metropolitan Library staff by October was 176. Meanwhile the audiovisual services of Metropolitan Libraries, Inc., largely a borough operation, was taken over on July 1, with the expectation that greatly increased financial support will begin to give Metro the film service it has so long needed. Meetings about interloan have led to arrangements for a much freer and faster system, with a daily delivery of both books and films among the public libraries of Metro. On October 1 a "slave" teletype network was instituted to see whether this kind of communication can further improve Metro interloan, and provide a useful channel for exchanging other kinds of information. The possible automation of the Bibliographic Centre is under study as are also research, workshops, role of consultants, questions of grants and debenture payments, role and support of city and borough regional libraries, training and exchange of staffs, centralized technical services, and liaison with school, community college, university, and special libraries.

Borough libraries are responsible for home reading services—reference, information, adult education, and regional reference—calling on the Metro services as needed. A common library card is honored by all. Metro has supplied considerable financial assistance. New branches have been erected by Toronto, Etobicoke, North York, Mimico, and Scarborough (see Figure 1). Salaries have been improved.

FIGURE 3. *Cedarbrae District Branch of the Scarborough Public Library, one of the borough libraries of the Toronto Metropolitan Public Library System. (Courtesy A. W. Bowron and Scarborough Public Library.)*

Ambitious building plans for headquarters for the Metro Public Library and the City of Toronto Library are under consideration.

In 1964 a library survey of Ontario was authorized by the Ontario Library Association (with funds supplied by the Minister of Education) by the firm of Francis R. St. John Library Consultants, Inc. "Ontario Libraries: a Province-wide Survey and Plan, 1965" analyzed the different types of libraries and the laws under which they are governed. The most urgent recommendations in this survey were changes in legislation and the Minister's regulations, the structuring of the Library Services Division, development of a reference and research library for the staff of the Department of Education, and the total integration of the resources of all types of libraries in the province. There were sixty-three specific recommendations as to the

Provincial Library Service, public libraries, elementary and secondary school libraries, higher education, special and government libraries, personnel, and legislation and the trustee. The survey was released at a press conference at which the Minister of Education, the Honorable William Davis, was present, and he announced that additional provincial aid of $5,000,000 would be made available to public libraries and noted also the favorable attitude of his department to many of the recommendations. The report proved controversial and attracted news reports, comment, and editorials, not only in Ontario but throughout Canada.

Several of the St. John recommendations were incorporated into the new Public Libraries Act of 1966, which rescinded the former act and the amendments. The new act is in four parts: I. Public library service; II. Provincial library service; III. Regional library service; and IV. County library service.

It established the Provincial Library Council and legislated that on January 1, 1967, each public library association then in existence was dissolved and its assets and liabilities became the assets and liabilities of the regional library system having jurisdiction in the area. It set 100,000 as the population for a regional library and ruled that the eleven regional library cooperatives be deemed regional library systems, although eventually boundaries may be altered.

For a county library it demanded a population of 25,000, and on its establishment any county library cooperative and every public library board is dissolved and their assets and liabilities vested in and assumed by the county library board unless otherwise provided in the bylaws establishing the county library. Thus the small, ill-financed public libraries with meager collections are incorporated into either regional or county libraries. Within a few months fourteen regional library systems linked within and without by telecommunications and with resource centers within the constituent municipal libraries were organized. These are under the management, regulation, and control of boards of nine members representing the area libraries, who are charged with the responsibility of improving standards of library service and of providing a plan for developing and coordinating library work within the region.

The fourteen regions are Eastern Ontario (10 counties), Lake Ontario (9), Central Ontario (3, exclusive of Metro), Metropolitan Toronto (the city and 5 boroughs), South Central (3), Niagara (3), Lake Erie (4), Southwestern (3), Mid-Western (4), Georgian Bay (4), Algonquin (3), North Central (3), Northeastern (3), and Northwestern (3 regions). Each regional library system develops its organization to suit its clientele. Thus the bilingual Eastern Ontario Regional Library System, including forty-nine libraries scattered over a territory of 10,000 square miles divided into ten counties, was established in 1965. Its main resource library is the Ottawa Public Library; the secondary resource libraries are in Cornwall, Pembroke, and Brockville. It is not yet a library service but rather an organization created to bring the various libraries together into closer operation, to develop further service, and to provide it where none exists. Out of 300 requests in one month to the Ottawa Public Library, 200 were for books in languages other than English and French—Dutch, Polish, Russian, and German—and all were supplied.

The Northwestern Regional Library System established in 1956 has successfully included a nonbook program to the multilingual population it serves in fourteen languages. Pieces of sculpture (originals and copies) are loaned to the libraries and schools for circulation as well as to individual patrons at the bookmobile stops. Pictures, films, and phonograph records are also included.

The Mid-Western Regional Library System (formerly the Mid-Western Regional Library Cooperative) commissioned Francis R. St. John Library Consultants, Inc., to conduct an in-depth study of the library situation in the region which includes the counties of Huron, Perth, Waterloo, and Wellington, and to develop a feasible plan of operation taking into consideration existing libraries, unserved areas, methods of financing, and such other necessarily related items as should be included in the preparation of the long-term plan. The resulting report gives a vivid picture of the problems faced by all Ontario library cooperatives automatically transferred by the 1966 act into regional library systems. It recommends a plan for the future, including the employment of a qualified director, a headquarters building, the employment of staff, a regional reference center, and conferences with local officials as to future financing. Its objective should be the establishment of four county libraries as provided for in the act, and inaugurating service to the unserved parts of the area.

The act has placed the training and certification of professional and supporting library staffs under the jurisdiction of the Provincial Library Service.

With the population of Ontario flocking into the urban areas, the urban public libraries face new situations and the necessity of planning for the future. Among its activities the Toronto Public Library Board included consideration of the advice in the Shaw Report that it merge its reference and circulation departments into a single subject-departmentalized library, move to a new building in a more central location, and employ specialized staff and subject specialists. This program began in 1960 and was completed in 1966. The whole, designated the Central Library Division, included twelve specialized departments and some 350,000 volumes. The decentralization and the growth of the new subject sections raised many questions and pointed to the need for a systematic review of the holdings of the Central Library toward reporting on its deficiencies and developing a plan for strengthening its resources. Accordingly, Mr. Lee Ash was engaged by the library board to carry out this review, to include the analysis of the entire collection and a thorough appraisal of its weaknesses and strengths. "The Scope of Toronto's Central Library; a Review of the Nature of the Book Resources of the Central Library Division, with Notes on the Use of Nonbook Materials and on Some Related Studies" by Lee Ash summarized the findings and suggested a sum to be spent exclusively on books, new serial publications, back issues of serials, and related reference materials, if the library was to bring itself up to the standard set by the board and take its place as Canada's most important community reference library. With the transfer of this collection to the Metro Public Library Board, the responsibility regarding the collection is no longer with the City of Toronto Public Library Board.

The Toronto Public Library since its establishment in 1883 has been administered by four distinguished librarians—Dr. James Bain, Jr., to whom it owes the glory of its Canadiana collection; Dr. George Herbert Locke, who developed its far-flung branch system; Dr. Charles R. Sanderson, who consolidated the pioneer work of his predecessors and carried the library forward into the age of radio; and Mr. Henry Cummings Campbell, who piloted the system toward and into its metropolitan era, and investigated and pioneered modern automated techniques and the computer control of knowledge. Now that the City of Toronto is a borough, work in adult education and community involvement is receiving more attention. This library's work with boys and girls under Lillian H. Smith and Jean Thomson has been an inspiration to all children's librarians. The choice of Toronto to receive the Osborne collection of children's books collected from the earliest times by Edgar Osborne was a mark of international approbation.

The Hamilton Public Library reflects the needs of an industrial, multilingual, multicultural city. Its great organizer, Mrs. Lorene Macdonald Lyle, was followed by Dr. Freda Farrell Waldon under whom the city acquired an extensive branch system and a notable sense of community translated into numerous special collections. Dr. Waldon was succeeded by Mr. Charles Brisbin, chief librarian, Waterloo, Ontario, Public Library.

Windsor was the first Ontario library to request a Carnegie building. It pioneered the *Canadian Periodical Index* and developed specialized collections of interest to industry and art. Memorable names are Agnes Lancefield, Angus Mowat, Eleanor Barteaux, and Dr. Anne Hume, who was the first chief librarian following the amalgamation of neighboring towns into the modern city of Windsor. Under Dr. Hume and her successor, Miss Gladys Shepley, the branch organization has burgeoned. The healthy emulation of Windsor with its neighbor across the river, Detroit, has insured a dynamic program.

The Ottawa Public Library in eastern Ontario had an uneasy birth in the late nineteenth century, for the citizens voted down the public library in 1895. The library's sponsors appealed to Mr. Carnegie, who donated $100,000 on condition the city tax itself to the extent of $7500. The gift was accepted and Mr. Carnegie attended the opening ceremonies. The first three librarians were noted bookmen— L. J. Burpee, W. J. Sykes, and F. C. Jennings. They also developed a branch system and built up the collections in the French and English languages (for Ottawa is a bilingual city), and under Mr. Jennings a bookmobile service was inaugurated. Mr. Claude Aubrey, his successor, has had to deal with an exploding urban population as the neighboring townships join the city. He has developed shopping center branches and is also responsible for the bilingual regional library system of East Ontario for which Ottawa is one of four resource libraries.

The London Public Library has been a Mecca to all interested in programs of adult education, work with groups, and the combined services of a library and art gallery. A documentary film, *New Chapters,* and two histories of the library, compiled respectively by Miss Eleanor Shaw and Miss Jean Gorwill, trace its development under chief librarians Robert J. Blackwell, a signer of the 1900 Canadian Library Association resolution; W. O. Carson, later inspector of libraries; Fred Landon, who moved on to be librarian and eventually a vice president of University of Western Ontario; and Richard E. Crouch, under whose guidance the

Elsie Perrin Memorial Library was built and the library's extensive cultural and community services were promoted and established—an inheritance being consolidated under Charles Deane Kent, the present librarian, and his staff.

These five municipal centers of Toronto, Hamilton, Windsor, Ottawa, and London are the traditional "big five" which have influenced library development within the province. Some of the new areas, such as North York, now a part of Metro Toronto, have had a phenominal rise of population, and an equally rapid development of central and branch library services under the direction of William Graff and John Dutton. On one memorable evening North York opened four branches at the same moment using the same ceremony transmitted by radio. The audiovisual experimentation by Scarborough, another Metro unit, under Albert W. Bowron, has been of value to the entire Canadian profession.

Within smaller municipal centers such as Kitchener, Guelph, Sault Sainte Marie, Fort William, Sudbury, and Kingston to name but a sampling, are distinguished community services, modern buildings, and forward looking programs. More than half the public libraries of Canada are in Ontario. All are working toward the goal of universal public library service with mandatory replacing the present permissive legislation.

School Libraries. School libraries present a great problem to this large, sprawling province. Both Shaw and St. John made recommendations in their surveys. Within the cities some experimentation is taking place, such as the City of Toronto Department of Education Library. There is no adequate province-wide system. One inspector of school libraries was appointed in 1954. In addition to the school library courses at the three Ontario university library schools, a course in school library work is given by the Ontario College of Education. In 1964 a supervisor of elementary school libraries was appointed and certificate summer courses were established. At present a coordinated school library program is being organized by a team of five school librarians, English- and French-speaking, in the Department of Education.

Special Libraries. Toronto possesses many industrial, business, professional, research, and association special libraries, as well as special collections within its university and public libraries. There is a Toronto chapter of the Special Libraries Association which meets regularly and to which special librarians in other centers belong.

College and University Libraries and Library Education. In the study on the *Resources of Canadian Academic and Research Libraries* by Robert B. Downs there is a section on profiles of colleges and universities. Included for Ontario are the universities of Brock in St. Catharines; Carleton in Ottawa; Guelph; Lakehead in Port Arthur; Laurentian in Sudbury; McMaster in Hamilton; Ottawa; Queen's in Kingston; St. Michael's in Toronto; Saint Paul in Ottawa; Toronto; Trent in Peterborough; Trinity in Toronto; Victoria in Toronto; Waterloo; Waterloo Lutheran; Western Ontario in London; Windsor; and York in Toronto. Also included are the colleges of Huron, Kings, and St. Peter's, all three in London, and the Royal Military College in Kingston. This makes a total of nineteen universities and four colleges. The oldest university with the most extensive library is the University of Toronto, founded in 1827 as the Anglican King's College of York; it was secularized and its name changed to Toronto in 1849. Toronto has five recently formed constituent colleges—Innis, New, Erindale, Scarborough, and Massey, the latter a graduate residential college—all with their own libraries. To accelerate book ordering and cataloging, unit collections of 90,000 titles were ordered, processed, and cataloged by automation, and printout catalogs were supplied by the University of Toronto, while the colleges collected and cataloged the specialities under their domain. A large graduate library complex for the humanities, rare books, and the School of Library Science is under construction. The collections will be at the disposal of graduate students of all Ontario universities. To accelerate university interlibrary loans, three vans cover the province daily bringing books to the libraries. The National Library, Ottawa, is also included.

The three surveys by Williams, Bonn, and Downs, discussed earlier, give a summarized report on various aspects of university and college library work in Ontario. The cooperation between the university and college libraries and the larger public libraries is marked. The present Minister of Education is also the Minister of University Affairs, and under him come the distribution of federal funds to universities as well as provincial university financing.

The education of librarians has been undertaken by three of the universities— Ottawa, Toronto, and Western Ontario.

Library Associations. The Ontario Library Association, established in 1901, has been active in promoting the welfare of libraries and librarians. An association for professional librarians has been organized, the Institute of Professional Librarians of Ontario. There are also library associations within cities, such as the Library Association of Ottawa, and numerous staff associations. There is a chapter of the Special Libraries Association in Toronto. The Ontario Library Association is a chapter of the American Library Association. The Canadian Library Association has its Executive Office in Ottawa.

Publications. The first library periodical in Canada, the *Ontario Library Review,* appeared in June 1916, published quarterly by the Ontario Department of Education. It has guided librarians professionally concerning library techniques; it has a book selection guide, a list of government documents, special booklists, and library news and is an excellent source of Ontario library history. The Ontario Library Association and the Institute of Professional Librarians of Ontario publish mimeographed newsletters periodically, as do several of the staff associations and many of the regional libraries. Annual reports and publicity brochures and announcements are issued by the municipal libraries and some of the university libraries. A joint list of periodicals in Toronto was undertaken for many years by the University of Toronto and the Toronto Public Library. From January 1938 to December 1947 the University of Toronto and the *Ontario Library Review* cooperated in compiling and publishing the *Canadian Periodical Index* originally initiated by the Windsor Public Library and eventually taken over by the Canadian Library Association. The Toronto Public Library has issued a distinguished list of bibliographies including the work of Frances Staton and Marie Tremaine, and before the existence of the National Library, published the current national bibliography annually under the title the *Canadian Catalogue of Books Written in Canada, About Canada and by Canadians.* In recent years an active publishing program has marked the services of the Toronto Public Library. The London Public Library is issuing a series of Occasional Papers.

Toronto is the center of publishing in the English language. Several publishing firms have issued valuable additions to professional library literature, for example *The Public Library* by E. A. Hardy (William Briggs); the bibliography *Canadian Imprints to 1800* by Marie Tremaine (University of Toronto Press); *Canadian Quotations . . .* by Robert M. Hamilton (McClelland and Stewart); and *The Republic of Childhood* by Sheila Egoff (Oxford University Press). There has been enthusiastic liaison between publishers and librarians in compiling and publishing needed works of reference about Canada, such as the *Encyclopedia Canadiana,* compiled and published by the Canadiana Company Limited, a subsidiary of the Grolier Society of Canada Limited; and the *Dictionary of Canadian Biography,* compiled and published under the direction of the University of Toronto Press.

BRITISH COLUMBIA

(Area 366,255 square miles; third largest province)

In 1849 Vancouver Island was created a colony with Victoria as its capital. The mainland of the present province became the crown colony of British Columbia in 1858 with New Westminster as its capital. James Douglas, the governor of the Vancouver Island Colony, was appointed governor of British Columbia. In 1866 the two colonies were united as British Columbia. Victoria became the capital after 1869. In 1871 British Columbia joined the Canadian Confederation.

The first library in British Columbia, as far as can be ascertained, was that of John McKay, surgeon on the *Experiment,* a vessel in a fur trading expedition to the northwest coast in 1786, who remained for some time at Nootka Sound. As was the usual practice the fur trading company supplied books and there is mention in 1805 by Daniel William Harmon, a trader with the North West Company, of his reading pleasures.

In 1858 a library for the Legislative Assembly was opened, as was also a short-lived reading room and library of W. F. Herne of Victoria. Associations such as the Y.M.C.A. began opening libraries for their members. In that same year, 1858, a company of the Royal Engineers arrived in New Westminster complete with a library chosen by Sir Edward Bulwer-Lytton for which the company had subscribed £200. When the Corps of Engineers was disbanded in 1863, since many elected to remain in the new colony, the library was given to this group and eventually became a part of the New Westminster Public Library founded in 1865.

In 1864 a Mechanics' Library Institute was formed in Victoria with a library of 475 books and a few newspapers, with privileges for men only for a fee of $1.00 a month or $10.00 a year. Later women were admitted for $5.00 a year. This became a part of the Victoria Public Library; the referendum for this as a tax supported institution was agreed to in 1887.

Vancouver's public library began through the interest of three men who organized themselves into a library committee to salvage the collection of the Hasting Literary Institute. By December 1887 the subscribers to this Vancouver Reading Room were electing officers and in 1888 received a City Council grant of $150.

The Free Libraries Act was passed in 1891 but there was little immediate development except for the municipal libraries of Victoria and Vancouver. Provincial traveling libraries were set up in 1894. A second act came into force in 1911. After considerable agitation, the Public Library Act of 1919 was passed. It created a Public Library Commission whose function was to supervise all public library services in the province including the traveling libraries, and to apportion moneys annually appropriated by the legislature for the aid of public libraries and to promote the extension library facilities. Both Mr. Herbert Killam, in charge of the Provincial Travelling Libraries, and Miss Helen Gordon Stewart, chief librarian of the Victoria Public Library, worked for the various provisions of the act. Its passage ushered in a new era for British Columbia libraries.

The Commission of Enquiry's Report *Libraries in Canada,* published in 1933, in the chapter "British Columbia: Definite Library Plans in Process of Achievement" notes:

> Public indifference and lethargy have been replaced by responsiveness, by an aroused interest every year growing more widespread and intelligent. This has been the fruit of fifteen years of education by a group, at the outset less than a dozen in number, partly lay, partly professional, who did not merely subscribe to the doctrine that the library was an essential part of the protective equipment of modern civilization, but really believed it, with something of a passionate fervour. They wrote, they gave addresses, they debated with others contrary-minded; they made friends for their cause—some of them politically influential, among them members of the cabinet.

It was the commission's good fortune in 1926 that Dr. Norman F. Black, a well-known and energetic educator, was appointed chairman. He took it as basic that the commission's first duty was to discover all the essential facts regarding provincial library requirements for the establishment of future policies. Assisted by a research board of six professional librarians, a member of the British Columbia Teachers Federation, and three members of the Library Commission, findings were presented to a Survey Council of thirty representative laymen appointed by the commission, the executive of which included three members of the legislature and the chairman, Robie L. Reid, lawyer, historian, and book collector. The provincial-wide survey used volunteer librarians and laymen. Dr. Black obtained funds from the province and the Carnegie Corporation of New York to engage a library consultant, Mr. Clarence B. Lester, Free Public Library Commission of Wisconsin. Probably no library documents have been studied more carefully throughout Canada than the commission's 1929 report of the *British Columbia Library Survey, 1927–1928,* followed by its reconsideration in 1940, the programs of library development of 1945 and 1950, the survey of the union libraries in 1950, the report of the special survey committees of 1956, and the implications for British Columbia in *The Public Libraries of the Pacific Northwest Library Association,* edited by Morton Kroll in 1960.

Within the pages of these documents are outlined the development of all types of libraries under the commission, and that body's reiterated recommendations culminating in 1956 for increased provincial financial support, shared construction costs, mechanized routines, urban metropolitan systems, encouragement to the public library associations to become tax-supported municipal or regional systems, adequate school libraries, adequate headquarters for the Public Library Commission, correction of the shortage of professional librarians, and endorsement that "the Provincial Government and the University of British Columbia give careful consideration to the establishment of a graduate library school within the next three years."

The 1930–1933 regional library demonstration financed by the Carnegie Corporation of New York of regional library service in the Fraser Valley under Dr. Helen Gordon Stewart promoted the idea of the larger unit throughout Canada. The library received streams of visitors, many of whom pondered what adjustments would have to be made in their areas with a less hospitable climate to insure continuous service in the winter months when bookmobiles might be impossible. The National Film Board's documentary film, *Library on Wheels,* 1944, carried this pioneer story around the world. Recently a later film, *Journey from Zero,* demonstrated British Columbia's library service on the Alcan Highway from the commission's Peace River Regional Library headquarters at Dawson Creek to the Alaska boundary.

British Columbia is notable among the provinces for the completeness of its documentation. The commission's publication, *Library Service in British Columbia; a Brief History of Its Development* by Marjorie C. Holmes, issued in 1959, is a valuable short form outline.

In November 1962 the commission announced a survey of the province, to provide a current assessment of the status, extent, and quality of public library service, and to provide the commission with guidelines for public library development in the midsixties and the decade ahead. The British Columbia School of Librarianship, now well established, included research projects in its terms of reference. A provincial grant was made to its newly organized Public Libraries Research Study, under Dr. Samuel Rothstein, director of the school, to insure that as objective a view as possible might be provided and to take advantage of the university's research facilities. The survey was the responsibility of Dr. Rose Vainstein, an associate professor of the school and a public librarian of varied and extensive experience, assisted by Dr. Ronald Hagler, who assumed editorial work in the final phase of the publication which appeared in 1966. The report's appendices are exceedingly valuable and include a map of the proposed plan of development for public library service, using 1963 data, showing 13 proposed library service areas with the school districts, the nonschool districts, the unorganized areas, the municipal and association libraries, and the regional libraries carefully indicated. The text illuminates all the problems before British Columbia public libraries, several of which are shared by other provinces such as the population movement from the rural to the urban areas. In discussing metropolitan and urban areas—special problems and prospects—a carefully argued case is set out for these areas to receive a fair share of provincial aid, both, financial and advisory.

The commission's *Annual Report 1967* emphasized that the aim of the survey was to produce guidelines only—not a finished blueprint of library service—to show clearly and briefly the state of each aspect of public library service and to discuss measures which might be adopted for improvement. The commission notes: "The advent of the report has so far produced a kind of sustained rolling motion toward the goal of universal library service."

The City of Vancouver celebrated its centenary of library service in 1969, taking as its start the opening of the New London Mechanics' Institute in January 1869 by J. A. Raymur, the manager of Hastings Mill. Its tumultuous early history has been written by Elizabeth Walker in "Vancouver Public Library—before Carnegie" in the *British Columbia Library Quarterly,* October 1966, with a definitive history in preparation promised by the publishers in late 1969. The Carnegie building erected in 1903 was replaced on a more central city site with a splendid new building in 1957. The progressive and tireless efforts of Edgar S. Robinson, chief librarian from 1924 to 1957, and of his successor, Peter Grossman, have developed an outstanding city system. The north-south pull of geography is strong in this part of Canada, and Vancouver has benefited from the library experimentation of the Pacific states of Washington, Oregon, and California, making ingenious adjustments to suit British Columbian needs. Several Vancouver Public Library branches have won architectural awards. The Vancouver Public Library's prison work demonstrated to the provincial government the needs of libraries in provincial prisons.

The city of New Westminster, incorporated in 1860, established its Library and Reading Room on August 15, 1865. The library's history, *New Westminster Public Library 1865–1965* by Amy M. Hutcheson, the present chief librarian, is a faithful record of a century of maneuvering with economic and political forces to obtain the excellent public library service complimented by the Honorable Vincent Massey when he opened the new library building on November 19, 1958. Miss Hutcheson ascribed this success to "the enthusiasm and the idealism which both volunteer board members and working staff members have brought to the service. . . ." The success of the present service is based on the work of Miss Ruth Cameron and Miss Amy Hutcheson.

The Victoria Public Library dates back to 1864 when the Mechanics' Literary Institute was established. It became a municipal public library in 1887. In 1911 it appointed its first trained library assistant, Helen Gordon Stewart, who became chief librarian the following year. Away went the closed stacks and the indicator system. Open shelves, apprentice classes in librarianship, the Dewey Classification, the card catalog, and separate reference and children's rooms followed rapidly, while in the provincial field she aided in library legislation reform and in the provincial survey of 1929 and became director of the regional library demonstration in the Fraser Valley and other areas. Later her work for library education in Louisiana and for regional work in the West Indies made her career international. She was succeeded in the Victoria Public Library by Miss Margaret Clay, whose work included the extension of library service on a contract basis to the neighboring townships, the establishment of the music and film collections, and the extension of the Carnegie Building of 1904 by practically a new buiding, opened in 1951. The present librarian, Mr. John Lort, formerly chief librarian of the Vancouver Island Regional Library, is busy with a program of consolidation and extension.

Municipal public libraries exist in Burnaby, Comox, Kamloops, Nelson, Prince George, Prince Rupert, Quesnel, Trail, and West Vancouver. There are three regional libraries—the Fraser Valley, Okanagan, and Vancouver Island—and fifty-eight public library associations.

The thirteen public library areas proposed in the Vainstein Report are Greater Victoria, Vancouver Island Regional, Vancouver-Ocean Falls, New Westminster-Burnaby, North Shore-Sunshine Coast, Fraser Valley Regional, Kamloops, Okanagan Regional, West Kootenay, East Kootenay, Prince George, Prince Rupert, and Peace River. This scheme would care for 1,598,340 people living on 366,255 square miles and with 30,742 Indians living on reservations.

At present the Public Library Commission is responsible for five units—the Open Shelf Division and the Travelling Libraries Division, both based in Victoria; the East Kootenay Branch in Cranbrook; the North Central Branch in Prince George; and the Peace River in Dawson Creek. These five have been organized as temporary measures to assist areas which at the time of founding were too small or too isolated to organize for regional library service.

The Provincial Library of British Columbia developed from the Legislative Assembly Library founded in 1863. Its policy was set by R. E. Gosnell, the first permanent librarian who took office in 1893. His aim was to "create a library which would anticipate not only the requirements of the Legislative Assembly . . . but . . . of the Province at large," i.e., a provincial library. His successor, E. O. S. Schofield, continued this policy of being able to ensure inquiries from all over the province. The special department on British Columbia was created the Provincial Archives in 1908. The two departments were under Mr. Schofield and his successors John Forsyth, John Hosie, and W. Kaye Lamb who was also superintendent of the Public Library Commission. On Dr. Lamb's moving to the University of British Columbia Library, Mr. C. Keith Morison became provincial librarian and superintendent of the Public Library Commission and Mr. Willard E. Ireland became archivist. In 1946 the Provincial Library and Archives were combined under Mr. Ireland and Mr. Morison continued as superintendent to be succeeded by Mr. Robert Davison. The collections of the Provincial Library and Archives are exceedingly rich, especially in Northwest history and provincial newspapers.

School Libraries. The Commission of Enquiry, 1930, makes no mention of the school library other than to note that of the 500 traveling libraries sent out by the Provincial Government, 95 were sent to remote rural schools. In 1949–1956, summer school courses in school library work were available in Victoria.

In its "Programme for Library Development in British Columbia, 1956," the

British Columbia Public Library Commission recommendations included the following: "The provision of adequate libraries in schools is a pressing problem and should receive further study."

British Columbia was included in the survey of elementary and secondary school libraries of the Pacific Northwest by Morton Kroll in 1960 and in the survey undertaken by the Research and Information Division of the Canadian Education Association in 1962–1963, with an intensive survey by the British Columbia Department of Education by a survey committee under the chairmanship of Franklin P. Levirs, assistant superintendent of education (instructional services) with cooperation from members of the British Columbia Library Association. The report was transmitted to the Minister of Education on November 1, 1964; the information collected pertained to the school year 1961–1962 and subsequent years. Under Part A on elementary schools: quarters, librarians, book collections, and administration were studied. Nine recommendations about quarters, six about librarians, five about book collections, and seventeen about administration were made. The *Standards for School Library Programs* of the American Library Association were used and schools were divided into the same categories used by Mr. Kroll. The survey showed that the elementary school libraries, where they existed, were in many instances in need of a complete reorganization. There was no computation of the cost which this would entail and no recommendation that the department should appoint a fully qualified and experienced provincial supervisor of elementary school libraries.

Part B on secondary schools followed the same pattern. Seven recommendations about quarters, five about librarians, five about book collections, and sixteen about administration were made. Again there was no computation of costs to bring about reform and no recommendations that the department appoint a fully qualified experienced supervisor of secondary school libraries.

Part C dealt with school district information and included the 82 large school districts and 8 of the unattached school districts. Thirteen recommendations were made, again without reference to cost and without any recommendation that the Department of Education appoint a fully qualified and experienced provincial supervisor of school district libraries. The survey shows the variation of school library service in the province and the dependence of some libraries on the municipal, regional, and library services of the British Columbia Public Library Commission. The discussion of the collections is quantitative, with generalizations on the importance of reference books, etc. The study met the British Columbia Library Commission's request of 1956 for further study of the "pressing problem" of school libraries.

Included in the study of public libraries directed in 1963 by Miss Vainstein was the relationship of school and public libraries.

> (1) We need a centralized library in every school, to be used concurrently with the teaching programme, a collection of such diversity in subject content and grade level as to meet everyday needs in every subject of the curriculum. Children and students need books, audio-visual materials, magazines, newspapers, maps, and pamphlets—to name only some of a school library's materials.

(2) We need a centralized library in every school to provide a basic core from which varied small collections can be selected by each teacher, throughout the year for use within the classrooms.

(3) We need a large central school library in every school in which students can be taught, as in a living laboratory, the many necessary life-long skills required for the effective use of books and libraries. If, as we insist, we are teaching students how to learn and not just what to learn, then we must equip them to locate, evaluate and use sources of information. This cannot be done in a school system which does not provide an adequate full-time centralized school library programme within the school's premises, fully integrated with everyday teaching, and staffed by fully qualified school librarians, one for each five hundred students.

(4) We need both school and public libraries which serve children and students. The public library provides for a further extension of resources in several important ways. Even the best of school libraries, whether serving elementary or secondary students, cannot provide all the materials in depth which are necessary in today's teaching programme. Nor is the school library designed to provide a collection which will satisfactorily estimate and meet the insatiable curiosity of today's child. Nor can the school library meet the needs of the pre-school child, the school drop-out, and the student completing his education through correspondence and home study.

Then follows a discussion of school and public library cooperation and of academic excellence and library use. Four recommendations are made:

(1) The immediate appointment, in the provincial Department of Education of a full-time school library consultant.

(2) Every school district to appoint at least one qualified full-time school librarian to direct and co-ordinate efforts at the district level.

(3) School library development demonstrations and experiments to help devise the different patterns of organization and service which would best serve local student needs.

(4) Encouragement of continued cooperation between the Department of Education and the Public Library Commission.

The chapter concludes with the paragraphs for the need for action, and notes that the cost per pupil for education annually is over $400 and the average school library expenditure is $5.00 per pupil.

Miss Mary Mustard and Miss Doris Fennell in their review of school library service, 1946–1967, note that in British Columbia the quality of library service varies with the geographical region, the greatest challenge to improvement being in the interior of the province.

College and University Libraries. The university and college libraries of British Columbia are those of the Universities of British Columbia in Vancouver, Notre Dame in Nelson, Simon Fraser in Burnaby, and Victoria (formerly Victoria College) in Victoria. They are included in the "Profiles of Colleges and Universities" in the Downs Report. The University of British Columbia opened in temporary quarters in September 1915 with John Ridington appointed librarian. The library building was one of the first on the Point Grey campus. Its history was the subject of a special January 1, 1966, issue of the *British Columbia Library Quarterly* titled "Scrapbook for a Golden Anniversary; the University of British Columbia Library, 1915–1965." *Library Service in British Columbia* by Marjorie C. Holmes includes summary histories of the University of British Columbia and of the Victoria College Library, established in 1902, and now the University of Victoria Library housed in the fine McPherson Lbrary on the new campus. The Simon Fraser University Library is housed in ample quarters in the massive architectural style of this university. The application of recent developments in automation are under continuous study by the universities of British Columbia, Victoria, and Simon Fraser. To keep the province and others informed about their activities and progress, a regular publication has been issued since 1967 entitled *Recent Developments in Automation at British Columbia Libraries.* Notre Dame University has a new library building in blueprint and is developing its collection for the undergraduate courses presently given.

The collections of the University of British Columbia Library have been strengthened by purchases from a 3-million-dollar gift for books by H. R. MacMillan, MacMillan Bloedel, Ltd., inspired by the findings of the Williams report. This library has had a notable group of chief librarians who have made national contributions to the Canadian library scene, such as John Ridington, W. Kaye Lamb, and Neal Harlow.

Special Libraries. The number of special libraries is increasing with the rapid development of business, industry, research, and the professions. The British Columbia listings in "Special Libraries in Canada; a Directory" by Beryl L. Anderson; Chapter 7 of *Library Service in British Columbia* by Marjorie Holmes; an article by Theodora G. Rhodes in the *British Columbia Library Quarterly,* July–October 1957; and the 1968 "Directory of Special Collections in Canadian Libraries" by Janet Fyfe and Raymond H. Deutsch round out the picture of the British Columbia situation and holdings.

Library Asssociations. The driving force behind many of the library accomplishments of this province has been the members of the British Columbia Library Association founded September 6, 1911, in Victoria in the office of the provincial librarian. At this first meeting nine British Columbians and the chief librarian of the Calgary Public Library were present to discuss library legislation and the extension of library services throughout the province. An action program followed and finally resulted in the 1919 Act for the Establishment and Maintenance of Public Libraries. "The British Columbia Library Association; a Brief History" by Margaret Clay in the *Canadian Library Association Bulletin,* April 1956, and "So Far—So Good; BCLA at the Crossroads" by Elizabeth Jupp in the *British Columbia Library Quarterly,* January 1965, place the work of this association in perspective. With the growth of professionalism, the Institute of Professional Librarians of Victoria, and later the Association of British Columbia Librarians, were established in the 1960s.

Publications. The *BCLA Bulletin* was succeeded by the *British Columbia Li-*

brary Quarterly, which has received various honors for its general excellence and format. The association also issues a mimeographed newsletter, program notes, etc., as do the more recently formed professional library associations. The municipal and regional libraries issue annual reports, book lists, and special publications. The British Columbia Public Library Development Board, formerly the British Columbia Public Library Commission, is notable for the frequency and excellence of its publications.

Certification and Library Education. The certification of professional librarians is under the Department of the Provincial Secretary under Section 58 of the Public Libraries Act. The education of librarians has been entrusted to the University of British Columbia School of Librarianship.

PRINCE EDWARD ISLAND

(Area, 2,184 square miles; smallest province)

The early library history follows the pattern already described for Ontario and British Columbia of short-lived subscription or social libraries and a mechanics' institute in Charlottetown, the provincial capital. The Religious Circulating Library and the Prince Edward Island Subscription Library were established in 1824 and 1825, respectively. The Mechanics' Institute continued from 1838 to approximately 1858. Legislation to establish school district libraries was included in the 1877 Education Act. Few libraries, even for schools, were formed. In 1900 the Honourable Walter Dodd left $5000 for public library use. The collection purchased with these funds was amalgamated with the Legislative Library which had been established in 1773, and had allowed access to the citizens since 1890. It now became the Legislative and Dodd Library. Later $20,000 was willed by Mrs. Robert Harris for a building, opened in 1930, as the Legislative and Public Library with an art gallery on the upper floor. Summerside, the largest town, had library service from 1908 to approximately 1914, with a revival in 1932 by the Imperial Order Daughters of the Empire.

In the summer of 1930 the Commission of Enquiry into Library Conditions and Needs of Canada visited the province and discussed the good features of Prince Edward Island as a library demonstration area similar to the demonstration then in progress in British Columbia's Fraser Valley, under Dr. Helen Gordon Stewart.

The analogy of the Fraser Valley seemed inappropriate to many observers. Nothing in Prince Edward Island reflected the careful community styled library survey of British Columbia, the hard work of the British Columbia Public Library Commission, the leadership of Dr. Helen Gordon Stewart and Dr. Norman Black, and the long established British Columbia Library legislation. On learning of the recommendations by the Commission of Enquiry there was an exchange of letters between Robert Lester, secretary of the Carnegie Corporation, May 24, 1932, and Carl Milam, executive secretary of the American Library Association, July 18, 1932, both expressing doubt as to the suitability of Prince Edward Island as a demonstration area. However, Dr. F. P. Keppel, president of the Carnegie Corporation, had a deep interest in education in the Maritimes and was favorable. The

Honourable W. J. P. Macmillan, who had become premier as well as minister of health and education, promised cooperation. Dr. Keppel visited Prince Edward Island and was impressed. He invited Dr. G. R. Lomer, librarian of McGill University and director of the McGill University Library School, to visit the island and draw up a scheme for a three-year demonstration of regional library service. The Lomer report presented in October 1932 was accepted; the sum of $60,000 was appropriated by the Carnegie Corporation for the first year with renewal of the grant contingent on the merits of the demonstration of a "modern system of library service on Prince Edward Island and thereby to set an example for corresponding development in Nova Scotia and New Brunswick and possibly Newfoundland." Miss Nora Bateson, a librarian with public and regional library experience, was placed in charge.

Premier Macmillan accepted the plan proposed by Dr. Lomer and Miss Bateson and agreed to by the Carnegie Corporation. The Demonstration Office opened on June 1, 1933. Miss Bateson toured the island to promote the library and took a sample collection of the type of books for branch use. Public meetings were held. Branch arrangements to serve the community and districts were discussed. All services to the readers were free. All materials were purchased, processed, and maintained with Carnegie funds. In the first six months five branches were opened with five more added before the spring of 1934. Twenty-two were in operation when the demonstration ended on June 1, 1936. Book collections were forwarded to rural schools but less than 50% of the teachers made use of this service. Ninety-three clubs, studying fox farming, oyster culture, credit unions, etc., were organized as part of the adult education program. The Carnegie Corporation granted additional funds for 1935 and 1936 bringing the total grant to $95,000. The Prince Edward Island legislature appropriated $2000 toward support in 1935. A Public Library Act received assent on April 4, 1935, providing for a Library Commission, its powers, and the appointment of a superintendent.

The question of continuing the library at the Demonstration standard had to be considered by the provincial government in 1936. In the opinion of Dr. H. H. Shaw, the chief superintendent of education and later premier, the period of three years was "too short to overcome the innate resistance against increased taxation." In August 1935 there was a change of government. The Library Act was repealed on the grounds that government funds should be administered directly and not through a commission. The Provincial Legislature assumed the financial and administrative responsibility of regional library service, voting $12,000 for 1936–1937. The budget requested had been $30,000 or 34 cents per capita of the population. Direction of the system was transferred to two Islanders, Mr. H. Bramwell Chandler assisted by Miss Dorothy Cullen, both trained at the Pratt Institute. The system became the responsibility of the Minister of Education under the Department of Education Act, which reads:

> The Minister through his Department shall have the execution of the laws and orders of the Province and the administration of public business relating to . . . (7) The Prince Edward Island Libraries.

At the conclusion Miss Bateson wrote a very full report, *The Carnegie Demonstration in Prince Edward Island, Canada, 1933–1936*. With the growing interest in regional libraries in the 1960s the Prince Edward Island demonstration was studied by Marjorie Morley, who reported in *Regional Libraries: Nova Scotia, New Brunswick and Prince Edward Island* and by Violet L. Coughlin in *Larger Units of Public Library Service in Canada with Particular Reference to the Provinces of Prince Edward Island, Nova Scotia and New Brunswick*. The Coughlin study is the more complete because of access to the files of the Carnegie Corporation of New York as well as manuscript material in the possession of provincial library officials.

The Demonstration in its influence on other Maritime Provinces achieved the end envisaged by the commissioners of enquiry and the Carnegie Corporation. Marion Gilroy reports of Nova Scotia:

> In spite of these reverses on the Island, the Demonstration impressed a great and original adult educator in Nova Scotia, Dr. J. J. Tompkins. His interest and that of the small but zealous group in Halifax, members of the Maritime Library Institute, got the attention of the Superintendent of Education and of the Premier, the Honourable Angus L. Macdonald. Miss Bateson was engaged to survey library conditions and needs in Nova Scotia.

In 1964 Prince Edward Island Libraries headquarters was moved to the new Confederation Building. The professional staff has been increased and provides service to 485 rural schools and 25 public library branches, several of which are housed in interesting library buildings financed in part by the provincial government.

School Libraries. Under the Demonstration and the subsequent Prince Edward Island Libraries Organization, rural schools were included in the service. Some public library branches were established in schools and there gave students a wider selection. Both Mr. H. Bramwell Chandler and Miss Dorothy Cullen, successive librarians of the Prince Edward Island Libraries, were former teachers and deeply interested in the school libraries. There is an active school libraries group in the province. It is hoped that eventually school libraries will be organized in schools with four or more classrooms, that an enrollment of 200 or more will each have a trained librarian and a book collection of between 2000 to 5000 books, that schools with an enrollment of 120 to 200 will have their own collections with a trained children's librarian from the Prince Edward Island Libraries staff, and that all will be organized and supervised by a director of school libraries in a central agency, possibly part of the Prince Edward Island Libraries system. This scheme is dependent on future action of the Department of Education.

College and University Libraries. Prince of Wales College and St. Dunstan's University have libraries and have been included in the Downs report. A University of Prince Edward Island has been organized with the collections of Prince of Wales and St. Dunstan's amalgamated to form the nucleus of the university's library collection.

Special Libraries. Other than some specialized libraries in government departments these do not exist.

NOVA SCOTIA

(*Area, 21,425 square miles*)

Reference has been made earlier to the first private library in Nova Scotia— that of Marc Lescarbot in 1606. Records of the legislature show that between 1758 and 1819 the government made small appropriations for the purchase of books. Thus by 1819 the Legislative Library had 200 volumes, the cornerstone of its present rich collection of legislative materials, Americana and Canadiana.

In 1797 Chief Justice Sir Thomas A. L. Strange donated his library to the province for a law court library. In 1793 the dean of Christ Church, Oxford, drew up a list of books for a proposed public library in Halifax. It was 1824 when the library began operations. The Garrison Library has already been noted. In 1806 Halifax had a short-lived circulation library with another formed in 1808 that lasted until 1831. In the meantime, in 1820 a subscription library had been opened at Newport, followed by libraries in Amherst, Yarmouth, and Pictou. These were short-lived. By 1876 the collections of the Central Agricultural Society and the Mechanics' Institute formed in 1831 were taken over by the City of Halifax and the Citizens Free Library gave service until the present Halifax Memorial Library was built in 1951. In 1880 the Nova Scotia Historical Society Collection and the Legislative Library were amalgamated and placed under joint management. This continued until 1954 when the Historical Society Collection was transferred to the new Nova Scotia Archives building. The Legislative Library became a part of the Provincial Library.

In 1930 the Commission of Enquiry summarized its Nova Scotia findings in Chapter III of *Libraries in Canada,* mentioning the traveling box libraries to the rural schools, the public libraries in Yarmouth, Amherst, Truro, and Halifax—all insufficiently supported financially and inadequately housed—and the bookmobile service of Acadia University (financed by an anonymous donor) which circled the Maritime Provinces every three weeks. It recommended a Library Commission for Nova Scotia to work in close cooperation with a similar commission in New Brunswick because of the similarity of needs and conditions, "competent professional advice leading up to the framing of definite provincial library policies," "new legislation with necessary taxing powers." It omits mention of the strong extension department library under Sister Marie Michael McKinnon which supported the cooperatives sparked by Dr. J. J. Tompkins in 1927 and carried out under Dr. M. M. Coady of the Extension Department of the University of Saint Francis Xavier, Antigonish, to aid the people of Nova Scotia both socially and economically. From this resulted the internationally known Antigonish Co-operative Movement, which among other undertakings established the People's Library at Reserve Mines. When a request came from Cape Breton County for the Joint Expenditure Board to appoint a library committee, the board did so. Its committee reported to the Municipal Council, which forwarded resolutions to the Nova Scotia Legislature. In 1937 the Provincial Government passed an enabling act, the provisions of which allowed municipalities, towns, and cities either singly or jointly to establish regional libraries and to take the necessary steps for their maintenance.

In conformity with this act, the government authorized the Department of Education to initiate a survey of libraries. Miss Nora Bateson, formerly director of the Prince Edward Island Library Demonstration, did so in cooperation with the department and its officials. Miss Bateson visited many parts of the province giving addresses on regional libraries, their purpose, scope, and organization. In particular, she stressed library service as an effective instrument of adult education. Miss Bateson was received favorably at meetings where resolutions requested more information. Her report, *Library Survey of Nova Scotia,* proposed a library commission with detailed powers, a director of libraries, and a regional library for Cape Breton, and advocated that Nova Scotia be served by seven or eight county and regional libraries, unified and coordinated by the commission and its executive officer, the director of libraries. A central provincial library department would serve as a general clearinghouse for the province arranging interlibrary loans between counties and regions, calling when needed on the special collections in universities, building a union catalog, and doing on a small scale what the National Central Library does for Great Britain. She warned that such a plan could not be put into effect immediately because "although many feel the need keenly, the necessity and the way in which it can be effectively met are not yet generally recognized."

The survey was carefully studied and legislation was passed providing provincial financial aid and a Regional Library Commission. Miss Bateson was appointed regional director by Order-in-Council. Promotion, persuasion, and organization were tackled in several parts of the province, with enthusiasm, courage, and the experience gained by Miss Bateson in British Columbia and Prince Edward Island. Where the local enthusiasm for libraries was greatest, local taxation support was time and again refused by the Nova Scotia Department of Municipal affairs, on the grounds of economic inability to pay. The library commission revised the Regional Libraries Act making the conditions of establishment, management, and support more specific and authorizing the Provincial Government to give annual grants to regional libraries using the same formula established for public schools, i.e., one-third of the amount contributed or paid by the regional library. The next year (1940) the Provincial Legislature increased the grants to equal the amount contributed by the local authorities up to $1.00 per capita.

The interest of the Carnegie Corporation of New York was aroused. When the dollar for dollar legislation was passed the Corporation's trustees made $50,000 available from the British Dominions and Colonies Fund payable $10,000 in 1939–1940 and the balance on receiving a satisfactory plan of operations. The plan was not forthcoming until 1948–1949 due to World War II and local factors resulting in the departure from the province of Miss Bateson and her first assistant, Miss Marion Gilroy. In 1947 Miss Marion Moshier, head of the Extension Division of the New York State Library, Albany, New York, was invited to meet with interested groups and eventually to resurvey the province for a system of regional libraries. Her investigations showed that the highest per capita tax possible at that time was below the 50 cents per capita advocated earlier. Miss Moshier's report was a closed document for the use of government officials. However, it is known to have advised revisions to the existing library act, greater provincial financial assistance, and the setting up of centralized services at the Provincial Headquarters Office in Halifax. The next year a provincial librarian was appointed, Mr. Peter Grossman, formerly the head first of the Vancouver Island Union Library and later of the Fraser Valley Union Library in British Columbia. Mr. Grossman advertised widely for staff, declaring the work in Nova Scotia to be probably the most difficult, but the most rewarding, in Canada.

By 1949 the Annapolis Valley Regional Library was organized with regular bookmobile service. In 1950 followed the units of the Cape Breton Regional Library and the Colchester-East Hants Regional Library. In 1951 came the Pictou County Regional Library. Halifax had erected a public library as its war memorial in 1951 and in 1954 this urban area became the Halifax Regional Library. Halifax Municipal County Library followed in 1960, Dartmouth in 1963, and Cumberland in 1967. Some 30% of the province is still considering regional library organization. In 1952 the Libraries Act was rewritten and cooperation with the National Library was added. The Provincial Library came under the Department of Education and assumed all the functions of the Regional Library Commission. The financial aid given by Nova Scotia is generous. In 1967 the provincial government grants for public library service paid to councils which provide regional library service amounted to two-thirds of the cost of the public library service in the province. This support was allowed by the revision of the Libraries Act, 1966. Grants to buildings as well as the services were being given for the first time. Budgeted for grants was 1 million dollars. Scholarships were also provided for training at accredited library schools.

The interrelation between the Provincial Library and all libraries in the province, Canada, and abroad is close. The province has been generous in sharing its library experiences with other Canadian provinces and in giving its director of libraries, Miss Alberta Letts, leave of absence to advise the Republic of India on a regional library plan in 1957 and in creating observation working tours for librarians in Nigeria, South Africa, and other countries.

Visitors to Nova Scotia interested in visiting public libraries will find some of the municipal library buildings of interest, such as the Halifax Memorial Library and its New North End Branch; the Sydney, Cape Breton, City Library and Regional Library Headquarters; the Isaak Killam Library at Yarmouth; the Cumberland Regional Library headquarters at Amherst; and the Truro Public Library.

School Libraries. The impetus to develop school libraries comes from the tenure of Dr. Henry F. Munro. By 1929 a regional system of book distribution had begun to thirteen counties with exchanges between schools. With the formation of regional libraries in 1949, schools with little library material received help. In 1960 a supervisor of school libraries was appointed. Agreement was reached that school libraries should provide material related to the curriculum and regional libraries types of recreational reading. In 1964 legislation provided $100 for each school library. This is no solution. Massive organization grants are needed. A 1967 survey of the Halifax schools by Miss Kathleen Bowlby showed that the collections do not include the necessary reference works and supplementary material to support the present curriculum. There is the occasional well-organized library with a trained librarian, library clerk, and other help, but this is exceptional.

College and University Libraries and Education for Librarianship. Profiles in the Downs report include the Universities of Acadia (Wolfville), Dalhousie (Halifax), King's College (Halifax), Mount St. Vincent (Rockingham), St. Francis Xavier (Antigonish), and St. Mary's (Halifax), the Nova Scotia Agricultural College (Truro), Nova Scotia Technical College (Halifax), and Xavier College (Syndey). Not included was the College Sainte-Anne, which is also a member of the Association of Universities and Colleges of Canada. Donald A. Redmond in "Some College Libraries of Canada's Maritime Provinces; Selected Aspects," 1949, discusses the physical plant, resources, personnel, administration, use of the library, standard plans, and the dual problem of the individual utilization of resources and regional resources of the Acadia and Dalhousie-King's libraries. John P. Wilkinson in "A History of Dalhousie University Main Library, 1867–1931" has made an exhaustive study of this period. Both Redmond and Wilkinson include valuable historical and background discussions of unsuccessful efforts to federate the Maritime universities and their library resources. The Downs survey shows that the libraries in 1967 have suitable quarters, either new buildings or good space with a new building being erected for Dalhousie. Four out of six of the libraries are meeting personnel standards. Two out of six are meeting the standards of a minimum collection of 100,000. None of the libraries is receiving the minimum financial support of the university's budget. By 1967 the Nova Scotia university and college libraries had moved from the dangerous starvation funds situation of the midcentury to one of semistarvation as to funds to improve their collections, personnel, facilities, and services.

In 1963 a new body called the Associated Atlantic Universities was organized and a special committee was set up at the request of the university presidents to discuss cooperation between the Atlantic universities libraries. Later a Council of Library Resources was established; it meets regularly to devise, plan, and recommend action. It includes all types of libraries interested in research.

The education of librarians was first undertaken under the direction of Mrs. Mary Kinley Ingraham by Acadia University as elective courses for the Bachelor of Arts degree. Next a course for university graduates was offered by Mount St. Vincent under the direction of the chief librarian, Sister Francis de Sales. This included an experimental public library for the Rockingham area. Scholarships to train out of the province was the next experiment. With the growing demand for librarians, and pressure from the Atlantic Provinces Library Association, Dalhousie University has organized a graduate school at the master's level. The first class was for the academic year 1969–1970.

Special Libraries. These are not numerous. There are special collections but these are chiefly in government, college, university, and public libraries as may be seen in the directories already referred to compiled by Anderson, Fyfe, and Deutsch.

Library Associations. Nova Scotia is fortunate in having strong library associations. The Maritime Library Institute founded in 1935 is now the Atlantic Provinces Library Association. There is also an active Halifax Library Association. These discuss needs, publish bulletins, and initiate action.

Publications. Ambitious bibliographies such as the *Atlantic Provinces Checklist* have been undertaken. Both the Atlantic Provinces Library Association and the Halifax Library Association issue bulletins as well as special publications. The regional and individual libraries issue annual reports, book and film lists, and special local brochures.

The spirit of optimism which Miss Bateson detected in 1937 has grown with the years. The four Atlantic Provinces have set up an Atlantic Provinces Economic Council to better conditions. The four premiers of the Atlantic provinces are acting in concert whatever their political parties. New industries are being sought and found. Education is being improved. Research is being fostered. New cultural blossomings in Nova Scotia have been the successful establishment of the Neptune Theatre, an increased body of good writing, and the steady development and improvement of all types of libraries. By now every area could have its regional system were it not for the shortage of librarians, and in some areas a native reluctance to invest in public education through the public library.

The type of library in greatest need of establishment and enrichment is the school library at both the elementary and secondary level.

NEW BRUNSWICK

(Area, 28,354 square miles)

New Brunswick shares with Nova Scotia a common tradition until 1784, when Nova Scotia was divided to form the two provinces.

New Brunswick's early library history begins with the private library of the Loyalist, Jonathan Odell, provincial secretary from the formation of the province in 1784 until 1812. What remains of the collection is now in Saint John at the New Brunswick Museum. Social libraries, supported by membership fees, were established in Saint Andrews in 1815, in Fredericton in 1816, and in Saint John, the Eclectic Library, in 1821. A mechanics' institute appeared around 1838 at Hillsborough, followed in 1839 by one in Saint John, in 1844 by one in Miramichi, and in the next year by one in King's County, with others following. As in the Canadas, they were incorporated under provincial acts and there is record of a government grant of £500 to the one in Saint John.

The 1854 Commission to Study Educational Problems introduced a recommendation on the advantages of school district libraries. The revised Education Act of 1858 therefore provided a grant of 50% raised locally, not to exceed five pounds. Only fourteen libraries were formed. Urban public libraries were established with varying success in Fredericton (ceased in 1859), in Saint John in 1883 (now the Saint John Regional Library), in Moncton, incorporated in 1928 (now part of the Albert, Westmorland, Kent Regional Library), and in Woodstock incorporated in 1912 (still in service); and two small association libraries were established in Port Elgin (lasted three years) and in Sussex (still in service).

In 1928 New Brunswick authors formed a branch of the Canadian Authors

Association and set up a committee chairman, Major Henry C. F. Christie, to investigate library service for the province. The committee surveyed New Brunswick and the best library practices in other parts of Canada, the United Kingdom, the United States, and abroad. They were particularly interested in California, Great Britain, and British Columbia. Their report was discussed with Premier J. B. M. Baxter, himself a noted book collector. The result was an act which became law on March 25, 1929—a very general act patterned somewhat on the British Columbia Act of 1919 with powers and duties assigned to a library commission. No legal provision was stipulated as to financial support, neither was it specified which minister of the crown was responsible for the administration of the act. Annual reports were to be submitted to the provincial secretary to be laid before the legislature. A unique feature of the act was the creation of a library council to cooperate with the commission both to supply information about the province and to assist the commission in carrying out the provisions of the act. This was an innovation for Canada.

By the spring of 1930 the government had named the commission—Major H. C. F. Christie, Mrs. Margaret E. Lawrence, both of Saint John, and Mr. Angus MacLean of Bathurst. Major Christie was elected chairman and a professional librarian, Miss Elizabeth H. Morton, was appointed secretary-treasurer. An office was opened in Saint John and a budget for preliminary work was authorized. The premier placed the commission under the provincial secretary-treasurer, the Honourable Antoine J. Leger of Moncton. Major Christie and Mrs. Lawrence met to prepare an agenda for the first council meeting, to develop plans along the thinking of the committee's report to the premier, and to set up a budget. By coincidence the chairman of the Commission of Enquiry, Mr. John Ridington, arrived in town when all three commissioners were available and a meeting was held at which Mr. Ridington preached the gospel of regional libraries and the excellent publicity gained through bookmobile service. He sparked the imagination of all and particularly of Mr. Angus MacLean. Mr. Ridington decried encouraging any more tiny local libraries and felt the day of the box library was long past. He spoke of Prince Edward Island as an ideal demonstration unit for the Maritime Provinces.

Following this session the commissioners worked with the secretary on regional plans for the whole province and postponed the council meeting until the revised scheme and its budget could be discussed with Premier Baxter. The second and third members of the Commission of Enquiry, Dr. George H. Locke, and Miss Mary J. L. Black arrived during the following months. The New Brunswick Library Commission's revised plan was developed after study of reports of other areas supplied by Miss Julia Wright Merrill of the American Library Association, and incorporated local information garnered by Mrs. Lawrence from her years of reportorial experience in New Brunswick. It was presented to the government on October 31, 1930, and at that time was the only province-wide plan for library service in Canada. The province was divided into seven library units using existing libraries where possible as resource centers. Centralized ordering, cataloging, classification, and a union provincial catalog with shared expenses by area and commission were based on the experience of the ordering and cataloging divisions of the

Toronto Public Library whose annual book acquisitions for its main libraries, branches, settlement deposits, foreign collections, etc., seemed to supply an adequate working scheme.

While awaiting a reply from the government regarding this submission the commission, at the request of the premier, did a survey of the Legislative Library in Fredericton and other libraries in that area and forwarded this report to Fredericton. Through an error in Fredericton, this report was tabled in the legislature and the commission's "Annual Report and Plan" remained filed. The spring of 1931 had set in with stringent government economics decreed by the economic depression. The commission received 10% of the budget requested; this allowed it to pay its bills, close its office, and release all staff. Major Christie resigned. Soon after Mr. Angus MacLean and Premier Baxter died. The commission, now consisting of Mrs. Margaret Lawrence and Mr. A. B. Brooke of Sussex, completed their terms and no reappointments were made. Because the act decreed action through the Library Commission all provincial government encouragement ceased.

During the next twenty years library developments were not forgotten. The *Telegraph-Journal* carried news and editorials about Prince Edward Island and Nova Scotia. The superintendent of education, Dr. Fletcher Peacock, always incorporated space for a community library into each of the thirty-two regional high schools built during his term of office and kept in communication with the former secretary of the commission, who had returned to the Toronto Public Library. Mrs. Hugh John Flemming developed school and community library service in Juniper. With the increase in the number of professional librarians in the province, chiefly in the libraries of the University of New Brunswick, St. Joseph's College, and Mount Allison University and in the Legislative Library, a New Brunswick Library Association was formed in 1951, quite separate from the Maritime Library Association, at the call of the University of New Brunswick librarian, Mrs. Majorie Jardine Thompson, formerly librarian of the Moncton Public Library. Maurice Boone, chief librarian of the Legislative Library and formerly librarian of Acadia University, was elected president and A. Robert Rogers, University of New Brunswick Library, secretary. Resolutions were passed and forwarded to the proper government officials, one going to the Legislative Library Committee which invited the director of libraries for Nova Scotia, Mr. Peter Grossman, to speak at its meeting on March 26, 1952, after which discussion followed. The result was that the Department of Education invited Mr. Grossman to survey library facilities throughout the province and outline a suitable plan for future library development.

Mr. Peter Grossman spent five weeks of the summer of 1952 in the province and presented his report, *Library Service in New Brunswick; a Report and Recommendations* on December 24, 1952, which was tabled by the Legislative Assembly in the spring and was published and widely distributed by the Department of Education. Mr. Grossman proposed eight regional library units, stressed the need for comprehensive enabling legislation, and listed what should be embodied in the proposed act. He emphasized the early appointment of a director, a library council, and a publicity campaign. He made practical suggestions on the organization of regional libraries including features not included in Nova Scotia but which he felt

would benefit New Brunswick. The plan was accepted. A director, James F. Mac-
Eacheron, formerly on the staff of the Cape Breton Regional Library, was appointed and took office January 1, 1954; the Library Services Act was passed
April 14, 1954; the 1929 act was repealed; and the Central Library Services Office,
responsible to the Minister of Education, was opened, with four divisions charged
with central cataloging, reference, children's work, and regional libraries, replacing
the commission. Financial support was authorized, and a library council was
named.

The development of the New Brunswick Regional Library Service is discussed
at considerable length by Dr. Violet Coughlin and Miss Marjorie Morley in their
studies of the Maritime Provinces. The York Regional Library was set up as an
experimental demonstration for the province as a whole, with assistance from the
Canada Council and was supported by the City of Fredericton and the County of
York, November 21, 1958. Service began January 1, 1959, from the Fredericton
Public Library, and bookmobile service to rural areas began in May. Albert-
Westmorland-Kent Regional Library had been set up in 1957 with the Moncton
Public Library as the center of a bilingual system. Promotion, advice, and discus-
sions were undertaken continually with other areas.

On May 19, 1967, the Library Services Act of 1954 was repealed, to be replaced by the Libraries Act, 1967. Anyone familiar with New Brunswick library
developments of the intervening years and with the major recommendations of the
"Report of the Royal Commission on Finance and Municipal Taxation in New
Brunswick, 1963," commonly called the Byrne Report will note that the act incorporates proved library experience within the province and brings libraries into
line with the major recommendations of the Byrne Report that:

> All libraries and other such facilities of a local service nature should be taken
> over by the Municipal Affairs Commission and operated and maintained by it,
> on behalf of the appropriate local service districts and as a charge on the rate-
> payers who benefit from such services.

The Royal Commission came to this conclusion because:

> There are several other reasons for the variation in per capita spending, but size
> is a persuasive factor. . . . Second, the residents of small towns do not always
> demand some services, such as libraries, which are demanded by the residents
> of large cities or, more important, as high a standard of such facilities as roads.
> But by far the most important reason is that the smaller centres do not face as
> many of the problems of the large centres, or do not face up to them.

The Libraries Act of 1967 places libraries under the Minister of Education. The
Central Library Services is now the New Brunswick Library Service which is to
support and enhance public library and school library service. The Library Council
is changed to include, in addition to three representatives of public libraries, three
representatives of school libraries, with the director of the New Brunswick
Library Service as chairman. The council's terms of reference are widened to
include school libraries. The province may be divided on authority of the Min-

ister into *a maximum of eight* library regions. The Regional Library Board has its powers and duties carefully detailed, as has also the Public Library Board. Provision is made for training, examination, and certification of library personnel on the authority of the lieutenant-governor in council. Financing is covered by Articles 4 and 5:

> 4. The service shall support and enhance public library and school library service in the Province.
> 5. From money provided by the Province, or from bequests, gifts, or otherwise, the Service may acquire, hold, and lend materials.

In the *Annual Report, 1967, of the Albert-Westmorland-Kent Regional Library* the librarian notes that the proclamation of the act "marked an important development in this regional library." No longer does the regional library go to its concomitant parts for its tax support but directly to the province.

Five regions are now set up in the province: in the north, Restigouche with Campbellton as the central library, and Nepisiguit with Bathurst as the central library; in the east, Albert-Westmorland-Kent, centered in Moncton; in the south, Saint John centered in Saint John City; and in the central portion and the west, York centered in Fredericton.

The push forward of the period 1966–1968 has been the result of steady work by the central provincial office. The centennial celebrations of 1967 gave a focus for accomplishments; for example, the establishment of the Restigouche Library Region with new centennial public library buildings in Campbellton and Dalhousie, and of the Nepisiguit Library Region centered around the new centennial Bathurst Public Library.

The *1967 Annual Report of the Saint John Regional Library* reflects the benefits the province's longest established public library has received through the change from a municipal to a regional system. The population is now 89,000 instead of 55,000; two new branches have been organized in shopping centers; new borrowers have been registered and the staff increased. This library is rich in its Canadiana collection and rare New Brunswick items.

School Libraries. School libraries received careful attention from Mr. Peter Grossman in his 1952 survey. He wrote that measured by *The Teacher-Librarian's Handbook* by Mary Peacock Douglas,

> . . . it is doubtful if any school in the province meets these standards, but as more teachers from the larger schools take professional training and as more teachers from smaller schools take the library courses at summer school the improvement which is already obvious will continue.

With regard to the Department of Education Library he pointed out the lack of use by the teachers and he advised full-time service for the librarian of the Teacher's College Library. His evaluation of the school and community libraries at Centreville, Juniper, Milltown, Petitcodiac, and Saint Stephen showed that "joint service depends entirely on local conditions and no rules can be laid down that will apply in all cases."

In the discussion of school library developments of 1946–1967 Mustard and Fennell report that during 1960, courses in school library work and children's literature were given at the Teacher's College. New Brunswick library service now provides a mail service to teachers and children as well as graded book lists. The province provides central library service through each school district library. The provincial school library grant is 60 cents per student—far below the Canadian School Library Association standard of $7 to $12 per pupil for books and other printed and audiovisual materials. Though the larger city school library service presents a more rosy picture, there are only three trained school librarians in the province.

In line with the recommendations of the Royal Commission on Finance and Municipal Taxation in New Brunswick 1963 that

> . . . all libraries and other such facilities of a local service nature should be taken over by the Municipal Affairs Commission and operated and maintained by it, on behalf of the appropriate local service districts and as a charge on the ratepayers who benefit from such a service,

the Library Services Act of New Brunswick of 1954 was repealed and the Libraries Act of 1967 passed into law. Among its provisions the act states: "The [New Brunswick] Service shall support and enhance public library and school library service in the province," that the Library Council may include "three representatives of school libraries appointed for a term of three years . . . ," and that the Library Council

> . . . shall study and review public and school library service in the province and make recommendations to the Minister and . . . subject to the approval of the Minister, shall make rules for the establishment and operation of public libraries and school libraries in the province.

The Regional Library Board, of which there may be a maximum of eight, includes:

> . . . representatives from each school district in the library region to equal the number of representatives appointed under clause (a) [which requires a minimum of five] to be appointed by the school boards of those districts for a term of one year.

> Each school district under the Schools Act shall provide library facilities as part of the library region subject to section 9 (4) of the Schools Act.

The act has not been without criticism. The director of the New Brunswick Library Service points out that the act

> . . . while retaining the essential regional idea for public libraries, extends it to include schools in the belief that school libraries must eventually belong to

a library system as the public libraries do, that the Act does not substitute one type of library for another, nor does it make provision to combine types of libraries, that the Act regards the school library and the public library as educational entities and at no point are they considered similar in function.

College and University Libraries. There are three university profiles for New Brunswick in the Downs report—the Université de Moncton (Moncton), formerly St. Joseph's College (College Bridge); Mount Allison University (Sackville); and the University of New Brunswick (Fredericton with a branch in Saint John). The Redmond study of 1949 includes Mount Allison and New Brunswick. All three universities are now housed in fine new buildings. They are a part of the joint undertakings of the Atlantic Provinces, such as the Associated Atlantic Universities, noted in the section on Nova Scotia.

Special Libraries. The most distinguished is the group of libraries in the New Brunswick Provincial Museum, a private undertaking.

Library Associations. On accomplishing its purpose of a new library act and encouraging a scheme of regional libraries by the province, the New Brunswick Library Association, mentioned earlier, disbanded. New Brunswick librarians are members of the Atlantic Provinces Library Association, the Canadian Library Association, and L'Association Canadienne des Bibliothécaires de la Langue français.

Publications. A most valuable annual list of New Brunswick publications is compiled and edited by Mr. Maurice Boone, legislative librarian. The New Brunswick Library Service issues book lists, releases, etc., as do regional libraries. Annual reports are distributed. There is active cooperation with the compiling of the *Atlantic Provinces Checklist* including editorial time and of the *Atlantic Provinces Library Association Bulletin.*

Bilingual Aspects. With the growth of its French-speaking population, New Brunswick is rapidly assuming importance as a bilingual and bicultural province and is in a unique position in Canada. Its progressive legislation following the Byrne Report is designed to upgrade educational, library, social, and welfare opportunities for all.

NEWFOUNDLAND

(Area, 156,185 square miles; 43,385, islands; 112,826, Labrador mainland)

Canada's tenth province entered Confederation March 31, 1949, after a long history as a colony, as an independent dominion from 1931 to 1934, under a Commission government 1934 to 1949. The province has the highest percentage of English-speaking people in Canada. Economically Newfoundland was the poorest province when it entered Confederation, chiefly because of isolation and because its natural resources remained undeveloped. By 1967 this was changing rapidly.

During the nineteenth century there were two public subscription libraries, one at Harbour Grace and one in St. John's—the Atheneum Library—destroyed by fire in 1892 and not restored. A Mechanics' Institute was established in 1827 and lasted until 1928. In 1926 the Newfoundland Bureau of Education applied and received from the Carnegie Corporation financial assistance to set up traveling libraries for lighthouses, ships at sea, and remote and near outposts, to support the adult education movement. The library boxes served communities other than St. John's and were distributed chiefly through public schools. The question of improving literacy was arousing government concern.

The commissioners of 1934 took up the proposal of public library service. The work was inaugurated in 1934 with Mr. Harold Newell appointed as librarian. In January 1935 a Public Libraries Act was passed giving the Public Libraries Board power to establish libraries in St. John's and throughout the island. The latest revision of the act passed in 1959 works out in careful detail all powers, relationships, and funds and is supplemented by Rules and Orders of Procedure. By January 1936 the Gosling Memorial Library was opened in St. John's; it was named for a former mayor whose books formed the nucleus of the collection, and in addition there were handsome gifts from Lord Rothermere and Sir Edgar R. Bowring. Part of the former Legislative Library collection was incorporated and the whole undertaking supported by government funds to maintain collections, technical processing, administration, accounting, and services to the province as a whole. The traveling libraries were transferred to the Public Library Service, expanded, and completely reorganized. In 1940 the board adopted a plan of regional libraries which was approved by the government and put into operation in 1942 with a grant for books of $10,000 from the Carnegie Corporation. The plan called for 25 regional or central libraries, branches, and deposit stations, all to work in the closest cooperation. Each regional library would have its own board, affiliated with the Public Libraries Board but with a large measure of autonomy. Each regional board would receive an annual grant, a stock of books, and technical and reference assistance from the Public Libraries Board and was expected to contribute to the maintenance of its libraries. There would also be a matching building grant of monies raised locally for library buildings.

The reason 25 regions were adopted stemmed from the geography of Newfoundland with its deep fiords which in some situations made only communications by sea possible because of the then lack of a transisland system of roads and the need to provide service to Labrador. Professional staff problems were solved in part by sending Newfoundlanders to Canadian library schools. Custodians from the branches were brought to St. John's for short term training sessions annually or biennially.

The administration center for the Public Libraries Service was organized into three divisions:

1. The Gosling Memorial Library, which had the double duty of servicing the City of St. John's and of supplying reference service to the entire system.

2. The traveling libraries, which serviced schools, adult education groups, and points without regional library service.

3. The regional libraries, which developed so rapidly both on the island and in Labrador that in 1965 the system included some sixty libraries in active service

(fifty-seven in the island and three in Labrador) and some two hundred deposit stations.

The Public Library Services have developed plans periodically and systematically for the betterment of the system, but until recently were limited and frustrated by lack of adequate financing. The latest plan is to divide the province into six regions with at least one professional librarian to develop the work of each region. There are 700 communities scattered throughout the province without library service, and only five of the sixty libraries are open full-time. The others operate from six to sixteen hours a week and are administered by a local custodian with some spare time and an interest in books. The south coast and the northern peninsula have few libraries due to the small population and the isolation of the area for there are no roads on the south coast, an irregular plane service because of fog, and only a weekly boat service. In the isolated area in much of Labrador and the north coast, the traveling library is still largely used. The use of a book-boat such as is used to service the islands of Sweden has been advocated for southern Newfoundland by the head of the regional libraries system who had an opportunity to study library services in Finland, Sweden, Norway, and Denmark under a Canada Council grant. One Newfoundland bay has over three hundred islands (not all populated), some of which are important fishing centers and will always need library servicing.

The Newfoundland Public Libraries Board, "32nd Annual Report, 1967–1968," announces:

> The year 1967–68 witnessed the beginning of a great expansion in Public Library Services in Newfoundland made possible by the significant increase in grant from the Provincial Government, which was most encouraging after such a long period of marking time. No major projects were completed but the increased grant made it possible for large stocks of books to be ordered, thus laying the foundation for the building of a better service. Indeed, it is noteworthy that the book budget alone for the year was almost as large as the entire grant for the preceding year.

New professional and other staff were engaged and bookmobile service was initiated. The Arts and Culture Centre Library, housed in a new building erected at a cost of eight million dollars was opened. The headquarters of the Public Library Service was moved to the Arts and Culture Centre. Memorial library became a downtown branch, to be moved later into the new City Hall building. Nineteen new libraries were built as centennial projects, eleven in communities which formerly had no library, so the Public Library Service has had to supply book collections, all processed and ready to go on the shelves. Not since the early days of Regional Libraries Service has there been such an expansion, for no fewer than eight new libraries were established.

Thus the service has expanded steadily since its inauguration but it continues to need funds, staff, and collections to meet its objective of providing library service suitable to the needs of every man, woman, and child. There are difficult problems of book selection. Not only are suitable books needed for the undereducated but also for the sophisticated, for the province contains internationally known authors, historians, painters, and sociologists.

The Royal Commission on Education and Youth of Newfoundland and Labrador, commonly called the Warren Commission (Dr. Philip J. Warren was chairman), in its report devotes Chapter IV of Volume 2 to library services, concluding with twenty-three recommendations, now under study.

School Libraries. The schools of St. John's were the first to have libraries. Outside the capital, the schools have been supplied entirely or supplemented by the regional libraries or the traveling libraries of the Public Library Service. In the autumn when school reopens, circular letters advise all teachers in areas where a regional library does not service the school about the traveling library services. About two hundred schools request a box of some forty or fifty books; this is sent by coastal boat, train or truck and may be exchanged. Some schools are now building their own collections, using a small grant from the Department of Education of thirty-nine cents per pupil, probably the lowest grant in Canada. Recently a Royal Commission on Education and Youth has surveyed Newfoundland and has strongly recommended the adoption of the financial standards of the Canadian School Library Association of $5 and $8 per student for books and other printed materials, and $2 to $4 per student for audiovisual materials. It also advised the appointment of a school library supervisor, which recommendation has been implemented. Mrs. Sally Davis is organizing several undertakings.

Library manuals and book lists have been prepared by the Public Library Service and published by the Department of Education. By 1965 there were twelve teacher-librarians in the elementary schools and fifteen in the central and regional high schools, one of whom had a degree in library science. The bulk of these are in urban centers. A School Library Council was formed in 1966. A program to help teachers and to encourage the government to increase the school library grants has been undertaken.

College and University Libraries. Memorial University of Newfoundland is included in the Profiles of Colleges and Universities of the Downs Report. The library building was completed in 1961 but is proving inadequate as to seating and other facilities due to the increased enrollment. Its financial support is the third best in the Atlantic provinces but below the Canadian Association of College and University Libraries standard.

Special Libraries. Corner Brook and St. John's have special libraries which are listed in Anderson.

Publications. An interesting *Newsletter* goes out quarterly to the regional libraries. Annual reports, lists, and special brochures, and, from Memorial University Library orientation films, are issued.

PRAIRIE PROVINCES AND THE TERRITORIES

The prairie provinces share with the territories a common early history and tradition, for it was not until the late nineteenth and early twentieth century that the present boundaries were settled for the three provinces—Manitoba, Saskatchewan, and Alberta—and two territories—Yukon and the Northwest, which continue under the federal government. The provinces have been dominated successively by the fur trade, wheat, minerals, and manufactures; the territories by the fur trade, fisheries, and minerals. The population is more multicultural and multilingual than the rest of Canada with a higher proportion of the native Indian and Eskimo races.

Many of the fur traders from Europe brought books with them; evidence of this is found in the journals of explorers and traders and in the remains of the post libraries now at Hudson's Bay House in Winnipeg.

The Northwest Territorial Ordinances show encouragement of Mechanics Institutes and Library Associations in 1890 and the School District library in 1901.

MANITOBA

(Area, 251,000 square miles)

By 1700 there were books at the Hudson Bay post of York Factory, in line with this company's policy of supplying books, periodicals, and newspapers for the use of the staff. Lord Strathcona, a former factor in the northwest, reminisced once about the daily opening of a newspaper one year after date of issue in the outpost in Labrador where he was located, and later in the territories. Books were available on arrival. It is safe to surmise that the Scottish Selkirk settlers would have the Bible, the Psalms, and the Paraphrases in Gaelic among their personal belongings. The British army provided garrison libraries for the use of officers in the district— also available to the local population. In 1847 this led to the organization of the Red River Library, dissolved in 1857 with half the books retained at Lower Fort Garry for the use of the settlers and the rest sent to Winnipeg where eventually they were incorporated into the Legislative Library.

Special and academic libraries were formed in Winnipeg in the 1870s and 1880s: for example, the Legislative Library in 1870, Manitoba College and St. John's College in 1871, and the Isbister Library in 1877, all free; the Law Society of Manitoba, and the Historical and Scientific Society libraries were by subscription.

The Winnipeg Public Library was organized free to all under a city charter of 1879. The Mechanics' Institutes and Library Associations legislation was passed in 1890. The Earl of Aberdeen became governor-general of Canada in 1893. Lady Aberdeen, a most public spirited woman, was inspired by a group of Winnipeg women to found the Aberdeen Association to

> . . . collect good and attractive periodicals and other literature, and to distribute it in monthly parcels to settlers who apply for it from outlying parts of Canada.

Although subscriptions were requested to an amount of whatever the recipient could afford, the work was largely philanthropic. Its importance lies in setting a pattern of what eventually developed into the traveling library services of Manitoba, Saskatchewan, and Alberta.

A Manitoba Library Act was passed in 1899 by the legislature and was modeled on the 1883 Ontario Act. Although it allowed municipalities to cooperate with each other for library service, for some reason this was later rescinded. A 1925 amendment created a commission named the Manitoba Library Board, which was given neither authority nor money. The appointees were the provincial librarian, the head of the traveling library system, and the assistant deputy attorney general.

By 1930, when the Commission of Enquiry visited the province, there were some forty institute libraries as well as small libraries in Brandon, Portage la Prairie, Dauphin, and Virden. The city of Winnipeg Public Library was limited financially due to the library one-third mill rate on city assessment, which showed a steady decrease just when the city's population was increasing. The result in 1930 was a rate of just under 40 cents per capita. With no board of trustees, the library reported to the overburdened Health Committee of the City Council. When queried by the Commission of Enquiry, the newly appointed trained librarian, Mr. Jamieson, could not consider under these circumstances any extension of service beyond the city. The City of St. Boniface depended on a parish library established in 1911. The traveling libraries of the Department of Education included 242 collections of 50 to 100 books, mostly fiction, with a small Open Shelf Collection to reinforce resources; the Manitoba Wheat Pool loaned books to its members; there was a collection (chiefly donations) in the Winnipeg General Hospital.

The Commission of Enquiry recommended the appointment of a provincial organizer, a revision of the act, the reorganization of the Library Commission—in power, funds, personnel—and stressed the need of the Winnipeg Public Library for financial assistance. These recommendations were issued in 1933, the darkest year of the Economic Depression, and nothing happened.

In 1935, through strong leadership from the University of Manitoba libraries, the Legislative Library, the Winnipeg Public Library, and half a dozen special and government libraries, the Manitoba Library Association was formed with a membership of 60. Committees to study pertinent problems were appointed, two of the most active being Library Extension and Library Legislation.

The legislature repealed the 1925 Manitoba Library Act in 1940 and the province was without library legislation until 1948 when an act, thanks to the efforts of the Library Legislation Committee of the Manitoba Library Association and the legislative librarian, Mr. Leslie Johnson, reached discussion and consideration by the Legislative Assembly and finally became law. The act provided for the establishment of public libraries in municipalities and of regional libraries. It continued the limitation of one mill of the tax assessment and it failed to provide for establishment and provincial grants. Since assessment of property outside of Winnipeg is low, this lack of financial assistance by the province was serious. Later, provincial establishment grants and annual grants were made available to municipal and regional libraries. Six municipalities established public libraries under this act— Dauphin, St. Boniface, St. Vital, St. James, Fort Garry, and West Kildonan. Community interest increased. A Library Development Committee on which the Manitoba Library Association was represented was appointed. The committee prepared a brief to the Minister of Education which recommended a survey of libraries later conducted by Mr. George Noble. Various traveling library services had developed in government departments—in Education, Agriculture, and the Extension Department of the University of Manitoba. When the Manitoba Wheat Pool library had been discontinued, the Provincial Government purchased it and Mr. Noble was appointed head of the Extension Library of the University of Manitoba with a collection of some 12,000 volumes. The legislative and provincial librarian became director of libraries under the Public Libraries Act, responsible for the general coordination of library service throughout Manitoba, the stimulation of interest in regional libraries, and the approving of the annual establishment grants.

The government began to promote the larger unit of library service. The size of the unit had been hotly debated as some advisors warned of the evils attendant in setting up too small a unit (less than the standard advocated by the American and Canadian Library Associations) while others argued that Manitoba was in a special situation and with its widespread, isolated population, it would be expedient to allow miniregional libraries and to hope that eventually these small units would federate or amalgamate into units of standard size. This course was followed.

Thirteen miniregionals were set up—Assimiboine River, Boissevain and Morton, Evergreen, Glenwood–Souris, Henderson, Jolys–St. Pierre, Lakeland, Morden–Winkler, North-West, Russell and District, Sainte Rose, Southwestern, and Virden–Elkhorn. The largest, Henderson, serves a population of 43,024 while the smallest, Southwestern, serves 2206.

The 1964 revision of the Public Libraries Act included a Part IV devoted to federation of regional and municipal public libraries, thus legislating toward the formation of a more standard size limit if and when possible. The act notes that the Brandon War Memorial Public Library is a municipal library within the meaning of the act, since this library is pre-1948 and was organized under a charter. The area around Brandon was considered a most likely one for a federation. All federations would be administered by federation boards to govern, supervise, control, operate, and manage the library federation, make rules and regulations, appoint a librarian, keep accounts, and furnish an annual report to the minister, who is the member of the executive council designated as the minister responsible for the administration of the Public Libraries Act.

In 1962 the Canadian Library Association held a special workshop on metropolitan library systems as part of its Annual Conference in Ottawa. Among possibilities discussed were Winnipeg and its surrounding towns of St. Boniface, St. Vital, St. James, Fort Garry, and West Kildonan.

In a memorandum of September 20, 1967, prepared for a Manitoba Library Association meeting, Mr. Easton writes regarding the provincial situation:

> The factor which makes it supremely difficult to plan province-wide service is not distance, or geography, or weather or lack of money, although we have them all; it is the exaggerated unevenness of the distribution of population. Well over half of the people live in or near Metro Winnipeg. Apart from this area, it is not possible to find a grouping of people sufficiently large within a manageable area, with the doubtful exception of the south-west corner of the province.
>
> Under these circumstances the achievements of the provincial library services deserve to be called miraculous. By persuasion, legislation, financial stimulation and direct help it has succeeded in creating a dozen or more small "regional"

libraries in rural Manitoba with more on the way. It has also aided the formation of municipal libraries and individual libraries in Greater Winnipeg, and has encouraged the small amount of inter-relationship which exists there.

Mr. Easton proceeded to advocate a public library "system to provide library service in those situations where locally based service is not feasible." He suggested that some of the small municipal libraries in time might like to become branches of such a "system." Already the contractural arrangements between St. James Public Library and the Assiniboine River Regional Library had been significant. Grants for special services or to add personnel with special experience and training to the staff of what may eventually become resource libraries, for example Brandon and Winnipeg, were advocated.

The Winnipeg satellite municipal libraries, all in modern buildings and well organized, are giving excellent service. Winnipeg City needs a new central library, and if it is to become a resource library some massive sums for its collections and staff. In the 24 public libraries of the province as of 1967 there were 17 graduate librarians, 10 with other library training, and 36 with university degrees. They serve areas of one square mile (Flin Flon) to 448 square miles (Morton) and populations varying from 2206 in Southwestern Regional to 254,844 in the city of Winnipeg. Situations in rural and particularly in northern Manitoba bear comparison with the Yukon and the Northwest Territories.

To guide developments with the care and diplomacy already demonstrated by the Minister responsible for libraries, the Honourable Stewart E. McLean, the provincial librarian, Miss Marjorie Morley, and her staff, it might be of value to establish a library planning and development group within the Provincial Library.

School Libraries. School libraries in Manitoba are under the direction of a provincial supervisor, who is a graduate librarian. Before 1946 the Brandon secondary schools were the only schools outside of Winnipeg to have central libraries. Information for 1961–1962 collected by the Canadian Education Association lists central and classroom libraries in Winnipeg, St. James, Flin Flon, Portage la Prairie, and Brandon. Manitoba has a Teachers' Professional Library which lends for one month and mails books and periodicals free of charge to rural teachers. Only three librarians had professional training in 1961–1962 but the number increases annually. Some schools are served by the regional and public libraries where these exist. Two school divisions had school library supervisors in 1967 with an increase to eight divisions within months. In 1967 grants from the Department of Education had been increased to $60.00 per teacher.

In 1945 a group of Winnipeg teacher-librarians formed a Library Club. Their efforts resulted in summer courses in 1950 and 1951 and the appointment in 1963 of the first supervisor of school libraries for the city, Mr. Harry Newsom, who made a survey and drew up a ten-year plan including in-service training for school librarians; development of central libraries in the elementary schools; the organization of central library service. By 1965 the School Service Centre began operations processing materials for 87 schools, and providing a teacher's professional library, a reference library, and a display library. Supported by the Manitoba Association of School Librarians, a prairie regional conference on school libraries was held in April 1964.

College and University Libraries. Manitoba profiles of colleges and universities in the Downs Report are Brandon College (Brandon), University of Manitoba with its affiliated colleges, some of which—St. Paul's and St. John's—are on the Fort Garry campus (Winnipeg), and the University of Winnipeg (listed in Downs under its former name of United College) (Winnipeg). The Elizabeth Dafoe Memorial Library of the University of Manitoba built in 1953 and extended in 1963 was the first modern university library in the west built without permanent partitions, and was the results of years of planning by the university's School of Architecture and Miss Elizabeth Dafoe, under whom the great expansion of the library's collections and services began. St. Paul's and St. John's are of architectural interest. Under the present librarian, Mr. David Wilder, a reorganization of faculty deposit libraries has been initiated as well as general administrative practices.

Special Libraries. Fast growing business and financial Winnipeg has numerous special libraries. From the point of view of the province's history, the Hudson's Bay Library is of unique interest.

Probably in no other part of Canada have the special libraries played so enlightened and interested a role in the development of general library welfare. Special librarians have been leaders in Manitoba Library Association and have been supported by their firms and associations in their efforts in cooperation with public, university, college, school, and government libraries for the passage of legislation and the present program of library extension through the Provincial Library. They have also been active in producing union lists of Manitoba serials and other holdings. For information of individual special libraries the compilations of Anderson and Fyfe and Deutsch are most useful.

Library Associations. One of the great strengths of the library situation in Manitoba is the Manitoba Library Association with which are associated the Manitoba Library Trustees Association and the Manitoba Association of School Librarians. Reference to their work for legislation and library promotion appears throughout this article.

Publications. The *Manitoba Library Association Bulletin,* union lists of serials in Winnipeg libraries, annual reports of municipal, regional, and university libraries and the Provincial Library, and special publications such as the *Handbook of the University of Manitoba Library* guarantee good library liaison within the province.

SASKATCHEWAN

(Area, 251,700 square miles)

In 1906, one year after becoming a province, Saskatchewan enacted a Public Libraries Act modeled on the Ontario Act as well as legislation dealing with mechanics' institutes and library associations. In 1915 the act was amended and the Travelling Libraries Branch was established by the provincial government. This was followed in 1922 by the Open Shelf Library with books from the Legislative

Library selected to meet specific requests and provide reference service to all parts of the province. By 1930 when the Commission of Enquiry visited the province the act was reported as providing for the opening of public libraries and allowing municipalities to levy sufficient taxes for their maintenance, no special amount or limit being mentioned. A dollar for dollar grant up to $200 was made by the province for books purchased. Rural libraries were given special consideration, the provincial librarian being empowered to provide them with special amounts of reading material. There was no provincial official responsible for the development of libraries. There were twenty-three public libraries, sixteen of which received the government grant. There were approximately twenty mechanics' and literary institutes, each with a small library as part of its organization. The provincial government, through its Department of Publicity, operated a Travelling Libraries Department with 1500 collections in circulation and an Open Shelf Collection with some 20,000 volumes, a printed catalog with supplements and used by some 3500 borrowers, and a circulation of 1000 volumes per year. The diagnosis of the commission was the necessary employment of an organizing librarian backed by a commission of interested laymen to make a study followed possibly by a demonstration library which would serve as a model to all three prairie provinces. Prince Albert was suggested as a strategic location.

By 1940 after studying experiences in British Columbia, Prince Edward Island, the United Kingdom, and the United States, the concept of the larger unit of library service was recognized for rural library service in Saskatchewan. A Library Advisory Council under the chairmanship of Dr. Carlyle King was appointed in 1945 with Mrs. Jessie Bothwell, the legislative librarian, as secretary. A regional libraries supervisor, Miss Marion Gilroy, was appointed in 1946. A Regional Libraries Division was set up in the Legislative Library, now also responsible for the Travelling Libraries and the Open Shelf Library.

In 1948 the Saskatchewan government agreed to pay an initial book stock grant of $1.00 for every person in the library area as well as operating costs. Miss Gilroy points out that:

> The province needed substantial grants to weld its innumerable small local government units into library regions. Its great distances and sparse population impeded library development; but the first regional library on the Prairies started in 1950 with headquarters in Prince Albert.

This first unit was named the North Central Saskatchewan Regional Library.

In 1953 the Provincial Library was organized by combining the Regional Libraries Division, the Public Information Library (the former Open Shelf Library), the Travelling Libraries, and a new unit, the Technical Processing Division, directly responsible to the Minister of Education with the second title of Minister-in-Charge-of-Libraries under "An Act to Provide for the Establishment and Maintenance of Libraries." A provincial librarian, Miss Mary Donaldson, was appointed. The creation of this new library agency, with its relatively substantial grants for regional libraries, had created demands from all areas of the province for provincial grants for regional library service by 1964. Urban centers, such as Regina and Saskatoon, also felt entitled to a proportion of the provincial funds.

After careful consideration and on the recommendation of the Library Advisory Council, the government decided that a Library Inquiry Committee should be appointed to survey library service in Saskatchewan and to make recommendations. The death of Miss Donaldson in June 1966 deprived the government of its most experienced consultant, for Miss Gilroy was on the teaching staff of the University of British Columbia School of Librarianship, and her successor, Miss Donalda Putnam, had accepted a university appointment in Prince Edward Island. The Library Inquiry Committee was appointed on June 29, 1966.

Its terms of reference were to investigate the adequacy of existing library facilities, public and regional, in the Province of Saskatchewan; to study organization for administration of library services in the Province of Saskatchewan; to examine financing of public and regional library services; to make recommendations to the government of Saskatchewan regarding developments of public library services, finances, and administration; and for these purposes to consult with all organizations and individuals interested, to accept for consideration articles, submissions, or other representations, and to hold public hearings.

An *Interim Report December 15, 1966,* conveyed the recommendations requiring immediate attention. The final report was issued under the title *Library Service in Saskatchewan: the Report of the Library Inquiry Committee (a survey with recommendations), August, 1967,* Judge John H. Maher, Chairman, Dr. W. A. Riddell and R. M. Macdonald, members. The *Interim Report* dealt with:

> emergent requirements and recommendations, a plan of action for improving the Provincial Library and regional and public libraries in the province.
>
> The recommendations represent a holding operation which will serve to retard deterioration of library services in the province and will fit them to better serve in the overall plan which the Library Inquiry Committee will describe in its report-in-chief.

In its General Remarks the committee noted:

> There was perhaps a day when local initiative was enough but that day is gone. The information explosion is upon us and it is clear to the Library Inquiry Committee that, unless this fine province is to fall far behind in the struggle for enlightenment, provincial aid in fair and growing measure must be brought up in support of the loyal and hard working forces in the cities, towns and rural areas. Neither is Saskatchewan alone. Other provinces in Canada and almost all the States in the United States are facing the problem, studying it, and devising methods of attack. The problem is not necessarily the product of past neglect, rather it is a sign of the times. The challenge is great but, with proper organization and assistance and a pinch of our legendary "prairie ingenuity" it will prove to be far from insurmountable.

Recommendation A, regarding the provincial librarian's status and access to the Minister, salary competitive with that of the national librarian in Ottawa and the chief librarian at the provincial university, and career incentives to guarantee a challenge and a future for a talented person, was discussed with the Minister. Agreement was reached. A provincial librarian, Mr. Harry E. Newsom, was appointed. Recommendation B, regarding facilities, stock, and staff of the Provincial Library, requested additional funds in the 1966–1967 appropriations to meet minimal needs, that establishment grants to regional libraries be increased, and that the annual per capita grant be increased from 75 cents to not less than $1.25. Recommendation C, regarding Regional Headquarters, was that buildings be provided for new regional libraries as in the past. Recommendation D advised more flexibility in the regulations dealing with the formation of regions and recommended that the Minister-in-Charge-of-Libraries assume more responsibility regarding the formation of regions, and that such formation be pursued with all possible despatch.

The committee noted that the urban public libraries were limited to a provincial grant of $400 annually, and recommended that substantial grants be immediately made. It also recommended that the Provincial Library be included in a feasibility study regarding the use of the computer.

The final report dealt with long-term and short-term situations, based on public hearings, field surveys, private interviews, and a consultant. Carefully planned preliminary hearings led to overwhelming public support, resulting in 106 briefs and 96 letters read and discussed, opinions tested, problems aired, and ideas accepted at the hearings held in Saskatoon, Prince Albert, North Battleford, Kindersley, Swift Current, Moose Jaw, Yorkton, Weyburn, and Regina. The twelve chapters of the report are packed with information of past, present, and the possible future of libraries in Saskatchewan and lead to a series of recommendations dealing with a proposed plan for province-wide library service; the Provincial Library; the development of regional public libraries and municipal public libraries; library cooperation in Saskatchewan; government support for library services; library personnel; library legislation; and the establishment of a Library Development Board to work closely with the provincial librarian and the Minister.

Seven regional library units were proposed: North Central Saskatchewan Regional Library, North West Saskatchewan, Wheatland, Parkland, South West Saskatchewan, Palliser, and South Eastern Saskatchewan, with populations varying from 70,930 in South West to 133,730 in Parkland.

The provincial librarian reported as of December 31, 1967, the significant steps taken to carry out the recommendations of the Library Inquiry Committee. An additional $250,000 had been provided by the government to the budget of the Provincial Library. These funds had been used to strengthen the Provincial Library by adding staff and books, to increase grants to municipal libraries in the cities, to increase grants to regional libraries from 75 cents to $1.00 per capita, and to establish the Wheatland Regional Library. With the additional funds the Provincial Library had taken the first steps toward coordination of library services throughout the province. Meetings had been held and agreement reached on interlibrary loan procedures, central cataloging practice, specialization among libraries, and priorities in library development.

The Wheatland Regional Library with headquarters in Saskatoon and twenty branches was opened within nine months. Additional branches of South Eastern Saskatchewan Regional Library, now totaling forty, had been opened, as had also branches of the North Central Saskatchewan Regional Library. Parkland was planning to open in July 1968, while Palliser had completed organizational undertakings and early organizational plans were in progress for the Chinock (South West) Regional Library. All regions now have the necessary framework to enable the larger unit library systems to provide quality library service to all residents. Steps are also being taken by the Provincial Library to encourage library service in the northern areas, where small isolated communities pose a distinct problem.

In short, the situation at the end of 1967 was most heartening to the provincial librarian now completing his first year in office and to the Saskatchewan Library Advisory Council completing twenty-two years of service. The council has played a significant part in the development of libraries in Saskatchewan, and has led to the establishment of the Provincial Library as a separate government department, to the acceptance of the concept of the larger unit of library service, and to the development of the North Central Saskatchewan Regional Library and the system of Provincial Library grants, all under the chairmanship of Dr. Carlyle King, who, supported by a distinguished staff of Marion Gilroy, (chief: regional division), Mary Donaldson (provincial librarian), and Donalda Putnam (who succeeded Miss Gilroy), initiated the plans and programs that changed the entire structure of library services in the province. In place of the council, the Library Development Board, a policy-making body for the development of libraries as recommended by the Library Inquiry Committee, had been appointed.

Both the Regina Public Library and the Saskatoon Public Library (see Figure 4) recommended by the Library Inquiry Committee to serve as resource centers have celebrated fifty years of service. Both cities have erected fine main buildings recently, have extended their branch systems, and are giving notable city service. The new public library building at Weyburn is admired for its architecture.

School Libraries. The Commission of Enquiry in 1930 reported approvingly of the three Normal School libraries, all in charge of full-time librarians, whose col-

FIGURE 4. *Regina Public Library.* (*Courtesy Marjorie Dunlop and Regina Public Library.*)

lections were open not only to the students but to teachers in the field. In 1944 the Department of Education had consolidated the province into sixty larger school units, designed to provide equal educational opportunity for rural students, thus making a centralized school library service possible. A supervisor of school libraries, the first in Canada, Miss Lyle Evans, was appointed in 1946. In the next three years came the revision of the secondary school curriculum with an emphasis on reading and library materials. Each school unit office had a central library, each school a core collection of basic books, and each rural library a box of books circulated from the center or from school to school. Committees of teachers, school librarians, and superintendents, chaired by the provincial supervisor of School Libraries compiled book lists—three elementary and two secondary—issued by the Department of Education. Teachers were encouraged to obtain library training. Summer courses in school library work were given by the University of Saskatchewan. In 1959 the College of Education revised its curriculum to provide for an undergraduate major in library science.

In 1966 a survey of school libraries, with information supplied by the super-intendents of schools, produced a checklist of all school libraries in Saskatchewan, noting name of school, whether public, separate, or private, type of library quarters, and personnel. Except in the urban areas an overwhelming number of schools were without librarians.

The Saskatchewan Association of School Librarians undertook a survey of library conditions in 1962 as a basis for setting up school library standards for the province. The survey showed that the role of the unit library needed reviewing with the changing school pattern, and the need for trained school librarians, better financial support, standards, etc., were all of major concern. In 1964 the Stan-dards for School Libraries in the Province of Saskatchewan were issued. In 1966 the Saskatchewan Association of School Libraries presented a brief to the Library Inquiry Committee hearing in Saskatoon on October 4. The question of school libraries was discussed by other groups. As a result the inquiry recommended: "That the Department of Education be encouraged to evaluate the policies of the Department in relation to the development of school libraries." In addition co-operation regarding a card cataloging service was under discussion between the provincial librarian and the school library supervisor.

Saskatchewan school libraries were resurveyed in 1967. Of the 1290 operating school plants reporting, 49% had enrollments of 150 students or more, 75% had centralized libraries, 40% of which were of classroom size or larger. In charge of 641 schools were 407 individuals, 200 of whom had no scheduled time for their library duties. Of the remaining schools (enrollment less than 150), 188 had centralized libraries and 104 had an official in charge. The survey showed that 40% of all elementary schools, 67% of public schools (grades 1–12), and 92% of all high schools had centralized libraries.

In June 1967 all provincial school library supervisors met in Quebec City for two days on invitation of the Quebec supervisor of school libraries to discuss school library problems of mutual interest—the first nation-wide meeting of pro-vincial school library supervisors outside of meetings at the conferences of the

Canadian School Library Association during a Canadian Library Association conference.

The matter of education for school library work has received great consideration. With the formation of a prairie library school at the University of Alberta, Mr. John Wright, who had succeeded Miss Evans, left Saskatchewan to assume a teaching position as a school library specialist.

What of the future? It is to be hoped that the recommendation of the Library Inquiry Committee will receive careful consideration and implementation, that the presence of a library school in Edmonton will begin to fill the empty school library positions, and that some form of consolidated school library service will be devised to bridge the inadequate present with the services desired under the School Library Standards as propounded both by the Saskatchewan School Library Association and the Canadian School Library Association.

College and University Libraries. Saskatchewan universities included in Profiles of Colleges and Universities in the Downs Report are the University of Saskatchewan in Saskatoon (with one federated college, Sir Thomas More College, and seven affiliated colleges) and the University of Saskatchewan in Regina. Both have splendid new library buildings.

Special Libraries. Special libraries are scattered throughout the province and are listed in Anderson and Fyfe and Deutsch.

Library Associations. Because of the distances and local interests the Saskatchewan Library Association, organized in the 1940s, has two active chapters—the Saskatoon and the Regina Library Associations, which meet frequently. The Saskatchewan Library Association meets annually, publishes a bulletin, and is a channel for discussions with the provincial government. The Saskatchewan Association of School Librarians has been discussed under School Libraries.

Publications. The Provincial Library publishes a newsletter *Focus on Saskatchewan Libraries,* annual reports, special reports, publicity brochures, etc. The *Saskatchewan Library Association Bulletin* is issued quarterly since 1945 and is a rich source of information about library affairs. The university libraries issue miscellaneous publications. In addition to annual reports, publicity releases, book lists, etc., issued by the municipal libraries, both Regina and Saskatoon published histories of the library to mark their fiftieth anniversaries. The Saskatchewan School Library Association publishes a bulletin regularly and various miscellaneous publications.

ALBERTA

(*Area, 255,285 square miles*)

The early libraries followed the same pattern as in Manitoba and Saskatchewan, being the collections of the fur trade companies and their men; for example, Roderick Mackenzie in 1788 had a collection of books at Fort Chipewyn, now in Alberta, which circulated among the traders.

Alberta received a grant of money in lieu of its share of the North-West Territories Library and established the Alberta Legislative Library in 1906. A legislative librarian was appointed in 1907. In 1908 a Mechanics' Institute and Library Associations Act was passed. The Public Library Act had come into force in 1907 providing for the organization of public libraries and the appointment of boards; it stipulated that one mill and no more should be levied by any municipality for library maintenance. A grant of $300 was given to libraries based on book purchases. Branch libraries were treated as separate units.

An inspector of schools, Mr. E. L. Hill, was deeply interested in library work and through his influence Calgary opened the first public library, bringing the librarian of Ontario's Fort William Public Library, Alexander Calhoun, to be in charge. Mr. Hill became the librarian of the Edmonton Public Library. Public libraries in the towns of Lethbridge, Red Deer, and Medicine Hat followed. By 1930 an additional twenty small libraries or more had been formed and by 1967 the number was over one hundred.

In 1946 the Alberta Library Board was established with Alexander Calhoun as chairman, and there was considerable interest in the organization of regional libraries. Two miniregionals were organized at Lacombe and Barrhead using the school district as the unit and have continued in service. Library developments in the five cities of Calgary, Edmonton, Lethbridge, Medicine Hat, and Red Deer have expanded with the growing population, enriched services, and professional leadership. Splendid main library buildings have been erected in Calgary, Edmonton (see Figure 5), Medicine Hat, and Red Deer with fine new branches in Calgary, Edmonton, and Lethbridge. Chief librarians directing the recent thrust forward have been William R. Castell, Calgary; Morton Coburn, Edmonton; Phyllis Lapworth, Medicine Hat; and MacDonald Coleman, Red Deer.

The act respecting libraries has been amended several times and the 1966 consolidation includes sections on the Alberta Library Board and Central Library Services and provides for a director of libraries whose duty it is to supervise the Central Library Services, direct its staff, promote and encourage library services

FIGURE 5. *Main building of the Edmonton Public Library.* (*Courtesy Morton Coburn. Photograph by Charles H. Machtans.*)

thoughout the province, supervise libraries and library support under the act, and cooperate with the National Library and any other cultural or educational organization. The Alberta Library Board, with the approval of the Minister, may carry out surveys, encourage community activities, call public meetings, promote publicity campaigns, etc.; it has for its purpose the promotion of library service. The act has sections on municipal, regional, and community libraries and financial assistance to libraries, and provides by order-in-council for varying any of the forms in the schedule.

In his 1967 Report of the Libraries Division of the Provincial Secretary's Department, the Supervisor of the Public Library Service, Edward T. Wiltshire, writes:

> Centennial year had a marked and favourable effect on Alberta's Public Library Service. Eighteen communities chose new library buildings as their official centennial projects and all but one have been completed, officially launched and are now in full operation. Three others were completed as locally sponsored projects. This activity gave strong impetus to library development in an area which had been badly neglected in the past. A side effect has been the good example set for neighboring communities who can now see what should and can be done to develop their own libraries.

> The cooperative leadership shown by the three levels of government, Federal, Provincial and Municipal, in this one phase of library service has gratifying results. It can be a pointer to the same cooperative action in regard to library service generally and thus eventually bring libraries to the level of service required by today's social conditions . . .

> All these activities served to engender much useful publicity for libraries in many of our communities, and the results are beginning to show in increased local appropriations for 1968 and an upsurge in patronage. Both being very gratifying to the dedicated Albertans who for many years have struggled along with shoe-string operations for far too long.

> The Provincial Government has taken part in this upsurge in library activity. Library legislation was amended in 1966 to increase the government financial support to local Public Libraries, and this came into effect during the year under review. The total of grants paid to Public Libraries in 1967 was $242,470.00 which represents an increase of almost 100 per cent over the previous year. This large increase and the growth in service provided incentive to local authorities which, in many cases, raised their appropriation for library purposes. With the consequent increase in library budgets, library boards have been enabled to offer better services to their communities: more books of a higher quality, overhauled book stocks, more staff, and libraries having much longer hours for public use.

With the emphasis on technical education which in Alberta affects employment on the large farms, the mines, and industry, public library service outside the cities and towns may develop more speedily. A landmark in library architecture and service planning is the Edmonton Public Library, officially opened in the autumn of 1967.

School Libraries. With regard to school libraries the *Report, May 1957* to the

Alberta Department of Education by the Library Subcommittee found on the basis of questionnaire returns that:

> . . . library service on the whole is inadequate. That some schools lack books, others lack the necessary organization and personnel to use the books they have properly, while others are unable to organize library service because they lack space.

The Alberta Royal Commission on Education, 1959, revealed a lack of trained personnel and a lack of adequate library quarters. Since 1959 regular summer courses in school library work have been given by the Faculty of Education at the University of Alberta. In 1964 a graduate school librarian was appointed to the faculty as a full-time instructor in school library services, and the Alberta School Library Council was organized and held two workshops. It has issued a periodical regularly, and cosponsored a workshop on education for school librarians with the Canadian School Library Association in June 1968. In September 1966 a Provincial School Libraries Consultant was appointed. Seven local supervisors had been at work, one since 1945. Although school libraries in Alberta have been on the whole inadequate, the school library system of Calgary under enthusiastic graduate librarians has been of such competence as to inspire the surrounding area. A full-time professor of school library work was an early appointment to the University of Alberta School of Library Science.

College and University Libraries and Library Education. Alberta institutions included in the Down's Report profiles are the University of Alberta in Edmonton, with which is affiliated four junior colleges and the University of Calgary. Both have spendid new buildings and are growing so rapidly that Calgary is now planning a second building. Alberta's two libraries are the Rutherford and the Cameron. Lethbridge is the latest college library to be organized.

The University of Alberta Extension Department Library is responsible for the provincial Travelling Libraries and an Open Shelf Reference service. It includes special assistance; for example, to dramatic groups it not only supplies multiple copies of plays but also makes available original plays by Alberta authors for acting and experimentation. The Extension Department has a system of field visitors—two of its most remarkable leaders being Edward Corbett, the founder of the Canadian Association of Adult Education, and Donald Cameron, the founder of the Banff School of Fine Arts, both great believers in books, who kept the Extension Library alive to the needs of continuing education at every level. Responsible for recent university literary progress have been Donald Ewing Cameron, Marjorie Sherlock, and Bruce B. Peel.

In 1967 a director, Miss Sarah Rebecca Reed, was appointed to the University of Alberta School of Library Science. Much time and energy was devoted to collecting a staff and library commensurate with the standing of a library school suitable for accreditation. The first class graduated on May 28, 1969, with the degree of B.L.S.

Special Libraries. The special libraries of the oil industry are limited to company personnel or by special permission. In Calgary the oil companies cooperated in setting up an open collection in the Technical and Reference Department of the Calgary Public Library.

The largest and most valuable library is the Glenbow Foundation, Library and Archives, in Calgary, open to anyone interested in serious research. The collection on the history and development of the Canadian west is particularly strong on materials about the native peoples of western and northern Canada and studies of the pioneer settlers. In addition there is reference material on archaeology, military matters, horses and horsemanship, art and fine arts, and natural history, including some rare and beautiful works. In 1965 the Museum, Archives, and Library became the Glenbow Alberta Government Museum, being formally presented in 1966 by the original owner and collector, Mr. Eric Harvie, with an endowment of $5 million dollars to the province which made a similar grant of $5 million dollars, the whole being the Glenbow Alberta Institute. There are the usual professional, association, hospital libraries, etc., which are listed in Fyfe and Deutsch and in Anderson.

Library Associations. The Alberta Library Association and its various committees have been active since 1944. It publishes a bulletin and book lists, conducts training for custodians, and has undertaken many campaigns for an improved library program. Its two chapters are the Calgary Library Association and the Edmonton Library Association. The trade union organization of some of the public libraries is of interest.

Library Literature. Annual reports, book lists, and the library association bulletins constitute the bulk of the publications.

The Future. Alberta library planners are faced with metropolitan problems in the fast-growing cities of Calgary and Edmonton combined with the rural problems described for Manitoba and in the north situations similar to the territories.

The development of a province-wide plan lies ahead.

YUKON TERRITORY

(Area, 207,076 square miles)

This part of Canada was the last to be explored, the date being 1840 and by Robert Campbell of the Hudson's Bay Company. In 1895 the Yukon became a separate district and in 1898, with the finding of gold in the Klondike, was made a separate territory, with Dawson City its capital. In 1951 Whitehorse was recommended as capital, a recommendation confirmed by federal legislation in 1955. The territory is governed by a Territorial Council of seven elected members and with a commissioner appointed by order-in-council as its chief administrative officer, the whole coming under the Canadian Department of Indian Affairs and Northern Development. It is represented in the House of Commons by one member.

In October 1957, in reply to repeated requests from voluntary workers in the existing association libraries and from citizens interested in library organization, information, and aid, the librarian of the then Department of Northern Affairs, Miss Doreen Bailey, after consultation with the Canadian Library Association, recommended to the department that a survey of the Yukon be made with the possibilities of a regional library system under consideration. Miss Bailey, who had regional library experience in Nova Scotia, was appointed to undertake this survey and visited Mayo, Elsa, Dawson City, Whitehorse, Carcross, and Haines Junction, followed by a visit to neighboring Alaska to see the public and university libraries at Fairbanks and to consult with the Alaska Territorial Librarian. While in the Yukon, Miss Bailey was greatly impressed with the work being done by chapters of the Imperial Order Daughters of the Empire, the Parent-Teacher Clubs, and other voluntary groups. She noted that the Carnegie Building in Dawson City had been vacated and the books stored for a period, and that at this time the best of them were in a room in the Commission Building, but the library was without funds for future support. In summary, she concluded:

> Only when money is forthcoming to organize these struggling units into one system, and to hire a trained librarian can the people of the Yukon have the books they need and desire so much.

Miss Bailey's Report to the Department of Northern Affairs was considered officially, and eventually a scheme for a library demonstration was placed before the Canada Council and received an establishment grant of $15,000. A regional librarian, Mrs. Elizabeth Colyer, was appointed and the Yukon Territory Regional Library was established in 1961. A small library headquarters was built and financial arrangements drawn up. There were endless problems of establishment, promotion, and library programming. General public support had to be aroused. The library as a "cultural center" had to become a part of the Yukon way of life in the absence of universities, galleries, concert halls, museums, and film centers.

The provision of books for every resident of the territory was the priority and this meant ordering them from Central Canada, British Columbia, and abroad, and processing and distributing them. There was no existing pool of books for a nucleus other than some 5000 books at Whitehorse, well chosen but out of date. Small branch libraries were organized. Deposit stations with equipment on wheels and locked shelving were established. Boxes of books for isolated families and individuals were shipped by whatever means were available. The regional librarian was the only trained staff member. There was no provision for salaried staff except at Whitehorse. Volunteer library custodians had to be sought and the regional librarian found herself faced with hazardous and often time-consuming travel to make adequate arrangements. Eventually a library chain of seven branches (Dawson City, Whitehorse, Elsa, Haines Junction, Mayo, Watson Lake, and Takhini) and thirty-six deposit stations were set up. The communities served were along the Alaska Highway from Mile Post 635 to Mile Post 1220 on the Alaska border, and along the Whitehorse-Dawson City Highway. Takhini Branch in Camp Takhini, a governmental housing community in the Whitehorse area, became part of the system in 1967. The more isolated localities frequently were to be reached only by small bush plane, riverboat, and canoe. The system began to grow rapidly, and with demands on its services by the residents, a substantial increase was made to the book budget, operating funds, and supporting staff in Whitehorse.

In January 1966 a permanent library building was opened at a cost of $168,000, designed to house both the Regional Headquarters and the Whitehorse Library Branch and planned for cultural center activities (see Figure 6). The hours were extended to 52½ on a seven-day-a-week basis so as to involve all the community. Story hours and family sing-songs held beside the beautiful stone fireplaces, lectures by visiting experts, and interfaith church services—all were incorporated into the library program. The small fireproof art gallery with its excellent appointments offered exhibits from well-known galleries, as well as private showings by A. Y. Jackson of the Group of Seven fame, and others, whose northern paintings command international interest. Art displays by Yukon, neighboring British Columbia, and Alaska painters were frequently exhibited. For the musically minded

FIGURE 6. *Yukon Regional Library Headquarters and Whitehorse Public Library.* (*Courtesy Garth Graham and Yukon Regional Library.*)

there was a special soundproof music room with the latest in approved recording and listening equipment, and an extensive collection of records and music books, all of which could be borrowed. In 1967 films were added and the library now houses and administers the Yukon Film Society collection. Statistics for the month of November 1967 show that 9500 people viewed films provided by the library. For special events news is carried by the radio, and people fly in or drive hundreds of miles to attend them. For example, the display of Best British Book Design was loaned through the Canadian Library Association's International Displays Project for one month. It was still drawing audiences from a radius of 300 miles at the end of this time, so the loan was lengthened. Many viewers wanted to know where these beautiful books might be purchased, while others returned repeatedly to handle them and enjoy browsing. When this appreciation was told to the British Council, the owner of the exhibition, the books were presented to the Yukon. Eventually they were divided between the branches and deposit stations on an exchange basis. When the Regional Librarian flew north to Old Crow, an Indian village eighty miles north of the Arctic Circle, she took with her illustrated volumes from the collection to deposit there.

The example of the Best British Book Design exhibit illustrates two factors: first, the ability to pay for and own expensive books once a book-selling agency (of which there is none in the Yukon) was known, and second, the delight in books on sports, on design, and on fine illustration by an Indian village.

The section of greatest interest for research on the north is the Regional Library's Yukon Room, carefully organized and cataloged. It is as complete a collection as can be assembled quickly and was fortunate in obtaining the books on the Yukon of Senator and Mrs. Black of Dawson City. This includes many unique privately printed accounts of Gold Rush days. An examination of the library's general collection showed it to be well rounded by all the tenets of book selection with the emphasis on the interests of the community in the outdoors, the artistic, and the various northern pursuits. Never have there been such splendidly printed, illustrated, and written books in these fields as were collected for the library from the book markets of Canada, the United States, the United Kingdom, and abroad. From a publishing point of view 1961–1967 was a most favorable time in which to build the collection. No figures of the cost of the library have ever been publicly released and probably it is impossible to compile them as so many costs are shared with other government departments such as telecommunications, transportation to the distant north made in government planes on many missions, etc.

Although trained staff was advertised for, at first the only appointments made were of a cataloger who was in Whitehorse for the summer, who cataloged the Yukon collection, and a general librarian who stayed a short time. The opportunities of life in the Yukon were yet to be impressed on professional librarians. Eventually, an assistant librarian was recruited from British Columbia.

The social and economic life of Whitehorse is akin to that in a capital town in Canada. The civil service, the army until 1964, the air force until 1968, mining, ecclesiastical, and old Yukon society include people of learning, culture, and sophistication to many of whom reading, in the words of E. B. White, "is the work of the alert mind, is demanding and under ideal conditions, produces finally a sort of ecstasy." In addition, the population includes the unlettered, the unemployed, and the frustrated jetsam and flotsam of many a nationality. It includes the week-enders who arrive on Friday from their isolated posts and stay until Sunday. For all of these groups the regional librarian and the Friends of the Library Group of over ninety have worked indefatigably and in many different ways, ordering, listing, cataloging, processing, talking on the radio, storytelling, singing, designing posters, and describing the library to visitors. Their ranks include the commissioner's lady, the bishop's wife, and all strata of society. Such an amazing group as the Friends of the Library Group is not organized overnight. It began, for example, in Whitehorse in 1921 with a chapter of the Imperial Order Daughters of the Empire, who sponsored the association library, and who later petitioned for government attention to library needs, and who welcomed the leadership of Mrs. Colyer, a most versatile, imaginative bibliophile and administrator with a keen interest in all the arts, who had the understanding and assistance of an able engineer-army husband, Major Harry Colyer, and her six gifted children who brought the schools, the University of Alaska, and all the interests of young people to her daily attention.

The library is part of the Canadian Library Telecommunications Network and through the National Library, Ottawa, is connected by TWX with libraries in the United States. It has special arrangements about interlibrary loans as these perforce have to be for a longer period than in southern Canada, since the loan may leave Whitehorse for an isolated borrower in an area with infrequent transportation. At the request of the Yukon this was drawn to the attention of the Canadian Library Association Information Section Committee working on a revised interlibrary loan code for Canada.

The statutory basis of the Yukon Regional Library Department is the Appropriations Ordinances of the Yukon. Unlike the federal government, in which each department has its own enabling legislation, the departments of the government of the Yukon do not have individual statutes. The various libraries which existed prior to 1961 were incorporated under the Societies Ordinances of the Yukon Territory but these have been completely absorbed into the Yukon Regional Library System.

By 1967 the Regional Library system was succeeding in carrying out the functions for which it had been established, from serving towns like Whitehorse and Dawson City, to the isolated hunter and trapper. To quote Mrs. Colyer:

> The character of the Northerner is different from the people of southern Canada. By nature reticent and unassuming, by environment fiercely independent, Northerners want no ideas from the South foisted upon them. To win their approval and cooperation, it was necessary for the librarian to carry out a quiet and continuing public relations programme in order to persuade Yukon residents of the value of good library service and to convince them that such service should be and could be theirs.

In addition to her public relations program, Mrs. Colyer might have mentioned her program by which, through the National Library's Union Catalogue, she located desired books for particular readers, even if it meant borrowing them from the far ends of the continent. She was always anxious to meet new people, to discuss how the library could serve, and she worked days of amazing length to establish the library as a cultural center. Her interest in newspapers led to the microfilming of the Whitehorse newspapers of historic interest by the Canadian Library Association.

School Libraries. In 1948 the territory had 13 schools, 500 students, and 20 teachers. In 1967 this had grown to 22 schools, 3527 students, 176 full-time teachers, and some part-time teachers. Only one Indian residential school, with the children returning to their families for the long summer vacation, remains. It teaches up to Grade 6 and will soon be changed to a local elementary school. This is in line with the territorial policy of integrating all children in the local schools.

The school libraries, especially in the rural areas, with few exceptions were most inadequate. The Department of Education gave a grant of $3.00 per capita but not less than $100.00 per year per school for the purchase of library books; however, much of this money was being used for textbooks and school supplies. The selection was left to the teachers, none of whom had any library training and little knowledge of book titles. Few schools had a circulation system or mended their books. The situation was ready for change.

As schools were often used as deposit stations for the Regional Library, the Yukon Department of Education and the Regional Library consulted and agreed that a plan must be evolved for school library service. It was therefore agreed that the Department of Education transfer the rural school library grant to the Regional Library, and in return the library would undertake to provide a basic reference collection according to need for each school; would send out twice a year, or oftener if desired, a rotating collection of recreational and supplementary reading with the books processed for circulation; would pay all transportation costs to and from schools; and would place all resources of the Regional Library as well as interlibrary loans, reference, consulting services, etc., at the disposal of the rural school teachers. This scheme proved successful and in 1965 the per capita grant was raised to $5.00 per pupil. As the Regional Library's book budget was also increased, the school library service gradually reached a more adequate level. In the urban areas, for example Whitehorse, the schools have adequate libraries administered by teacher-librarians, several of whom have taken provincial school librarian's summer courses. They work closely with the regional librarian and school library visits are organized to the Whitehorse Public Library and Regional Library Headquarters, either by classes or small groups working on a particular project.

Special Libraries. There are special collections in various federal government departments and in private industry. They are of three types: working collections for the department or industry; archival and public document collections under the official most concerned, many of which collections are now being microfilmed; a recreational collection devised to meet the needs of National Defense personnel and their families. Liaison is maintained between those responsible for these collections and the regional librarian, except for the closed collections for defense, industrial research, medical and hospital personnel, etc.

College and University Libraries. There are no college and university library collections. Extension students (frequently teachers) borrow from the University Extension department library where registered, or have interlibrary loans arranged through the Regional Library.

The Future. To the far northern Canadian librarian it is of greatest interest to visit the Alaskan system and to learn what the USSR, with its similar climatic conditions, is doing across the Bering Strait. Siberia has the advantage of a larger population, but its permafrost problems are similar to those of the Canadian North. It is the far northern areas of Canada that promise some of the most experimental and challenging aspects of library service with the Yukon probably cast for a leading role. Organized first, it has certain advantages over its eastern neighbor in that its capital, Whitehorse, is a natural center for the territory, its climate is less rigorous, its communications are more complete. Like the Northwest Territories, one of its problems is to make the optimum use of that part of the population which is transilient rather than sedentary. In 1967 it lost its first librarian because of a career transfer of her husband to northern Manitoba. In the six years of her tenure,

Mrs. Colyer and her Friends of the Library developed a service which has been accepted by the Territory with enthusiasm as a truly Yukon Service. The assistant librarian, Mr. Garth Graham, has succeeded and under him the future holds great promise.

NORTHWEST TERRITORIES

(Area, 1,304,903 square miles)

Administration is under a commissioner. The council meets twice a year. The capital is Yellowknife. Following the report of the Advisory Commission on the Development in the Northwest Territories, 1966, steps have been taken to give a greater measure of self-government to the Territories. Representation in the House of Commons is by one member.

In 1959 the Department of Northern Affairs, after considering the importance of books in an isolated community, the success demonstrated by the school libraries already organized and requests from the existing associations libraries, decided on a territorial library survey. The Canadian Broadcasting Commission was supplying radio programs, the U.S. Armed Forces Radio stations were listened to, and the USSR was beaming programs to the Territories. Handicrafts among the Eskimos had shown them to have marked artistic ability. A large unit library system designed as a community cultural center promised valuable returns to the territorial community.

After careful consultation, Marion Gilroy, head of the Regional Division, Saskatchewan Provincial Library, was appointed. The summer of 1959 was spent on a series of trips to different sections of the Territories with interviews and consultation locally and in Ottawa. Following the terms of reference of the department, Miss Gilroy submitted recommendations for a twenty-year plan. The report is a closed one for the information of the government and has never been released. Miss Gilroy summarized her summer observations in the *A.L.A. Bulletin,* April 1960, as follows:

> In spite of obvious needs the very presence of libraries so far north indicates concern and interest. In Aklavik books in the school and community libraries were combined, and although crowded into a tiny room, they were well read by a cross section of the community. A special effort had been made to buy books on the North. One of the teachers told me that her fourth-grade Eskimo children liked best of all to have fairy tales told or read to them. At Fort Simpson the board members wanted to start a story hour for children, and were looking for adequate space for a reading room because so many of the Indians live in overcrowded homes. The small grants which the Territorial Government has given the libraries for books for the last ten years have helped; but all of the libraries —and communities with none—desperately need the advantages which would accrue from being served by a regional library. In another connection the Commissioner for the Territories referred to the need for a "crash operation." Such is needed simultaneously for libraries and for fundamental adult education—a flexible program geared to the needs of all the people of the North. It should explore all sorts of possibilities for satisfying those needs. Radio can help. A Library on Wings would be an ideal part of the service for a immense country riddled with transportation hurdles.

The Yukon Territory Regional Library was successfully established in 1961 and its librarian, Mrs. Elizabeth Colyer, was invited to submit a complete and detailed report on its organization, problems, and achievements. This report was studied by Commissioner Sivertz and his staff and a recommendation was presented to the Territorial Council in November 1964. A plan was adopted as the centennial project of the Territories government; a centennial grant of $250,000 was obtained from the Centennial Commission of the federal government for a headquarters building at Hay River; and a librarian with regional experience both in British Columbia and in England, Miss Patricia Smith, was appointed in July 1965. Her first three immediate undertakings were a tour of the north, the purchase and processing of the necessary collections using Edmonton, Alberta, as headquarters, and serving as architectural consultant to the Edmonton firm of Bittorf-Wensley on the library building plans. The building was officially opened early in 1968. It contains 8600 square feet of which some 4000 are the public area—adult, children's and reference sections. A meeting room accessible both from the public area and from the main entrance is self-contained and is available for small community group meetings or for art displays, being provided with burlap covered walls and special lighting. The rest of the building is occupied by the regional operations of the Public Library Service. New library buildings have been opened at Inuvik in the Western Arctic and at Frobisher Bay in Baffin Island—the eastern counterpart of Inuvik.

The Public Library Service began with 26,000 volumes, of which some 55% were allocated to Yellowknife, Hay River, Inuvik, Fort Smith, Cambridge Bay, and Fort Franklin; 25% went to deposit and traveling libraries; and 20% consisted of a central pool including a permanent reference collection at the headquarters in Hay River. A collection of phonograph records has been provided for both adults and children, as well as a collection of films. The library centers are at Yellowknife, Inuvik, Fort Smith, and Frobisher Bay. There is a system of deposit and traveling libraries. Residents of Keewatin have books delivered through Edmonton, Winnipeg, and Montreal pending the organization of an "across the north" air service.

All public library services are free of charge to all residents of the Territories. Radio programs will be adopted when staff and time permit. The system is part of the Canadian Library telecommunications network and its interlibrary loans outside the system are expedited by the National Library in Ottawa through its National Union Catalogue, not only to other parts of Canada but to the United States and abroad. Figures on costs and on circulation are not yet available. The service is a division of the Department of the Territorial Secretary and is directly responsible to the territorial secretary. The library ordinance received assent on November 10, 1966.

School Libraries. Education in the nineteenth and early twentieth century depended on the missionary schools which taught in English for the most part, or in French. In the Eastern Arctic there was some instruction in syllabics. The federal government assumed responsibility for schools in 1946. By 1966–1967 there were 65 federal schools with some 7700 children in attendance in the Northwest Territories and in the Eskimo settlements of Arctic Quebec (1332 Indian, 3366 Eskimo, and 3054 others).

School library services were organized when the federal school system was established in 1946. The first teacher to be appointed was Miss Marjorie Hinds, who established the school with its library at Tuktoyaktuk in 1947. Subsequently the mission schools were taken over by the government. By 1958 the large schools at Fort Smith, Fort McPherson, Yellowknife, Inuvik, Aklavik, and Hay River had central school libraries and smaller schools had classroom collections. The school libraries receive $6.00 per pupil to grade 6, $8.00 for grades 7–12, and $10.00 per pupil for a new school or additional classroom.

Various guides are supplied to the northern teacher-librarians. Thus the *Librarians' Handbook* notes:

> In Federal Schools for Indian children and for children in the Northwest Territories, the school library is, if possible, even more important than in other Canadian schools since the great majority of these children have no other source of books and no pre-school acquaintance with picture books. New worlds are being opened . . .

There are two lists of books recommended for school libraries. *Library Books* compiled by Kathleen Bowlby, designed for school libraries in the Northwest Territories and Arctic Quebec, gives extensive coverage of the north and its people. *List of Library Books, 1968* compiled by Edith Adamson selects 700 of its 3000 titles to inform Indian children of their heritage and to help to develop pride in their own culture.

Further assistance is given to teacher-librarians to attend a summer course in school librarianship given in Ottawa by Miss Kathleen Bowlby, who is in charge of School Library Services, Curriculum Section, Department of Indian Affairs and Northern Development, and is available at the department's headquarters in Ottawa to assist with library problems and in particular with book selection. For the benefit of teachers wishing to do professional reading, *Recommended Reference Lists for Educators* is supplied to every teacher in the system. Transportation of books is still under study. Books for the Eastern Arctic are now sent by air since water transport, although cheaper, has proved too uncertain.

Adult education programs are discussed in the *Education Review, 1966–67: Northwest Territories and Arctic Quebec* in this introductory paragraph:

> In northern Canada Adult Education provides the education, training and guidance which adults require to face the complex social, economic and cultural problems encountered in their rapidly changing environment. Such problems are most acute for those of Indian and Eskimo ancestry. Many of these adults have little or no schooling and as their children advance in school, the gap between children and parents increases. By developing suitable programs for the adult community we are trying to overcome these problems.

One adult education program centered on housing. There are others on homemaking, carpentry, welding and woodwork, typing, shorthand, bookkeeping, various secondary school subjects, current affairs, the operation of small engines, and in academic upgrading. In all of these the school and the newly organized Public

Library Service can play an important part given adequate staff with time to cooperate.

Eskimo Linguistics. The Public Library Service also can support the planning and research in Eskimo linguistics and the distribution of titles in the new Eskimo orthography which is now recognized as the most precise, systematic, and efficient medium to express the Eskimo language and culture. Small booklets are now in preparation and an Eskimo dictionary is being compiled.

In the Eastern Arctic a system of syllabics was taught by the missionaries after the Reverend E. J. Peck adapted to Eskimo the work James Evans did in syllabics for the Cree language. At present the changeover is made difficult in that the older Eskimo citizens use the syllabics and their children are being instructed in English and eventually in the new orthography, thus creating a serious communications gap. Storytelling is the Eskimo art par excellence and has been used by government teachers to bring Eskimo storytellers to the schools and to arouse their interest in modern education.

Special and Departmental Government Libraries. Special library collections are available in the Hudson's Bay trading posts for the use of the post's personnel and include newspapers, periodicals, and books—a practice dating back to the days of the earliest post establishments. In the mining center of Yellowknife the early public library service received help from the mining company which owns a professional collection for the use of the company's personnel. The U.S. Army has libraries containing both closed professional collections and recreation collections. Canadian government libraries in the Northwest Territories include nucleus reference collections in the Area Adminstrator's Office. The Royal Canadian Mounted Police are supplied with basic reference collections on professional and miscellaneous topics. One volume is a health manual to meet every occasion; there have been instances when the Royal Canadian Mounted Police have used it to perform emergency operations in isolated communities. The Department of National Health and Welfare supplies professional reading to its medical, dental, and nursing staff. The Department of National Defense has both closed and open collections. In short, any government department is supplied with nucleus reference collections and may request by telex special volumes from the Departmental Headquarters Library in Ottawa to be delivered by air. When the Public Library Service is completely established a union list and directory of Territorial holdings would be of great value to the area and beyond.

College and University Libraries. There are no colleges and universities in the Territories. Students attend the universities of the nearest province. Territorial secondary schools therefore follow the provincial curriculum in preparation for the students writing provincial university matriculation examinations. During vacations the Public Library Service will borrow books for them on interlibrary loan. Citizens taking courses by extension are supplied by the extension library of their university.

Library Users. In addition to the Eskimo and Indian populations there are the old Canadians on the Mackenzie and new Canadians in the mining towns; some are captivated by the freedom and spaciousness of the north and even uneasy about living elsewhere, and others are made unhappy by this very spaciousness and long for the warmer southern Canada, United States, or Europe, with their crowded neighborhoods, their theaters and TV, their sports, their many amenities. Then there are groups of occupational migrants on terminal undertakings. For all of these the library can become a center not only for books and mass media, but eventually as an organization to entice plays, concerts, etc., to the north as was so successfully done through the Canada Council in the Centennial Year of 1967 and is being done in Western Quebec by the Bibliothèque Regionale du Nord de l'Outaouais. A "Library on Wings" service would speed deliveries throughout this vast area to its less than 30,000 inhabitants since there is no natural geographic center to the Territories. The ever-present problem of mobility within the population—not only of the Eskimos and Indians but of those who have brought their skills to the north for the duration of a special undertaking and then pass on to another area or another country—must be realized in all development planning. Of this latter group, Anthony H. Richmond writes in *Post-war Immigrants in Canada* ". . . it will be important to make the optimum use . . . for the duration of their stay and to facilitate the rapid assumption and relinquishment of social ties." Thus, society in parts of the Northwest Territories has had to be adapted to the needs of transilient rather than sedentary populations. This factor affects the library service. In this transilient group are many of the more highly educated and professionally trained members of the population. Among the public library users there is more variety in education, interests, and mobility in the Northwest Territories than in any other part of Canada.

Library Education in Canada

Because of its national implication, the education of librarians transcends provincial boundaries and interests.

The 1933 Report of the Commission of Enquiry praised the important contribution by the McGill University Library School, directed by Dr. G. R. Lomer, and noted that it had been accredited by the American Library Association. The problems faced by the University of Toronto Library School, directed by Miss Winifred G. Barnstead, and of education for librarianship in Ontario were discussed, terminating with the following observation: "While every effort should be made to improve the professional technique of librarians, it is even more important that very high cultural standards should be insisted upon." In "Education for Librarianship Today" in the *CLA Bulletin,* February 1956, Dr. Bertha Bassam, director of the Toronto School, states the situation in the midfifties.

In 1966 the library schools organized formally as the Canadian Association of Library Schools, affiliated with the Canadian Library Association and associated with the Association of Universities and Colleges of Canada. To the Canadian Association of Library Schools belong the eight library schools:

The Graduate School of Library Science, McGill University
School of Library Science, University of Toronto
School of Librarianship, University of British Columbia
School of Library and Information Science, University of Western Ontario

Ecole de Bibliothéconomie, Université de Montréal
Library School, Ecole de Bibliothécaires, University of Ottawa
School of Library Science, University of Alberta
School of Library Service, Dalhousie University

Of these, the first five have been accredited by the American Library Association whose decisions are accepted by the Canadian Library Association.

The goal of education for librarianship has been defined by the School of Library Science, University of Toronto, Committee on Curriculum, as follows:

> The ultimate goal of education for librarianship should be to educate students who are able to think and act upon the issues presented to them as administrators, planners, or practitioners. The emphasis of the education should be intellectual and theoretical so that librarians can think creatively about whatever area of librarianship they may be concerned with. Because of the continual change in the nature of libraries and librarianship it is not possible for library educators today to foresee all the needs of the future. Therefore, they should endeavor to educate librarians who can analyze problems and then work out their own solutions. Library education should provide a methodology which will enable librarians to function in any situation.

The Canadian Association of Library Schools at its Annual Meeting in Jasper, in June 1968, confirmed a resolution passed by a majority of the schools at an April 23, 1968, meeting in Toronto:

> Resolved that this meeting endorse the principle of a four-term graduate program leading to a Master's degree in library science as the basic preparation for the professional practice of librarianship in Canada, and that Canadian library schools attempt to implement the new basic Master's program within five years, i.e., by 1973.

The implementation of this resolution should resolve the situation which has existed since 1964 when the McGill University Library School instituted a two-year program with the M.L.S. as the first professional degree. By this action the standard degree program in Canada of awarding the B.L.S. for a one-year course of study ended. In 1967, a three-semester graduate program of eleven months leading to the M.L.S. as the first professional degree was introduced by the newly formed School of Library and Information Science at the University of Western Ontario. Dalhousie University, scheduled to open a School of Library Service in 1969, has proposed the three-semester program leading to the master's degree. The Université de Montréal, which currently offers a one-year program leading to the degree of Baccalauréat en bibliothéconomie, plans to drop its bachelor's program and switch to a two academic-year M.L.S. program by September 1970. On the other hand, the new School of Library Science at the University of Alberta, which opened in September 1968, offers a program of one academic year leading to a B.L.S. degree.

A measure of standardization would benefit the library schools, university administrators, trustees, students, graduates, library employees, and certification boards, which are confused somewhat by the variation of programs and degrees offered in the 1964–1968 era. Another and more cogent reason for the change is that one academic year no longer suffices to cover the field of knowledge. New areas of concern and new methods require treatment impossible in the two semester year.

In addition to the regular library schools, courses for library technicians are currently being offered in Ontario, Alberta, British Columbia, Manitoba, and Quebec in institutions of applied arts and technology. This new class of library employee makes it mandatory for the graduate library schools to concentrate their efforts on educating librarians in greater depth than heretofore and to drop any vestiges of a "technician approach" that might remain in their curricula.

The master's course following the B.L.S. has been given by the Universities of McGill, Toronto, and Ottawa for many years. Preparation for the doctoral courses has been under discussion by four of the schools.

Notes on National Development

Municipal Library Service. The municipal public library with its branch system compares favorably with those of the United States, the United Kingdom, and Scandinavia. Work with boys and girls had had a distinguished history thanks to the imaginative leadership of Lillian H. Smith, Toronto; Louise Riley, Calgary; and others. It was 1906 when children were admitted to the Sarnia (Ontario) Public Library. In 1907 other libraries followed with instruction in children's library work given throughout Ontario in 1908. In 1911 the Westmount (Quebec) Public Library built a separate entrance to the children's room, and Toronto topped it all with a separate building, the Boys and Girls House at 40 Saint George St., under Miss Smith's direction. Research in children's literature was made possible by the Osborne Collection given to Boys and Girls House and by the complementary Lillian H. Smith Collection of twentieth-century children's books. Both collections have increased annually with new purchases. Children's books of historical interest are collected by the McGill University Graduate School of Library Science and a number of public libraries in Western Canada. A distinguished collection on *Alice in Wonderland* is in the University of British Columbia and available for research to the University of British Columbia School of Librarianship.

Work with young people, which followed after the establishment of work with children, is now under scrutiny as the modern young Canadian prefers the full selection of the adult departments both for research and circulation. In the latter department responsibility is now felt for the aged and infirm with various solutions adopted.

Friends of Libraries. Friends of Libraries organizations have been used in all types of libraries, for example in the University of British Columbia Library, the Yukon Regional Library, city libraries, and schools where the Home and School and Teacher-Parent Associations have worked assiduously. In 1967 the centennial project of the Canadian Home and School Association was the promotion of school libraries. The Canadian Federation of University Women give a grant of $500 annually as a reading stimulation award to a public or regional library.

Legislative Libraries. In the past the unsung hero of the provincial library development program frequently has been the Legislative Library and its chief librarians—men and women of recent times such as Leslie Johnson of Manitoba, Maurice Boone of New Brunswick, Mrs. Austin Bothwell of Saskatchewan, and Jean-Charles Bonenfant of Quebec. John Robert Beard in *Canadian Provincial Libraries* has produced a valuable study in this area.

Work with the Blind. Work with the blind began in 1906 with the Canadian, later the Toronto, Free Library for the Blind. Many public libraries had collections until 1919 when this service was centered in the Canadian National Institute for the Blind library system which looks after Canada, and certain Central and South American countries. The University of British Columbia has a special library for blind students.

Hospital Library Work. Hospital library work is organized in three ways—the hospital's own libraries for staff and patients with professional librarians in charge; as a branch of the public library; or as a project of the Hospital Aid Society or a service club using volunteer help. All modern techniques to assist patients are used such as overhead projectors for books and films, and story hours and puppet plays for children.

Academic Libraries. These are among the earliest libraries and possess some unique collections such as Acadiana in the universities of eastern Canada and on the history of the North-West in British Columbia. The present concern is building collections to support a rapidly developing program of graduate studies. School libraries are organizing rapidly. An outstanding system is in Calgary, Alberta.

Automation. In this modern period of automation considerable research and practical experimentation has been taking place, notably at the Université Laval, the University of Toronto, the universities of British Columbia, several public libraries of metropolitan Toronto, the National Library of Canada, the National Science Library, and in the School of Library and Information Science at the University of Western Ontario.

The Future

The outline of library development discussed under the provinces and territories highlights the need for more funds, more trained professional staff, more book and nonbook materials, more buildings, and an enhanced sense of the urgency to provide information to the people that Canada may become a knowledgable nation. Titles about Canada, its many sided cultures, its folklore, arts, and sciences, were issued in the Confederation year of 1967, but many works of a reference and informational character are still to be written, compiled, and published. Library work is inhibited because of this lack as is also the development of a national sense of unity and loyalty because of ignorance and lack of communication about the twelve parts which make up the whole nation.

Library conditions in 1968 showed marked improvement in several quarters. It is noticeable, however, that although political-economic-social conditions in Canada as a whole have improved, this improvement is not reflected in the libraries in proportion to the national change of the last half century. Consequently the next decade will demand the use of all means, intellectual and mechanical, to overcome past lethargy and limited financing. With imaginative leadership, funds, and informed research, 1967–1980 could develop adequate service to the entire population.

Libraries have been accepted in Canada as resource centers of public and private education and of assistance to government and private enterprise at all levels— local, provincial, and national. Reliable statistics supplied by provincial library officials show that only 60% of the population of Canada in 1965 had public library service available. No statistics recently gathered present an accurate picture of the school library situation. Visits to libraries show that the Ash findings of Toronto exist elsewhere. Since Canada expects to educate and train her citizens for the technological age and entrusts much national research to the colleges and universities, it is an urgent necessity that the federal government:

1. Increase funds to the university libraries to carry out the recommendations of the surveys that have evaluated conditions.

2. Make funds available for research by the graduate library schools, by professional experts, specialists, and scholars informed about the use of library materials, to aid in finding solutions to problems and to advise on programs of importance to the future progress of libraries in the rapidly changing environment of late twentieth century Canada.

3. Join with the provinces, regions, and municipalities following agreement at a Dominion-Provincial Conference in supplying funds:

(a) To initiate and carry through studies regarding the selection and appraisement of informational and quality materials in the public and school libraries of the nation.

(b) To compile lists of basic works of information which should be in libraries, and enriched lists of holdings for resource libraries.

(c) To report on the book procurement situation in Canada, and to make recommendations regarding means of organizing the prompt delivery of books.

(d) To report on architectural plans and specifications for college, university, public, and school libraries to insure adequate planning for future needs of enrollment and population growth.

4. Establish an Office of National Education and Cultural Affairs with a strong Libraries Division under the proposed new national constitution.

This Office of National Education and Cultural Affairs should have financial grant distribution authority and work cooperatively with provincial departments including those responsible for library legislation, promotion, and extension, particularly in the fields of public and school libraries to provide universal library service of a satisfactory standard.

In Quintessence

The foregoing pages show that there is no one pattern for the Canadian library be it public, regional, college, university, school, or special. Each library has been developed to meet the particular need of its users and the interests of its particular community in a country described by W. L. Morton in *The Canadian Identity* as existing "in America by the operation of geography . . . and the conscious will of the Canadian people . . . an attempt to develop in a particular North American environment a civilization European in origin and American in evolution . . . an endeavour to allow two cultures to flourish in one political nationality."

SELECTED BIBLIOGRAPHY

Adamson, Edith (Kirk), "Library Service to the Indian Population of Canada," Swedish-Canadian Workshop on Mutual Problems, Opinicon Inn, September 23–24, 1967, Canadian Library Association, Ottawa, 1967 (mimeographed).

Adamson Edith (Kirk), and Kathleen Bowlby, (compilers), "Librarians Handbook," Canada, Department of Indian Affairs and Northern Development, Northern Administrative Branch, Ottawa 1968 (mimeographed).

Albert-Westermorland-Kent Regional Library, "Annual Report," Albert-Westmorland-Kent Regional Library, Moncton, 1967 (mimeographed).

Alberta, Department of Education, Library Subcommittee, "Report, May 1959," Department of Education, Edmonton, 1959 (mimeographed).

Alberta, Department of the Provincial Secretary, Cultural Development Branch, Libraries Division, "Report of the Supervisor, 1966," Libraries Division of the Cultural Development Branch, Edmonton, 1966 (mimeographed).

Alberta, laws, statutes, etc., "The Libraries Act," in *Canadian Public Library Laws, 1966* (compiled by Canadian Library Association, Library Legislation Committee), Canadian Library Association, Ottawa, 1967.

Anderson, Beryl Lapham (compiler), "Special Libraries in Canada; a Directory Compiled for the Research and Special Libraries Section of the Canadian Library Association," Canadian Library Association, Ottawa, 1968 (mimeographed).

Ash, Lee, "The Scope of Toronto's Central Library; a Review of the Nature of the Book Resources of the Central Library Division, with Notes on the Use of Nonbook Materials and on Some Related Studies," Toronto Public Library, Toronto, 1967 (mimeographed).

Aubry, Claude, "Regional Libraries," Swedish-Canadian Workshop on Mutual Problems, Opinicon Inn, September 23–24, 1967. Canadian Library Association, Ottawa, 1967 (mimeographed).

Bain, James (compiler), "Public libraries in the Dominion of Canada," *Lib. J.*, **12**, 217 (June 1887).

Bassam, Bertha, "Education for Librarianship Today," *Can. Lib.*, **12**, 139–142 (Feb. 1956).

Bateson, Nora, *The Carnegie Demonstration in Prince Edward Island, Canada, 1933–1936,* Prince Edward Island Libraries, Charlottetown, 1936.

Bateson, Nora, *Library Survey of Nova Scotia,* Department of Education, Halifax, 1938.

Beard, John Robert, *Canadian Provincial Libraries,* Canadian Library Association, Ottawa, 1967.

Bibliothèque régionale du Nord de l'Outaouais, Inc., "Rapport Annuel des Activités du 1 Avril, 1967 au 31 Mai, 1968," La Bibliothèque régionale du Nord de l'Outaouais, Inc., Hull, 1968 (mimeographed).

Blackburn, Robert Harold, "Financial Implications of the Downs Report on Canadian Academic and Research Libraries," Association of Universities and Colleges of Canada, Ottawa, 1969 (mimeographed).

Bonenfant, Jean Charles, "Progrès des bibliothèques au Canada français," in *Librarianship in Canada, 1946 to 1947* (Bruce Braden Peel, ed.), Canadian Library Association, Ottawa, 1968.

Bonn, George S., *Science-Technology Literature Resources in Canada; Report of a Survey for the Associate Committee on Scientific Information,* National Research Council, Associate Committee on Scientific Information, Ottawa, 1966.

Bosa, Réal, "Université de Montréal École de Bibliothéconomie," *Can. Lib.,* **22,** 226–228 (Jan. 1966).

British Columbia, Department of Education, Survey Committee [on School Libraries], "Survey of British Columbia School Libraries." Department of Education, Victoria, 1964 (mimeographed).

British Columbia, Department of the Provincial Secretary, "Certification of Professional Librarians," Queen's Printer, Victoria, n.d. (mimeographed).

British Columbia, laws, statutes, etc., "Public Libraries Act," in *Canadian Public Library Laws, 1966* (compiled by Canadian Library Association, Library Legislation Committee), Canadian Library Association, Ottawa, 1967.

British Columbia, Public Library Commission, *British Columbia Library Survey, 1927–28,* Public Library Commission, Victoria, 1929.

British Columbia, Public Library Commission, "Libraries in British Columbia, 1940; a Reconsideration of the Library Survey of 1927–28," Public Library Commission, Victoria, 1941 (mimeographed).

British Columbia, Public Library Commission, "Programme for Library Development in British Columbia, 1956," B. C. Public Library Commission, Victoria, 1957 (mimeographed).

British Columbia, Public Library Commission, *Report for the Year Ending March 31, 1967,* Queen's Printer, Victoria, 1968.

British Columbia, Public Library Commission, Survey Committee, "Survey of Union Libraries in British Columbia," Public Library Commission, Victoria 1950 (mimeographed).

Burpee, Lawrence C., "Modern Public Libraries and their Methods," *Royal Society of Canada, Proceedings and Transactions,* Secs. II, VII (1902), p. 45.

Canada, Bureau of Statistics, *Canada One Hundred, 1867–1967,* Queen's Printer, Ottawa, 1967.

Canada, Bureau of Statistics, *Canada Year Book, 1967, 1968,* Queen's Printer, Ottawa, 1967–.

Canada, Bureau of Statistics, Education Division, *Survey of Libraries, 1946–48,* King's Printer, Ottawa, 1950.

Canada, Bureau of Statistics, Education Division, "Survey of Libraries; Part I: Public Libraries, 1964," Queen's Printer, Ottawa, 1966 (mimeographed).

Canada, Bureau of Statistics, Education Division, "Survey of Libraries; Part II: Academic Libraries, 1965–66." Queen's Printer, Ottawa, 1968.

Canada, Department of Indian Affairs and Northern Development, Education Division, "Library Books," Department of Indian Affairs and Northern Development, Ottawa, 1968 (mimeographed).

Canada, Department of Indian Affairs and Northern Development, Education Division, "Recommended Reference Books for Educators," Department of Indian Affairs and Northern Development, Ottawa, 1968 (mimeographed).

Canada, Department of Indian Affairs and Northern Development, Education Division, "Education Review, 1966–1967," Queen's Printer, Ottawa, 1968 (mimeographed).

Canada, Royal Commission on Bilingualism and Biculturalism, *Report,* Queen's Printer, Ottawa, 1965–.

Canada, Royal Commission on Canada's Economic Prospects, *Final Report,* Queen's Printer, Ottawa, 1958.

Canada, Royal Commission on Dominion Provincial Relations, *Report,* Queen's Printer, Ottawa, 1940.

Canada, Royal Commission on National Development in the Arts, Letters and Sciences, *Report, 1949–51,* Queen's Printer, Ottawa, 1951.

Canada, Royal Commission on Patents, Copyright, Trade Marks and Industrial Designs, *Report on Copyright,* Queen's Printer, Ottawa, 1957.

Canada, Royal Commission on Publications, *Report,* Queen's Printer, Ottawa, 1961.

Canadian Association of College and University Libraries, "Forecast of the Cost of Academic Library Services in Canada, 1965–1975; a Brief to the Bladen Commission on the Financing of Higher Education," University of Waterloo Press, Waterloo, 1964 (mimeographed).

Canadian Association of College and University Libraries, University Library Standards Committee, 1961–64, "Guide to Canadian University Library Standards," Canadian Library Association, Ottawa, 1964 (mimeographed).

Canadian Association of School Superintendents and Inspectors, *Education North of 60; a Report Prepared by Members of the Canadian Association of School Superintendents and Inspectors in the Department of Northern Affairs and National Resources,* Ryerson Press, Toronto, 1965.

Canadian Education Association, Research and Information Division, *Libraries in Elementary and Secondary Schools in Canada, 1962–63,* Canadian Education Association, Toronto, 1963.

Canadian Library Association. *Public Library Standards,* Canadian Library Association, Ottawa, 1967.

Canadian Library Association, Library Legislation Committee, "Canadian Public Library Laws, 1966," Canadian Library Association, Ottawa, 1967 (mimeographed); "Supplement," May, 1968 (mimeographed).

Canadian Library Association, Microfilm Committee, "Canadian Newspapers on Microfilm Catalogues," Canadian Library Association, Ottawa, 1959 (mimeographed).

Canadian Library Association, Provincial Libraries Committee, "Provincial Library Service, 1965; a Résumé of the Survey," Provincial Library Service, Quebec, 1966 (mimeographed).

Canadian School Library Association, Standards Committee, *Standards of Library Service for Canadian Schools,* Ryerson Press, Toronto, 1967.

Carter, Mary Duncan, "A Survey of Montreal Library Facilities and a Proposed Plan for a Library System," unpublished Ph.D. dissertation, Graduate Library School, University of Chicago, 1942.

Cartier, Georges, letter, January 23, 1969.

Caswell, Edward S., "Early western libraries," *Ontario Lib. Rev.*, **12**, 12–14 (Aug. 1926).

Colyer, Mrs. Elizabeth, "Library Development in the Far North," in *Librarianship in Canada, 1946 to 1967* (Bruce Braden Peel, ed.), Canadian Library Association, Ottawa, 1968.

Commission of Enquiry into Library Conditions and Needs of Canada, *Libraries in Canada; a Study of Library Conditions and Needs*, Ryerson Press, Toronto, 1933.

Commission Sponsored by the Canadian Association of University Teachers and the Association of Universities and Colleges of Canada, *University Government in Canada; a Report*. University of Toronto Press, Toronto, 1966.

Coughlin, Violet L., *Larger Units of Public Library Service in Canada with Particular Reference to the Provinces of Prince Edward Island, Nova Scotia and New Brunswick*, Scarecrow Press, Metuchin, 1968.

Creighton, Donald, *Dominion of the North; a History of Canada*, rev. ed., Macmillan Co. of Canada, Toronto, 1966.

Downs, Robert B., *Resources of Canadian Academic and Research Libraries*. Association of Universities and Colleges of Canada, Ottawa, 1967.

Drolet, Antonio, "La Bibliothèque du College de Québec à l'Université Laval," *Can. Lib. Council Bull.* **1**, 49–50 (June 1945).

Easton, Harry H., "Library Development; a Preliminary Essay," unpublished manuscript (Sept. 20, 1967).

Fyfe, Janet, and Raymond H. Deutsch, (compilers). "Directory of Special Collections in Canadian Libraries," Canadian Library Association, Ottawa, 1968 (mimeographed).

Gagnon, Gilbert D., "Découpage du Territoire Québécois en Régions de Bibliothèques," Ministère des Affaires Culturelles, Service Bibliothèques Publiques du Québec, Quebec, 1967 (mimeographed).

Gale, Phyllis, "The Development of the Public Library in Canada," unpublished M.A. dissertation, Graduate Library School, University of Chicago, 1965.

Gilroy, Marion, "With Parka and Sleeping Bag," *ALA Bull.*, **14**, 294–99 (April 1960).

Gilroy, Marion, "Regional Libraries in Retrospect, 1927–1967," in *Librarianship in Canada, 1946 to 1967* (Bruce Braden Peel, ed.), Canadian Library Association, Ottawa, 1968.

Grad, Tamara E., "The Development of Public Libraries in Ontario," Unpublished M.S. in L.S. study, School of Library Science, Drexel Institute of Technology, Philadelphia, 1952.

Graham, Garth, letter, January 27, 1969.

Great Britain, laws, statutes, etc., "The Statute of Westminster," in J. J. Talman, *Basic Documents in Canadian History*, Van Nostrand, Princeton, N.J., 1959.

Great Britain, laws, statutes, etc., "British North America Act," in *Canadiana Encyclopedia*, Grolier of Canada, Ltd., Toronto, 1966.

Grossman, Peter, "The Cape Breton Regional Library; a Highlight in Library Promotion in Nova Scotia," *Can. Lib.*, **6**, 186–188 (March 1950).

Grossman, Peter, "A New Library Act," *Can. Lib.,* 9, 34 (Sept. 1952).

Grossman, Peter, *Library Service in New Brunswick; a Report and Recommendations,* New Brunswick Department of Education, Fredericton, 1953.

Harris, Robin S., *Quiet Evolution; a Study of the Educational System of Ontario,* University of Toronto Press, Toronto, 1967.

Holmes, Marjorie C., *Library Service in British Columbia; a Brief History of Its Development,* Public Library Commission of British Columbia, 1959.

Joint Committee of the British Columbia Library Association and the Public Library Commission, "Programme for Library Development in British Columbia, 1945," Public Library Commission, Victoria, 1945 (mimeographed).

Joint Committee of the British Columbia Library Association and the Public Library Commission, "Programme for Library Development in British Columbia, 1950, being a Condensation and Revision of the Programme for Library Development in British Columbia, 1945," Library Commission, Victoria, 1950 (mimeographed.)

Jupp, Elizabeth, "So Far—So Good; BCLA at the Crossroads," *British Columbia Lib. Quart.,* 28, 3–8 (Jan. 1965).

Kroll, Morton (ed.), *The Public Libraries of the Pacific Northwest Library Association* (Pacific Northwest Library Association, Library Development Report, Vol. I), University of Washington Press, Seattle, 1960.

Kroll, Morton (ed.), *Elementary and Secondary School Libraries of the Pacific Northwest* (Pacific Northwest Library Association, Library Development Project, Vol. II), University of Washington Press, Seattle, 1960.

Land, Brian, "University of Toronto School of Library Science," *Can. Lib.,* 22, 223–225 (Jan. 1966).

Land, Brian, "New Directions in Education for Librarianship in Canada," *Can. Lib. J.,* 26, 36, 39 (Jan.–Feb. 1969).

Lomer, Gerhard Richard, *Report on a Proposed Three Year Demonstration of Library Service for Prince Edward Island,* McGill Univesity Library, Montreal, 1932.

McCombs, Charles F., "Report on Canadian Libraries to the Carnegie Corporation of New York," typescript on deposit with the American Library Association.

MacEacheron, James F., letter, Nov. 18, 1868.

McKinnon, Sister Marie Michael, "Extending Extension Frontiers," *Atlantic Provinces Lib. Asso. Bull.,* 115–119, 135–136 (Dec. 1966).

Manitoba, laws, statutes, etc., "An Act to Provide for the Establishment and Maintenance of Public Libraries," in *Canadian Public Library Laws, 1966* (compiled by Canadian Library Association, Library Legislation Committee), Canadian Library Association, Ottawa, 1967; *Supplement,* May 1968.

Manitoba, Provincial Library, *Report of the Director of Libraries, 1955,* Queen's Printer, Winnipeg, 1955.

Martin, Gérard, "Legislation on Public Libraries in Quebec," International Federation of Library Associations, Section on Public Libraries, Frankfort, 1968 (mimeographed).

Mifflin, Jessie Beaumont, "Regional Libraries—Terra Nova Style," *Can. Lib.,* 11, 97 (Dec. 1954).

Mifflin, Jessie Beaumont, "Newfoundland Regional Library System; Distribution of Books in Sparsely Populated Areas," *Can. Lib.,* **25**, 92–96 (Sept.–Oct., 1968).

Morisset, Auguste-Marie, "University of Ottawa Library School—École de Bibliothécaires, Université d'Ottawa," *Can. Lib.,* **22**, 219–222 (Jan. 1966).

Morley, Marjorie, *Regional Libraries: Nova Scotia, New Brunswick and Prince Edward Island,* Canadian Library Association, Ottawa, 1961.

Morley, Marjorie, "Report of the Director of Libraries," in Manitoba, Legislative Library, *Annual Reports of the Legislative Library of the Province of Manitoba, 1953–63,* Queen's Printer, Winnipeg, 1964.

Morton, Elizabeth Homer, "Libraries in the Life of the Canadian Nation, 1931–1967, unpublished M.A. dissertation, Graduate Library School, University of Chicago, 1969.

Morton, William Lewis, *The Canadian Identity,* University of Wisconsin, Madison, 1963.

Mustard, Mary I., and Doris P. Fennell, "Libraries in Canadian Schools," in *Librarianship in Canada, 1946 to 1967* (Bruce Braden Peel, ed.), Canadian Library Association, Ottawa, 1968.

New Brunswick, laws, statutes, etc., *Libraries Act,* Queen's Printer, Fredericton, 1967, Chap. 14.

New Brunswick, laws, statutes, etc., "Library Services Act, 1954," in *Canadian Public Library Laws, 1966* (compiled by Canadian Library Association, Library Legislation Committee), Canadian Library Association, Ottawa, 1967.

New Brunswick, laws, statutes, etc., *Public Libraries Act,* King's Printer, Fredericton, 1929.

New Brunswick Library Commission, "The Legislative Library; Report of a Visit with Suggestions, January 24, 1930" (manuscript).

New Brunswick Library Commission, "Preparatory Notes for Annual Report, Sept. 1930" (manuscript).

New Brunswick Royal Commission on Finance and Municipal Taxation, 1963, *Report,* Queen's Printer, Fredericton, 1963.

Newfoundland, laws, statutes, etc., "Public Libraries Act," in *Canadian Public Library Laws, 1966* (compiled by Canadian Library Association, Library Legislation Committee), Canadian Library Association, Ottawa, 1967.

Newfoundland, Public Libraries Board, "32nd Annual Report, 1967–68," Newfoundland Public Library Board, St. John's, 1968 (mimeographed).

Newfoundland, Royal Commission on Education and Youth, *Report,* Queen's Printer, St. John's, 1967–1968.

"Newfoundland Travelling Libraries," *Can. Lib.,* **6**, 207 (March 1950).

Northwest Territories, laws, statutes, etc., "An Ordinance to Provide Public Library Services in the Northwest Territories," in *Canadian Public Library Laws, 1966* (compiled by Canadian Library Association, Library Legislation Committee), Canadian Library Association, Ottawa, 1967.

Nova Scotia, laws, statutes, etc., *Libraries Act,* King's Printer, Halifax, 1937, Chap. XI.

Nova Scotia, laws, statutes, etc., *Libraries Act,* King's Printer, Halifax, 1938, Chap. LVII.

Nova Scotia, laws, statutes, etc., *Libraries Act,* King's Printer, Halifax, 1939, Chap. LXII.

Nova Scotia, laws, statutes, etc., *Libraries Act,* Queen's Printer, Halifax, 1966.

Nova Scotia, laws, statutes, etc., "Libraries Act," in *Canadian Public Library Laws, 1966* (compiled by Canadian Library Association, Library Legislation Committee), Canadian Library Association, Ottawa, 1967.

Ontario, laws, statutes, etc., "The Public Libraries Act, 1966," in *Canadian Public Library Laws, 1966* (compiled by Canadian Library Association, Library Legislation Committee), Canadian Library Association, Ottawa, 1967.

Parkhill, John, letter, Jan. 25, 1969.

Parkhill, John, "Metro Toronto Library Board" (manuscript).

Prince Edward Island, laws, statutes, etc., "Department of Education Act," in *Canadian Public Library Laws, 1966* (compiled by Canadian Library Association, Library Legislation Committee), Canadian Library Association, Ottawa, 1967.

Quebec Province, laws, statutes, etc., "An Act Respecting Public Libraries," in *Canadian Public Library Laws, 1966* (compiled by Canadian Library Association, Library Legislation Committee), Canadian Library Association, Ottawa, 1967.

Quebec Province, laws, statutes, etc., "Quebec National Library Act," in *Canadian Public Library Laws, 1966* (compiled by Canadian Library Association, Legislation Committee), Canadian Library Association, Ottawa, 1967.

Québec Province, Ministère de l'Éducation, Bureau des Bibliothèques Scolaires, "Statistiques au 31 janvier 1966 d'après les renseignements fournis per les commissions scolaires locales," Ministère de l'Éducation, Québec, 1966 (mimeographed).

Quèbec Province, Ministère des Affaires Culturelles, *Rapport, 1966–67,* Imprimeur de la Reine, Québec, 1968.

Recent Developments in Automation at British Columbia Libraries, University of British Columbia Library, Vancouver, 1967–.

Redmond, Donald Aitcheson, "Some College Libraries of Canada's Maritime Provinces; Selected Aspects," unpublished M.S. thesis, Graduate College of the University of Illinois, 1950.

Roedde, William A., letter, Jan. 22, 1969.

Ross, Vernon, "McGill University Graduate School of Library Science," *Can. Lib., 22,* 215–216 (Jan. 1966).

Rothstein, Samuel, "University of British Columbia School of Librarianship," *Can. Lib., 22,* 226–228 (Jan. 1966).

St. John Library Consultants, Inc., Francis R., "Ontario Libraries; a Province-wide Survey and Plan, 1965," Ontario Library Association, Toronto, 1965 (mimeographed).

St. John Library Consultants, Inc., Francis R., "Mid-Western Regional Library Cooperative; a Plan for Library Development," Francis R. St. John Library Consultants, Inc., New York, 1966 (mimeographed).

Saskatchewan, Department of Education, "Annual Report; School Libraries, 1966–1967" (mimeographed).

Saskatchewan, Department of Education, School Libraries Division, "Check List of Elementary and Secondary Schools in Saskatchewan," Department of Education, School Libraries Division, Regina, 1967 (mimeographed).

Saskatchewan, laws, statutes, etc., *Public Libraries Act,* Government Printer, Regina, 1906, Chap. 37.

Saskatchewan, laws, statutes, etc., "Libraries Act," in *Canadian Public Library Laws, 1966* (compiled by Canadian Library Association, Library Legislation Committee), Canadian Library Association, Ottawa, 1967.

Saskatchewan, Library Inquiry Committee, "Interim Report," Provincial Library, Regina, 1966 (mimeographed).

Saskatchewan, Library Inquiry Committee, *Report, 1967,* Queen's Printer, Regina, 1967.

Saskatchewan, Provincial Library, *Annual Report, 1967,* Queen's Printer, Regina, 1968.

Saskatchewan Association of School Libraries, *Standards for School Libraries in the Province of Saskatchewan,* The Association, Saskatoon, 1964.

Shaw, Ralph, *Libraries of Metropolitan Toronto,* Library Trustees' Council of Toronto and District, Toronto, 1960.

Simon, Beatrice V., *Library Support of Medical Education and Research in Canada; Report of a Survey of the Medical College Libraries of Canada, Together with Suggestions for Improving and Extending Medical Library Service at the Local, Regional and National Levels,* Association of Canadian Medical Colleges, Ottawa, 1964.

Smith, Patricia, "Public Library Services, Northwest Territories," *Can. Lib.,* **24,** 19–20 (July 1967).

Smith, Patricia, letter, Feb. 4, 1969.

Sutherland, Mrs. Doreen (Bailey), "A Journey to the Yukon, October, 1957," *Can. Lib.,* **14,** 187–191 (April 1957).

Thomas, Lewis, "Books and Reading in the Fur Trade Days," *Saskatchewan Lib. Assoc. Bull.,* **11,** 10 (Dec. 1957).

Tompkins, James J., "Experiment in Reserve Mines," *Can. Lib.,* **5,** 172–173 (March 1949).

Vainstein, Rose, *Public Libraries in British Columbia; a Survey with Recommendations,* Public Libraries Research Study, British Columbia; Victoria, 1966.

Wade, Mason, *The French Canadians, 1760–1967,* rev. ed., Macmillan Co. of Canada, Toronto, 1968.

Wallace, William Stewart, *Report on Provincial Library Service in Ontario,* Department of Education, Toronto, 1957.

Wilkinson, John Provost, "A History of Dalhousie University main library, 1867–1931," unpublished Ph.D. dissertation, Graduate Library School, University of Chicago, 1966.

Williams, Edwin E., *Resources of Canadian University Libraries for Research in the Humanities and Social Sciences; Report of a Survey for the National Conference of Canadian Universities and Colleges,* National Conference of Canadian Universities and Colleges, Ottawa, 1962.

Wilson, Mrs. Marion Conroy, June E. Munro, and John M. Marshall, *Summary of a Survey of Library Technician Training Courses in Alberta, British Columbia, Manitoba and Ontario, 1967–68,* Canadian Library Association, Ottawa, 1968.

Wiltshire, Edward T., letter, Dec. 3, 1968.

Wright, John, "Looking at Libraries," *Saskatchewan Assoc. of School Lib. Newsletter,* **5,** 10–13 (Spring 1964).

Yukon Territory, laws, statutes, etc., "Yukon Regional Library Appropriation Ordinances," in *Canadian Public Library Laws, 1966* (compiled by Canadian Library Association, Library Legislation Committee), Canadian Library Association, Ottawa, 1967.

Elizabeth Homer Morton

CANADA. LIBRARY OF PARLIAMENT, OTTAWA

See also *Canada National Library*

The Library of Parliament was initially the product of the amalgamation of the legislative libraries of Upper and Lower Canada after these two provinces, now Ontario and Quebec, were united in 1841. In Canadian terms, therefore, it has a long history, for the library in Quebec City was established in 1792 and that in York (Toronto) at about the same time.

Unfortunately, few, if any, of these original volumes remain, for when the Americans destroyed York (Toronto) in 1813 the books of Upper Canada contributed to the flames. And when the ultraloyalists of Montreal burned the Parliament buildings there in 1849, the 7300-volume collection of the Library of the Legislative Council was totally destroyed, and only 200 volumes of the 12,332-volume collection of the Library of the Legislative Assembly were saved. Another fire in 1854 severely damaged the 17,000-volume collection existing at that time, though more than half were saved. Naturally, other volumes disappeared over the years, and further losses occurred when this book collection became one of the earliest of traveling libraries as it followed Parliament from Kingston, to Montreal, to Toronto, to Quebec City, to Toronto again, and then to Quebec City, until the decision to settle in Ottawa was implemented in 1865. Even then, one may reasonably assume that there was some damage and further loss when the 55,000 volumes were moved by barge from Quebec City to Ottawa in 1865.

The library building, however, was not ready. Although planned, it was not begun until 1872 and not opened until 1876. In the meantime, temporary quarters were found in the new centre block of the Parliament Buildings and service recommenced.

Alpheus Todd, the first real parliamentary librarian, served until his death in 1884. His fame endures as the author of two books still cited today, *Parliamentary Government in England* (1867) and *Parliamentary Government in the British Colonies* (1880), but he also wrote many others.

The present library building (Figure 1), designed by Thomas Fuller and Chilion Jones, was formally opened in splendid style with a ball organized by the members

FIGURE 1. *The present library building.* (*Courtesy National Film Board of Canada.*)

from Quebec, attended by the then governor general, the Earl of Dufferin, and Lady Dufferin, and enjoyed by no fewer than 1500 costumed guests, many of whom arrived at eight o'clock and danced until half-past three with time out for supper in the Parliamentary Dining Room at one o'clock. Surely no other library has been so well and truly launched!

The next extraordinary event was the infamous fire of 1916 (still considered by many as an act of German sabotage), which destroyed the noble centre block of the Parliament Buildings on the night of February 3. Though the library itself was saved by a fierce north wind, by the prompt closing of the fire doors connecting it with the main parliamentary buildings, and by the heroic efforts of the fire department, some 20,000 volumes stored in the centre block (housing the Senate and House of Commons) were destroyed.

Until recently, the Library of Parliament has been serving an ambiguous role. Shortage of space and money, and a divided administration from 1885 to 1956, reflected this and hampered the library in properly fulfilling either of its roles, that of Acting National Library or that of Parliamentary Library.

The most important recent event allowing the Library of Parliament to concentrate on its prime function was the establishment, in 1950, of the Canadian Bibliogiaphic Centre from which the National Library emerged in 1953, to settle into its fine new building in 1967. The National Library has now accepted from the Library of Parliament some 250,000 seldom-used volumes, and certain useful, but essentially nonparliamentary, functions which had been carried out previously in the Library of Parliament. Many volumes of theology and Canadiana, general books, duplicates, and foreign documents received on exchange were in the former group; the searching of *Book Auction Records* and *American Book Prices Current* and the answering of the question "How much is it worth?" are a sample of the latter. Over 7200 volumes of bound Canadian newspapers have also been trans-ferred. These newspapers, frequently used by academics, represent the most exten-sive collection in Canada, and their transfer released time and energy for more direct service to parliamentarians. The required microfilms, of course, and three microfilm readers have been retained.

The time-consuming chore of establishing and maintaining international ex-change has also been partially transferred to the National Library. For example, it was agreed that the National Library will obtain, store, and circulate Parliamentary Papers from the newer Commonwealth and other states, while the Library of Parliament will continue to be responsible for France (from 1945), Great Britain, the United States (federal), Australia (federal), New Zealand, the Union of South Africa (federal), and the West Indies Federation (now dissolved). The Library of Parliament will always obtain and maintain what it requires, but the National Li-brary will increasingly attend to the national interest.

The National Library became the legal deposit library under the new National Library Act proclaimed September 1, 1969, thus relieving the Library of Parliament of responsibility for copyright deposit material. This means that the Library of Parliament no longer need accept unnecessary items such as children's books and comic books formerly received under the provisions of the Copyright Act.

Certainly, if the National Library did not exist, it would have been exceedingly difficult for the Library of Parliament to move into the field of serving members in depth. The routine of warehousing, and the resultant overcrowding, was not only taking an unhealthy toll of time and energy from direct service to parliamentarians, but it was also causing some confusion regarding goals and priorities. When ware-housing demands are excessive, the service function almost certainly suffers.

The earlier fires were certainly not welcome, but, all things considered, the latest fire (1952) was a good thing as it finally brought drastic action and nearly three million dollars' worth of repairs and improvements, which were long overdue. The catacombs were transformed into well-lighted, modern, air-conditioned stack areas, surrounded by clean and convenient storage and office rooms, and a small reno-vated bindery which has since been air-conditioned. The main reading room, all that most visitors see of the library, was also air-conditioned and better illuminated, and adjustable metal shelves unobstrusively replaced the older wooden ones. Nevertheless, when the library was reopened in 1956, the overall reading room in-terior was much the same as it originally appeared in 1876, though brighter. This was made possible by the removal, refinishing, and replacement of the original white pine paneling for which the library is famous, for its beauty and its comforting appeal. Fortunately, also, the beautiful white marble figure of the young Queen Victoria continues to dominate this room (see Figures 2 and 3).

The increasing complexities of modern life, and the consequent lengthening of parliamentary sessions to deal with them, have made the parliamentarians most anxious to participate effectively and to be even more aggressive in demanding research facilities, and this, combined with the appointment of the first professionally trained parliamentary librarian in 1960, has created a climate favorable to both the broadening and deepening of service. Previous efforts for substantial improvement had been frustrated by overcrowding, the Depression, and war, but by 1960 a fortuitous combination of factors, including receptive Speakers, paved the way for new services, and opposition lessened.

Even before 1960, however, the improved working conditions, enlarged staff, and increasing effectiveness of the National Library had made possible the beginnings of improved service. In late 1953, work began on classifying the whole collection by the Library of Congress scheme; this massive undertaking is now nearing completion. Combined with this was the trying task of translating and adapting the Library of Congress Subject Headings into French for the separate French Catalogue. The result of this was published by the Queen's Printer in 1963,* but is, of course, a continuing project. The "K" Classification also had to be developed to suit the large law collection, and copies of a "working" scheme have been provided to other librarians requesting it.

A mimeographed *Selected Additions List* was first issued in 1959, in response to

FIGURE 2. *The main reading room.* (*Courtesy National Film Board of Canada.*)

* Canada, Library of Parliament, *Répertoire des vedettes-matière, Subject Headings used in the Catalogue,* Queen's Printer, Ottawa, 1963 (348 pp.).

FIGURE 3. *The beautiful white marble figure of Queen Victoria.*

a resolution from the Joint Committee on the Library of Parliament. This list has been expanded and improved until it now consists of some nine or ten pages, about six in English and three in French. It is now arranged by subject and annotated, and appears every two weeks during the Session and monthly when Parliament is not sitting.

In 1956, the professional positions were more clearly spelled out, and it was decided that library school graduates would, in the future, fill these positions as they became vacant. The old system of on-the-job learning, which had worked in the past, was felt to be inappropriate in the modern world with its rising flood of publications. Not only were university graduates needed, but also those with professional library education. Adequate salaries being paid, these could be secured even during a time of increasing demand.

The parliamentary librarian is directly responsible to the Speakers of both Houses as defined in Section 3 of the *Library of Parliament Act* (Chap. 166 R.S., 1952):

> The direction and control of the Library of Parliament, and of the officers and servants connected therewith, is vested in the Speaker of the Senate and the Speaker of the House of Commons for the time being, assisted, during each session, by a joint committee to be appointed by the two Houses.

The Joint Committee now consists of 22 members and 14 senators, and must meet at least "once per session." These meetings, though not well attended, are useful and frequently lively.

The parliamentary librarian and the associate parliamentary librarian are appointed by the governor-in-council to serve "at pleasure," but, in practice, have usually served beyond the normal Public Service retirement age of 65. Under the *Library of Parliament Act* the parliamentary librarian "has the rank of a deputy head of a department,"* and this has social and administrative advantages which need not be further considered here except to say that it gives a highly desirable degree of independence. Under the *National Library Act* the parliamentary librarian is an ex officio member of the National Library Advisory Board.

From 1885 to 1956 there were two equal administrative heads, an English-speaking parliamentary librarian and a French-speaking general librarian. In theory, the parliamentary librarian was to concentrate on service to parliamentarians and the general librarian on building up a general collection to form the basis of the National Library collection. In fact, the parliamentary librarian administered the English staff, book collection, and services, and the general librarian looked after the French staff, book collection, and services. That such a system was administratively awkward eventually became evident to those responsible for it, and finally resulted in the act being changed, in 1955, to provide for one chief, as in the years 1870–1884, and the separate staffs have now been successfully integrated.

In 1961, the Joint Committee on the Library of Parliament wisely decided to severely restrict the use of the library, which at one time had served almost as a public library for Ottawa's more important citizens. An "adults only" rule was adopted and enforced, and though scholars are assisted (and necessarily because of the quality of the collection), it is a cardinal rule that service to others must not interfere with service to parliamentarians. This has resulted in some unpleasantness, of course, but the local universities do not really suffer, and the parliamentarians never do. The latter are given the priority they have the right to expect from the only library established specifically to serve them.

Another difference between the Library of Parliament and the National Library is that the Library of Parliament lends to individuals; since 1961, those with the right to borrow are "the Governor-General, members of the Privy Council, members of the Senate and of the House of Commons, officers of the two Houses, Justices of the Supreme Court of Canada and of the Exchequer Court, members of the Press Gallery, and other persons in accordance with the written authorization of either Speaker or of the Parliamentary Librarian." Only a handful of "other" individuals have the privilege, however, and almost all are distinguished academics locally resident.

The location, halfway between the Senate and the House of Commons Chambers, is ideal, and the importance of this is underlined by the heavy use made of services. Nearly 90% of all senators and members of the House of Commons had borrowed from the collection when the files were last checked, and most of these and the nonborrowers consult the library for information.

The collection, though a "general, catholic" one, as decided at a meeting of the

---

* The equivalent in general Commonwealth usage is permanent secretary heading a government department, or in the United States, the undersecretary of a department.

Joint Committee on the Library of Parliament in 1956, is not well rounded but specializes in books of particular interest to parliamentarians. There is maintained, of course, a large law collection, and monographs on politics and economics supersede literature and mystery novels on the shelves. Every effort is made to provide any volume requested and, if not obtained for permanent retention, interlibrary loan is naturally used. Far more is still loaned than borrowed, however, and the bedrock of service is the collection of some 300,000 volumes, including newspapers and periodicals. Nearly one-third of this collection consists of official government publications; roughly 10% is history and about 15% law, political science, and international affairs. Over 10% is economics, and this percentage will certainly grow at the expense of literature, religion, and philosophy.

The present library reference services include the following:

1. *The location and supply of specific information,* frequently by telephone, and quickly done. The most numerous requests are for statistical, historical, and biographical information. There is a large collection of city and telephone directories, *Who's Who*s, and other quick reference sources to help supply this information.

2. *The location and supply of general information* after a more extensive search. Copying facilities are extremely useful for this in providing, for example, information on the divorce laws of foreign countries, the treatment of Indians in the United States, and the office of ombudsman.

3. *The preparation and provision of bibliographies* in addition to the regular *Selected Additions List.* Special lists are issued, for example, *Background to Parliament, Parliamentary Procedure, Canadian Dualism, Health Insurance,* and *Capital Punishment.* Special bibliographies are prepared on request.

4. *The Parliamentary Reading Room* has been administratively part of the library since 1954, and is the only place where all the daily, and nearly all the weekly, newspapers of Canada are assembled. And this is no small accomplishment, for this means 109 daily newspapers and 634 weeklies, in addition to 41 foreign newspapers and 211 periodicals. The library proper receives additional newspapers and 1216 periodicals, only some of which duplicate those in the Parliamentary Reading Room.

Within the last six years the following services have been added:

1. *Indexing:* (a) Committee Reports of the Senate and the House of Commons are now fully indexed in English and French.

2. *Chronology of legislation in process* provides a history of all legislation introduced and is up-dated each day during the parliamentary session.

3. *Photocopying:* If practicable, copies of information or articles desired are now sent, rather than the sometimes several volumes involved, directly to the member's office, in order to keep the book and its information accessible for use in the library. There is also much copying of newspaper comment. Three different machines are available for this purpose.

4. *Vertical file and clipping service:* This much-used service is based on 19

promptly clipped Canadian daily papers and two weeklies, supplemented by the eventual clipping of the editorial pages of nearly all other Canadian daily newspapers plus a selection from some of the 634 weekly newspapers. This service covers subjects of prime interest to parliamentarians, including themselves, and provides as comprehensive a coverage of the issues of the day as do the collective journalists. Increasing research value is obtained by compiling volumes by means of Xerox copying when the clipping files fill with newspaper or periodical articles. A master and circulating copy are made, gathered together, indexed, and cataloged, and a unique new volume added to the resources.

5. *Manuscript or typescript material* of published books by or about parliamentarians is now being actively collected in order to preserve it for scholarly parliamentarians and parliamentary scholars. Five members of the House of Commons, one senator, two members of the Parliamentary Press Gallery, and one journalist are now represented.

6. *Abstracts of selected periodical articles* on subjects of current interest to senators and members of the House of Commons are prepared when time permits and irregularly disseminated.

7. *Information Centre for Canadian Parliamentary Information:* This service answers inquiries addressed directly to the library (by letter, telephone, or telex), but now also replies to letters formerly handled by the clerk of the House of Commons. In addition, the parliamentary librarian is the Canadian correspondent for the Inter-Parliamentary Union's International Centre for Parliamentary Documentation at Geneva, and also Canadian correspondent for Parliamentary and Administrative Libraries for the International Federation of Library Associations, Sevenoaks, England.

8. *Research facilities for members:* The most expensive improvement, the establishment of a Research Branch, was begun in 1965, following the twelfth report of the House of Commons Special Committee on Organization and Procedure, which formally recommended research facilities for members. Though its ideal of at least one research assistant for every ten members of Parliament has not yet been reached, their function is clearly established, and includes the preparation and interpretation of statistical data, the investigation of the pros and cons of any argument referred to them, and the provision of notes for speeches. The Research Branch is hard-pressed even though the three opposition parties now have research officers of their own paid for with public funds. Funds have also been provided for special research assistance to the Government Caucus. In any case, the Research Branch carries reference work beyond the stage of providing the books, pamphlets, articles, chapters, and information desired by actually preparing the information in concentrated readable form. About 200 reports were produced each year during 1966, 1967, and 1968, and though the Research Branch includes only 17 persons out of a staff of 88 at present, it will clearly be the most rapidly increasing part of the library.

9. *Specialist staff* is also provided in important nonlibrary areas. The chief of the Research Branch has assisted three House of Commons Special Committees on procedure; he was secretary to the last such committee and is secretary to the

present one. He also served as secretary to the Canadian Delegation attending the Inter-Parliamentary Union meeting in Majorca, 1967. A former member of the Research Branch was the secretary of the Canadian Group, International Association of French-speaking Parliamentarians. (The former associate parliamentary librarian, M. Guy Sylvestre, now national librarian, was secretary of the Canadian Section of the Association Internationale des Parlementaires de langue Française and also secretary of the Canadian Section of the Association Interparlementaire Canada-France.)

Though hopes to establish a computer-assisted service comparable to that of IBM's SDI (Selective Dissemination of Information) have failed to materialize after some three years' effort, interest has not lessened in utilizing machine methods to help with the job of assisting parliamentarians to be well informed. Recent discussions should lead to more fruitful studies of machine-assisted improvements within the foreseeable future.

Finally, the Prime Minister's statement early in July 1968 that the president of the Privy Council (also government house leader in the House of Commons) "will immediately assume direction of special studies and projects relating to [amongst other things] Provision of adequate research facilities and modernization of the Parliamentary Library, for the benefit of all Members and with special regard to Party Leaders" suggests a new era of truly significant improvement of facilities.

ERIK J. SPICER

CANADA NATIONAL LIBRARY

The need for a national library in Canada first received serious consideration in 1883, sixteen years after the creation of the Canadian Confederation. The character and functions of the Library of Parliament were under discussion in the House of Commons, and the prime minister, Sir John A. Macdonald, stressed the fact that it was "technically merely a Parliamentary library" and added: "Canada really ought to have a National Library, containing every book worthy of being kept on the shelves of a Library. . . . It ought to be a quite separate and distinct question, which should be taken up at an early day." Nothing, however, was done. Proposals that aroused some interest and had some prospect of being implemented were made in 1913 and again in 1938, but in each instance a world war intervened.

The turning point came in 1946, with the founding of the Canadian Library Association. The association placed the establishment of a national library very high on its list of objectives, and in company with the Royal Society of Canada and four other learned societies it presented a brief to the government of Canada. The approach taken was a novel one. The association contended that certain essential services that only a national library could provide could start immediately, and that they could be furnished, in the first instance, without a special building, and, indeed, without any great supply of books. Initially the services would be chiefly bibliographical, and would include the publication of a current national bibliography and the compilation and servicing of a national union catalog. This eminently reasonable program met with general approval, and in June 1948 the Joint Library Committee of the Senate and the House of Commons, the governing body of the Library of Parliament, recommended in its report "that as a first step toward the creation of a National Library, the planning of a Bibliographic Centre be commenced. . . ." Later in the year, when Dr. W. Kaye Lamb, librarian of the University of British Columbia and formerly Provincial Archivist of the province, was appointed Dominion Archivist, he was given the extra assignment of preparing the way for the establishment of a national library.

The link with the Public Archives requires a word of explanation. Although no national library existed in Canada, some of the functions of such a library were already being performed, in varying degrees, by other institutions. In 1948 the government's book resources in Ottawa, scattered through many collections, totaled about 1,800,000 volumes. Half a million of these were in the Library of Parliament, which had long recognized the need for a comprehensive book collection by a purchasing policy that extended far beyond its own special needs, especially in the humanities and the social sciences. The library of the National Research Council had not only served the needs of the council itself, but was building up the best library in Canada devoted to science and technology. The Public Archives was another institution that performed functions associated elsewhere with a national library. It had in its own library an outstanding collection of printed materials of all sorts relating to the history of Canada; and its manuscript, map, and picture divisions corresponded to those found in the British Museum, the Bibliothèque Nationale, and the Library of Congress. Quite as important, although the stack rooms of the archives building were crowded, it would be possible, by invading the museum area, to find space in which to begin national bibliographic services.

In this space the Canadian Bibliographic Centre came into existence in 1950. Work on a national union catalog began in earnest in 1951. The first step was to provide a central key to the government's own libraries in the Ottawa area; next came the task of copying the catalogs of a select list of libraries all across the wide expanse of Canada. The initial copying program was completed in 1958; at that time the catalog represented the holdings of 136 libraries. This total has since been increased to nearly 300, and the catalog consists of more than 10,000,000 entries. Telex links it with the larger libraries in Canada, and TWX gives access to many of those in the United States.

The library's work in the field of national bibliography has been a continuation and considerable expansion of that carried on for many years by the Toronto Public Library. From 1923 to 1949, the Toronto Public Library published annually *The Canadian Catalogue of Books Published in Canada, About Canada, as Well as Those Written by Canadians*. Although incomplete, this catalog had become an indispensable reference work for Canadian libraries. The Canadian Bibliographic

Centre assumed responsibility for the *Canadian Catalogue* from January 1, 1950, and entries for that year were published in installments in the *Bulletin of the Canadian Library Association*. In January 1951 it appeared as a separate monthly publication entitled *Canadiana*. In the first year listings were confined to trade and nonofficial publications, but in 1952 the publications of the government of Canada were added, and in 1953 a third section listed the publications of the provinces and territories. Films and film strips have since been included and the addition of further categories of material is in prospect.

Just as the Canadian Bibliographic Centre was coming into existence the government of Canada appointed the Royal Commission on National Development in the Arts, Letters and Sciences (better known as the Massey Commission), and the ultimate character and extent of the national library was one of the matters upon which it was asked to comment. The commission's report, submitted in 1951, strongly favored the development of a national library and the government thereupon proceeded to prepare legislation to bring it formally into existence. The National Library Act was passed by Parliament in June 1952, and came into effect by proclamation on January 1, 1953. On that date the library absorbed the Canadian Bibliographic Centre and the author was appointed national librarian.

The National Library Act included a book deposit law, under the terms of which the library was entitled to receive two copies of all publications offered for public sale or distribution in Canada, except the official publications of provinces and municipalities. The first book deposit regulations approved under the terms of the act came into effect on February 15, 1953.

The urgent need for an adequate fireproof library building in Ottawa was emphasized in August 1952 when fire broke out in the Library of Parliament. Most of the damage was caused by water, but it was clear that a major catastrophe had been very narrowly averted. As an immediate result a commanding site on Wellington Street, the main thoroughfare of Canada's capital, was assigned to the National Library and architects were appointed to prepare plans for a structure that would house both the library and its sister institution, the Public Archives. By 1955 the basic design had been completed. Construction of the new building was then delayed by a familiar impediment—the fact that the site was occupied by a temporary frame building erected to meet a wartime emergency. After many delays this building was finally vacated in the fall of 1958, but an explosion that wrecked the interior of other government premises made it necessary to reoccupy it, and five years passed before the construction contract was awarded in the spring of 1963. The building (Figure 1) was completed in 1967 and was formally opened by the Right Honorable L. B. Pearson, then prime minister of Canada, in June.

Meanwhile the library had long outgrown its first quarters in the archives museum. In 1956 a large Records Centre was completed for the archives in Ottawa West, and the library moved to these new quarters which, although still makeshift and temporary, provided about an acre of floor space. As the years passed this area in turn became inadequate and lack of space seriously hampered the development of collections and services. Quite as disturbing, the long delay in the construction of the new building gave rise to doubts about the library's

FIGURE 1. *National Library and Archives Building, Ottawa, Canada.*

future, and this added greatly to the difficulty of recruiting well-qualified professional staff. It is significant that the library was never able to recruit its full authorized establishment until it finally took possession of attractive permanent quarters.

Although the book deposit requirement has only been in force since 1953, the Canadian publications acquired under its provisions already constitute a substantial and valuable collection. Shortage of staff and space unfortunately made it impracticable to extend the deposit regulations to periodicals until 1966, but all titles published in Canada are now being gathered and preserved systematically. A basic reference collection has been acquired, and this includes many items, such as foreign national bibliographies, that are not available elsewhere in Canada. When the Library of Parliament was rebuilt after the 1952 fire it was decided to restrict its collections much more closely to parliamentary materials than formerly, and many thousands of volumes were transferred to the National Library. Although appropriations for the purchase of books have been very modest in scale, the library now possesses a valuable and useful book stock of about half a million volumes, plus many additional titles available in microform.

In round numbers, in 1969 the staff numbered 200; an additional 50 persons, technically on the staff of the Public Archives, were engaged in providing services common to both the archives and the library, such as photoreproduction facilities of all kinds, the bindery, and personnel and financial services. The total annual budget was about $2,000,000, which was supplemented by many costs borne by service departments of the government. The National Union Catalog was dealing with location requests at the rate of over 80,000 inquiries per annum, and new entries reported to the catalog in 1968–1969 by participating libraries numbered more than 1 million per annum. The National Library and Archives Building, completed at a cost of $13,000,000 and providing a floor area of 520,000 square feet, about equally divided between the library and the archives, was providing attractive and convenient quarters for both institutions. In time it will be out-grown, and either the library or the archives will then seek new accommodations. It is intended that this additional building, when required, will be on an immediately adjacent site, in order that common services may be continued and scholars may continue to enjoy the unique convenience of being able to consult books, maps, pictures, manuscripts, and a great variety of other materials in one location.

Throughout its development the library has been acutely conscious that it serves a bilingual country. *Canadiana* and its other bibliographies and catalogs are either bilingual or appear in separate English and French editions. There have been exceptions, such as the checklist of the writings of Stephen Leacock, compiled by Dr. G. R. Lomer and published by the National Library in 1954, but all publications that now originate within the library itself are bilingual. The same is true of the library's subject catalog, which is a classed catalog with separate subject indexes in English and French.

Important developments took place in 1968–1969. On June 1, 1968, the administrations of the National Library and the Public Archives were separated and Mr. Guy Sylvestre, formerly associate librarian of Parliament, was appointed national librarian. In 1969 a revised National Library Act was passed that made important new provisions for the future development of the library. For some time studies have been in progress with a view of ascertaining how automation and computer techniques can best be applied to the library's operations; the index to *Canadiana* and a union list of serials currently received by Canadian libraries have already been produced by computer. In recent years the Treasury Board has been anxious to have the National Library provide advice and assistance to the libraries of some of the government's departments and agencies. Reflecting these developments, the new act includes the following provisions for the "coordination of certain library services:"

> Subject to the direction of the Governor in Council, the National Librarian may coordinate the library services of departments, branches and agencies of the Government of Canada including (a) the acquisition and cataloguing of books; (b) the supply of professional advice, supervision and personnel; and (c) the provision of modern information storage and retrieval services including photocopying and microfilming services, electronic and other automated data processing services and facsimile or other communication of information services.

In these and other developments the National Library will work closely with the library of the National Research Council, which has become the National Science Library of Canada. It may well be that most of the government's many book collections will by degrees become part of two centralized systems supervised by the National Library or the National Science Library, whichever would be the more appropriate authority.

WILLIAM KAYE LAMB

CANADIAN LIBRARY ASSOCIATION

The Canadian Library Association was founded in 1900, established in 1946, and incorporated in 1947. Its address is 63 Sparks Street, Ottawa 4, Canada.

Preestablishment History

On June 11, 1900, nine Canadians met in the office of the chief librarian of McGill University during the Montreal conference of the American Library Association to discuss action to obtain cooperation for Canadian libraries through a Dominion library association. Present were Charles H. Gould, librarian, McGill University; James Bain, Jr., chief librarian, Toronto Public Library; E. A. Hardy, trustee, Simcoe (Ontario) Public Library Board and in the twenty years to come the devoted secretary-treasurer of the Ontario Library Association; W. T. J. Lee, trustee, Toronto Public Library Board; R. J. Blackwell, chief librarian, London Public Library; E. A. Geiger, chief librarian, Brockville Public Library; Robert W. McLachlan, honorary curator of the Numismatic and Antiquarian Society of Montreal, curator of the Chateau de Ramesay Museum, and prominent in the Royal Society of Canada; and the Misses Brock and Fairbairn of McGill University Library.

At the conclusion it was moved by Mr. Lee, seconded by Mr. McLachlan, and unanimously carried that "we do now form the Canadian Library Association." An organizing committee was named as follows: chairman, James Bain, Jr.; secretary, E. A. Hardy; members, Charles H. Gould, R. J. Blackwell, and R. T. Lancefield (librarian, Hamilton Public Library). The committee met on October 19, 1900, in the Toronto Public Library. Present were Mr. Bain and Mr. Hardy and, by invitation: H. H. Langton, librarian, University of Toronto Library; A. B. Macallum, Canadian Institute, Toronto; and A. H. Gibbard, librarian, Whitby, Ontario, Public Library. The discussion was on the scope of the proposed Canadian Library Association. It was unanimously decided that the organization at present should be the Ontario Library Association (OLA) rather than a Dominion association. A draft constitution was considered, agreement was reached, and a draft program for a conference of all interested in library work was called for Easter week of 1901 in Toronto. The constitution, with changes, was accepted and is of interest. It had no provincial limitations and was an excellent pattern for national development. In the years to come OLA frequently had to lead discussions on national library affairs.

Other provincial library associations followed: British Columbia in 1919; Quebec in 1932; Maritime (now Atlantic) Provinces in 1935; Manitoba in 1936; Saskatchewan (a reorganization) in 1940; Alberta (a reorganization) in 1944; and New Brunswick in 1951. Library associations devoted to special interests were organized: Ontario Regional Group of Cataloguers in 1927; Canadian Association of Children's Librarians in 1932; Montreal Chapter of the Special Libraries Association in 1932; Toronto Chapter of the Special Libraries Association in 1940; L'association canadienne des Bibliothèques Catholiques, now L'association canadienne des Bibliothécaires de langue française, in 1943.

The organization of the Canadian Library Association was under continual discussion. In 1925, W. O. Carson, inspector, Public Libraries Branch, Ontario Department of Education, presided over a meeting of Canadians at the Seattle Conference of ALA followed by two meetings in Vancouver. These meetings were devoted to reaching a clear understanding of the needs and difficulties of forming a nationwide organization. In 1927 at the Toronto conference of the American Library Association at a meeting convened by Fred Landon, president of the Ontario Library Association and librarian, University of Western Ontario, London, at which 300 librarians and trustees from every province except Prince Edward Island were present, it was determined to establish the Canadian Library Association. It was

> projected as a society that would be a national rallying point for all Canadian library activity, a clearinghouse for library information, a forum for library discussion, an organization that might co-ordinate, and perhaps do somewhat to unify, the library work of the several provinces. Its programme was to be principally educational, but partly executive, for it was hoped it might undertake, on behalf of library interest throughout Canada as a whole, the working out of certain special and primarily Canadian problems, in which all friends of libraries in the Dominion are interested.

John Ridington, librarian of the University of British Columbia, was appointed president. It was the general view that more knowledge of the differing needs and situations throughout Canada should be obtained by a survey conducted by personal visitation and consultation. Mr. Ridington made personal representations to the president of the Carnegie Corporation and was supported by Mr. Carl H. Milam, executive secretary of the American Library Association, who suggested that a Commission of Enquiry be set up to study the library conditions and needs of Canada—the commissioners to be George H. Locke, chief librarian of the Toronto Public Library and a past president of the American Library Association; Mary J. L. Black, librarian of the Fort William Public Library and a member of the Extension Board of ALA; with John Ridington, librarian of the University of British Columbia and president of the Canadian Library Association, as chairman. The grant was made to the American Library Association, whose officials worked closely with the commissioners. The final report, issued in 1933 by the Commission of Enquiry and the American Library Association, includes fourteen chapters: one devoted to the commission and its undertaking, eight to the provinces, two to government libraries, one to university libraries, one to public library legislation, and the last to final comments and observations.

The commissioners traveled separately so that some localities were visited three times in the summer of 1930. The commissioners were all strong-minded individualists full of enthusiasm, charm, and experience. As tried administrators they gave considerable local assistance in addition to collecting the material for the national report. Mr. Ridington preached the gospel of the regional library as well as university library improvement. Dr. Locke held meetings in public library centers giving aid to trustees and librarians. Miss Black's interests in adult education and the smaller library and her easy approach to the untrained "librarian" enriched all those who came in touch with her. As a former newspaperman the chairman worked closely with the press, and the commission aroused universal interest as its members traveled across the land. The commission visited the heads of government and community leaders, and many of the quotations in the report mirror these conversations.

When the report appeared it caused controversy, disappointment, and approbation. Appearing in the midst of the economic depression, to the reform wing of the library group it appeared to lack a courageous attitude toward library needs, particularly in the section on the Canadian Library Association, which it handled as follows:

> This commission has strong convictions as to the value of such an Association, with a small but thoroughly competent, technical staff, co-operating with other educational workers and agencies throughout the Dominion. For it can clearly be seen splendid avenues of usefulness. This Commission firmly believes that such an Association, properly organized and staffed, would do much to speed up library progress, and give to library workers incentive and enthusiasm. The scope of its proposed activities has been discussed, planned and accepted by those interested, from Atlantic to Pacific. But this Commission reluctantly and regretfully reports that the organization of such an Association is out of the question, at least for the present.

In 1934 Canadians held a meeting at the American Library Association Conference in Montreal at which an interim step was taken through the setting up of a Canadian Library Council. No report of this council's interests or activities was ever made, and to quote Miss Margaret Gill, ". . . nothing was done by this Council." When at the beginning of World War II a national meeting was called to consider library service for the armed forces, librarians were omitted as Canada had no active national library association. This blow to the profession's pride helped to arouse dormant interest in a national association of some kind. Miss Margaret Gill, chief librarian of the National Research Council of Canada, held informal conversations across Canada. Miss Margaret Clay, chief librarian of the Victoria Public Library, did likewise in a cross-country tour. Both believed the moment was ripe for the launching of such an association. During 1940–1941 as president of the Library Association of Ottawa, Miss Gill persuaded her association to take the initiative in sponsoring the organization of the Canadian Library Association and research on the need for a National Library. Letters and questionnaires went out to library associations and representative librarians across Canada. Replies with few exceptions encouraged organization as soon as possible of both institutions.

While the Ottawa group was organizing its campaign another group had proposed to the American Library Association that it set up a Committee of Canadian Consultants; this committee, with Charles R. Sanderson, chief librarian of the

Toronto Public Library, as chairman, was announced by ALA in December 1940. There was concern expressed as to whether the Ottawa "movement" should be considered anti-ALA. Such was not intended. A conference of librarians working with the Canadian Legion Education Services met in Ottawa. Dr. John Robbins, Dominion Bureau of Statistics and conference organizer, arranged a free evening for January 27, 1941, so that the members of the ALA's Committee of Canadian Consultants and the Library Association of Ottawa might meet at dinner, hear the plans of both groups, have a discussion, and come to some conclusion. At the end of the evening this motion was carried unanimously: "That this meeting of librarians from every part of the Dominion feels that the proposal for the establishment of a Canadian Library Council offers the best prospect for the advancement of Canadian librarianship and for the development of a Canadian Library organization."

The Canadian Library Consultants Committee, on February 3, recommended to ALA that it be replaced by a Canadian Library Council, that Margaret S. Gill be added to the committee, and that certain projects be undertaken, e.g.:

> The submission of briefs or petitions to the Canadian Government on any matters which concern the interests of Canadian librarians. The forwarding of the establishment of a Canadian National Library. . . . The establishment of a Canadian library bulletin. . . . The establishment of a central bureau of information for and about Canadian libraries. The publication of bibliographical material . . . e.g. . . . The establishment on a permanent basis of a Canadian Index to periodicals. . . . That one of the aims of the Canadian Library Council shall be the establishment of a permanent and self-supporting Canadian Library Organization.

Thus came into being the Canadian Library Council, Inc. It received universal Canadian library support. It was accepted by ALA as also functioning as the ALA Advisory Committee on Canada. The council was incorporated under Part II, Companies Act, Secretary of State of Canada, and arranged with the Carnegie Corporation of New York and the Rockefeller Foundation for funds for a central office, library visits, and the microfilming of Canadian newspapers of historic importance; prepared a brief for the Reconstruction Committee (Principal James, McGill University, chairman); distributed widely "Libraries for Today and Tomorrow" by Nora Bateson (1943) and "Canada Needs Librarians" (1944) to the members of the House of Commons Special Committee on Reconstruction and Rehabilitation; opened its executive office in Ottawa; in May 1944 appointed as executive secretary and editor Elizabeth H. Morton of the Toronto Public Library, who for seven years had been the part-time secretary-treasurer of the Ontario Library Association; issued the *CLC Bulletin* bimonthly; and cooperated with the National Film Board's film, *Library on Wheels*.

Establishment

In 1945, following a cross-Canada tour by the executive secretary and on the suggestion of Elizabeth Dafoe, chief librarian of the University of Manitoba, Winnipeg, the council decided to call a conference in June 1946 at McMaster University, Hamilton, Ontario, to organize the Canadian Library Association. The conference, "Libraries in the Life of the Canadian Nation" chaired by Margaret S. Gill, was marked by a sense of good comradeship and a oneness of purpose. Discussion was everywhere—both indoors and out.

Miss Margaret Clay was elected chairman of the committee of the whole to discuss the proposed activities, constitution, and financial support. The activities were accepted without change; the constitution received various amendments in addition to its name of the French equivalent of Canadian Library Association (Association canadienne des Bibliothèques); the financial report was received. The incoming executive was requested to have the association incorporated as a private corporation without share capital under Part II of the Companies Act of the Department of the Secretary of State of Canada. Incorporation under an act of Parliament would have been simpler and would have allowed more freedom in the constitution, but the cost for the young association was prohibitive.

Freda F. Waldon was elected the first president of the association with Margaret S. Gill retained as honorary past-president; William Kaye Lamb, president-elect; Joseph-Antoine Brunet, second vice-president; Hugh Gourlay, treasurer; these to be the executive board and on incorporation as a company the board of directors. The members of the Canadian Library Council were elected councillors for one year pending the election of 1947.

The message of Dr. G. R. Lomer, librarian of McGill University, was the keynote to the future: "Let this day be the V-Day of our profession in Canada in its war against apathy, ignorance, narrow-mindedness, selfishness, and regionalism of any kind."

By December 1947 the association was incorporated. After this, changes in the bylaws of the corporation as set forth in letters patent were proposed by a constitutional committee appointed by the directors, and confirmed by the annual meeting of the members and forwarded for assent to the Companies Branch of the Secretary of State of Canada. The revised constitution is printed and available to all. Government is by a board of directors and a council, the directions of which are carried out by an executive office in Ottawa responsible to an executive director. The first executive director was Elizabeth Homer Morton, who served 1946–1968; the second, Clifford Currie, 1968–.

The association makes use of special committees both to take action and to advise on policy and supply guidelines to the council, executive board, and executive office. These include a committee on committees, constitution, elections, finance, grants-in-aid, membership, nominating, publications, and resolutions, and in addition liaison committees with ALA, ACBLF, the provincial and special library associations of Canada, the Canadian Citizenship Council, and the Joint Planning Commission of the Canadian Association for Adult Education, and a delegation to IFLA headed by a chairman appointed for a term of three years to provide delegation continuity. Special committees are also appointed to investigate current problems, e.g., the Activities Committee. To provide liaison with affiliates and others a special interlibrary association liaison committee was organized of the presidents and editors of provincial and special library interest associations with a chairman appointed for three years for continuity. This was changed in 1967 to an Council Advisory Group meeting with the CLA Council and including the presidents of the aforesaid organizations, all of whom may speak to the council agenda but do not vote.

Activities

The Activities Report accepted in 1946 was analyzed by the first board of directors and its implementation was considered a twenty-year program. In fact it was completed in eighteen and a half years.

The association immediately assumed all the activities of the Canadian Library Council, the executive office in Ottawa, the *Bulletin,* other publications, briefs to the government, the microfilming of the newspapers, the library clearinghouse, library visits, and liaison with (1) library associations within Canada, (2) the federal government on matters of national concern, (3) organizations with mutual interests, and (4) the ALA and library associations within the British Commonwealth and beyond, for library public relations and conferences at the national level.

In addition it was proposed that the association develop three varieties of library standards: for the community, for librarianship, and for library legislation; a system of library placement; library exchanges within and beyond Canada; interlibrary loans of professional library information; the establishment of a list of library surveyors; the encouragement of the compiling of Canadian reference books; and support efforts to promote library training.

NATIONAL LIBRARY

In 1946 in the opinion of the members, the council, and the executive board, the first association priority was a request to the federal government for immediate consideration toward the esbtalishment of a National Library. A brief was compiled by an interassociation committee on which there was representation from the Royal Society of Canada, the Canadian Historical Association, the Social Science Research Council, and the Canadian Political Science Association, the chairman being Freda F. Waldon, president of the Canadian Library Association. Provincial library associations lent support as did more than twenty associations with mutual interests. The brief was forwarded to the prime minister, the Right Honourable William Lyon Mackenzie King, on December 18, 1946, and was discussed with the secretary of state, the Honourable Colin Gibson, on January 25, 1947, by a committee of representatives from the interassociation committee led by Miss Waldon. Action followed swiftly with the appointment in September 1948 of Dr. W. Kaye Lamb, librarian of the University of British Columbia and a former British Columbia provincial archivist, as dominion archivist with the special assignment of preparing the way for the establishment of a National Library for

Canada. In March 1949 the National Library Committee was appointed and in 1950 the Bibliographic Centre was established. The Royal Commission on National Development in the Arts, Letters and Sciences received numerous briefs regarding the National Library, including one from the CLA presented by Kathleen Jenkins, president 1949–1950. In its remarkable report issued in 1951, the Royal Commission advised the immediate establishment of the National Library. In 1952 the National Library Act was passed by the Canadian Parliament; it became law in January 1953. W. Kaye Lamb was appointed the national librarian. During the years 1946–1953 the association worked unceasingly to further this service by publishing articles about national libraries in other countries, by detailing its place as the cornerstone in the arch of Canadian library service, by arranging full cooperation from all its members such as cheerfully giving up staff to the Bibliographic Centre, by assisting with compiling the national bibliography and the microfilming of library catalogs for the National Union Catalogue and a nationwide interlibrary loan system, by interviewing key personnel whose goodwill would help, and by mailing literature to all members of the House of Commons, Senate, and provincial legislatures to keep them abreast with the need.

This program meant diverting attention from other activities, but such were the directions of the membership, who recognized the need for national library services to assist the local services and in particular bibliography, cataloging, and interlibrary loans. In time a National Library building was designed. Frustrating building delays were met by the association once more releasing publicity regarding the importance of this structure for the inauguration of public services, study, and research. The building was officially opened in June 1967 during the Ottawa CLA conference (with members from every province and territory present) by the Honourable Lester Bowles Pearson, prime minister of Canada. As a mark of appreciation the association presented a portrait in oils by Lawren Harris, Jr., of the first national librarian, Dr. W. Kaye Lamb, whose sagacity, unswerving persistence, diplomacy, leadership, and scholarly distinction had brought the national library service into being. New national library services have been requested to meet the expanding collections and services of the scholarly libraries. Prior to his retirement as national librarian on May 31, 1968, Dr. Lamb appointed the first official to the Office of Library Resources, requested by the university and research libraries of the association and recommended by Edwin Williams in his survey of some fourteen university libraries in Canada. Dr. Lamb was succeeded by Dr. Guy Sylvestre, associate parliamentary librarian, Library of Parliament, distinguished author and editor.

MICROFILMING OF CANADIAN NEWSPAPERS OF HISTORIC IMPORTANCE

This project, which had a high priority, was instituted by the CLA Council in the autumn of 1946 under the chairmanship of Robert Hamilton, assistant librarian of the Library of Parliament. Earlier work had been done for the Canadian Library Council by Alexander Calhoun, chief librarian of Calgary Public Library. Funds to expedite the project had been arranged by the Rockefeller Foundation through

ALA on the recommendation of Charles McCombs of the New York Public Library. An advisory committee of librarians, historians, and archivists was set up and by June 1948 the first catalog of newspapers microfilmed was issued. The project has filmed some 300 titles and is self-supporting except when very costly filming has to be undertaken; in these instances the Canada Council for the Encouragement of the Arts, Humanities and Social Sciences, created in 1957, has given some financial assistance. This assistance has allowed the filming of widely scattered files, such as Canada's first newspaper, *The Halifax Gazette* and the rare and scattered files of some of the Eastern Township, Quebec, papers. Cooperation has come not only from many organizations in Canada, but also in the United States, Britain, and France. Its intrinsic value is unquestioned. Its need to be carried on by the association grew out of four facts: (1) the laborious research to find all possible copies since newspaper files were seldom complete, loans on occasion having to be requested from fourteen sources in three countries; (2) the sales on completion were limited, particularly in the 1940s and 1950s to two to six copies per title; (3) high standard of filming had to be maintained; and (4) frequently the files were in poor condition or badly bound, demanding great attention. The kind cooperation of the Dominion Archives provided camera space until the early 1960s, binding assistance, and research facilities; the enthusiasm, knowledge, and technical experience of Robert Hamilton, Elsie Jury of the University of Western Ontario, and Martha Shepard of the Toronto Public Library and later the National Library solved all difficulties. The cooperation of the New York Public Library for consultation was another valuable factor. Robert H. Blackburn of the University of Toronto Library, Willard E. Ireland of the Provincial Library of British Columbia, Victoria, and James Talman of the University of Western Ontario Library in London have served as chairmen and have added new features to the undertaking. As a centennial project all papers in the Atlantic Provinces, Quebec, and Ontario for 1862–1873 were filmed. To make this possible a grant was obtained from the Centennial Commission and several interested libraries assisted by prepayment of orders.

CANADIAN PERIODICAL INDEX

Among the major forces that led to the organization of the association was the need to establish an indexing service for Canadian periodicals and documentary films. Initiated in 1928 by the Windsor Public Library, lapsed, then continued, lapsed, and reorganized through the cooperation of the University of Toronto Library and the Ontario Department of Education Public Libraries Branch, it was a priority for the CLA. A plan was put forward at the 1947 conference, a three-year grant was received from the Carnegie Corporation of New York, and Vol. 1, No. 1 appeared in January 1948 titled *Canadian Index to Periodicals and Documentary Films,* a monthly author and subject service with annual cumulations. Eventually a cumulation for 1948–1959 and a cumulation of the pre-CLA volumes for 1938–1947 were issued by the association. The service designed in 1948 was a bilingual one. The number of subscribers was disappointing and explains why no commercial organization would be responsible for this publication. It was only in 1967 with the growing interest in information and documentation that subscribers increased to over 600. To assist costs the National Library until 1968 paid for printing the annual cumulation. Each period of expansion has received assistance from the Canada Council for a limited term. The publication is sold on a service basis and is self-supporting. In 1968 some eighty-two periodicals in English and in French, out of the two hundred and fifty considered needed, were being indexed. With the listing of documentary films transferred to *Canadiana,* Canada's national current bibliography, the name was changed to *Canadian Periodical Index.*

REFERENCE PUBLICATIONS PROGRAM

At the 1946 McMaster conference some forty needed works of reference on Canada were listed. For some of these, texts were available in the libraries. The association undertook to assist in finding publishers and in soliciting prepublication orders if these were needed, as well as to encourage the compilation of needed new works and to advise on content. This program has been very successful. By 1968 over thirty of the works had been compiled and published, among which were the *Encyclopedia Canadiana,* compiled and financed by the Canadiana Company Limited, a subsidiary of the Grolier Society of Canada Limited; *Canadian Book Prices Current,* published by McClelland and Stewart; *Canadian Imprints Before 1800, Dictionary of Canadian Biography,* published by the University of Toronto; and *Canadian Periodical Index,* published by the association.

CLA MISCELLANEOUS PUBLICATIONS

In addition the CLA brought out needed library publications at cost plus service for the use of specific members and interested groups. These include the compilation of Canadian public library laws, a Canadian library directory, a series of Occasional Papers, proceedings of conferences, reports of the work of special committees, annual reports of the association, and materials for book weeks. A catalog of publications is available from the association's office.

WELFARE OF LIBRARIANS

The 1946 conference requested the immediate setting up of a study on the salaries of librarians and a recommended salary scale. The first committee, with Juliet Chabot of the Montreal Civic Library as chairman, included every type of librarian and every region of Canada. This proved too diverse for the task in hand and in 1947 the revised recommendation was to begin with public libraries and then follow with university, government, special, and school libraries; it was also recommended that the committee have a core membership in one center with corresponding members and consultants across Canada. This pattern proved successful and has been used since for many CLA committees. The Public

Library Salaries Committee with Flora Macleod of the University of Alberta Extension Library as chairman issued a Report and Standard which was accepted by the 1950 conference, and was followed by reports for other types of libraries in subsequent years. Pensions for librarians were carefully studied. A scheme sponsored by a life insurance company, a trust company, and a bank with direction from a firm of group insurance consultants was accepted in 1958 following studies by special committees under Mrs. Gordon Kerr of the Windsor Public Library Board and Newman Mallon of the Toronto Public Library. An income replacement scheme was accepted in 1965 in cooperation with the Ontario Library Association. Tenure cases have been defended by the association's executive board and executive office. The appointment of fully qualified librarians to professional positions has been watched and on occasion unqualified appointments have been questioned officially and resolutions passed by the Annual General Meeting.

Intellectual freedom has had years of study, debate, and articles and finally resulted in a workshop, in Banff in 1966, which produced a statement ratified by the association at the Calgary conference in 1966. To safeguard this statement a special committee chaired by the past president of the year is appointed annually.

The certification and the education of librarians have been handled by special committees, publications, and workshops. Cooperation between the Canadian library school directors and staff was inaugurated by a luncheon meeting in 1950 and in 1967 an independent Canadian Association of Library Schools, affiliated with the association, was established. The training of library technicians has been studied and a Canadian survey completed with a published report by Marion Wilson and June Munro in 1968. The use made of professional staff has been investigated and efforts made among librarians to promote a greater awareness of the importance of their professional status and responsibilities. Scholarships for library education have been raised by membership donations and special conference events. Professional qualifications have been stated, the latest revision approved in 1968 by the Jasper Park conference. Recruitment campaigns have been carried on by a film produced for CLA, *The Librarian,* leaflets, booklets, posters, face-to-face recruitment, talks, and receptions, resulting finally in more qualified recruits than the space of Canadian library schools allowed. The association then turned its attention to the university presidents to urge larger schools, more schools, and more assistance to unaccredited schools to encourage their meeting the accreditation standards of the ALA's Committee on Accreditation. This campaign, together with the shortage of university librarians and the progressive climate of the library schools, has resulted in extensions to the existing schools (more faculty, enlarged quarters, etc.) and the establishment by 1968 of two new schools and the proposal of a third.

To assist librarians from abroad the association has established an International Libraries Hospitality Committee. The CLA representative on the Canadian National Commission for UNESCO, Edna Hunt, and her international committee have worked closely with the External Aid Office, and the executive office has cooperated with visitors sponsored by organizations in the United States.

WELFARE OF LIBRARIES

The association's major work for the welfare of libraries has centered in its committees on standards for public and university libraries, public library legislation, government reference libraries, library-publisher relations, architecture and building, library mechanization, provincial libraries, art libraries, administrators of large public libraries, and statistical research. The Public Library Standards Committee began work under Marion Gilroy, then head of the Regional Libraries Division, Saskatchewan Provincial Library, Regina, in 1950. The standards were completed under Mary Cameron, Halifax Public Library's chief librarian, and accepted by the association in 1955. By 1960 the standards were out of date. Part I of the new standards produced by a committee under Alberta Letts, provincial librarian of Nova Scotia, was accepted by the Calgary conference and published in 1966, French edition 1967.

The interim university library standards were discussed in 1963, in which year a university libraries section, the Canadian Association of College and University Libraries, was formed and the final publication was confirmed and published by it.

The Legislation Committee, inaugurated in 1946 under C. Keith Morison, director of the British Columbia Public Library Commission, has been most active, its committees being responsible for the compiling of "Canadian Public Library Laws" with supplements; a discussion in English and French of the problems of library legislation; and special compilations on school library legislation, national library legislation, etc. There is also a committee on copyright.

The Provincial Libraries Committee program has increased from a single meeting to a full-day workshop at the annual conference and active correspondence between members during the year. In the group now belong the two territorial library systems that were organized during the 1960s. The new government reference libraries program is centered in the functions, the services rendered from the holdings maintained, the related activities, the personnel, the educational needs, and the general problems of the legislative and departmental libraries of the provincial, territorial, and federal governments, as well as those departments in public and university libraries specifically concerned with the collection and distribution of government documents. Important liaison with much cooperative bibliographic work has resulted from this group and its directing committee. Originally the committee was a Legislative Libraries Committee sparked by J. L. Johnston of the Legislative Library of Manitoba.

Groups and committees to deal with special types of libraries such as music and art libraries have in time developed into sections or have merged their work with specific sections as a section committee.

The Architecture and Building Committee, inaugurated by Edgar S. Robinson of the Vancouver Public Library, meets to exchange experience and plans and also maintains a central depository of plans and photographs in the Kitchner (Ontario) Public Library.

The Mechanization Committee has sponsored a national telex code and directory and also a subcommittee on high-speed transmission of cataloging data. Its newsletter is an exchange of the experiments reported to the committee.

The Statistical Research Committee has worked in liaison with the Dominion Bureau of Statistics to the advantage of both groups in the devising of forms and the collection and reporting of library statistics in Canada. During 1946–1968 several important surveys based many of their results on the reports of *Libraries in Canada,* published by the Dominion Bureau of Statistics and assisted informally by the committee.

The Library-Publisher Relations Committee, inaugurated under Peter Grossman, provincial librarian of Nova Scotia and now chief librarian of the Vancouver Public Library, has promoted the Co-operative Book Centre now established in Toronto; promotes reforms in book ordering and other techniques; keeps librarians and publishers informed on the problems of excessive Canadian prices of books published abroad and the reasons behind buying directly from foreign countries, particularly the United States, the United Kingdom, and France; promotes interest in book weeks, book fairs, traveling book displays, etc.; and studies, makes recommendations, and acts as a watch and word committee in respect to areas of mutual concern to libraries and publishers.

The Large Public Libraries Committee, inaugurated by Charles R. Sanderson, chief librarian of the Toronto Public Library, meets to discuss matters of interest to chief and deputy chief librarians in populations of 100,000 or more, with proceedings confidential.

Various special committees have been appointed as needed and have successfully met such emergencies as the abolition of the sales tax on books and the materials going into their production in 1953; trade union relations and library service to labor in 1961; and library postal rates, 1946.

Sections

At the organizational conference in 1946, requests were made for sections to act for the association within special fields of responsibility. The first group to request this was the University and College Libraries; the second, the Canadian Associations of Children's Librarians, independently organized in 1932. Faced with establishment and financial problems, the council requested that sections be deferred until the association was incorporated, had a membership, and knew what its annual income would be. This was agreed. In the bylaws incorporating the association in 1947, sections were included as Article 8. In 1946–1968 ten sections were established: Adult Services, Canadian Association of Children's Librarians, Canadian Association of College and University Libraries, Canadian Library Trustees' Association, Canadian Music Library Association, Canadian School Library Association, Information Services, Research and Special Libraries, Technical Services, and Young People's. The agreed-upon division of responsibility between CLA and its sections is that while the purposes of the association often can best be served by the association acting as a corporation through decisions and resolutions by its annual general meeting, the council, and the board of directors, there are particular interests of certain types of libraries and certain types of library service that call for the grouping of like members into sections. Each section has its own constitution, sets its section fees, plans its conference program, keeps its membership informed of developments in its field by newsletters and bulletins, and prepares special material for the association to publish. To provide continuing liaison, section chairmen are automatically members of the CLA Council, with full voting rights and privileges on all council matters.

The purposes of the various sections are as follows:

Adult Services: To be responsible for the study and discussion of the selection, promotion, and circulation of books and other materials used in service to adults (other than specialized services such as reference, or specialized materials such as music, already provided for by other sections) and for library adult education programs, group services, and individual advisory services for adults. To promote a community of interest and the exchange of ideas and information between librarians and others concerned with service to adults.

Canadian Association of Children's Librarians: To further children's library work in Canada with a national committee appointed for Young Canada's Book Week to arouse interest in good books for boys and girls; to encourage the reading of worthwhile books at home, at school, and at the library; to make adults aware of the fine children's books available today; to remind adults of the important place good books have in a child's life; to stress the need for good library service to boys and girls wherever they may live; and to maintain a Book of the Year for Children Award Selection Committee with carefully worked out award directions.

Canadian Association of College and University Libraries: To further college and university library work in Canada. CACUL decentralizes its work under subcommittees on such topics as academic status, automation, cost finding, position classification and salary scales, salaries and budget, and library standards; it issues briefs on the financing of higher education with special regard to the costs of academic libraries services up to 1975; it cosponsors, with the Association of Universities and Colleges of Canada, a study of Canadian academic and research libraries.

Canadian Library Trustees' Association: To inculcate into each member the responsibilities assumed by a library trustee; to promote and foster the development of libraries and library service; to provide for the exchange of ideas and experience among library board members through conferences and library publications; cooperation with associations of library trustees within and outside Canada.

Canadian Music Library Association: To promote library service and librarianship in the field of music by: providing for the exchange of ideas and information; stimulating public interest in, and encouraging the improvement and expansion of, such library services; promoting and participating in bibliographical projects, especially with regard to musical resources and activity in Canada; assisting in the recovery, preservation, and documentation of the records of Canadian musical history; promoting the work of the Canadian composers; cooperating with the parent association and other organizations, Canadian and foreign, devoted to the advancement of enterprises in library or related services.

Canadian School Library Association: To further school library service in Canada with subcommittees on liaison with the Canadian Teachers Federation, and with school library awards, publications, standards, and workshops on specific problems.

Information Services: To encourage interest among the librarians of Canada in matters pertaining to all aspects of reference work; to promote library service in this specific field; to provide for the exchange of ideas and experience among the members of this section. There are subcommittees on bibliographies, indexes, library mechanization, liaison with bibliographical projects of other countries, interlibrary loan code, telecommunications code, and standards of service.

Research and Special Libraries: To further the interests of research and special libraries with committees on directories of special collections in Canadian libraries and special libraries in Canada. Formerly responsible for certain codes, this work has been transferred to the Information Services Section.

Technical Services: To encourage interest among the librarians of Canada in matters pertaining to technical services; to promote library service in this specific field. Its subcommittees cooperate with the international conference on cataloging principles and with the committee on revision of the Anglo-American cataloging rules, list of Canadian subject headings, and basic cataloging tools for use in Canadian libraries.

Young People's: To arouse, encourage, and further interest among librarians, school administrators, teachers, and others who work with youth in the provision of adequate library facilities for young people throughout Canada; to promote library service in this specific field; to provide for the exchange of ideas and experience among the members. It has a subcommittee on book selection, an annual list of Canadian books to serve young people in public libraries and secondary school libraries for reference, study, and recreation, and standards for work with young people.

The accomplishments of the sections may be read in the annual report volume, which appears in May of each year in the CLA publication *Feliciter,* Part 2, and in the "History of the CLA" issues of *Canadian Library,* issued in: Vol. 11, June 1955; Vol. 17, May 1961; Vol. 23, May 1967; Vol. 24, May 1968; as well as in the issues of the section newsletters: *Agora* (Research and Special Libraries); *CACL Bulletin* (Canadian Association of Children's Libraries); *CACUL Newsletter* (Canadian Association of College and University Libraries); *Canadian Library Trustee* (Canadian Library Trustees' Association); *CMLA Bulletin* (Canadian Music Library Association); *Moccasin Telegraph* (Canadian School Library Association); and *Young People's Section Newsletter* (Young People's Section).

Liaison With Organizations in Canada With Mutual Interests

With the complete cultural and education services given by the modern library, the association has been under compulsion to establish liaison with such bodies as the Canadian Citizenship Council, the Canadian Education Council, the Canadian National Commission for UNESCO, and the Joint Planning Commission of the Canadian Association for Adult Education, and to keep itself informed of the work of the Canada Council. This is done by exchange of reports, by attendance at meetings, and in some instances by membership on the executive council.

Liaison With Government

This responsibility has been handled in many ways, such as the submission of briefs and hearings before royal commissions of the federal government and on occasion of provincial governments, for example, the Royal Commission on Bilingualism and Biculturalism, the Royal Commission on the National Development in Arts, Letters and Sciences, and the Royal Commission on the Status of Women; letters to royal commissions, for example, the Royal Commission on Patents, Copyrights, Trade Marks and Industrial Designs, and the Royal Commission on Broadcasting; delegations to the prime minister and to cabinet ministers, for example, to discuss the National Library, the sales tax on books, or provincial library affairs; delegations to senior government officials to discuss, for example, the library postal rates, distribution of government publications, censorship, salaries of government librarians, or statistics; cooperation with government departments regarding the publishing of pamphlets, film-strips, and documentary films of library interest; visits from the executive director to provincial library officials during field trips across Canada.

Direction by the Presidents

In discussing the history of the association's accomplishment we have already made mention of its first president (1946–1947), Dr. Freda F. Waldon, chief librarian of the Hamilton (Ontario) Public Library, "a good personnel manager with business experience, a woman of broad interest, and most practical ideas." A scholar and an astute politician, she steered CLA through its first difficult year, confident in her belief that "library service is . . . almost a preliminary condition of a distinctive national culture." Freda Waldon will ever be associated with the inauguration of the association's four great projects—the promotion of a National Library, the microfilming of the newspapers of historical importance, the indexing of Canadian periodicals and films, and successful conferences—the 1947 one in Vancouver. The presentation of a doctor of laws degree by McMaster University honored her contribution to the nation, to the community, and to her profession.

William Kaye Lamb, second president (1947–1948), librarian of the University of British Columbia and first national librarian of Canada, on being presented for an honorary degree by the University of Toronto was described as a "constructor" and a "national builder" under whom the National Library "will be at once an intelligence post and a light house." Under Dr. Lamb the association was incorporated, the committee structure outlined, the *Canadian Index* financed, the first catalog of the microfilming of the Canadian newspaper issued, the promotional work for the national library continued, and the March of Books for the Canadian Book Centre for war-damaged European libraries inaugurated; also, there was a successful conference in Ottawa.

Elizabeth Dafoe, third president (1948–1949), librarian of the University of Manitoba, brought to the association poetic diction, historic perspective, exact scholarship, and a sense of values. Her view of Canada was national and her intention, "before we draw new designs, let us perfect those we have," resulted in a presidential year with a strengthened membership, an improved *Bulletin* and *Canadian Index,* a brief presented to the Royal Commission on National Development in the Arts, Letters and Sciences in both English and French, the committees codified, the March of Books successfully conducted, a multicultural conference in Winnipeg, a strengthened newspaper microfilm project, and great expectations for the national library.

Kathleen R. Jenkins, fourth president (1949–1950), chief librarian of the Westmount (Quebec) Public Library, continued perfecting the association design through her remarkable energy, enthusiasm, clear thinking, and sense of humor, adding as well support for Young Canada's Book Week and the first statement on salary standards for public libraries. The conference met in Montreal and heard the plans for the newly organized Bibliographic Centre, a first step toward National Library service. The members of the National Library Advisory Council attended the conference. Miss Jenkins has been honored for her national, provincial, and local contribution to public life and librarianship by an honorary doctoral degree from Sir George Williams University.

William Stewart Wallace, fifth president (1950–1951), librarian of the University of Toronto, devoted his year "to consolidate the position of the Association and to build up financial reserves." A noted administrator, teacher, and encyclopedist, renowned for his tenacity of purpose and intensity of conviction, President Wallace set up a Planning Committee to consider future expansion, and personally reorganized the finances of the *Canadian Index.* By the end of the year the association was self-supporting, the fund of the Toronto Conference showing a favorable balance with a Development and Endowment Fund campaign launched under the Budget and Finance Committee. The Report of the Royal Commission on the Arts, Letters and Sciences had been issued and recommended that a National Library be established immediately and commended the work of the association. The Right Honourable Vincent Massey, chairman of the Royal Commission and chancellor of the University of Toronto, received the delegates at a reception. For his contribution to librarianship, Mr. Wallace was presented by the University of Toronto with an honorary doctor of laws degree.

Marion Gilroy, sixth president (1951–1952), director of the Division of Regional Libraries, Saskatchewan, with a flair for the unusual in word and deed, a sparkling wit, an abiding faith in adult education, and a practical approach, presided over a year of "mission accomplished" and new plans. The Development and Endowment Fund campaign under the chairmanship of Mr. R. D. Hilton Smith and the patronage of Mr. Leonard Brockington reported its successes, the National Library Bill had been passed, and the moment had come for a change in emphasis for CLA from promoting the National Library to concentrating on library needs and professional standards. At the Banff conference a special committee was set up to review library-publisher relations.

Edgar S. Robinson, seventh president (1952–1953), chief librarian of the Vancouver Public Library and the second treasurer of the association, presided over the forward march of the new program. Time and thought were given at the fall council meeting at Université Laval to the wisest expenditure of the Development and Endowment Funds now that it was apparent the full target would not be reached, and to analyzing the Grossman Report on Library-Publisher relations. CLA joined a delegation of publishers, booksellers, and authors to the minister of finance, the Honourable Douglas Abbott, to request that the sales tax on books and the materials going into their making be canceled. This was granted. The Ottawa Conference Book Fair was opened to the delighted citizens of Ottawa and an institute on school libraries was held. Mr. Robinson's interest in public and international relations and in library architecture was mirrored in the improved developments in these fields of association activity. The work of the association was recognized by the bestowal of a Coronation Medal by Her Majesty, Queen Elizabeth, on the association's executive secretary, who was chosen to receive it for the association.

Peter Grossman, eighth president (1953–1954), director of libraries for the Province of Nova Scotia, an expert in library extension and regional work in British Columbia and the Atlantic Provinces, a raconteur, rhymster, and humorist of no mean fame, devoted his year to an examination of the quality of trained library personnel needed if the nation was to extend its library facilities. The topic was so timely and so urgent that it was studied throughout the association and its sections. The entire Halifax conference was devoted to it, resulting in the establishment of committees to prepare recruitment materials and to investigate a nationwide pension plan and a study regarding library education in Canada.

Anne I. Hume, ninth president (1954–1955), chief librarian of the Windsor (Ontario) Public Library, a leader both in special library services to industry and in county extension services, a notable community leader in the Windsor-Detroit area, brought political and public relations expertise to the association. Her drive continued the work begun in Halifax and added surveys of reference, information, and documentarian work. The Saskatoon conference adopted the Public Library Standards of the committee, which had worked steadily for five years under the successive chairmanships of Misses Marion Gilroy, Ruth Cameron, and Mary E. Cameron; accepted the study on library education by Mrs. Dorothy Chatwin, adopting several of its recommendations; and considered various reports on bibliographical developments. Miss Hume's work received national recognition with the bestowal of a doctor of laws degree, *honoris causa,* by Queen's University, Kingston, Ontario.

Willard E. Ireland, tenth president (1955–1956), provincial librarian and archivist of British Columbia, was scholarly, merry, and astute. His memorable speech calling on the membership for courage, industry, loyalty, and honesty created the climate for moving into the association's second decade in venturesome spirit. The association now had a heavy load of undertakings which it continued and in addition gave particular attention to the larger unit of library service, the role of the library trustee, library financing, and better communications with the membership through a newsletter, *Feliciter*. Attention was given to the executive office staff pension and salary welfare.

Mary E. Donaldson, eleventh president (1956–1957), provincial librarian of Saskatchewan, placed the accent upon library resources—the supply of books, films, music, trustees, and trained librarians available in Canada. Gifted with the faculty of inspiring personal devotion, the members under her happy direction continued on their many undertakings. The Victoria conference received the report of the incorporation of the Canadian Library Resources Foundation to assist library research and scholarship in Canada from John Corcoran, Toronto Public Library Board, chairman; received the report of the establishment of the Canada Council for the Encouragement of the Arts, Humanities and Social Sciences for the government of Canada for which the association had asked in its brief to the Royal Commission on National Development in the Arts, Letters and Sciences, and saw a steady forwarding of section and committee projects.

Miss Alberta Letts, twelfth president (1957–1958), provincial librarian of Nova Scotia, chose five areas for exploration through workshops, discussion, and conferences in Montreal (January) and Quebec City (June), and called in the assistance of experts—Dr. Ralph Shaw, Dr. Harold Laucour, the National Film Board of Canada, and Miss Mary Gaver—to assist in exploring new methods and techniques for the communication of knowledge, library education, current film problems, and education for school librarians, while the role of the library in communications was entrusted to Dr. E. A. Corbett, Mrs. Harold Wilson, Miss Marion Gilroy, and Mr. Pierre Berton. This year was marked by the bestowal upon CLA of the National Citizenship Award of a beaver skin and citation "in recognition of distinguished services in the field of citizenship." Six members of the association won Canada Council and Ford Foundation scholarships. The association decided to sponsor Canadian Library Week, deplored any definition of obscenity in the Criminal Code that might limit freedom of inquiry or restrict pertinent library materials, inaugurated a study on federal financial aid, approved a scheme for a national pension scheme for librarians, and decided upon the handling of comparative library education, accreditation of library schools, standards of library education, and the establishment of additional library schools. Appreciation was expressed to the Canada Council for financial grants for the extension of the association's newspaper microfilming and periodical indexing projects.

Robert H. Blackburn, thirteenth president (1958–1959), librarian of the University of Toronto, poet, dramatist, and public and university library administrator, shared with Mr. Edgar Robinson the benefit of having been treasurer of the association for three years before being elected president. So many resolutions and recommendations having been forwarded by the Quebec conference, his acceptance speech in which he stated, "Next year's country—the ideal beyond reality," was most inspiring. The year was devoted to completing the many undertakings of the association to free the members to work on the joint conference of ALA and

CLA scheduled for June 1960 in Montreal and in stepping up the recruitment campaign with *The Librarian,* the documentary film produced for the association and the *Encyclopedia Canadiana,* and with the special leaflets and releases illustrated with scenes from the film (whose script had received professional assistance from a committee of Ottawa librarians). An experiment of the Edmonton conference was the many intense but informal group discussions to assess and further the immediate and pressing problems of the association. This was successful, as was the postconference workshop held by seven national associations interested in school library service and attended by 200 delegates. In recognition of his contribution to so many levels of library service, Robert H. Blackburn has been honored by a doctor of laws degree, *honoris causa,* by the University of Waterloo.

Bertha Bassam, fourteenth president (1959–1960), director of the University of Toronto Library School, gifted with wit, patience, perseverance, and decisive action, with professional experience gained both in the United States and Canada, was the ideal president for the year of the joint conference of ALA and CLA on "Breaking Barriers." In spite of Mr. Blackburn's efforts to clear the decks of CLA business by autumn 1959, unexpected new business required presidential action. Miss Bassam led a delegation in November 1959 to meet with Prime Minister Diefenbaker to discuss library matters of mutual concern to the federal government and the association, and in particular the delay in erecting the National Library building and the Canadian book titles for distribution abroad. A statement on Canadian library qualifications was issued by the council for distribution throughout the world for better understanding regarding Canadian standards of library education. Miss Bassam took part in discussions on comparative library education at the University of Illinois and attended the White House Conference on Children and Youth and the meetings of the National Council of the Canadian Conference on Education and of Canadian Library Week.

At the annual general meeting of the association at the University of Montreal a resolution requesting the federal government to appropriate funds for the National Library building was forwarded. The association invited ALA members that evening to celebrate at dinner the sixtieth anniversary of library association work in Canada, the fifteenth conference of CLA, and the passage of public library legislation for Quebec. From then on the joint ALA-CLA conference swung into action and assumed an international aspect.

Miss Bassam's educational and library leadership was honored by the University of Waterloo with an LL.D. honoris causa.

Neal Harlow, fifteenth president (1960–1961), librarian of the University of British Columbia, was faced by an association somewhat exhausted by its efforts for the joint conference and with a program that had lost impetus in preparing for Montreal. "Abraham Lincoln," as Mr. Harlow is affectionately called by his admirers, diagnosed and prescribed an eightfold program under the title "Every Idle Silence;" it included a library inquiry, chiefly by questionnaire, of every phase of Canadian library work and culminated in reports that served as working papers for the Saint Andrews (New Brunswick) conference entitled "RX: Inquiry—Consultation—Action." The intensity of the individual participation in the conference was due to the wide-ranging scope and "gloves off" policy of the inquiry. The resolutions passed were more than corporate gestures. The individual members were committed about the future as to federal financial aid, statistics, standards, school library service, shortage of librarians, the National Library, and the enunciation of a long-range program. An Activities Committee was requested to work in conjunction with the provincial library associations. Mr. Harlow's year exposed many areas where effort should be directed.

Robert M. Hamilton, sixteenth president (1961–1962), assistant librarian of the Library of Parliament, organizer of the association's newspaper microfilming project, compiler, author, and theater buff, established the Planning and Action Project and subcommittee to carry through the multitudinous recommendations of the Saint Andrews conference. Used to coping with the multiplicity of demands made by parliamentarians, he was very much the man of the hour. In addition to the plethora of committees requiring his attention, he organized a joint conference with the Ontario Library Association in Ottawa and dealt with the continuing frustrations to the profession of delays in plans to erect the National Library and regarding federal aid.

Ruby Wallace, seventeenth president (1962–1963), chief librarian of the Cape Breton Regional Library, Sydney, Nova Scotia, was a blithe spirit. A directors meeting with Ruby in charge was an occasion for rejoicing. Her capacity for hard work and devotion to the highest standards of personal library service were inspiring, as were her wide humanitarian interests, her international outlook, and her fund of amusing tales. It was her decision that a wider view would be salutary for the association. Through the cooperation of the Canada Council this was provided by having as Winnipeg conference guest of honor Mr. Bengt Hjelmquist, of the Department of Education of Sweden, who advised on the larger unit of library organization, government aid to libraries, and financial reimbursement to authors for titles circulated. The work of the Planning and Action Project instituted under Mr. Hamilton was continued and pressure continued regarding the National Library. The outcome was a series of findings from workshop meetings organized by Mr. Harry C. Campbell of the Toronto Public Library at Winnipeg, the recommendations of which were referred to the final annual session for resolution and action. A letter from the Honourable John Pickersgill and the Honourable Jean-Paul Deschatelets was received notifying that $10 million had been appropriated for the National Library building. A project under the expert guidance of Dr. Lowell Martin of New York was set up to compile public library standards.

The Reverend Edmond Desrochers, S.J., eighteenth president (1963–1964), librarian of La Maison Bellarmin, Montreal, scholar, social scientist, and expert in work with young people and library education, requested the opinion of the final session at Winnipeg regarding a study on libraries and Canadian dualism. This suggestion received ready agreement. The new association program was now in full swing and throughout the nation there was an unprecedented development of new services and the erection of new buildings. The association started the preparation of a brief to the Royal Commission on Bilingualism and Biculturalism with which some eight hundred members actually participated as critics of the first draft. New membership fee scales were accepted. The Halifax conference on libraries and Canadian dualism advocated new points of view and presented opinions being debated throughout Canada but now applied to library situations.

David W. Foley, the nineteenth president (1964–1965), librarian of the University of Manitoba, scholar, poet, and librarian, presided over the International Year library program and the submissions and hearings to the Royal Commission on Bilingualism and Biculturalism, to the Committee on Canadian Broadcasting, and to the Bladen Commission on the Financing of Higher Education of the Canadian Universities (a brief prepared by CACUL) and supported by a formal resolution of CLA directors. He visited the USSR, Sweden, Finland, Britain, and Iceland as part of the International Year program and cooperated in international library publications. In May 1965 the cornerstone of the National Library building was laid. The Toronto conference experimented by having workshops on particular topics and decreasing the number of general sessions. It recognized the ecumenical spirit in the land by holding a singularly beautiful interfaith service. The closing general conference sessions were electric with controversy.

William Rentoul Castell, twentieth president (1965–1966), chief librarian of the Calgary Public Library, bibliophile, library architectural expert, no-nonsense business executive, and librarian, presided over a year of notable accomplishments including the long-desired Activities Report (John Archer, chairman), the Public Library Standards Report (Alberta Letts, chairman), the statement on intellectual freedom prepared by a group attending a workshop in Banff, and the acceptance in principle of school library standards. He saw the inauguration of a comprehensive study of academic library resources; the appointment of a group of committees to deal with professional library topics, copyright, and improved interlibrary association liaison; and a Canada-wide study of all aspects of library service and related matters. There was a tonic quality to the wide spaces of the western air of this Calgary conference, which induced all to "make no small plans."

John Hall Archer, twenty-first president (1966–1967), director of libraries at McGill University in Montreal, historian, archivist, and a former treasurer of CLA, reigned over the CLA centennial celebrations. From sea to sea he traveled to obtain the point of view of Canadian librarians at provincial and special library conferences regarding the implementations of the Activities Report. The Annual Conference in Ottawa included invitations to the official opening of the National Library, at which Mr. Archer represented CLA. The original 1946ers echoed the sentiments of Simon as Prime Minister Pearson cut the ribbon. On behalf of the united library interests of Canada, Mr. Archer presented to the National Library an oil painting of Dr. W. Kaye Lamb by Lawren Harris, Jr. The Ottawa conference was lively, controversial, and critical, as became CLA's twenty-first anniversary and coming of age. In August Mr. Archer welcomed the IFLA Council to Toronto, its first Canadian meeting (Dr. Robert Blackburn, chairman of arrangements), at which delegates from five continents were present.

Amy M. Hutcheson, twenty-second president (1967–1968), chief librarian of the New Westminster Public Library, endowed with a flair for experimentation, a logical mind, the exact use of words, and an abiding interest in Japan, a specialist in library work with the young as well as a successful library administrator, ushered in the consolidated program of new and revised association activities including a 1968 work-study type of conference amid the beautiful surroundings of Jasper Park, Alberta. In the interest of liaison the Council Advisory Group, representing provincial and special library associations, now meets with the CLA Council with full voice but no vote. A "dialog" with the Association Canadienne des Bibliothécaires de Langue Française has brought into focus the problems held in common. Ten members of the association were honored with Centennial Medals for their contribution to the nation. The association was thanked by the Canadian Library Week Council for its sponsorship and cooperation. This council, having completed its purpose, has surrendered its charter and no longer exists. In March Miss Hutcheson, on behalf of the directors, organized a dinner in Ottawa to honor the first executive director, Miss Elizabeth Homer Morton. Wishing to recognize Miss Morton's leadership in librarianship, the association also published *Librarianship in Canada—Le Bibliothécariat au Canada de 1946 à 1967; Essays in Honour of Elizabeth Homer Morton,* edited by Bruce Peel. The twenty-two contributions cover most aspects of Canadian library development since the founding of CLA and are of value in evaluating progress made in these subject fields during this period. From some seven hundred members Miss Morton also received a fellowship to continue her library research at the University of Chicago. At the Jasper conference Miss Hutcheson introduced the second executive director, Mr. Clifford Currie.

SELECTED BIBLIOGRAPHY

Blackburn, Robert Harold, "Canadian Library Association," *Stechert-Hafner Book News,* **14,** 29–30 (Nov. 1959).

Canada, Bureau of Statistics, Education Division, *Survey of Libraries, 1946–48,* King's Printer, Ottawa, 1950.

Canadian Library Association, "Annual Reports, 1946–47 . . . 1967–8," Canadian Library Association, Ottawa, 1947– (mimeographed); issued separately or in *Feliciter,* April, May, and June issues prior to Annual Conference.

Canadian Library Association, "Annual Report of the Board of Directors," *Can. Lib.,* annually, issue prior to the Annual Conference.

Canadian Library Association, *Annual Conference Proceedings,* 1946–68, Canadian Library Association, Ottawa, 1946–68; partly printed in some years in the autumn issue of *Can. Lib.*

Canadian Library Association, "Annual General Meeting; Summary Report," *Can. Lib.,* annually, Autumn (1946–1968).

Canadian Library Association, "Decennial and Quinquennial Histories of the Association, Its Projects, Sections, Committees," *Can Lib.,* **11** (July 1955); **17** (May 1961); **23** (May 1967); **24** (May 1968).

Foley, David William, "The C.L.A. as Publisher," in *Librarianship in Canada, 1946 to 1967* (Bruce Braden Peel, ed.), Canadian Library Association, Ottawa, 1968.

Gill, Margaret S. "C.L.C. to C.L.A.," in *Librarianship in Canada, 1946 to 1967* (Bruce Braden Peel, ed.), Canadian Library Association, Ottawa, 1968.

Lomer, Gerhard Richard, "The Background of the Canadian Library Association," *Can. Lib.,* **20**, 299–302 (May 1964).

Morton, Elizabeth Homer, "The Canadian and the American Library Associations," *ALA Bull.,* **54**, 282–285 (April 1960).

Morton, Elizabeth Homer, "Twenty Years A-Growing, 1944–64—CLC Bulletin, CLA Bulletin, Canadian Library," *Can. Lib.,* **20**, 291–293 (May 1964).

"National Citizenship Award to the Canadian Library Association," *Can. Lib.,* **15**, 73 (Sept. 1958).

Waldon, Freda Farrell, "The CLA—The First Twenty Years," *Librarianship in Canada, 1946 to 1967* (Bruce Braden Peel, ed.), Canadian Library Association, Ottawa, 1968.

ELIZABETH HOMER MORTON

CARNEGIE, ANDREW

Andrew Carnegie (1835–1919) lived during the greatest period of growth in the United States. Born to a humble family of weavers in Dunfermline, ancient capital of Scotland, he was to become a great businessman, entrepreneur, innovator, and philanthropist.

Except in Pittsburgh and Dunfermline the name of Andrew Carnegie is commonly mispronounced. The accent is on the second syllable. His intimates called him "Naig," a testimony that refutes accent on the first syllable as impractical, even by those who work for organizations bearing the Carnegie name.

Led by a remarkable mother, the Carnegie family left hard times in Scotland in 1848 to join relatives in Allegheny City, now a part of Pittsburgh. Here in a muddy district was a nursery of millionaires, nearly all of them Scots. Robert Pitcairn and David McCargo of later railroad fame, Henry W. Oliver in ore fields, and Henry Phipps in iron and steel, were active in this coterie of bright young boys who were contemporaries of Andrew Carnegie.

The Carnegies were poor, so that before he was 14 young Andrew was a bobbin boy in a cotton mill at $1.20 a week. Although small in stature, he was capable of intense industry. A new life began as telegraph or messenger boy, along with the Allegheny boys mentioned above. This employment was a turning point in Carnegie's great career. A literary enthusiasm, particularly for Shakespeare, developed as young Andrew delivered messages to the Pittsburgh Theater and tarried in an unoccupied seat to watch professionals. He was now making $4 a week.

Next he mastered telegraphy and was the third operator in the United States to take messages by sound. His public work was the natural outcome of personal experiences. Col. James Anderson, retired manufacturer, had assembled a library of more than 300 volumes and was disturbed that young working boys had little access to good reading. So Anderson shared his books with the boys of Allegheny, with young Andrew as one of the most active beneficiaries. One day young Carnegie would acquire wealth and imitate Col. Anderson and establish free libraries. He would erect a monument to Col. Anderson in front of his first library as a gift to the City of Allegheny.

Carnegie soon came to the attention of Thomas A. Scott of the Pennsylvania Railroad. He earned $35 a month and was known as "Mr. Scott's Andy." Successive promotions were made and in 1859 Carnegie was named superintendent of the Western Division of the Pennsylvania system. He spent 12 years as an active railroad executive. His railroad career was important. Here he mastered self-reliance, quickness of decision, and absolute confidence in himself.

The basis of his future comes in this period of his life. It starts with homely Scotch thrift. At 20 he purchased 10 shares of Adams Express Company stock. His mother mortgaged their home to obtain the money. The real beginning was a chance meeting with an inventor of a sleeping car. At 25 Carnegie received annual dividends of $5,000 from his participation in this pioneer business.

The outbreak of the Civil War affected Superintendent Carnegie's job. The movement of troops to defend the Federal City led to Carnegie's supervision of all military railroads and telegraphs in the East. At the Battle of Bull Run he suffered a sunstroke. This led to a leave of absence to revisit Scotland for three months. Ever after he was to spend at least half of every year in Scotland or some cool country.

The Civil War income tax caused Carnegie to prepare a statement of his earnings in 1863. This document reveals that at 27 his annual income was nearly $48,000. His salary was $2,400; the remainder came from prudent investments, principally the new Pennsylvania oil fields. Another investment was an iron firm, destined to become an exclusive interest. As telegrapher and railroad executive, Carnegie's life was cramped by office routine. After he was 30 he became a roving spirit. He organized industries and left the drudgery to others.

Carnegie resigned from the Pennsylvania Railroad in 1865. He had pioneered in sleeping cars before Pullman and made a small fortune in oil before Rockefeller. He abandoned railroading before the great names of Vanderbilt, Gould, Huntington, and Hill loomed in the post-Civil War years. He next turned to an old and competitive industry—the iron trade. He saw that iron railroad bridges would supplant wooden structures and proceeded to organize the Keystone Bridge Company. Keystone bridges soon spanned every large American river in the Middle West.

The business of iron for bridges now began to assume other forms. Carnegie organized one company to manufacture rails and another for locomotives. The ever-extending railroad was the economic basis of Carnegie's career. Another interest was the Kloman forge, famous for its axles. Orders from the War Department assured this firm's prosperity; $1,620 invested grew to $50,000,000. Having conquered the iron trade in Pittsburgh in its early days, Carnegie sailed off to Europe for a holiday. This was characteristic of the man. His biographers are careful to note that the business of life was not the manufacture of iron but rather to round out his mind and character. Pittsburgh associates carried on the work.

In 1867 Andrew Carnegie returned to New York City, where there were wider opportunities for his literary and business interests. Regard for Pittsburgh was to remain constant, but the greater metropolis was to be his settled abode. By the time he was 33 his income was $56,110. He dreamed of settling in Oxford for a thorough education. He wanted to know literary men and to learn to speak in public. He began to formulate his "Gospel of Wealth." Millionaires should hold their capital in trust for public benefit. In formulating this scheme Andrew Carnegie was a pioneer. However, he did not retire yet. Industrial forces were too strong. Henry Bessemer interrupted Carnegie's plan. The new steel would supplant cruder materials.

The dawn of Bessemer Steel led to the transfer of economic leadership from Great Britain to the United States, and the man chiefly instrumental was himself British born. The zest for this adventure was in Carnegie's blood. The brillance of the invention of the Bessemer converter transformed Andrew Carnegie's plans for early retirement. He now lived for the manufacture of steel, and first for the steel rail. He organized the Edgar Thomson Steel Company on the site of Braddock's defeat. Here he made no claim as inventor, chemist, or mechanic. He was not equipped for technical work. His contribution was on the human side. He knew how to select men.

Carnegie's biographer, Burton J. Hendrick, thinks there were many Carnegies. Here was a complex, many-faceted man. He was devoted to his youthful companions and took them along on his journey to success. He was devoted to his mother and did not marry until after her death, when he was 52. With his mother he rebelled against the stern Calvinism of Scotland. He ultimately was a mixture of agnostic and nonpracticing Unitarian. His distaste for sectarianism led to a later exclusion of church-related colleges from his charitable trusts.

Pittsburgh terrain and geography were well suited for the production of iron. The forks of the Ohio provided water transportation to the area. Coke mines in nearby Connellsville added to the industrial climate for Andrew Carnegie's rise in the right place at the right time.

Carnegie kept building the Braddock Works during the depression years. He sold his other interests and poured his own resources into the mills. He backed confidence in his country's recovery and the future of railroads and steel. He was generous to his associates, called partners. From 1880 to 1900 Carnegie dominated the steel industry and ultimately had 40 partners. The split with Henry Clay Frick left 39 at the time the Carnegie Steel Company was absorbed by the United States Steel Corporation. Even those with minute fractional shares emerged as millionaires. Mr. Frick did even better on his own.

There were two great stars in the Carnegie constellation. One was Henry Clay Frick and the other was Charles M. Schwab, both born in Pennsylvania. Frick became Carnegie's leading partner and Schwab later became president. It was Schwab who negotiated the sale of the Carnegie Company to J. Pierpont Morgan in 1901. The Carnegie profits were extraordinary. Carnegie leased ore lands from Rockefeller, fought railroad battles, and made Pittsburgh a lake port by rail connections with Conneaut, Ohio.

There was a gypsy spirit in Carnegie. Foreign travel added to his intellectual experiences. As an independent gentleman he traveled widely. He especially enjoyed coaching trips through England and Scotland. His travel diaries were published. These led to his first adventures in authorship. He was a frequent contributor for 40 years to important American and British periodicals. The main currents directing English thinking were the evolutionary philosophy of Herbert Spencer, the liberal statesmanship of William E. Gladstone, and the literary and social criticism of Matthew Arnold. These three men were close friends of Andrew Carnegie.

In his expanding years Carnegie was, in the words of Burton Hendrick, a "star-spangled Scot." Carnegie wanted to devote some of the profits of his Pittsburgh business to the task of transforming Great Britain into a republic! His letters to Lord Rosebery criticize the British monarchy, aristocracy, and House of Lords. In 1885 he wrote *Triumphant Democracy*. It was a kind of admonition to his mother country. Republicanism made America great after the Civil War while the remainder of Europe, chained by monarchical principles, was slipping. The future of the world lay in America, the land of equal opportunity. Carnegie gave a systematic defense of the order of things at a time when the United States was plagued with depression, strikes, and riots.

As Carnegie's amazing life evolved, the fires of Pittsburgh and its environs were burning steadily. The name of Andrew Carnegie after 1880 meant the top leadership in the American steel trade. Carnegie Brothers and Company Ltd. was the great milestone of his worldly fortunes. This new firm gathered in a single organization the various iron and steel works associated with the Carnegie name. It was big business, built on brains, enterprise, and industry rather than wealth, social status, or business prestige. Carnegie rails built the elevated railroads in New York City and the Brooklyn Bridge, and the American transportation system has the Carnegie name imbedded in it. The geography of Pittsburgh also played its part; it was cheaper to bring the ore to the coal than the coal to the ore. So the Carnegie organization was an economic marvel.

Carnegie once remarked, "Mr. Morgan buys his partners; I grow my own." And he always kept his hand on the pulse of Pittsburgh, whether he was resting in his Scottish castle or riding a camel in Egypt. He also was careful to keep aloof from speculative management.

The new American navy was built of steel. Steel barbed wire was closing in the herds of Western cowboys. American steel tools were flooding the world. American business was transacted largely on steel typewriters. Southern planters were bundling their bales with steel ties. Oil went to market through steel pipelines. And then came skyscraper office buildings. Most of these have every beam and girder underneath the encasing brick and mortar imbedded with the word "Carnegie."

In 1887 Andrew Carnegie married a friend of many years, Miss Louise Whitfield, daughter of a New York merchant. For 10 years their summer home was Cluny Castle in the Grampian Hills of Scotland. He never recognized any conflict between his love of Scotland and his love of America. "Return to Scotland was ever to be the prize of life."

In 1889 Carnegie wrote an article which he called "Wealth" and sent it to the *North American Review*. Up to then Carnegie was known as an American ironmaster who made a great fortune—by grace of high tariffs—from which he now and then gave a public library. He now said, as close friends already knew, that he felt it was disgraceful to die rich. Here, then, was a phenomenon new in human annals. The Vanderbilt wealth was already great. Socialists foresaw the day when individual wealth would be severely concentrated. What was America to do with its rich men? Was Carnegie overpaid? He concluded that surplus wealth should be returned to society, that excessive accumulations in the hands of millionaires were not ethically their own property. The Pittsburgh millionaire solemnly suggested that there was fun in apportioning one's wealth to public causes and watching the results. Here was exhilaration not to be missed.

The duty of the man of wealth, Carnegie believed, was to set an example of modest living, to provide moderately for his dependents, and then to consider all surplus revenues as trust funds to produce beneficial results for the community. This was his "Gospel of Wealth." For Carnegie, philanthropy did not mean support from private fortunes for asylums and remedial institutions. These were appropriate matters for the State. Carnegie was kind. His own private pension list was long, but he preferred to spend great sums for the principles of prevention and cure rather than charity. He wanted to help what he called "the swimming tenth," not the submerged tenth. Private benefactions then were aimed at root deficiencies. He approved more of the establishment of universities, such as Leland Stanford's gift, and the strengthening of existing universities. He approved of William Thaw endowing a poor millright, John A. Brashear, who later became the world-famous grinder of optical instruments. He liked Mrs. Schenley's park in Pittsburgh and Mr. Phipps' conservatory for the same city. These were some of the proper outlets for millionaires, in his opinion.

He argued with Gladstone and numerous religious leaders that he did not favor charitable relief but preferred to better society. When the "Gospel" appeared, Carnegie was rich, but not nearly as rich as he was to become. He possessed few stocks and bonds except those in the Carnegie Steel Works. By 1890 Carnegie's fortune was in excess of $15 million. He planned, and pledged publicly, to give an eventual $30 million.

The year 1892 was painful for Carnegie. He had been sympathetic to labor. Henry Clay Frick, strong with property sense, had become manager of the Carnegie operations as the most famous strike in American history loomed. Carnegie left the country, as was his usual custom, and was prepared to shut down his plants and suffer when there was a dispute with the men. "Make no attempt to start again until a majority by secret ballot vote to return to work." Homestead became a battleground with the workmen in control. Violence was met with violence. The story is long and complicated. Carnegie suffered. Many Americans turned against him. A thousand Carnegie libraries, editorialized the *St. Louis Post Dispatch,* would not compensate for the evils resulting from the Homestead lockout. Republicans were worried about the coming Presidential election. Carnegie wrote his English friends, "This is the trial of my life." Later he wrote, "No pangs of any wound received in my business career save that of Homestead. . . ." Carnegie supported Frick personally and publicly, but it appears he was unhappy with Frick's behavior.

In the closing years of the nineteenth century, when American industry zoomed, Carnegie's life as a manufacturer came to a climax. Here was a man who spent half his time out of the country, yet at the same time kept close touch with the Carnegie Company so that it surpassed all its rivals. He brought to the American economy cheap steel, a boon to the nation's industrial success. Reasonable profits and a huge output were the secrets of Carnegie's success.

The Carnegie domain grew with the activities of Henry Oliver in the Mesabi Range. This transaction for ore marked an important date in the story of Pittsburgh steel. Like Frick with coke in Connellsville, Oliver turned to Carnegie for ore leases which were to mean cheap steel and the Carnegie Steel Company loomed as a giant. Then followed arrangements with John D. Rockefeller over leasing ore properties and a battle over freight rates with the Pennsylvania Railroad which made Pittsburgh the best point for manufacturing and marketing steel. Carnegie freed himself of the Pennsylvania Railroad by joining Lake Erie with Pittsburgh. He bought the whole lake shore front of the town of Conneaut, Ohio, and connected it by railroad to his various plants around Pittsburgh. The Pittsburgh, Bessemer and Lake Erie Railroad took ore from the Conneaut docks to all the Carnegie furnaces and returned loaded with coke for the Northern market. "This railroad saved our property," Carnegie wrote in 1896.

This epoch brought his fortune to flood tide. The adoption of the basic open hearth process in the United States was his achievement. While he was tardy in appreciating the Bessemer converter, he took it up as an innovator and developed it on the grand scale. Carnegie was the trail blazer in the mechanism of the steel trade. His long summer vacations were criticized, but Carnegie, away from his desk-bound partners, operated on the theory that the master of industry gets results when stimulated by his fellow man on foreign tours, at the dinner table, or by chance conversation on a boat or railway train. While Carnegie hammered his way, without the opening of a single industrial door, he out-distanced all competition, leaving no ruins or shattered fortunes in his rise to eminence. He was simply first among a prosperous group. In 1900 the steel output of Great Britain was 5 million tons. One American plant, The Carnegie Steel Company, was manufacturing almost 4 million tons. Steel, turned out by the pound before the Civil War, was now turned out by the train load. Carnegie found America made of wood and iron and turned it into steel.

But there were tribulations. What was to become of this industrial power? He told Frick in 1894 he wanted to sell, and they quarreled. Like Theodore Roosevelt he was dynamic and compulsive. He admired Frick's executive capacity but Frick was not dazzled by Carnegie's brilliance. The Carnegie business was not a corporation, but an "association." Carnegie held 58% of the stock and was intolerant of any speculation by the partners. From the time he was 33 he planned an early retirement and the dispersal of his fortune. A lawsuit between the steel kings, Carnegie and Frick, revealed the many contributions that had been made by the latter.

Carnegie then reorganized his firm with no touch of Wall Street. The Carnegie Company still was a close family affair, with Charles M. Schwab as president. Capitalization was enlarged after the departure of Frick.

American steel now developed "integration," a plan for centering in one organization all the materials and mechanisms for making steel. The Carnegie Company was an outstanding example of tying ore fields and railroads to furnaces and mills. Amalgamations were now the practice of the day. Scattered units were grouped into new combinations. This setting was a prelude to Carnegie's sale to J. P. Morgan. It was engineered by Schwab in Morgan's library. Carnegie's price was $400 million. No American had ever ended his business career with such large capital in liquid form. Carnegie took bonds. He was no longer an owner but a creditor. Capital was necessary to endow public institutions. He would give most of it away. This was self-abnegation on a heroic scale. He shifted the burden to Morgan, thus dividing it among thousands of shareholders.

Now Andrew Carnegie could have a new occupation as "The laird of Skibo." From his summer castle in Scotland in his declining years he was ready for the "making of his soul." He became entranced with organ music. He knew his Shakespeare backward. He was honored with 52 "Freedoms" from cities. He received prime ministers, literary men, clergymen, editors, musicians, and ambassadors at his Highland home. Still others came, old friends and associates from Pittsburgh, as well as persons of moderate means. The "American-British flag" flew from Skibo's tower.

At 65 Carnegie engaged to improve mankind. The first important agency, the one synonymous with his name, was the free public library. Here was the blow to fight ignorance with the light from books. Existing monuments range from the great Carnegie Institute in Pittsburgh to a tiny granite library on the Island of Iona. Carnegie declined Gladstone's appeal to improve the library at Oxford. Bodleian was for scholars, not common people. Carnegie moved from his own restricted area in Allegheny City with Col. Anderson's books loaned to working boys to library extension on an intercontinental scale.

Of course, Carnegie never gave libraries, only buildings. Even his riches were inadequate for endowment. He had a formula. Libraries were a state function, like public schools. His was a one-time gift; the community was required to store the building with books and pay for perpetual maintenance. As with steel, he formulated general policy and left the details to lieutenants. In time there were 2,509 Carnegie public libraries costing more than $56 million. Of these 1,681 were actually built in the United States.

Next he turned to Scottish education with an endowment of $15 million to improve four Scottish universities. He gave both endowment and scholarship aid.

In the domain of pure science he contributed more than $30 million over a period of time to create the Carnegie Institution of Washington, D.C. Astronomy was a favorite subject, and Mount Wilson in Southern California received a $10 million endowment.

Carnegie's ego had a sentimental side. Both Dunfermline and Pittsburgh, which were part of his early life, have imposing Carnegie monuments. The "sweetness and light" of his friend Matthew Arnold was to become what Carnegie called his "cathedral work." Pittsburgh contributions were embodied in the Allegheny Library and the Carnegie Institute—the latter cost him more than $36 million for art, music, books, and education.

The Carnegie Technical Schools in Pittsburgh became the Carnegie Institute of Technology and, more recently, Carnegie-Mellon University. The women's college was named for his mother, Margaret Morrison Carnegie.

Carnegie's last years in the United States were spent at his New York residence at 91st Street and Fifth Avenue. Here he received and consulted with the great and near-great on how to give away the remainder of his fortune. He gave nearly $7 million to provide organs to about 8,000 churches of all faiths. Not always trusting what came from the pulpit, he remarked, ". . . but you can always depend on what the organ says." He preferred to give to struggling colleges rather than to Harvard, Yale, or Princeton. He favored libraries and science laboratories. He made gifts of $10,000 to $100,000 to more than 300 institutions in little towns throughout the nation. His gifts aided Berea and the mountaineers of the South, and Hampton and Tuskegee Institutes for Negroes. He liked trade schools like Cooper Union in New York. He provided pensions for college professors. This interest led to the Carnegie Foundation for the Advancement of Teaching and ultimately the Teachers' Insurance and Annuity Association.

All this activity produced many anecdotes about Andrew Carnegie. The Carnegie fellowship was indeed large: Mark Twain, Theodore Roosevelt, John Hay, Elihu Root, plus a whole host of poets, writers, educators, and public figures in American and British society. Carnegie had long and close associations with Herbert Spencer from 1890 to 1903. He visited the German Emperor in the vain hope of stopping the Prussian menace. He spent much of his time campaigning for peace in the first decade of the twentieth century. The Carnegie Hero Funds, $5 million for the one in Pittsburgh and another $5 million for others in Europe, were part of his campaign against war. He wanted personal acts of heroism to have medals for peace like Victoria Crosses and Congressional Medals for war. The Peace Palace at The Hague was his idea. His great contribution to the cause of peace was a $10 million gift to create the Endowment for International Peace. This perpetual body works to create public sentiment for reason and justice, to bring nations into closer relations, and to stimulate the will to peace as against the will to war.

As Carnegie neared his end as a living donor and practicing philanthropist, Elihu Root advised him to transfer the bulk of his fortune during his lifetime to establish The Carnegie Corporation. Hereby he took a long look ahead. He wrote a famous letter to his trustees. He wanted his beneficial work to continue during future generations. "Conditions upon the earth inevitably change; hence no wise man will bind Trustees forever to certain paths, causes, or institutions. . . . I give my trustees full authority to change policy . . . from time to time. . . ." This great counsel by a great donor to his trustees is a landmark in the history and operations of modern philanthropy. With it the Carnegie inheritance passed out of family control. It began with an initial gift of $25 million and ultimately reached $125 million. There was another trust of $10 million for Great Britain. The family fortune was decreased to $15 million. Others of wealth, like Rockefeller and Harkness, have followed the Carnegie example of eliminating the dead hand.

There were other Carnegie gifts, for the Church Peace Union, wartime grants to the Red Cross and other agencies, pensions for ex-Presidents and their widows, and his private pension list to the famous and the humble unknowns. When Carnegie was a witness before a government commission to study working conditions, he was asked what his business was. "My chief business is to do as much good as I can in the world; I have retired from all other business."

Andrew Carnegie's final years were quiet. The war and old age kept him from Skibo in Scotland. His last summers were spent in Lenox, Massachusetts. Here he died in 1919. He is buried in Sleepy Hollow Cemetery near Tarrytown, New York.

The creation of the Carnegie Corporation was perhaps Carnegie's greatest work. While it continues to provide money for a multitude of works, here is a new agency in American life. A huge liquid capital, with no strings attached, for public distribution was not previously known. This seed idea was truly Andrew Carnegie's. Other men continue to emulate him.

The benefactions of Andrew Carnegie to improve mankind totaled $350 million. He called himself a "distributor" and disclaimed the word "philanthropist." He persuaded others to give. This gave him great satisfaction. He changed the attitudes of millionaires and even set an example for those of lesser means. The Carnegie Corporation of New York was the prototype of the great modern foundations.

"My heart is in the work" truly describes the life of Andrew Carnegie. It is quite a story, from Dunfermline to Pittsburgh to New York to Skibo to Tarrytown.

The life and works of Andrew Carnegie were examined anew in 1968 in a volume entitled *The World of Andrew Carnegie* by Professor Louis M. Hacker. He studied the growth of the United States following the Civil War, and assays the legend of the "Robber Barons" popularized in Depression and New Deal days. He calls Carnegie an "entrepreneur" and believes his world has been superseded by one more complicated and sophisticated. Businessmen are still a power, but the greatest power is Big Government. He concludes on the sombre note that ". . . the United States will never behold an Andrew Carnegie again."

STANTON BELFOUR

CARNEGIE CORPORATION OF NEW YORK

The Carnegie Corporation of New York was established by Andrew Carnegie in 1911 with an initial endowment of $25 million, later to be increased to $135 million through additional gifts and legacies. As stated in its charter, it is an educational foundation "to promote the advancement and diffusion of knowledge and understanding among the peoples of the United States . . ." and of certain areas then known as the British Dominions and Colonies. (Only 7.4% of the Corporation's income may be used for its program in the Commonwealth.)

To put the Corporation in perspective and explain its name, a few historical facts are needed. Andrew Carnegie was born in Dunfermline, Scotland, in 1835, the son of a linen weaver. The family emigrated to Pennsylvania when Andrew was 12 years old. His formal schooling ended then and he began to work, first as a bobbin boy at $1.20 a week, then as a Western Union messenger, a railroad superintendent, and finally head of the great Carnegie steel empire. In 1901 he sold the steel company to J. P. Morgan for $400 million and devoted the rest of his life to philanthropy in accordance with the philosophy expressed in his famous essay, "The Gospel of Wealth" (first published in the *North American Review* in 1899).

In addition to hundreds of personal gifts for public library buildings, church organs, colleges, and cultural organizations, Mr. Carnegie endowed a number of continuing organizations which bear his name, all but one of these founded before the Carnegie Corporation. These were:

> Carnegie Institute (Pittsburgh), 1896, comprising a music hall, museums of art and natural history, and a division of education.
>
> Carnegie-Mellon University (Pittsburgh), formed from the merger in 1967 of Mellon Institute and Carnegie Institute of Technology, which was founded in 1900 as a division of Carnegie Institute and later became an independent university.
>
> Carnegie Trust for the Universities of Scotland (Edinburgh), 1901, for assistance to students, expansion of the Scottish universities, and stimulation of research in science, medicine, history, economics, English literature, and modern languages.
>
> Carnegie Institution of Washington, D.C., 1902, for the encouragement of scientific research.
>
> Carnegie Dunfermline Trust, 1903, for the betterment of social conditions in Mr. Carnegie's native town.
>
> Carnegie Hero Fund Commission (Pittsburgh), 1904, for recognition of heroic acts performed in the peaceful walks of life.
>
> Carnegie Foundation for the Advancement of Teaching (New York), 1905, to provide pensions for retired college teachers and to conduct educational studies.
>
> Carnegie Hero Fund Trust (Dunfermline), 1906, for recognition of heroic acts performed in the peaceful walks of life in Great Britain and Ireland.
>
> Carnegie Hero Funds in Europe, established during 1909–1911 in France, Germany, Norway, Switzerland, the Netherlands, Sweden, Denmark, Belgium, and Italy. (Some of the Funds are no longer active.)
>
> Carnegie Endowment for International Peace (New York), 1910, to serve the purpose indicated by its name.
>
> Carnegie United Kingdom Trust (Dunfermline), 1913, for the improvement of the well-being of the people of Great Britain and Ireland, chiefly through aid to educational institutions and agencies of the drama, music, social services, and so forth.

When Mr. Carnegie decided to place the bulk of his remaining fortune in one large, general-purpose foundation, he had already used all the conventional labels. The Carnegie Corporation thus has a name which is far from descriptive of its purpose, and is often thought to denote a steel company or other industrial enterprise.

From 1911 until his death in 1919, Mr. Carnegie was president of the Corporation and this foundation was primarily a corporate structure for his personal giving. His favorite gift was a library. As has been noted, he had little formal education, but he was a well-educated man, thanks to books. When he was 16 years old he was one of a small group of working boys permitted to use the private library of Colonel James Anderson, a wealthy citizen in Allegheny, Pennsylvania, now part of

Pittsburgh. This experience left an indelible impression and in providing public libraries he was, in his words, giving communities "the ladders upon which the aspiring can climb."

Starting in 1881 with the gift of a library to his birthplace, Dunfermline, Mr. Carnegie and later the Corporation gave $56 million to build 2509 public libraries. Of these, 1681 were built in the United States. The rest were located in many other parts of the English-speaking world. The Corporation continued Mr. Carnegie's formula of giving money for a building if the community would provide a site and would appropriate annually from tax funds at least 10% of the amount of the gift to maintain a free public library.

In 1917, with the advent of America's entry into World War I, grants for buildings were discontinued, except to honor previous commitments.

Concurrent with their grants for public libraries, Mr. Carnegie and the Corporation financed 108 library buildings on college campuses.

After Mr. Carnegie's death, the Corporation was restructured. Elihu Root became chairman of the board and the president was a salaried chief executive. James R. Angell was appointed president in 1920 and resigned in 1921 to become president of Yale University.

In that brief period large commitments were made for academic buildings and endowments which were to be a drain on the Corporation's income for many years to come.

Following Mr. Angell's resignation, Henry S. Pritchett, president of The Carnegie Foundation for the Advancement of Teaching, was acting president of the Corporation for 2 years.

A new era began when Frederick P. Keppel became president in 1923. He molded the Corporation's program until his retirement in 1941. The major areas of activity during that period were library service, fine arts, and adult education.

Following a number of studies and conferences on library needs and opportunities, the Corporation in 1926 embarked on a library program which was to cost about $12.5 million or approximately one-sixth of its total income for the next 15 years. Many of its grants, including a $2 million endowment fund, were made to the American Library Association to strengthen its services to the profession and for special projects.

The training of librarians was another need to which the Corporation gave high priority. Mr. Carnegie and the Corporation had made grants to library schools prior to 1926 but after the new program was launched grants totaling $1,896,700 were made for the endowment or support of 17 existing library schools. An endowment of $1 million established the first graduate library school, at the University of Chicago, which received an additional $662,000 for general support and other purposes. Over $100,000 was devoted to fellowships for training Americans in the various library schools and a number of grants were made to provide professional education for librarians in Africa, Australia, and New Zealand.

The development of academic libraries was an important part of the program prior to 1941. In 1928 the Corporation formed the Advisory Group on College

Libraries under the chairmanship of William W. Bishop, then librarian at the University of Michigan. This group devised standards for libraries of liberal arts colleges, was responsible for the preparation, by Charles B. Shaw, of a list of books for such libraries, and selected 83 colleges to receive grants from the Corporation for the purchase of books for undergraduate reading. Other advisory groups in the United States and Canada recommended similar grants to junior colleges, teachers colleges, Negro colleges, land-grant colleges, technological colleges, and colleges and universities in Canada. The Corporation appropriated approximately $2,400,-000 for this series of grants, related administrative expenses, and attendant studies. In addition to this special program for book purchasing, some 30 academic institutions received Corporation grants totaling nearly $2 million for library endowment or development. Assistance was also given to college and university libraries in the British Overseas Commonwealth.

Among small but potentially important grants in the 1930s were those for support of the American Documentation Institute and for several experiments with the use of microfilm.

In the fine arts the Corporation provided support for the American Federation of Arts and for special programs of the College Art Association and many other art organizations. Between 1928 and 1931 it operated a graduate fellowship program to train art teachers and museum directors. It encouraged the teaching of art history by selecting and distributing collections of photographs, books, and color slides. A number of colleges and universities received grants to expand their art departments and art libraries. Sets of music study material were also distributed to colleges, schools, and a few libraries. Organizations such as the National Orchestral Association received continuing support over a number of years. Funds were provided for circulating exhibitions and scholarly publications. In the 1930s museums in both the United States and the Commonwealth were helped to develop educational programs for children and adults. The arts, including music, museums, and allied fields, received nearly $10 million prior to 1941.

The Carnegie Corporation was one of the first foundations to take an interest in adult education. In 1918 it initiated a series of studies of Americanization which included a volume on the education of the immigrant. During Mr. Keppel's presidency, the Corporation spent some $5 million for a variety of projects. The first conference on adult education in the United States was called by Mr. Keppel in 1924. A later meeting resulted in the establishment in 1926 of the American Association for Adult Education (AAAE), which received substantial support from the Corporation through 1941. In 1951 it merged with the Department of Adult Education of the National Education Association of the U.S.A. The AAAE was not only established and supported by the Carnegie Corporation, but it also recommended and administered the majority of grants made during this period for experimental projects, studies, and conferences, including some concerned with library service and the reading habits of adults.

Another organization established by the Corporation, to encourage a particular medium for adult education, was the National Advisory Council on Radio in Education, which was active between 1930 and 1940. It worked primarily to improve the educational programs on commercial stations, and experimented with radio listening groups for adults and special programs for schools.

A landmark study, initiated under Mr. Keppel but not completed until 1943, was the study of the Negro in America directed by Gunnar Myrdal. Mr. Myrdal's comprehensive report was published under the title *An American Dilemma*. Four other books on special aspects of the problem were written by his collaborators and staff members.

After Mr. Keppel's retirement, Walter A. Jessup, President of The Carnegie Foundation for the Advancement of Teaching, was an interim wartime president of the Corporation. He died in office in 1944.

Since 1945 the Corporation has had four presidents: Devereux Josephs (1945–1948), Charles Dollard (1948–1955), John W. Gardner (1955–1967), and the present incumbent, Alan Pifer, who became acting president in 1965 when Mr. Gardner was given a leave of absence to serve as Secretary of Health, Education and Welfare. Mr. Pifer was elected president in May 1967.

The Corporation has always operated with a relatively small staff. When Mr. Keppel became president, he inherited a secretary and a treasurer from Mr. Carnegie. He later added an assistant to the president and these posts comprised the total executive staff, except for an investment office, until 1938. Needless to say, Mr. Keppel relied heavily on outside consultants and advisory committees, and the Corporation officers still do today. The staff has increased gradually to 12 executives; administrative, editorial, secretarial, and other backup personnel brings the total to about 40. The Corporation has always had its offices in midtown Manhattan and now occupies the 38th floor of the ITT building at 437 Madison Avenue.

In addition to handling voluminous correspondence, the officers spend a large portion of their time reading, listening, and traveling. They must be aware of needs and trends, be open to new ideas, and get to know the leaders in the fields in which the foundation operates. Like most foundations, the Corporation concentrates its grants in a few fields at a time, for two major reasons: its limited funds will have more impact if not spread too thinly, and its officers can make competent judgments only when they learn to know a specific area in some depth. Although each officer has certain primary areas of responsibility, the staff is not departmentalized and all proposals which are recommended to the trustees are first read and discussed by the entire executive staff.

The Corporation has an active board of 15 trustees. The full board meets four times a year and the executive committee at least five. Although most grants are made in response to specific proposals, ideas for programs and projects emanate from many sources: the trustees, the staff, and numerous organizations and individuals.

During the post-World War II decade, the emphasis of the Corporation's program was on the social sciences. The Corporation provided, and continues to provide, substantial sums for the administrative expenses and fellowship programs of the Social Science Research Council. It made grants to several universities for research and graduate training in these fields.

The United States entered World War II almost totally ignorant about other parts of the world, with the exception of Western Europe. America's position after this war demanded that the situation be corrected and the Carnegie Corporation, along with some other foundations, began to make grants to universities to develop area study centers where the work of scholars in separate disciplines was brought to bear on a country or region. An outstanding example is the Russian Research Center at Harvard University which the Corporation helped to establish in 1948 and continued to support for some 15 years thereafter.

Most of these area study grants included funds for the purchase of books and magazines to strengthen university library collections. A small grant in 1950 provided initial support for "The Farmington Plan" under which a group of university libraries agreed to specialize in certain world areas so that at least one university would purchase all important publications of a certain country or region and make them available to others by interlibrary loans. Another Corporation grant in 1959 established an Africana section in the Library of Congress in support of the growing interest in Africa on the part of scholars in the United States.

Although the Corporation did not consider libraries a major area of interest after World War II, it continued to make occasional grants. It provided $750,000 toward the building and equipment of the Midwest Inter-Library Center in Chicago (now Center for Research Libraries). Assistance was given to ALA committees for the development of standards for public libraries, school libraries, and state libraries. Film collections in public libraries were encouraged through support of ALA's Film Advisory Service and demonstrations of "film circuits" in Cleveland and Missouri.

The major study financed by the Corporation in these postwar years was the Public Library Inquiry administered by the Social Science Research Council and directed by Robert D. Leigh. A modest experiment in the use of photoclerical processes in libraries led to widespread use of these techniques. More recently a grant of $250,000 to Massachusetts Institute of Technology provided "startup" funds for a major experiment in library technology known as Project Intrex.

The Corporation established the Foundation Library Center (now Foundation Center) in 1955 with a grant of $500,000 and, along with other foundations, continues to support its operation.

In the Commonwealth the Corporation helped to establish the first library school in West Africa, at the University of Ibadan, Nigeria. In 1954 it undertook a special project to send to public and academic libraries in the Commonwealth a collection of books about the United States. The "American Shelf," consisting of 350 volumes, was presented to 250 libraries.

How the human brain acquires, processes, and retrieves information is still somewhat of a mystery but our understanding of the phenomenon has been increased by a number of research projects supported by the Carnegie Corporation and others during the late 1950s and 1960s. The development of the computer has enabled psychologists to simulate certain thought processes and thus learn more about cognition in human beings. Grants for basic research in this field were made in Carnegie-Mellon University; the University of California, Los Angeles; the University of Texas; and Wayne State University. The Corporation also supported the Center for Cognitive Studies at Harvard University. Closely related, but with a greater emphasis on teaching, is the work of Patrick Suppes at Stanford University which has received substantial assistance from the foundation.

Experiments with computer-assisted instruction at the college level have been supported at the University of California, Irvine; at Dartmouth College; and at a number of institutions in North Carolina, the latter coordinated by the Triangle Universities Computation Center.

Although traditionally interested primarily in higher and professional education, the Carnegie Corporation made a number of grants in the 1960s for research and demonstration programs at the preschool level. It planned and shared in the financing of the Children's Television Workshop, which produces "Sesame Street."

Early in 1967 the Carnegie Commission on Educational Television issued its report, *Public Television: A Program for Action,* which resulted in the establishment by Congress of the Public Broadcasting Corporation to be supported by a combination of public and private funds. The Carnegie Corporation gave this new body $1 million in 1968.

From its beginning the Carnegie Corporation has supported research on practically every aspect of the educational system. In the 1950s, however, it undertook a special series of studies which resulted in a large number of books, most of which were published by the McGraw-Hill Book Company in its Carnegie Series on American Education. In 1967 The Carnegie Foundation for the Advancement of Teaching founded the Carnegie Commission on Higher Education with Clark Kerr as executive chairman. The Commission receives its major financing from the Carnegie Corporation.

The predominantly Negro colleges always received a share of Corporation grants but all America realized belatedly that a "share" was not enough to provide truly equal opportunity for students from minority groups. In 1963 the Corporation appropriated $1.5 million to be allocated to the United Negro College Fund and several of its member colleges. A grant of $300,000 in 1966 financed the work of the Commission on Equal Opportunity in the South of the Southern Regional Education Board. The Southern Association of Colleges and Schools received $350,000 to help the predominantly Negro institutions meet accreditation standards. The American Association of Junior Colleges undertook a special project to help its members in the Southern states to improve their services to Negro students. Summer institutes for Negro college teachers and several projects to develop new curricula and teaching materials were supported by Corporation grants. Funds were made available to national scholarship and fellowship programs specifically for Negro, Puerto Rican, Mexican-American, and American Indian students. Several universities received grants for graduate fellowships for minority groups.

The Corporation's program in the Commonwealth since 1959 has been concentrated primarily on strengthening educational institutions in the developing African countries. A major study of postsecondary education in Africa, made by a commission headed by Sir Eric Ashby, was financed by the Corporation in 1960. Since then teacher education and educational research have been emphasized. The Corporation has established or supported Institutes of Education in African universities, and financed the Afro-Anglo-American Teacher Education Program which had its headquarters at Teachers College, Columbia University. Other central services for African and other overseas universities supported by the Corporation are the Overseas Liaison Committee of the American Council on Education and Overseas Educational Service, a division of Education and World Affairs.

Among other major interests of the Corporation, current or historical, are international communication, expressed chiefly through the Institute for International Education and the Corporation's own Commonwealth travel grant program; humanistic studies, primarily through support of the American Council of Learned Societies; and improvement of state and local government. In the latter category, experiments with data collection and retrieval have been supported by a grant to the San Gabriel Valley Municipal Data System and grants to develop information systems for community health care. The Corporation has also made major grants to other organizations established by Andrew Carnegie, either to increase their endowment or for special projects. In cooperation with The Carnegie Foundation for the Advancement of Teaching, it established the Teachers Insurance and Annuity Association, to which it made grants totaling $17 million between 1918 and 1957.

As of September 30, 1969, the Carnegie Corporation has spent $398,366,985 from income for the advancement and diffusion of knowledge.

FLORENCE ANDERSON

CARNEGIE LIBRARY OF PITTSBURGH

Pittsburgh, Andrew Carnegie's home city, was the first one for which he offered to erect a library building if the municipality would furnish the land and assume the cost of operation—the formula that became standard in all of his later offers of buildings. The offer was made in 1881, but Pittsburgh had to await legislation authorizing it to use tax funds for library services, and it was not until 1890 that the offer could be accepted.

The then independent city of Allegheny, across the Allegheny River from downtown Pittsburgh, now Pittsburgh's North Side, was empowered to accept Mr. Carnegie's offer of 1886 at once and did so. The Carnegie Free Library of Allegheny was opened February 13, 1890, and thus became the first municipally owned and operated "Carnegie Library" (see Figure 1). It is now the Allegheny Regional Branch of Carnegie Library of Pittsburgh.

Pittsburgh's own building was opened November 5, 1895. It housed the library,

FIGURE 1. *Allegheny Regional Branch, Carnegie Library of Pittsburgh, formerly Carnegie Free Library of Allegheny. (Courtesy Carnegie Library of Pittsburgh.)*

a 2000-seat music hall, an art gallery, and a museum of natural history. It was soon outgrown, and the greatly enlarged building, as it stands today, was opened in 1907. It covers four and one-half acres, and provides fourteen acres of floor space on all floors (see Figure 2). The cost of reproducing it today is estimated at $30 million.

It was located at the entrance to Schenley Park, three miles from the business district, because at that time attractive surroundings, quiet, and natural light were thought to be paramount factors in locating a library. The University of Pittsburgh and Carnegie Institute of Technology (now Carnegie-Mellon University) later chose nearby sites, making the area the educational center of the city.

Pittsburgh offered the advantages of a new and well financed library, in which services and methods—the best that were known at that time—could be introduced. These conditions attracted some of the nation's most promising librarians, who accepted the challenge to give Pittsburgh the model public library of 1895.

Among the early directors were two future presidents of the American Library Association: Edwin H. Anderson and Harrison W. Craver. Mr. Anderson later became director of the New York Public Library, as did Franklin F. Hopper, an early order-librarian. Mr. Craver went on to become director of the United Engi-

FIGURE 2. *Carnegie Library of Pittsburgh and Carnegie Institute.*

neering Center of New York. Miss Margaret Mann was perhaps the best known cataloger of her time. Miss Frances Jenkins Olcott and Miss Elva S. Smith were pioneer children's librarians of the first rank. Miss Effie L. Power became a recognized authority on school library services. Elwood H. McClelland became widely known as a science and technology librarian. These librarians, and other staff members, set standards of service that have served as basic guidelines throughout the years.

The library grew rapidly. Five branches, all gifts of Mr. Carnegie, were opened between 1898 and 1900; three additional ones, by 1910. Also by 1910 the book collection had grown beyond 300,000 volumes, and circulation exceeded 1 million.

The library soon became widely known through its publications. The *Classified Catalogue* (1895–1916) recorded all acquisitions and was used throughout the English-speaking world as a guide to classification and cataloging. *Rules for Filing Cards in a Dictionary Catalogue* went through many editions. The *Technical Book Review Index* was published by the library from 1917 through 1928; it is now a publication of the Special Libraries Association. The *Review of Iron and Steel Literature* first appeared in 1919, and has since been published annually.

In its earlier years Carnegie Library was the recognized leader in services to children, due largely to the Training School for Children's Librarians, established by the library in 1901. At a time when other library schools gave scant attention to work with children, this school gave instruction in this one field only. In 1916 it became the Carnegie Library School, with a broadened curriculum but with a continuing strong emphasis on children's service. It was an integral part of Carnegie Institute of Technology from 1930 until 1962. It was then transferred to the University of Pittsburgh and is now that university's Graduate School of Library and Information Sciences which continues, as one of its major specializations, library work with children and young people.

The Carnegie Free Library of Allegheny continued as a separate institution until 1956, when it was merged with the Pittsburgh library system, thus bringing unified service throughout the city.

In the same year the library contracted with the County Commissioners to extend free borrowing privileges to all residents of Allegheny County. Three bookmobiles cover those parts of the country that are remote from a Pittsburgh branch library. Regional reference centers, chiefly for the use of students, and located at strategic points in the county outside Pittsburgh have been proposed. Funds for the establishment of one such unit—a "pilot plant"—have been allocated.

The library's service area was further extended by the State Library Code of 1961, which divided the state into 27 library districts. Pittsburgh was designated the District Library Center for Allegheny County and part of an adjoining one. District library centers in Pennsylvania are service, not governing, agencies. They offer interlibrary loans, advisory services, and workshops for the staffs and trustees of smaller libraries, of which there are fifty in the district.

The State Library Code also designated four of the state's largest libraries as Resource Centers, each one to serve the libraries of the state in the fields of its greatest strength. Carnegie Library was named Resource Center for science and technology. Its specialization in these fields began in 1900, and the Science and Technology Department was formally organized in 1902. It is believed to be the first such department in any municipal library. It started with a gift of $20,000 from Mr. Carnegie. Low prices at that time enabled the library to purchase a large number of complete sets of basic journals and transactions.

The department's own book funds are supplemented by the income from an endowment fund of $358,000 raised by the Pittsburgh Section of the American Chemical Society. Substantial periodic gifts from the Association of Iron and Steel Engineers enable it to maintain a virtually complete collection on iron and steel. The department's aim is to provide information in the pure and applied sciences, with emphasis in industrial technology, especially chemistry, and metallurgy. Teletype, photocopier, photostat, and Xerox equipment speed information to the libraries of the state.

Other specialized subject departments are: Pennsylvania, organized in 1928; Art, 1930; Business Branch, 1930; Music, 1938. All departmental and the general reference collections are strong enough to support intensive research.

The Pittsburgh Photographic Library contains about 30,000 photographs, all indexed, of Pittsburgh's past and present. The Snowdon slide collection includes 49,219 classified slides on a variety of subjects.

Carnegie Library's services also extend beyond the county limits in providing books for the blind and films. Its Library for the Blind, started in 1907, is now operated under contract with the State Library, and serves the western part of Pennsylvania. A supplementary contract with the West Virginia Library Commission extends its services to the blind of that state. The Regional Film Center, also operated under contract with the State Library, supplies films to the libraries of western Pennsylvania.

Informal cooperation among the libraries of the city was initiated by Carnegie Library in 1947, and developed into the incorporation of the Pittsburgh Regional Library Center in 1967. Membership is open to public, academic, and special libraries of the area. Its purposes are to improve the information-handling capabilities of the libraries; to help solve research, administrative and service problems; and to coordinate local efforts with larger library and information systems elsewhere. With support from a grant from a local foundation, the Pittsburgh Regional Library Center was organized by Thomas L. Minder. Its continued operation is financed by the member libraries. Its first task was to supervise the automating of the Pittsburgh Union List of Periodicals.

Pittsburgh's school libraries are operated cooperatively by the Board of Public Education and Carnegie Library under a contract first adopted in 1916.

Branch libraries include the Allegheny and East Liberty regional branches, the downtown Lending and Business branches, and thirteen neighborhood branches. There are a city bookmobile, three county bookmobiles, and a children's book van which give saturation coverage in underprivileged districts.

At the end of 1968, the book collection numbered 2,136,375 volumes; circulation for the year was 4,381,625; total expenditures were $4,037,725; and the staff, excluding the maintenance force, totaled 610 (479 in equivalent of full-time).

RALPH MUNN

CARUSO

CARUSO is an acronym for a series of conversational and reactive user-oriented search operations that have been developed at the Knowledge Availability Systems Center at the University of Pittsburgh since 1967 as part of a continuing effort to discover user-interaction patterns which are effective in on-line retrieval systems.

The programs are written in PIL (Pittsburgh Interactive Language) (1), a JOSS-like interpretive language, and in CATALYST (2), a capable CAI (Computer Assisted Instruction) language which interfaces with PIL. They operate under PTSS (University of Pittsburgh Time Sharing System), implemented on the IBM 360 Model 50, and use 8 to 32k core memory. Most operate on any small files containing from ten to more than 100 documents in an indexed sequential organization of variable length records. The semi-interactive program (see below) is an exception; it operates only on the file of infrared spectral data prepared by the Sadtler Research Laboratories of Philadelphia.

The IBM 2741 typewriter console and the Sanders 720 display scope are used as input/output stations at various locations on the campus.

Four basic program types comprise the series, and reflect some of the variations of user–system interaction which might be considered practicable with present technology:

(1) The purely "conversational" approach, with verbose tutorial messages or brief prompting messages available as options, and inseparable from the search program itself.

(2) A semi-interactive approach, a variation of (1) above, which incorporated long and short tutorial message schemes with a preliminary search of a subset of the Sadtler tape files of infrared spectral data prior to a search of the complete file.

(3) The generalizable strategy program which teaches the user the basic concepts of Boolean logic, their reduction to symbolic form, and illustrates their application in a tutorial which is separable from the search and output program. The search and output program itself contains extensive diagnostics for errors in the construction of the symbolic strategy statement.

(4) The tutorial for profile construction which teaches principles of logical coordination of terms, but does not attempt to introduce symbolic representation of the search strategy.

The development of the programs was heuristic; no controlled experimental testing (with one exception, see Ref. 3) has been attempted since no rigorously definable principles of the interactive processes have been isolated. Conclusions drawn to date, based on development and use of the four programs of the series, can be summarized, however.

The conversational system contains elements of similarity to such programs as System Development Corporation's ORBIT (4) and C. H. Kellogg's CONVERSE guided mode option (5). The user is prompted to describe his search interest and possible logical coordination of search aspects by programmed questions. Feedback is limited to system display of alphabetically-near terms when nonsystem vocabulary is used, and to a report of the number of postings to each search term which does match the stored file. Logical strategies of conjunction, disjunction, and negation are created by the program, using user responses to such questions as "Are there any search terms which MUST occur in a given document to assure you of its value to you?"

Use of the program is long and tedious, even when the shorter message pattern is chosen. Worse, flexibility of search strategies is severely limited, not only by the programmed interaction, but also by the lack of insight into possible uses of that logic gained by the user during operation of the program.

The second program in the series, the semi-interactive search, attempts to remedy this problem by giving more explicit feedback on postings to requested search keys and the possible effects of logical conjunction and disjunction of those keys. The basic pattern of the interaction is still the guided or directed input, however.

This program also attempts to deal with the problem of handling large files in an environment of a small core memory. Since the subject scope of the file is very narrow (infrared spectral data), a sample of its content was selected for a preliminary on-line search. The user perfects his strategy on the basis of results obtained by examination of the file subset and requests completion of the search off-line, if he has not found sufficient information in the on-line search. Such filed requests are batched and searched at times when the system load is reduced; final results are distributed to the user by messenger.

Experience with the "guided" mode of input led us to believe that more flexible searches could be developed by users who understood the construction of the logical statements and the methods of matching stored index vocabulary. Furthermore, log dialogs between system and user could be much shortened if the user had sufficient sophistication to type his strategy in a computer executable form. Symbolic representation of the query terms was adopted; each search term was to be represented as A, B, . . . , while the logical operations of conjunction, disjunction, and negation were to be represented as $+$, $\times$ or $\cdot$, and $-$. It was felt that the compact string of symbols, rather than an unwieldy concatenation of search words, provided a more visually comprehensible entity, and that requirement of this level of abstraction could result in more generalizable understanding of the logical concepts.

A third program type was therefore written. It accepts user query terms in natural form, provides statistical feedback on the density of postings for each term, and displays terms alphabetically close to the query terms, but it requires the user to present his final query version in a simple symbolic form. A separable tutorial program was then prepared which develops the Boolean concepts and gives practice in their use.

Results of a controlled experimental test showed that the on-line program did teach users to create symbolic statements of the form $(A + B + C) \times D - E$, which reflected accurately the intent of the verbal search requests they were given, and which were executable by the search program. Most of the thirty-eight experimental subjects spent over 2 hours at the task, which, while not an inconsiderable period of time, would be well spent if it provided a skill that could be applied in any machine searching situation.

No precedent for this approach was found in the literature. The AUDACIOUS (6) experiment required the user to write complex symbolic statements but did not attempt to instruct him in their creation or use. RECON (7), the National Aeronautics and Space Administration experimental interactive retrieval system, uses simple symbolic logics which can be combined into more complex statements. Since the user group for this system consists of scientists and engineers, there is no felt need for instruction in the logical construction which uses the functionally obvious $+$, $*$, and $-$ to represent the logical sum, product, and difference strategies.

The only reported attempts to create separable tutorials, either superimposed on or preliminary to existing systems, are those of the Mitre Corporation (8), operating as an adjunct to the AESOP data management system, and an instructional subsystem for a military information system reported by Mayer (9).

The idea of separable tutorial and search modules was adopted in a very specialized program for training chemists to construct interest profiles for biweekly searching of the Chemical Abstracts Service's bibliographic tapes. The use of truncation and logical disjunction to cope with uncontrolled system vocabulary was stressed, together with terminology as used by CAS in documenting their services. The program is freely used by university students and faculty as an alternative to the introductory seminars that are irregularly scheduled to introduce new users to CAS services.

REFERENCES

1. The Computer Center, University of Pittsburgh, *PIL/L, Pitt Interpretive Language for the IBM System 360 Model 50,* University of Pittsburgh, February 1969. v.p.

2. Ibid., A Lesson Designer's Guide to CATALYST and the CATALYST/PIL Interface, University of Pittsburgh, October 1969, 47 pp.

3. D. E. Caruso, *An Experiment to Determine the Effectiveness of an Interactive Tutorial Program, Implemented on the Time Sharing IBM System 360, Model 50, in Teaching a Subject-Oriented User to Formulate Inquiry Statements to a Computerized On-Line Information Retrieval System,* Ph.D. Thesis, University of Pittsburgh, 1969, 185 pp.

4. System Development Corp., "Man/Machine: A Contemporary Dialogue," *SDC Magazine,* **10,** 13–19 (September 1967).

5. C. H. Kellogg, *An Approach to the On-Line Interrogation of Structured Files of Facts Using Natural Language,* System Development Corp., Santa Monica, Calif., April 29, 1966, 86 pp. (SP-2431/000/00).

6. R. R. Freeman and P. Atherton, *An Experiment With an On-Line, Interactive Reference Retrieval System Using the Universal Decimal Classification System as the Index Language in the Field of Nuclear Science,* American Institute of Physics, UDC Project, New York, April 25, 1967, 34 pp. (Report no. AIP/UDC-7).

7. D. Meister and D. J. Sullivan, *Evaluation of User Reactions to a Prototype On-Line Information Retrieval System.* Bunker-Ramo Corp., Canoga Park, Calif., October 1967, 58 pp. (NASA CR-918).

8. C. S. Morill, "Computer-Aided Instruction as Part of a Management Information System," *Human Factors, 9,* 251–256 (June 1967).

9. S. R. Mayer, "Computer-Based Subsystems for Training the Users of Computer Systems," *IEEE Trans. Human Factors in Electronics,* HFE-8, 70–75 (June 1967).

ELAINE CARUSO

CASE STUDIES AND CASE METHOD

A case study in librarianship or information science is a descriptive record of circumstances and events relating to the emergence of a particular issue or problem in a specific library or information center. As in other disciplines, the case study in librarianship is *inclusive* in character as a data-recording instrument, in that it incorporates all relevant information or material about the problem-environment that has significance for the issue under consideration. The case study, then, is a vehicle for presenting a problem in the total context of its human and institutional setting.

The case history centers on an individual, group, or institution; the case study centers on a specific issue or problem. The case study usually covers a shorter time span than the case history, and is generally briefer. Case studies may describe and identify actual library situations, or they may disguise the prototypes on which they are based. A case study may be based on a single prototype, or be an amalgam of several related problem situations. The case writer may employ a narrative style exclusively or in combination with dialog, source documents, etc. Although a majority of case studies in librarianship and information science are in written form, other media such as tape, film, or videotape may be utilized for presentation.

Case studies vary in form depending upon the purposes for which they are intended. In general, they are of two types: the research case study and the instructional case study. The *research case study* is employed in many disciplines as a tool of inductive investigation. As a research technique, it makes possible incorporation of multiple variables in the data-gathering process. A body of case studies may serve as the basis for generalization or for the testing of a hypothesis. Such use of case studies is common, for example, in the field of clinical medicine. With a few exceptions, such as Phinney's *Library Adult Education in Action,* the case study has been comparatively little-used for research purposes in librarianship up to this time.

The instructional case study, on the other hand, has been employed widely in recent years in both formal education for librarianship and in in-service and post-graduate training. Two major kinds of instructional case studies may be distinguished. The *exemplary (or illustrative) case study,* as found in *Case Studies in Reference Work* by the British library educator, Denis Grogan, and in S. R. Ranganathan's *Reference Service,* is intended either to provide a model of excellent (or less than excellent) practice or to illustrate a general principle. Exemplary and illustrative case studies appear to have been employed thus far in library education chiefly to supplement more familiar instructional methodologies such as lectures, readings, and examination of source materials, rather than as a substitute for these.

In the United States, the emphasis in the past twenty years has been on the development and utilization of a different type of instructional case study, which may be termed the *problem case study.* The problem case study is like the research case study and the exemplary case study in that it presents a specific issue or instance in a particularized library setting. It differs from these other types of case studies in being intended primarily for the purpose of posing a problem effectively, rather than for the purpose of either providing a basis for generalization or illustrating a principle. Accordingly, the facts are ordered in a problem case study so as to point up the central issue in the form of a question that must be answered, a crisis that must be resolved, or a decision that must be made. Once the central issue has been clearly presented in its individualized library setting, the problem case study is complete and ready for use instructionally.

Problem case studies are employed in courses taught by the case method of instruction. The case method of instruction has emerged in American higher education in the twentieth century as a partial or complete substitute for the lecture-textbook-required reading method in several disciplines. The case method should not be confused with casual or incidental use of case studies to supplement traditional lecture method, content-centered instruction. Case method teaching is not primarily content-centered in character. It does not emphasize transmission of a body of information from teacher to student. The case method is a type of problem-centered instruction where the student is judged, not in terms of the ability to reproduce a body of factual material on demand, but chiefly or solely in terms of the ability to produce viable and defensible solutions to very specific problems posed in case study form. In addition to its use of problem case studies as the chief vehicle of instruction, the case method of teaching is also distinguished by a strong emphasis on independent decision making. This normally involves a choice by the student between two or more alternate solutions to a case problem. Thus, an essential requirement of the problem case study is that it state a problem in such a way that at least two different solutions are possible. A problem to which there is only one acceptable solution, or a question that has only one possible correct answer, is not suitable for presentation in problem case study form.

The distinction between content-centered and problem-centered instruction is crucial to understanding the rationale of the case method. A major objective of case method teaching is to liberate the student from dependency on the teacher and the textbook, by developing the ability to identify, analyze, judge, and resolve problems independently. Case analysis demands a highly disciplined research methodology wherein the student must determine independently the amount and kind of information needed to make an adequate response to a case problem, locate all pertinent data, and present and defend a solution under the rigorous scrutiny of other students and the instructor.

The origins of case method instruction lie in the field of legal education, where it was introduced late in the nineteenth century. It subsequently spread to medical education, and was later adopted widely in other professional curricula in the United States and overseas, including business administration, public administration, and education. More recently, problem case studies and the case method have been employed instructionally in such diverse fields as the teaching of human relations, government, and administration of physical education and school athletic programs. Outside of law and medicine, perhaps the best-known use of the case method is in the graduate professional curriculum at the Harvard Business School.

The earliest systematic use of the case method in library education, by contrast with mere addition of illustrative or exemplary case studies to courses or texts that were basically content-centered in character, appears to have been at Simmons College School of Library Science in the early 1950s, under Kenneth R. Shaffer. Modifying and adapting the case method approach then in use at the Harvard Business School, and incorporating an adversary system borrowed from legal education for classroom presentations of case analyses, Shaffer fashioned a series of problem-centered courses in library administration. In 1956, he received a grant from the United States Steel Foundation for preparation of further case studies in library administration. Four collections of such cases, written by Shaffer, have been published since 1960. In 1968, a large collection of case studies in library administration was issued by Mildred H. Lowell of the Graduate Library School at Indiana University, these having been compiled, in part, under a grant from the Council on Library Resources.

The popularity and success of case method instruction in library administration led to experiments in the application of problem-centered techniques to other areas of the graduate library school curriculum. At Simmons College, the author of this article has adapted the case approach to the requirements of an introductory course in reference method. Kenneth F. Kister of Simmons and Thomas P. Slavens of the University of Michigan have subsequently extended variants of the case method into the subject literature portion of the library education curriculum. Published collections of problem case studies now exist in both general reference method and policy, and in subject reference work and materials selection in social science literature. Work currently in progress at Simmons College and other library schools in the United States includes both development and testing of case materials in the humanities and science literatures, and experimentation with case studies and the case method of instruction in such diverse curricular areas as machine applications in libraries, organization of technical services, and school library/media center administration. In summary, the case method of instruction appears at present to be well established and widely accepted as a teaching technique in library administration in American library schools, and to be generally recognized as readily adaptable to instruction in other curricular areas, either in combination with, or as a substitute for, more familiar methodologies.

The case method offers some distinct advantages over traditional approaches in library education. If librarianship is correctly described as an *applied* discipline, then its general principles become meaningful chiefly in their application. The case study has the advantage of presenting professional problems in their total environmental context to students, thus more closely simulating the world of practice, where a multiplicity of complex variables influence professional decisions. With the case method, the emphasis in instruction shifts from mastery of a body of material for its own sake to problem solving through adaptation and modification of general principles of library and bibliographic management in the context of specific library situations. The case method aims to replace perfectionism with realism, and to discriminate carefully between ideals and realities in professional practice.

Case method instruction places a heavy burden of independent decision making directly upon the individual student. Adjustment to the method is often difficult for students whose previous academic experience has failed to prepare them psychologically for a classroom environment where there are no "right answers" that can be predicted in advance. There is a general need, both in library education and in other disciplines where case method instruction is utilized, for further objective study of both the educational and psychological consequences and effects of problem-centered instruction. There is also a need for descriptive studies in which the many individualized approaches to case method instruction are identified and compared, since it is clear that teachers will vary considerably in their manner of using case materials, just as there are innumerable individual variations on the lecture method. Finally, there is a need to produce instructional case studies in far greater numbers than exist at present, and to enlarge the body of available case materials, so that those wishing to experiment with case method instruction may draw readily upon the work of other case writers. Plans for establishment of a center for case studies in librarianship, comparable to the Case Clearing House at Harvard, which collects and distributes cases in business administration, are now under consideration at Simmons College.

In addition to the use of case studies and the case method in formal education for librarianship, the case technique has been employed widely in recent years in a variety of formal and informal programs of continuing education for librarianship. Among the more interesting of these were the problem case studies emanating from the Advanced Seminar for Library Administrators held at the Graduate School of Library Service at Rutgers University in 1956. Eight of these case studies with accompanying analyses, based on actual current problems in academic and research libraries, are included in Metcalf's *Studies in Library Administrative Problems.*

In 1961–1962, a case method approach was employed in a middle-management seminar for librarians from eight countries of Europe, Asia, and Latin America conducted by the School of Library Science at Simmons College, under sponsorship of the American Library Association and the U.S. Department of State. The Special Libraries Association and the Medical Library Association are among national professional organizations which, since 1960, have utilized case studies in conference settings. Case studies are also being used extensively at the present time in workshops, institutes, and local or regional programs of in-service training for both professional and nonprofessional library and information center personnel. Because the case study affords a focal point for application of general principles, and a common basis for discussion among a group of individuals with differing backgrounds of experience and varied points of view concerning professional issues, it seems particularly well suited to postgraduate continuing education and in-service training.

SELECTED BIBLIOGRAPHY

I. THE CASE STUDY IN RESEARCH

Good, Carter V., *Introduction of Educational Research,* 2nd ed., Appleton, New York, 1963, Chapter 7.

Hillway, Tyrus, *Introduction to Research,* 2nd ed., Houghton Mifflin, Boston, Mass., 1964, Chapter 16.

Phinney, Eleanor, *Library Adult Education in Action: Five Case Studies,* American Library Association, Chicago, 1956.

II. THE CASE METHOD OF TEACHING

Andrews, Kenneth R., ed., *The Case Method of Teaching Human Relations and Administration,* Harvard Univ. Press, Cambridge, Mass., 1960.

Copeland, Melvin T., *And Mark an Era: The Story of the Harvard Business School,* Little, Brown, Boston, 1958.

Galvin, Thomas J., "The Case Technique in Education for Reference Service," *J. Educ. for Librarianship,* 3, 231–263 (Spring 1963).

Galvin, Thomas J., "A Case Method Approach in Library Education," in *Proc. Conference on Library School Teaching Methods: Courses in the Selection of Adult Materials,* Graduate School of Library Science, Univ. of Illinois, Sept. 1968 (in press).

Hewitt, Roy, "Case Studies and Their Place in Education for Librarianship," *Lib. World,* 69, 8–10 (July 1967).

McNair, Malcolm P., ed., *The Case Method at the Harvard Business School,* McGraw-Hill, New York, 1954.

Shaffer, Kenneth R., "The Case Method in Library Education," *Coll. and Research Libs.,* 19, 487–490 (Nov. 1958).

Shaffer, Kenneth R., "Personnel Administration: The Case Method of Teaching," *Bull. Med. Lib. Assoc.,* 53, 546–551 (Oct. 1965).

Sherwood, Frank P., and William B. Storm, eds., *Teaching and Research in Public Administration: Essays on the Case Approach,* School of Public Administration, Univ. Southern California, Los Angeles, 1960.

III. COLLECTIONS OF CASE STUDIES IN LIBRARY SCIENCE

Galvin, Thomas J., *Problems in Reference Service,* Bowker, New York, 1965.

Grogan, Denis, *Case Studies in Reference Work,* Archon Books, Hamden, Conn., 1967.

Kister, Kenneth F., *Social Issues and Library Problems,* Bowker, New York, 1958.

Lowell, Mildred H., *The Management of Libraries and Information Centers* (3 vols.), Scarecrow Press, Metuchen, N.J., 1968.

Metcalf, Keyes D., *Studies in Library Administrative Problems,* Graduate School of Library Service, Rutgers—The State Univ., New Brunswick, N.J., 1960.

Ranganathan, S. R., *Reference Service,* 2nd ed., Asia Publishing House, New York, 1961.

Shaffer, Kenneth R., *Twenty-five Cases in Executive-Trustee Relationships in Public Libraries,* Shoe String Press, Hamden, Conn., 1960.

Shaffer, Kenneth R., *Twenty-five Short Cases in Library Personnel Administration,* Shoe String Press, Hamden, Conn., 1960.

Shaffer, Kenneth R., *The Book Collection,* Shoe String Press, Hamden, Conn., 1961.

Shaffer, Kenneth R., *Library Personnel Administration and Supervision,* 3rd ed., Shoe String Press, Hamden, Conn., 1968.

Slavens, Thomas P., ed., *Library Case Studies in the Social Sciences,* Campus Publishers, Ann Arbor, Mich., 1967.

Thomas J. Galvin

CASE WESTERN RESERVE UNIVERSITY, SCHOOL OF LIBRARY SCIENCE

During the early years of the present century, when leading librarians were discussing the educational needs of the profession, they were responding to a growing awareness that the old "on-the-job training" sponsored by the larger public libraries would no longer meet existing needs, and that universities might well assume some responsibility for library education that could profit from affiliation with an academic environment. In the vanguard of this movement was William Howard Brett, librarian of the Cleveland public library, who urged Charles F. Thwing, president of Western Reserve University, to establish such a school at his institution. Accordingly, President Thwing, who was then on the board of advisors to Andrew Carnegie, proposed to this distinguished library benefactor that funds be made available for the establishment of a library school at Western Reserve University. Carnegie made this first grant for library education in February 1903. The original gift of $100,000 was increased in 1923 by a grant of $25,000 from the Carnegie Corporation of New York, in recognition of the school's success.

Brett was appointed the first dean of the new school, a position he held until his untimely death in an automobile accident in 1918. The basic planning and operation of the school were begun by Electra C. Doren, followed in 1905 by Julia M. Whittlesly, who was to play a leading role in the formation of the Association of American Library Schools, and Alice S. Tyler. Bessie Sargeant Smith was acting director in 1912, and Miss Tyler became director in 1913, although she was not given the title of dean until 1925. Thus, Miss Tyler's regime encompassed the period of growth in American library education that followed the publication of the Williamson report of 1923, the establishment of the ALA Board of Education for Librarianship, and the beginning of ALA accreditation of library schools.

Also it was under Miss Tyler that the school awarded, in 1927, its first bachelor of library science degree. During these early years the faculty of the school included, in addition to those already mentioned, such distinguished people as Linda A. Eastman, Azariah S. Root, Harriet E. Howe, Effie L. Power, Bertha R. Barden, and Thirza E. Grant. Among the members of the first graduating class of 1904 were Ernest J. Reece and Carl Vitz.

Miss Tyler retired as dean in 1929 and was succeeded by Herbert S. Hirshberg, previously state librarian of Ohio and director of the Akron public library, who was appointed dean of the school and director of the university library. He remained in office as dean for 15 years, through the dark days of the Depression, when not only the school but the entire university was struggling with serious financial problems. During this period, however, the school achieved graduate status, first through the introduction of a program in training for high school library service, for which the baccalaureate degree was a requirement. This requirement was extended to all programs, except for outstanding students of Adelbert and

Mather Colleges, who were allowed to enroll in the library school as seniors in absentia. Also, in 1930, during Dean Hirshberg's administration, the program in library service for children was expanded under Helen Martin Rood to include a sixth year leading to a master's degree. Both this sixth-year program and the undergraduate program were phased out in the late 1930s. The program in school library service continued as a specialization from 1929 on, under the guidance of a succession of outstanding leaders, including Edith Cook, Lucile F. Fargo, Margaret Cleaveland, Helen B. Lewis, Hannah Hunt, and, currently, John A. Rowell. Dean Hirshberg also inaugurated a summer-session program that enabled a student to earn the degree through attendance at successive summer sessions.

Thirza E. Grant, who had been acting dean for a year, was appointed dean in 1944, a position she occupied until the summer of 1952, when the present incumbent, Jesse H. Shera, came from the faculty of the Graduate Library School of the University of Chicago to assume the deanship. At the present time the school has two associate deans, Margaret Kaltenbach and A. J. Goldwyn; the latter also serves as director of the school's Center for Documentation and Communication Research.

In its first catalog the officers of the school stated that its purpose was "to give a thorough course in training for library work. While, as is eminently proper in a school so established and endowed, special attention will be given to training for work in our rapidly developing system of public libraries, the interests of college, endowed, and other libraries will not be neglected." There seems good reason for believing that in the minds of the school's early administrators the institution was seen primarily as an agency for the preparation of staff to serve in the Cleveland Public Library, and, indeed, a program of supervised practice work in that library was a feature of the school's program.

It was not long, however, before the curriculum was expanded and the school began to draw students not only from other sections of the country, but from abroad as well. Today it is truly international in scope, though like most library schools, the majority of its students are attracted from its own and contiguous states. In the more than 65 years of its existence the nineteenth-century idea of "training" for library work has yielded to belief in the need for professional education for, as the current catalog says, those "who are competent in subject knowledge, qualified for positions of responsibility, and aware of the social importance of libraries." Research in library and library-related problems was unthought of in 1903, but today it is a major activity of the school's faculty and its advanced students.

In 1948, Western Reserve, along with many other accredited library schools, abolished the degree of bachelor of science in library science and instituted the master's degree in the same field. Initially a master's paper was required of all students but, largely because of the growth of the student body, this requirement was dropped as impractical some ten years later. Students may, however, elect to prepare a minor research study if they so desire. Also in 1948, a course in research methods was added to the curriculum, and for a time provision was made for graduates of the school to convert the fifth-year bachelor's degree to the new master's degree.

Library service to children has been a serious interest of the school virtually ever since it was established, but in 1920 an agreement was reached between the school and the Cleveland Public Library by which the former assumed responsibility for the training program in children's work that the public library had been operating since 1909. A special department of the school was established at that time to provide an extended program in children's work. The new activity was under the supervision of Effie L. Power, Director of Children's Work in the Cleveland Public Library, and provided an unusual opportunity for students to engage in practice work in the library while taking courses in the school. Though independent, this program was closely associated with the training of school librarians, then under the direction of Annie Spencer Cutter, also of the public library staff. The school has maintained this specialization in work with children throughout its subsequent history, under the direction of such distinguished children's librarians as Harriet G. Long, Elizabeth H. Gross, Dorothy Broderick, and Arlene Mosel. Today, it and the Graduate School of Library and Information Sciences at the University of Pittsburgh are the only schools in the country offering such an advanced specialization.

The Cleveland Public Library followed the lead of its sister institution in Newark, New Jersey, by establishing a Business Information Bureau. Rose L. Vormelker was its founder and for many years its director. During the deanship of Herbert Hirshberg, the need for a course in special librarianship at Western Reserve that would be somewhat comparable to Linda Morley's offering at Columbia University was recognized. In the late 1930s Miss Vormelker instituted such a course. She withdrew from the school in 1965 to accept a combined library and library school position at Kent State University, but her course has been continued by Jessica Melton.

The trend at Western Reserve toward the new nonconventional methods of librarianship can be traced to a course in abstracting and indexing first offered during the academic year 1949–1950 by Helen M. Focke. The following year the title of the course was changed to "Documentation" and its content was extended to include punched-card techniques and other innovations in the storage and retrieval of recorded information. This was the first course of its kind in the country.

The curriculum of the school is under constant review and revision. Two important changes have been made in recent years. The appointment of John Rowell, formerly school library supervisor for the state of Pennsylvania, has made possible a substantial expansion of the program for the education of school librarians, including a sixth year of study. He has also contributed substantially to the research and professional activities of the faculty. In the summer of 1966 the school inaugurated its "Foundations" course, a six-semester-hour course of intensive introduction to all phases of librarianship, required of all entering master's degree candidates. The course, of which Helen Focke and Margaret Kaltenbach were the architects, requires the services of all members of the faculty in presenting an organized overview of librarianship with a sound introduction to its basic principles and techniques. The course has yielded a variety of benefits. It provides the student with a substantial foundation for his advanced study and ensures that all students come to subsequent programs with a common background of professional knowledge. It is of material assistance in helping the student to reach a decision, if he has not already done so, as to the area of librarianship in which he wishes to specialize, or even if he is at all interested in a library career. It makes possible the review and revision by the faculty of all other courses so that by consolidating the basic elementary skills, more time can be devoted to advanced study. It has also been of substantial assistance in developing a community of understanding among the several members of the faculty for each other's subject specializations.

Center for Documentation and Communication Research

The appointment of Jesse H. Shera as dean brought to the school a man who, during his years at the University of Chicago and earlier at the Library of Congress and at the Office of Strategic Services, had been very involved with the rising field of documentation. He was one of the active participants in the reconstitution of the American Documentation Institute after the end of World War II. In the spring of 1955, with the support of the faculty of the school and President John S. Millis of Western Reserve University, he established the Center for Documentation and Communication Research as a department of the school. James W. Perry and Allen Kent came to this new organization as director and associate director, respectively. Both men had been heavily involved in research in the nonconventional methods of information storage and retrieval, first at the Massachusetts Institute of Technology and later at the Battelle Memorial Institute. Margaret E. Egan, who had been engaged in research and teaching in the area of bibliographic organization at the University of Chicago, joined the faculty in the autumn of that same year. More staff, both academic and supportive, was added as the operations of the center developed.

Basically, the responsibilities of the center were twofold: (1) to conduct an intensive program of research in the newly developing nonconventional methods of information storage and retrieval, and (2) to enrich the educational program of the school by introducing new courses and seminars in this area and to provide opportunities for students to become engaged in the research and operational program of the center itself. Shortly after the center was established the American Society for Metals gave it a grant of $75,000 to conduct research on the application of machine methods to organize and abstract the literature of metallurgy. Assistance in the center's research program was also received from such agencies as the National Science Foundation, the Office of Education, the U.S. Air Force, the Union Carbide Corporation, and the National Institutes of Health.

At Western Reserve, James W. Perry refined his theories of semantic factoring, a form of linguistic analysis applied to scientific literature and semantic codes, and continued work on the use of "telegraphic abstracts" for machine searching. The entire system, including the semantic code thesaurus, has been published (1). Also, with the aid of the center staff, Perry built a prototype of a mechanical searching selector, an elaborate system of electric relays activated by punched

FIGURE 1. *Prototype searching selector built at the Center for Documentation and Communication Research, Case Western Reserve University.*

paper tape that not only proved the validity and practicability of Perry's theories, but also was used in an actual literature searching service operated by the center for the American Society for Metals (see Figure 1). This machine aroused the interest of the Computer Division of the General Electric Co., which, after a protracted period of study and experimentation, devised a modified form of the G-E 225 general-purpose computer for machine literature searching. This mechanism, supplemented by a substantial amount of auxiliary equipment, is still in use in the school.

Publishing and Related Activities

Over the years the research program of the center and the school has generated a substantial body of published reports and related materials. For examples, see Refs. 2 to 5. With the cooperation of the American Society for Metals and educational television station WQED of Pittsburgh, the center also produced a 15-

minute motion picture in color, "The Metals Information Center of Tomorrow," which featured the Western Reserve system of telegraphic abstracting and the prototype searching selector.

In January 1956, the center sponsored a conference on "The Practical Utilization of Recorded Knowledge," the object of which was to bring together a substantial number of representatives from a wide variety of academic disciplines, librarians, and people from business and industry to consider the growing problem of controlling the recorded knowledge that advances in science and technology were generating. The audience numbered some 700, and the proceedings were published that same year (6). All registrants to the conference were sent a series of working papers before the meetings. These papers served to stimulate discussion and to prepare all those present for active participation in the program.

The conference itself, which lasted 3 days, was addressed to such areas of concern as the present state of the documentation art, requirements, methods, and problems; programs for the future; cooperation; and the definition of areas of needed research. These deliberations also provided some guidelines to the new documentation center in the formulation of its own program of activities, but perhaps the most important contribution was the facilitation of communication among quite diverse and disparate groups of individuals who had never before considered the growing problems raised by the proliferation of recorded knowledge. With this communication came some awareness of "the new librarianship" and the vital role it could play in all areas of political, social, and economic endeavor. It was the first conference of its kind, and although its impact can never be measured in any absolute sense, it certainly was to establish a pattern for many subsequent conferences, not only in Cleveland but elsewhere in the nation.

Several other major conferences sponsored by the school should be mentioned briefly. As a direct outgrowth of its first conference the center sponsored a symposium in 1957 on "Systems for Information Retrieval," the proceedings of which were published (7). In 1959, with the assistance of the Rand Development Corporation, an international conference was held on "Standards on a Common Language for Machine Searching and Translation," and the proceedings were published in 1960 and 1961 (8). This conference brought to Cleveland representatives from all parts of the world—Asia, South America, and Europe—including the Iron Curtain countries. In 1962, at a somewhat smaller conference, the program of the documentation center was reviewed and research then in progress was discussed. The presentations at this meeting were published by the Western Reserve University Press (9).

An invitational conference on "The Future of Library Education," sponsored jointly by the school and the U.S. Office of Education under the direction of Ruth Warncke and Frank Schick, was held in Cleveland in 1962. Its proceedings appeared in the summer issue of the *Journal of Education for Librarianship* that year. This conference was followed in 1964 by a second invitational meeting on "The Education of Science Information Personnel," the proceedings of which, edited by Associate Dean A. J. Goldwyn and Professor Alan Rees, were published by the school in 1965.

Other major monographic volumes are given in Refs. *10* to *19* and include two collections of essays by the dean of the school (*15,16*). Also, since 1966 the documentation center has been compiling, for the National Institute of Arthritis and Metabolic Diseases, the monthly and cumulated annual *Diabetes Literature Index,* published by the Government Printing Office, Washington, D.C.

James W. Perry resigned from the school in 1960 to accept a position with the Numerical Analysis Laboratory of the University of Arizona, and in 1963, Allen Kent was invited to the University of Pittsburgh to become a member of the faculty of the School of Library and Information Science and head of its Knowledge Availability Systems Center. A. J. Goldwyn was made executive director of the documentation center and a short time later was appointed an associate dean. The center has continued its research in nonconventional methods of information retrieval and other aspects of automation, but has, in recent years, broadened its scope to include exploration of library service in a variety of social problems, especially those relating to the inner city and the disadvantaged. Participation in the instructional program of the school, especially at the level of the doctorate, has increased substantially during the past five years. The appointment of James V. Jones as director of the university libraries has also made possible the cooperation of the center with the university library system in developing and testing new methods for the application of automated techniques to library routines and, with the assistance of LaVahn Overmyer, Robert Hazelton, and William Goffman, students will have an opportunity to gain experience with these new techniques in an operating situation. Under the direction of Alan Rees of the documentation center and Robert Cheshier, director of the Cleveland Health Sciences Library, and with support from the National Library of Medicine, an advanced program for the education of medical librarians was inaugurated in 1967. Three visiting scholars, Jacobus Verhoeff of Delft, Robert A. Fairthorne of the Royal Air Force establishment, and A. D. Booth, dean of the College of Engineering at the University of Saskatchewan, contributed greatly to the work of the school.

Doctoral Program

The doctoral program of the school was initiated in 1954, and the first doctorate was awarded in 1959. Under the direction of Dr. Conrad Rawski, the program is research oriented, terminates in the degree of doctor of philosophy in librarianship, and is interdisciplinary, sponsored by both the School of Library Science and the School of Graduate Studies. Its goal is to produce librarians, especially those who anticipate careers in library education, who combine the intellectual attainments and competencies required to earn a Ph.D. with an adequate mastery of present problems, patterns, and practices in librarianship and information science.

Technical requirements (foreign languages, examinations, and the dissertation) for the degree are identical with those for the School of Graduate Studies, by which the degree is awarded, and all candidates must meet the same standards of proficiency demanded of the students in the cognate subject field, or fields, with which librarianship is combined. Provision is also made for students to elect an interdisciplinary program in information science, for which curricula and course work have been developed by Professors Goffman and Booth. Increasing recognition of the school's program within the university community has facilitated the development of curricula in a variety of cognate subject areas that are meaningful not only in terms of subject concentration, but also in terms of library activities and responsibilities pertaining to those subject areas. In addition, new areas of application and new resources have been developed for the information science curriculum, to which the resources of the former Case Institute of Technology have added great strength. All programs are characterized by great flexibility, and throughout allowance is made for effective articulation between study and research in librarianship and in the cognate field; curricular flexibility and interdepartmental dialog are basic. Thus, a ground structure is provided that encourages a maximum of student initiative and free inquiry within a wide spectrum of instructional and research opportunities. The interdisciplinary program in information science encourages study and sophisticated operational implementation of applications throughout the university.

Federation of Case and Western Reserve

On July 1, 1967, the Case Institute of Technology and Western Reserve University were federated to form a single institution, Case Western Reserve University. In the new administrative pattern of the federation, the School of Library Science is recognized as part of the group of social and behavioral sciences, which reflects its increasing orientation in this direction. The new union greatly strengthens the resources of the school by facilitating cooperation between the members of its faculty, students, and research personnel and those involved with the engineering and related programs of the former Case Institute, including its Computing Center and the newly established School of Management. The continuing growth of the student body and the enrichment of the teaching and research programs should ensure that the contribution the school makes over the years to the advancement of education for librarianship will be even greater in the future than it has been in the past.

REFERENCES

1. J. W. Perry, A. Kent, and J. Melton, *Tools for Machine Literature Searching,* Wiley (Interscience), New York, 1958.
2. J. W. Perry, A. Kent, and M. M. Berry, *Machine Literature Searching,* Wiley (Interscience), New York, 1956.
3. R. S. Casey and J. W. Perry, *Punched Cards,* Reinhold, New York, 2nd ed., 1958.
4. J. W. Perry and A. Kent, *Documentation and Information Retrieval,* rev. ed., Western Reserve Univ. Press, Cleveland, 1957.
5. A. Kent, *Textbook in Machine Literature Searching,* rev. ed., Wiley (Interscience), New York, 1962.

6. J. H. Shera, A. Kent, and J. W. Perry, eds., *Documentation in Action,* Reinhold, New York, 1956.

7. J. H. Shera, A. Kent, and J. W. Perry, eds., *Information Systems in Documentation,* Wiley (Interscience), New York, 1957.

8. A. Kent, ed., *Information Retrieval and Machine Translation,* 2 vols., Wiley (Interscience), New York, 1960–1961.

9. *Information Retrieval in Action,* Western Reserve Univ. Press, Cleveland, 1963.

10. J. H. Shera, *Historians, Books and Libraries,* Western Reserve Univ. Press, Cleveland, 1953.

11. J. H. Shera and M. E. Egan, *The Classified Catalog,* American Library Assoc., Chicago, 1956.

12. E. H. Gross, *Children's Services in Public Libraries,* American Library Assoc., Chicago, 1963.

13. D. Broderick, *An Introduction to Children's Work in Public Libraries,* Wilson, New York, 1965.

14. D. Sinclair, *Administration of the Small Public Library,* American Library Assoc., Chicago, 1965.

15. J. H. Shera, *Libraries and the Organization of Knowledge,* Shoe String Press, Hamden, Conn., 1965.

16. J. H. Shera, *Documentation and the Organization of Knowledge,* Shoe String Press, Hamden, Conn., 1966.

17. K. S. Warren and V. A. Newell, *Schistosomiasis: A Bibliography of the World's Literature,* 2 vols., Case Western Reserve Univ. Press, Cleveland, 1967.

18. G. Barhydt et al., *Information Retrieval Thesaurus of Education Terms,* Case Western Reserve Univ. Press, Cleveland, 1967.

19. B. Denison, *Selected Materials in Classification,* rev. ed., Special Libraries Assoc., New York, 1968.

JESSE H. SHERA

CASSIODORUS, FLAVIUS MAGNUS AURELIUS

Flavius Magnus Aurelius Cassiodorus was born about 485 at Scyllacium (now Squillace), of an influential family in southern Italy, a family that had long supplied the Roman imperial civil service with high officials. After a sound formal education in both Greek and Latin, Cassiodorus took a position as personal aide— *consiliarius praefecti*—to his father. By means of his own talents, Cassiodorus rose to the highest positions in government under the Ostrogoth rulers Theodoric, Amalasuentha, Theodahad, and Witigis. In about 537 he retired from civil service, no doubt because of the dissolution of the Ostrogothic kingdom that was taking place. His conversion to the religious life probably took place around this time, for his philosophical and religious works date from these years. It is quite possible that Cassiodorus left for Constantinople on a diplomatic mission around 540, and may have remained there until about 555, when he returned to his family estates in southern Italy and set up his monastic foundation at Vivarium for the systematic study of the Bible and the reproduction of its text and of works pertinent to its study. He spent the rest of his life industriously engaged in these pursuits, living at least to his 93rd year and probably a few years longer.

FIGURE 1. *Flavius Magnus Aurelius Cassiodorus.*

The known works of Cassiodorus include the following. *Laudes* (506), a pane-gyric written and delivered in honor of Theodoric—not extant. *Chronica* (519), a chronological list of important events in Roman history. *Historia Gothorum* (520s or 530s), a history of the Gothic peoples, now extant only in an epitome by Jordanes (551). *Variae epistulae* (538), revision and selection of Cassiodorus's official letters and formulas dictated while in public offices. *Ordo generis Cassio-dororum* (ca. 538), a brief family history, known only in an excerpt called *Anecdoton Holderi. De anima* (538), a brief philosophical work on the soul. *Expositio psalmorum* (538–548), a commentary on the Psalms, revised ca. 560. *Institutiones divinarum et saecularium litterarum* (ca. 560), an annotated, syste-matic bibliography for Bible study with instructions for scribes; final edition com-pleted after 578. *Expositio Epistulae ad Romanos* (ca. 575), a commentary on the *Epistle to the Romans. Codex de grammatica* (ca. 575), a concise grammar for his monks. *Complexiones Apostolorum* (after 578), a commentary on the latter books of the New Testament. *De orthographia* (ca. 578), a collection of excerpts from writers on spelling, said by Cassiodorus himself to have been composed in his 93rd year. Since the majority of his monks could not read Greek, Cassiodorus supervised the translation of Greek works including works of Josephus and the compilation of a Latin church history based on the Greek histories of Socrates, Sozomen, and Theodoret entitled *Historia tripartita.* These translations all date from the Vivarium period; and it can safely be stated that the death of Cassiodorus marks the final demise of Greek in the West.

A careful reading of Cassiodorus's works will reveal an almost professional interest in the technical aspects of books and documents and in their production and preservation. Undoubtedly this interest stemmed partly from his constant association with documents and files during the many years he spent in the imperial civil service, and from his consequent realization of the importance of properly arranged and carefully preserved documents. This interest, of course, carried over into the latter period of his life when his principal endeavor was to build up a library at Vivarium for the systematic study of the Bible. Probably the most influential of his works for library history was the *Institutiones,* consisting of two books principally containing annotated bibliographies of religious and secular works, respectively, for Biblical studies. The work also contains some chapters on scribal techniques. Since the arrangement of the items was systematic, one might say analogically that the later medieval monastic librarian had in it both his "Winchell" and "Dewey" as well as a kind of staff manual. Certainly the *Institutiones* was his most widely reproduced work during the Middle Ages, and its widespread influence probably accounts for the preservation of so many of the authors it mentions, both religious and secular. It should be added that the work probably represents the holdings as well as the "shelf" arrangement of the Vivarium library. But the influence of Cassiodorus would probably not have been what it was, if St. Benedict (q.v.) had not insisted upon holy reading in his rule; for it was the monks of the seventh and later centuries—particularly the English—who combined the ascetical ideals of Benedict and the scholarly prescriptions of Cassiodorus and formed the great libraries of Fulda, Jarrow, York, etc. It might be noted that a number of the original manuscripts of Vivarium are still extant and are listed in the work of Cappuyns.

BIBLIOGRAPHY

Cappuyns, D. M., "Cassiodore," in *Dictionnaire d'histoire et de géographie ecclésiastiques,* Vol. 11, Letouzey et Ané, Paris, 1949, pp. 1349–1408.

Courcelle, P., *Les lettres grecques en Occident de Macrobe à Cassiodore,* new ed., Boccard, Paris, 1948, pp. 311–388.

Jones, L. W., *Cassiodorus Senator, an Introduction to Divine and Human Readings, with an Introduction and Notes,* Columbia Univ. Press, New York, 1946; repr. Octagon Books, 1966.

Teutsch, L., "Cassiodorus Senator, Gründer der Klosterbibliothek von Vivarium," *Libri,* 9, 215–239 (1959).

Witty, F. J., *Writing and the Book in Cassiodorus,* University Microfilms, Ann Arbor, 1967. The latest editions of texts and translations of Cassiodorus' works are listed.

FRANCIS J. WITTY

CATALOGING-IN-SOURCE

The Cataloging-in-Source project is the title assigned to a Library of Congress experiment conducted from June 1958 to September 1959 to test the feasibility of publishers printing facsimiles of the Library of Congress cards in their current publications. This would be done by having these titles cataloged in advance by the Library of Congress from page proofs and data sheets provided by the publishers. The hypothesis was that all books could be cataloged once, at a centralized point, using standardized methods. The underlying purpose of the experiment, however, was to test the possibility of a full-scale program of Cataloging-in-Source in terms of financing, technical considerations, and usefulness.

The idea of centralized cataloging is an old one. In 1850 the Royal Commission on the British Museum suggested that Panizzi proceed not only with a catalog of the museum's holdings, but also with a catalog of all works published in the English language or printed in Great Britain and its colonies. William D. Cooley mentioned the process of stereotyping individual titles and pointed out that reduplication of titles could be avoided if each government printed its own catalog and then exchanged the stereotyped titles with the others. In August 1850 Charles C. Jewett, librarian of the Smithsonian Institution, submitted a more detailed plan along the same lines to the American Association for the Advancement of Science. He proposed the printing of a catalog by stereotyping the titles separately and preserving the blocks or plates in alphabetical order to allow insertions of new titles.

A closer approach to the specific concept of Cataloging-in-Source was made by Professor Max Müller, curator of the Bodleian Library. In an anonymous contribution to the March 18, 1876, issue of *The Academy,* he spoke of the waste involved when a hundred librarians each cataloged the same book, and recommended that cataloging slips be printed and exchanged between libraries, particularly the national libraries of Europe, each being responsible for its own national book production. He also suggested the possibility of authors preparing the slips for their own books, which the publisher could include, if libraries could agree on a common form.

The proposal that the cataloging information be actually printed in the book first appeared in the 1870s, a period when librarians were becoming increasingly concerned over the high cost of cataloging. The first suggestion was made in the early months of 1876 by Justin Winsor and by R. R. Bowker, editor of *Publishers' Weekly.* Mr. Winsor suggested that publishers should insert in the books they sent out a bibliographical record of the title, etc., on uniform-sized slips of stiff paper. These would serve the triple purpose of a registry for editors, libraries, and booksellers.

In the same year, C. A. Nelson added that each book published should contain a prepared slip bearing the author's name and the title page in full, carefully arranged as on general catalog cards of libraries. The slips were to be of thin paper and a little smaller in size than the cards used in libraries. When a book thus cataloged was added to a library, the slip could be pasted on a card and placed at once in the card catalog. Extra slips would be provided to be similarly mounted on cards and the necessary subject headings added on top.

A Committee on Publishers' Title Slips was formed in 1877, made up of Winsor, Bowker, and Dewey. Their first report appeared in the *Library Journal* of May 1878, and contained many recommendations, such as preparing a uniform title entry with headings and notes to be furnished to publishers for use in advertising circulars, catalogs, etc., and to journals desiring to use them for book lists. Another recommendation was to furnish to subscribers title slips prepared for immediate use as catalog cards. The slips were to consist of the headings, including title headings, subject headings in order of importance, and class numbers in the decimal system, and the author's name followed by the title entry and descriptive and explanatory notes. The committee proposed to make the New York office of the *Library Journal* and *Publishers' Weekly* a central office for library and book-trade records, but the title slips would be prepared under the supervision of the librarians of Harvard University and the Boston Athenaeum. It was thought essential that to maintain uniformity and to insure that the notes should be purely descriptive, all the slips should be prepared at one central office. Publishers were asked to forward to the office designated the first proof sheets or an advance copy of each book. The headings, title, imprint, and notes were immediately prepared, revised, and put in type, and an electro furnished to the publisher in time for use at the head of the flying sheet usually inserted in books issued, as well as for future use in catalogs. From this plate the catalog slip was then printed on stiff paper and mailed to every library and individual subscribing.

In 1879 R. R. Bowker reported that the first plan of the committee had proved impracticable, partly because all libraries did not use the standard card. Some libraries asked for an edition on thin slips for pasting, and the cost of handling so many individual slips increased the cost beyond the economic margin. The March 15, 1879, *Publishers' Weekly* announced the mailing of the January and February issues of the *Title-Slip Registry* printed on one side only of thin paper for pasting on catalog cards. Publication was planned for the last of each month and subscriptions were set at $1 per week. At the end of 1879 the title of this publication was changed to the *Book Registry,* and the price reduced. Even so the program did not prove sufficiently popular and came to an end in February 1880.

Although the practice of providing catalog information with the books seems to have halted, the idea remained alive. When the Library of Congress began its printed catalog card service in 1901, it was immediately suggested that a card should be distributed with each new book sold, and this suggestion has continued to be put forth to the present day. Some efforts were actually made during the years along this line, chiefly in connection with projects financed by grants from foundations. The most extensive effort of this sort took place during the years 1929–1938 in connection with a series of grants by the Carnegie Corporation to the libraries of 81 American colleges. Individual publishers have from time to time ordered Library of Congress cards in thousands of copies for a particular title and included them in their shipments to purchasers, but besides being costly, the cards could not be prepared by the Library of Congress until after the books had been published and received in the library, and this time lag detracted from their usefulness.

The United States was not alone in experimenting with these programs. For many years the Melbourne firm of F. W. Cheshire & Co. reproduced, in some of its books, catalog cards prepared by the University of Melbourne. There have also been similar attempts in New Zealand and Brazil, and in the USSR many publications contain cataloging data in the form of a colophon. A few agencies of the United States government, among them the Bureau of the Census, the National Advisory Committee for Aeronautics, and the Tariff Commission, have in recent years printed identification statements in certain of their publications.

A renewed interest in the idea of Cataloging-in-Source was supported by a grant from the Council on Library Resources to the Library of Congress in January 1958. Under this grant, Andrew D. Osborn, then assistant librarian of Harvard University, discussed with publishers and librarians some of the problems involved. As a result, he reported a favorable response on both sides and recommended a pilot project to test the feasibility of Cataloging-in-Source. The sum of $55,000 was then made available for a one-year experiment in prepublication cataloging.

The experiment had two main purposes. The first was to test the financial and technical problems involved in cataloging from final page proof and to discover whether such cataloging was feasible from the point of view of the publishers and the Library of Congress. This was to be tested by cataloging 1000 titles from presses of various sizes and types. The Library of Congress agreed to catalog each publication and to supply the publishers with printer's copy for a complete cataloging entry. The publishers were to print this entry in the finished book, on the verso of the title page, in the colophon, or in some other convenient place.

The second purpose of the experiment was to test consumer reaction, particularly the use libraries of various sizes and degrees of specialization would make of the cataloging entry appearing in the books they acquired. Esther J. Piercy of the Enoch Pratt Free Library was appointed director of the Consumer Reaction Survey. A field staff was assigned to investigate the effects in terms of the purchase of catalog cards, the cost of cataloging, the speed with which publications were processed for use, and the methods used to transfer catalog entries from books to card catalogs. The emphasis throughout the experiment was on determining as precisely as possible the conditions that would be required for the successful operation of Cataloging-in-Source.

The early months of the project were spent in securing the cooperation of publishers. The library's staff visited over 300 publishers including commercial firms, university presses, federal and state agencies, and associations. The response varied widely. Some publishers agreed to participate fully in the experiment, others agreed to only a limited and conditional participation, and a large number, although sympathetic to the needs of libraries, could not participate because of technical difficulties. The major difficulty was crowded schedules and the resulting strain on production. Another type of difficulty was illustrated by the situation in state publications. Some states do very little printing, their needs being taken care of by printing firms both within and outside the state. These firms operate on a bid and contract basis, so that the printer could change from year to year. A total of 244 publishers of varying types agreed to participate in the experiment, but only 157 of these had actually forwarded publications for cataloging when the project had ended.

Cataloging began in July 1958 with the processing of 25 titles from 8 publishers and reached its peak in January 1959 with the processing of 233 titles from 86 publishers. When this part of the project was terminated in February 1959, 1203 publications had been completed.

It was clear from the beginning that without the greatest speed in handling the page proofs, Cataloging-in-Source could not be fitted into the time schedules of the publishers. When proof was received, the schedule called for cataloging, printing the catalog entry, and mailing it to the publisher within twenty-four hours after receipt. Accordingly "rush" procedures for cataloging regular books were adapted and stepped up, and the resulting procedures were referred to as "nonstop rush." Each title received was given immediate and individual handling at every stage and hand carried to the succeeding stage. The only point at which there was group handling was in the actual printing of the cataloging copy. Naturally the Library of Congress was unwilling that speed should be allowed to interfere with the quality of the cataloging, except in those cases where cataloging from proof made it inevitable. The catalogers worked no faster and no less carefully on Cataloging-in-Source titles than on any other. Once assigned a title, the catalogers worked steadily on it, carried it to completion, and delivered it by hand to the next person in the chain of operations.

The experiment also tested the feasibility of using cooperative cataloging in Cataloging-in-Source. The Department of Agriculture library cataloged 100 titles published by agencies of the Department. The libraries of the Geological Survey, the Department of Labor, and the Department of Health, Education and Welfare cataloged a total of 116 publications issued by their agencies, and the libraries of the Universities of Illinois, Maryland, and Wisconsin, and of Harvard University cataloged 19 of the publications of their university presses.

The problems involved in Cataloging-in-Source were basically those caused by the experiment itself. It should be emphasized that the cataloger was faced with the task of cataloging something that was not quite complete and was still subject to change. In theory, the proof and data sheet should have presented a complete picture of the finished work, but in many cases they did not. The index was probably the cause of one of the most vexing problems. Production schedules were often such that when the publisher had to go to press with the copyright page, the index was still being set and its paging could not be determined exactly. A partial solution was found by omitting pagination in the proof of the card to be sent to the publisher but including instructions as to how to set the missing section when the index pages were completed. Another problem was that the timing of the project was such that many of the books cataloged were scheduled for publication at the end of 1958. Some of these were not actually published until 1959. In many instances when particular titles were being cataloged, the year of publication had become uncertain or was later changed from that printed on the page proof or the data sheet. There were sometimes other changes on the title page. The title itself seldom was changed but it was not unusual for subtitles and credits for editors, illustrators, and the like to be added, deleted, or changed at the last moment. The catalog entry then appearing in the work was usually not altered by the publisher to show these changes and the Library of Congress was not notified so that the cards could be corrected.

The cataloging that gave the least trouble was that for offset reprint editions when there was already a printed card for the original edition. In such cases, the publisher only had to supply the details of bibliographical differences between the two editions on a special data sheet.

When Cataloging-in-Source was first considered it was anticipated that one difficulty would be occasional dissatisfaction on the part of the authors and publishers with details of cataloging such as choice and form of entry. This was generally not the case. The details of descriptive cataloging created no great problem except that the variation in treatment of pagination was puzzling to many publishers. Questions of choice of entry were also few, but the form of name given in the heading presented more serious problems. Publishers strongly objected to real-name entries for works published pseudonymously or anonymously. Such entries proved to be unacceptable and were not printed in the books themselves. There was also considerable objection from authors on the use of their birthdates in the headings.

When the project was completed, the participating catalogers were asked for their reactions. Though they were sympathetic to the objectives of Cataloging-in-Source, they were unanimous in regarding this type of cataloging as unrewarding and taxing. It was unrewarding because, in spite of their best efforts, the end products was so frequently inaccurate and in Cataloging-in-Source, the error stands forever on the pages of the book. The work was taxing because of the over-all time limit, the necessity for recording the exact amount of time spent on each step, and the special difficulties involved in working with proofs and data sheets. These factors combined to produce a feeling of tension and considerably greater fatigue than regular cataloging. It was questioned whether catalogers could continue to work under such pressure, especially as the number of errors would increase and as a result the catalogers would be even more frustrated.

One of the principal purposes of the experiment was to find out whether Cataloging-in-Source could be performed with sufficient speed to meet the schedules involved in the complicated processes of publishing. Comments received from publishers made it clear that those books which publishers wished to get out at the earliest possible time could not receive Cataloging-in-Source treatment, because the time required for the proofs to be sent to the Library of Congress, cataloged, and returned with a cataloged entry could not be spared.

The experiment was least successful when assessing the accuracy of the end product. The records showed that 615 or 48% of the entries had some discrepancy with the book as published.

At the end of the experiment, when questioning publishers, the interruption of production schedules was reported by a great majority as being a very real problem. Most publishers reported that the problem of design had not been a serious one, although criticisms on aesthetic grounds were frequent. It is almost impossible to make the entry look unobstrusive without drastically changing its form, which would thereby end its usefulness. Estimates as to the average additional cost per title varied widely. About 10% of the publishers replied that there were no additional costs. About 25% incurred only negligible extra costs. By using offset lithography exclusively, it cost nothing to put the cards on a final page of repro proof and slide it under the camera. Most estimates were in the range of between $5 and $25.

Publications prepared from sheets imported from abroad were mentioned as a special problem, and it was also noted that proofs were frequently not available for fiction, juveniles, and a large number of publications that are printed by offset-lithography.

Most of the publishers concluded that although there were a number of serious problems that would have to be solved, most of them would be willing to cooperate in a continuing Cataloging-in-Source program, but only if it provided a useful service to libraries.

Right from the beginning, the anticipated goals for Cataloging-in-Source were getting new books to readers faster, cutting the high cost of cataloging, and providing greater standardization in the identification of books. It was felt that every area of library service would be affected, that the influence would reach beyond a given library into interlibrary relations and services and beyond libraries into the book world generally.

One of the goals of Cataloging-in-Source was furthering bibliographic standardization. The assumption that it would do so accounted for much of the enthusiasm for the service and much of its anticipated use. To achieve complete standardization, it was assumed that cataloging information would appear in each work published in the United States, that the author and title entry so established would be adopted by publishers in their announcements and catalogs, that this entry would be used in trade and bibliographical publications and in reviewing media, that it would be used by writers in preparing bibliographies, that it would be used by the book trade in advertising and billing, and that it would be used by all book people including librarians, in all forms of communication.

There was an assumption on the part of the majority of librarians that the cataloging information would continue to be that supplied by the Library of Congress. The printed catalogs and printed cards already made available bibliographic information for materials cataloged by the Library of Congress in the past. Most important was the fact that Library of Congress cataloging is built on a foundation of long-established and widely followed authority files.

Faced with varying cataloging practices, the Consumer Reaction Survey team attempted to find out how much of the provided cataloging information each library would use. Most librarians working with children wanted the materials used by children cataloged and classified for them. Although unhappy at the time spent in ordering and waiting for Wilson cards, they wanted cataloging like Wilson's:

simpler entries, briefer descriptions, shorter and more appropriate Dewey classifications, appropriate subject headings and annotations. On the other hand, the scholarly users of special collections wanted as much information as possible about the bibliographical and authoritative backing of a work and the most up-to-date technical and specific subject approach. Neither of these extremes could be fully served by the Library of Congress's cataloging, but even special libraries found the Library of Congress entry helpful as a starting place, since adaptation of an existing entry is far simpler than doing the work from the beginning.

To have the catalog information in the book was seen as a help in the selection and acquisition processes. Where selection is made from the book itself, the subject coverage could be found quickly, the authority for the work would be indicated by the main and other added entries, and relationships to other works might be indicated by series and other notes. In checking gifts and blanket orders such information would be equally helpful. When books were received, they could be sorted by a clerk for routing to subject departments or for departmental budget charges.

If publishers, trade and reviewing publications, and bibliographies followed the Cataloging-in-Source form of entry, it was anticipated that order requests might come from selectors with proper catalog entry, order cards could be prepared quickly and correctly, billing and other communications between library and dealer would be clearer, and inadvertent double ordering could be decreased or eliminated.

Public service librarians were as enthusiastic about Cataloging-in-Source as catalogers. They saw it as a possible aid in readers' advisory work since the subject tracings in the book would give a quick survey of the book's coverage while working with patrons. The tracings would also lead to other related material in the catalog. Reference librarians saw the service as a probable means for great improvement in making bibliographies. Writers and students would not have to guess at the author or main entry. Reference librarians were pleased with the idea of the catalog entry appearing in bibliographical works, bibliographies, or references in books or periodicals and the entry printed in the book itself all matching. Not only would they be saved hours of time in searching, they could trust much more checking to clerical assistants and they would feel more secure about giving better service.

For interlibrary loan requests and discussion of cooperative acquisition, much time, confusion, and error would be avoided if all parties to the transaction referred to the materials under the same terms and could easily identify editions. Cooperative acquisition could be extended and improved if agents responsible for locating and distributing material had a quick and easy way of determining its subject, i.e., from the classification numbers or subject tracings in the book. The work on union catalogs, in bibliographic centers, and on union lists and indexes would be considerably faster and more accurate.

The concept of a "cataloger's camera" was presented during the consumer reaction survey, and received an overwhelming response in favor of such equipment from librarians. Such a camera would be a dry-process, inexpensive, simple-to-operate unit, capable of reproducing positive copy directly onto catalog cards, and either enlarging or reducing the copy. The fact that such a camera was not available for use during the Cataloging-in-Source project had no direct bearing on the end result of the experiment. Even if a camera with such capabilities had been perfected within that period, the card printed in the book would still have had to be exact in form, and completely free from error. Other factors negating its usefulness for this purpose would be the obsolescence in subject headings and classification numbers, as well as the adaptation practices of many libraries. As it was, the Council on Library Resources continued to support the development of such a camera after the Cataloging-in-Source project was definitely ended, and by 1967 several models were available and being used by libraries. That these cameras are sometimes referred to as "bibliographers' cameras" indicates their wider application in libraries than just for catalog card copy.

A few bookstores were visited by the surveyors. Most of those saw help for themselves in the Cataloging-in-Source idea. They felt that the classification number and subject tracings might help them arrange their stock and that this information and the author entry would help them in preparing book lists or catalogs and in listing their stock for inventory purposes. They also thought this information would help the sales force in helping the customer to select the book he wanted. Bibliographic standardization was most attractive to them.

In theory, there are three strong arguments for a Cataloging-in-Source program. The first is the immediate availability, in the book itself, of a full catalog entry and the consequent possibility of getting the book into the hands of a reader at an earlier date. The second is the prospective saving in costs to libraries through the elimination of some operations, such as the ordering of catalog cards, and the simplification of other operations including the searching of gift items, checking and recording operations in order work, reporting to union catalogs, and interlibrary loan. The catalog entry in the book would make possible the transfer of some functions from professional to clerical staff, thereby freeing the professional staff for increased service in other areas. The third is the possibility of bibliographical standardization of entries in trade bibliographies, in reviews, in footnotes, in dealers' catalogs, and the like.

There are also strong arguments against such a program. Some of these are as follows:

1. Publishers might not be able to cooperate in a full-scale program.

2. The Library of Congress could not catalog all titles from page proofs with sufficient speed and accuracy.

3. Libraries would probably substitute a new set of time-consuming routines, such as adapting data to local conditions, or operating a camera, for previous procedures at no real gain.

4. The obsolescence of catalog entries would prove to be a major drawback. Names and subject headings could not be changed in the books themselves but would have to be changed in the card catalog.

The experiment demonstrated that the Library of Congress with the aid of a foundation grant and a great deal of overtime could, by an extraordinary effort over a short period of time and at the sacrifice of other work, catalog from page proofs and specification data sheets an average of 11 titles per working day. It was estimated that a permanent full-scale Cataloging-in-Source program would require the cataloging of 30,000 titles a year, at a cost of $750,000 or more. It was further estimated that 2000 of these titles would be publications which the Library of Congress would not otherwise have cataloged, chiefly additional analytical entries and some additional entries for series.

The survey also showed the overwhelming extent to which libraries would adapt the catalog entry to their local requirements rather than using it as given. Because of this, it was apparent that even entries in the format of a catalog card and without any errors would still not be used by librarians as they stood. Libraries with suitable photographic equipment might copy the entry from the book but they would then paste over certain items and add others, such as call number, additional author information, alternative or added subject heading, notes, and the like. The adapted card would then have to be rephotographed and reproduced in a sufficient number of copies to meet the library's needs. This would reduce the utility of the Cataloging-in-Source to the provision of cataloging information which would be checked, adapted, and then used as the partial basis for an individual library's own catalog cards. This in turn raised the basic questions as to whether such a program could be justified in terms of its very high cost to both publishers and the Library of Congress and whether the information provided could not be made available in some other way at a lesser cost. The Consumer Reaction Survey brought out the enthusiasm of a representative group of American libraries for Cataloging-in-Source information in the books, but it could not present any clear-cut evidence as to the savings that would result. A large number of libraries surveyed reported that they would continue to purchase Library of Congress or Wilson cards, but that it would be wasteful to operate both the Cataloging-in-Source program and the printed card program.

A Cataloging-in-Source program confined to American titles only would not meet the principal needs of the research library. On the other hand, the cataloging each year from page proofs of 30,000 American trade publications and government documents would be more than the majority of libraries would need. In the fiscal year 1959–1960 under the "All the Books" program, over 2000 publishers sent approximately 12,000 publications to the Library of Congress, the majority of them in advance of the date of issue, and they also printed the Library of Congress card numbers in the books themselves.

As a result of the experience gained through the experiment, it was decided by the Library of Congress that a permanent, full-scale program of Cataloging-in-Source would not be practicable from the point of view of technical considerations, financing, and utility.

Several alternatives to a complete Cataloging-in-Source program have been suggested. One of the forerunners to the whole concept was put forth by Ranganathan, and called by him "Prenatal Cataloging." In 1948 Ranganathan proposed that publishers should send the corrected galley proof to the National Central Library. The book would be classified at this stage and the call number could then be printed in the book on the back of the title page, and the call number tooled on the spine during binding. Using this method, there would be neither the pressure of rush on the classifier or on uneconomical holdup at the printing end. The complete cataloging could then follow. The publisher could send a complete set of the final proof, and the unit card could then be completed. Between the stage of the final proof and the release of the book after binding, there would be a period quite sufficient for the descriptive cataloging to be completed and the cards printed.

It had been suggested that the Cataloging-in-Source entry might be reduced to the elements of author, classification number, and subject heading. This did not prove workable, however, as it would still require an additional operation for the publisher and lengthen the schedule for many titles, and it would not relieve the objections to the use of dates for living authors, to the use of real names instead of pseudonyms, and to certain subject headings. The Library of Congress would still be required to catalog 30,000 titles a year using nonstop rush methods and to include several thousand titles to which it would not ordinarily have given author and title treatment.

The provision of cataloging information is of great assistance to the individual cataloger, but the final question still remains: Can it not be provided through some less costly method for a number of titles sufficient to meet the needs of most libraries?

In 1959 *Publishers' Weekly* started a new program that would provide full cataloging information in its "Weekly Record of New Books." It was arranged that Bowker would rush its advance review copies to the Library of Congress when Bowker received the book first. The Library of Congress would catalog the book and return it by the fourth day. *Publishers' Weekly* would then try to print the listing in the week of the book's publication. It was hoped that this program would provide, as far as the great majority of American libraries were concerned, most of the objectives of Cataloging-in-Source and at a minimal cost. Libraries would be provided with a Library of Congress catalog entry prepared from the completed publication for each title in the week of its publication. Copying cataloging information from a weekly listing would offer as many possible savings as copying from the book itself, and there would be the additional advantage of having the cataloging information before the book was in hand.

Because the method offered by the *Publishers' Weekly* program was to realize many of the objectives of the Cataloging-in-Source program in a much more economical way, the Library of Congress decided there should be no further experiments with Cataloging-in-Source.

The experiment ended in 1959, but the ghost of Cataloging-in-Source still haunts librarians, because the problem that was first discussed in 1850 refuses to be dismissed. In fact, by 1969, the problem has attained greater and more pressing proportions. In the ten years since the project was ended, the literature has shown that the *Publishers' Weekly* and Selection, Acquisition, Cataloging and Processing (SACAP) solution offered by the Library of Congress has not been a solution at all. With more material than ever being printed, and greater demands being made by the public for services undreamed of ten years ago, can the door be closed so completely on the idea of Cataloging-in-Source? Several questions should be raised by anyone reading the final report. On what basis was it ruled inoperable? Three groups were consulted during the experiment. The consumers were overwhelming in their enthusiasm for the project, even though in many cases they would modify the information for their own needs. The publishers admitted to some inconvenience and added expense, but expressed their willingness to continue if it would benefit libraries. And that it would benefit libraries in a great number of ways was clearly demonstrated by the project. The catalogers at the Library of Congress were the only ones who really registered a negative vote, and it would appear from the outside that their voice outweighed all the others. Their complaints were justified on a humanitarian basis. It is impossible to work under such extreme pressure for any length of time, particularly when there is also the frustration of uncertainty due to publishing changes. If any means of cataloging was contemplated other than the twenty-four hour marathon by Library of Congress catalogers, it was never mentioned.

It has been nearly a decade since the Library of Congress felt that the *Publishers' Weekly* program was the solution to the problem. Although this was a hope, the actuality was stated in an article by Joseph Wheeler, where he pointed out that the various methods adopted to solve the problem of immediate access to material by the public are still slow and expensive. *Publishers' Weekly* shows a time lag between publication of the book and listing it in the periodical; centralized processing centers with their variety of services still cannot provide materials quickly and inexpensively. Mr. Wheeler criticized the original Cataloging-in-Source project for its meagerness of funds, its sparseness of time, and the small number of volumes involved. It is a just criticism and further effort should be made by the library profession to see that this project be continued; the fine work done by the original research group serves as the foundation for a truly workable solution.

BIBLIOGRAPHY

Drewry, Virginia, "Consumer Reaction Survey of Cataloging in Source," *Lib. Resources & Tech. Services,* 3(4), 247–252 (Fall 1959).

Dunkin, Paul S., ed., "Cataloging in Source—A Symposium," *Lib. Resources & Tech. Services,* 4(4), 269–284 (Fall 1960).

Eastin, Roy B., "Cataloging in Source—The Viewpoint of Publishers," *Lib. Resources & Tech. Services,* 3(4), 253–256 (Fall 1959).

Kaser, Jane, "Venerable History of Cataloging-in-Source," *Missouri Lib. Assoc. Quart.,* **20,** 76–81 (Sept. 1959).

Mahoney, Orcena, "Cataloging in Source," *ALA Bull.,* **54**(3), 197–201 (March 1960).

Mallein, Marie-Elisabeth, "Le Catalogage à la source," *Bull. des Bibliothèques de France,* 7(7), 351–365 (July 1962).

Neelameghan, A., "Cataloging at Source and Standardization of Cataloguing, *Ann. Lib. Sci.,* 7(1), 13–15 (March 1960).

Piggott, Mary, "Cataloguing Experiments at the Library of Congress," *Lib. Assoc. Rec.,* 62(10), 325–327 (Oct. 1960).

Ranganathan, S. R., "Pre-natal Classification and Cataloguing on Its Way," *Ann. Lib. Sci.,* 6(4), 113–125 (Dec. 1959).

Spalding, C. Sumner, "Cataloging in Source—the Experiment from the Viewpoint of the Library of Congress." *Lib. Resources & Tech. Services,* 3(4), 239–247 (Fall 1959).

Trotier, Arnold, "Cataloging in Source—the Story Up to Now," *Illinois Librarian,* 41(6), 426–431 (June 1959).

U. S. Library of Congress, Processing Dept., *The Cataloging-in-Source Experiment: A Report to the Library of Congress by the Director of the Processing Department,* Supt. of Documents, Washington, D. C., 1960 (199 pp.).

Wheeler, Joseph L., "Top Priority for Cataloging-in-Source," *Lib. J.,* pp. 3007–3013 (Sept. 15, 1969).

Elspeth Pope

CATALOGS AND CATALOGING

Introduction

The story of catalogs and cataloging is only one phase of the broad panorama of library development. Traditionally the library has devoted its efforts to the acquisition, preservation, and promotion of graphic materials entailing the use of some system of bibliographic organization or control. Such organization is not unique to the library. History reveals the interrelationship between the activities of the bookseller, bibliographer, and librarian, all of whom sought to organize materials for effective location or retrieval. The methods employed are similar because they have a common goal, although they are inspired by relatively different purposes. Many attempts have been made to obtain some standardization of bibliographic entries among library catalogs, book trade publications, and published bibliographies. A substantial relationship exists between cataloging, designed to serve a definite library purpose, and bibliography, which has a more universal content and application. Cataloging in the United States has tended to be independent of book dealers' needs, while many European countries have coordinated bibliographic activities for centuries. Current efforts in international cataloging will no doubt serve to promote a closer working correlation of the two efforts. The Appendix lists the codes of cataloging rules in chronological order, the significance of which is the international character of standardization, still under way.

The library catalog is only one of the many forms of bibliography. It is generally defined as a list of books contained within a single library and is comprehensive rather than selective. In actual practice, although catalogs list the bulk of the monographic and at least part of the serial publications within a library, practices vary depending on the particular library. Jennette Hitchcock (*1*) in a study conducted in 1939 estimated that subject headings could be omitted for four-fifths of the ninety different types of material. The results of her survey indicated that a significant number of libraries had followed this practice of omission. Librarians customarily tend to list only books in the catalog, influenced apparently by the traditional definition, although today library collections include a wide range of graphic materials. The reverence accorded the monograph perhaps was due in part to the dominance of the codex during the early periods; it was not seriously rivaled by other forms until the seventeenth century. The origin of learned societies as a result of the scholarly endeavors of the Renaissance led to the founding of the first scholarly periodicals in the 1660s. The increasing emphasis upon science encouraged the publication of serial publications, and by the eighteenth century they were the principal vehicles for the dissemination of scientific information. Other disciplines and agencies readily adopted the new form; this led to the proliferation of government documents, proceedings of Congresses, annual reports, and popular magazines evident during the nineteenth century and reaching an all-time high by the midpoint of the twentieth century. Libraries, with their roots planted in the humanistic spirit of the past, failed to respond sufficiently and rapidly enough to the growing variety and numbers of publications outside the realm of the monograph, and proved inadequate to fulfill the expected industrial and governmental needs that now tended to dominate the national scene. As a result specialized groups became documentalists or information scientists in much the same way that librarianship and bibliography had separated years ago. The relationships were strong, but the methods and purposes varied to the point that each considered itself a separate discipline.

The movement to gain bibliographic control of serials has traditionally been of secondary concern to most librarians, although the efforts of Poole, Cutter, and Billings indicated a growing awareness which has continued to develop since their time. The number of periodical indexes from the nineteenth to the twentieth centuries attested to their dominant position in the bibliographic structure, even though librarians were confident that less effort was necessary and that bibliographic accuracy could be sacrificed in favor of more rapid processing.

The influence of the bibliographer on library cataloging was apparent as the position of librarian was generally relegated to a scholar or a man of letters. The librarian sought to organize the materials in a manner suitable to his needs or those of his immediate associates, without particular regard for ease of accessibility—this would come during the later years when the library was eventually recognized as an educational tool. With the rise of a pragmatic philosophy of education there came the rise of the librarian schooled in the technical aspects of practical organization rather than in bibliographical theories. The preparation of the catalog by the late nineteenth and early twentieth centuries ceased to be an immediate undertaking of the library administrator and was relegated to practitioners who were dependent upon codes and traditions rather than results. The problem, however, shortly became a concern of the total library, for the rising costs of cataloging forced both administrators and catalogers to reexamine their methods and question the need for bibliographic detail, with the hope of relying more upon the other available bibliographic tools. A period of reevaluation and technological change has brought about an increasingly pragmatic approach which attempts to fulfill the needs of the versatile user while minimizing the expense of processing time and effort.

The process of cataloging, in its narrowest sense, is the compilation of headings and bibliographic descriptions for use in the catalog. This could, perhaps, be considered the work of a pragmatic bibliographer, although catalogers are beginning to find other ways of determining the amount and kind of bibliographic descriptions necessary. In a broad sense the process encompasses descriptive cataloging which may include, in addition to bibliographic descriptions, the choice and form of author headings and subject cataloging which results in the assignment of classification numbers and subject headings. Catalogs may be distinguished as to purpose by such designations as public catalog, which serves the patron; official catalog, which serves the cataloging staff; and union catalog, which is a list of holdings of many libraries. Format or physical form is also .used as a basis of describing the catalog with the most common being card, printed book, sheaf (slip with loose leaf binder), guard book (slips mounted in a special book), computer, and visible file. The arrangement of the catalog is a third consideration. The three most popular approaches are the dictionary, which files authors, titles, subjects, and references in one alphabet; the divided catalog, which separates some of these headings; and the classified, which utilizes a systematic arrangement of subject entries supplemented by author, subject, and title indexes in alphabetical order. Other less frequently encountered variations are alphabetico-classed for subject headings, a combination of the alphabetico-classed and the dictionary catalog, and a number of single or combined arrangements of subject alphabetical and/or author and name catalogs. To this may be added a wide variety of variations of the divided dictionary catalog based on a horizontal (chronological) arrangement as well as vertical (type of entry) arrangement resulting in a separation of subject headings from author and/or title. Other combinations are possible with the printed book catalog serving as a supplement to the card catalog or vice versa. The correlation of shelf list and/or bibliographies with a printed book or card catalog present other possibilities.

The functions of the early catalog were comparatively simple, serving as an inventory list with progressive patterns of arrangement based on the order of accession, chronologically by date of publication or period of author. From these evolved a wide variety of approaches and an expansion of the inventory idea to include retrieval. The subject catalog, which employs a system of conceptual terms to depict the content of the material, has been the major outcome of centuries of development. The derivation of subject terms or headings may be dependent upon the title or content of the book and may be standardized through the use of a classification scheme or a specially prepared list. Cutter believed that "the ideal catalog would give under every subject its complete bibliography, not only mentioning all the monographs on the subject, but all works which in any way illustrate it, including all parts of books, magazine articles, and the best encyclopedias that treat of it; in short, the catalog would lay out just that course of reading which a man who thoroughly studied the subject, with a view not only to learn it, but to master the history of its treament by others, would be obliged to pass through" (2, p. 549). He continued by admonishing that "this can rarely be done because it is beyond the ability of librarians and the means of libraries." In addition, in *Rules for a Dictionary Catalog,* Cutter contended that the purpose or objects of the catalog were as follows (*3,* p. 12):

1. To enable a person to find a book of which either is known: author, title, or subject.

2. To show what the library has by a given author, subject, or in a given kind of literature.

3. To assist in the choice of a book: as to its edition (bibliographically) or as to its character (literary or topical).

These were restated in the *International Conference on Cataloguing Principles* of the International Federation of Library Associations as follows (*4,* p. 26):

> Functions of the catalog. The catalog should be an efficient instrument for ascertaining:
>
> 2.1 whether the library contains a particular book specified by
>   (a) its author and title, or
>   (b) if the author is not named in the book, its title alone, or
>   (c) if author and title are inappropriate or insufficient for identification, a
>   suitable substitute for the title; and
>
> 2.2 (a) which works by a particular author and
>   (b) which editions of a particular work are in a library.

The inventory list functioned as a catalog and only later developed into a retrieval device which became probably the most highly organized part of an inter-related bibliographic network. The expanding number of points of access in the catalog indicates the comprehensive approach now possible. As subject terminology is perfected and mechanized methods are developed and applied, new dimensions will further expand the catalog until the spectrum of organized knowledge will rest upon a combination of the total bibliographic force, not just one phase.

The catalog serves as the key to the functions of a library and is a communicative device based upon a long process of social habits, designed to provide methodical and effectual access to graphic materials (*5,* p. 6). Insight into the present practices can best be achieved by a survey of the catalogs of the past with particular attention to the developing forms and purposes that are reflected in our modern catalogs. Our major attention will be directed to the English-speaking countries, particularly Great Britain through the eighteenth century and the United States during the nineteenth and twentieth centuries.

Age of Inventory

ANCIENT TIMES

Primitive methods of bibliographical control have existed since the beginning of the first libraries. The original approaches were primitive, although Norris alleged that "the catalogs in use in the seventeenth century B.C. were very similar to those which are now in use in the twentieth century A.D." (*6*, p. 2). The archeological excavations at Assurbanipal (1668–626 B.C.) revealed that bibliographic information was recorded on tablets that were similar to a press guide or a very rudimentary shelf list. These tablets served as a crude location device by recording title (occasionally with opening words), number of tablets, number of lines, distinct subdivisions, and a location or classification symbol (*7*, p. 25). A similar method was employed at Edfu (200–300 B.C.), where a list of books was reputed to have been engraved on the wall.

The Alexandria Library supposedly had an extensive catalog compiled by Callimachus in the form of *Pinakes* in 250 B.C. There is, however, some element of doubt whether this was actually a catalog of the Alexandrian Library or merely a bibliography compiled by the celebrated first cataloger. Norris suggested the possibility that Hermippus, an assistant to Callimachus, may have actually compiled the catalog in 220 B.C (*6*, p. 5). It was described as a classified catalog complete in 120 books, but very few fragments are extant.

Witty was able to trace only about five true fragments, which were in reality only quotations from the original. The other conjectured remnants were found to be "oblique references" by ancient authors to the bibliographical work of Callimachus (*8*, p. 132). The term *Pinakes* (singular: *Panax*) was first used by the Greeks to indicate the tablets placed above the library press which served as a guide to its content and later denoted a catalog (*8*, p. 132). The actual title was "Tables of those who were outstanding in every phase of culture and their writings—in 120 books" (*8*, p. 133). The fragments reveal a newsy biobibliography of the works of the period with information more applicable for a biographical work than a catalog. Bibliographical information was comprised of a stoichiometric note (number of lines in text) and probably the first words of a work. The entries were subdivided by author or by chronological order.

The primal catalogs through the height of Greek civilization can be conjectured as quasiclassified with a broad subject and form arrangement that resembled an embryonic shelf list. The title concept was not firmly established so that opening words of text were of great importance and were always employed. The author was frequently cited without further reference, a practice that did not cause confusion in view of the paucity of works. As a result one of the most unique contributions of the Greeks may have been the first use of the author concept, for the traditional practice of the Orient has been under title (*9*, p. 257). The Tripitaka, the source of Buddhist scriptures, was organized only by title.

The Roman period was marked by scanty information regarding catalogs and cataloging. Public and private libraries were common during this period, depending largely upon the works of the Greeks, which were the foundation of Roman culture. Rolls were generally separated by Latin and Greek with general subject divisions used within both categories, and probably an attempt was made to retain all the works of a single author together under the relevant subjects. Two varieties of catalogs, the classified and the bibliographical lists, were prevalent with the former based on shelf arrangement and the latter seeking continuity through authors. Both ordinarily included titles and/or first lines, number of lines in work, and frequently appended biographical information. It was clear that the Romans continued the precedence as established by Callimachus adding nothing new to the art (*7*, p. 77). The beginnings of Christianity brought little change to the Roman conceptions of the library for the first seven centuries, except the addition of new works, and works of the church fathers supplementing or even supplanting the authors and philosophers of Greece and Rome (*10*, p. 43). Gradually, however, public or temple libraries began to decline, especially after the third century when Christianity became the state religion. In A.D. 336 with Constantinople now the center of the Roman empire, the libraries of Rome were rivaled by the collections assembled by a succession of emperors who as a whole supported libraries and scholarship until the conquest by the Turks in 1453. The great libraries of the empire slowly were dispersed or suffered the ravages of neglect. Few extant accounts actually depict the dispersal of the manuscripts and the razing of the temple structures.

MIDDLE AGES: EARLY PERIOD (FIFTH THROUGH ELEVENTH CENTURIES)

The fall of Rome in the sixth century brought about a decline in scholarship with the deliberate destruction and dispersion of the public or temple libraries as well as many private collections. The next ten centuries for the libraries of the Western world would be characterized by small collections of surprisingly similar manuscripts in the many monasteries established in this period. The austere life of the monastic orders was not entirely new; the tradition existed among the Essenes during the early days of the Christian period. The place of books in the monastery was important, for monks were admonished to read, meditate, and copy for the glory of the afterlife. One of the outstanding monastic clerics to whom libraries owe a debt was Cassiodorus (*11*), who after serving in public life retired and founded a monastery at Vivarium in Benevento (southern Italy). His respect for learning was clearly reflected in his famous *Institutiones,* which served as a scholarly model for the many orders and furnished an annotated guide to what he considered valuable.

These monasteries were the major instruments of education, such as it was, and were the primary vehicles in the preservation and production of books. The need for library catalogs, however, was limited during this early period, with efforts directed only toward an inventory record. One of the most elementary type was a list of books given by Gregory to the church of Saint Clements. It consisted of a marble tablet inscribed with an introduction or prayer and a few treasured Biblical works (*12*). The poetical catalog composed by Alcuin of York in the eighth century was a unique form that was in reality a list of famous authors or a bibliography, although it was reputed by some to be a catalog of the York monastery. Another simple listing of this period was Saint Augustine's *De Trinitate.*

This was merely a list of works transcribed on the final flyleaf of a book (*9*, p. 258). Emperor Louis the Pious (814–840) actuated the compilation of catalogs when he decreed that monasteries and cathedrals should make a list of all the books they possessed (*13*, p. 615). These early catalogs or inventory lists were thus fashioned by the immediate need for a list of material possessions. The books were generally arranged not by author but by the importance of the work, with precedence given to the Bible and other religious works and with secular works placed last. In addition, these terse lists were not indicative of the full contents of the works included, because it was common practice during this period to bind several works by the same author, or treatises by various authors but on similar subjects, within one cover as an economy measure. Thus a small collection of ten volumes may contain actually nearly double this number of distinct works. The purpose of the list was to identify the book rather than analyze the contents of the physical volumes. Fortunately, Armarians realized the value of a more complete analysis of at least the distinct works. Several catalogs of the nineth century provided a listing of the works within each volume and the "number of volumes or rolls in which each work was contained" (*9*, p. 259).

One outstanding literary work, *The Myriobiblion,* is indicative of the bibliographic contribution of the period. It was compiled ca. A.D. 842–848 by Photius, patriarch of Contantinople. It bore a strong resemblance to the *Pinakes* of Callimachus and was a primitive but interesting review of approximately 280 works of the period with bibliographic, biographic, and critical information (*14*, pp. 568–572). The Upper Rhineland monastery at Lorsch in the tenth century produced a more typical catalog in the following order: liturgical works, the Testaments, theological and patristic works, lives of the saints, and last poetry, with a few of the classic authors (*13*, p. 616). Catalog production between the ninth and eleventh centuries was suprisingly active. Gottlieb listed twenty-four catalogs from the ninth century, seventeen from the tenth, and thirty from the eleventh (*15*).

The period of the early monastic and cathedral library catalogs may be characterized as a period of rudimentary methods. The earliest catalogs were crude lists, frequently inscriptions, without apparent order or sequence, which later became parchment inventories placed near the book presses, and further expanded into more distinctive works as the library grew. The manuscripts were arranged, or classified, by broad subjects. The most common order was: archives, scriptural texts and commentaries, constitutions, council and synodal proceedings, homilies and epistles of the fathers, lectionaries, and legends of martyrdom with secular literature frequently placed in a subsection divided by the seven liberal arts: grammar, rhetoric, logic, arithmetic, geometry, music, and astronomy (*13*, p. 617). This arrangement reflected a utilitarian as well as a philosophical aspect. As long as the collections were small the divisions were simple. Frequently secondary arrangements were by order of acquisition or size. The widely varying catalogs of the early Christian period were most nearly like the modern shelf list and provided an inventory designed to facilitate record keeping while showing the location of the work.

MIDDLE AGES: LATE PERIOD (TWELFTH THROUGH FOURTEENTH CENTURIES)

Twelfth Century

Catalog arrangement of this century continued in the same casual manner. The extant portion of the 1158 catalog of the monastery at Prüfening indicated a chronological sequence for all books which were grouped after the Biblical works. The compiler was foresighted enough to provide space for the collection of later acquisitions (*13*, p. 617).

The Christchurch catalog, 1170, was the first to use a system of reference letters placed both within the catalog and the books (*16*, p. xix). The Lincoln Cathedral Library Catalog of ca. 1200 continued the practice of including opening words as well as the title and added another feature, an introduction (*6*, pp. 20–22).

Although only a few catalogs have been discussed, the twelfth century was characterized by a large number produced on the continent with Gottlieb listing sixty-two examples (*15*). The typical catalog, however, remained an inventory list compiled with a general lack of system on a two-column parchment page. The broad subject arrangement was the accepted pattern with titles generally sub-arranged in chronological order rather than alphabetical by author. Author's names served primarily as a means of identification with little attention given to form and accuracy. The information listed was extremely brief, composed of author's name and short title, frequently with the opening words of the work and occasional statements concerning physical conditions, color, or number of items in the volume. The addition of the beginning words of the text was necessary to aid in distinguishing anonymous works and works with identical or similar titles. As a whole the information included was so vague that it offered little aid outside the context of the individual library.

Thirteenth Century

The thirteenth century found a continuation of the shelf or press arrangement with short titles and opening words. The Glastonbury catalog of 1247 (*6*, pp. 29–30) employed a unique and remarkable classification. Books that were by obscure authors but yet valuable for subject information were placed under the subject. Those by well-known writers were placed under the author. This system, in effect, was an attempt to select an entry that would best serve the needs of the user. The beginnings of union catalogs can be traced to the *Registrum Librorum Angliae,* 1250–1296, which was an unfinished attempt to record the holdings of 183 English monastic libraries.

The earliest information regarding the libraries of the universities came to light in the catalog of the Sorbonne at the University of Paris in 1289. It contained over 1,017 Latin titles but only 4 in French, arranged by ten major divisions: the seven liberal arts (or the trivium and quadrivium) plus theology, medicine, and law. Authors were arranged alphabetically within each division followed by the title and the beginning words of the text (7, pp. 122–123).

Fourteenth Century

The fourteenth century provided an abundance of examples although few new innovations. Subject arrangement was common; five of the seven catalogs described by Norris had this arrangement. The catalog of Christchurch, Canterbury, 1313–1331, was considered to be the first to adapt an alphabetical order under at least one subject heading, theology. In addition a system of press marks was present as well as an inept attempt to list the works of each volume (6, p. 38).

The Exeter Cathedral Library catalog of 1327 was an author catalog with only one subject heading. It listed the value of each book, as it was probably intended only for the inventory of church property.

The catalog of the Saint Martin's Priory at Dover of 1389 had an unusual three-part arrangement by location number. The first section was intended for the use of the librarian, consisting of a tabular shelf list; the second was a duplicate of the shelf list with enumeration of the individual works bound within each volume; and third was a crude alphabetical-analytical index designed to indicate the location of an individual treatise in a volume (17, pp. 105–106). The addition of the author index to this inventory list added the dimension of a true catalog which was not evident in many of the examples up to this time. The catalog of the Leicester Abbey in 1394 exhibited a similar characteristic with a double catalog of authors and subjects (13, p. 620).

The catalog of the Library of Meaux Abbey, 1396, was arranged by the location of the bookshelves, which were scattered about the abbey. It did have a more distinct feature, however, in its introductory remarks concerning the origins of the catalog; these were later to become an interesting addition to book catalogs as late as the nineteenth century.

The catalogs of the fourteenth century were the familiar inventory lists arranged by broad subjects with books assigned to a designated or fixed location on the shelves. In effect this was merely the classification of shelf space within the presses which were marked as to content. This concept encouraged the use of press marks which could readily be added to the books as an aid in reshelving. Each individual library devised a unique mark generally relying upon alphabetic characters and upon Roman and Arabic numbers. The Dover (1389) and Durham (1391) catalogs established the practice of recording the "opening words of the second leaf of each book," which was to become an almost universal method in the next few centuries (16, pp. xix–xx).

MODERN PERIOD

The fifteenth and sixteenth centuries were a period of sweeping sociological, economic, and cultural changes that reverberated throughout the whole social structure. The Reformation shifted the power from the old universal church to a wider range of authorities with secular organizations assuming more responsibility in many of the nations. In England the decline of the monastic orders tended to shift the collections of books to the private, college, and university libraries impelled by the suppression of the monasteries during the reign of Henry VIII, 1536–1539. The collegiate libraries were to suffer some of the same harassment in 1549 from the Commissioners of Edward VI, who sought to root out "superstitious literature." In spite of these difficulties the influence of the Renaissance on scholars, who were nurtured within the academic community, caused them to emphasize the collection and preservation of books as the mark of gentlemen and valuable assets for a nation. The beginning and rapid development of printing from movable type assured a wide distribution of multiple identical copies of a work, a technological advance hitherto unknown to the world. The expensive manuscript books with parchment pages, beautiful and unique, ceased to be the primary form of communication. Printed books were the beginning of a revolution with which bibliographic organization had to keep pace. No longer would the written word be controlled by a central authority that closely guarded the use and distribution of ideas. The existing few and soon numerous libraries, though still in monasteries, cathedrals, universities, and private palaces, began to acquire universality. The stagnation of the preceding centuries ended. The private libraries of the past had represented a broad range of tastes but were limited in number due to the cost and paucity of the manuscript codices. The church had reluctantly retained the works of the ancients, primarily as a method of education rather than for their contribution to Christian ethics. The university libraries and expanding private libraries began to seek a wide representation of works and assumed the role of conveyors of human knowledge rather than the preserver of a few standard works. Leaders such as Naude and Dury recognized the value in retaining all types of works as the tools of the scholars and the links to the past. The printers and booksellers, albeit with large economic motivation, provided the substance of libraries as well as forging a major link in the bibliographic chain through the efforts of such giants as Maunsell. As the libraries developed, the methods of bibliographic organization slowly evolved despite poor communication, a lack of clear objectives and functions, minimal economic resources, traditionalism, and the relegation of library usage to a selected few. By the end of the sixteenth century the dawn of the new era was at hand and blossomed fully in the next three centuries.

Fifteenth Century

The beginning of the century brought the *Catalogus Scriptorum Ecclesiae* by John Boston, a monk at Bury Saint Edmunds. Apparently he intended to continue the *Registrum* of the previous century, as identical code numbers were employed in both (*18*, p. 10). He increased the list of authors' names from 85 to 700 and included additional libraries as well as biographical information (*17*, pp. 58–59).

The catalog of the private library of Amplonius Ratinck de Berka, 1410–1412, which was later given to the University of Erfurt, represented one of the more carefully classified catalogs of the period. Arrangement was by broad subjects such as grammar, poetry, logic, rhetoric, mathematics, natural philosophy, metaphysics, moral philosophy, medicine, law, and theology, with the contents of each volume fully listed and frequently extending to ten or more items (*19*, p. 17).

The collegiate catalog of Peterhouse Library, Cambridge, 1418, was arranged by the traditional subjects and indicated two distinct collections, one for reference, which consisted of chained books, and one for lending to the "fellows." Its unique feature lay in the use of the last word of the second folio in addition to the widely accepted practice of indicating the first words. This pattern was also followed by the Cambridge University Library catalog of 1424 (*6*, pp. 91–93).

The Vatican Library catalog of 1481 depicted the accepted practice of placing the books in bookcases by broad subject arrangement. The catalog was simply an inventory device to show the locations of the materials within the bookcases of the Latin, the Greek, and the Inner libraries, and the Bibliotheca Pontificia (*10*, pp. 214–217).

The most outstanding catalog of this century was that of the Saint Augustine's Library of Canterbury, 1497. It was comprised of three parts: first, a location list indicating in tabular form the exact place where the books were located and/or the name of the borrower; second, an unfinished alphabetical listing of all books in the library with a reference to the page number of the catalog where the full entries and the press marks could be found; and third, the main section of the catalog (*6*, pp. 113–114). The latter was a model of uniformity with the general title or that of the first treatise, the name of the donor, the contents (titles) of other works in the volume, the traditional first words of the second work, and the press mark (*17*, p. 104).

The alphabetical approach with its problem of interfiling was more common on the Continent than in England during this period. Several catalogs that originated in Austria and Germany revealed the efforts to achieve more logical points of access to the shelf arrangement. An alphabetical catchword index to the shelf list was formulated at an Austrian monastery at Aggsback; a list of authors, subject designations, and catch title anonymous works were employed as special indexes to the catalog at Melk Monastery in 1483; and dictionary type catalogs with a multiple-entry approach through author and title catchword were reported at the monasteries of Rebdorf at Eichstaett and Aegidian at Nurënburg (*20*, pp. 220–221).

The most obvious change during the fifteenth century was a break in the traditional bibliographic organization both within and outside the libraries. Generally the university catalogs were not as well developed as those of the monasteries. The subject arrangement of the inventory was still the dominant order, but the finding list concept was slowly evolving through the addition of author indexes. Extent of description remained fairly constant with bibliographic comments at a minimum, but exceptions were evident in the Durham Catalog of 1416 which had such information as value, size, doubtful authorship, stolen books, and location (*6*, pp. 78–87). Thompson reported that the earliest entry of the pages in a work appeared in 1465 (*13*, p 621) Press marks were used to some extent as in the fourteenth century while the use of the last word as well as the first of each treatise was an innovation. The Saint Augustine Catalogue was perhaps the most outstanding product, with its analysis of the parts of volumes through the use of rather advanced cross references which were given the status of entries (*18*, p. 562).

Before leaving this century some attention should be given to an important approach devised by Johann Tritheim, who began his bibliographic career with the reorganizing and cataloging of the German monastic library at Sponheim. While engaged in this undertaking, he apparently realized the value of a bibliography of ecclesiastical writers, which he completed in 1494. The *Liber de scriptoribus ecclesiasticis* enumerated 277 works, recorded about 7,000 books, and reflected a considerable amount of investigation (*19*, pp. 7–8). The inclusion of an alphabetical index of authors, arranged by their Christian names, was appended to facilitate the use of the chronological arrangement and established a principle that was to continue as a bibliographical method for many centuries to come (*19*, p. 10). Thus recognition of multiple access to books was clearly emerging as standard bibliographic procedure with the finding list theory becoming a recognized element within the catalog.

Sixteenth Century

The sixteenth century found a continuation of the concept of the inventory device. Some catalogs, such as Saint Martin's Priory of Dover, had gone beyond this by developing shelf lists and analytics. The value of analyzing each part of the physical volume was evident in many catalogs but was by no means universally accepted.

The entry had little resemblance to that of the modern catalog with only title and first words and perhaps last words of each work. This, however, was to be modified somewhat during this century and substantially during the next as the printed book became relatively commonplace. Catalog production shifted from monasteries to collegiate and private collectors. The century was truly productive with some of the most positive influences for the catalog attributed to Gesner, Triflerus, and Maunsell. Their efforts stimulated a systematic approach rather than the individualistic methods of the past.

Only two monastic catalogs are of particular value during this century. First, the Syon catalog of 1526 was important because it was the first English catalog to incorporate the idea of Tritheim by including an alphabetical index of authors. It utilized a subject arrangement within the main section with letters of the alphabet denoting subjects. These were then combined with Arabic numbers, which represented accession numbers, to form a complete press mark. Donors and opening words of the second work in the volume are recorded as well as the traditional abbreviated entry. The second was the 1558 catalog of the library of the Bretton Monastery, which was the first to include in the entry the names of editors and translators.

One of the greatest contributions of this century, however, was made by Konrad Gesner, who in 1545 issued the first volume of a comprehensive international bibliographical dictionary entitled *Bibliotheca Universalis.* The work was divided into several distinct parts. First, the main section was comprised of a listing of all the Latin, Greek, and Hebrew authors that were known to the compiler. The arrangement was by the author's Christian name with an added "summary list" of author's names in inverted order (*19,* p. 15). The second volume was the *Pandectarum,* in which the works of the first volume were rearranged under twenty-one subject headings that were more extensive than ordinarily found in a typical library catalog up to this point; this represented a marked improvement. The scheme, however, gives the ". . . impression that it was drawn up empirically and then forced into a pseudo-logical system" (*19,* p. 16). The use of copious subdivisions and an alphabetical index of headings were features that were truly remarkable. As an added bit of information for the book collector, Gesner provided instructions for arranging books in a library. He suggested that books be divided by size and then by some order on the shelves. A catalog of books in shelf order and an alphabetical author index were considered sufficient, although a record by accession number with acquisition and value was also contributory. In addition to these suggestions he pointed out that his *Bibliotheca* could be readily used as a catalog to any library by the addition of press marks.

Additional support for a logically organized library catalog was expounded in 1560 in a manual published in Augsburg by Florian Treflerus, a Benedictine monk. He stressed the value of a catalog and suggested that five catalogs were desirable: first, one arranged alphabetically by the name of the author; second, one arranged in classed order or shelf list order; third, one serving as a subject index to the various contents of all books; fourth, an alphabetical index to the third; and fifth, one intended to list books held in reserve because of age or condition. He suggested a shelf mark comprised of a letter designation for size, color, and subject. The first two were represented by abbreviations, but the subject scheme was delineated by the first seventeen letters of the alphabet (*6,* pp. 135–136).

The last provocative work of this century was done by Andrew Maunsell, a London bookseller who in 1595 compiled a bibliography of books published in English. He adopted new methods and shunned the examples of "the learned men that have written Latine Catalogues" (*21,* [p. v]). A dictionary arrangement was followed with a single alphabet of authors, limited added entries such as translators, and subject words. Individual entries were arranged alphabetically by author's surname rather than the Christian name, and the anonymous works were entered under title, subject, or sometimes both if it would facilitate location. When subject was used it was as a "see" reference to the main entry. This practice was continued in library catalogs and encouraged the custom of distinguishing the main entry. All Bibles or books of the Bible were listed together under the designation Bible to facilitate their location and no doubt influenced later use of uniform headings. The form of entry had a completeness of description lacking in most earlier library catalogs. It was composed of author's names, translator if present, sufficient name of printer or bookseller, imprint date, and type of format.

It is readily seen that this century witnessed great strides in bibliographical organization, with two of the most important contributions emanating from out side the library itself. The two library catalogs described were significant since they incorporated some of the concepts that were later suggested by Treflerus, Gesner, and Maunsell. Gesner and Treflerus clearly championed the need for several points of access through multiple indexes. Maunsell's direct and simple approach to the problems of entry word, arrangement, anonymous works, and completeness of description would have a decided influence upon the codes of the succeeding centuries. As the century closed it was clear that a recognition of the need for uniformity and a systematic approach to catalogs and cataloging would soon be a reality rather than just the vague promise of a few erudite bibliographers.

Age of the Finding List

MODERN PERIOD

Seventeenth Century

The dawn of the seventeenth century found a continued lack of understanding regarding the nature and purpose of library cataloging. The familiar concepts persisted with shelf arrangement designed for administrative reasons rather than the needs of the patrons. The classification by size as well as subject gained in popularity. The finding list idea, however, was clearly established with author indexes widely advocated. The development of the printed catalog was a highlight of this century. The old manuscript catalog had been laboriously produced while the new lists lent themselves to extensive production if the need should arise.

The number of libraries continued to increase, but cataloging methods changed only slightly although there seemed to be some standardization during the first quarter of the century (*23*, p. 37). The gulf between the medieval and the modern methods of cataloging could be discerned in the precocious instructions given by Naude, Dury, Baillet, and the Bodleian Catalogue of 1674. The first general library catalog that served primarily as a finding list was the Bodleian Catalogue of 1620. The combined efforts of Thomas James and Sir Thomas Bodley produced a catalog that was arranged by the author's surnames and catchword titles for anonymous works. The functions of the catalog had finally come to the forefront, although it was in an unintentional manner. Bibliographers would continue to extend the points of access which would be valuable to students and scholars. The major philosophical issues involved in catalog construction were in the offing and only in the nineteenth century were they explored more fully.

The Bodleian catalogs are one of the dominant influences of the seventeenth century and would continue to affect all succeeding study of cataloging procedures. The principal figure behind the reorganization of the Oxford University Library was Sir Thomas Bodley, a retired English diplomat, who dominated the cataloging efforts of Thomas James, the first librarian. The initial printed catalog of 1605 was primarily a shelf list of printed books and manuscripts. The arrangement was typical of the sixteenth century, with groupings by the four academic disciplines of theology, medicine, law, and art. Size separated the books further with the folios chained to the reading desks and the quartos and octavos shelved in special locked cases. Individual entries were listed under subjects alphabetically by the author when known. Anonymous and pseudononymous works were placed under the most significant word of the title or else under the first word. The entry was somewhat more complete, with author's name in natural order, title, place, date, size, and location, but lacking edition. To the main catalog was appended an alphabetical index of authors and lists of commentators. The original intent was to print the contents of a single shelf on one page, which would allow extra pages to be used as shelf guides. Recent additions were to be included within an appendix (6, pp. 142–147).

In 1613 an alphabetical author catalog was compiled in manuscript form. It was never printed but rather formed the draft for the second catalog.

The 1620 catalog was a milestone in catalog arrangement, as it used a single sequence of authors' surnames (Christian name first), with anonymous works placed under the first or most striking word of the title. This in effect was our modern dictionary catalog in its embryonic stages without the benefit of uniform subject headings. The idea here, as in other earlier catalogs, was to provide a single entry for each book with the author considered the most logical approach. The anonymous works had created serious problems in other catalogs as indicated above. Entries for them frequently were made under title, under form heading, or under the most striking word of the title. This catalog utilized the latter method, not in the sense of a systematic coverage of subject information but rather as an attempt to establish some assemblage of materials lacking authors by subject words or forms that might be remembered by the catalog user. The titles of the ancient works had never been a unique form of identification and even at this time were considered of doubtful value in their natural order. The catchword seemed to be the logical way to supplement the author list by serving to group materials of a like nature (form or subject) rather than to scatter them by title. Other practices were separation of author's name from title, books by several authors entered under each name, cross references used, and initial or pseudonym constituted an anonymous work.

The last Bodleian catalog of the century was issued in 1674 under the direction of Thomas Hyde; it kept the alphabetical sequence of authors with catch titles for anonymous works as well as making provisions for the assembling of literary units. The preface contained a number of rules that were the most innovative cataloging procedures formulated until the middle of the nineteenth century. Many of the rules had been previously followed in the earlier Bodleian catalog, but now the rules for main entry clearly supported three continuing concepts. First, the literary unit principle was expressed by the fact that only one form of the author's name was selected for use in the catalog. Second, an assumed name with cross references was used if the author's name was not given. Translations were entered under original author. Finally, anonymous works were entered in one of four ways: (1) under selected form headings for widely used works, (2) under place or edition for less used works, (3) under biography referred to for biography, and (4) under the most striking or subject word of title (*6*, p. 151). The recognition and assemblage of authors known by different names, under a single form, constituted the first principle of modern cataloging (*22*, p. 58).

The catalog of the Lumley collection, compiled by Anthony Alcock in 1609, was a typical private library compilation. It was comprised basically of a classed catalog of 2,500 printed books and 400 manuscripts which were arranged within eight classes ranging from theology to music, to which was appended an alphabetical index of authors (*23*, p. 140).

The catalog of the Sion College Library, 1650, was one of the early dictionary catalogs with names of authors and subjects filed in a single alphabet. Subject headings and authors' surnames were printed in italics, while guide letters were placed at the top of each column of a two-column page with press marks indicating press, shelf, and order of books on the shelf. The general practice of a single entry per book prevailed, with entry either under author or under subject for anonymous works, as used in the Bodleian Catalogue of 1620 (*6*, p. 163).

In addition to the catalogs cited, the status of cataloging was depicted through the contribution of five authors of the period. Gabriel Naude included valuable hints to the librarian regarding the catalog in his *Instructions* . . . (*24*, pp. 74–75). He commented on the desirability of the catalog and suggested the compilation of two: the first, arranged according to classes (morals, sciences, and devotion) and the faculties (theology, physics, law, mathematics, humanities, etc.) with subdivisions; and the second, an alphabetical author catalog (*24*, p. 80). He pointed out the need for a miscellaneous class, criticized the single access of some catalogs, and exalted the superiority of the systematic arrangement over the fixed location.

John Dury, a protestant clergyman and later Royal Librarian, in 1650 published in England a small pamphlet devoted to library economy. He contended that "the proper charge then of the Honorarie Libraric Keeper in an Universitie should bee thought upon, and the end of the Imploiment in my conception, is to keep the publick stock of learning which is in Books and Manuscripts, to increas it, and to propose it to others in the waie which may bee most useful unto all . . ." (*25*, pp. 45–46). A catalog was the first step. It should be divided by sciences (subject or classes) and languages. He concluded that space on the shelves and in the printed catalog should allow for the "increase of number" and that a reference to the location of the book on the shelves be included. He spoke of the printed catalog as though it were commonplace and called for an annual supplement compiled for use in the library and "made common to those that are abroad," through printing every three years. He suggested other methods such as acquisition by exchange, faculty opinions in selection and cataloging, and the selective cataloging of doubtful publications through the use of an alphabetical author catalog with notes regarding subject. Treflerus in 1560 had suggested a similar list but limited it to books that had been superseded or that were worn.

Adrien Barillet, a French librarian and teacher, achieved two distinctions in the field of cataloging: first, the compilation of a catalog in 1682 of the library of

Chretien-Francois de Lamoignon with an alphabetical subject index; and second, the formulation of a set of rules for the multi-entry, alphabetical catalog (subjects and titles for anonymous works). He advocated the use of major subject categories for shelf arrangement which could be further subdivided by chronological, geographic, or more minute subjects; upheld extensive use of cross references; lamented the traditional single-dimensional approach of the present shelf arrangements as being too restrictive; championed the subject index as the key to the collection through a multidimensional approach; supported the need for an alphabetical index of author's surname; and differentiated between the entry of biographical works under specific name or subject (*20,* pp. 225–230). In general his remarks exhibited a firm grasp of the value of the catalog for the location of all materials of the library.

Near the end of the century another provocative publication appeared on the construction of the library catalog. The author was a Danish book collector by the name of Frederic de Rostgaard. His somewhat complicated arrangement of a double page, divided into columns, which designated size and the chronological arrangement of entries within each column with accession number and a letter to designate the subject, provided a varying approach to the grouping of books. He also included instructions for an alphabetical index of subjects and authors arranged by surname with reference to size, accession number, and subject.

The seventeenth century was one of growth, experimentation, and expression. The catalog had progressed to the finding list stage, but still was beset by an absence of universally accepted principles although the many manuals indicated a more systematic attempt. Cross references were now accepted practice and analytical entries were used, especially in the alphabetical subject catalogs as suggested by Baillet. The imprint was now a standard item of the catalog entry, although still limited to place and date. That the subject arrangement was becoming much more refined was due in part to the publication of Bacon's system of classification of human knowledge. The classification that had been used for centuries in the catalogs seemed necessitated by the shelf arrangement rather than by a proven need for a classified catalog forming a systematic arrangement of subjects to provide access to collection. Classification continued to play a more important role as knowledge became more systematized. The value of the subject and author indexes as a means of expanding the approach to the single-dimension shelf arrangement was recognized and discussed by the theorists of the period, but they continued to remain as adjuncts rather than an essential part of the catalog. The use of catchword titles for anonymous works added a limited subject dimension to the catalog which would progress beyond its original intent. The use of the surname had largely replaced the archaic practice of entry by Christian name, although some vestige of the former remained with the Christian name frequently recorded before the surname. The question of arrangement was still in doubt, with a full range of possibilities. For example, the catalog of the Norwich City Library of 1658–1883 illustrated the shifting trends in concepts of arrangement. The initial catalog followed the subject method but shifted to the author approach in the eighteenth century, then adopted the division by language and size, and finally returned again to the author catalog in the nineteenth century (6, p. 178). In addition to the question of arrangement the use of the original language of the book for title, the treatment and analysis of composite works, indication of size, inclusion of eminent printer with date and place, designation of first edition or best edition, assemblage of different editions of every author together in chronological order, and designation of the value of the book were all problems which confronted the cataloger of the century according to Humphrey Wanley, an assistant librarian at the Bodleian (6, p. 152). Many problems would be answered only to be replaced by more perplexing ones brought on by an expanding society; however, the question of arrangement would persist to the present day. The cataloging process slowly developed from the evolutionary examples and rudimentary codes of this century to the more theoretical and logical efforts of the eighteenth and nineteenth centuries.

Eighteenth Century

The eighteenth century was a time of stabilization rather than one of innovation. The expanding university and private collections, augmented by a few municipal libraries, grew in size but only slightly in organizational methods. The French code of 1791, which was the first national code, represented the only major contribution of the century toward a solidification of cataloging procedures. The arrangement of the catalog was still dominately by subject or by size, with the author approach gaining since the publication of the Bodleian of 1620. The spread of new ideas was slow as each individual library approached the preparation of a catalog greatly restricted by local conditions and attitudes. The printed catalog that became so abundant after the seventeenth century did allow for a distribution of examples highly susceptible to the apprenticeship status of the early bibliographers, who were ordinarily not too concerned with theory.

The inventory or shelf list approach had slowly yielded to a more erudite product, the catalog, although the persistent concern for books on the shelves, not the indexing of knowledge, inhibited the process. Some of the methods of classification developed beyond the simple arrangements of the past and expanded the major classes and subdivisions. The Philadelphia Library Company of 1789 exploited the suggestion of Naude, Baillet, and Dury by classifying under three major divisions and thirty-one classes, which were then subdivided by size. The purely artificial arrangement by size was frequently used during the seventeenth and eighteenth centuries in accord with the suggestions of Gesner and Rostgaard, and perpetuated the major concern for shelf arrangement. Size is still utilized today as a secondary shelf arrangement, although the storage libraries have recognized its value as well as the accession number approach.

The increased information included in the entry was evident in the catalog of the Friends' Library of 1708, which added place of birth and residence, time and place of death, edition information, and number of sheets in work. Although it was primarily an alphabetical catalog arranged by authors' surnames, a few subject and form divisions as well as titles for anonymous work were included (6, pp. 181–184).

The fourth Bodleian Catalogue of 1738 continued the tradition of the alphabetical arrangement by author and catch title for anonymous titles subarranged in chronological order. The addition of the name of the printer indicated that one of the problems suggested by Wanley had been solved.

The catalog of the Sion College Library departed from its former alphabetical arrangement of 1650 and was reissued in classified order in 1724 (6, pp. 184–191). The artificial scheme was similar to many of the period, which was simply a designation of letters to represent not necessarily subjects, but rather book presses and their contents.

Compilers frequently contended that a catalog by shelf order was most suitable, as missing items could be readily detected and the donors could more quickly determine which presses needed books (6, p. 188). The latter reason was legitimate at that time and was reflected in the later library laws of Great Britain and in such American catalogs as that of Harvard, 1723.

The Chetham catalog of 1791 attempted to utilize a "judicious and scientific" arrangement under the divisions of theology, law, history, sciences and arts, and humanistic literature, which could in turn be subdivided as necessary. The lack of an index badly hampered its use until 1826, when some relief was afforded through the addition of an author index, which gave the title of anonymous works (6, pp. 193–195).

Harvard College had the distinction of issuing the first printed library catalog in America in 1723. Its expressed purpose was not for the improved use of library facilities, but rather as a solicitation device to be circulated "to friends abroad." The catalog served as an inventory and was arranged by size with subdivision by author and catchword titles for anonymous works, although the later editions were in alphabetical order.

Twenty years later, in 1743, Yale produced an excellent catalog composed of three parts: a manuscript shelf list, an alphabetical list of authors, and a classified guide or index for student reading that was divided by approximately twenty-three major classes with appropriate subdivisions. Books were listed under as many as five subjects in order to bring out the various contents of the volume (26, p. 10).

Generally the catalogs produced in America during the eighteenth century favored the size or author arrangement or a combination of both, with only three out of approximately twenty-four relying upon the subject approach. Of these, only the Philadelphia Library Company Catalogue of 1789, with its three divisions and thirty-one classes which were subarranged by size, and the Harvard catalog of 1790, with its sixty-four classes which chose subarrangement by author, are of particular significance. The use of the index was slowly evolving as a valuable asset and was frequently found in the American catalogs. The catalogs of the Philadelphia Association Library Company of 1765 and the Library Company of Philadelphia, 1770, frequently made entries under the first or substantive word of the title in addition to the author (26, pp. 8–9), which would later develop into accepted practice. The information contained in the entry was approximately the same as the British successors. In spite of the unique innovations which have been described, the early American catalogs as a whole could be characterized as rudimentary devices primarily serving as an inventory or index, arranged in a single sequence with generally only a single entry for each work.

Near the end of the century the French revolutionary government confiscated a large number of books and manuscripts from a countless number of institutional and private libraries. The code of 1791 was formulated to provide simple but comprehensive rules for organization, beginning with the assembling and numbering of the books and continuing through the mailing of the completed cards to Paris. Playing cards or slips of paper were suggested as a format which was the first mention of such an approach in any code. The completed code was to contain an accession number, title exactly as recorded in the book unless extremely long, imprint (place, printer, date), size, and other exceptional features. The authors' name, as it appeared on the title page or elsewhere in the work, or a word that was most indicative of the subject if anonymous, was underlined for emphasis. Cards were then arranged alphabetically and fastened together by a thread through the lower left-hand corner. The name of the parish or district was recorded at the bottom of the card. A copy was then made on ordinary paper for retention within the district, and the cards were forwarded to Paris. It was reported in 1794 that approximately 1 million cards had been compiled as a record for roughly 3 million volumes (*27*, pp. 329–331).

The close of the century witnessed few new innovations in cataloging procedures. Author, size, and subject or a combination of any two dominated the arrangements with preference to author and size. A chronological subarrangement rather than alphabetical by title was frequently used in the author catalogs, although the size of the collection dictated the practice in this regard. Completeness of description varied, with the catalog of the Friends' Library being the first to use the number of sheets. Analytical entries continued to gain in popularity, as shown in the Yale catalog of 1743 and in the catalogs of the two society libraries of Philadelphia in 1765 and 1770. The inverted form of the author's name was now a reality, in spite of the use of the possessive form by some of the less progressive libraries.

Nineteenth Century

At the beginning of the nineteenth century some vestige of the old inventory concept still persisted. Generally, the catalog was considered a finding list but occasionally was further refined to include the newest Bodleian concept of assembling literary units together. The purpose of the catalog had evolved through two distinct phases: first, the inventory or content of shelves, which was prevalent in the monastic period; second, the finding list, which began with the author indexes and attained recognition with the alphabetical catalog of the Bodleian in 1620. In addition, Akers (*22*) acknowledged a third state, that of assembling literary units, which was originally expressed and practiced in the Bodleian Catalogue of

1674. She further contended that the stage demanded a highly developed instrumentation with differentiation between author, subject, and title entries, with main entry determined by authorship, and with the finding list function assigned to secondary entries in the event that the main entries were inadequate for quick location of the book (*22*, p. 286). The catchword title continued to be used throughout this century, but was dominated by Edwards's statement that "of necessity such catalogues must deal rather with the phraseology of title pages than with the subject of book" (*28*, vol. 2, pp. 155–156). As a result of strict adherence to this and the idea of only one entry per book, the development of subject headings was retarded. Cutter very philosophically avowed that after the introduction of the title entries for anonymous books, "the next step was to make the title-entries not merely for anonymous books but for all which had any good word in the title from which to refer, the object being to provide a means by which anyone who had heard of the book could easily find it" (*2*, p. 533). Apparently catch titles were considered as an adjuvant means of grouping materials on certain subjects together, and were used by at least nineteen catalogs in the United States between 1815 and 1854 (*2*, p. 534). It should be pointed out that Cutter in 1876 codified the practice of entry by author, subject, title, and form and refuted the notion that "a catalogue must of necessity confine itself to titles only of books" (*2*, p. 571).

This was a century of codes, with fifteen major works originating in Great Britain, France, and the United States, not to mention the individual rules as expounded in the introductions of countless catalogs. The number of catalogs produced during the first three-fourths of this century numbered over 1,000 (including supplements) in the United States alone. This was the age of the printed book catalog, which was to continue until the waning years of the century, largely replaced by the card catalog in the early twentieth century only to be revived later.

Our discussion for this century will be directed mainly toward the American catalog and the codes developed by the British Museum, Jewett, and Cutter.

Considerable attention was devoted during this century and the early years of the twentieth to the relative merits of the alphabetical author, the dictionary, the classified, and the alphabetical-classified catalogs. The alphabetical author catalog consisted primarily of the surnames of the authors while anonymous titles were entered by one of the Bodleian code suggestions. Only one entry per book was considered necessary, although deviations from this occurred quite early in the Philadelphia Association Library Company catalog. The dictionary catalog evolved from the author catalog and is an alphabetical sequence of duplicate entries for authors, titles, subjects, and forms. Frequently the name is used in a narrow sense to apply only to a single alphabetical sequence, while in the broadest connotation it indicates the mere alphabetical arrangement of several separate files. The main distinction lies in the arrangement of specific subjects that are in alphabetical rather than systematic order.

The classified catalog is limited to subjects that are arranged in a systematic order so that related objects are grouped together or in close proximity. The subject-arranged catalogs discussed up to this point were habitually arranged in an unsystematic order so the value of a subject, author, and title index was readily seen although not always present at the preliminary stages. Just when the true classed catalog developed is open to debate, since the early subject arranged shelf lists were pseudoclassified. The assumption that the classified catalog developed before the alphabetical is misleading, for without the modern classification schemes and indexes of the twentieth-century classified catalog, it would fall far short in achieving the usability of the dictionary form (29, p. 30). The early works of Gesner, Naude, Dury, and later Brunet were instrumental in an attempt to systematize the approach to knowledge in the library catalog. The lack of suitable classification schemes retarded the full use of the classified catalog, but the nineteenth century brought some alleviation. For the sake of clarity, the term classed catalog rather than subject arrangement or subject catalog will be used in the discussion of the nineteenth and twentieth centuries. The term subject catalog in its broadest sense does not refer to the arrangement, but rather to the inclusion of subject entries.

The alphabetico-classed catalog, which became popular during the middle of the nineteenth century, was basically a merger of the best points of the dictionary and classed catalogs. Cutter indicated that ". . . the subjects are grouped in broad classes with numerous alphabetical subdivisions" (3, p. 13). This definition was somewhat limited and has been expanded by Shera to include two possible arrangements: first, major divisions in alphabetical order with subdivisions classified in an "appropriate manner," or second, classified order for major divisions with subdivisions in alphabetical sequences (30, p. 13). The catalog of the New York Public Library was strongly influenced by the alphabetico-classed concept, although recent subject headings tend toward greater specificity.

In addition, the combined catalog mentioned by Cutter was composed first of a classified catalog and second of a dictionary catalog, with author and anonymous-title entries, subject entries, other title entries, and subject references to classed catalog (2, pp. 541–542). This approach would be similar to the combined use of a dictionary catalog and shelf list.

In the early part of the century, the popularity of the alphabetical catalog continued despite the fact that the classified catalog was developing into a sophisticated device with systematic classification schemes and author and/or subject indexes. In 1810 (2nd ed., 1820), Jacques-Charles Brunet published a classified bibliography or *catalogue raisonné* of books for booksellers and private bibliophiles; it consisted of an alphabetical author index with full entry to which was appended a classified abbreviated entry catalog or *"table en forme de catalogue raisonné"* (29, p. 30). The latter was devoid of a separate index, although it did have a brief summary outline which provided a cumbersome but nonetheless systematic access.

The *Catalogue of Printed Books* of the Society of Antiquaries of London, 1816, was reputed to be the first true dictionary catalog; it used the duplicate entry approach within a single alphabet, including catchword or subject word for anonymous works as well as for those the authors of which were known (31, pp. 26–27). This practice, however, was followed to a limited extent in the Philadelphia Association Library Company Catalogue of 1765. Eight years later, Robert Watt issued the *Bibliotheca Britannica,* a two-part bibliography with one alphabetical sequence for authors and a second for subjects. His deviation from the phraseology of the title page as the only source of subject headings was to have a profound effect on indexing methods, ultimately producing a dictionary arrangement (29, p. 31). Panizzi acknowledged the influence of R. Watt's work on his proposed plan, but pointed out that insufficient information had been given "to the titles of books or to the index" (32, Question #9869).

As the purpose of the catalog became more clearly defined, libraries began to reintroduce the classified catalog, which incorporated such refinements as systematic classification schemes devised by Bacon, Horne, Brunet, and others. Indexes were not considered an essential part and were comprised primarily of authors, although the Providence Athenaeum catalog of 1837 included editors and translators (2, p. 585). Thus new means of access were evolving through the index, which served to provide added entries for the book catalog.

At the same time supporters of the alphabetical arrangement sought to improve the subject approach. The Andover Theological Seminary catalog, compiled by O. A. Taylor in 1838, was one of the best alphabetical catalogs of the period and was based on the German practice that provided for two separate alphabetical catalogs arranged by author and by subject. He managed to complete the author section but never finished the systematic index (26, p. 28). Taylor was aided by Charles Jewett, a student, who would later adapt his example at Brown University. The subject index of 1843 to the author catalog of Brown was to serve as an alphabetical and a pseudoclassed index and was comprised of a single sequence of subjects or catchwords, broad subject entries, and specific entries (26, p. 29). Although Jewett only infrequently deviated from the phraseology of the title page, the departure from the traditional concept of Panizzi and Edwards was significant enough to foster a movement that would in time free the subject index from the restraint of title terminology. "The way was now open for the compilation of a full dictionary catalog" (26, p. 29). Three years later a similar catalog was issued by the Linonian Society of Yale, using a single alphabet with author, title, and subject word (2, p. 588).

Another form of alphabetical catalog, issued in 1844 by the New York Mercantile Company, was comprised of an author catalog with an alphabetico-classified index. The index was divided into 69 subjects arranged in alphabetical order, with individuals works listed beneath each heading in a similar arrangement (26, p. 29).

The first half of the nineteenth century was characterized by a variety of combinations of arrangements and indexes. The first major group was comprised of catalogs that were arranged primarily by subject or classified order. The most elementary form was by broad classes or subjects in a shelf list order, with works subarranged by accession and chronologically by imprint date, title, or author. An extension of this was close classification with classes or divisions subdivided into more minute facets by a systematic scheme. Both were considered indexes with single or variant combinations of author, title, or subject as optional features, but their presence became commonplace as librarians recognized the need for a multi-dimensional approach and stopped arguing about whether the patrons sought material primarily by author or subject. The classified approach was considered more difficult to use, which was true until the development of classification schemes and indexes. The problem of looking in two places, however, always will tend to be somewhat of a disadvantage of this arrangement.

The second broad group of catalogs had a primary arrangement in alphabetical order. They were in many cases indexes to a secondary classified order, but the major emphasis was placed upon the ready accessibility of an alphabetical, rather than a systematic, approach. In other words, both were complementary to one another, with a classified system being rather limited without an alphabetical index and the alphabetical system badly limited because of extreme dependency upon the occurrence of letters. Some of the most common types of arrangements in alphabetical order were: subject list or combinations of subject, author, and title to a classified catalog; subject list with works listed beneath each heading with possible indexes for author and/or title; classes with subdivisions in alphabetical order or classified order; and author list with appended subject list in alphabetical or classed order. Some of the more sophisticated types actually developed shortly after the turn of the century. It is easily seen that the distinctions are not always too clear. The recognition of the value of each type of arrangement precipitated some rather unusual combinations which testify to the ingenuity of American bibliographers and librarians. The emergence of the dictionary catalog unquestionably demonstrates the growing influence of the public library in American society. The development of a new form, the card catalog, seemed to parallel the new arrangement during the second half of this century.

In 1853 in an introduction to a classified catalog compiled by Ezra Abbot for the Cambridge High School, the changing concepts of authorship were reflected in the placing of anonymous works under the first word of the title if not an article or preposition, societies under name, periodicals under title, and collections under editor (*33*, pp. 133–134).

The continuing effort to utilize the key words of the title as a source of information slowly led toward the development of the dictionary catalog. In 1854 Sampson Low issued an *Index to the Titles* for the *British Catalogue of Books Published in 1854*. The former classified index with its thirty-four classes was now arranged in one alphabetical sequence. This new "concordance of titles," which supposedly presented the "author's own definition" of his book, was concerned not with subject information but rather with a more ready location device for the booksellers (*2*, p. 535). The idea was further developed in 1856 by Crestadoro, a former assistant to Low.

Frederick Poole in 1854 compiled a dictionary catalog at the Boston Mercantile Library with a single sequence of authors, titles, and subjects. The use of subject words rather than independent subject headings continued the obedience to wording of the titles. The catalog was limited to a single line for each work and was one of the first condensed catalogs produced as an answer to the overwhelming costs of the comprehensive printed form. The lack of cross references was unfortunate, as the related subject words were further obscured just as failure to provide for multiple subjects of composite works further limited the subject value. The catalog continued the tradition as employed in Poole's *Index to Periodical Literature,* which was first begun at Yale for the libraries of the Linonian and Brothers' Society in 1848.

After leaving the Smithsonian, Jewett became librarian at the Boston Public Library in 1857 and 1 year later issued a catalog for the Lower Hall; it continued the title entry idea with synonymous words scattered but strengthened it with a wider variety of subject words employing duplicate entries to bring out the various aspects of polytopical books. It also included cross references, which were considered the "greatest improvement of all," from many subjects to others that were of a similar nature (*2*, p. 538). The authors' names were placed first under the headings, thus allowing for easy alphabetical arrangement and greater importance for subject emphasis. Jewett thus ". . . took the first steps, somewhat wavering steps, it is true, in a different direction" (*2*, p. 538). He recognized the informational purpose as well as the need for a specific citation and sought to bring about some distinction between subject and title entries. "The idea was not thoroughly carried out, but it had been conceived" (*2*, p. 839). The prominence of the subject idea continued to develop in the later Bates Hall Index and its supplements. The dictionary catalog was now an immature but accepted method; however, the idea of specific entry was still in a formative stage though regimented by the title page.

Ezra Abbot entered the catalog scene once again in 1861 by embarking upon an alphabetico-classed card catalog for the Harvard University library, where cards had formed a "private card supplement" since 1833 (*34*, p. 483). This practice was not entriely new, as libraries for years had maintained files of "slips" which were integrated into supplements or new editions of the printed or manuscript catalog and served the staff as a supplementary list. Their use was not an American innovation, as they were employed by Abbe Rozier in 1775 for the compilation of an index of publications of the Paris Academie des Sciences; again in 1791 as described in the French code; then by the Society of Telegraph Engineers in London in 1820; and continuously since 1827 by the Trinity College in Dublin (*35*, pp. 332–333). The British Museum used an 11- by 4-inch slip, which formed the basis for a sheaf catalog begun in 1841 (*35*, pp. 332–333). The first catalog designed for public use within the United States was reputed to be at the Philadelphia Library Company in 1857 (*36*, p. 79). Bates Hall at Boston Public Library instituted a public Card Catalogue in 1871 with two rods across the top of each drawer to hold the cards securely (*35*, p. 333). The University of Rochester was reported to have used them temporarily as early as 1846 (*2*, p. 559). In addition to the use of cards, the Harvard Catalogue was the first time a librarian had undertaken a subject catalog that would include true subject headings for each book that were derived from the content of the book rather than the words of the title (*26*, p. 70). The subjects would not be scattered by accident of alphabet but rather would be grouped together under a common form. To Abbot the most logical approach was to compile two separate catalogs or indexes, one for authors and one for subjects. The former would follow the usual pattern and be primarily intended as a finding list for determining the availability of a particular book. The second would be made up of subjects, arranged in alphabetical order, which were subdivided by various aspects in a second alphabetical sequence, thus allowing for some of the advantage of the classified catalog. In addition to entries for books, analytical entries for academy proceedings and periodicals were included. He reasoned that none of the three approaches presently used were feasible: first, the closely classified catalog required a knowledge of a complex classification scheme; second, the broadly classed catalog tended to be too general an approach; and third, the dictionary scattered materials in every part of the catalog (26, pp. 70–71). Abbot's efforts were to have a decided affect upon the cataloging procedures, particularly upon the extensive application of cards. His suggested subject arrangement was not widely accepted, although it was in part adopted for the dictionary catalog with its many subdivisions which became a part of the latter. Cutter commented that Abbot's system was ". . . best adopted for the thorough investigation of comprehensive subjects"; while the dictionary catalog was for "finding quickly what relates to a person, a place or other specific topic" (2, p. 540).

The dictionary and classified catalogs were collocated in 1874 by J. Schwartz at the New York Apprentices Library (37, pp. 651–659); he believed that the "abstract" information or "objects," which must be "viewed in their relations to other objects, or as parts," can best be located by the classified catalog, while "concrete" information or "objects," which "may be viewed as complete" in themselves, can best be located by the dictionary catalog. Thus the information supplied by both was equally valuable but ". . . both methods cannot be united without doing violence to the principles on which each is based." The ideal catalog could be obtained by the acceptance of "both as co-ordinate parts of one whole." The results were first a classified catalog of all books (imprints omitted) arranged by twenty-four classes, 216 possible divisions, and about 2,000 subdivisions. This was prefixed by a synopsis of the classification scheme to facilitate ready location within each class. The second part was an alphabetical listing: authors and anonymous title entries with individual works subarranged alphabetically by title (complete with imprint); titles that do not clearly indicate subjects or topics "whether stated in title or only implied" followed by a list of all books thereon; class headings used as references to classified; and cross references. The subject headings adapted were frequently in inverted order with the noun or substantive first, then followed by an adjective. The catalog exemplified an attempt to use the best of both, but entailed a considerable effort to compile. The twentieth century would find a similar procedure being used with reference cards placed in the dictionary card catalog which directed the user to the shelf list for general and voluminous classes of information. This approach has never been extensively employed and certainly has great possibility for allowing more selective inclusion in the dictionary catalog while utilizing the ever-present shelf list as a systematic access.

The catalog of the Boston Athenaeum of 1874 was a monumental product of this period and embodied the most advanced thinking of Charles Cutter, who is most clearly identified with the dictionary catalog. The catalog was begun in

1856, the year that Poole assumed the post of librarian, and continued in various stages of development until Cutter became librarian in 1868. Cuttter was visibly displeased with the preceding efforts, as he sought to achieve high standards with complete and carefully constructed entries. Author headings were meticulously established with full names and identity of authors of anonymous works if possible; otherwise they were entered under the first word of the title. Unique subject headings were employed without regard to phraseology of the title, which had become accepted, if not universal, practice by this time. Contents notes were added for each collected work with analytics made for these under author, title, and subject as well as entries for periodical articles and society publications. This was a tremendous feat, but he considered the catalog to be the key to the library collection. At the other end of the spectrum during this same year, Poole published a finding list at Chicago Public Library that was simply a reproduction of the shelf list with brief bibliographic information. The popularity of such abbreviated lists persisted throughout the remainder of the century. The Boston Athenaeum catalog became the model of the period, with its dictionary arrangement by author, title, and subject with form occasionally denoted by references. The acceptance of the dictionary catalog was then almost universal within the United States, although a few classed catalogs were produced.

In addition to the publication of Cutter's *Rules* in 1876, four other events occurred that were to have an effect upon cataloging. First, the founding of the American Library Association united and concentrated efforts in the direction of cataloging with discussion and activities centering around the advantages and disadvantages of the card or book catalog, the merits of the dictionary or classified catalog, analytic indexing of periodicals, indexes for government publications, potential use of bibliographies, and other issues concerning bibliographic organization. Maddox concluded that the most widely discussed library topics of the period, 1876–1885, were classification and cataloging (*38*, p. 1). The second was the publication of the Dewey Decimal Classification with subject index by the young Amherst librarian. This scheme was designed for a classified catalog and supplied a long-awaited standard index to subjects which would tend to solve one of its major disadvantages. Librarians quickly recognized the value of the scheme, utilizing it first for the classified catalog and later primarily as a shelf arrangement for the dictionary catalog. The third was the planned publication of the *American Library Journal,* which was to serve as "a periodical supplement" to the 1876 Report (*39*, p. XXIX). In addition, the editors solicited copies of catalog cards or slips to be used as examples of methods and catalogs in the many libraries and hinted at possible cooperative cataloging ventures by the *Journal* through the "printing of accurate titles of new books in such a way that they can be used for the card catalogs of libraries" (*39*, p. XXIX). And the fourth was the founding of the Library Bureau, which both standardized the dimensions of the catalog card and later was one of the first organizations to offer printed catalog cards for sale.

The catalog of the Brooklyn Mercantile Library, 1880, was based on the alphabetico-classed concept which attempted to bring some semblance of order to the subject headings rather than scattering them throughout the dictionary catalog. It occurred at a period when the book catalog was beginning to wane and at a time when the Boston Athenaeum catalog overshadowed other contributions. S. B. Noyes, the compiler, sought a systematic approach to authors, titles, and subjects within a single alphabet by forming certain general classes or class lists, such as BIOGRAPHY (individual subjects), COUNTRIES (alphabetical arrangement), or FICTION (alphabetically by author and title), within the general alphabetical sequence. Specific headings were then grouped primarily under thirty such class lists, which were interspersed among authors, titles, and cross references in traditional alphabetical order. Topics that were too fragmentary, complex, or many-sided would be placed in the general alphabet rather than under the general classes for easy location. Analytics for collections, miscellaneous essays, and some periodical articles were included. The purpose of the catalog was aptly described by Noyes: "The catalogue is designed to secure as far as possible, in one alphabet, an index to authors, titles, class headings, subject class headings, specific subjects and subheads, so that the inquirer may at once be directed to what he is in search of" (40, p. 649). Although it was well received, Cutter criticized the catalog as a "mixture of partial dictionary and incomplete classification . . ." (2, pp. 543–545). The user must know the degree of comprehensiveness of subject, which was generally a varying process as clearly pointed out by Oliver Lilley (41, pp. 45–50) in the next century. Cutter further contended that with such classes the arrangement was a "return to the dictionary plan by specific entry," and certain important classes were lacking which had for instance been used as subjects for a separately published class list for the Lower Hall at Boston Public Library. He conceded that perhaps this irregular selection of classes might "correspond to the public's unsystematic association of ideas" with the reader possibly looking "in the right place at first" and avoiding extensive use of cross references. He concluded that: "Never the less it may prove a most successful catalogue" (2, pp. 543–545). Nearly 80 years later the comment was made that "its (alphabetico-classed) possibilities have never been adequately explored" (30, p. 13).

The Index-Catalogue of the Library of the Surgeon-General's Office, 1880–1895, compiled under the direction of John S. Billings, was another monumental product of the period, requiring over 20 years to complete. The title, "index-catalog," was used to denote the inclusion of books and periodicals. The consistent use of specific headings which were independent of title words and a systematic employment of aspect subheadings which were separated by brackets rather than dashes were outstanding features of this sixteen-volume classic (29, p. 29).

Centralized cataloging or the preparation of catalogs or cards by a centralized agency or library for distribution to other libraries was first suggested shortly after the middle of the century by William D. Cooley, an English geographer, and Charles Jewett, through the use of stereotyped plates. Photographic techniques were suggested in 1835 by Albert Blor (42, p. XI) and again at the Librarians Conference in 1877 by Henry Stevens, who speculated that centrally produced cards might include a photographically reduced title page for each entry (43). F. Max Müller, former librarian at the Bodleian, had suggested the use of printed slips that could be distributed with each book in an article in the *Times* (London) of March 1876. He contended that national libraries should assume the responsibility for cataloging publications produced within their borders and pointed out the desirability of requesting each author to compose a "proper slip of his own book." He also proposed that printed slips could be used to maintain three or four kinds of catalogs such as alphabetical by authors, chronological, local, and classified by subject (*44*, p. 513). Similar proposals regarding the use of printed slips had been made by Otis Robinson, librarian at the University of Rochester, 2 years previously, and in 1876 by Justin Winsor, the librarian of Harvard (*44*, p. 516). The first successful, but short-lived, attempt was by *Publishers' Weekly* in the form of slips that could be cut apart and pasted on cards. This was followed by a similar venture in 1887 by the American Library Association, which sought to supply cards. The Rudolph Indexing Company in 1893 planned to supply cards for over 100,000 volumes, but this failed to materialize (*45*, p. 319). The Library Bureau issued cards from 1893 through 1896 until the project was shifted to the American Library Association Publication Section, where it was quickly dropped although efforts continued through the production of cards for serials and composite books. As the century ended, plans were in the offing to expand the publication of cards by the American Library Association but in July 1898, the Library of Congress began to print catalog cards for American copyrighted books. A short time later cards were exchanged with two or three large libraries which were also printing catalog cards at that time. A printed card service has been available to all libraries since 1901. Failure of the early attempts at cooperative cataloging were largely attributed to the inability of librarians to accept such a radical innovation; failure of cards to conform to individual practices such as author headings, size of card, and bibliographic information; and the long delays in shipment (*45*, p. 318).

The early catalogs had occasionally utilized a supplementary alphabetical subject index which was the forerunner of our present subject lists. After the freeing of subject words from the phraseology of the title, librarians quickly became conscious of the lack of uniformity among the subject headings selected by the various catalogs. The dictionary catalog made the problem even more acute, as now the subject headings were words that would be suggestive of content, not the title. It was soon observed that they must utilize a syndetic structure to be effective in covering the many possible approaches by the user. A committee was established in 1879 by the American Library Association to study the problem of an index to subject headings which would serve as an appendix to Cutter's *Rules*. Cutter, the chairman, reported 2 years later that an impasse had been reached as "we can't agree" (*46*, pp. 114–115). The efforts of the committee continued with numerous reports and membership changes attesting to the difficulties. In 1895 the project culminated in the publication of the *List of Subject Headings for Use in the Dictionary Catalogue*. The work was a composite listing of terms used by several large catalogs and other sources which had been carefully screened and was complete with "see" and "see also" references. It was considered a standard list for all types of libraries and found wide acceptance in three editions until the final issue in 1911, when it was largely replaced by the Library of Congress list of subject headings, which was issued in parts between 1909 and 1914. The popularity of the latter was assured by the widespread use of printed catalog cards. Its failure to include references until 1943 was a decided drawback, although supplements were a distinct asset in keeping up to date on new terminology.

Three other important bibliographic tools, which would affect catalogs, were issued during this period. The first was the third edition of *Poole's Index to Periodicals Literature,* which extended coverage to 1882. The second was the *A.L.A. Index* of 1893, which was designed to index collections and composite works and free the catalog of innumerable analytics for this type of material. The third was the *Catalog of the A.L.A. Library, 1893,* which was to serve as a selection aid, cataloging guide, and printed catalog. It is interesting to note that all three of these have continued to be issued, although under different names and publishers, until the present time.

Codes: British Museum. Before the merging of the Royal Library with the Cottonian, Harleian, and Sloan collections in 1753, early individual cataloging attempts were as a whole poorly planned and executed. In 1759 the trustees expressed the desirability of a catalog and further suggested in 1807 that a separate alphabetical catalog for each collection be compiled as well as a general classed catalog (*6,* p. 201). These efforts culminated in the issuance of seven volumes between 1813 and 1819, during the tenure of Sir Henry H. Baber as Keeper of Printed Books.

The current emphasis on scientific classification was skillfully presented by Thomas H. Horne, who submitted his *Outline for the Classification of the Library* in 1825 to the trustees, who engaged Horne temporarily to accomplish such a catalog at the British Museum. Although the project came to an impasse, this proposal and his *Observations on the Manner in Which Titles of Books are to be Entered and Classed* were valuable additions to cataloging literature. The latter contained a few rules which pertained to bibliographic descriptions such as content notes, forms of authors' names, and the need for several indexes to the classified catalog.

The work on the classified catalog begun by Horne was suspended in 1834, at which time Mr. Baber proposed a plan for an alphabetical author catalog based on sixteen rules which provided for uniform cataloging slips, entry under author if it appeared any place in the work, form of name taken from title page, anonymous works placed under "prominent or leading word" with name of possible author inserted at end of titles in brackets, pseudonymous works cataloged under pseudonym with real name inserted after title in brackets, entry under editor for collected works, and translations entered under original author (*47,* pp. 32–33). In addition he proposed that Panizzi, an impetuous Italian political refugee, should be given the task of editing the new work. The proposal was rejected and then followed by committee studies in 1834 and 1836, during which time the arguments for the classified and alphabetical catalogs were vehemently expressed with few concrete results. In 1837 Panizzi was appointed the Keeper of the Printed

Books in spite of strenuous objections. The work on the new catalog was authorized by the trustees in 1838 with a projected completion data of 1840, but with the stipulation that each letter of the alphabet was to be published individually instead of the original "shelf by shelf" plan of Baber and Panizzi (6, p. 207).

The so-called "Ninety-one Rules" employed in the compilation of this catalog were not the work of Panizzi alone but were accomplished by the unique method of having Edward Edwards, J. W. Jones, J. H. Parry, and Thomas Watts compile codes which were then studied and criticized. The resultant code was thus formulated by the effort of five men who carefully collaborated to express the best in cataloging philosophy of the period. It was approved by the Board of Trustees in 1839 and published two years later (6, p. 207). The final product consisted of ninety-one rather than the originally suggested seventy-nine rules and was decidedly inferior because of the meddling of the trustees (48, p. 7). Work on the catalog, however, was not progressing as smoothly with the first volume so marred by omissions that the printing was suspended in 1841, although the manuscript project continued. A rash of criticisms and investigations in 1847 ensued, with Panizzi defending the "Ninety-one Rules," but now questioning the feasibility of a printed catalog for such a large library. In 1849 a guard book catalog was devised with the entries copied on slips that were formed into a 150-volume catalog by 1851 (6, p. 24).

The influence of Panizzi may have been overemphasized, although his impact upon modern cataloging was decisive. An assessment of his contribution is obscured somewhat by the fact that the "Ninety-one Rules" were a product of collaboration, although the testimony before the commissions was assumed to be an expression of his ideas. He was a fervent supporter of the author catalog, contending that this was the most natural approach by the user. An "index of matter" or title subject words, which were severely limited by the admonition that only the title page was to serve as a source, was appended. The authority of the title page was accepted as a means of attaining a consistent catalog in the typical tradition of the Bodleian Catalogue in 1674. The practice of using abbreviated references which guided the user to the main entry was considered a feasible method of gaining space in the book catalog and set a precedent which would be followed by future librarians even after the advent of the card catalog and the unit card should have negated such a concept. The treatment of anonymous works was a major concern and indicated Panizzi's feeling that the catalog must be more than a quickly prepared finding list. He sought to separate anonymous works into corporate bodies and form heading groups where possible, still leaving room for those entries that could only be called miscellaneous. The first were arranged in alphabetical order under the name of the country or place "from which they derive their denomination or for want of such denomination, under the name of the place from whence their acts are issued" (32, p. IX). Organizations such as academies, universities, and learned societies were entered under the form heading ACADEMIES, and were subarranged by continent and then country. The second group was designed to place special types of material where form was apparently considered essential under such headings as PERIODICAL PUBLICATIONS,

EPHEMERIDES, CATALOGUES, LITURGIES, and BIBLE. The final group was comprised of miscellaneous publications which lacked authors and were not covered in the other categories. They were listed in order of preference as possible alternatives: (1) enter under person if referred to in title, (2) enter under place if referred to in title, (3) enter under substantive if lacking both person or place, and (4) enter under first word if not substantive in title.

This elaborate structure clearly reflected the problem of anonymous publications, which included corporate and miscellaneous works lacking the name of a personal author on the title page. The rules were frequently divergent from Panizzi's opinions as revealed in the testimony by his preference for the first word which was not an article or a preposition rather than the first substantive (*32*, Question #9692), by his belief that the reader was expected to know the title of the book just as readily as the author (*32*, Question #9754), by his objection to class headings asserting that the most desirable situation would allow every title in its place without any other heading than "its own fixed and certain heading" with fewer titles under each entry (*32*, Question #9736), and by his contention that a cataloger must take the title as it occurs rather than forming it to suit his convenience (*32*, Question #9754). Many of his opponents advocated entry under the subject word rather than the first important word. One of the major contributions of the "Ninety-one Rules" was the concept of placing corporate bodies under the country or place, although the names were derived from the title and could be construed to have the quality of a subject rather than a corporate author. The system of form headings was a secondary approach relegating special types of works to a consistent location which supposedly made them more accessible than a wide variety of nondescript titles. This approach persisted in British cataloging practices to the twentieth century and was evident in all of the codes including the 1967 Anglo-American code. The reluctance to utilize the conventional title as an entry was evinced by the final group of miscellaneous anonymous work, although it was not indicative of Panizzi's philosophy.

The "Ninety-one Rules" were a monumental achievement, as they represented the first attempt to codify the rules for the compilation of an author catalog with logical guides for cross references. Many of the basic concepts originated from the Bodleian and other leading libraries. The "Ninety-one Rules" were to form a basis for future codes and had a particular affect upon librarianship in the English-speaking countries.

Codes: Jewett, 1853. The first distinct code of cataloging rules issued in the United States was compiled by Charles C. Jewett, librarian of the Smithsonian Institution. Jewett sought primarily to provide a set of uniform rules established on principles, and supplemented by explanations and examples. The "principal object" of the rules was to secure uniformity; however, he cautioned that even the most elaborate rules were inadequate to "provide for every case of difficulty which may occur" (*49*, p. 18). About one-third of the publication was devoted to a description of an ingenious system that had originally been proposed in 1850 at a meeting of the American Association for the Advancement of Science in New Haven and again at the Librarians Conference of 1853. Jewett's plan was truly remarkable for its day as it called for the compilation of a code of rules, the submission of catalog entries by individual libraries according to these rules, stereotyping of each single entry, and the production of catalogs according to demand by simply interfiling and printing. The project failed, however, as it was too far advanced for the period to achieve widespread support as well as being hampered by technical problems which developed in the material used for the stereotype plates. The advantages described by the author were: elimination of duplicate effort, source of location for books, useful bibliographic information, guide for exchange, increased uniformity, possible American bibliography, and a future universal bibliography. The possible list of American literature embodied the concept that was later used in the Library of Congress printed catalogs. He pointed out that copyright books were required by law to be deposited at the Smithsonian and that these could be listed in monthly bulletins, annual lists, and quinquennial catalogs which would form a record of American publications.

He asserted that a catalog was a list of titles of books that a library contained and was generally not expected to give any further information "than the author gives or ought to give in the title page, and the publisher, in the imprint, or colophon; except the designation of form which is almost universally added" (49, p. 10). He admonished that "the catalog is designed to show what books are contained in a particular collection, and nothing more. Persons in want of further information, are expected to seek for it in bibliographical dictionaries, literary histories, or similar works" (49, p. 10).

The alphabetical catalog according to Jewett was the best type and he supported this with many of the arguments previously advanced by Panizzi. He proposed an alphabetical rather than a classified index as it was considered easier to use.

The rules themselves are basically those formulated by Panizzi but with a few changes such as the simplified treatment of anonymous works. The corporate concept was more clearly established in Rule 23 which placed all corporate bodies in one category and provided that they be entered under the name of the body. Cross references were to be made from "any important substantive or adjective, to the principal word" (49, p. 52). United States government publications were to be placed under *United States*. To secure uniformity, anonymous works were to be entered under the first word of the title which was not an article with cross references made from other words that might be sought. The librarian would be relieved of problems and the reader would no longer have to search in two places for a book. "Any rule for selecting the most prominent word of a title, or for entering a book under the name of its subject, would be found fatal to uniformity . . ." (49, p. 56). Pseudonymous works were to be placed under the assumed name followed by *pseud* but were not considered pseudonymous if the author had ". . . published any edition, continuation, or supplement under his name" (49, pp. 54–55).

The contribution of this small pamphlet should not be underestimated. The plea for uniformity would prove to be somewhat idealistic although the suggested rules were widely accepted, exerting a strong influence on future development of catalogs and codes.

Codes: Crestadoro, 1856. Four years after the publication of Jewett's rules, Andres Crestadoro issued an informative pamphlet (*50*) which advocated an extension of the subject word concept. He objected to the classified catalog because of its dependence upon an artificial arrangement and suggested a detailed entry catalog arranged by accession number which would be supplemented by a rather comprehensive alphabetical index of authors and subjects. He believed that the cataloger should add the author, subject, and "nature" or form of each book to the index even though the title failed to yield this information. An extensive system of cross references was proposed to overcome the lack of standardized terminology by referring from as many terms of the title as necessary, by connecting synonymous terms, and by interrelating class headings with subordinate or "partially synonymous" terms. Title terminology was always preferred with supplied information, only as a last resort supplied by the cataloger. This would scatter similar subjects in several locations, although at least a recognition of the need for a subject approach was expounded.

Codes: Cutter, 1876. The most comprehensive rules formulated during this century were by Charles Cutter. They were issued as part two of the Bureau of Education Report *Public Libraries in the United States . . .* (*2,* pp. 526–622). The rules evinced the influence of Panizzi, Jewett, Perkins, Abbot, Poole, and other leading librarians of the century. The first edition was issued in 1876 and was continued through a fourth in 1904 which Cutter suggested was actually unnecessary in view of the success of Library of Congress cataloging (*3,* p. 5). The rules covered the full range of cataloging procedures including a section of definitions; another on entry (where to enter) which contained subsections pertaining to authors, title, subject, and form catalogs as well as analysis; a section on style (how to enter) which included aspects of descriptive cataloging such as headings, body of card, collation, contents, notes, capitalization, and punctuation; and other minor sections pertaining to other catalogs and cataloging of special materials. Some of the major points regarding entry were: entry under personal or corporate author or substitute for it, bodies of men considered as authors, corporate bodies under name, anonymous works entered under title including periodicals, entry under original title for anonymous works when variant titles appear in successive volumes, specific subject heading rather than inclusive class, and subject entry under words expressing content of book rather than under terminology of title.

The rules were the epitome of the cataloging "art" of the period and were complete with copious notes which discussed the problems and suggested possible alternatives. Cutter's pragmatic approach was based primarily upon three principles. First, the principle of convenience and habit of the user. System and simplicity should be sacrificed when strict adherence to rules and uniformity create practices which are at odds with the "general and deeply rooted" habits of the public (*3,* p. 6). Second, the principle of specific and consistent subject entries. Each term used was to be applicable to innumerable books as it was derived from the content and not the title. It should consist of a specific heading, not the class, to which it was subordinate. To this was added the syndetic structure to connect related and synonymous terms (*3,* p. 67). Third, the catalog was more than a mere finding list "for a given book by an author's name" and should facilitate the location of all books of an author by placing them together in one place (*3*, p. 31).

The rules for the subject catalog represented the first attempt at such a codification and were to serve as the basis of American subject cataloging practices until the present day. Although they were designed to establish principles and practices with alternative solutions, they reflected the occasional uncertainty of the author and are marred by inconsistencies which still haunt cataloging theoreticians today. The Vatican code of 1931 was the only other completed codification of rules for the subject catalog and included one section on general principles and forms and a second on specific areas of application.

Many of the problems of the present dictionary subject catalog may be attributed in part to the context in which Cutter compiled his rules. The book catalog was still the dominant tool although the card catalog was gaining stature and was recognized by his last edition of the *Rules* as the way of the future. The *Rules* were compiled for a book catalog, dependent upon the main entry concept, and were designed for the relatively small popular library with a collection of information sources in the traditionally monographic format rather than the highly specialized texts in varying forms, and promulgated the developing concept of subject analysis that was generally regarded as a convenience rather than a necessity (*41*). The lack of direction that has persisted in the subject catalog may be attributed in part to the unquestioning adherence to Cutter's Rules and a failure to expand the few principles which were presented. Similar issues were still visible in the twentieth century when Frarey enumerated the eight major problems of the subject catalog: the principle of specific entry, terminology, form and structure of headings, choice among alternatives (place or subject), confusion of title and entry, size and complexity, reference structure, and maintenance (*51*, pp. 31–47). Without a doubt, little progress had been made since the days of Cutter except the addition of a new obstacle, the size of the subject catalog that aims at thorough analysis.

The rules as a whole proved to be a valuable addition to library literature and provided a codification of policies so badly needed by American libraries. Many of the issues raised by Cutter were to become the subject of intense debates in the next century. On the negative side the rules supplied a refuge for tradition and tended to reduce cataloging to a routine rather than make it the application of principles. Akers commented that since the 1876 issuance of the rules ". . . there has been no further development in principles although an enormous amount of work has been done in amplifying, codifying, and clarifying rules, which has contributed to a needed uniformity of practice" (*22*, p. 286).

The nineteenth century had been a productive year in catalogs and in cataloging procedures. The beginning of the century found both the classified and alphabetical author catalog in use with a variety of subject arrangements and indexes. Panizzi and Jewett both proclaimed the author catalog the most useable and reasonable form. The newly developing author catalogs eventually evolved into the dictionary form when subject headings were recognized as independent forms and no longer dependent upon the phraseology of the title page. In 1876 Poole reported that "the plan of the catalogue with references under authors and subjects, in one alphabetical arrangement, is the one which is now most universally used and is preferable to the classified plan" (*52*, p. 498). By 1893 catalog arrangement was still divergent with the single alphabetical order for authors and subject dominating, although some libraries still separated authors and subjects in two distinct parts with the latter in dictionary classified or alphabetico-classified order. In Europe the classified catalog tended to be more popular although the subject catalog was never strongly advocated in Great Britain during this century. The Germanic countries tended to develop comprehensive catalogs divided into an alphabetical catalog of authors and anonymous titles and a separate subject catalog or "schlagwortkatalog" which was arranged alphabetically by subject or catchword or the "systematischer katalog" arranged in classified order (logically or alphabetically) by subject.

The form of the catalog was manuscript or printed book at the beginning of the century. The use of slip catalogs, which were maintained originally only for preparation of the printed catalog, slowly began to evolve beyond their original intent. Cards had originally been suggested and used by French libraries in the eighteenth century, but failed to achieve widespread application until expanding book production and changing concepts of bibliographic organization stimulated the need for increased flexibility. Slip catalogs were frequently only accessible to librarians, but the Boston Public Library and the Philadelphia Library Company opened their slip catalogs to public use during the 1850s (*53*, pp. 284–285), while the former introduced a public card catalog in 1871. By 1893, Lane reported that the card catalog (forty-three reported) was the dominant form and was conceded a necessity although it infrequently served as a supplement for the printed book (thirteen reported). He also found that "most libraries still employ a running hand, generally preferring an upright and round to a slanted or angular one" (*54*, p. 841). He reported that the typewriter was now being used by over forty libraries and that printed cards from the Library Bureau were used by three. He ascertained that catalog cabinet drawers were generally designed for one instead of two rows of cards which were divided in size between 12.5 × 7.5 cm. (U.S. Postal Card) and 12.5 × 5 cm. although other unusual sizes were in use.

The need for the catalog was now recognized with the subject cataloging evolving from the shelf inventories, to the anonymous title, to the subject word, and eventually the subject heading as advocated by Jewett, Abbot, and Cutter. Lane found a consensus that every book should have an author or title entry and that most should have subject cards. Out of 191 libraries surveyed, 171 reported subject catalogs in one form or another (*54*, p. 837). Subject headings were still a matter of catalog's choice and varied widely, but the subject approach to books aided by the syndetic structure was firmly established and awaited further development.

The form of author or title entry progressed considerably during the century. Anonymous works were originally treated by intricate form headings, subject or place entries, or a host of alternatives. Jewett and Cutter advocated the separation of corporate bodies from the anonymous category and established a simple and logical framework. Corporate bodies by the end of the century tended to be entered primarily by first word of title or place depending upon the inclusion of the name within the title or whether it was a local British or American group (*54*, p. 845).

Varying opinions continued to govern pseudonyms at both the beginning and the end of the century.

The entry of descriptive elements had continued to increase. In the book catalog there are wide variations depending upon whether the entry was subject, author, or title as abbreviated forms were used to economize printing space. Lane determined this practice was still present in 1893 even though cards were now widely accepted (*54*, p. 837).

Throughout the century the title page continued to be the basis for the description, with brackets later used to indicate supplied information. The publisher or printer was recognized as an important part of the imprint early in the century. The use of size continued to be standard procedure although methods varied somewhat. Inclusive paging began during the early years and was widely accepted by the end of the century. Editors, translators, and now artists were all recognized as essential parts of the bibliographic description.

By 1893 Lane discerned that libraries tended to agree on the following: diminishing use of capital letters but no uniform practice, Arabic rather than Roman numerals, compound names under last part for English and first part for others, English and French names under prefix, and periodicals under title unless too generic. The use of contents notes evolved more fully during this century and were widely used during the last quarter. Analytics also developed more widespread use as bibliographers sought to increase the usability of the catalog and included periodicals and society publications as in the Harvard card catalog of 1861 and in the Boston Athenaeum Catalogue of 1874.

Codes were accepted during this century as the guides for cataloging compilation rather than the individualistic ideas that had dominated. Panizzi, Jewett, and Cutter were the major leaders of the century with Cutter's influence still dominating today's scene. Lane found that the majority of libraries used Cutter, with infrequent or supplemental use of codes by Linderfelt, Library School Rules (Dewey), and ALA (*54*, pp. 841–842).

The nineteenth century was a period of prodigious growth in cataloging procedures and codification. This was the era of numerous catalogs beginning with initiatory inventories and finding lists and culminating in the monumental printed dictionary catalogs. American cataloging had passed through a pioneer period while Europeans experienced stabilization. The lack of rules for the construction of catalogs during the early years stimulated local ingenuity, and techniques were crude with uniformity at a minimum. The situation was greatly improved by midcentury, and in the last two decades codes were a standard part of the cataloging process. The freedom from restraint during this century had nurtured innovative and conflicting ideas, pragmatic and idealistic approaches, and enhanced interest by bibliographers and scholars who slowly began to recognize the necessity for at least some semblance of bibliographic organization. Cataloging activities ceased to be the major concern of the administrators and were relegated to trained practitioners. The differentiation in staff assignments became more pronounced. Cataloging could be considered the first recognized specialization within libraries with Harvard establishing a distinct department devoted to this endeavor in 1859 (*48*, p. 8). Personnel training and recruitment, however, were largely based on expediency for Poole suggested that "there are ladies in the eastern cities who have had much experience in cataloging, and who devote themselves to this speciality . . ." (*52*, p. 490). The opening of the Columbia School of Library Economy in 1887 assisted development by supplying personnel with previous technical training.

Age of Sovereignty and Scrutiny

MODERN PERIOD

Twentieth Century

The cataloging activities of the twentieth century may be divided into two distinct periods: first, a period of traditionalism which extended approximately to 1941; and second, a period of reevaluation and rebirth.

The survey of cataloging practices by Lane in 1893 was followed by a similar report in the opening years of the new century. He attempted to review some of the then current cataloging tendencies which faced the profession. He began by pointing out that the catalog had been a simple author list but now every library needed as perfect a subject catalog as possible. The debate over the relationship between subject bibliography and subject catalog persisted intermittently when Raynard Swank renewed the discussion in the 1940s. American librarians such as J. C. M. Hanson tended to seek wide coverage for the subject catalog while the European librarians frequently relied heavily upon subject lists. Lane was further concerned by the growing size of the catalog and suggested that certain sections of the catalog could be printed, that selected lists could be compiled for use by the general reader, and that existing bibliographies could be checked to denote library holdings and to provide for omission of older imprints by libraries attempting to compile a subject catalog. He maintained that classification was used basically as a shelf arrangement, was designed primarily for the popular library, and had contributed little to the subject catalog. He pointed out the values and problems of certain enriching devices of the catalog such as subject headings, annotations, and analytics. He concluded that the card catalog was here to stay although national libraries still relied upon the printed catalog, and that codes tended to "become longer the oftener they are revised," although the object was to seek simplicity and uniformity with specific instructions for more cases. Lane expressed hope for international uniformity in bibliographic matters and card publication by foreign governments, and he contended that the catalog was a finding list and not a bibliographic dictionary, but expressed the need for cooperation and centralization and described some of the cooperative projects such as printed cards and local union lists of periodicals (*55*).

Two events that were to have a decided effect occurred during the early part of the century. The reorganization of the Library of Congress revitalized its cataloging department with an influx of qualified personnel such as James Christian Meinert Hanson and Charles Martel who later became leaders in the field of cataloging and classification. The second was the appointment of a committee by ALA in 1901 under the chairmanship of Hanson to revise the old 1883 catalog rules so that they were in accord with those of Library of Congress. A draft or advanced copy was issued a short time later and circulated for comments and criticisms. At the same time the Library Association (Great Britain) was also in the process of revising their cataloging rules and it occurred to Dewey that this was an opportune time to establish some uniformity among the English-speaking countries of the world. A committee was formed and in 1908 the code was completed and published in two separate editions although there were only eight rules upon which agreement could not be achieved. Within the United States the reconciliation of the rules with Library of Congress was not as complete as hoped for; the codification of their practices was still in the developmental stage and efforts had to be continued in this direction (56, p. 72).

Cooperative cataloging, which is defined as the compilation of catalog cards through a joint effort by a number of libraries in an effort to reduce duplication of operations (57, p. 26), continued during this century. The Library of Congress began the printing of catalog cards submitted by other government libraries in 1902, and this was further extended to include several large libraries outside the government structure in 1910. By 1932 the Cooperative Cataloguing Committee of the ALA had opened an office at the Library of Congress with a subsidy from the General Education Board. Two years later the Cooperative Cataloguing and Classification Service became a division of the library and by 1941 it was largely absorbed by the Descriptive Cataloguing Division (58, pp. 8–9). Efforts at cooperative cataloging were never as intense as those directed toward centralization, which would afford more concentration of staff and tools, maximum standardization of procedures and codification of rules, and substantially improved supervision and administration.

The dictionary form of the catalog continued to dominate the scene with some exceptions such as the 1903 Classed Catalogue of the Carnegie Library of Pittsburgh, which was compiled by Margaret Mann and was to be remembered not only for its arrangement but also for its printed format. The debate over the relative merits of the classified and dictionary catalog continued although the issue was largely closed in the U.S. In 1905 Fletcher intimated that the dictionary catalog ". . . has the character of a superstition in so far as it is accepted and religiously carried out on grounds that are traditional, rather than on intelligent conviction that it meets present needs and is good for the future needs for which we must make provisions." He warned that changes had occurred in the size of libraries, methods of administration, and the attitude toward the library patron which must be considered in catalog construction, and he suggested that the subject catalog be supplemented by the shelf list, bibliographies, reading lists, and indexes (59, pp. 141–144). Rider later renewed the discussion, contending that librarians lacked imagination in approaching the problem of bibliographic organization and should examine such alternatives to the dictionary catalog as classified catalog, microphotography, book catalogs, and smaller sized catalog cards. He contended that a philosophy of the catalog was necessary and cited Hanson and Mudge as believing the catalog was an end in itself while Richardson and Currier believed it existed only to put the reader in contact with the library's holdings. He criticized the bibliographic method of cataloging as practiced by the Library of Congress which was slavishly adhered to by the majority of the libraries in the U.S. (*60*). Interest in the classified catalog was somewhat stimulated at an institute on subject analysis of library materials in 1953 when Harry Dewey and Kanardy Taylor supported its excellence. Dewey succinctly outlined the ease of converting the dictionary catalog to the classified (*61*). Kanardy Taylor contended that the alphabetical was best for public use while the classified was more adaptable to scientific research and concluded by agreeing with Gjelsness who contended in 1931 that "perhaps we have gone too far in accepting a standard product and applying it to all purposes" and called for a "universal re-evaluation" (*62, p. 112*).

Continued interest in the classified catalog in a few special libraries, the mounting pressures for improved bibliographic organization, experimentation with new approaches to classification, and the recognition of the underdeveloped potential of the classified catalog precipitated the publication of a manual in 1956 that sought to depict the functions, characteristics, and necessary procedures (*30*, pp. IX–X). Although well done, this manual failed to stimulate the production of classified catalogs, as a survey made in 1962 listed only sixteen classified catalogs in use in the U.S. and Canada (*63*, pp. 274–275). Today exemplary classified catalogs are found at John Crerar, the Engineering Societies Library of New York, and Boston University Library, and the National Library of Canada. Some libraries did produce duplicate shelf lists which were used as adjuncts to the dictionary catalog but further development of the classified catalog in the U.S. must await another era.

Advocates of the dictionary catalog attempted to facilitate more rapid use and maintenance in the 1940s by separating the subject and form entries and the author and title entries into two distinct files although other combinations were possible. The separation was reputed to alleviate searching by the user and to make filing by library personnel considerably easier. A number of college and university libraries such as the University of Denver adopted the divided catalog but interest was limited with only twenty-four divided catalogs found out of 457 academic libraries surveyed with the majority of them developing between 1938–1947 (*64*). Later the discussion shifted from the author-subject division of the catalog to the horizontal division by date of publication as large research libraries sought to devise a solution to the problem of the mass of entries under some headings.

Size became a topic of discussion as book production soared. The major virtue of the card catalog soon became a detriment as catalogers continued insertion of added entries in the form of analytics, numerous subject headings, title cards, series cards, and catch-titles as well as a host of references for both authors and subjects. Each new edition of the subject lists tended to multiply the number of references until librarians began to question their use. The traditional form of descriptive cataloging continued to necessitate the inclusion of items which some librarians thought should have been relegated to biographical and bibliographic sources outside the catalog.

Library administrators began to bewail high cataloging costs while catalogers struggled to evaluate their methods. As a whole, cataloging departments of the early twentieth century were poorly organized and administered, regimented by tradition rather than by objective analysis of the situation, and dependent upon Library of Congress cataloging practices. To complicate matters the number of catalogs also increased with duplicate cards filed in official, departmental, and union catalogs being maintained at unknown expense. Library of Congress cataloging policies continued to expand with supplementary rules or decisions printed on cards after 1911. Numerous special publications such as a guide for cataloging periodicals issued in 1918 (*65*) and another for serials in 1919 (*66*) were characteristic of the growing complex of rules. The ever increasing arrearage at the Library of Congress, which was due in part to the mass of rules, precipitated an extensive study by Joeckel in 1940 (*67*). The survey clearly indicated that the proliferation of rules must be arrested and the present body reduced and simplified. This was followed by further studies during this decade which evinced the desired simplification of cataloging procedures and would reach its climax in the revision of the code a few years later. Librarians were beginning to demand that the principles of cataloging be recognized rather than attempting to provide rules for every situation.

Outside the Library of Congress the use of centrally prepared catalog cards were clearly a time saver, but the constant rechecking and adherence to minutia tended to keep the cataloging costs at a high level. In an effort to counteract the growing size of the card catalog, selective and simplified cataloging were suggested as possible solutions. Selective cataloging was suggested by Dury in 1649 and was thoroughly discussed by Van Hoesen in 1928 (*68*). Selective cataloging is an attempt to limit the number of catalog entries by designating library materials for varying degrees according to their potential use. Generally full cataloging is accorded reference works while at the other end of the scale pamphlets or government documents are usually completely excluded from the cataloging process. The economic feasibility of this method was recognized although the cataloger was required to be aware of the users' methods and demands. Simplified cataloging denotes an effort to omit or greatly simplify elements of the catalog card that are not considered essential. It is intended to achieve economy by an abbreviated entry, less effort for verification of author's name, fewer added entries, or similar steps which are not considered essential in a small public library or a childrens collection. The Library of Congress instituted cataloging categories in 1947 and limited cataloging in 1951. Both are examples of selective and simplified cataloging as certain types of materials were relegated to full bibliographic description while others were described less fully. Added entries were made only after a careful scrutiny of their potential value. In spite of the objection by some catalogers that every book in the library should be subject to the same rules, all libraries practice some form of simplified or selective cataloging. Some of the more recent innovations are the omission of subject entries for older works, limited use of added entries, and simplified entry for materials in storage. The widespread use of printed cards by commercial companies such as H. W. Wilson and *Library Journal* attest to the acceptance of simplified cataloging by public and school libraries.

The use of the card catalog was also a subject of discussion and represented an attempt to utilize empirical research in offering a more logical approach to one of Cutter's basic principles, the user. Early studies were primarily discussions of inadequacy, complexity, and organization of catalogs based on traditional impressions and theories of the user and his approach to the catalog (*69*, p. 148). During the thirties the studies began to become more concerned with the users point of view and continued to develop in outlook and method. A survey of twenty-seven catalog use studies completed between 1930–1956 revealed some shortcomings in methodology and tended to relate only to the quantitative use of the catalog. Some of the more significant findings were: catalog used by 50–60% of all library users; nonspecialist tends to use catalog more than specialist; subject catalog infrequently used to find all material in library; English language material of recent date most widely sought; author, title, call number, and subject heading most widely used information; problem of use stems largely from lack of understanding and application of principle of specific entry, preferences for subject or place, and inability to deal with obsolete terminology; subject catalog considered effective about 70% of the time; need for better instruction in use of catalog; and possible modification into a more selective tool as some evidence supports dispensability in present form (*69*, pp. 162–163).

Active revision of the 1908 code began in 1930 with the appointment of a committee on code revision by the ALA. The preliminary edition of the revised code was issued in 1941 and was divided into two sections: the first dealt with form of entry and heading, and the second was concerned with the description of the book. The code was received with a rash of complaints, largely due to the elaborate rules suggested in part two which was dropped in the final publication of the second edition. It was immediately apparent that a reevaluation or reappraisal of cataloging policies was needed. This call for reevaluation marked the end of the traditional period and the beginning of the new.

In 1941 the "crisis in cataloging" was succinctly depicted by Andrew D. Osborn who called for an end to the slavish adherence to codes which tended to obscure reasons and principles and maintained that cataloging was an art which was based upon a few simple rules. He continued by discussing the four types of cataloging: legalist theory (an expanding complexity of rules); perfectionism (effort to catalog a book once and for all); bibliographic (cataloging molded into a branch of descriptive bibliography); and pragmatic theory (rules and decisions serving a practical purpose). He soundly condemned the continuance of the three tradition-bound methods and called for recognition of a need for the pragmatic cataloger. He contended that card catalogs frequently failed to achieve their goals because of meaningless practices, a need for three distinct grades of cataloging with the standard less detailed than advocated by the 1908 code, simplified rules even a necessity for the Library of Congress, self-cataloging methods advisable for little used materials, high quality for essential items but little for nonessential, practical interpretation of any point, and a review of the treatment of serials, documents, and nondocuments to determine cataloging needs. He concluded that the classical period was drawing to a close and that the change could be largely attributed to extreme systematization and standardization which had resulted from too much work (70).

Five years later the report of Herman Henkle on descriptive cataloging by the Library of Congress clearly reflected the changing concepts and sought to develop functions and techniques (71). The functions were aimed at presenting an accurate description of each book which would indicate its relationship to other editions and issues as well as entries for other books. The new rules, which were published in 1949, attempted to carry out the proposals of the study with brevity and simplicity (72). They were intended as an adjunct to the *ALA Cataloging Rules for Author and Title Entries* which were finally issued the same year. In spite of the years of discussion and the interest shown in the new codes, they tended to produce only a change in details, with the *ALA Rules* in particular tending to ignore the discussion, rather than reflecting it (56, p. 78). In any event, the period of discussion regarding the codes of 1949 tended to focus concern on the need to reevaluate the function of the catalog, to adapt time-saving methods within the cataloging department, to cope with mass acquisition, and to search for new approaches that would insure a less pronounced growth of the card catalog.

Within a few years after the appearance of the "twin codes" a movement for the simplification of author and title entries was afoot. The need for guiding principles was examined by Seymour Lubetzky in his study of 1953 which has exerted a major influence upon the actions of the resulting committees (73). As in the case of the 1908 code, the activities of the special committees appointed by the ALA were coordinated with a similar committee of the Library Association (Great Britain) and was further augmented by a committee of the Canada Library Association. International cooperation was afforded through the International Conference on Cataloguing Principles, Paris, 1961 (4). The results of the conference were encouraging as a relatively uniform consensus of opinion resulted in a statement of principles pertaining to the function and structure of the catalog and to the choice, form, and structure of entries. These principles clearly reflected the influence of Lubetzky's critique as well as his unfinished draft of 1960 (74) and were accepted by the Catalog Code Revision Committee in 1962. The Paris Principles "were seriously questioned by the large research libraries who were alarmed by the possible extensive recataloging as a result of their retrospective application." The Library of Congress conducted a detailed study of the "theoretical merits" of the statement and attempted to ascertain the proportion of change required in the retrospective application of the rules in its card catalog (75, p. 3). The results, as expected, provided support for the contention that the large research libraries were unable to accept the radical changes because of the heavy costs of revising the many catalog entries. The so called "Miami Compromise," which agreed to certain exceptions regarding the retention of the archaic entry under place rather than name of the corporate body, was approved and incorporated into the code Rules 98 and 99. The Library of Congress accepted the code only as it affects new author headings by adopting the practice of superimposition which allows the new rules to apply only in establishing entries not previously used while reverting to the old rules for all entries presently established in the catalog. As a whole the rules were a significant improvement for they were based upon a set of principles that freed them from some of the rigidity of the past. The inclusion of the rules for descriptive cataloging and for special material provided a single volume rather than the multiple works of the past.

Centralized cataloging became a primary concern during this century. Printed card production was largely limited to a few large public libraries and the Library of Congress. The card distribution service of the latter soon became recognized as a valuable asset with many libraries making extensive use of the somewhat limited number of available cards. In 1938 H. W. Wilson began the printing of catalog cards that were designed primarily for the needs of public and school libraries. The cards followed a simplified system, aimed at providing less bibliographic detail for the more popular titles with annotations and analytics adding another dimension for reading guidance.

The growing need for cataloging information and the dissatisfaction with the present services stimulated the movement for cataloging or processing centers that were occasionally established within large public libraries with small units contracting for services, or at the state level through the efforts of the state library commission, or at the regional level through an association of libraries.

Georgia was the first state library to initiate the distribution of printed cards in 1944. In the following years a number of similar centers were established as were commercial enterprises offering a variety of cataloging services. The major problems of availability and the delay in supplying cards stimulated a large amount of discussion which resulted in a number of cooperative plans such as the one suggested by Ralph Ellsworth in 1948 to assure the availability of printed cards for all books which were acquired by the Library of Congress and cooperating libraries (76). In 1953 the Library of Congress inaugurated the All-The-Book Plan in an effort to increase the number of titles for which printed cards were available. The library hoped to solicit prepublication copies of current American imprints from the publishers so that cards would be produced as soon as possible. The Library of Congress order numbers were also supplied to the publishers who placed them on the verso of the title page to assure ready accessibility in ordering cards. The services were further improved in 1959 when R. W. Bowker Co. agreed to lend to the Library of Congress review copies received by them for listing in *Library Journal* and *Publishers' Weekly* in exchange for cataloging information which would be included in the latter. Wholesale book dealers and commercial processing centers such as Alanar cooperated by lending copies which were not readily available (77, p. 40). Through this program the bulk of the trade books now had printed catalog cards available. It was estimated that in 1965 Dewey numbers were available on 80% of all Library of Congress printed cards because of this expanded coverage (77, p. 34).

The Library Service Act of 1956 with its state plans and federal funds added further impetus to the development of centers such as the Southwest Missouri Library Services, Inc. of 1957. The trend was apparent for by 1965–1966 there were sixty-three identified cooperative processing centers in forty-one states (*78*, p. 72).

School libraries enjoyed a similar interest with centralized processing, utilized as early as 1917 in one instance although by 1961 such services had expanded to include at least 3% of the elementary and 2% of the secondary schools (*79*, pp. 56, 62). The National Defense Act and the Elementary and Secondary Education Act of 1965 yielded increased book budgets which in turn actuated the need for cataloging services. Centralized centers for school libraries began to develop as did commercial services ranging from the *Library Journal* kits to complete processing. The charges for standard cataloging by the commercial centers in 1967 varied from $0.60 to $1.90, with custom or special cataloging costs much higher (*80*, p. 51). Card production at the centers and within individual libraries had developed extensively from the early heliotype method mentioned by Cutter in 1876 (*2*, p. 543). A study completed in 1965 outlined the following methods of card procurement or production: purchase, manual typing, stencil duplication (postcard size), fluid duplication, stencil duplication (full size), offset, addressing machine (fiber or metal stencil), automatic typewriter, Diazo duplication, electrostatic copying (Xerox, etc.), defusion transfer copying, and projection photocopying (*81*, p. 5). To this list may be added the newest computer produced cards which are generated by individual libraries as well as being available commercially from the Catalogue Card Corporation of America. Efforts of college and university libraries have been devoted primarily toward improving the program at the Library of Congress although Colorado recently embarked upon a state processing center. Junior and small four-year colleges frequently use commercial services in addition to the Library of Congress while infrequently relying upon the state and regional centers.

The Cataloging-In-Source experiment was the revival of a movement that was suggested and attempted during the nineteenth century and was designed to provide a copy of each catalog card within the book itself. The project was conducted by the Library of Congress between June 1958 and February 1959, with over 157 publishers cooperating through the provision of proof copies for 1,203 publications (*42*, pp. V–VI). The plan was well conceived but was hampered by a variety of factors such as a lack of cooperation by many publishers (only a little over 50% of those originally contacted actually participated) and dissatisfaction with the interrupted production schedules. Some reservations were also evident at the Library of Congress when the projected increases in staff and facilities were questioned in the light of the possible results. The results were well received by the libraries although an extensive consumer reaction survey failed to provide sufficient "clear cut evidence" of possible savings and of utilization of the information. The cataloging information contained in the *Publishers' Weekly* and SACAP, an acquisition and cataloging service instituted by Bro-Dart which would provide paper offset masters suitable for producing a sufficient number of catalog cards, were suggested as more economical methods of obtaining similar results. The project passed into oblivion with the following:

> In light of the experience gained through the experiment, it is concluded that neither a full nor a partial Cataloging-in-Source Program is desirable. The *Publishers' Weekly* and SACAP programs have suggested methods by which the potential promise of Cataloging-in-Source might be realized in a much more economical way. There should be no further experiments with Cataloging-in-Source. If the new programs fail to meet their objectives, further experiments should be conducted along the lines these programs have laid down (*42*, p. 52).

The Cards-with-Books-Program of 1961 was another attempt by the Library of Congress to get cards into the hands of librarians as quickly as possible. The major thrust of the program was to encourage publishers and book wholesalers to supply printed cards with their publications. Special arrangements were made at the Library of Congress to facilitate this operation and by 1967 over ninety-six wholesale distributors and publishers were annually distributing almost 10 million cards (about 2 million sets) (*82*, p. 53). Many were still hesitant, however, in spite of the fact that libraries purchase approximately 80–85% of all current American trade books through wholesale book distributors and recent card sales at the Library of Congress indicate that about 80% of all cards sold are for current American imprints (*83*, pp. 433–444).

Generally Library of Congress printed cards are available for only about 50% of the research library acquisitions with availability directly related to the acquisition and cataloging efforts of the Library of Congress and the cooperating libraries. The development of the Area Studies programs and the passage of PL 480 created an increased need for catalog cards in a wide variety of foreign languages which were simply beyond the capabilities of most cataloging departments. In 1962 a concerted effort was made to improve the availability of such cards by the Library of Congress adding several language sections to its descriptive cataloging division, cooperative copy being supplied by large libraries such as Princeton, and data sheets being compiled by personnel in the country of origin of each publication. A major step toward the systematization of centralized cataloging at the national and international level occurred in 1965 with the passage of the Higher Education Act, Title II-C. The Library of Congress was provided funds in 1966 to embark upon an unprecedented program of worldwide acquisition and centralized national cataloging aimed at alleviating the pressing needs of the research libraries (*82*, p. 36). The resulting National Program of Acquisitions and Cataloging, known in Europe as the Shared Cataloging Program, was to expedite acquisition through a carefully formulated plan of blanket orders and purchase arrangements. Cataloging operations were accelerated through the use of entries from national bibliographies which provide an international aspect although adjustments were made so that entries complied with existing standards. By the end of the first year of operations nine overseas offices were providing publications from twenty-one countries with cataloging information from seventeen foreign sources (*82*, p. 36). Catalog cards for over 150,000 publications were supplied to over ninety-two cooperating libraries in America within the first twelve months of its existence (*82*, p. 36). The impact of the program will be widely felt by the cooperating libraries as a preliminary analysis of the availability of cards for foreign titles indicated a record high of 73% opposed to the former 50% expectancy while the total number of all titles processed at the Library of Congress rose 20% (*82*, p. 39). The magnitude of the cataloging operation at the Library of Congress is clearly shown by a reported sale of over 74 million printed cards to approximately 20,000 libraries throughout the world by the Card Division in 1967 (*82*, p. 53).

Centralized cataloging operations were not confined to printed cards only, for in 1965 the Library of Congress published the first reports pertaining to a proposed plan for issuing cataloging information on magnetic tape. The first tapes for this experiment in Machine Readable Cataloguing Data (MARC) were issued in November, 1966, to sixteen participating libraries and resulted in over 16,000 records for current English-language monographs being provided by the end of the fiscal year (*82*, pp. 17–18). The results were carefully studied and a more highly developed standardized format was put into operational distribution recently under the MARC II designation.

Centralized cataloging has experienced tremendous growth during this century. The problems of individualism, time, and limited availability have tended to inhibit the universal acceptance although the situation improved considerably during the last decades. After over 100 years the visionary ideas of Jewett were nearing fruition.

The early 1930s witnessed the establishment of a number of local and regional union catalogs within the United States. The availability of personnel through the Work Project Administration exerted a strong influence upon their proliferation but the ensuing years proved difficult for many of them to endure because of soaring maintenance costs. Three bibliographic centers at Philadelphia, Denver, and Seattle today attest to the feasibility of the concept. The major reason for the survival of the latter two was probably the establishment of a broad base of regional membership held together by a strong moral belief in the cooperative idea as well as a definite need for such a service within an area rather sparsely populated and without extensive state library collections (*84*, p. 75).

The most notable union catalog is the National Union Catalog which was established in 1901 at the Library of Congress to provide a listing of governmental libraries in Washington and important libraries outside the city. The reciprocal exchange of cards soon became a reality and depository catalogs were established in many of the major libraries. The growth of the catalog continued and by 1926 it contained more than 2 million entries. From 1927 to 1932 a grant from John D. Rockefeller, Jr. financed the "Project B" program which was designed to expand the catalog to contain the location of all important reference books in American libraries. After 25 years of administration the Card Division was relieved of the Union Catalog project in 1932 when it was established as a separate unit. Continued efforts by librarians, particularly those working through the ALA, focused attention upon the venture which in turn led to increased financial support so necessary for expansion. The official name, National Union Catalog, was adopted in 1948 and by 1964 over 15 million cards represented approximately 8 million titles and editions (*85,* p. 77).

The pressing problem of maintaining the depository catalogs within the specially selected libraries and the need for wider distribution of cataloging information necessitated a more economical and feasible approach. The most logical solution lay in the revival of the book catalog which had continued as a standard in many national libraries in spite of abandonment by others. A *Catalog of Books Represented by Library of Congress Printed Cards Issued to July 31, 1942* was published in 1942–1946 in 167 volumes and was followed by a series of supplements for both authors and subjects. In 1956 the catalog was expanded to include the holdings of the National Union Catalog and the next issue was given a new title to reflect this increased coverage. The movement to encompass an extended retrospective period led to the publication of *The National Union Catalog, 1952, 1955 Imprints* . . . and the most recent, *The National Union Catalog, Pre1956 Imprints* which is presently being published by Mansell Information Publishing Ltd. (England) and will contain over 16 million cards. Thus the whole spectrum of the National Union Catalog will now be available through the use of the printed book catalog.

The success of the Library of Congress book catalogs and the advent of electronic hardware had a decided effect upon the return of the book catalog. In 1953 the Lamont Library at Harvard produced a printed catalog which was designed for wide distribution to students and faculty. The catalog was produced by a photo-offset lithographic process such as used by the Library of Congress catalogs, only each of the 40,000 titles were retyped, generally one line per title, in a classified order which was supplemented by an author index of approximately sixty pages and an index of the classification.

The Library and Information Service of Western Australia compiled a classified nonfiction book catalog in 1965 containing approximately 67,000 titles. The classified section was comprised of two volumes arranged by the Dewey Decimal System while the subject index was compiled from the Library of Congress subject headings which were carefully formulated into relative index entries. The entries were typed on strips which were then printed by a photolithographic process. Future revisions are planned by positioning new entries among the original strips (*86*, pp. 143–154).

A variety of other printing techniques are presently used with varying degrees of success depending upon the desired results and the amount of economic support. The linotype slugs method, used by H. W. Wilson, can be revised simply by interfiling new slugs and removing obsolete ones. It is expensive but is especially well adapted to the cumulative indexing scheme.

The shingled card technique with offset is inexpensive and especially adaptable for the smaller operation. The process entails the photographing of overlapping cards arranged like shingles, preparation of an offset plate from a reduced negative, and final printing. The sequential camera is a refinement of this technique and consists of a special camera capable of photographing only a part of the catalog card as it is placed before the lens. This method was used successfully in 1959 by the National Library of Medicine for the production of its *Current List of Medical Literature*.

The early Library of Congress catalogs utilized a photo-offset process based upon a photographically reduced negative produced by assembling cards immediately after one another in columns. Later a special card was printed which eliminated the blank spaces at the bottom, thus expanding the contents of each page considerably. Another offset process which utilizes microfilm and electrostatic or xerographic reproductions for plate composition has been extensively used by G. K. Hall since 1959 for the reprinting of a wide variety of library catalogs for commercial distribution.

One of the first catalogs produced by tabulating machines was that of the King County Public Library, Seattle, in 1951 and was issued on expendable IBM paper. The Los Angeles County Public Library employed a similar approach but went further and prepared multilith masters which were then used to print two extensive and carefully compiled catalogs in 1952 and 1954. The first was a four-volume children's catalog divided into separate alphabets for authors, titles, and subjects and an adult catalog of thirty-seven volumes which was divided into separate alphabets for authors (8 volumes), titles (6 volumes), conventional subjects (18 volumes), fiction subjects (4 volumes), and foreign books (1 volume) (*87*, pp. 203–204).

The New York State Catalog of 1956–1960 was designed principally for interlibrary loan and was a single line entry checklist of books and ephemeral material in three broad subjects issued in separate parts. The catalog was produced by the use of a tabulating machine and photo-offset printing.

The Baltimore County Public Library Book Catalog issued in 1965 was a completely computerized product containing approximately 55,000 titles with bimonthly and annual supplements. The shelf list was arranged in alphabetical order, then edited, and key punched on cards which were later transferred to magnetic tape for storage. The computer organized printout resulted in a divided catalog for authors, titles, and subjects. Simplified cataloging procedures were used as the main emphasis was a finding list rather than a bibliographic tool. Added entries were held to a minimum although no limit was placed on the number of subject headings (*88*, pp. 133–140).

Another recently developed computer-produced catalog appeared at Stanford University in 1966 with the first issue of an annual catalog containing about 25,000 titles arranged in a three part format: author and title, subject, and shelf list. The source of information was the basic Library of Congress cards which were keypunched and then converted to magnetic tape. The catalog sought to provide ". . . something more than reproductions of unit catalog cards" and rejected both the traditional main entry concept and unit card in an effort to gain space (*89*, p. 18). The final printouts were photographically reduced and placed on offset masters for printing.

The contemporary book catalog made tremendous strides in the last two decades of its revitalization. Generally production of the book catalogs falls into three categories. First, the photo-offset method based on the production of a photographically reduced negative by shingling or grouping individual cards, by a sequential camera, or by the use of microfilm and electrostatic printing. Second, tabulating machines with punched cards or tape equipment are used to produce printouts or multilith masters. The former may be used as copy for the photo-offset while the latter is immediately available for printing. Third, the computer now is capable of organizing information for catalog production which results in printouts for immediate use or for the production of photo-offset masters. Two other categories should be mentioned although they are an advance beyond the book catalog. First, the use of some form of microprint, suggested by Fremont Rider as early as 1940. Limited production of catalogs which utilize some form of microprint are available although accessibility has hampered extensive use. Another use is in such index-machines as Filmores, Flip, Fosdic, Media, Minicard, Rapid Selector, Verac, and Walnut (*90,* p. 30). Second, the futuristic computer-stored catalog as depicted by many current experiments may eventually become economically feasible. Presently the computer imput necessary to produce a book catalog could readily be adapted to direct user access and several libraries are making provisions for on-line, real-time terminal inquiries (*91,* p. 162).

Catalogs and cataloging will continue as in the past to vary considerably from one library to another depending upon needs, former practices, personnel, and financial resources. History clearly indicates that new methods are not unique to this century. A review of some of the so-called recent innovations reveals our debt to the past. The KWIC Index is nothing more than the old subject word concept which was revered by Edwards and criticized by Cutter. The finding list or limited entry catalog were used and strongly supported over 100 years ago by Poole. Arrangement of books in order of accession was practiced even in the most ancient libraries. The use of broad rather than close classification was employed for years. Size classification, so useful in storage libraries, was suggested hundreds of years ago by Gesner. The past can play an important role in future development if new practices are based upon a rational approach stemming from empirical research rather than tradition. The failure to define the functions of the catalog has created a framework of mythology regarding the needs of the users which was further promulgated by Cutter and accepted verbatim by catalogers as gospel. The method used to determine these potential needs during the time of Cutter has never been clearly enumerated although his philosophy has prevailed for almost 100 years and before that was adumbrated by the Bodleian and British Museum Rules which enounced dogma in the same authoritative tones. At that time, however, the position of the library was decidedly different from today as literacy was low and only the gentry had access to printed materials. As the libraries grew and assumed a prominent place in the educational structure, the catalog retained the nineteenth century rules for construction of the printed book catalog while slowly being filled with twentieth century acquisitions. The problem of determining the needs of the user is characterized by an infinite number of variables which are changing every day as the demands of society are modified. The few trends which are discernible from extant studies are difficult to translate into action which will fulfill all the needs at reasonable cost. The solution seems to lie in the formulation of catalog-centered criteria, as suggested by Taube, which would provide evaluation based on size, compilation and maintenance costs, amount of appropriate and relevant material, number of access points, extent of information about each item, inclusion of many types of information for various purposes, and a low rate of growth (*41,*

p. 58). These must then be assigned values with regard to the individual library in order to provide a statement of reasonable and attainable functions which can be interpreted into specific goals. The next step is the formulation of methods complete with suitable alternatives. These, however, are not an end in themselves but serve to carry out the specific goals and more inclusive functions.

It is impossible to foresee the many possible forms and methods which will characterize the catalog of the future because of the infinite variations existing from one library to another. General trends, however, may be conjectured upon the basis of events of the past although levels and extent of applications will vary widely.

The most advanced form of the catalog of the foretellable future will be the computerized catalog so aptly depicted by Swanson (92,93). This catalog will consider eleven performance goals: user dialogues (programmed interrogation), aids to browsing, user-indexed library, access to in-depth information, wheat and chaff identification, national "network" of libraries, national network of bibliographic tools, instant information, remote interrogation and delivery, active dissemination, and quality control over library services (improved feedback) (92, pp. 13–15). The basic system would be comprised of two-way communication with a computer-stored catalog such as the National Union Catalog through the use of a console that would permit the user to progress from simple bibliographic or limited subject information through a series of heuristic steps to the actual text. Many of the more specialized works such as periodical articles could be obtained as print-outs while the contents of monographs could be examined through a display of the table of contents or indexes by a type of cathode ray tube while the final examination would be dependent upon an actual physical perusal. The plan devotes sufficient attention to all of the performance goals. The cost, based on National Union Catalog size and use, is estimated at about $50 per minute which is clearly prohibitive with the primary problem created by the disproportionately large amount of information storage to that which is actually used (93, p. 124). The only solution seems to lie in the development of equipment that could economically surmount this problem and the utilization of more complex operations pertaining to subjects rather than simple descriptive searches involving the specific author, title, etc. (93, p. 125). The potential use of the computer in providing access to technical reports, government documents, periodical articles, and other highly specialized information has been clearly demonstrated and may be the most economically feasible area of immediate development. The failure of the present subject catalog to go beyond a cursory analysis could be greatly improved through such an application. Libraries will continue to seek wider coverage and will no doubt strengthen their positions through a more thorough subject analysis rather than by concentrating on the traditional monographic sources. Research libraries may find it feasible to store bibliographic information for all sources within the computer and produce printed catalogs only for the monographic materials which will be sought by a large number of users, while the computer information would be available for serious researchers desiring comprehensive searches. The inclusion of actual textual materials would be limited primarily to the units of a more manageable length rather than attempting to convert to total text storage for extensive monographic material.

A more immediate and universal application of the computer will be the production of book catalogs and catalog cards. As costs are reduced wider application will result in increased regional and national cooperation with catalogs being produced from state or regional union lists in much the same way as from the National Union Catalog. Wide distribution of cataloging information will in turn stimulate more sophisticated methods of card reproduction for those who seek to retain the card catalog.

Aside from the computer, less sweeping but significant changes will probably take place in the immediate future and would be more generally applicable to a large number of libraries. It seems likely that the book catalog will slowly become the dominant manual system with the card catalog serving as a supplement analogous to the old slip catalogs. The dichotomy of expanding the catalog beyond the monograph and limiting it to a reasonable size will continue as a major source of debate. Where computers are available the problem will be a question of input and storage, while both systems will strive to provide more information organized in such a way that the whole file must not be searched for each request. Horizontal division by date will allow older materials to be printed in a separate sequence, and the use of bibliographies will continue to prove useful. The use of the shelf list (conventional or printed) will serve as a source for large blocks of information that can readily be connected by references. The classified catalog will continue to gain new converts like the National Library of Canada where the Library of Congress system is applied. Centrally produced subject indexes for the classified catalog would greatly add to this movement, with several now available through G. K. Hall from such libraries as Boston University and John Crerar although much more needs to be done in this area. Classification will continue to rise above the shelf-location status which it was originally accorded in the U.S. and serve as a flexible subject device within the catalog. The use of the shelf list will be expanded, serving as a basis for computerization and as an expanded approach to subjects in the manual systems. Terminology will be of primary concern in all types of catalogs with emphasis given to logical development by specialists. Classified subject lists, as suggested by Mostecky (94, pp. 309–313), and thesauri will be prepared to replace the outmoded subject lists with complex and unsuitable terminology set in an illogical syndetic structure. Careful studies such as those done by Daily, Lilley, and Pettus all accentuate the need for a more realistic approach to the place of subject headings, descriptors, or indexing terms within the subject catalog. The intellectual process of converting a remote concept into a possible subject heading will be guided by improved lists with heuristic qualities rather than the chance inclusion of references. The present subject lists have been used to some extent as supplementary guides to the public catalog, but will be eventually replaced by the new lists which will convert the users concepts into catalog access points. The use of references within the catalog itself could be dropped with the lists serving as the first step to the subject approach. Libraries will continue to expand in-depth subject analysis within the manual systems. Analytics and wider coverage could be accomplished by separate indexes and bibliographies and by improvement of existing sources using a greater degree of more cooperative methods. The service basis approach by H. W. Wilson is indicative of the feasibility and economy of such action. Professional organizations have and should continue to make advances in this direction. Every possible effort should be made to extend cooperative indexing to its fullest potential so that it is available in usable formats, with reduced duplication and increased accessibility to the largest number of possible users. Professional organizations and the federal government will play an active role in such improvements with national planning developing far beyond present levels. Continued centralized efforts such as MEDLAR and MARC will be joined by a host of preparation centers to extend bibliographic control which is much less than popularly supposed. Use of centralized services and decentralized centers will combine a variety of approaches to produce and disseminate the guides to graphic materials. Regional cataloging centers will expand operations with the aid of centrally produced copy. Less deviation will be found between cataloging methods of the various libraries particularly in the areas of descriptive cataloging with a more pragmatic approach overcoming the traditionalism of the past. Major problems of the past will become minor ones of the future with the functions of the catalog clearly placed in a context of simplicity and usefulness.

The literary unit and main entry principle will undergo intensive study which will result in a restatement of their function within the context of the card catalog. The main entry and unit card concepts have both been eliminated from the computerized catalog, resulting in a substantial saving of space. The literary unit principle will be carried out logically by added entries which may again be accorded new prominence particularly within the computerized catalog. The verification process of the old methods will be modified to meet with a minimum amount of effort. The catalog will perform as a finding list rather than a bio-bibliographical tool which seemed so desirable during the early part of the twentieth century.

Other minor innovations will include a return to the use of guide cards rather than typing subject headings on each card, photographic reproduction of title pages which could be reduced for inclusion on catalog cards or left full size and placed in a loose-leaf binder serving as a supplement, sequential arrangement of books on shelves, and achievement of the original intentions of the *Anglo-American Rules* with names gaining precedence over locations. In regard to the arrangement of books, it is interesting to note that Dewey originally intended to provide classification numbers which would bring out other subjects of the book and suggested a sequential arrangement of books on the shelves rather than alphabetically by author.

The cataloging operation of the future will be based first upon a succinct statement of functions formulated in the light of needs; second, upon research, reevaluation, and experimentation which constantly provide alternative solutions and new methods; third, upon ideas, concepts, and machinery originating outside the library itself which will aid in the organizational process; fourth, upon professional personnel who plan, direct, develop, and evaluate the program and rely upon technicians who utilize the existing centralized services in the mechanical preparation of a catalog within a planned framework; and fifth, upon the combined cooperative effort of the professional, scholarly, and governmental units which benefit from increased bibliographic accessibility.

The twentieth century may be characterized as a period of growth and development of productivity. The emerging subject catalog developed within the context of the printed book catalog and retained many of the constraints until a new age of librarians began to rise above the technological phases of catalog production. Subject lists developed largely from existing library practices with the profession originating the quest in this direction only to be supplanted by the rather singular effort of the Library of Congress. The fate of the classified catalog was sealed in the U.S. when the Library of Congress adopted the dictionary catalog which resulted in the issuing of printed unit cards that set the pattern for the whole nation. Research was at a minimum with the appeal to authority exerting an overpowering influence. Catalogers followed the edict of Cutter and debated only his alternative suggestions. The lack of empirical research permitted the catalog to develop with regard only to the book although a secondary effort was given to the periodical indexes which strangely enough seemed to be outside the realm of the cataloger. The rules employed in the construction of the book catalog were perpetuated in such outmoded practices as the main entry. The card catalog eventually faltered under the weight of the increased number of books being printed with book budgets stretching its size far beyond original expectations. The newly formed administrative librarian, who had only recently relinquished the task of catalog construction to the practitioners, began to complain about the costs of processing. Catalogers sought to evaluate their own procedures but were hampered by traditional functions, outlooks, and methods. The codes continued to grow with each edition until finally the discontents of the 1940s brought some simplification first within the realm of descriptive cataloging which by 1967 had been expanded to include more logical approaches to author headings. Traditionalism and economic expediency once again caused some attrition but progress was made.

Cooperative and centralized cataloging were given impetus with expanding resources and federal funds largely responsible for their growth because the astute foresight of many librarians focused attention in this area.

The coming of the computer served to answer the immediate needs of the seeker of specialized information and is now being applied to conventional library situations with varying degrees of success. Its place in future development is apparent and is dependent upon pecuniary resources and logical applications.

By mid-century the subject catalog was the subject of considerable debate. User studies have failed to provide concrete answers for all situations but generally have indicated trends that aided in selecting methods. The role of the subject catalog, though generally recognized, has undergone more intensive study with its components, such as subject headings and the syndetic structure, receiving considerable attention. The results have been rewarding in a limited degree with some understanding gained through analytic studies of subject terminology and a burgeoning number of special subject lists or thesauri. Libraries, like other social institutions, have failed to keep up with new innovations and as a whole have retained old methods or hastily accepted practices which lead to unendurable problems. The subject catalog will continue to demand major emphasis during the remainder of the century which hopefully will be marked by scientifically sound experimentation and rational development.

Conclusion

The unfolding of the story of catalogs and cataloging has indicated general trends which may be succinctly summarized. The ancient period was a time of crude inventory lists which served only as a listing of property rather than an index to the library. The contributions of Callimachus to the cataloging field were typical of the early bio-bibliographic endeavors which were prepared by scholars in order to preserve a record of the leading literary works of the period. This method was characteristic of the attempts of the ancient civilizations which sought to perpetuate the culture for ensuing generations. The concept of authorship and title was confusing, with listings frequently a combination of author names, titles, and/or first lines although the Greeks were probably responsible for the use of the author in reference to individual works. Chronology or order of accession were the primary orders of arrangement. The rise of Christianity shifted the centers of learning to the monasteries where the codex was used and reproduced for distribution to other religious houses. Books were an exceedingly valuable commodity which necessitated a record of the holdings of each collection. Slowly the lists began to reflect a utilitarian aspect with books arranged not by the old chronological approach but by order of importance to the user which in turn led to broad subject and form arrangements which persisted for many centuries and later formed the basis for the more systematic classification schemes. As these lists lacked author or subject, and title indexes, they were not catalogs in the modern sense of the word but rather resembled our shelf list in character and use.

In the thirteenth century the first union catalog was attempted and college and university ibraries, which were to exert such an influence on later development, began to assemble comprehensive collections.

The fourteenth century brought the inclusion of an author index appended to an inventory list which could conceivably be designated as a true catalog.

The fifteenth century with the invention of movable metal type brought a new need for bibliographic organization with leaders such as Tritheim who appended an index of authors to his chronologically arranged bibliography of ecclesiastical writers and exhibited a concept of the main and added entry which was further developed by Gesner, Treflerus, Maunsell, and Sir Thomas Bodley.

The sixteenth century was marked by a number of leading bibliographies produced by Gesner and Maunsell who were joined by Treflerus in providing information on the construction of catalogs. Two astute bibliographers suggested that a bibliography could be pressed into service as a substitute for the catalog. Maunsell's use of the author's surname was indicative of the changing concepts regarding names. The addition of supplementary indexes was clearly emerging with the number of access points going far beyond the original inventory list and catalogs beginning to assume the retrieval function.

The seventeenth century brought the Bodleian catalogs. The author arrangement of the influential issue of 1620 advanced the concept of entry with considerable attention to the determination of the form of main entry and an expression of the literary unit principle. An early form of the dictionary catalog with authors and subjects filed in a single alphabet appeared although the single entry (author or title for anonymous) was the rule of the day. A number of codes of instructions by Naude, Dury, and Baillet indicated that interest in the catalog was increasing with methods taking on a few primitive signs of standardization.

The eighteenth century found a national cataloging project in France using cards as a basis of the catalog as well as a national cataloging code. Bibliographical description slowly increased and was assuming more of its modern aspects.

The nineteenth century was the high point of cataloging with a number of important codes produced, beginning with the British Museum and reaching a zenith in Cutter's *Rules* of 1876. Catalogs steadily developed under the concept of the subject word particularly within Germany and America as the single entry idea expanded beyond conventional application. The card catalog became more commonplace after 1860 and assumed a variety of arrangements reflecting a number of divergent opinions. The subject catalog was the major contribution of the era and was employed first in America by Jewett. Cutter was to provide the definitive work with the publication of his *Rules* in 1876 which were to serve for years as authoritative and final. The problem of catalog arrangement was still a controversial issue at this time and was never satisfactorily resolved although elements of the classified printed book catalog were readily adopted to the dictionary card form. The emergence of centralized cataloging at the Library of Congress, which was based upon a dictionary catalog, terminated serious debate and elevated the technological aspects of its catalog to a paramount place with little regard for its philosophical advantages over the classified systems (*41*). Classification became not a tool of the catalog but rather a location symbol. The catalog was dependent upon an alphabetical order which was supported by a syndetic structure, serving as a systematic guide to subject terminology. Subject headings and cross references, however, grew not by design but rather by chance until the burgeoning size of the catalog brought forth a deluge of criticism against Cutter's answer to the classified catalog. The lack of an acceptable classification scheme no doubt influenced the rapid growth of the dictionary catalog which came under close scrutiny during the twentieth century. The overemphasis on rules and a preoccupation with monographs in libraries stymied innovation to such an extent that seekers of specialized information and extraordinary services turned first to the documentalist and then to the information scientists. The mid-fifties produced a number of studies pertaining to the classified catalog, approaches and needs of the user, cost analysis, catalog division, book catalogs, and the relationship of bibliographies to the catalog. All of these reflected the failure to adequately study the fundamental design and purpose of the alphabetical subject catalog in card form (*41*). By the end of the nineteenth century the pattern of catalog construction was well defined with subject headings, main entry, literary unit principle, dictionary catalog, classification, unit cards, added entries, and adequate bibliographical descriptions all well-developed elements. Cooperative cataloging was in its beginning stage with the first efforts directed toward an early type of cataloging-in-source which advocated slips with the books.

The twentieth century brought an expansion of cooperative and centralized cataloging, three new cataloging codes for the English speaking world, numerous subject lists, and a general reevaluation of the cataloging process beginning with the descriptive phase. The junglelike growth in the size of library collections forced many librarians to seek simplified methods as well as expanding cooperative and centralized services.

Substantial sums of money have been used since the intervention of the federal government into the field of scientific information with primary efforts directed toward retrieval of specialized information but later expanding to encompass services of more immediate value to public and research libraries. The NAPAC Program is one example of the concerted effort which will result in a more comprehensive coverage of printed cards for foreign titles and will stimulate international cooperation in bibliographic control.

Continued technological advancements such as the electric typewriter, electrostatic copying, telefacsimile transmission, and computers will expedite cataloging activities.

The present and future hold great promise for the development of catalogs into a more useful, more functional, and more comprehensive tool through the formulation of attainable goals, continued experimentation, empirical research, and cooperative effort. So far there is no indication that the need for catalogs will ever diminish or be replaced.

Appendix: List of Codes of Cataloging Rules

1791   *Instruction pour procéder a la confection du catalogue de chacune des bibliotheques sur lesquelles les Directoires ont dû ou doivent incessaminent apposer les scelles* Imprimerie nationale, Paris, 1791.

1841   *The British Museum code of ninety-one rules,* adopted by the Trustees in 1839.

1852   C. C. Jewett, *Smithsonian report on the construction of catalogues of libraries . . . and their publication by means of separate, stereotyped titles, with rules and examples.*

1876   C. A. Cutter, *Rules for a printed dictionary catalog.* (Revised in 1889, 1891, and 1904.)

1878   Cambridge University, *Rules to be observed in forming the alphabetical catalogue of printed books.* (Originally contained 49 Rules but enlarged to 64 in 1925.)

1878   *L'Instruction generale relative au service des bibliotheques universitaires.*

1883   American Library Association, *Condensed rules for an author and title-catalog.*

1883   Oxford, Bodleian Library. *Compendious cataloging rules for the author catalog.*

1883   Library Association, *Cataloguing rules.*

1884   F. B. Perkins, *San Francisco cataloguing for public libraries.*

1886   American Library Association, *Condensed rules for a card catalog.*

1886   K. Dziatzko, *Instruction fur die Ordnung der Titel im alphabetischen Zettelkatalog der Koniel, und Universitatshibliothek zu Breslau*

1888   M. Dewey, *Rules for author and classed catalogs as used in Columbia College Library.*

1889   L. Delisle, *Instructions elementaires et techniques pour la mise et le maintien en ordre des livres d'une bibliotheque.*

1889   M. Dewey, *Library school card catalog rules; with 52 facsimiles of sample cards for author and classed catalogs.*

1890   L. Delisle, *Instructions elementaires et techniques pour la mise et le maintien en ordre des livres d'une bibliotheque,* Lille, 1890.

1890   K. Linderfelt, *Eclectic card catalog rules; author and title entries based on Dziatzko's "Instruction" compared with the rules of the British Museum, Cutter, Dewey, Perkins and other authorities,* Boston, 1890.

1899   Prussia, *Instruktionen fur die alphabetischen Kataloge der preussischen Bibliotheken, vom 1899.* Zweite ausgabe, 1908.

1902   Spain, *Junta facultativa de archivos, bibliotecas y museos,* Madrid.

1905   United States, Library of Congress, Catalog division. *Supplementary rules on cataloguing.* (First published as a monograph but continued on cards.)

1908   American and British Library Associations, *Cataloguing rules; author and title entries.*

1909   *Instruktionen fur die alphabetischen Kataloge der preuszischen Bibliotheken vom 10. mai 1889. 2. ausg. in der fassung vom 10. August 1908.* Berlin.

1912   Association des Bibliothecaires Francais, *Regles et usages observes dans les principales bibliotheques de Paris* . . .

1912   French Library Association, *Regles et usages observés dans les principales bibliotheques de Paris pour la rédaction et le classement des catalogues d'auteurs et d'anonymes, 1912.*

1913   Association des bibliothecaires francais, . . . *Regles et usages observés dans les principales bibliotheques de Paris pour la rédaction et le classement des catalogues d'auteurs et d'anonymes (1912)* . . . , Paris.

1916   Sweden, Kungliga biblioteket, *Katalogregler for Kungl, biblioteket samt anvisningar for anordnande av bokband,* Av riksbibliotekarien faststallda den 30 juni 1916, Stockholm.

1917   Denmark, Bogsamlingskomite, *Katalogisering; raad og regler til brug ved ordningen af bogsamlinger, udgivet af Statens bogsamlings-komite,* Copenhagen, 1917.

1921   Norway, Norsk bibliotekforening, *Forslag til katalogiseringsregler utarb. av Norsk bibliotekforenings katalogkomite,* Christiania, 1921.

1921   Vereinigung schweizerischer bibliothekare, *Entwurf zu einer Katalogisierungsinstruktion fur den schweizerischen Gesamtkatalog,* Zurich, 1921.

1922   Italy, Commissione incaricata di progorre un nuovo codice di regole (etc.), *Regole per la compilazi one del catalogo alfabetico,* Rome, 1922.

1922   Bayerische staabsbibliothek, *Katalogisierungsordnung. 2. ausg.,* Munich, 1922.

1922   Bodleian Library, . . . *Rules for the cataloguing of printed books published before 1920* . . . , Oxford, 1922.

1923   Bodleian Library, *Rules for the author-catalogue of books published in or after 1920.* Oxford, 1923.

1923   France, Bibliotheque nationale, *Usages suivis dans la redaction du Catalogue general des livres imprimes de la Bibliotheque nationale, recueillis et coordonnes par E. G. Ledos,* Paris, 1923.

1925   Norway, Norsk bibliotekforening, *Katalogiseringsregler for norske biblioteker utarb, av Norsk bibliotekforenings katalogkomite,* Oslo, 1925.

1929   Association des Bibliothecaires Francais, *Regles generales.*

1931   The Vatican code, *Norme per il catalogo degli stampati.*

1936   *Rules for compiling the catalogues of printed books, maps and music in the British Museum.* Revised edition.

1941   *A.L.A. Catalog rules: author and title entries,* prepared by the Catalog Code Revision Committee of the American Library Association, with the collaboration of a Committee of the (British) Library Association.

1949   *A.L.A. Cataloging rules for author and title,* 2nd ed., ALA, Chicago, 1949.

1949   U.S. Library of Congress, *Rules for descriptive cataloguing in the Library of Congress,* Government Printing Office, Washington, D.C., 1949.

1961   Germany (Federal Republic), Budestag, Bundestag, Bibliothek, *Instruktionen fur die Kataloge der Bibliothek des deutschen Bundestages,* 1961.

1961   U.S.S.R., *Glavone upravlenie kul'turno-prosvetitel' nykh uchrezhdenii. Edinye pravila opisaniia proizvedenii pechati dlia bibliotechnykh katalogov.* Chast' I. Vypusk 2. *Organizatsiia alfavitnogo Kataloga knig,* 2-e izdanie, ispravlennoe i dopolnennoe. (*Standard rules for the description of printed works for library catalogs.* Pt. 1, Section 2; *Arrangement of the alphabetical catalog of books.* 2nd ed., rev. enl.), Biblioteka im. Lenina, Moscow, 1961.

1964   Spain, Direccion General de Archivos y Bibliotecas, *Instrucciones para la redaccion del catálogo alfabético de autores y obras anónimas en las bibliotecas publicas del estado, dirigidas por el Cuerpo Facultativo de Archíveros, Bibliotecarios y Arqueólogos,* 3 ed. reformata, Dir. Gen. de Archivos y Bibliotecas, Madrid, 1964.

1965   Verein Deutscher Bibliothekar, Kommission fur alphabetische Katalogisierung, *Regeln fur die alphabetische Katalogisierung. Teilentwurf.* Kolstermann, Frankfurt, 1965. (A partial compilation of a new German code with Part I pertaining to corporate authorship and Part II covering alphabetical arrangement. This work clearly indicates the Paris principles.)

1965   Japanese Library Association, *Nippon Cataloguing Rules,* 1965. (This extensive code was clearly influenced by the Paris principles.)

1965   Zentralinstitut fur Bibliothekswesen, *Titelaufnahme fur die Kataloge der allegemeinbildenden Bibliotheken,* 2nd rev. ed., Bibliographis-ches Institut, Leipzig, 1965. (The Paris principles have strongly influenced this code although corporate bodies are not recognized as main entries.)

1967   *Anglo-American cataloging rules,* prepared by the American Library Association, The Library of Congress, The Library Association and the Canadian Library Association, ALA, Chicago, 1967.

REFERENCES

1. J. E. Hitchcock, "Subject Coverage in University Library Catalogs," *Lib. Quart.,* **10,** 69–94 (January 1940).

2. C. A. Cutter, "Library Catalogues," in U.S. Bureau of Education, *Public Libraries in the United States of America; Their History, Condition and Management* (U.S. Department of Interior, Bureau of Education Special Report, Part I), Govt. Printing Office, Washington, D.C., 1876, Chapter XXVII, pp. 526–622.

3. C. A. Cutter, *Rules for a Dictionary Catalog,* 4th ed., rewritten (U.S. Bureau of Education Special Report on Public Libraries, Part II), Govt. Printing Office, Washington, D.C., 1904.

4. International Federation of Library Associations, *International Conference on Cataloguing Principles, Paris, 9th–18th October, 1961,* London, 1963.

5. L. Jolley, *The Principles of Cataloguing,* Philosophical Library, New York, 1961.

6. D. M. Norris, *A History of Cataloguing and Cataloguing Methods 1100–1850: With an Introductory Survey of Ancient Times,* Grafton, London, 1939.

7. E. D. Johnson, *A History of Libraries in the Western World,* Scarecrow Press, New York, 1965.
8. F. J. Witty, "Pinakes of Callimachus," *Lib. J.,* **28,** 132–136, (April 1958).
9. R. F. Strout, "The Development of the Catalog and Cataloging Codes," *Lib. Quart.,* **26,** 254–275 (October 1956).
10. J. W. Clark, *Care of Books,* Cambridge Univ. Press, Cambridge, 1901.
11. Magnus Aurelius Cassiodorus, *An Introduction to Divine and Human Reading.* (L. W. Jones, ed.), Columbia Univ. Press, New York, 1946.
12. H. O. Serverance, "Three of the Earliest Book Catalogues," *Public Lib.,* **10,** 116–117 (1905).
13. J. W. Thompson, *The Medieval Library,* Hafner, New York, 1957.
14. L. Condit, "Bibliography in Its Prenatal Existence," *Lib. Quart.,* **7,** 564–576 (October 1937).
15. T. Gottlieb, *Über Mittelalterliche, Bibliotheken,* Harrassowitz, Leipzig, 1891. As quoted in J. Thompson, *The Medieval Library,* Hafner, New York, 1957, p. 614.
16. N. R. Ker, ed., *Medieval Libraries in Great Britain,* 2nd ed., Offices of the Royal Historical Society, London, 1964.
17. E. Savage, *Old English Libraries, The Making, Collection and Use of Books During the Middle Ages,* Methesen, London, 1911.
18. R. F. Strout, *Toward a Better Cataloguing Code; Papers Presented before the Twenty-first Annual Conference of the Graduate Library School of the University of Chicago, June 13–15, 1956,* Univ. Chicago Press, Chicago, 1957. [Reprints of papers originally published in *Lib. Quart.,* **26** (October 1956).]
19. T. Besterman, *The Beginnings of Systematic Bibliography,* 2nd ed., revised, Oxford Univ. Press, Oxford; Milford, London, 1936.
20. M. Verner, "Adrien Baillet (1649–1706) and his Rules for an Alphabetical Subject Catalog," *Lib. Quart.,* **38,** 217–230 (July 1968).
21. A. Maunsell, *The First Part of the Catalogue of English Printed Books: Which Concerneth such Matters of Divinities as Both Bin Written in Our Own Tongue, or Translated Out of Anie Other Language* (The seconde parte, etc.), printed by J. Windet, London, 1595.
22. S. G. Akers, *Simple Library Cataloging,* 5th ed., Scarecrow Press, Metuchen, N.J., 1969.
23. S. Jayne, *Library Catalogues of the English Renaissance,* Univ. California Press, Berkeley, 1956.
24. G. Naudeus, *Instructions Concerning Erecting of a Library Presented to my Lord the President De Mesme . . . ,* translated by J. Evelyn, Houghton Mifflin, Cambridge, 1903. (Originally printed in 1661.)
25. J. Dury, "The Reformed Librarie Keeper or two Copies Concerning the Place and Office of the Library Keeper, 1649," in J. C. Dana and H. W. Kent, eds., *Literature of Libraries in the 17th and 18th Centuries,* Vol. 2, McClurg, Chicago, 1906.
26. J. Ranz, *The Printed Book Catalogue in American Libraries: 1723–1900* (ACRL Monograph Number 26), American Library Association, Chicago, 1964.
27. G. W. Cole, "An Early French General Catalogue," *Lib. J.,* **25,** 329–331 (1900).
28. E. Edwards, *Memoirs of Libraries; Including a Handbook of Library Economy,* Franklin, New York. (Reprint of 1859 ed., 2 vols. in 1.)
29. J. Metcalfe, *Alphabetical Subject Indication of Information* (Rutgers Series on Systems for the Intellectual Organization of Information, Vol. 3), Graduate School of Library Science, Rutgers State Univ., New Brunswick, New Jersey, 1965.
30. J. H. Shera and M. E. Egan, *The Classified Catalog, Basic Principles and Practices,* American Library Association, Chicago, 1956.
31. J. E. Pettee, *Subject Headings; The History and Theory of the Alphabetical Subject Approach to Books,* Wilson, New York, 1946.
32. British Museum, Parliament, House of Commons, *Report of the Commission Appointed*

to Inquire into the Constitution of the Museum (Parliamentary Papers, 1850, Vol. 24), London, 1850.

33. W. J. Rhees, *Manual of Public Libraries, Institutions and Societies in the United States and British Provinces of North America,* Lippincott, Philadelphia, 1859.

34. J. Fiske, "The Librarian's Work," *Atlantic Monthly,* 38, 480–491 (1876).

35. M. S. R. James, "The Progress of the Modern Card Catalog Principle," in *The Library and Its Content* (H. P. Sawyer, ed.), (Classics in American Librarianship), Wilson, New York, 1925, pp. 331–338.

36. R. M. Heiss, "The Card Catalog in Libraries of the United States Before 1876," unpublished Masters Thesis, Graduate School of Library Science, Univ. Illinois, 1938.

37. J. Schwartz, "Catalogues and Cataloguing, Pt. III," in U.S. Bureau of Education, *Public Libraries in the United States of America, Their History, Condition and Management* (U.S. Department of Interior, Bureau of Education Special Report, Part I), U.S. Govt. Printing Office, Washington, D.C., 1876, Chapter XXVIII, Part III, pp. 657–660.

38. L. Maddox, "Trends and Issues in American Librarianship as Reflected in the Papers and Proceedings of the American Library Association, 1876–1885," unpublished Ph.D. dissertation, Department of Library Science, Univ. Michigan, 1958.

39. U.S. Bureau of Education, *Public Libraries in the United States of America; Their History, Condition and Management* (U.S. Department of the Interior, Bureau of Education Special Report, Part I), Govt. Printing Office, Washington, D.C., 1876.

40. S. B. Noyes, "Catalogues and Cataloguing, Part II," in U.S. Bureau of Education, *Public Libraries in the United States of America; Their History, Condition and Management* (U.S. Department of Interior, Bureau of Education Special Report, Part I), Govt. Printing Office, Washinigton, D.C., 1876, Chapter XXVIII, pp. 648–657.

41. O. Lilley, "Evaluation of the Subject Catalog, Criticisms and a Proposal," *Amer. Doc.,* 5, 41–60 (1954).

42. U.S. Library of Congress, Processing Department, *Cataloging-in-Source Experiment, a Report to the Librarian of Congress by the Director of the Processing Department,* Library of Congress, Washington, 1960.

43. H. Stevens, "Photo-Bibliography: or a Central Bibliographical Clearinghouse," *Lib. J.,* 2, 162–173 (November–December 1877).

44. O. H. Robinson, "College Library Administration," in U.S. Bureau of Education, *Public Libraries in the United States of America; Their History, Condition and Management* (U.S. Department of Interior, Bureau of Education Special Report, Part I), Govt. Printing Office, Washington, D.C., 1876, Chapter XXVI, pp. 505–525.

45. F. P. Jordon, "History of Printed Catalogue Cards," *Public Lib.,* 9, 318–321 (1904).

46. American Library Association Committee on an Index to Subject Headings, "Report on Subject Headings by the Chairmen of the Committee, Mr. Cutter," *Lib. J.,* 6, 114–115 (1881).

47. F. C. Francis, "A Reconsideration of The British Museum Rules for Compiling the Catalogues of Printed Books—I," in University of London, School of Librarianship and Archives, *Cataloging Principles and Practices; An Inquiry* (edited with an introduction by M. Piggott), The Library Association, London, 1954, Chapter III, pp. 26–36.

48. A. Osborn, *Descriptive Cataloging,* 2nd preliminary ed., Univ. Pittsburgh Graduate School of Library and Information Sciences, Pittsburgh, 1965.

49. C. C. Jewett, *On the Construction of Catalogues of Libraries and Their Publication by Means of Separate, Stereotyped Titles with Rules and Examples,* 2nd ed. (Smithsonian Report), Smithsonian Institution, Washington, D.C., 1853.

50. A. Crestadoro, *The Art of Making Catalogues of Libraries,* The Literary Scientific and Artistic Reference Office, London, 1856. As quoted in C. Cutter, "Library Catalogues," in U.S. Bureau of Education, *Public Libraries in the United States of America; Their History, Condition and Management* (U.S. Department of Interior, Bureau of Education Special Report, Part I), Govt. Printing Office, Washington, D.C., 1876, Chapter XXVII, pp. 526–622.

51. C. J. Frarey, *Subject Headings* (The State of the Library Arts, Vol. 1, Part 2), Graduate School of Library Service, Rutgers State Univ., New Brunswick, New Jersey, 1960.

52. W. F. Poole, "Organization and Management of Public Libraries," in U.S. Bureau of Education, *Public Libraries in the United States, Their History, Condition and Management* (U.S. Department of Interior, Bureau of Education Special Report, Part I), Govt. Printing Office, Washington, D.C., 1876, Chapter XXV, pp. 476–504.

53. M. O. Baker, "American Library Catalogs a Hundred Years Ago," *Wilson Lib. Bull.,* 33, 284–285 (December 1958).

54. W. C. Lane, "Cataloging," in *Papers Prepared for the Worlds Library Congress Held at the Columbian Exposition* (M. Dewey, ed.), (U. S. Bureau of Education, Chapter IX of Part II of the Report of the Commission of Education, 1892–1893), Govt. Printing Office, Washington, D.C., 1896, pp. 835–850.

55. W. C. Lane, "Present Tendencies of Cataloguing Practice," in *Papers and Proceedings of the 26th Conference at the Louisiana Purchase Exposition, St. Louis,* (Oct. 1904), American Library Association, Chicago, pp. 134–143.

56. L. Jolley, "Some Recent Developments in Cataloguing in the U.S.A.," *J. Doc.,* 6, 70–82 (June 1950).

57. American Library Association, *A.L.A. Glossary of Library Terms with a Selection of Terms in Related Fields* (compiled by Elizabeth H. Thompson), American Library Association, Chicago, 1943.

58. U.S. Library of Congress, Descriptive Cataloging Division, *Cooperative Cataloging Manual for the Use of Contributing Libraries,* Govt. Printing Office, Washington, D.C., 1944.

59. W. I. Fletcher, "Future of the Catalogue," *Lib. J.,* 30, 141–144 (1905).

60. F. Rider, "Alternatives for the Present Dictionary Catalog," in *The Acquisition and Cataloging of Books* (W. M. Randall, ed.), Univ. Chicago Press, Chicago, 1940, pp. 133–162.

61. H. Dewey, "Some Special Aspects of the Classified Catalog," in *The Subject Analysis of Library Materials* (M. F. Tauber, ed.), Columbia Univ. School of Library Service, New York, 1953, pp. 114–129.

62. K. L. Taylor, "Subject Catalogs vs. Classified Catalogs," in *The Subject Analysis of Library Materials* (M. F. Tauber, ed.), Columbia Univ. School of Library Service, New York, 1953, pp. 100–113.

63. American Library Association, "Resources and Technical Services Division, Cataloging and Classification Section. Classification Committee, Classified Catalogs," *Lib. Resources Tech. Services,* 6, 274–275 (Summer 1962).

64. I. W. Thom, "The Divided Catalog in College and University Libraries," *College Research Lib.,* 10, 236–241 (July 1949).

65. M. MacNair, *A Guide to the Cataloging of Periodicals,* 3rd ed., Govt. Printing Office, Washington, D.C., 1925.

66. H. W. Pierson, *A Guide to the Cataloging of Serial Publications of Societies and Institutions,* 2nd ed., Govt. Printing Office, Washington, D.C., 1931.

67. U.S. Library of Congress Librarian's Committee, *Report to the Librarian of Congress on the Processing Operations in the Library of Congress,* Library of Congress, Washington, D.C., 1940.

68. H. B. Van Hoesen, *Selective Cataloging,* Wilson, New York, 1928.

69. C. J. Frarey, "Studies of Use of the Subject Catalog: Summary and Evaluation," in *The Subject Analysis of Library Materials* (M. F. Tauber, ed.), Columbia Univ. School of Library Services, New York, 1953, pp. 147–166.

70. A. D. Osborn, "The Crisis in Cataloging," *Lib. Quart.,* 2, 393–411 (October 1941).

71. U.S. Library of Congress, Processing Department, *Studies of Descriptive Cataloging: A Report to the Librarian of Congress by the Director of the Processing Department,* Govt. Printing Office, Washington, D.C., 1946.

72. U.S. Library of Congress, *Rules for Descriptive Cataloging in the Library of Congress,* Govt. Printing Office, Washington, D.C., 1949.

73. S. Lubetzky, *Cataloguing Rules and Principles: A Critique of the A.L.A. Rules for Entry and a Proposed Design for Their Revision Prepared for the Board on Cataloging Policy and Research of the A.L.A. Division of Cataloging and Classification,* Library of Congress, Processing Department, Washington, D.C., 1953.

74. S. Lubetzky, *Code of Cataloging Rules, Author and Title Entry; An Unfinished Draft for a New Edition of Cataloging Rules Prepared for the Catalog Code Revision Committee,* American Library Association, Chicago, 1960.

75. C. S. Spalding, "Introduction," in *Anglo-American Cataloging Rules,* prepared by the American Library Association, The Library of Congress, The Library Association, and the Canadian Library Association, American Library Association, Chicago, 1967, pp. 1–6.

76. R. E. Ellsworth, "Mr. Ellsworth's Report," *Lib. Congr. Information Bull.,* November 16–22, 1948, Appendix.

77. U.S. Library of Congress, *Annual Report of the Librarian of Congress for the Fiscal Year Ending June 30, 1965,* Library of Congress, Washington, D.C., 1966.

78. P. Hiatt, "Cooperative Processing Centers for Public Libraries," *Lib. Trends,* 16, 67–84 (July 1967).

79. R. L. Darling, "School Library Processing Centers," *Lib. Trends,* 16, 58–66 (July 1967).

80. B. M. Westby, "School Library Processing Centers," *Lib. Trends,* 16, 46–57 (July 1967).

81. Fry (George) and Associates, Inc., *Catalog Card Reproduction* (Library Technology Projects Publication #9), American Library Association, Chicago, 1965.

82. U.S. Library of Congress, *Annual Report of the Librarian of Congress for the Fiscal Year Ending June 30, 1967,* Library of Congress, Washington, D.C., 1968.

83. J. H. Treyz, "The Cards-With-Books Program," *Amer. Lib. Assoc. Bull.,* 57, 433–434 (May 1963).

84. R. T. Esterquest, "Cooperation in Library Services," *Lib. Quart.,* 31, 71–89 (1961).

85. J. W. Cronin, "The National Union and Library of Congress Catalogs: Problems and Prospects," *Lib. Quart.,* 34, 77–98 (January 1964).

86. F. A. Sharr, V. Creasey, and C. L. Drake, "The Production of a New Book Type Catalogue in Australia," *Lib. Resources Tech. Services,* 10, 143–154 (Spring 1966).

87. R. Shoemaker, "Some American 20th Century Book Catalogs: Their Purpose, Format and Production Techniques," *Lib. Resources Tech. Services,* 4, 195–207 (Summer 1960).

88. P. Kieffer, "The Baltimore County Public Library Book Catalog," *Lib. Resources Tech. Services,* 10, 133–141 (Spring 1966).

89. R. D. Johnson, "A Book Catalog at Stanford," *J. Lib. Automation,* 1, 13–49 (March 1968).

90. C. D. Weber, "The Changing Character of the Catalog in America," *Lib. Quart.,* 34, 20–33 (1964).

91. D. C. Weber, "Book Catalog Trends in 1966," *Lib. Trends,* 16, 149–164 (July 1967).

92. D. R. Swanson, "Design Requirements for a Future Library," in *Libraries and Automation Proceedings of the Conference on Libraries and Automation* (B. E. Markuson, ed.), held at Airlie Foundation, Warrenton, Virginia, May 26–30, under the sponsorship of the Library of Congress, National Science Foundation, and Council on Library Resources, Inc., Library of Congress, Washington, D.C., 1964, pp. 11–21.

93. D. R. Swanson, "Dialogues with a Catalog," *Lib. Quart.,* 34, 113–125 (January 1964).

94. V. Mostecky, "Study of See Also References Structure in Relation to the Subject of International Law," *Amer. Doc.,* 7, 294–314 (1956).

BIBLIOGRAPHY

Abbot, E., "Statements respecting the New Catalogues of the College Library," in Harvard University *Report of the Committee of the Overseers of Harvard College Appointed to Visit the Library for the Year 1863,* Boston, 1864.

Avram, H. D., J. F. Knapp, and L. J. Rather, *The MARC II Format, A Communications Format for Bibliographic Data,* Library of Congress Information Systems Office, Washington, D.C., 1968.

Beck, F., "Zur Geschichte des Schlagwortkatalogs," *Praxis und Theorie, Zentralblatt für Bibliothekswesen,* **40,** 495–496 (1923). As quoted in M. Verner, "Adrien Baillet (1649–1706) and his rules for an Alphabetical Subject Catalogue," *Lib. Quart.,* **38,** 221 (July 1968).

Becker, G., "Catalogi Bibliothecarum Antiqui Bonn, Max Cohen 1885," as quoted in J. Thompson, *The Medieval Library,* Hafner, New York, 1957, p. 614.

Daily, J. E., "The Grammar of Subject Headings, A Formulation of Rules for Subject Headings Based on a Syntactical and Morphological Analysis of the Library of Congress List," unpublished Ph.D. dissertation, Columbia Univ. School of Library Service, New York, 1957.

Irwin, R. R., "Use of the Card Catalog in the Public Library," unpublished Master's essay, Graduate Library School, University of Chicago, 1949. As quoted in C. Frary, "Studies of the Uses of Subject Catalog: Summary and Evaluation" in *The Subject Analysis of Library Materials* (M. F. Tauber, ed.), Columbia Univ. School of Library Service, New York, 1953, p. 148.

Kingery, R. E., "Building Card Catalogs for Eventual Migration into Book Forms," in *Book Catalogs* (R. E. Kingery and M. F. Tauber, eds.), Scarecrow Press, New York, 1963, pp. 93–122.

Lilley, O., "How Specific is 'Specific,'" *J. Catalog and Classification,* **11,** 3–8 (January 1955).

Macray, W. D., *Annals of the Bodleian Library,* 2nd ed., Clarendon Press, Oxford, 1890. As quoted in D. Morris, *A History of Cataloguing and Cataloguing Methods 1100–1850 . . . ,* Grafton, London, 1939, pp. 152–153.

Metcalfe, J., *Subject Classifying and Indexing of Libraries and Literature.* Scarecrow Press, New York, 1959.

Morsch, L., "Cooperation and Centralization," *Lib. Trends,* **2,** 342–355 (October 1953).

"The National Union Catalogs," *ALA Bull.,* **63,** 39–41 (January 1969).

Osborn, V. J., "A History of Cooperative Cataloging in the United States," unpublished Master's Thesis, Univ. Chicago Graduate Library School, 1944.

Pettee, J. E., "The Development of Authorship Entry and Formulation of Authorship Rules as found in the Anglo American Code," *Lib. Quart.,* **6,** 270–290 (July 1936).

Pettus, C., *Subject Headings in Education, a Systematic List for Use in a Dictionary Catalog,* Wilson, New York, 1938.

Rostgaard, F., *Project d'une Nouvelle Methode Pour Dresser le Catalogue d'une Bibliotheque,* 2nd ed., Paris, 1698.

Runge, S., "Some Recent Developments in Subject Cataloging in Germany," *Lib. Quart.,* **11,** 46–68 (January 1941).

Shores, L., *Origins of the American College Library, 1638–1800,* Shoe String Press, Hamden, Connecticut, 1966.

Swank, R. C., "Subject Catalogs, Classifications or Bibliographies? A Review of Critical Discussion, 1876–1942," *Lib. Quart.,* **14,** 316–322 (October 1944).

EUGENE R. HANSON AND JAY E. DAILY

CATEGORIAL GRAMMARS

Categorial grammars (CGs) as a system for the description of the syntactic structure of natural languages were first suggested by Bar-Hillel (1) in 1953. This proposal stemmed from Leśniewski's theory of semantical categories (2), originally intended for formal languages of the "Polish" parenthesis-free type, and from a later modification of this theory by Ajdukiewicz (3).

Because determining sentence structure according to a categorial grammar involves only repeated application of a simple cancellation operation, CGs have been suggested as particularly suitable for use in machine translation or in any other task requiring mechanized parsing. However, there has been no large-scale attempt to construct a CG for any natural language or to apply this descriptive device in such areas as automatic indexing or information retrieval, primarily because CGs have been shown to be fundamentally inadequate to characterize the syntactic structures of natural language.

In a categorial grammar each word (or morpheme) in the lexicon is assigned to one or more syntactic classes called *categories*. Recursive application of a small number of *rules of operation* (or *resolution*) determines the groupings of contiguous units into phrases, clauses, and sentences together with their category assignments. A CG can be considered a formal characterization of traditional immediate-constituent analysis (4), the essential feature of which is that the complete syntactic structural description of any sentence is given by a proper labeled bracketing, or, equivalently, a phrase-structure tree ($5,6$). In contrast to grammars having syntactic classes such as *adjective, intransitive verb,* or *manner adverbial,* a CG typically employs only two simple categories—s for *sentence* and n for *noun* or *noun phrase*—and derives all others from these by the following recursive definition:

(a) s and n are categories.
(b) If α and β are categories, then so are α/β and $\alpha\backslash\beta$.
(c) There are no other categories.

Thus a CG might contain, among others, categories denoted as s/n, $(n/n)\backslash(s/n)$, and $(s\backslash n)/((s\backslash n)/s)$. (Parentheses are used only to avoid ambiguity in the notation.) There are two rules of operation, which are formally analogous to the right- and left-cancellation rules of arithmetic:

(1) A constituent composed of a category sequence of the form (α/β), β can be assigned category α.

(2) A constituent composed of a category sequence of the form α, $(\alpha\backslash\beta)$ can be assigned category β.

The assignment of a syntactic structure by a categorial grammar is illustrated below for the sentence: *John smokes a pipe*.

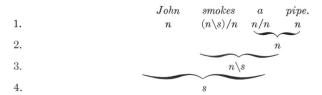

In Line 1 the category assignments for each word are given. Line 2 shows that Rule (1) has been applied to resolve the sequence (n/n), n into n. Line 3 represents the resolution of $(n\backslash s)/n$, n into $n\backslash s$, and in Line 4, an application of Rule (2) yields s from the sequence n, $(n\backslash s)$. The resulting description contains information of the following sort: *a pipe* is a constituent of type n; *smokes a* is not a constituent; *smokes a pipe* is a constituent of type $(n\backslash s)$ (which other grammars would call a *verb phrase* or *predicate phrase*); and the entire string is an s, i.e., a well-formed grammatical sentence.

In this illustration only one category has been assigned to each word, but in general a word must have more than one. For example, *smokes* will also be assigned the category $n\backslash s$ in order to allow the sentence *John smokes* to be correctly resolved to s. Therefore, all combinations of category sequences must be taken into account in applying the rules of operation. Given a categorial grammar G, a sequence of words w_1, w_2, . . . , w_n is a *grammatical sentence of G* if and only if there is at least one sequence of categories c_1, c_2, . . . , c_n (for all i, c_i is assigned to word w_i) which reduces to s by application of the rules of operation. The set of all grammatical sentences of G is said to be the *language generated by G*.

Bar-Hillel, Gaifman, and Shamir (7) have investigated the formal properties of CGs and found that they have the same *weak generative capacity* as context-free phrase-structure grammars (8). That is to say, for every categorial grammar G_c there is a context-free phrase-structure grammar G_p that generates exactly the same set of sentences, and conversely. However, categorial and context-free phrase-structure grammars are not equivalent in *strong generative capacity*, i.e., in the sets of structural descriptions they assign to sentences. If all the derived categories of a CG are of the form α/β or if all are of the form $\alpha\backslash\beta$, the grammar is said to be *unidirectional*. If it contains categories of both types, it is *bidirectional*. It is rather surprising that unidirectional CGs have the same weak generative capacity as bidirectional CGs (7), although the structural descriptions assigned to a given sentence will typically be quite different.

Lambek (9–11) has proposed various modifications within the basic framework of categorial grammars and studied their properties. At least one of these systems has now been proven by Cohen (12) to have the same weak generative capacity as the CGs of Bar-Hillel, Gaifman, and Shamir (7).

CGs are limited by the defects inherent in all versions of immediate-constituent analysis (*13*), and thus they cannot serve as grammars for natural languages. Interest in CGs is now sporadic and confined chiefly to their formal properties.

REFERENCES

1. Y. Bar-Hillel, "A Quasi-Arithmetical Notation for Syntactic Description," *Language,* **29,** 47–58 (1953).
2. S. Leśniewski, "Grundzüge eines Systems der Grundlagen der Mathematik," *Fundamenta Mathematicae,* **14,** 1–81 (1929).
3. K. Ajdukiewicz, "Die syntaktische Konnexität," *Studia Philosophica,* **1,** 1–27 (1935).
4. R. Wells, "Immediate Constituents," *Language,* **23,** 81–117 (1947).
5. N. Chomsky, *Syntactic Structures,* Mouton, The Hague, 1957.
6. N. Chomsky, "On Certain Formal Properties of Grammars," *Information and Control,* **2,** 137–167 (1959).
7. Y. Bar-Hillel, C. Gaifman, and E. Shamir, "On Categorial and Phrase Structure Grammars," *Bull. Res. Council of Israel,* **9F,** 1–16 (1960). Also published in Y. Bar-Hillel, *Language and Information,* Addison-Wesley, Reading, Mass., and Jerusalem Academic Press, Jerusalem, 1964, pp. 99–115.
8. N. Chomsky, "Formal Properties of Grammars," in *Handbook of Mathematical Psychology,* Vol. 2 (R. D. Luce, R. R. Bush, and E. Galanter, eds.), Wiley, New York, 1963, pp. 323–418.
9. J. Lambek, "The Mathematics of Sentence Structure," *Am. Math. Monthly,* **65,** 154–170 (1958).
10. J. Lambek, "Contributions to a Mathematical Analysis of the English Verb Phrase," *J. Can. Linguistic Assoc.,* **5,** 83–89 (1959).
11. J. Lambek, "On the Calculus of Syntactic Types," in *Structure of Language and Its Mathematics Aspects, Proc. 12th Symp. in Appl. Math.* (R. Jakobson, ed.), American Mathematical Society, Providence, R.I., 1961, pp. 166–178.
12. J. Cohen, "The Equivalence of Two Concepts of Categorial Grammar," *Information and Control,* **10,** 475–484 (1967).
13. P. Postal, *Constituent Structure: A Study of Contemporary Models of Syntactic Description.* Mouton, The Hague, 1964. Also published as *Intern. J. Am. Linguistics,* **30,** No. 1, Part III (1964).

ROBERT WALL

CATHOLIC LIBRARIES AND COLLECTIONS

Collections are attached to Catholic institutions ranging from elementary schools to universities, novitiates to abbeys, parishes to the Vatican, and including seminaries, information centers, and hospital libraries. Since the word *catholic*—with or without the initial capital—suggests several shades of meaning, it should be noted that the adjective was applied to the Christian church in its earliest period by Ignatius of Antioch (d. 110) in his letter to the Church at Smyrna (8.2). Thus, for the purposes of this article, *catholic* will apply to church-connected libraries prior to the Reformation, but only to those associated with Roman

Catholic institutions for the subsequent period. No statistical or geographical survey will be presented here, since the emphasis of this article will be on historical and administrative aspects. Articles on specific Catholic libraries (e.g., Vatican) will be found under their individual names.

Since the principal goal of the Church is the spread of the Christian message, the preservation and organization of documents was early recognized in ecclesiastical circles as essential for its purpose, as well as for the better understanding of the inspired word of the Sacred Scriptures, and furthermore for the defense of Christian tenets (apologetics) against the philosophical and religious doctrines of the Hellenistic world. Thus the early collections associated with the churches of Alexandria and Caesarea were strong in biblical and philosophical texts, and bring to mind the names of such giants of the early Church as Clement, Origen, Pamphilus, and Eusebius, whose work of collecting, preservation, and synthesis would result in the scholarly contributions of Jerome in the fourth century.

Probably the most influential figure in the development of Catholic libraries in the Middle Ages was Cassiodorus (q.v.), whose *Institutiones* (Instructions for Religious and Secular Reading) laid the foundations of a library for the systematic study of Scripture. Since his work included a book on secular literature, he was undoubtedly instrumental in influencing Carolingian and later scholars to collect and preserve the works of the classical writers of Greece and Rome. Thus monastic and church-connected libraries of the Middle Ages would not infrequently contain works representing the seven liberal arts as well as the expected Bible texts and writings of the Fathers.

Since the Church was so early in recognizing the importance of the written word, it is not surprising to find ancient official documents concerning acceptable and forbidden books—a matter of no small importance to the library administrator. The earliest such text extant is the so-called *Muratorian Canon,* a list of the canonical books of the New Testament dating possibly from the time of Hippolytus in the latter second century. Although many individual writers such as Origen, Eusebius, and Athanasius published biblical canons of their own, the one famous document from the early Church listing acceptable and forbidden books is the so-called *Gelasian Decree* (see *Decretum Gelasianum*) anciently attributed to Pope Gelasius (492–496); but this first *Index* probably was not wholly the work of Gelasius. It contains, among other items, a list of apocryphal and heretical books, the canonical books of the Bible, and recommended works of other writers. However, book censorship was not practiced on a large scale until after the Reformation when all sides employed it vigorously. And so the two principal bibliographic guides for the medieval librarian were the two books of Cassiodorus' *Institutiones* and the *Gelasian Decree,* with the first book of Cassiodorus (biblical texts and commentaries, with a guide for scribes) being the most popular.

The concept of ecclesiastical sanctions associated with the infringement of library circulation rules is probably one that is unique to medieval and Renaissance Catholic libraries. The precious manuscripts of a monastic library were at times secured against unauthorized borrowing or tampering with the threat of excommunication. This extreme measure of library administration was condemned by the reforming Council of Paris (1212) but seemingly without lasting effect, for in the latter sixteenth century we note a decree of Pope Sixtus V (1585–1590)—still epigraphically prominent in the Vatican Library—which utilizes this same stringent method:

> In accordance with this everlasting decree of Sixtus V, Supreme Pontiff, regarding the preservation of Vatican Library books, the rules inscribed below shall be thus solemnly binding and shall be inviolably observed: No one shall have the authority to remove or draw out therefrom, or carry away elsewhere the books, manuscripts, and rolls of this Vatican Library—neither the librarian, the custodians, the scribes, nor any others of whatsoever rank or office—except by the hand-written permission of the Supreme Roman Pontiff. If anyone harms the books, or removes, draws out, steals and carries off, tears or destroys some portion thereof with malice, he shall be forthwith cast out from the communion of the faithful, condemned, and bound with the bond of anathema. By no one save the Roman Pontiff shall he be absolved.

Needless to say, such measures have passed out of use in Catholic library circles in the twentieth century.

Interlibrary cooperation during the early and medieval period was almost non-existent, with the exception of the great Franciscan union catalog effort in fourteenth-century England, the *Registrum librorum Angliae*. Certainly the exchanging of desiderata lists, like those of Lupus of Ferrières, hardly is representative of medieval library practice. Really effective and consistent cooperation among Catholic libraries has been seen only in these latter days of the twentieth century, notable examples of which are the Vatican film library at St. Louis, the Catholic Microfilm Center project described in the article of Alhadef (*1*), the Monastic Manuscript Microfilm Library at St. John's University (Collegeville), and the Ambrosian Library Microfilm Project at Notre Dame. Such recent efforts at cooperation in the United States have been generated and/or fostered by the Catholic Library Association (q.v.) which showed an institutional membership of 934 for the year 1968–1969. It should be noted, however, that other countries have their own such professional organizations; e.g., Association des Bibliothèques de Sciences Religieuses, Association des Bibliothèques Ecclésiastiques de France, and the International Committee for Coordination of Associations of Catholic Theological Libraries.

Renaissance enthusiasm for classical manuscripts was not lacking in Catholic library circles, as can be seen by the phenomenal growth of the Vatican Library in the latter part of the fifteenth century, but it should be noted that Cassiodorus in his second book of the *Institutiones* had recommended secular authors for the better understanding of Scripture. Thus the acquisition of nonreligious literature by Catholic libraries had a precedent that reached back officially at least to the sixth century, and probably centuries earlier, since the great Fathers frequently reflected in their works a thorough knowledge of the pagan classics.

The Reformation and Counter-Reformation movements of the sixteenth century opened a new era of Catholic library history. Certainly it is not necessary here to recount again the widespread confiscation and destruction of monastic and other church affiliated libraries that took place during the sixteenth century, especially in Great Britain, nor even of the later, similar vicissitudes of Catholic libraries during the French Revolution. While the Reformation emphasis on the printing of Bibles both in the original languages and in the vernacular was expressed in all religious camps, dogmatic intolerance was equally shared and particularly manifested in the censorship of literature. This aspect of the controversy appeared in its Roman Catholic form as a result of the Council of Trent by the publication in January 1559 of the first *Index librorum prohibitorum* (q.v.) under Pope Paul IV. This work, which appeared in many subsequent editions (the last in 1948), constituted a very tangible restricting force upon Catholic librarians until its happy demise early in 1966. Not only did the reading of such works as were on the *Index* require special permission from the local bishop, but the librarian had to keep all such items segregated and secured from general use. A further official restriction on graphic materials is found in Canon 1399 of the *Code of Canon Law* (1918). This, theoretically, still (1969) constitutes something of a deterrent for the Catholic librarian in spite of the "fresh air" of Vatican II. This regulation lists twelve categories of forbidden books and graphic materials ranging from editions of the Bible in the original tongues published by non-Catholics down to printed pictures of sacred and religious personages "foreign to the mind and decrees of the Church." Canons 1400–1405 explicitly spell out the restrictions and their exceptions. The prolonged and rather successful attempt of the Council of Trent (1545–1563) to restore and preserve orthodoxy and the later, similar efforts of Vatican I (1869–1870) have had no small effect upon Catholic library administration, especially in the areas of acquisition, cataloging, and classification. A representative work of typical U.S. Catholic library practice of the pre-Vatican II era can be found in the work edited by Martin (*2*). Problems in cataloging and classification faced by the Catholic librarian can readily be surmised by a glance at the works of Kapsner (*3,4*) and Lynn (*5*), and can easily be understood when one considers the separate development and nomenclature of liturgical and vernacular biblical books, the continuation of Latin as the official language, the place of the deutero-canonical books (apocrypha) of the Bible, and the many distinct theological features that resulted from the decrees of Trent. Thus the Catholic librarian had been faced with administrative, cataloging, and classification problems similar to those of the librarian of any special collection.

Looking to the future of Catholic libraries, the writer hesitates to make any predictions with absolute confidence. The goal of the post-Vatican II Church is still to spread the message of the Gospel, thus its libraries will naturally be associated with this aim; only the ways, means, and emphases will differ. And so the writer sees continued cooperation among Catholic libraries in making important religious, theological, and historical collections available on microfilm or other means, and in pooling resources—perhaps through systematic, cooperative acquisition—and further cooperation with non-Catholic libraries, as has been seen at least in Washington, D.C., where the Catholic University Library has participated in cooperative efforts with the other university libraries of the Consortium. It seems likely, also, that the Catholic libraries of the near future, as many now do, will generally adopt acquisition policies emphasizing honest, scholarly research rather than ecclesiastical chauvinism in the purchase of works in religion, theology, and church history. Finally, certain cataloging and classification problems of the past will surely disappear as a result of the fluorescence of ecumenism (e.g., adoption of common vernacular Bible texts and nomenclature), but certainly new problems of subject terminology and classification will continue to develop from the new theological and liturgical outlooks of Vatican II.

REFERENCES

1. J. J. Alhadef, "The Sharing of Catholic Library Resources," *Catholic Library World,* 39, 25–30 (1967).
2. D. Martin, *Catholic Library Practice,* Univ. Portland, Portland, Oregon, 1947–1950.
3. O. L. Kapsner, *Catholic Subject Headings,* 5th ed., St. John's Abbey Press, Collegeville, Minnesota, 1963.
4. O. L. Kapsner, *A Manual of Cataloging Practice for Catholic Author and Title Entries,* Catholic Univ. of America Press, Washington, D.C., 1954.
5. J. M. Lynn, *An Alternative Classification for Catholic Books,* 2nd rev. ed. by G. C. Peterson with a Supplement by T. G. Pater, Catholic Univ. of America Press, Washington, D.C., 1954–1965.

BIBLIOGRAPHY

Burke, R. A., and B. Connolly, "Libraries, Modern Catholic," in *New Catholic Encyclopedia,* Vol. 8, McGraw-Hill, New York, 1967, pp. 724–728.

Mierzwinski, T., "A Catholic Philosophy of Librarianship," *Catholic Library World,* 35, 75–78 (1963).

Sparn, E., *La riqueza de las bibliotecas pertenecientes a la iglesia cristiana en incunables al sobrevenir la secunda guerra mundial,* Imprenta de la Universidad, Cordoba, Argentina, 1947.

Sparn, E., *La riqueza de las iglesias cristianas en bibliotecas al sobrevenir la segunda guerra mundial,* Palumbo, Cordoba, Argentina, 1945–1946.

Thompson, J. W., *The Medieval Library,* Univ. Chicago Press, Chicago, 1939; reprinted by Hafner, New York, 1957.

FRANCIS J. WITTY

CATHOLIC LIBRARY ASSOCIATION

Begun in 1921 as the Library Section of the Department of Colleges and Secondary Schools of the National Catholic Education Association "to deal with library problems as they affect education," the Catholic Library Association is now, after almost 50 years of existence, an incorporated institution organized on a national scale and composed of over 4000 members from the U.S. and 20 foreign countries. In 1931, affiliation with the National Catholic Education Association was terminated and an independent organization known as the Catholic Library Association began functioning with a broader purpose: "to initiate and encourage any movement toward the progress of Catholic literature and Catholic library work." The original aims, though expanded, are reiterated in the Association's purpose: (1) to cooperate in the improvement of Catholic book collections and services in all libraries; (2) to stimulate the writing, publishing, and reading of good Catholic literature; (3) to stimulate the production of Catholic bibliographic tools; (4) to provide for the official publication of the Association; (5) to encourage the formation of Interest Sections and Regional Units; (6) to cooperate with standardizing agencies in the development of Catholic Library Schools; (7) to represent the ideals and interests of Catholic librarians before secular and governmental organizations; (8) to collaborate with other organizations having problems of mutual interest; (9) to radiate interest in scientific research and technical advances and developments relating to libraries and librarianship; and (10) to assist in the establishment and development of foreign Catholic libraries and library schools.

According to the present constitution and by-laws of the Catholic Library Association, the object of the association is the promotion and encouragement of Catholic literature and library work through cooperation, publications, education, and information.

In 1921, at the National Catholic Education Association's Cincinnati meeting Rev. Paul J. Foik, C.S.C., proposed that

> the cumulative efforts of Catholic librarians for improvement of conditions in our universities, colleges and secondary schools is best accomplished by a centralization of responsibility. The necessity for a section or at least a librarians' round table within the NCEA where those interested can come to discuss informally their experiences and their difficulties in library practice and administration, should indeed be obvious to all.

This proposition resulted in the establishment of a library unit within the NCEA and, at the association's meeting in Philadelphia in 1922, Father Foik, acting as chairman, a position he held for 7 years, announced that 86 interested librarians had positively signified their intentions by sending representatives to this convention.

As a result of this meeting, the Library Section to the Department of Colleges and Secondary Schools of NCEA was established. After the Library Section had been in existence 8 years, its chairman, Father Foik, recommended the preparation of a tentative constitution and by-laws for it. To this end, a committee of three members—Rev. Henry Regnet, chairman, assisted by Mr. Francis E. Fitzgerald and Rev. Coleman J. Farrell, O.S.B.—who would continue to have a vital interest in the association, were appointed. After the committee met twice, Father Foik asked the general assembly of NCEA to consider and approve discontinuance of the Library Unit of the NCEA College Department. The separation and newly devised constitution were approved.

The new independent organization assumed the name of Catholic Library Association. Elected as first president of CLA was Rev. William M. Stinson. He was assisted by the following officers: Vice-President, Rev. Paul J. Foik; Secretary, Rev. Peter J. Etzig; and Treasurer, Mr. Francis E. Fitzgerald. A resolution, which was the final recording of library section activities in the NCEA proceedings, was submitted to the College Department of the NCEA. The statement and resolution asking for a discontinuance of the section and the approval of the establishment of the Catholic Library Association was favorably acted upon at the closing general meeting of the NCEA on June 25, 1931. It officially marked the termination of NCEA control and the inauguration of the Catholic Library Association. The Catholic Library Association was launched with the hearty endorsement and the generous blessing of the dean of American Hierarchy, His Eminence, William Cardinal O'Connell, Archbishop of Boston.

As a national association with a widespread membership, meeting only once a year, the CLA had difficulties with communications and continued activity. A system of units and regional conferences was devised and, in 1938, definitions were accepted by the membership for a unit and regional conference. A unit was defined as "a group of members of CLA within a defined area such as the locality, a diocese, or where members are few and scattered, a larger geographical area." A regional conference was defined as "a meeting made up of a number of Units within a rather large geographical area such as eastern states, midwestern states, southern states, etc." By 1968, the CLA was composed of 44 units throughout the United States and Canada. Each unit holds two meetings during the year, sponsors library programs, and, in general, carries out the policies and plans of the CLA within a clearly defined area. The chairman of each unit is a member of the CLA Advisory Council and has a voice in making policies for the Association. Units are recognized as a vital and sustaining factor of the CLA; it would be difficult to estimate the total contribution from the units as a generating power for the association's unity, growth, and achievements.

The CLA holds an annual convention. At the time the association withdrew from the NCEA, it was decided to hold the annual convention of the CLA concurrently with the convention of the NCEA. For several years, NCEA and CLA met at the same time and place, but in 1932, CLA held its first independent annual convention in Cincinnati.

Except for the years of World War II, when travel was restricted, the CLA has held its annual conventions in cities across the country. Meetings have been held from New York to California, and from Minnesota to Texas. The annual conventions, held during Easter Week, attract 1000 to 1200 delegate members, and programs are planned around the professional activities of librarianship.

From the very beginning of the CLA, round tables were formed to permit members with like interests to meet with one another and to discuss common problems. Also, the constitution and by-laws of the CLA provide for sections—groups formed by members having common interests. Each section elects its own officers, sets its own dues, and issues a publication several times a year to inform members of its activities. During the annual convention, each section is responsible for a portion of the convention program. In the past, sections have contracted with nationally known speakers in the library field and have attracted large numbers of members to the section meetings. Interest sections that have been formally established as component parts of the Association are the Children's Libraries Section, College and University Libraries Section, High School Libraries Section, Parish and Lending Libraries Section, Library Education Section, Seminary Libraries Section, Cataloging and Classification Section, Health Sciences Libraries Section, and, most recently, the School Libraries Supervisors' Section.

Another noteworthy activity of the CLA is the promotion of observance of Catholic Book Week. Established over 29 years ago, the intention of Catholic Book Week was to focus attention on good Catholic reading and good books. Once celebrated in November, for the past several years it has been observed during the last full week of February. A slogan is adopted and attractive posters dramatizing the slogan, bookmarks with reproductions of the posters, and quotations from the Regina Medal Award winners, the annual *CLA Booklist,* and other assorted materials encouraging the celebration of Catholic Book Week are mailed to members interested in this observance.

A major contribution of the CLA to the library profession has been its publications program. Almost from its very beginning as a separate organization in 1931, the association planned its most important publication, *The Catholic Periodical Index.* Through many vicissitudes and trials, *The Catholic Periodical Index* achieved a prominent place in library literature. Second to this is *The Guide to Catholic Literature,* which was purchased from its founder, Walter Romig, in 1959. In 1968 the membership of the CLA voted to combine the two publications into one, *The Catholic Periodical and Literature Index.* The combination took effect in July 1968, providing, in one reference guide, an annotated author-title-subject index to books by or of interest to Catholics as well as an alphabetic index to articles appearing in over 100 Catholic periodicals.

On a smaller scale the association has published a number of booklets designed for use by all librarians, especially Catholics. The first of these is the *CLA Booklist,* known at one time as the *Catholic Booklist.* Edited by a competent board of contributing editors, the annual *CLA Booklist* lists books by, about, and of interest to Catholics in major subject areas. Of special value in the annual *CLA Booklist* is the extensive listing of books for elementary and secondary school libraries.

The Parish and Lending Library Manual was developed to meet the need of parish libraries. This movement to establish libraries within parishes was started to complement, but not duplicate, the local public library collection of religious material. The Parish and Lending Libraries Section still holds to its original intention to buy for its clientele books that would not be purchased by the local public library. Thus the parish library is in no instance in competition with the local public library. Parish libraries are primarily in the hands of volunteers, with occasional supervision by a qualified librarian, so for them the CLA published *The Parish Library Manual* in 1959. It contained detailed instructions on how to set up the parish library, how to obtain books, where to purchase books, and how to catalog and classify in a very simplified way the books received for the parish library. It also included a basic list of books recommended for first purchase. Updated in 1965, it was given a more inclusive title, *The Parish and Lending Library Manual*. In this edition, the basic purchase list was omitted.

The official publication of the CLA is the *Catholic Library World*. Begun in 1929 as a mimeographed paper, it has developed into a substantial journal, carrying articles of interest to the Catholic librarian and to the library profession in general. Published monthly from September to May-June, it features new books recommended for children's libraries, high school libraries, professional reading, and parish libraries and contributed articles on developments in the library profession.

For the Catholic high schools, *Basic Reference Books for Catholic High School Libraries* was first printed in 1959. A second edition was published in 1964, and an updated listing of reference books was published in 1968. The CLA has also compiled the titles for *The Catholic Supplement to the Senior High School Library Catalog* since 1940, in cooperation with the H. W. Wilson Company.

Besides working on its own publishing program, the CLA has sponsored a number of other important library publications. As a sponsor the association promoted and advertised *Catholic Bookman's Manual* by Sister M. Regis, I.H.M.; *An Alternative Classification for Catholic Books* by Jeanette Murphy Lynn and Rev. Gilbert C. Peterson, S.J.; *Books for Catholic Colleges* by Sister Melania; and *Catholic Religious Orders* and *Catholic Subject Headings* by Rev. Oliver Kapsner, O.S.B.

In 1967, by vote of the membership, the Catholic Library Association asked for and was granted affiliation with the American Library Association, giving it a permanent representative on the ALA Council. The Catholic Library Association has had representatives on the Council of National Library Associations since its founding. Some of them have served as chairmen of the council and members of the Board of Trustees.

Activities of the CLA, especially Catholic Book Week, have been cosponsored by the National Council of Catholic Men, the National Council of Catholic Women, the Catholic Press Association, and the National Office for Decent Literature. Materials from the Children's Book Council, National Library Week, and the National Council of Christians and Jews have been included in Catholic Book Week kits.

Perhaps the major contribution to the library profession is the annual scholarship granted by the CLA to an individual for study toward a graduate degree in library science. Promise of success based on collegiate scholastic record and evidence of financial need are the criteria for the award. The scholarship was established in 1959 with a grant of $600, and was increased by 1966 to $1000.

In 1967, Rev. Andrew L. Bouwhuis, a loyal member of the CLA, died. He had served as president of the association from 1943 to 1945, as a member of the CLA Executive Board, and as chairman of the Children's Libraries Section, and enjoyed national prominence in the library profession. To honor Father Bouwhuis, the CLA renamed the scholarship The Reverend Andrew L. Bouwhuis Scholarship.

Another important contribution has been the annual award of the Regina Medal to an individual who has contributed a lifetime to the field of children's literature. Established by an anonymous grant in 1958, the Regina Medal, inscribed with the words of Walter De la Mare, "Only the rarest kind of best in anything can be good enough for the young," has been given each year since that time. The winners have been Eleanor Farjeon (1959), Ann Carroll Moore (1960), Padraic Colum (1961), Frederic Melcher (1962), Ann Nolan Clark (1963), May Hill Arbuthnot (1964), Ruth Sawyer Durand (1965), Leo Politi (1966), Bertha Mahony Miller (1967), and Marguerite de Angeli (1968). The award is given without regard to the recipient's religion, country, or nature of contribution (author, publisher, editor, illustrator, and so on).

The CLA has also given testimony on federal legislation before Senate and House Appropriations Committees. With the advent of Title II of the Elementary and Secondary Education Act, the children attending Catholic schools were given an opportunity to read more books, and school libraries expanded. To encourage continued support for such a program the CLA has taken an important part in promoting federal legislation and the continuation of Title II. Members of the CLA have been invited to offer testimony to Senate and House committees and the association has cooperated with the ALA and the U.S. Catholic Conference in spearheading campaigns to influence the decision of the appropriations committees.

BIBLIOGRAPHY

CLA Handbook and Membership Directory.

Catholic Library World, various issues.

Donleavy, Sister Consolata Maria, "The History of the Catholic Library Association, 1921–1961," unpublished master's dissertation, Dept. of Library Science, Catholic University of America, Washington, D.C., 1964.

MATTHEW R. WILT

CATHOLIC PERIODICAL AND LITERATURE INDEX

One of the prime motives for forming the Catholic Library Association was to publish bibliographic tools of specialized interest that were not published commercially. The *Catholic Periodical Index* was discussed in 1923, at the Cleveland meeting of the Library Section of the National Catholic Education Association, but it was not until 1931, when the Catholic Library Association became a separate organization, that the *Catholic Periodical Index* became a reality. The purpose then, as now, was to index articles that appear in representative Catholic magazines. Although it was begun as a cooperative venture, the Catholic Library Association soon realized that this highly technical indexing must be performed by a permanent staff.

From 1921 to 1931, the fledgling association's main endeavor was the compilation of the *Index,* a venture which, because of its ambitious scope, necessitated extensive expenditures. In 1930, the Catholic Periodical Index Committee named Francis Fitzgerald as editor and contracted the services of the H. W. Wilson Company, and the initial issue was published. Between 1930 and 1938, the task of keeping the publication going became an ever-increasing concern of the Catholic Library Association. In 1938, Laurence A. Leavey was named editor of the *Catholic Periodical Index* and its permanency was established. In 1939, the long-awaited 1930–1933 basic volume of the *Index* was published by the H. W. Wilson Company and distributed on a service basis to subscribers. Before the end of 1939, the second volume, covering the period from January to June 1939, was published. Mr. Leavey continued as editor until 1952, when he was succeeded by Joseph Sprug. Under Mr. Sprug's editorship, the volume covering 1934 to 1938 was published. Subsequent volumes under the editors have appeared on schedule. The *Index* is now in its fourteenth volume, covering the years 1966–1968.

Now on a bimonthly issue basis with a bound cumulation every 2 years, the *Catholic Periodical Index* is still the only reference guide to Catholic periodicals of the time.

In 1958, the Catholic Library Association purchased from Walter A. Romig the publication rights for the *Guide to Catholic Literature* and assumed the responsibility of editing, publishing, and distributing it. At that time, the *Guide* was published on an annual basis with a 4-year bound cumulation.

At the 1967 Catholic Library Association Convention, a special ad-hoc committee was named to examine the *Catholic Periodical Index* and the *Guide to Catholic Literature* for content, inclusiveness, and production techniques, and to recommend any necessary changes. A vote from subscribers revealed that some publications currently indexed needed to be dropped, while newer, more important publications needed to be added to the list. Further deliberation of the committee resulted in the proposition to merge the two publications to form a unified bibliographic tool covering Catholic periodicals and Catholic books.

In July 1968, the first issue of the new *Catholic Periodical and Literature Index* was published by the Catholic Library Association. The new publication appears every 2 months and will be cumulated every 2 years in a bound volume.

MATTHEW R. WILT

CATHOLIC UNIVERSITY OF AMERICA, GRADUATE DEPARTMENT OF LIBRARY SCIENCE

There had been an insistent demand that a library school be established at the Catholic University of America long before the inauguration of the Department of Library Science in 1938–1939. More and more religious communities were founding houses of study at the university (more than 50 by 1938). Bishops and superiors were reluctant at that time to grant permission to attend secular library schools. The two existing Catholic library schools were located in undergraduate colleges for women.

The annual report of the rector, James Hugh Ryan, in 1928–1929 summarized well the several references to the subject made in previous years.

> Considerable thought has been given to the organization of a Graduate School of Library Science. There is no such school in the U.S. under Catholic auspices. The need for trained librarians is acute, especially in our high schools. The demands of State Departments of Education and various accrediting agencies are such that no school will be accepted as standard unless the librarian has been trained especially for such work. During the summer sessions a number of courses have been offered. While useful, these courses do not meet adequately our educational situation. Nothing short of a well-organized and well-conducted School of Library Science will suffice.

The summer session courses referred to by Bishop Ryan had actually been offered during the very first summer session of the university, July 2–Aug. 8, 1911. They were taught by members of the university library staff and librarians from the District of Columbia Public Library. Under the leadership of the university librarian, Joseph Schneider, and Mother Agatha, O.S.U., of Wilmington, Delaware, from 1920 to 1929, the development of the program continued in successive summer sessions, so that by 1930 a complete four-summer training program was offered and a special certificate awarded. Subsequent summer sessions offered additional courses and more faculty members were recruited from local libraries as well as from Catholic school libraries in various cities of the country.

It was not until 1937 that the hopes of the rector in his annual reports from 1928 to 1932 for a program of studies during the academic years began to be realized. Rev. Francis A. Mullin had been selected to be the director of the university library, and had spent 2 years at the University of Michigan working under the special guidance of William Warner Bishop, director of the university library and of the Library Science Department at Ann Arbor. Under the guidance of Bishop and members of the Board of Education for Librarianship of the ALA a B.S. in L.S. degree program was begun in the fall of 1937. Thirty credit hours beyond the bachelor's degree and a reading knowledge of French or German were required for graduation. For the first 2 years faculty still consisted for the most part of part-time lecturers.

In September 1939, a permanent organization was given to the department. It was included in the Graduate School of Arts and Sciences with Father Mullin as head of the department. A full-time faculty of four was added and the number of available courses was increased. In 1941 an evaluating team from the ALA inspected the department and granted provisional accreditation.

Father Mullin suffered a severe heart attack in 1941 and recurrent illnesses prevented him from full-time activity in the library and the Library Science Department. Rev. James J. Kortendick, S.S., was appointed assistant librarian in the spring of 1941, and served as acting librarian and acting head of the department during the absences of Father Mullin until the latter's death in 1947. In the fall of 1946 Father Kortendick was appointed head of the department.

In 1948 the accreditors were invited to inspect the department again. The program had been considerably enlarged to include among its objectives the training not only of school and college librarians, but also of public, special, and governmental librarians. Full accreditation was granted the same year.

Meanwhile, the faculty of the department was laying plans for a complete revision of the curriculum to meet the changes affecting the library profession and, as in a number of the other larger library schools, set up a program of studies leading to the M.S. in L.S. in place of the former graduate degree, a B.S. in L.S. The first M.S. in L.S. degree was granted in June 1950.

The revised program brought with it two special new features, the dissertation and the required minor of six credits in another field of graduate study. A basic core curriculum of 20 credits was supplemented by additional courses to prepare the student for specialization in various types of libraries as well as in various types of service in libraries. The new program was fully re-accredited by the standards issued by the ALA in 1952.

The department has kept pace with succeeding developments in the field of librarianship. Courses are regularly reviewed and revised and new courses added to provide more opportunities for specialization and to reflect the latest approaches to discovery, selection, and acquisition of the wide range of library materials; their organization for more effective retrieval; and the needs for broader and more extensive service to users.

The library science program for the master's degree requires 34 hours of course work, 20 of which constitute the basic core courses. These are organized to introduce the student to the historical, philosophical, and technical background of professional library service and to prepare him for the more specialized courses selected to meet his own particular career interests and goals. These courses represent advanced study in the areas of information sources and services, administration and organization of types of libraries (school, college and university, public, special, and governmental libraries), building and control of collections, and special services.

The student maps out his program in consultation with his faculty adviser. In doing so he is encouraged to select from a wide variety of courses from other departments of graduate study those adapted to further his special needs. Flexibility in the individual program is achieved through adaptation to the student's academic background, his special requirements, and his choice of career.

The library science courses are designed to maintain a balance of theory and practice. Emphasis is on understanding the principles of technique and service; these will most likely endure in a rapidly changing profession that must adapt itself to and adopt modern technological tools. The student is introduced to these principles in appropriate general courses; he becomes more conversant with them in specialized courses in automation of library processes, computer science, systems analysis, and information retrieval.

The national and, indeed, international character of the university, its location in the greatest bibliographic center of the world, the large number and variety of libraries and library networks in the area, and the fact that until recently the university had the only accredited library school in the Washington, Maryland, and Virginia area all help to account for its ability to attract students. The local libraries, federal, public, and private, have from the beginning been cooperative and helpful in providing laboratory experience and observation facilities for students and faculty and in providing highly qualified regular and special lecturers to supplement the full-time faculty.

Many of these libraries, in cooperation with the department, have set up part-time or full-time programs so that students can gain practical experience in connection with professional training and receive financial assistance at the same time. More than half the enrollment consists of part-time students thus employed. In recent years a growing number of graduate librarians employed in local libraries are enrolling in advanced and special courses to update their knowledge and expand their competence.

As many as a fourth of the students enrolled possess other graduate degrees, including doctorates, in special subject fields. There have been registrants from every one of the 50 states and from 56 foreign countries. The number of students has continued to grow, but since 1960 has leveled off to approximately 250 to 260 each year. The total number of degrees granted is 1453; 249 received the B.S. in L.S. degree; 1204 received the M.S. in L.S. degree between 1950 and 1969. The largest graduating class, 117, was in June 1969. The department has served more than 2000 additional students in selected courses. Of the 1453 graduates, 1022 are women and 431 men. Religious sisters, brothers, and priests among the alumni number 425.

Current records of graduates show that approximately one third are employed in libraries of institutions of higher education; another third in government and special libraries; the remaining third are fairly equally divided among school libraries and public libraries; several are with publishing firms; and 25 are engaged in library education, four of them as directors or deans of library schools. The proximity of great libraries has proved to be reciprocally advantageous. Area libraries, federal, public, academic, and special, each year recruit approximately one half of the graduates. This parallels the percentage of area residents enrolled. Few libraries of any size in the greater Washington community do not have at least one alumnus on the professional staff, frequently at the top supervisory level.

Through the department, the university has fulfilled its objective to serve the local, national, and international communities, and, as an arm of the National Catholic University, to serve the Church. This has been accomplished not only by supplying leadership in staff but also by participating actively in programs of development, survey, and faculty and student research related to the improvement of library service in most types of libraries.

Workshops and other intensive training programs have been offered for foreign librarians in service in binational and information centers in Latin America; for parochial school librarians; for theological seminary library staff members; for middle managers in libraries; for national library school faculty members in federal library resources, projects, and services; and for area librarians in automation of library services. Several of the faculty have visited extensively and served as consultants to foreign libraries and library schools. Fellowships for foreign students have been secured from the Rockefeller and Ford Foundations, the Organization of American States, and the Foreign Area Fellowship Program. A course in comparative librarianship has been introduced, enhanced by the fact that many foreign librarians visiting the National Libraries have included on the agenda prepared for them by the Department of State and the Library of Congress a visit to the university and the Department of Library Science. These occasions provide an opportunity to exchange information and to have the foreign librarians address or talk informally with the students and staff. All of this has helped significantly to extend the influence of the department here and abroad.

Funded research and development currently under way look toward the enlargement of the library science program to include post-master's certification in specialized areas of service, and ultimately a doctoral program, further utilizing the uniquely rich library resources of Washington, D.C., and further meeting the needs for developing leaders in the profession.

JAMES J. KORTENDICK

CAXTON CLUB

The Caxton Club of Chicago was established in 1895 by a group of local bibliophiles who were doubtless inspired by the example of the Grolier Club in New York. Among the 15 founders were men prominent in business, in education, and in connoisseurship. They included Edward E. Ayer, noted for his collection of books and manuscripts on the Indian, whose collection is now at The Newberry Library; John Vance Cheyney, poet and librarian; Charles L. Hutchinson, president of the Art Institute of Chicago; George Millard, the leading Chicago bookseller of the day; Herbert S. Stone, partner in Stone and Kimball; W. Irving Way, bookseller and publisher; and John H. Wrenn, the noted collector and friend of T. J. Wise whose library, rich in Wise forgeries and thefts as well as in more respectable books, is at the University of Texas. The announced purpose of the

Club was "the literary study and promotion of the arts pertaining to the production of books," which was loosely interpreted from the beginning. The Club's publications and exhibitions have treated book bindings, prints, Americana, printing, and even a printed facsimile of an alphabet stone cut by Eric Gill. The speakers at the monthly dinner meetings (varied by an occasional luncheon or field trip) have also reflected the wide and eclectic interests of the membership.

The most recent *Yearbook,* issued in 1965, lists 53 publications, as well as a great many ephemeral pieces distributed to members. It is difficult, and perhaps invidious, to select from these the handsomest or most important of the Club's books. The following brief selection must suffice to indicate their scope: Cyril Davenport's *Thomas Berthelet* (1901), *Samuel Mearne* (1906); and *Roger Payne* (1929); Gordon Duff's *William Caxton* (1905), a pious gesture which remains one of the best books on its subject; A. W. Pollard's *An Essay on Colophons* (1905); James Westfall Thompson's *The Frankfort Bookfair* (1911); Frederic G. Kenyon's *Ancient Books and Modern Discoveries* (1927); Berthold Laufer's *Paper and Printing in Ancient China* (1931); Lloyd Brown and Howard Peckham's *Revolutionary War Journals of Henry Dearborn* (1939); George Ade's *Stories of the Streets and of the Town* (1941); *John McCutcheon's Book* (1948), designed by McCutcheon's college friend, Bruce Rogers; Harry Owens's translation of a popular puppet version of *Dr. Faust* (1953), with woodcuts by Fritz Kredel; and *The Crockett Almanacks* (1955), edited by Franklin J. Meine, a former president of the Club. In addition, there has been an attempt to make the announcement of each meeting a piece of fine printing and design, worthy of being saved as a keepsake.

The Caxton Club does not, unfortunately, have its own rooms; meetings are usually held at one of the downtown clubs, with occasional side trips to local institutions. The meetings (restricted to the membership, all male, and their male guests) have a long tradition of conviviality; it is the proud boast of the Club that even during the drought of Prohibition the high spirits of The Caxton Club flowed undiminished. The membership, the majority drawn from Chicago, numbered some 200 in 1969. Drawn together by a common love of books and talk about books, they have included during its 75 years most Chicagoans prominent in design, typography, publishing, bookselling, librarianship, and book collecting.

JAMES M. WELLS

CAXTON, WILLIAM

William Caxton (1422?–1491) printed the first book in English, *The Recuyell of the Historyes of Troye,* Bruges, 1473/74 and printed the first book in England, *The Dictes or Sayengis of the Philosophres,* Westminster, 1477. Before he was a printer he had pursued a successful career for thirty years in the Low Countries as a member of the Mercers' Company, eventually becoming Governor of the Merchant Adventurers of England, in which capacity he was entrusted with important commissions for the Crown. He spent the last fifteen years of his life as translator, printer, and publisher in Westminster, England.

William Caxton was born in Kent about 1422, but the town of his birth remains obscure. That he was from a well-to-do family is evidenced by his superior education and the fact that he was apprenticed to a successful mercer, Robert Large, later Lord Mayor of London, at whose home he no doubt lived as one of the family. The untimely death of Large led Caxton to join the Company of Merchant Adventurers in Bruges about 1441 where he became most successful. In 1462 he was Governor of the English Nation beyond the sea and as such he had important duties in regulating affairs among the merchants, negotiating with town councils, and upholding the rules of the company. He acted as ambassador for Edward IV in the affairs that concerned the Duke of Burgundy and the Hanseatic League and was involved in the delicate political maneuvers fostered by the Earl of Warwick.

Upon the marriage of Charles the Bold and Princess Margaret, sister to King Edward IV of England, the English King selected Caxton as one of three of the Mercers' Company to renew trade with Burgundy. The successful fulfillment of this mission was one of Caxton's last official acts. On March 1, 1469, "having no great charge of occupation . . . to eschew sloth and to put myself into virtuous occupation and business," he began to make a translation into English of one of his favorite tales, the French *Le Recueil des Histoires de Troye*. After he had translated sixty pages or so he tired and laid it aside. He showed the translation to his employer, the Duchess Margaret, who made suggestions as to how it might be improved and urged him to finish it. Since he had business in Cologne, he finished his translation there on September 19, 1471. It was in Cologne that Caxton learned the art of printing so that he could furnish additional copies of his translation without having to write them tediously out by hand. He helped his printer instructor produce the book *De Proprietatibus Rerum* in 1472. That Caxton learned to print in Cologne is confirmed by his foreman, Wynkyn de Worde, in the prologue to his edition of the same book issued about 1495:

> And also of your charyte call to remembraunce
> The soule of William Caxton first prynter of this boke
> In Laten tonge at Coleyn hymself to avaunce
> That every well disposyd man may theron loke

Caxton secured type, press, and other accessories and began printing in Bruges in 1473. Colard Mansion, a scribe, worked for Caxton and was not his instructor in printing, as claimed by Caxton's biographer, William Blades (*1*). He probably finished printing his first book, *The Recuyell of the Historyes of Troye,* in the same year.

Much information about Caxton is to be gleaned from the prologues and epilogues to the books he printed. In the epilogue to Book III of the *Recuyell* he wrote: "Therfore I have practysed and lerned at by grete charge and dispense to ordeyne this said book in prynte after the maner and forme as ye may here see, and is not wreton with penne and ynke, as other bokes ben, to thende that every man may have them attones, for all the bookes of this storye named the Recule of the Historyes of Troyes, thus empryntid as ye here see were begonne in oon day, and also fynysshid in oon day." Caxton also printed in Bruges his English translation of *The Game and Playe of The Chesse* by Jacobus de Cessolis, which is a kind of guide to living rather than a compendium of rules for playing chess, and a devotional book, *Les Quatre Derrenières Choses*.

Caxton left Bruges and established his press in England in 1476. In December of that year he printed a Latin indulgence issued by the Abbot of Abingdon. Practically nothing is known of his equipment or printing procedure except that which is gathered from the external evidence of the printed sheets. He rented space in a house close by the Chapter House of Westminster Abbey. Later he expanded his operation to the Almonry nearby, identified by the Red Pale. He undoubtedly kept his original location as a bookshop since it was near the entrance to the Abbey where it would attract the patronage of the important passers-by. The first dated book printed in England was *The Dictes or Sayengis of the Philosophres,* dated November 18, 1477, in the epilogue. It was translated by Earl Rivers who may be presumed to have borne some of the cost of printing.

Caxton printed books of worship for use in Salisbury Cathedral. The printing of missals involved the use of red and black ink on the same page, a skill that Caxton never perfected. In fact, in order to satisfy the clergy, he was known on at least one occasion to have had a book of worship printed in Paris by Guillaume Maynyal, the *Sarum Missal* of 1487, the first book to bear his well-known printer's mark (see Figure 1).

To Caxton, printing was a means to an end rather than an art. His main interest was to provide books in English, so that the enjoyment of literature could become more widespread. Compared with the Gutenberg Bible, his best work could be called shoddy, but then so could most other printing then and now. His first types no doubt came from Bruges and probably resembled his handwriting; he invested in new types only when forced to meet competition. He endeavored to dress up his work by having a rubricator add colored initials and he did use wood engravings to illustrate some of his books.

The Golden Legend, issued sometime after November 1483, is probably his most ambitious work. It is a book of 449 leaves and Blades (*1*) says that it "may be considered the most laborious as well as most extensive of all Caxton's literary and typographical labours." He used many woodcuts and they are more artistically executed than those used in his other books. Whereas most of the paper used by Caxton came from the prolific mills of Normandy, the paper for *The Golden Legend* had to be of a larger size and was of a higher quality. According to Allan Stevenson (*2*): "This was an exception, apparently due to the fact that few other mills down the Rhine or Moselle could supply the full royal sheets that Caxton needed for his golden book. As in the first Latin *Legenda,* Eggestein's of about 1472, Bull's heads sanctified by taus look forth from the windows. Perhaps Caxton specified this famous mark rather than the Seal of the Gallizians, which would have

FIGURE 1. *Caxton's device from* The Mirrour of the World, *2nd ed.* (*Courtesy of Frick Fine Arts Library, University of Pittsburgh.*)

had little meaning for Englishmen. Because of the patronage of the Earl of Arundel, Caxton could afford fine royal paper brought from a considerable distance."

Caxton printed more than 100 editions, totaling more than 10,000 copies or an average of about 100 copies. Choosing for the most part to print books written in English, he had to provide his own translations or search out the best version of such classics as Chaucer's *Canterbury Tales* and Thomas Malory's *Morte d'Arthur.* Caxton first printed the *Canterbury Tales* in 1478, an edition that probably sold quickly, but when he learned that he had used an inferior version as copy, he reissued a new edition in 1484. He made available books on English history, which up to that time had never been printed. In 1480 he published the *Chronicles of England* and reprinted it in 1482, the same year that he produced the *Polychronicon,* a lengthy work to which Caxton added a whole book, bringing history down to 1460. He was also responsible for the only known example of a printer's advertisement in England in the fifteenth century. This was undated, but known to have been printed prior to 1480. It refers to separately published portions of the common "Directorium seu Pica Sarum" (see Figure 2).

The manuscript of Caxton's translation of Ovid's *Metamorphoses,* Books 10 to 15, has long been in the Pepys Library at Magdalene College, Cambridge. In 1966 the first part of the text, containing Books 1 to 9, appeared on the market and was sold at Sotheby's to Lew David Feldman for $252,000, the highest price ever paid for a manuscript or printed book at public auction, but through contributions

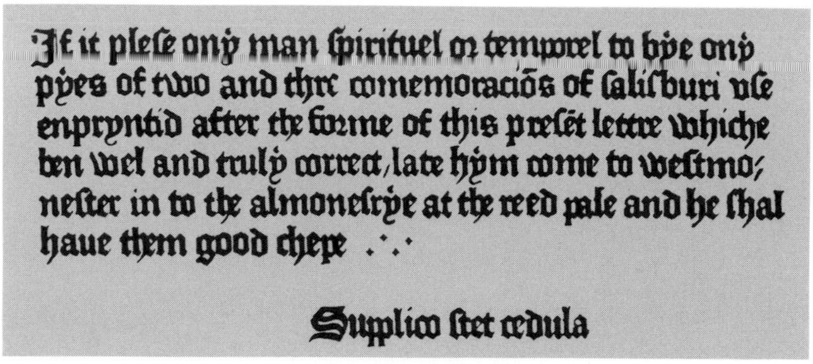
Jf it plese ony man spirituel or temporel to bye ony
pyes of two and thre comemoracios of salisburi use
enpryntid after the forme of this preset lettre whiche
ben wel and truly correct, late hym come to westmo-
nester in to the almonesrye at the reed pale and he shal
haue them good chepe .:.

Supplico stet cedula

FIGURE 2. *Caxton's handbill advertisement.* (*Courtesy of Frick Fine Arts Library, University of Pittsburgh.*)

of friends and the proceeds of the publication of both parts in color facsimile, it was possible to reunite the two parts in the Magdalene College Library. If Caxton printed the *Metamorphoses,* no copy has survived nor is there any evidence of such an edition. The possibility that the manuscript is written in Caxton's own hand cannot be excluded. If not in his hand, it was certainly produced under his close supervision by an English scribe trained in the Netherlands and working in Caxton's establishment at Westminster.

Caxton, through his translation and printing of texts in English, created an interest in and filled a need for English literature. For better or worse he succeeded in producing a uniformity in spelling that had not been achieved theretofore. Many of his publications were subsidized by patrons, but he financed the more popular books himself.

Most of the information about Caxton has been derived from the prologues and epilogues to his books in which he set down his philosophy of translation and publication. The other sources of information are found in the official record books, particularly those of Bruges and Westminster Abbey.

George Parker Winship (*3*) closes his book, *William Caxton,* with the following: "The annals of literary history offer to the imagination no more fascinating picture than that of the first in the long line of English publishers who have also been men of letters, a man who was likewise one of the earliest in the succession of English merchants and men of affairs who have found recreation and fame in the production of literature. When William Caxton went to his reward in the year 1491, he completed a career of widely varied activities, regarding which we have much more than the average of record left by the public men of his age—records preserving not one single hint of any untoward incident to qualify our admiration for one of the greatest of Englishmen."

REFERENCES

1. W. Blades, *The Life and Typography of William Caxton,* 2 vols., J. Lilly, London, 1861–1863.

2. A. H. Stevenson, *The Problem of the Missale Speciale,* Thomas C. Pears III, Pittsburgh, 1967. New information on paper used by Caxton.
3. G. P. Winship, *William Caxton,* Doves Press, Hammersmith, England, 1909.

BIBLIOGRAPHY

Aurner, N. S., *William Caxton: Mirrour of Fifteenth Century Letters,* Houghton, Boston, 1926.

Bühler, C. F., *William Caxton and his Critics,* Syracuse Univ. Press, Syracuse, New York, 1964.

Crotch, W. J. B., *The Prologues and Epilogues of William Caxton,* The Early English Text Society, Oxford, 1928.

Moran, J., "William Caxton and the Origins of English Publishing," *Gutenberg Jahrbuch, 1967,* pp. 61–64.

Ibid., "William Blades," *The Library* (The Bibliographical Society, London), 16(4), 251–266 (December 1961).

Sheppard, L. A., "A New Light on Caxton and Colard Mansion," *Signature,* 15 (1952).

Tanner, L. E., "William Caxton's Houses at Westminster," *The Library* (The Bibliographical Society, London), 12(3), pp. 153–166 (September 1957).

THOMAS C. PEARS III

CENSORSHIP

Fire has been used since its first discovery as an agent to combat contrary opinion. Men and books have been burned when their teachings were distasteful to the prevailing authority. The censorship of books has had a long and varied history and lists of *librorum prohibitorum* have existed since before the birth of Christ.

The term censorship is of Latin derivation, *censere,* "to assess." In ancient Rome, censor was the title of the two magistrates who took the census. In addition to registering individual citizens and property, they assigned burdens and duties to the different classes of society and checked to see that the responsibilities were executed. The censors had great power; they had no superior except their own consciences and Roman tradition. Eventually the office was raised above the consulship in dignity and was considered the crown of a political career.

The Roman censors as arbiters of morality could prevent citizens from attending public functions on moral grounds. They could invade family life and check into personal conduct and could investigate the exercise of political duties of the individual. The elder Cato was the most famous of the censors.

In modern thought, censorship is an effort by a government, private organization, group, or individual to prevent people from reading, seeing, or hearing what may be considered as dangerous to government or harmful to public morality.

Censorship may be exercised on political, religious, or moral grounds, making the offense one of treason, heresy, or obscenity. At different times censorship has been undertaken by the state, by the priesthood, and by unofficial groups.

In a restricted sense censorship refers to the work of a person or agency with the authority to come between the producer to publish, and the consumer to acquire knowledge of, the censored materials. In a looser interpretation the term is used to describe the enactment and enforcement of laws that restrict the freedom to publish unless these laws deal with the protection of the rights of others, as in cases of slander, libel, or copyright infringement.

Freedom of the press does not exist in Communist countries, where the press is considered an instrument of the state. A noncritical attitude toward the government is enforced by the government and the press functions primarily as an agent to report and support decisions of the government.

Countries that have a free press, on the other hand, believe the citizen should know what his government is doing and must be free to criticize it. This coincides, with the democratic belief that a democracy can exist only so long as an enlightened citizenry is contributing new ideas for the guidance of the government—and is participating in shaping the decisions that are being made.

Historical Background

Historically religion was the first target of censorship, with punishment for blasphemy and heresy; political ideas came next, with persecution for treason; later, the subject of sex led to persecution for obscenity. Censorship has operated continuously from antiquity to the present day, in every period, in various environments and climes.

It may be that the Greeks were the first to emphasize the value of freedom of speech and to emphasize the fact that persuasion is better than coercion. But there have been numerous instances of persecution in every country in the world. In the fifth century B.C., in Athens, the philosopher Anaxagoras was fined for impiety; his books were burned and he was exiled. The books of Protagoras were burned after he fled from Athens, having been accused of blasphemy. Euripides was charged with impiety. The most famous martyr to freedom of speech was Socrates, who was put to death in 399 B.C. on charges of impiety and corruption of youth. His pupil Plato, however, was a censor; and in his *Republic* declared that he would censor fables and would prohibit bad tales and anything that might be harmful to the young. Moreover, he would censor the plays of dramatists who tell untruths about the gods.

In spite of the fact that censor is of Latin derivation, censorship was not prevalent in ancient Roman history. During the reign of Caesar political pamphlets were circulated and epigrams were written against Caesar and Pompey by such writers as Lucilius and Catullus. The tradition of free speech was strong in that period, but examples did occur, and in the second century B.C. restraints were imposed on seditious speech and writing. In 8 A.D. Augustus banished Ovid. Caligula, Nero, and Domitian punished writers and burned their books.

During the period of the Holy Roman Empire, Rome became more tolerant, especially in the area of religious opinions. However, this tolerance did not extend to the Jews and Christians. The persecution of Christians ended in 313, when Emperor Constantine issued an edict expressing tolerance of Christianity. In 380, Emperor Theodosius I declared Christianity to be the state religion. In 445 Theodosius II decreed that the pope was the final authority in the church and that the state would use force to compel obedience to the pope. This Christian orthodoxy and persecution of heresy were maintained for more than 1000 years. The first formal banning of a book was done by the Council of Nicaea in 325, when it condemned a book by Arius as heretical. In the year 400 the books of Origen were condemned and other heretical writers suffered the same fate. In 1233 the Inquisition was established and heretics were often burned at the stake.

During Medieval times, the Roman Catholic Church forbade the circulation of heretical works, but after the invention of printing a more formal and systematic method had to be devised to deal with the great multiplication of books. In 1501 a papal bill was issued that provided for the licensing of all printing. The first Roman index of prohibited books was published in 1559.

In 1564 a report of a committee of the Council of Trent was issued under the title *Index Librorum Prohibitorum*. With periodic revisions this list has continued through the years to designate the books Catholics are prohibited from reading except under very special conditions.

Leaders of the Protestant Reformation in the sixteenth century, like the Roman Catholic church, emphasized obedience to authority and preservation of the social order. John Knox, Martin Luther, and John Calvin persecuted heretics and papists. In England Henry VIII displaced the pope and became head of both the church and state with authority over both and power to punish heresies. He burned copies of William Tyndale's *New Testament* and had Thomas More beheaded because More refused to recognize the king's supreme power over religion. Each of the rulers who followed Henry VIII also attempted to coerce conformity. These included Edward VI, who persecuted Catholics; Mary, who denounced Protestants and Anglicans and had such heretics as the Archbishop of Canterbury and the Bishop of Worcester burned at the stake; and Elizabeth, who persecuted both Puritan reformers and Catholics.

During the period of the Reformation in England licensing was transferred from the Catholic church to the monarch. Elizabeth I authorized Messengers of the Press to enter and search houses for unlicensed presses and publications. The Long Parliament continued to enforce this policy until, as a revolt against the 1643 parliamentary ordinance, Milton published *Areopagitica,* the classic work on freedom of publication. Because of increasing resistance, the Licensing Act was abandoned in 1695. This date highlights the establishment of freedom of the press in England; in the eighteenth century the emphasis changed from censorship and persecution to tolerance and freedom.

Censorship and the Law

A society for the suppression of vice was formed in England in 1809. The modern law of obscenity began with Lord Campbell's Act (Obscene Publications Act, 1857).

In the Hicklin case (1868) in London, Justice Alexander Cockburn ruled that the test for obscenity under the statute was "whether the tendency of the matter charged as obscenity is to deprave and corrupt." The test of literary morality was what a father could read aloud in his own home. As a result of this law literary works were often prosecuted and books were seized and destroyed. The law was criticized on the grounds that it reduced literary standards to the level of what was morally proper for the young and forced authors to falsify social realities.

In the U.S. two laws passed by Congress affected printed materials. One dealt with importing books and forbade customs officials from allowing the works of such classic writers as Voltaire, Rousseau, and Boccaccio to be brought into the country. But in 1930 the law was changed to allow for the importation of classics and books of recognized scientific and literary merit. The second law was enacted through the efforts of Anthony Comstock, who went to Congress in 1873 and lobbied through both houses, with less than a total of one hour of debate time, the law that still governs obscenity in the mails. It was rushed through in the last hours of a hectic session, the final vote coming about 2:00 A.M. on a Sunday morning, although the clock was stopped to preserve the fiction that it was still Saturday.

Notable advancement has been made by certain judges. Justice W. N. Stable, in a case in London (1954), set aside the Hicklin test of obscenity, making a distinction between "filth for filth's sake and literature." In a work of literature the author has "an honest purpose and an honest thread of thought." Literature should not be condemned because it deals with the realities of life, love, and sex. He told the jury that sex is not dirty or a sin that the literary-moral-legal test ought not to be what is suitable for a 14-year-old schoolgirl to read.

Further progress was made in 1954, with changes in Lord Campbell's Act, followed by a new Obscene Publications Act (1959). This provided that a work was to be read as a whole; that the testimony of expert witnesses could be admitted as evidence in relation to the literary, artistic, scientific, or other merits of the work; that a person should not be convicted if publication was "in the interest of science, literature, art, or learning;" and that book publishers and authors could speak in defense of the work even though they had not been summoned in the case.

In 1933 an effort was made to prevent the entry into this country of *Ulysses,* by James Joyce, but Judge John Woolsey of the Federal District Court in New York ruled that the book was not legally obscene. He said ". . . in any case where a book is claimed to be obscene it must first be determined, whether the intent with which it was written was what is called, according to the usual phrase, pornographic—that is, written for the purpose of exploiting obscenity. . . ." He continued by saying "although it contains . . . many words usually considered dirty, I have not found anything that I consider to be dirt for dirt's sake."

In 1959, *Lady Chatterley's Lover,* by D. H. Lawrence, caused a furor in the U.S. It had been published in Italy in 1928. Pirated editions had been distributed in England and the U.S. When it was published in New York, the Federal Post Office Department banned it from the mails, but the Federal court ruled that the book was not hard-core pornography and dismissed the banning restriction.

Judge Curtis Bok, in *The State of Pennsylvania vs. Five Booksellers,* in 1949, expressed his opinion:

> I believe that the consensus of preference today is for disclosure and not stealth, for frankness and not hypocrisy, and for public not secret distribution. That in itself is a moral code. It is my opinion that frank disclosure cannot legally be censored even as an exercise of the police power, unless it is sexually impure and pornographic. . . . Who can define the clear and present danger to the community that arises from reading a book? If we say it is that the reader is young and inexperienced and incapable of resisting the sexual temptations that the book may present to him, we put the entire reading public at the mercy of the adolescent mind and of those adolescents who do not have the expected advantages of home influence, school training, or religious teaching. Nor can we say into how many such hands the book may come . . . If the argument be applied to the general public, the situation becomes absurd, for then no publication is safe. . . .

Supreme Court judges in the U.S. have, in recent years, protected and defended intellectual freedom. Justice J. G. Shapiro of the New York Supreme Court in the *New York Law Journal* of Sept. 10, 1963, in referring to a trial involving censorship of books, said:

> It is of the utmost importance in this field that judges be not motivated to assume the guise of censors by reason of personal predilections, and that decisions be not dictated by their personal whims with little consideration given to the fact that liberty is not divisible and that when we deny its privileges to others we place our own in jeopardy, or by pressure subconsciously exerted by groups of well-meaning vigilante guardians of the public morals who often refuse to recognize that free societies are dynamic and that literature and art, and badly written books too, are merely the mirror reflections of some phase of existing life.

William O. Douglas, Justice of the U.S. Supreme Court, blames our mass system of communication media for avoiding controversial topics. In his book *Freedom of the Mind,* Douglas says that the communication media—newspapers, press, radio, television—in an effort to reach the largest audience, sink to the lowest common denominator and in so doing fail in a responsible role, the role of information and education.

The famous Roth opinion in the Supreme Court of the U.S. amended the law of obscenity to the extent that a publication is now considered obscene if its "dominant" appeal is to the "prurient interests" of the "average person"—applying "contemporary community" standards. It also said that any work conveying "ideas having even the slightest redeeming social importance—unorthodox ideas, controversial ideas, even ideas hateful to the prevailing climate of opinion—have the full protection of the guaranties."

Recent Cases

Three obscenity cases have been of popular concern since 1963. These are *Ginzburg vs. United States, Mishkin vs. New York,* and *John Cleland's Memoirs of a Woman of Pleasure vs. the Attorney General of the Commonwealth of Massachusetts.* In 1963, a publisher, Ralph Ginzburg, was found guilty in the U.S. District Court of Philadelphia of distributing obscene materials through the U.S. mail. The publications in question were a magazine, *Eros;* a newsletter, *Liaison;* and a manual of sexual information, *The Housewife's Handbook on Selective Promiscuity.* In December of 1963 Ginzberg was sentenced to 5 years in prison and a fine of $28,000. On Nov. 6, 1964, the U.S. Supreme Court of Appeals in Philadelphia upheld the decisions of the District Court. Ginzburg declared his intention of appealing to the Supreme Court, and received support from 111 interested citizens, who filed *amici curiae* briefs in his behalf.

Edward Mishkin was found guilty of violating Section 1141 of the New York penal code by the Court of Special Sessions of the City of New York. About 50 books of an admittedly sadistic and masochistic nature were involved. His conviction and sentence of 3 years and $12,000 in fines were upheld by the U.S. Court of Appeals.

In the case involving the novel *Fanny Hill,* reissued in this country under the title *The Memoirs of a Woman of Pleasure* by G. P. Putman's Sons, the book had been declared obscene in a suit brought by the attorney general of Massachusetts. The decree was upheld by the Massachusetts Supreme Judicial Court and the novel's publishers filed an appeal to the Supreme Court. The Court was asked to decide whether or not *Fanny Hill* was obscene in light of the definition of obscenity handed down in the Court's 1957 ruling in *Roth vs. the United States:* "Whether to the average person, applying contemporary community standards, the dominant theme of the material, as a whole appeals to prurient interest."

On Mar. 21, 1966, the Court ruled to uphold the convictions of both Ginzberg and Mishkin. The unexpected factor in the Court's decision in the Ginzberg case was the introduction of a new determinant of obscenity, one involving the promotion and advertisement of the works in question. The problem of promotion and advertisement also figured in the decision on *Fanny Hill.* The Massachusetts ruling banning the book was reversed, but Justice Brennan, speaking for the majority, implied that the Court's decision might not have obtained had evidence regarding the promotion for the novel been admitted.

The publications of Ginzberg and Mishkin were the first the Supreme Court ever found to be obscene and the two publishers the first persons to receive a Federal prison conviction on the strength of such a finding.

A victory for defenders of intellectual freedom was won in California in the November 1966 election with the defeat of Proposition 16, an antiobscenity measure promoted by an *ad hoc* organization called CLEAN, Inc. (California League Enlisting Action Now). The proposition was an initiative measure that had been certified for a statewide vote by more than 468,000 signatures obtained by CLEAN on petitions circulated earlier in the year. Specifically, the initative sought to have the "utterly without redeeming social importance" phrase eliminated from the present State definition of obscenity. This was one of the major objectives of the CLEAN proposition, whose backers said the present law favored the pornographer. The CLEAN proposition sought "to proscribe all obscene matter and conduct that is beyond the protection of the free speech and free press guarantees of the First and Fourteenth Amendments of the United States Constitution." Obscenity was defined as appeal to "prurient interest," namely, "a shameful or morbid interest in nudity, sex, or excretion which goes substantially beyond customary limits of candor. . . ." The definition was continued, but it carefully omitted the qualification that to be declared obscene the material must be utterly without social importance.

Proposition 16 was opposed by such people as the district attorney of Los Angeles, the District Attorneys Association of California, the California Library Association, the California School Library Association, the California and Nevada Councils of Churches, Governor E. G. Brown, and the *Los Angeles Times*. Many of those opposing the proposition warned that if it passed, it would amend existing laws, but if the amended laws were then declared unconstitutional, California would be left without any obscenity law. It was fortunate that the proposition was defeated.

Pressure Groups

Local and state officials and citizens' groups have organized from time to time in various parts of the U.S. to have books withdrawn from libraries or from dealers' shelves; or, in other cases, to force libraries to stock specific titles. Among titles that have come under attack are *The Scarlet Letter* by Nathaniel Hawthorne, *The Good Earth* by Pearl Buck, *Brave New World* by Aldous Huxley, *The Catcher in the Rye* by J. D. Salinger, *To Kill a Mockingbird* by Lee Harper, and *The Last Temptation of Christ*. State legislatures have investigated textbooks in almost a third of the states. Textbook committees have been subjected to pressures from religious, political, racial, and other groups. Issues that have been subjects of controversy include evolution, communism, attitudes toward the American Civil War, Russia, racism, religion, and morality. Textbooks have sometimes been changed in response to pressures. In some states the selection of textbooks is made by committees of local school boards, school faculties, or individual teachers; in others the selection is done by state textbook commissions.

Organizations that have worked in defense of intellectual freedom are the American Library Association, The American Book Publishers' Council, the National Education Association, the National Council of Teachers of English, the American Civil Liberties Union, the American Association of University Women, the American Studies Association, Phi Beta Kappa, and the American Association of University Professors.

Tolerance and Intellectual Freedom

Although the history of censorship has been a story of repression and persecution, it has also been a chronicle of tolerance and freedom. Some of the basic premises relating to intellectual freedom have been variously expressed by different people and groups. One of the first philosophers to express a rational defense of freedom of speech was Socrates, who asserted the supremacy of his conscience over the decision of the jury and declared that he was a public benefactor when he exercised freedom of inquiry. Another classic principled argument for freedom from censorship was that of John Milton in *Areopagitica*. Milton believed the first freedom was the liberty to know and to argue freely according to conscience. He said:

> We should be wary therefore what persecution we raise against the living labours of publick men, how we spill that season'd life of man preserv'd and stor'd up in Books; since we see a kind of homicide may be thus committed, sometimes a martyrdome; and if it extend to the whole impression, a kind of massacre, whereof the execution ends not in the slaying of an elementall life, but strikes at that ethereall and fift(h) essence, the breath of reason itselfe, slaies an immortality rather than a life.

John Locke's *Letter Concerning Toleration* (1689) argued that states should have no control over the religious beliefs and observances of men and that tolerance should be extended to noncomformists and pagans; however, he excepted Catholics and atheists. Much of American constitutional law relating to the freedoms of religion, press, speech, and assembly has been an outgrowth of Locke's theory.

John Stuart Mill believed that every man is the best judge of his own actions and welfare and is competent to choose for himself what he will read or hear. In his essay *On Liberty* (1859) Mill expressed his conviction that bold expression of thought is important:

> Who can compute what the world loses in the multitude of promising intellects combined with timid characters, who dare not follow out any bold, vigorous, independent train of thought, lest it should land them in something which would admit of being considered irreligious or immoral? . . . No one can be a great thinker who does not recognize that as a thinker it is his first duty to follow his intellect to whatever conclusions it may lead. . . . There is always hope when people are forced to listen to both sides. It is when they attend only one that errors harden into prejudices and truth itself ceases to have the effect of truth, by being exaggerated into falsehood.

At the end of the eighteenth century several documents advanced the cause of freedom. These were the American Declaration of Independence (1776), the French Declaration of the Rights of Man (1789), and the Bill of Rights to the U.S. Constitution (1791). In 1800, Thomas Jefferson wrote to Benjamin Rush, "I have sworn upon the altar of God eternal hostility against every form of tyranny over the mind of man." From an amendment to the Constitution of the U.S. comes the principle that has protected citizens of this country since 1789:

Freedom of religion, of speech, of the press, and right of petition—Congress shall make no law respecting an establishment of religion, or prohibiting the free exercise thereof; or abridging the freedom of speech, or of the press; or the right of the people peaceably to assemble, and to petition the Government for a redress of grievances.

Libraries and Intellectual Freedom

The American Library Association has fought efforts at library censorship. The Library Bill of Rights adopted by the ALA in 1948 stresses the need to resist "all abridgment of the free access to ideas and full freedom of expression." The Bill has its basis in the first and fourteenth amendments to the Constitution of the U.S. It takes an unequivocal stand on the freedom to read and it supports democracy in full measure in the principle, "There should be the fullest practicable provision of material presenting all points of view concerning the problems and issues of our times, international, national and local."

In 1953 great consternation was caused by the "book burnings" in approximately 200 U.S. Informational Libraries overseas. Early in 1953 a committee headed by Sen. Joseph McCarthy was investigating the activities of the International Information Administration of the State Department. A number of confusing directives from the State Department were interpreted differently in libraries in the various countries. The resultant book banning caused serious damage to U.S. prestige abroad. On June 14, 1953, Pres. Dwight D. Eisenhower made his famous speech at Dartmouth College, "Don't Join the Book Burners." On June 24 he wrote a letter to the president of the ALA that he concluded with:

The libraries of America are and must ever remain the homes of free, inquiring minds. To them, our citizens—of all ages and races, of all creeds and political persuasions—must ever be able to turn with clear confidence that there they can freely seek the whole truth, unwarped by fashion and uncompromised by expediency. For in such whole and healthy knowledge alone are found and understood those majestic truths of man's nature and destiny that prove, to each succeeding generation, the validity of freedom.

Part of the responsibility of the Committee on Intellectual Freedom of the ALA is guarding, protecting, defending, and extending intellectual freedom. It performs a "backstopping" function for the Library Bill of Rights and stands firm on the ALA statement that "Censorship of books, urged or practiced by volunteer arbiters of morals or political opinion or by organizations that would establish a coercive concept of Americanism, must be challenged by libraries in maintenance of their responsibility to provide public enlightenment through the printed word."

In 1953 the ALA endorsed a "Freedom to Read" statement against groups that seek to remove, censor, or label books. The statement expressed the ALA's responsibility for making "available the widest diversity of views and expressions, including those which are unorthodox or unpopular with the majority." Concern was also voiced about the danger of suppressing ideas. The point was made that freedom had given the U.S. the elasticity to endure strain, but "Every silencing of heresy, every enforcement of an orthodoxy, diminishes the toughness and resilience of our society and leaves it less able to deal with stress."

Other propositions affirmed in the Freedom to Read statement are: (1) Publishers and librarians do not need to endorse every idea or presentation contained in the books they make available. . . . (2) It is contrary to the public interest for publishers or librarians to determine the acceptability of a book solely on the basis of the personal history or political affiliations of the author. . . . No society of free men can flourish which draws up lists of writers to whom it will not listen, whatever they may have to say. (3) It is the responsibility of publishers and librarians, as guardians of the people's freedom to read, to contest encroachment upon that freedom by individuals or groups seeking to impose their own standards or tastes upon the community at large. . . . No group has the right to take the law into its own hands, and to impose its own concepts of politics or morality upon other members of a democratic society.

Perspective

Censorship is a negative factor, whereas the basic freedoms are positive and are mandatory in a democratic society. President Eisenhower said in 1953: "As it is an ancient truth that freedom cannot be legislated into existence, so it is no less obvious that freedom cannot be censored into existence. And any who act as if freedom's defenses are to be found in suppression and suspicion and fear confess a doctrine that is alien to America." Speaking for liberation and against repression, with specific application to books, Pres. Whitney Griswold of Yale said, "Books won't stay banned. They won't burn. Ideas won't go to jail. In the long run of history, the censor and the inquisitor have always lost. The only sure weapon against bad ideas is better ideas."

BIBLIOGRAPHY

Blanchard, P., *Right to Read,* Beacon Press, Boston, 1955.

Bryson, L., "Freedom of Information," in *Freedom and Culture,* UNESCO, Columbia Univ. Press, New York, 1950.

Bury, J. B., *History of Freedom of Thought,* 2d ed., Oxford, Toronto, 1952.

Chafee, Z., Jr., *The Blessings of Liberty,* rev., Lippincott, New York, 1956.

Craig, A., *The Banned Books of England,* Macmillan, New York, 1940.

Downs, R. B., *The First Freedom,* American Library Assoc., Chicago, 1960.

Douglas, W. O., *The Right of the People,* Doubleday, New York, 1958.

Ernst, M. L., and A. U. Schwartz, *Censorship, the Search for the Obscene,* Macmillan, New York, 1964.

Fellman, D., *The Limits of Freedom,* Rutgers Univ. Press, New Brunswick, N.J., 1959.

Gellhorn, W., *American Rights,* Macmillan, New York, 1960.

Haight, A. L., *Banned Books,* 2d ed., rev. and enlarged, Bowker, New York, 1955.

Hocking, W. E., *Freedom of the Press,* Univ. Chicago Press, Chicago, 1947.

Konritz, M. R., *Fundamental Liberties of a Free People,* Cornell Univ. Press, Ithaca, N.Y., 1957.

McKeon, R. P., et al., *Freedom to Read,* Bowker, New York, 1957.

MARTHA BOAZ

CENSORSHIP, CONTEMPORARY AND CONTROVERSIAL ASPECTS OF
See *Censorship*

In the foregoing review of the history of censorship, the attitude of librarians at present was assumed to be in strong opposition. Such an assumption is valid, but it did not always hold. Librarians have generally been in accord with the intellectual leaders of their times. They favored censorship up to the end of World War I (*1*). They were both for and against censorship as the so-called sexual revolution took place (*2,3*). They rejected censorship through the medium of the American Library Association, at times effectively, until the beginning of the 1960s (*4*). Now they are faced with the problem of selection of materials for libraries on a massive scale, leading to a reevaluation of their own and their intellectual peers' viewpoints.

At its annual conference in 1968, the American Library Association went beyond a verbal position and voted to support any librarian faced with a censorship problem with both expert help and such financial assistance as might be needed (*5*). It might almost have been predicted that the association would do so. It was again following the general direction of its intellectual peers by taking an activist role where formerly it had relied upon the power of propaganda to furnish support. The question remains whether the association will not find itself in the role of supercensor, like the Supreme Court (*6*, pp. 115–180), having to defend the librarian who builds up a collection that fits his community but displeases some elements in it, as—to take a farfetched example—in the case of a public library in the center of a community of disaffected persons experimenting with sex and drugs. Such books as Philip Barrow's *Whores, Queers, and Others* (*7*) and such periodicals as *Jaybird Gallery* (*8*) would seem more appropriate than, say, *Vogue* and Taylor Caldwell's *Grandmother and the Priests* (*9*).

The purpose of the present article is to examine the positions of both censors and anticensors, to ascertain whether some censorship is always necessary, to distinguish between selection and censorship—as much as the scant illumination of this gray area will permit—and to examine the limits that have been reached in the publication of materials. Librarians should be able to deal with any printed material with as little emotional response as a physician conducting a genito-urinary examination. How this can be possible, what psychological adjustments are necessary, reaches the point of challenging many of our accepted ideas of librarianship and of information handling. Not even the information scientist is free from this problem, for the storage and retrieval of psychiatric records, to give one ready example, involves rights of privacy which conflict with freedom of access, and may contain verbatim statements that cause genuine emotional problems in those who have to transmit them, copy them, analyze them, or abstract them.

Research Libraries and Censorship

Censorship may be divided into two major areas at present—political and moral—and is very difficult to separate from what may be labeled suppression. Almost all the countries of the world have given up the attempt at *censura praevia,* censorship before publication, because of the cost involved and the scant gains to be derived from it, except for those countries where the government owns the means for the production of all literary material. In this form of government, a kind of state capitalism, the official role of censor is blurred by the accepted role of the editor, so that what is printed popularizes governmental views. Even in these countries control can never be complete except by the exercise of terrorism, so that mimeographed papers may maintain the freedom of inquiry while printed works reiterate the accepted view. Typically, complete control of printed material includes rather severe moral restrictions as well as political restraints (*10*). No one can question the virtue of marriage or describe its intimacies too graphically, just as the philosophy of the communist theory in practice at a given time must not be questioned nor its logic too closely analyzed. Such control, during the era of Stalin, affected all avenues of thought, from the textbooks used for instruction in reading to disquisitions on biology and linguistics (*11*). The pressure for liberalization, which has more or less affected all countries following Marxist theories of economics, generally derives from intellectuals at odds with constraints that blunt the purpose of their inquiry (*12*).

Censura praevia is odious to countries that espouse the freedom of the press, but governments achieve the same result by withholding information or publishing only distorted views that coincide with official policy. An example is the reporting on the war in Vietnam, and the reporting of the foreign policy of the United States as it relates to Burma from 1962 until the time of this writing (1968). Vietnam and Burma are very similar, with the exception that Burma has adopted a kind of independent form of "socialism" that vests all power in the government, especially the Chairman of the Revolutionary Council, and this form of state capitalism extends through the country, while in Vietnam it is limited to the area established by the agreements of 1954 (*13*). Partly because of the secretive nature of the Burmese government since 1962, partly because of the obvious questions that would arise if it were widely debated why the United States opposes the policies of the Viet Cong and North Vietnam to the extent of military intervention yet assists the policies of the Burmese government to the extent of providing it with foreign aid, very little can be read in print about the extent of communism in Burma and the means the U.S. foreign policy utilizes to support the regime in power.* Perhaps the independence of the Burmese government, and its neutralism since 1948, is an embarrassment both to the Russian and Chinese styles of economic development as well as to the American style.

Moral censorship has been effective in the United States and England and creates another gray area where the distinction between moral and political censorship is hard to discern (*14*). *Night* by Francis Pollini was first published by the Olympia Press, Paris, and appears in two forms at present (*15*). One is in the edition that includes works described as hard-core pornography by the Kronhausens (*16*). The other is reprinted by Bantam Books and reflects the editorial policy of the house. A line-by-line comparison shows that no change has been made in the text. The subject matter is the imprisonment and brainwashing of United States soldiers during the Korean War and their reaction to their captors. Like other war novels, the speech of the soldiers is reported with considerable accuracy, but no more frankly than many other works. The theme of homosexuality is not given the slightest attention, and one is left with the belief that a passage reflecting a soldier's remembrance of sexual intercourse with a girl-friend, before he began his Army career, is included to establish the heterosexual orientation of the character. A typically pornographic work would have included some kind of sexual activity on the part of the soldiers, in the manner of *The Sexual Life of Robinson Crusoe* (*17*) by Humphrey Richardson, if not to the same degree. *Night* was banned by the U.S. Customs either as a reflex or as a result of fear of political consequences, both of which reasons seem inadequate to account for the financial loss Mr. Pollini has suffered as a result.

In the period up to 1953, although opposition to censorship was established, there were no hard cases for librarians to consider. But afterward, especially with the conclusion of the *Tropic of Cancer* and *Fanny Hill* cases, the problem has grown intense. The difference arose because the anticensors found an effective means of challenging the views of the censors and because of a man who was willing to undergo the harassment necessary to establish a publishing policy at variance with the accepted canons of taste. Maurice Girodias has reported the history of the Olympia Press without attempting to draw any further conclusions than that he was interested in publishing as a profession and did not agree with the climate of moral censorship established in the English-speaking countries of the world (*18*). Until there was a sufficient body of material on which to base an investigation, the censors had pretty much their own way. They fulfilled their role of protecting the public by citing the dangers if their protection lapsed.

Up to 1933, when the Woolsey decision replaced the Cockburn rule as the standard to be applied in a test of obscenity (*6*, pp. 99–101), the viewpoint of the

---

* *The New York Times Index,* Jan. 16–31, 1969, listed 3 articles pertaining to Burma and 357 pertaining to Vietnam.

censors was adequately expressed by Anthony Comstock. At core was the New England proverb, "Reading rots the brain," and the Roman Catholic injunction against "curiosity" that Thomas a Kempis reflects in *The Imitation of Christ* (*19*). Inquiry itself is dangerous and likely to cause confusion, leading us to establish, as the first benefit of censorship, the maintenance of the status quo. Where there is no inquiry, there is no reason to challenge the established views so that the only effective means of propaganda is that which includes censorship as an extension. A research library may collect censored material to establish a propaganda line (*20*).

In *Traps for the Young,* Comstock asserts that reading brings thoughts to mind that cannot be avoided, like an evil companion, but that tend to "captivate fancy and pervert tastes" and rob the individual of a desire to study. Fiction, he says, tends to trend downward rather than upward. He doubts whether a person who begins with Alexander Dumas will make his way upward to Sir Walter Scott (a progress that would seem horizontal rather than vertical to most modern readers). The worse the literature, the more rapid the descent into hell with crime the only result (*21*, p. 11). Although Comstock would have thought that few people who ever read the sort of literature he opposed could come away with morals undamaged, for him the reading of such books constitutes a sin in itself, with damaged morals the sinful interest that led the affected to investigate the writing at all (*21*, pp. 20–42). This view is reflected by all modern proponents of censorship in whatever degree from Wertham (*22*) to the official publications of the Citizens for Decent Literature.* As cited by Harold C. Gardner, a Catholic commits a mortal sin by reading a work that is *ex professo* obscene, that is, has as its central purpose teaching the reader about sins of impurity and arousing sexual desires (*23,* p. 61). The implication is that once taught a person will certainly act out what he has learned.

This is questionable and readily tested. A group of men might be given a diet of homosexual novels to find if the last they read is as repugnant as the first. The degree to which they would engage in homosexual activity would remain a question of opportunity and personal proclivity. It is widely assumed that only male homosexuals read novels about male homosexuality (unless they make a study of the genre for whatever obscure purpose), but there is nothing to suggest that this is invariably true, nor that all novels dealing with male homosexuality are written by male homosexuals. The evidence being compiled of male homosexuality as a psychosexual aberration tends to support the view that its members are enlisted rather than recruited (*24*). Most heterosexually oriented men find novels dealing with graphically depicted sexual activity between males loathesome in the extreme and far from inciting to such activity, it rather warns against it (*16*).

The investigation of sex offenders conducted by the Kinsey Institute, by far the most authoritative to date, concludes an investigation on the influence of pornography on sex offenders by stating, "Men make the collections, collections do not make the men" (*25*, p. 678). It would be even more farfetched to assert that a

* Citizens for Decent Literature, Inc., 3300 Carew Tower, Cincinnati, Ohio.

sex offender is driven to commit a crime because he has read a single work that caused sexual arousal. Indeed, what causes sexual arousal in male human beings, who respond to psychological influence more rapidly than female human beings, remains an insoluble puzzle (*25*, pp. 659–692). There is no way to state conclusively that the work alone and not the fantasy that accompanies it causes the sexual arousal, and good reason to state that whatever causes sexual fantasy is usually accompanied by masturbation which, far from inciting to further sexual activity, rather makes it impossible. We might conclude that the problem with sex offenders arises not because they have pornography but because they do not have enough (*25*, pp. 486–514).

No research librarian can accept the idea that inquiry should be restrained; he can only provide the circumstances that make the inquiry valuable to the user. Hence a person who wishes to read a novel by Dumas would not be treated to encouraging lectures on Sir Walter Scott, nor would a man who reads *Eustace Chisholm and the Works,* by James Purdy (*26*), be warned against becoming an active homosexual as a result of the baleful influence of the work.

There is a general principle of the marketplace of ideas that seems to direct that the most popular works establish a level of acceptability, so that Gore Vidal's novels have each set a kind of standard for acceptability, as evident from the change of plot in the initial *The City and the Pillar* and in its revised version. The research of the Kinsey Institute supports the view, if it does not conclusively establish it, that the climate of literary acceptance has virtually nothing to do with establishing the rate of homosexual experience among men (*27*, pp. 610–666). What has changed is the literary view of male homosexuality from a heinous crime to a forgiveable aberration. As Vidal explains in his "Afterword" in the revised version, the cautionary ending involving the murder of Ford in the first version, evidence of one crime leading to another, has become the rape of Bob Ford by his adolescent chum, Jim Willard (*28*). The change is significant, for murder seemed to be the only method of asserting Jim's essential manhood in the first version, while homosexual rape much more deftly portrays it in the second. Popular culture would like to find all effeminate mannerisms as evidence of male homosexuality, but very importantly this is not the case. The "homosexualist" as Vidal describes him in the character of Jim Willard is protective of his masculinity, a characteristic anyone experienced in psychiatric work can validate (*29*). It is generally not the effeminate homosexual male who commits sex offenses against children, but the masculine aberrant who cannot face the challenge which an adult represents (*25*, pp. 272–297).

No challenge has been raised in the courts to works such as *The City and the Pillar* and *Eustace Chisholm.* They are not, in the farthest reach of imagination, *ex professo* obscene, but one wonders how *Naked Lunch* by William Burroughs can be, if these are not (*30*). The subject of several trials, which have resulted in establishing its graphic descriptions of sodomy as acceptable community standards that separate the obscene from the acceptable, *Naked Lunch* is far more explicit than *Last Exit to Brooklyn,* by Hubert Selby, Jr. (*31*). Banned in Great Britain at a now-famous trial, this collection of short stories may well become the

Lady Chatterly's Lover of the present generation of Britons—excepting those who buy the book with impunity in the United States *(32)*. *Myra Breckinridge* by Gore Vidal extends the standards by utilizing them. Devoted to sex change and with the theme of homosexuality dominant throughout, this novel, if not *ex professo* obscene, vindicates the wealth of novels that deal with the subject at various levels of literary competence but are not noticeably different so far as setting and actions are concerned *(33)*. A scene in *Myra Breckinridge* is reminiscent, not derivative, of *Naked Lunch*.

The choice of fiction dealing with male homosexuality is intentional, for in no other area of controversy are the lines so clearly drawn and the differences so noticeable. Female homosexuality cannot be used, because books graphically describing sexual activity among women are likely to arouse purely heterosexual libidinous feelings among men, and in any case the absolutism of physiology prevents male participation in any lesbian activity, other than by means of fantasy. If obscene literature causes sex crimes, we must ask how many homosexual men have derived their orientation from such books. No specialist in the field even hints that literary works "cause" homosexuality.

There is good reason to doubt that any work describing heterosexuality in literary terms, however graphic, would be judged obscene if no taboo words were used *(34)*. What the banned works of previous decades have in common is a sense of taboos violated. In the period when Comstock wrote and worked for the suppression of vice, any discussion of sexuality between members of the same sex was strictly taboo. It had been commonplace during the Renaissance; later, during the period of the seventeenth century up to the middle of the eighteenth century, thinly veiled allusions were not only permissible but enjoyable and the stage reflected this *(16*, Pt. I). In the period that followed, the prize of virginity became so greatly valued that a woman was thought to be corruptible and led to excitement by allusions to genital functions. Up to the end of World War I there was much opinion but little science regarding the procreative capacities and their gross anatomy in human beings. At this time, scholarship consisted largely in quoting what had been said before. It was soon discovered that science could advance only by direct testing, but it was thought that certain areas of human knowledge were beyond the reach of science. As the philosophy of science broadened the horizons of the testable elements in the objective environment, as scientists found new measures of objectivity, many of the taboos were questioned and none more successfully than the taboo against masturbation *(35)*.

This was originally a purely religious taboo, but beginning with Tissot's medical work dealing with the "treatment of onanism" *(36)* it became a matter of scientific investigation by physicians, the only group of scientists who could influence, at all widely, the mass of people. *Sexual Self-stimulation,* edited by R. E. L. Masters, a collection of essays regarding the subject, accurately portrays in the words of contemporary authors their attitudes at the time they wrote *(37)*. When it was found, however, that organic ailments were not the result of masturbation, a perfect case of the logical fallacy, *post hoc, ergo propter hoc,* the taboo relaxed and has finally disappeared, except as a matter of sexual ethics and religious precept. Masturbation is now regarded as not harmful. Even the injunctions against "excessive" masturbation have been dropped, especially since, as reported by Masters and Johnson, the average individual would define excessive as something more than the attempts. Physiologically, masturbation to orgasm cannot be carried to excess in men or in women (*38,* pp. 200–203).

However, much of the literature of censorship, especially the statements of those who believe that censorship for moral purposes is essential, relies on conclusions reached at a time when masturbation was considered the cause of homosexuality, in the case of Krafft-Ebbing (*39*), or of insanity (*40*) or of hundreds of other diseases (*41*). If graphic descriptions of sexual acts lead to erotic arousal, this may lead to masturbation, and the whole consequence of social ills would seem to follow. Although it is undoubtedly true that those persons who regard masturbation as sinful deplore the availability of literature that stimulates men to the act, and sometimes, women (*42*), there is no reason for the research librarian to regard these members of the community as having more right to determine the character of the collection than a group that considers the policies of a given political party as likely to cause irretrievable harm.

There is no uniformity of opinion about masturbation, homosexuality, or birth control. To some members of the community all are sinful and wrong, and any information concerning them is to be removed from a place where it might wrongly influence the young, within or outside the library. To others, any one of these areas of interest is wrong, if not criminal, and the others at least of total disinterest. The majority of the community would find homosexuality evidence of either invincible ignorance or immorality, while the members of the community who are fixated homosexually in their psychosexual orientation would find literature on birth control of no interest whatever, or possibly sickening. Where there is no agreement, the librarian must exercise his judgement on whether the book budget can afford an item of limited interest if no research applications are decisive. This applies as much to the literature of sexuality as to the literature of economics. The librarian's personal viewpoint is of no consequence, and it would be unethical for him to impose his views on the community, however slightly his bias might influence the development of the collection.

If the laws were perfectly clear in this regard, it might be less troublesome, but they are clear enough. Whatever is published and withstands a test in court establishes the community standards (*43*). Most states in the United States have laws regarding obscenity at least as it affects the young. For a librarian knowingly to give a young person an obscene book would constitute a crime. The age varies from state to state and the wording of the law varies, but the laws exist (*44*). Research libraries generally have been free of this kind of intervention and library associations have reacted when the professionalism of their members is questioned.* If an overriding reason were needed, it might be found in the fact that librarians have very faithfully been in accord with their times. The National

* A review of censorship reports in *Library Journal* failed to reveal a case of censorship in a research library.

Commission on Obscenity and Pornography, established after two attempts, was directed to conduct tests that would show the influence of reading on persons (45). The test is available as stated above, but it would show nothing, for it is now regarded as an established fact of communications that individuals read to confirm their ideas, not to change them (46). In an era where the totality of psychosexual development is involved, no book, not even *The Loon Songs Trilogy* by Richard Amory (47), could turn a man from a happy life as a heterosexual to sexual activity exclusively with members of his own sex. The idea repels the majority of the male population (48, pp. 100–120).

The question is yet to be solved as to what is immoral about immoral literature. In an essay derived from a speech that was frequently given, Corinne Bacon attempted to establish this for the profession in the United States in the era of Prohibition. She asks, "What Makes a Novel Immoral?" and then gives her ideas (3). In his Preface to *The Picture of Dorian Gray,* Oscar Wilde states just as flatly that art cannot be moral or immoral. It is either good or bad (49). This is in accord with the opinion of most writers and editors, who would like not to have to consider the opinions of the least cultured readers or the vague strictures of the law but only the force and direction of the art they pursue (50). It is a cliché among proponents of intellectual freedom that condemnation of a piece of library material does not necessarily imply that it has been read by those who most anxiously describe its dangers.*

Tests of obscenity can be applied by reviewers to identify "pornography," which is, by the definition of Gebhard et al., ". . . that literature or art which is expressly intended to cause sexual arousal in the beholder and has no other primary purpose." These tests of obscenity will also locate erotic material, but in agreement with the Institute for Sex Research, Inc., it seems wise to allow that a work may be obscene (25, p. 669). Obscenity is that which is offensive to the modesty and decency of any individual. If the adjective "obscene" is to be used with anything like its original force, then such a statement as "the obscene music of Bruckner" enables this author and his fellows to make comparisons that would otherwise be impossible. Obscenity is a private matter that becomes public when offense may be imputed from the nature of the material itself. The music of Mendelssohn was "obscene" in Nazi Germany because the composer was a Jew (51). A picture of black and white rabbits together is "obscene" in the southern United States because it implies that the surface color of an individual is of no importance in social life (52).

Obscenity that offends everyone against his will is primarily an invasion of privacy, and in this sense it enjoys no protection from the First Amendment to the U.S. Constitution (21, pp. 208–237). The Supreme Court of the United States cannot protect by one amendment what would nullify another, and despite the quarreling that attends each decision reflecting the Bill of Rights, the Supreme Court has as its first duty the maintaining of the integrity of the Constitution as

---

* For example, the late Justice Musmanno fought a highly unsuccessful war against obscenity in works he would not himself read.

it is used to preserve law and order at a given time in history (53). Such protection, written into the Constitution of India (1949), is as much as anything else an explanation of the viability of the U.S. Constitution since its adoption, making the government of the United States the oldest constituted authority in the world. Such protection has evidently provided the least change of system with the maximum development of the economic and social life of its citizens. However, an act of volition is necessary to read—where it is not to view or to hear—and in this sense literary works are protected by the First Amendment to the Constitution, but obscene letters are not. One is forced, against his will, to peruse a document that offends his decency and modesty, when he receives a letter that contains the commonly recognizable features of obscene writing. Such a distinction is essential if the privacy of an individual is to be protected by public law, but it seems an extension beyond the powers of government to assume that any obscene correspondence between consenting individuals is illegal, especially when carried in the most protected of common mailing arrangements, "first class" in the United States (54). The Ginzburg decision does not adequately establish this principle, but it shows the trend of modern legal thought. Ginzburg was finally convicted primarily on the basis of his own words; he advertised *Eros* as pornography to persons whose decency and modesty were offended even by the envelope bearing their personal names (55). Hence a research librarian who suggests a pornographic work to a reader as a part of his investigative plan may be liable for some kind of punitive action, if it is only the intense displeasure of the reader. In the practice of his profession, where it most attains the characteristics of other professions that serve the public, the librarian cannot substitute intelligent understanding of literary material with any combination of technical competence and technological education.

Erotic literature has the purpose of depicting sexual acts for a specific, and not necessarily sexual, purpose. In this sense, the passage in *Naked Lunch* depicting troilism, which includes sodomy, between John, Mary, and Mark may be erotic to some persons and sickening to others, so that sexual arousal that is possible to some and not others is shocking and offends the modesty of many who read the book. Hence the passage is obscene. Its primary purpose is to utilize the emotional reactions of the reader and transfer them to the subject of capital punishment because the author opposes it. Whether an individual is sexually aroused or not is inconsequential, because even if one part causes libidinous feelings another will in all probability cancel them. The author was so intensely desirous that this scene be correctly interpreted that his Introduction, which includes an intelligent and useful description of drug addiction, contains an explanation of the scene (56).

The test of pornography is rather simple; utilizing the methods of content analysis, the text is examined for certain words, particularly taboo words. These are counted (as offered at the Los Angeles trial of *Naked Lunch*) and their context noted. It will be seen that erotic literature depicting sexual acts may contain no taboo words at all, utilizing sex-related words or even a figure of speech, such as metonymy, but that pornography to be so labeled must contain taboo words. Second, descriptions of setting and of persons (characterization) are noted. It will be seen that erotic literature contains carefully established settings and details of characterization that require many more words than whatever is found in pornographic literature. Finally, the structure of the work is examined and the sequence of scenes depicting sexual activity is noted. A pornographic work relies on the piling of scene on scene, so that each, more intense in the author's view than the last, keeps the reader in a state of constant sexual arousal. Erotic literature is under no such constraint of technique and achieves its artistic purpose by means that vary with whatever the purpose might be (*16,* pp. 17–24).

As readers may have observed, this method utilizes those principles of pornographic writings established by Eberhard and Phyllis Kronhausen in their book, *Pornography and the Law* (*16*). This book, along with Olympia Press and its founder, Maurice Girodias, may be credited with furthering the scientific investigation of literary materials beyond what has been possible before.

Erotic literature may be obscene in the view of one person and simply dull to another. When *Lady Chatterly's Lover* was published as written by D. H. Lawrence, reviews appeared in many periodicals commenting judiciously on the value of the work as seen from the point of view of the critic (*57*). Reviews are always likely to show the special interest of the periodical that prints them. Because pornographic literature may be obscene to a certain person, it does not follow that all pornography should be banned. Research libraries have always retained material that was contrary to the law, and even the famous book banning of the Hitler regime in Germany did not affect the great collections of German universities. Types of material from the kiosk libraries that was specifically prohibited, removed, and burned was simply locked in cages in German university libraries (*58*). The Institute of Sex Research at the University of Indiana founded by Alfred C. Kinsey has a very valuable collection of pornographic materials essential to research in several areas.* The change of attitude that has begun the contemporary period in the history of censorship now imposes upon the individual librarian decisions that were left to the courts before. It is impossible to think of a literary work that is utterly without redeeming social value to someone, even if only to a doctoral candidate looking for a topic for a dissertation. Libraries in institutions dealing with social problems are deficient if they do not contain controversial works regardless of the nature of the controversy.

As previously stated, as repeated endlessly throughout the library profession, as taught in schools of librarianship, the highest professional task of the librarian is the development of a collection that fits the community he serves (*60*). Although any member of the community may criticize a particular selection, no one but the librarian should presume to speak for the users of the library. The librarian is ethically bound not to overrepresent one group at the expense of another with funds that almost always are limited. Various disciplines for the study of com-

---

* L. Ash and D. Lorenz, comps., *Subject Collections:* "Sex: all disciplines, emphasis on behavior . . . Extensive folklore collections incl. books, manuscripts, illustrative and photographic materials, tapes, and disc recordings. Rich in French, German and American sources, and much Oriental . . . bawdy limericks, double entendre and puns; slang and special dictionaries; graffiti . . . research materials of the Kinsey studies, etc." (*59*).

munity organization will reveal the character and research requirements of a local group and show its diversity as well as its uniformity (*61*). Content analysis is an established technique, which, within the constraints imposed by the need for objectivity, can assist in the evaluation of a work, so that the librarian who is asked why he bought a particular work can give an effective and professional answer. Such refined methods are usually unnecessary, but if a case should develop where sanctions may be imposed either on the librarian or the library itself, it being the privilege of a professional organization (or union) to reprimand institutions, some objective means of study is required. The tests described show one type of material, but once the essential characteristics of a body of literature are known, other tests may be devised (*62*).

These tests relate only to printed matter. A much more difficult area is that of audiovisual information sources. Picture books and illustrations would be judged obscene, quite within contemporary views, because they make explicit at a glance what hundreds of words could only inadequately convey. The test of pornography that the author assumes to be different from erotica still applies, and is still in accord with the distinction drawn by various individual writers of all viewpoints save the dedicated proponent of censorship. A group that cannot adequately be defined is often labeled a censorship organization, e.g., the Citizens for Decent Literature. But even this organization, which is most fearful of the influence of erotic literature on the state of society, does not advocate censorship. Their viewpoint might be stated as favoring only the laws now in force in most places interpreted as strictly as possible (*63*). It would be quite unfair to equate their standards with those of Anthony Comstock, though there are points of similarity. Comstock, in *Traps for the Young,* includes "infidel" traps among others and assails the ideas of Robert Ingersoll, whose writings he would cheerfully have banned if he had a chance (*21*, p. 200). The Citizens for Decent Literature is much more an ethical than a religious group, and however their viewpoints are at odds with professional opinion, their contribution to the subject must be welcomed and appreciated, if only because their writers portray at times untenable ideas supported with questionable logic.

A picture or a sound recording is *ex professo* pornographic and obscene if it has no other purpose than depicting sexual acts for the purpose of causing sexual arousal among those who view or hear the work. Various attempts have been made to arrive at a consensus view of obscenity in motion pictures (sound recordings seem to have escaped censorship proceedings so far, although erotic recordings are advertised in various places). Community standards apply here with considerably more force, because the community may be confronted with, and forced to glance at, a picture that is shocking to the decency and modesty of the members of the group. One does not include in this idea of obscenity motion pictures that are shown to persons who must pay to be admitted and who are warned that the picture is likely to cause emotional disturbance. Vivid pictures of sexual activities have been available for all of human experience, since man first started to draw pictures in caves. What makes the picture obscene is the status of taboos regarding it (*64*). The "House of the Bachelors" in Pompeii contains paintings, preserved from Roman times, of heterosexual activity, just as ancient Chinese and Japanese paintings depict heterosexual activity (*64, pp.* 240–312). Pictures of homosexual activity, except among women, are quite rare, but exist in Grecian vases, Incan pottery, and so forth (*64,* pp. 89–94). One of the first pictures made with the motion picture camera was of sexual activity; the author has not seen it, although it is described in various sources (*65*).

Since that time, motion pictures that are explicitly sensational have been made with great dedication and very little profit, by individuals whose interest must be primarily that of a voyeur rather than an entrepreneur (*66,* p. 43). In these films, explicit detail is captured with little or no attempt at cinematographic artistry. The same technique of piling taboo on taboo is utilized so that films of executions of actual criminals were made, including beheadings and hangings (*66,* p. 41). Such films are far from rare, nor are their showings unusual to male audiences. Various organizations for men, once their membership has proven to be receptive to such entertainment, show the films with impunity, frequently with members of the local police force in the audience (*66,* p. 95).

This "doublethink" was amply demonstrated to the author when he attended a "carnival" given by the church in his parish in New York City only to discover that craps, lotteries, blackjack, and other illegal games of chance were being conducted under the benevolent eyes of the priests and members of the local police force. In the same place, somewhat later, the author attended a meeting of a Yorkville group made up of a priest, several devoted mothers, and the members of the local parish club for men. In the course of the meeting, the films produced by the Citizens for Decent Literature were shown and examples given of obscene works available for sale at the stationery and candy store at the corner. These "obscene" works included *The Second Sex* by Simone de Beauvoir in a paperback edition, a copy of *Playboy,* and a copy of *Tomorrow's Man.* Each was meant to show that the kind of dangerous material the films elaborated upon was readily available at the corner store where impressionable youth could buy it. It was unfortunate that these examples were chosen, because it was soon obvious that no one had read *The Second Sex* and no one was able to judge the appeal of *Tomorrow's Man* to males with homosexual inclinations. The only effective portion of the display was the revelation of the centerfold picture in *Playboy* of a very attractive girl in the nude. "What would your son do if he had this to look at?" one of the mothers asked the men accusingly. Very likely the men in the audience silently remembered having to confess masturbation at one time or another in their lives and wisely made no comment. Possibly everyone had used less beautifully photographed and printed illustrations, which may not have been in color and could not have been so glowingly printed, as the source of their fantasies that accompanied their self-stimulation.

Certain canons exist for vice squads that govern their decision that one film is obscene and another is not. Community standards, in the Roth decision, are not given a point in time; rather, the opposite is true, so that what is allowable to many members of the audience is not to others. The U.S. Customs represents perhaps the most restrictive ideation in this field, far greater than the average young adult who, having read works that have survived the test of censorship in the courts, cannot see why a film should be judged differently. A long battle was fought to permit the showing of *491,* a Swedish film based on the novel of the same name, by Lars Gorling (*67*), and the film *I Am Curious (Yellow)* made by Vilog Sjoman was shown to adult audiences in the United States only after a successful appeal from the U.S. Federal Court decision. A description in *Evergreen* whets the appetite of those interested in the development of the cinema as an art form (*68*). *Fireworks,* a film made by Kenneth Anger, concludes a rather horrifying sequence of scenes depicting in a surrealistic fashion the masochistic homosexual inclinations of a young man with a brief shot of a sailor with an erect penis thrusting from his white uniform. The penis is transformed into a Roman candle and the film ends with the audience realizing that the anguished dreams of the main character must be lived out in real life because of his misinterpretations of male sexuality. At the showing the author attended, a young man in the front row fainted as the concluding scene began. None of the many young women attending the showing, in a university meeting room, were similarly affected. This film figured in several censorship attempts, possibly as a reflex based on the old Hays code, which forbade any mention of male homosexuality whatever.

Research libraries, especially those making a collection of motion picture films with both examples and descriptions, can scarcely be considered complete unless they contain films of all descriptions. That the librarian might faint as he views the film must be considered an occupational hazard, but there is little reason to deny serious scholars the privilege of viewing such films, for the obscenity does not exist to a person who is impelled by reasons other than prurient interest to investigate such examples of film making. A film that includes scenes of sexual intercourse is of no more and no less interest to a scholar than one that includes scenes of gambling, drunkenness, or intoxication with substances other than alcohol. Nor have the censors anything to say about such a collection; that all persons do not follow the particular moral code of a censor is not regrettable to one who either does not follow it at all or who, with full dispensation, investigates such materials for a moral purpose. The priest who reviews a film in Italy for showing in the local village is not guilty of a sin if the film is to his mind obscene. His purpose in viewing the film was not to be aroused sexually but to consider whether it would have such an effect on the members of his parish (*23*, pp. 57–58). There can be no official board of censors that is not made up of those who are old enough to utilize the material for purposes other than sexual arousal. Even if the intent of the producer or publisher is to appeal to prurient interest, research must not be obstructed because a researcher might have to battle his own emotions in order to make the judgments necessary to carry on his research.

So far it is apparent that the advance of knowledge cannot be determined by censorship proceedings, nor has this ever been proposed. The censor, who is a scholar in his own right, is understood not to be affected by what he judges. When this privilege is granted to one qualified person, it must be granted to all who are qualified even in countries where censorship is still actively enforced, as in Ireland, the United States, and Spain. The customs officials who review material are not considered homosexually inclined after having passed on a film dealing with the subject, however graphic it might be (69). The essence of the rule established by Lord Cockburn in the Hicklin case is that obscenity becomes a matter for police action when it is found to be probably dangerous to persons likely to be influenced by the material. The actual material that brought this decision is uncomfortably close to *The Autobiography of a Flea,* depicting the dangers encountered by young women in the confessional, one of the favorite topics of anti-Catholic literature (70). Until the relaxation of censorship as the result of trials of books originally published by Olympia Press and widely distributed abroad, investigation of erotic literature was impeded by the legal philosophy that the morals of the public must be protected lest those readily affected by prurient literature be activated to the point where they commit sex crimes (23, pp. 192–193). It now seems evident that no such simplistic cause and result can be shown, for the only sexual activity that may commonly result from sexual arousal as a result of reading erotic literature, or actual pornography, is self-stimulation, which is probably the least harmful sexual act that society may ever consider (25, passim). It cannot be denied that reading sexually stimulating material may be a part of the etiology of a sexual criminal, but no person with training in psychiatry, whether to be a physician, clinical psychologist, or social worker, can accept such a one-to-one relationship as anything but evidence of poor research and biased conclusions. It has generally been found that pornography has played only an incidental role, if any at all, in the history of sex criminals, and it is clear that those who commit heterosexual crimes against adults are the least likely to have any extensive familiarity with pornographic or erotic literature (25, Table 115, p. 692). Smokers and stag parties of affluent men ought to have produced a far greater number of sex criminals among their strata of society in the United States than can be shown. Generally the sex criminal is a "loner" with intense guilt feelings to be worked out in violence.

A further danger is seen in the statement, uttered with remarkable faith, that civilizations are destroyed by wanton sexuality, and Rome is given as the example where this occurred. Even if this were the case, no other country is Rome at the same time in history, and the argument scarcely deserves comment. Civilizations are not destroyed, they are changed. The "barbarians" who conquered Rome considered their regime an improvement. This statement conceals a much more vital question, whether the unfettered publication of material that was considered obscene in the past will have the effect of disrupting society. There seems to be no question that the fight against censorship has been waged in the name of change, as a challenge to the status quo. Hence, whatever character the change takes may to some extent be blamed on the liberalization of censorship restrictions. A vital part of the reforms in Dubček's Czechoslovakia was the removal of censorship restrictions on press, radio, and television (71). Whether this extended beyond the political sphere is unknown, but where people are free to think as they please and communicate their thoughts and writings, there is a broad area of change that follows. If change is dangerous, if a social position must be maintained in the view of governmental authority, then censorship practiced as discreetly and quietly as possible is the only means of retarding change while propaganda works whatever magic it is supposed to achieve. It has always been the case that the society with the most stable organization is the one that has the least to fear from freedom of the press and of speech (*72*).

In this section the position of the censor and the anticensor have been examined, not without bias, because the implication that anything more than blind faith may be considered as evidential is considered anticensorship by those who seek to impose it. The proposal that objective tests for pornography exist, that erotic literature is not obscene in a legal sense, whatever the person who proclaims it so may think, is not meant to support or defeat the view that censorship is necessary or not necessary. Until it is determined who can censor effectively for everyone, it is not possible to determine whether censorship is valid. The choice must be made on another basis. Is censorship desirable? That can only be determined by various communities and societies, but the decision to restrict or constrain expression almost invariably causes intellectual and artistic stagnation, whatever good effect it may also have (*69*). For the research librarian, whether in a special library or dealing with a special collection, no instrument of censorship may ever be tolerated.

The College Library and the Extent of Freedom

In the previous section, the research librarian and the effect that censorship has had upon the development of collections was not considered. Rather, the emphasis was placed upon the use of prohibited materials for research purposes, one of which, through content analysis, was demonstrated. The research librarian, by definition, is not concerned with the attitudes of the general public toward his collection, nor is he primarily concerned with the nature of the material itself. This section is devoted to discussion of the dividing line between what is and what is not acceptable for college libraries, where the emphasis is not so much on research as on the materials that provide a broad liberal education. In distinguishing between the erotic as it tends toward the pornographic, we must cover the extent of materials available on the open market and what purposes they serve. It would be facile, and rather untrue, to say that material by reputable publishers is the only thing that the nonsectarian college library need be concerned with. This is virtually never pornographic in the objective sense the tests would establish. Whether it is obscene or not, in a nonlegal sense, depends upon the individual using the material. Obscenity is a "high-order abstraction" in a semantic sense, having no necessary relationship to the objective environment. What is obscene depends on what the individual concerned regards as obscene.*

To what extent does the college librarian include erotic literature and pornography in his collection as a part of a board liberal education? In asking this

---

* Obscenity, even in the legal definition, assumes a consensus of individual views. A consensus, here, is as meaningless as would be a vote on the true religion.

question, we also include the adult circulating collection of a public library. There is no need to investigate whether youngsters up to the postadolescent age are harmed by reading such material. As with the question of pornography as the "cause" of sex crimes, there are too many other factors to be considered, not the least important of which is the nature of parental control. In any case, below the age of eighteen, the young person is responsible to his parents and represents a privileged area of influence for them. The laws are quite specific in protecting the young on behalf of the parents, and in any case the librarian would be interested in the general reading of his young patrons, not in their special instruction. Below the age of eighteen, there seems to be no question that the young person must accept his instruction in sex as left for the parents to control.

But as an individual enters college for education beyond the level of the majority of his fellow citizens, the question must be asked whether the nature of the college program is aided or impeded by collections of erotic literature. Such practical excuses as not buying "dirty books" because they are always stolen, or keeping them locked up, begs the issue and need not be considered. Unless there is a policy of strictly limiting what a young person should learn of the world, then the question is raised. Cleland's *Memoirs of a Woman of Pleasure* (*73*), Friedman's *Totempole* (*74*), James Baldwin's *Another Country* (*75*), J. D. Salinger's *The Catcher in the Rye* (*76*) do not qualify as pornographic. The use of taboo words is slight, if not absent altogether; the settings and characterizations occupy much more verbal space than the scenes depicting sexual activity; and the structure is remote from that of standard pornography. Such books, it would seem, belong in a college library where the exposure of the student to even more detailed and explicit works may be taken for granted. The question becomes more problematic when works by the Marquis de Sade (*77*) and such works as *My Secret Life* (*78*) are considered.

At core is a basic difference in philosophy that is very great though hard to determine precisely. First, we must ask what degree of diversity in opinion and morals we are able to tolerate. In some church-related schools, little diversity would be considered licit, and in some none at all. We are not concerned with the right of an institution to set its limits; we are concerned with the nonsectarian college in which the limits are those of the community and lie somewhere between the total freedom of Denmark and the narrower and more recently gained freedom of the United States. Thomas Beer, in the *Mauve Decade,* considers a Harvard baccalaureate to be a certificate of literacy (*79*). How informed is the liberally educated man; of what importance would erotic literature be in his life; and are there significant dangers to be found in exposure to pornography as a postadolescent?

Robert H. Rimmer's novel, *The Harrad Experiment,* deals with an experiment in educationally directed heterosexual community living. The students in the college live as roommates, but there is no sexual segregation; the purpose of the college is to bring young men and women together sexually as well as socially, and to deliver them from all consequences of shame and guilt. Gymnastic exercise and swimming are in the nude, and detailed birth control information as well as contraceptive measures are furnished the students. The author supposes that the general result of this will be most beneficial and depicts the characters achieving success not only in their marriage but also in their careers and social life (*80*). No better treatment for homosexuality has ever been described, and in a society that is equally permissive and guilt-free of homosexual experience, it is very likely that intensely fixated individuals will at least gain an understanding of themselves, as seen in many "hippie" communities (*48*, pp. 292–323). Rimmer, however, does not touch on homosexuality, preferring to explore in depth the psychology of heterosexual understanding (*80*).

The Harrad Experiment is erotic literature of a very didactic type but it deserves consideration because it proposes an entirely different concept of morals from that which sustains home and church in the popular view. Simone de Beauvoir, in one of the most perceptive essays written on the subject, considers whether the works of the Marquis de Sade should be burned (*81*). That they were not is one of the more fortunate events of an otherwise destructive period. (A constant rumor exists that Lord Byron was the author of several erotic works, which his publisher systematically destroyed after he received word of the author's death in Greece (*82*).) De Beauvoir's answer is that these appalling works should not be destroyed, because understanding the passions that drove the Marquis de Sade illumines the nature of human beings as few other writings can hope to do (*81*). One cannot, as a librarian, decide that the moral code proposed and explained by the Marquis de Sade is more worth shelf space than that proposed by Anthony Comstock. The one favors sexual license, the other reviles it, but both regard crimes for which only personal consequences are the result of unfettered sexual activity. De Sade worships depravity, but the result is not what he most deplores, personal happiness, but what he cannot enjoy, personal freedom. If the Marquis de Sade and Anthony Comstock are considered moralists, then it is hard to say which has the more perverted view of human beings. The slightest misstep is utter depravity to Comstock, who cannot bring himself even to use the appropriate medical terms for what will result from reading erotic literature. In *Justine* the moral perfection of Justine is incessantly punished, fitting the ideas of the Marquis de Sade (*77*). A view of morality that does not conform to accepted view is still morality, despite the fulmination of Anthony Comstock (*21, passim*).

If the college librarian can accept this point of view, and he may as well admit that his efforts at book selection are special pleading if he does not, then the question is nearly resolved. (Where erotic materials are freely available, a certain amount of theft will continue because some users would rather steal a book than have to admit to a bookstore salesman that they want to read it.) The writings of Jean Genet represent a harder case more readily resolved, as do some of the writings of Jean Cocteau and other authors. As the object of the extensive critical research of Sartre, Genet becomes a literary study in itself (*83*). To many persons it would seem that college students would sit with bulged eyes reading literature that would have been incredibly filthy, in all likelihood, to Anthony Comstock. Many students are frankly bored when they can make fragmentary sense out of the writings of Genet or of Sartre. These works are in no way more erotic than, for instance, the *Droll Stories* of Balzac (*84*) or the *Satyricon* of Petronius (*85*).

Beyond this point of view is the haste with which youngsters are pressed to accept the responsibilities of society in the United States, to the point of dying in support of a foreign policy, but are guarded from an awareness of what is in the world besides the sweetness and light his education up to college has provided. The rebellion of the young against injustice and hypocrisy ought to delight everyone, and if hypocrisy is evident in many of the censorship decisions, then one cannot blame the best-educated generation so far if they scorn their elders. Indeed, a course might be instituted on the characteristics of nineteenth-century social attitudes and actual practice that would require the reading of pornographic works produced in such quantity during those years. Certainly no other work clearly shows the English gentleman's utilization of the class structure so well as *My Secret Life* (78). The only thing that mitigates against such a course, if it is not already being given somewhere, is the sad fact that reading which delights because it seems forbidden would be boring because it is required.

In order to understand the freedom the new generations will enjoy, we have to inquire into the possible motivation of censors. An irate parent may insist that a son withdraw from college because his morals are being corrupted by the holdings of a college library. If so, the struggle must be between the parent and his offspring. The librarian must, though, maintain his dignity as a specialist in the area of information handling to the point of promptly resigning if his integrity and professionalism are impugned, as did Daniel Gore when members of the MacMurry College Library Committee ordered that the library's subscription to *Evergreen Review* be canceled (86). In general, anything that challenges an established conclusion in any field—science, literature, the arts, philosophy, or politics—is likely to face severe criticism by those whose vested interests or beliefs are undermined. All the conclusions that deal with the objective environment, that is, that are not based on faith, must be founded on reliable knowledge, with its requirement of showing that we know what we know. Where censorship is not possible, suppression may be employed, as in the case of the academic response to Velikovsky's theories of cosmology.* Another constant rumor persists that a major publisher was warned by several professors that other publications would be boycotted if a second work by Velikovsky were published. The publisher, who relied heavily on textbooks, acquiesced to their demands.

Although few people with more than an average knowledge of books would be willing to enforce the destruction of a work in fact or by making it illegal to sell (and in some cases own) the work, the censorious person has precisely this in mind. It was supposed that a kind of moral superiority motivates the censor, but it seems more likely that he is motivated by intense guilt and is subject to the mental mechanism of projection (88, pp. 160–177). This is a common feature of human thought and accords to others the faults we would not admit in ourselves. The person who sees everyone as possessing some blemish of character or morals is probably suffering from guilt over the very thing he condemns. An illustration is available in the popular conception of men who read homosexual novels; the

---

* "It is and may long be regarded by most scientists as mostly fiction in so far as the scientific theories it advances are concerned. The reviewer is unconvinced that any scientist of repute would give it his confirmation" (87).

average man concludes that only a homosexual fixation can motivate such a person, when the opposite might be the case (*16*). The censor must destroy what threatens him as a person because his interest in the work might be suspected or revealed. A kind of self-righteousness is necessary to conclude that another would be harmed by what was found displeasing to oneself, especially when the guilt concerns some relatively insignificant malefaction, such as masturbation, voyeurism, or a single homosexual experience (*23,* pp. 49–51).

The attitudes of the previous century, especially those insisting that virtuous women had no sexual desires, were largely destroyed by what has come to be called "the sexual revolution" (a particularly depressing term, as if human beings had learned to procreate by a means other than genital). This occurred after World War I, as much with the popularization of psychoanalysis as with the reconstruction of scientific opinion regarding masturbation and homosexuality (*89*). The present view would be more reasonably stated as considering sexual excitement and fulfillment the essential right, if not necessity, of every woman (*90*). The taboos that prevented discussion of sexual matters in groups made up of both sexes have largely been destroyed as well (*91*). At a time when society began to take notice of "immorality" in works of literature and stage presentations, those who proposed strict codes of propriety looked forward to a period when their rules would bring safety, sanity, and security to all. That this does not occur by wishing and probably has very little to do with private morality has not bothered those who now look back upon a period of propriety and decorum and wish it reinstituted. "Why must everyone talk of sex? Is there no other subject of discussion?" Few subjects interest human beings so much, if the subject matter of literature in all its forms is considered (*92*). The reason given for censoring works of erotica in modern Communist China is that such writing distracts workers and prevents them from doing efficient work (*93*). The purpose of modern censors, as they state it, is to preserve public morality (*94*).

It seems reasonable to assume that if freedom of the press implies that the average citizen may be trusted to determine his own political future, then freedom to read whatever pleases an adult implies a trust that he can determine his moral future as well. Several writers on sex have found positive merits in work that would be obscene outside the bedroom and recommend them as a means of stimulating married couples to more enjoyable sexual experience (*95*). The idea itself would be obscene to the Puritan, who admits the necessity of procreation but would deny its pleasure (*96*). In a work that church censors may not have had the opportunity to review and that in any case bears no imprimatur, Father James Kavanaugh questions whether the holy ignorance required of professing Catholics during the period of their lives up to their marriage really serves the individual well (*97,* pp. 113–118). The problems so often observed during the nineteenth century, when the moral code of Roman Catholics served everyone except the strongest adherents of the double standard, are repeated today when a considerable number of men and women live in bleakest misery, performing acts of heroic virtue every moment, because of their ignorance of human sexuality and its influence on human lives (*97,* pp. 119–145). This virtue is dubious and is the kind of behavior the Church would deplore as excessive penance, but if it is in the name of the holy purity then all can be forgiven (97, pp. 85–89). The Church does not forbid all mention of sex but requires that the unmarried not dwell upon the subject (97, pp. 105–106). Instruction is patient and adequate to explain what constitutes the Catholic idea of sin in the area of sex and how to avoid it. Confessional manuals of an earlier time went into much explicit detail about the sexual activities of married couples,* much in the manner of police descriptions of sex crimes for official use.†

The moral future would be interpreted by the majority of the young adults over eighteen as having nothing to do with sexual acts but everything to do with an awareness of the consequences of these acts. The distinction is subtle but important. Morality consists not in chastity but in forebearance when one would offend another person, not in sexual innocence but in knowledge controlled (98), so that a sexual act, per se, is neither immoral nor moral. The person participating or affected governs the morality of the deed. Virginity, therefore, has the sole virtue of permitting a young woman to have the widest choice of mates, among those who regard virginity as an anomaly and those who prize it highly. It seems highly unlikely that many men would refuse to marry a girl who is a virgin. A man who has never had experience with women and whose only sexual experience has been involuntary (nocturnal emissions) could demand a girl who is a virgin as his bride (98, pp. 163–164).

As Kinsey noted, those men with less than a high school education tend to reflect the moral code of their elders, those with a high school education tend to veer from that moral code, and those with a college education tend to formulate their own. These codes of behavior are at greater variance with those of their parents as the education of the individual widens his knowledge of different opinions of sexual morality (99). The code of men with the least education tends to reflect the actual, not stated, moral code of the nineteenth century, in permitting men sexual intercourse with women of easy virtue but requiring that the virtuous wife be a virgin at the time of her wedding (27). Masturbation or homosexual experience is considered unmanly and feminizing, if not actually criminal. Among individuals with more education, masturbation is considered normal and unimportant, and very likely a casual homosexual experience is regarded as insignificant, an experiment that proved such behavior to be without enjoyment (25, pp. 500–503). The college-age group tended to have (or admit) fewer homosexual contacts and tended to believe that masturbation served the useful purpose of a sexual release so that the virginity of girls would not be endangered (27). Virginity was considered a matter of physiology, not experience, so that a girl who had no experience of actual sexual intercourse with a man, whose hymen was intact, might still have had considerable sexual experience of a nonvaginal kind. This was considered permissible if not by society, at least by the person most involved (100).

---

* For example, translations of portions of St. A. M. di Liguori's manual of confession formed the basis of *The Confessional Unmasked,* the book at issue in Cockburn's decision in *Queen* v. *Hicklin,* 1868.

† Private communication of law enforcement official.

The morality reported by Kinsey is more than twenty years old as of the publication of this volume. Many of his interviews were conducted in the 1930s so
that we can register all of the above as the morality that largely affects parents
now (*100*, pp. 185–190). With the development of effective birth control measures—the pill—and the relaxation of strictures on birth control and abortion
in many states, the danger of sexual intercourse to young women is largely reduced
so that all sexual activity seems relatively harmless to the body, if not to the
psyche (*101*). Modern youngsters are much more aware of psychological factors
than their parents were—reflecting, we can hope, adequate courses in human
relations if not abnormal psychology (*100*).

The change of attitude is reflected in novels and periodicals dealing with male
homosexuality. As noted above, *The City and the Pillar* exists in two versions. The
first, written when the author was twenty-one, even with its cautionary ending,
scandalized critics who had hoped for different subject matter differently treated
by the author of *Williwaw* (*102*). At the time it was published, 1946, no periodical
would have dared admit that is was directed primarily toward male homosexuals,
although many posed behind art or body-building in order to show the unclothed
or undraped male, at times, especially when the dorsal aspect of the figure was
portrayed completely nude.* The male genitalia, however, were never depicted
in photographs because such photographs would have been promptly ruled obscene
by the large number of reviewing authorities that had this power. Other novels,
as well as *The City and the Pillar,* described sexual activity in vaguest terms so
that a person with no experience of homosexual activity would not be able to
divine precisely what occurred (*103*). Even to have mentioned the possibility, to
have described the setting and the characters, and to have indicated that some
kind of genital activity took place between two males was daring, probably more
for the author than for the censors, who would most likely miss the import of the
passage. Such books as *This Finer Shadow* (*104*) and *The Divided Path* (*105*)
were equally obscure, and the punishment that followed criminality was evident
in the ending of the novels. Those who did not change their orientation either
were murdered; murdered someone else and were made ready to be tried, convicted, and executed; or committed suicide.†

That these books were wide of reality became evident as other novels depicting
the actual extent of homosexual activity were published. One of the first to portray
homosexual society in the manner of Gide's proselytizing *Corydon* (*107*) was
Quatrefoil, by James Barr (*108*). The present author derives his views from his
experience as a psychiatric social worker during and immediately after World
War II, as a sergeant in the Army and later as an employee of what was then the
War Department: what was reported by patients and what made up the substance

---

* Several authors, Rembar (*57*) and Richards and Irvine (*96*), for example, consider the
decision of the U.S. Supreme Court in the Roth case to be the deciding factor in the defeat
of obscenity laws.

† A definite turning point can be seen in the sexual realism of the most recent of novels
with a homosexual theme which equates with the sexual realism of such heterosexual novels
as Roth's *Portnoy's Complaint* (*106*).

of these novels had in common only the fact of male homosexual activity. Psychiatry, at the time, equated homosexual activity with psychopathy, and patients who protested their fixated homosexual orientation were discharged as undesirable (*109*), but the author soon learned to keep in confidence a casual homosexual experience lest an overeager and possibly guilt-ridden psychiatrist, as a medical officer, should fall upon this as a reason for a discharge other than honorable.

As part of in-service training, the author and another soldier read through the literature of male homosexuality as it existed at the time and presented a two-hour summary to a seminar of other military social workers, male and female. The result of this exercise was precisely summarized by one man at the Convalescent Center for psychiatric cases where we worked. The summary had drawn no conclusions; it reported areas of agreement, which were few, and continents of disagreement among the authors who had written on the subject. Our colleague remarked that from what he had gathered, no one knew "borscht" about the subject. Under the guidance of the chief social worker, a captain who had practiced in New York City before he was commissioned, we worked out a reading list for other social workers, including a glossary of male homosexual argot, which vastly reduced the work of those of us who were trying, with no experience to guide us, to distinguish between the fixated homosexual orientation and the casual homosexual experience. A useful rule of the thumb was that the convalescent soldier who had actually had little experience other than what we called "battlefield romances" would rarely use any of the terms in the glossary we employed. We made it a practice, as well, to advise those soldiers who had served honorably abroad, at times having obtained a decoration for bravery, that we would not describe their homosexual experience, especially if the only official knowledge of it would come from the case histories and summaries of therapy we wrote, knowing that official attitude was capable of discharging as unfit for duty and undesirable a man whose only mistake was in reporting his homosexual orientation in confidence to a person who was ethically bound to try to assist him to an understanding of himself. It was not common to find such men (they made up less than ten percent of the case load), but it was not so unusual as might be imagined. It was our custom, under the direction of the chief social worker, not to attempt therapy, even at our primitive level, for those with fixated homosexual orientation, except where other problems of adjustment existed.

With those who had misinterpreted a battlefield romance as fixated homosexuality, we utilized all the expertise at our command to generalize the problem and remove the sting of guilt by an attitude of acceptance verging on nonchalance unless the patient had allowed his feelings of love for his comrade in arms to be mistaken for a change of psychosexual orientation. The author was frequently reminded by his supervisor that an attitude of acceptance toward the sexual history of the patient would help solve otherwise refractory problems. His fellows counseled him to restrict his practice to women because he would never be able to pick up the delicate hints that indicated that the patient wanted to discuss a problem of homosexuality. In becoming a librarian, the author was struck by the similarity of attitudes displayed toward the fact of homosexuality as a psychosocial problem and the attitudes of the proponents of censorship toward erotic literature. The same logic prevailed: false generalization, *post hoc, ergo propter hoc,* argument from analogy, false syllogism, and premises that are untestable in the objective environment. It was only after organizing a collection dealing with interpersonal relations that the author came to the conclusion that prejudice of whatever kind must utilize false logic because the hard method of science will not sustain beliefs held against all evidence to the contrary.

It has been noted that the sexual revolution is really a change of attitude toward minority groups of all kinds, to which each person belongs in one or another of the vital areas of his life, and which include persons who call themselves "homosexuals" as they might describe themselves as "the handicapped" or "Catholics" or "liberals" (*100*). It has been generally established that fixated homosexuality is not a syndrome but a symptom of other underlying emotional problems (*110*), so that to describe a person as homosexual is rather like saying that a person is a "sinusitis" or even a "measles." This is common medical jargon: the "appendectomy in ward A" is a person readily located by the nurse where a lengthy description would waste time and be subject to misunderstanding.

This rather elaborate excursion into autobiography seemed the only way to describe briefly how society develops instruments of understanding from the raw material of the objective environment only if each area of knowledge is subjected to the scalpel of truth in the light of logic. The attitudes of professional (or subprofessional) personnel at the Convalescent Center were developed from such knowledge as was available, a desire to assist those who needed assistance and could utilize it, and an awareness that official attitudes lag behind practical understanding.

How far behind is wonderfully revealed by John Gerassi in *The Boys of Boise.* Gerassi studied the scandal arising from newspaper publicity regarding homosexual acts with adolescents committed by certain men in Boise, Idaho. This began on the morning of Wednesday, November 2, 1955, with a headline on the front page of *The Idaho Daily Statesman:* THREE BOISE MEN ADMIT SEX CHARGES (*111*, p. 1). In his attempt to account for the "Furor, Vice, and Folly in an American City," as his subtitle describes, Gerassi's work was impeded by veiled warnings and threats, including the ransacking of his motel room about which he had been warned by an anonymous telephone call (*111*, p. xiii).

Since 1955 there has been a steady deterioration of the attitudes that enabled those involved in the scandal to profit from it, however briefly or inequitably. *Combating Crime,* the November 1967 issue of *Annals of the American Academy of Political and Social Science,* advocated the repeal of laws emanating from the nineteenth-century position of official hypocrisy and the adoption of the American Law Institute's Model Penal Code (*112*). Where crimes have no victims, as in sexual activity between consenting adults, and are usually undetectable except on the basis of evidence much like that supplied at witchcraft trials in the Middle Ages, the authors have shown that they may be used for unjust purposes, just as the charge of heresy was used for financial gain during the reign of Ferdinand and Isabella and the institution of the Holy Office of Inquisition under Tomas de Torquemada (*113*). Connecticut and other states have recognized this and changed old Puritan laws or repealed them* in accord with what Thurman Arnold had observed a generation earlier when he stated that such laws "are unenforced because we want to continue our conduct, and unrepealed because we want to preserve our morals (*114*). In like fashion, the governor of Indiana vetoed measures passed by the legislature that would have liberalized abortion laws.† As the comments on the Model Penal Code put it, "Dead letter laws, far from promoting a sense of security, which is the main function of the penal law, actually impair that security by holding the threat of prosecution over the heads of people whom we have no intention to punish (*115*).

The attempt to stifle an exchange of information among those interested in male homosexuality, whether as a matter of personal concern or research interest, by ruling that such material came under the purview of the "Comstock Law," was defeated by the U.S. Supreme Court in *Manual Enterprises, Inc.* v. *Day* (*116*) and in subsequent trials in lower courts. In the first case it was ruled that even though appeal was primarily to those men who participated in homosexual acts, even though there were photographs of nude men with the genitals either covered or thinly veiled, even though the ideas expressed were repugnant to the majority of the citizenry, the publications are protected by the First Amendment to the Constitution. This has led to publication of homosexual classics such as *7 in a Barn* (*117*), which the Kronhausens describe. It should be noted that the publisher was the plaintiff in *Manual Enterprises, Inc.* v. *Day*.

Certainly the periodical *Grecian Guild Pictorial* was devoted to high ideals, as stated on the inside cover, and included information concerning a Greek boy who was supported by voluntary contributions by members of the Grecian Guild. The periodical included drawings ranging from the very detailed and skillful draftmanship of "Quaintance" to rather cruder drawings (*118*). Beginning in 1963, *Grecian Guild Pictorial* included reviews of books that would be of interest to readers of the periodical.‡ This service has resulted in several bookstores devoted to material on homosexuality and sexuality generally.§ The reviews are literate, are generally innocent of special pleading, and on the whole present the subject matter fairly. At present they appear to be published by the same organization and are used as promotional material by a New York bookstore.¶ Needless to say, the reviews are not indexed in *Book Review Digest*. There is no question that a research library in an institution serving social workers, physicians, psychologists, anthropologists, and other professional personnel, either in training or in

---

* Canada recently followed the lead of Great Britain in putting sexual acts between consenting adults outside the scope of criminal law.

† Such veto power may be politically fatal. According to an informant, a former governor was not reelected because of his veto, and even his rather limp quest for the presidential nomination failed.

‡ E.g., "Bulletin No. 23," which included unsigned reviews of *The Gay Flesh* by Joe Leon Houston, *Celebration of Fools* by Lawrence Hughes, and *Abnormals Anonymous* by Stella Gray.

§ Trojan Bookstore in Philadelphia and Village Books and Press in New York City.

¶ Possibly Village Books and Press and other elements of H. Lynn Womack's enterprises. He is listed as president of the Grecian Guild in the issues cited.

practice, serving the general public should know of periodicals of the type as *Grecian Guild Pictorial* and could make highly valuable use of the reviews. Indeed, the college librarian should make arrangements to obtain the reviews of books if only to decide which books belong in the collection and which do not.

Recently obscenity decisions have been made by lower courts and the cases never reach the Supreme Court. Previous decisions enabled a verdict in favor of the distributor and publisher by the federal court judge before whom the case came. These decisions have been harmful to the publishers of nude male periodicals, because men with erections can be shown in frontal views. A great many were published, at consistently lower prices, so that the older periodicals became valueless, and sales have been announced listing "any 15 for $10" (*119*). This is a sign that the market is glutted.

The male genitalia were not considered erotic during the nineteenth century. Medical textbooks that were retouched so that the pubic area of the female figure was never represented in an artistic fashion included photographs of the male genitalia as frank and revealing as those found in DSI* periodicals. To the majority of men, the male genitalia are still not the subject of eroticism though they may be of vital interest. Of the several fears to which a male adolescent is subject, one is that his genitalia are abnormal because they are different, despite the lack of any such evidence as cryptorchidism, and that he is somehow defective as a male (*120*). Periodicals such as those published by DSI can show the post-adolescent that his anatomical development fits within the very wide pattern of normality as understood by physical anthropologists (*121*).

Some of the early DSI publications were little better than hard-sell advertisements of motion pictures,† but one of the periodicals, *Rugged,* contains a very useful article on obscenity, providing the viewpoint of the publishers, whose stated intention is to provide male figures for art studies and examples of the art of posing and photographing the male figure (*122*). The views of the unsigned author coincide with those of the author here and it was rather a shock to realize that several years of devoted research could be so neatly summarized by an anonymous person writing for a periodical that had been attacked by the postal authorities as evidently obscene. The passage deserves quotation fully, in the spirit of fair use of copyrighted material. After asking what the nature of obscenity is, the author continues (*123*):

> If a belief in the objective reality of obscenity is wholly illusionary, then its general acceptance must be due to the high degree of widespread suggestibility on the part of the masses. This suggestibility is promoted by the psychotic mode of thinking which controls our education and moral development. It imposes an artificial intensification of the childish conflict between the lure and fear of sex. So our educators and moralists push the learner ever nearer to (or beyond) the psychopathic borderline. It is there in the shamefully intense conflict of emotions over the' sexual problem where the illusion about the objectivity of obscenity acquires its familiar pattern and dynamics.

* Distributor Services, Inc., Minneapolis, Minn.
† See, e.g., the periodical *Butch,* No. 1 (1965?).

This passage is opposite a photograph of a young man wearing a Marine cap. The most interesting feature of this page is what appears to be a peacock tattooed on the skin over the gluteus maximus of the visible buttock (*123*, pp 10–11).

Psychopathy, in the classic study of Robert Lindner, is characterized by the lack of deep emotional response. The psychopath is breezy, often amusing, shallow, unpredictable, at conflict with the law even when there is no necessity for conflict, and unaware of the consequences of his act. Social psychopathy is a character neurosis, which can be treated but with not great hope of success. Psychopaths are dangerous not because they wish to be but because they cannot see the other point of view; they feel nothing when harm is done another person; they lack compassion (*124*).

Sexual psychopathy is a different matter and involves all those whose actions do not conform to the active standards of the community. Persons with a fixated homosexual inclination are not necessarily included, but male and female prostitutes usually are. A vivid sequence of pictures of sexual psychopathy is given in *City of Night* by John Rechy (*125*). The distinction to be drawn between the narrator of this story and some of those he observes is to be found in a second novel, *Numbers* (*126*). In the latter novel, the character of the narrator is identifiable as a compulsive neurosis, beautifully depicted in scenes in which the character personifies his compulsion as some external, godlike figure. Violence is a characteristic of the sexual psychopath, as are robbery, sadism, and even masochism (*48*, pp. 275–280). Hence the main figure in a novel like *Born to Be Gay,* by J. X. Williams (*127*), is victimized by psychopaths who wish to experience homosexual relations without bearing the consequence of having to consider themselves homosexually oriented.

Just as in other fields where a minority under blind penalty of the law, often without justification, may be victimized, so may the person be victimized who is unaware of extortion and brutality as a possible concomitant of casual homosexual experience. It is ironically the person who is least likely to be fixated in his sexual inclinations who is most often victimized. When this comes to be known, men who have had casual homosexual experience can evaluate whether further experience is too dangerous and may then utilize homosexual literature as an outlet for mild homosexual impulses. Equally, those persons who feel intense anger and hatred toward homosexually inclined men may utilize the literature to remove or blunt these feelings and replace them with understanding and compassion. So, too, may the protected individual come to know of a characteristic of human nature that he finds so frightening and repugnant that he cannot recognize it when it is thrust upon him, sometimes as a direct accusation by a sexual psychopath (*48*, pp. 199–238).

There is much more reason to argue that such literature fills a social need than that it will convert males to homosexuality. A patient and frustrating search of the literature has failed to reveal a case where an individual was converted to seeking homosexuality as an outlet because of his reading. The opposite is the case. A psychologist can use a novel with the theme of homosexuality as the means by which the tongue-tied patient and the busy therapist can come to a discussion of the problem without great waste of time.* Frequently such novels make plain the social ostracism facing the fixated individual. This exists even in modern Denmark and Sweden where sexual freedom is the privilege of the citizenry, apparently without any danger whatever to the society there (67). To rule that homosexually inclined males are by their nature outside the law is no different from ruling that persons of African descent are, by their nature, not entitled to the social benefits awarded other persons in the social fabric. Equally, to rule that novels dealing with homosexuality are *ipso facto* obscene, as being shocking to the decency and modesty of all who read them, is to conclude that one can make judgments about another person's psychosexual development that he would deeply resent. The usual response of a heterosexually oriented person to such a novel is either revulsion or clinical interest, something a dentist understands when he begins to treat a patient with a badly abcessed and foul-smelling tooth.

Clinical interest extended to literary and dramatic subjects explains the theater of the absurd. That some do not like such an art form is understandable; not everyone likes the taste of Stilton cheese, but to forbid either the cheese or the dramatic form to a person who wishes to see if he likes it, is to prevent examination of a harmless nature of something that might be enjoyable. The college librarian must therefore exercise judgment of a very professional kind when he determines what suits the community he serves. The faculty come from one generation, the students from another, but it is the student body who will determine the ultimate fate of the college and its library. In the poetic image of John Donne death is already rushing to meet the members of the faculty as they rush toward it (128); the future, life and its continuance, belongs to the students. The preservation of the status quo seems less to be sought as a goal than the enlargement of those admirable human qualities of interest, compassion, enjoyment, understanding, and diversity.

Members of the younger generation view the hypocrisy of censorship cases as an acknowledgment that what their elders do is rather remote from what they say. In effect, anything is permissible to a district attorney, provided it accomplishes his ends. Murders go unsolved, robberies and burglaries are committed with impunity, while the police search madly for evidence of sexual vice. The college librarian, then, is likely to establish rapport with the students to the extent that he enables them to explore the world through the materials the library has collected in an environment at once protected and literate. Librarians with sufficient professional understanding, with no moral axe to grind, and with a willingness to discuss reading matter with the student can do much to develop their taste at a critical time. It is doubtful that such as remains of the present laws of censorship will survive the openness and logic of the best educated generation to date.

The rapid decline of censorship in the United States has encouraged creativity and will probably also be the incentive toward the dispersal of the publishing

* Private communication with practicing clinical psychologist.

industry. Los Angeles, as well as New York City, and Atlanta, Georgia, have become publishing centers in a manner that is oddly reminiscent of the highly successful method used by the Franklin Books Program to encourage the development of a publishing industry in countries beginning to industrialize (*129*). The method depends upon the available material in the language of the country. Both Los Angeles and Atlanta found such material in the swift publication of material originally put out by Olympia Press in Paris, during the years it was permitted to operate by the French government (*130*). Because of the copyright laws of the United States, material not copyrighted in this country at the time of publication in English cannot be copyrighted later except for changes and additions.

The college librarian must keep in mind that what he prohibits for his bookshelves may be readily available at a college bookstore or another bookstore nearby. The attitude of the past was that material dealing with human sexuality was best kept to the privacy of the bedroom; but the modern generation discusses the whole subject with considerable frankness and little or no guilt. Coming from an earlier period of social attitudes, the librarian often has to fight down his own impressions of a work in order to purchase it at all. This is one of the requirements of a librarian; one orders books not because they suit his prejudices but because the community needs them. It is the opinion of many authors that guilt over sexual misdemeanors, if they are such, is likely to have a highly deleterious effect upon the development of the individual as a responsive, joyful adult, capable of assuming responsibilities because he values the rewards they bring. The opposite is apparently the case as well. Where there are no values, there can be little sense of responsibility, and in a climate of instense frustration, aggression is almost always the direct result (*131*, pp. 142–231).

Erotic literature cannot be equated with violence. Violence in literature has been established by Leslie Fiedler, in a series of essays, and in his book *Love and Death in the American Novel* (*132*). Scenes of sadism that lack only the sexual element to equate with *The Story of O* and *The Image* abound in highly moral novels, especially war novels and novels of police work. It is very likely that capital punishment and corporal punishment are retained in the law because of the sexual thrill involved for those who participate in the grisly proceedings. Certainly a huge literature on the subject validates the immense sexual importance that corporal punishment had in British schools in the nineteenth century, and in society generally (*133*).

Nor can riots be equated with censorship or with the freedom to read. Demonstrations are probably encouraged by censorship, especially where the persons who participate have no other means of showing their point of view. It is significant that during the riots in France, the United States, and mainland China, there were no riots in Denmark, Spain, and Ireland. The freedom to express a point of view is a safety valve that minimizes the need for terrorism and other brutal forms of restraint. A cold impersonality on the part of the governing authorities, an unwillingness to act, and intense devotion to the state of society as it stands leaves a suppressed majority with no opportunity to introduce change except through violent action (*131*, pp. 232–260).

The baby boom in the United States following World War II has brought a large number of young men and women to maturity at a time when industrial and social change has reached its peak. In this perfervid air of change, censorship has no place. There is as much evidence that repression of information causes mental illness of the most debilitating type as there is that it causes sex crimes (*48*, pp. 155–198; *88*). Both explanations are simplistic and dangerous. The decision of the college or public librarian in building a collection should be to select material that fits the community he serves and its standards of education. The change of educational method must govern his decision as much as the availability of material forbidden those educated at an earlier time. Modern educative techniques would have rote learning mechanized as much as possible so that the student and his teachers can devote their time more profitably to the development of hypotheses and to tests of them, using original data. A college library can build up considerable collections at low cost by regarding much material as "documentary" rather than treating it to the formal cataloging procedures that reflect the characteristics of information and printed communication in the last century. The methods of coordinate indexing can be utilized for government documents, for collections of paperback books, and for many other purposes to serve as the original material on which students can exercise their creative abilities.

For the study of sex in literature and the resolution of many of the problems of censorship that remain, certain reference books are essential. In addition, the college library should obtain the two works by Alfred C. Kinsey and the succeeding one by Paul Gebhard et al.: *Sexual Behavior in the Human Male* (*27*) and *Sexual Behavior in the Human Female,* which were written under the direct supervision of Dr. Kinsey, and *Sex Offenders, An Analysis of Types* (*25*) (probably entered in the card catalog under the *Institute for Sex Research*). Requisite as well are the Kronhausens' *Pornography and the Law* in both its editions; Sagarin's *The Anatomy of Dirty Words; The Olympia Reader,* edited by Maurice Girodias; and the complete works of the Marquis de Sade, available in the Grove Press edition (*77*), which includes Simone de Beauvoir's essay. All of these should be considered reference material, with possibly another copy available for home loan. A collection of pornography seems highly useful if the college wishes to provide the broadest education possible.

Such a program would require that there is someone on the college staff who has studied the principles of interviewing and similar subjects in the area of social work so that students who are disturbed can talk with qualified college personnel who will explain the mechanisms of repression, projection, shame, and guilt. A college psychiatrist should be available for those students who have major problems that such a collection will probably bring to the surface. A parent who is disturbed over the collection should have the same opportunity to discuss his mental mechanisms with a psychiatrist as the students, for it is quite clear that an attitude of deep shame and guilt over human sexuality is as much evidence of emotional problems as other aberrant thinking and behavior. No major religion would demand that its adherents regard sex as a universal evil.

In this rather tortuous pursuit of these conclusions, the argument has not been for uniformity of collections, nor even that a college which wishes to teach particular moral codes along with the understanding of human sexual functions, or wishes to leave this entirely to the parent, should desert this position. A nonsectarian college, however, should develop a program in cooperation with psychiatric and counseling personnel, so that misinterpretations of human sexuality will not be a source of danger to the mental health of the students. The argument has proceeded through a general discussion of what is available and how this affects some individuals to the statement that a valid collection in the college library might be made of materials which were taboo before the various cases established the limits of censorship. As the motivations of the censors become clearer, theft of books out of shame or worry will be rare enough to indicate the problems that arise in the minds of students who have endured a childhood of lies and evasions, and a passage through puberty without sound parental guidance, on meeting the range and force of erotic literature.

Variant forms of sexuality offer a danger to society in only three instances: complete continence by members of both sexes, complete reliance on solitary self-stimulation by all members of society, and utilization of homosexual acts as the only form of participatory sexual behavior. If society can avoid these possibilities, the race will continue. The rampant heterosexuality on the campus is our insurance against such a disaster. Rimmer's *The Harrad Experiment* is acted out unofficially by some members of the modern college today as before in the past. The difference is that hypocrisy is no longer an adult virtue.

The innocence which the older members of community would legislate into obscenity laws is best preserved by only vicarious exposure to the aberrant sexual behavior that exists on all sides today, as in the past. *Therese and Isabelle,* by Violette Leduc, serves his function for women, showing the transitory nature of homosexual love and the general impossibility of building a human relationship on behavior that serves only to placate emotional pressures (*134*).

Contrary to what must seem the case to those who have not made a systematic investigation of the literature of male homosexuality, the emphasis is on rather strict moral and ethical codes, requiring the individual who wishes to make a practice of homosexual activity not to force his predilections upon another person or to make another person suffer because of them.* Violence is regarded with genuine horror, except as it comes within the nebulous area of what Freud called "The Pleasure-Plain Principle" (*135*). A novel such as *The Black Angel* by Carl Corley (a prolific author of novels in this genre), set in some future time, indicates that the main character by constantly expressing aggression to his partners invites equal and finally fatal aggression on the part of others (*136*). Told in the simple fashion of routine science fiction, *The Black Angel* is much less involved than *Myra Breckinridge,* by Gore Vidal (*137*) and *Couples,* by John Updike (*138*).

Myra Breckinridge contains one clinical scene of the rape of Rusty Godowski

---

* See articles in *Rugged, Grecian Guild Pictorial, Vagabond, Drum,* etc. H. Hefner's "Playboy Philosophy" (*Playboy,* 1962–1965) is in accord. See also the pamphlet "Towards a Quaker View of Sex," issued by the Literature Committee of Friends Home Service Committee of England, 1963.

by Myra, which leads Rusty to work out his aggressions on another character before he becomes the star, Ace Mann. Myra herself is revealed as changed from Myron to Myra and at the end of the novel back to Myron again. The novel is repulsive to many people, but Vidal achieves his artistic purpose in working out physically what he believes is true psychically of Americans. *Couples* (*138*) deals with the shadowy morality that governs a group of married couples in Tarbox, Massachusetts. Utilizing a brilliant style fixed entirely on the details of life, Updike is grossly frank throughout the novel, using taboo words in the way they are now employed in certain strata of society, but using them not only as quotations but also in direct descriptions. In each of these novels, the changing pattern of American morals is viewed not from the fixed ground of a moral position but from the shifting position of those who are working out moral structures and ethical codes from no ground whatever. There is a curious similarity in the novels, and one has the uneasy feeling that a change of sexual orientation would have little or no effect on the basic structure and development of either novel.

The anonymous author of the quotation from *Rugged* (*123*) uses the term "psychotic" to describe the behavior of persons who believe all manifestations of sexuality to be shameful and any discussion of sexuality to be dangerous. Psychosis is often defined as consisting of symbolic and substitutive behavior. In this sense, a dedication to the pursuit of vice may have psychotic motivation, quite typical of paranoid schizophrenia where the underlying homosexual factor is projected to other members of the society in which the afflicted person finds himself. The author, as a librarian not a psychiatrist, is unable to test the hypothesis that a person who is dedicated against manifestations of homosexuality is not suffering from paranoia to some degree. Certainly we must wonder what the person has to hide if he feels he must guard the public morals. Is it likely that his private morals or his interior dialogue would not bear investigation? A belief in the virtues of censorship of material dealing with sex does not, despite the claims of the censor, confer moral superiority. To quote the crude remark of an informant in this regard, who must remain nameless, "Don't fool yourself. Those guys get a bang out of seizing the films and showing them for themselves. Censors can get erections just like anyone else. If they can't, maybe that's their trouble."

Censorship and the Information Center

Society keeps many records that are not for public usage. When the censor moves into the area of mass communication, he establishes a standard of artistic effort that more or less restricts the creative urge of those engaged in producing material. In the self-regulation of the television industry in the United States, the argument is used that children watch what is shown and may be affected in a way the parent does not wish. Censors, however, are likely to be motivated by the preferences of the sponsor as much as they are by consideration of public morals. Every station must be mindful of laws regarding libel, and some censorship is inevitable, but exercised by the authorities that pay for the work, there seems to be little recourse for those whose taste is not suited by a diet of material for those of a mental age to first start watching television.

Johnny Carson, the star of the "Tonight Show," has invented a name for the censor on the National Broadcasting Company. This is Miss Priscilla Goodbody, who, during a series of broadcasts from Hollywood, was working overtime. The show is recorded earlier in the evening, and the studio audience sees a version denied the general public. Sometimes scenes are omitted, as in the last part of a sketch satirizing "the make friends and influence people" school of social development, but the most common form of censorship is the blanking out of any unacceptable words on the recording tape. From lip movements the attentive viewer can sometimes see an occasional hell or damn purged from the public record. Sometimes other words are employed, possibly in a very suggestive fashion. Equally suggestive material, which relies on a knowledge of jargon, is likely to escape Miss Goodbody's attention.

When several persons must cooperate in the production of material, it is impossible to hide accidents that occur which may be highly suggestive. Miss Goodbody, in a famous oversight, failed to attach the importance to Ed Ames's demonstration of hatchet throwing which the cast of the "Tonight Show," as well as the studio audience and many viewers at home, did not miss. Ed Ames threw his hatchet at an outline of a man and, with an accuracy he could not have planned, sank the blade into the drawing at a spot where it resembled an erect penis. The bewilderment, the shock, the raw edges of castration complex, and other subtle influences could only be relieved by hysterical laughter among those who understood and the rather worried question, "What was so funny?" among those who had missed the joke. This episode has now passed into the oral history of show business.

What happens to this material? What becomes of material seized in raids, refused admittance to the country, donated by persons who have no use for it? Many rumors exist of special collections which include obscene material not for sale on the open market. (This essay is limited to a discussion of that which is on the open market for sale.) Usually a research library will maintain a special collection, a rare book room, or other completely controlled repository for such material, limiting the use to those who are intellectually qualified. At times, such material becomes vitally interesting to researchers pursuing literary and social history to its original sources, as discussed above. The laws forbidding "possession" of obscene material were among those that were unenforceable, and have now been overturned by the U.S. Supreme Court. At present, a person so inclined could build up a large collection of obscene material simply from advertised sources which escape postal regulation or from utilizing equipment which he can operate without the need for another processor. Polaroid cameras and videotape recorders would make any person his own pornographer, and there is little that local authorities can do about it unless they receive information of its existence and are willing to chance a suit for false arrest if they pursue the lead. The police force that is too eager to take action is likely to err through design as criminal elements offer false leads, the enemies of a person provide information that is not tenable or cannot be confirmed, and the individual himself is forewarned by another person. Furthermore, such laws may be used in a totally unjust way, aiding extortioners either by accident or design (*139*).

Significantly, research organizations engaged in a study of human sexuality have been left alone when the local authorities are aware of the dangers they run in attempting to stop the experimentation and observation. Those who suspect that large collections of pornographic material exist in such studies are wrong. The conventions necessary for a pornographic work are absent or if present represent coincidence rather than design. The films of heterosexual activity and of self-stimulation reported by Masters and Johnson would include a great deal of scientific data which could not interest the pornographer, although some individuals viewing the work might find the gauges and clocks more obscene than the highly repetitive activity being measured (*38*).

Institutions dealing with human sexuality have long ago learned to keep their records in strictest confidence, reflecting the attitude of hypocrisy of many years ago. When a record is used as an example in a written report, the name of the person is blanked out or altered to protect the individual. If the name were used, the permission of the person whose right of privacy was invaded would have to be secured. A lengthy film set up across the street from a spot where male homosexuals met for purposes of making assignations could not be shown publicly because of the invasion of the rights of privacy. *The Titticut Follies* has been censored on the same grounds, which, sadly enough, also serve to keep secret the scandalous condition of mental institutions in Massachusetts. Where activities may be criminal, the individual who engages in them for the purposes of scientific research, or who admits them in order to obtain understanding of himself, is unwillingly put in the position of having to place himself outside the protection of the Fifth Amendment to the U.S. Constitution, which covers self-indictment.

The right of privacy is concerned with the freedom of U.S. citizens from unreasonable searches and seizures, as guaranteed in the Fourth Amendment. This amendment, more than any others, assures the individual that even though the law rule against his written works, if he retains them in private and utilizes them for his own purposes, then a search may not be made on suspicion alone or on the hope that there might be something actionable in his collection. A person who collects pornographic works, even those beyond the scope of this essay, is safe from governmental interference. Formerly, if a legal vendetta was planned, he would have been the subject of a warranted search, and one case was tried on the basis of possession of obscene works. Subsequent appeals produced the prevailing rule of law. The sex laws that are unenforceable are in the same category as other laws that rule against the person rather than the act, much as the heresy of the Renaissance, where the tendency of the individual to commit heresy was offered as proof that heresy had been committed and the fact of an espousal of Jewry, for instance, was prima facie evidence.

An individual, to control his own destiny, must keep some matters secret. Almost everyone is reluctant to describe his sexual experiences and fantasies except to competent medical or religious authority, and any person with some feeling of guilt over some action in the past must expect that his confidant, whether medical, legal, or religious, will keep his confidence. This has lead, in U.S. law, to the establishment of privileged conversations, by extending the right of the Fifth Amendment to cover situations where the individual could only be convicted on the basis of an involuntary confession. That such confessions are invalid has been shown through the years. Inviolable records, if not legally, at least ethically obtain in many fields, and were a matter of great importance when the membership rolls of supposedly communist organizations were subpoenaed in a kind of net meant to catch all who could be guilty of association with persons under suspicion of violating the law (140). The right of privacy becomes important with the acknowledged possibility that a large data bank available to the federal government could keep a kind of dossier on everybody, revealing personal habits, financial status, and any proclivities that might appeal to a blackmailer.

Included in this is the need for secrecy in much of the operation of government which concerns defense and foreign relations. It would be unwise to use censorship to describe either activity, but it seems reasonable that suppression, which is akin to censorship in preventing the public utilization of information, serves as a kind of *censura praevia*. The desirability of suppression over public awareness is often questionable and is readily misused, but no one could argue that it is always wrong, as far as the argument that has been developed so far on the censorship of various openly published materials is concerned. Suppression of information is commonplace with children and adolescents up to the age of eighteen, and librarians at present are generally not so much willing to support this view as unwilling to challenge it. Suppression has prevented the publication of many works, where censorship has simply made them difficult to obtain.*

It is too early, and too little is known, both technologically and legally, about the collection of data in information centers and the utilization of material that might affect the life of a person who offered in confidence what becomes the data of research. Suppression of revealing facts as well as the name and address of the individual is commonplace, but much more is at stake, for in the hands of unscrupulous persons very revealing data may be utilized for extortion unless suppression is effective at the outset, as in the case of records obtained for the various projects of the Institute of Sex Research. It is likely that the label of censorship will never be applied in this area, because the individual has a right to let his past die, especially if it no longer affects him, and there is no reason for any individual in public life to be subjected to revelations that are inconsequential.

Censorship and Professionalism

The controversial aspects of censorship have reached the point where the librarian cannot afford to be passive in his life in the community. A strong position, taken early, is the best defense against self-appointed voluntary groups, but only

---

* Several of the late Teilhard de Chardin's works are still unpublished as a result of the opposition of elements of the Papal Curia to his views.

with a rationalization of the laws—a prospect that seems far more likely than ever before—can much of the hypocrisy be shown for what it is. Librarians owe the school and public librarians aid in a particularly difficult position, for the privilege of parents to determine the kind of education a child receives is beyond the scope of law and an area into which the school and the public librarian moves with great caution.

School librarians are in the position of needing much clearer understanding of their role in order to explain what motivates the library to keep books on its shelves of which some parents disapprove. Where there is controversy, the library serves its greatest function by providing the information which brings the issues into focus and prevents the triumph of propaganda over a balanced understanding of the whole problem. The community is led to deprecate the profession if there is no clear understanding that the librarians are motivated by a desire neither to change society nor to prevent change but to insure the freedom of access to libraries and to library collections by those qualified to use them. Librarians are now closer to the swift flow of communication than ever before; consequently, they enter into controversial areas much sooner than they have done in the past. The librarian's protection is participation in the affairs of the community, utilizing his special knowledge for the benefits that society hopes to achieve. University administrators recognize that the university itself is becoming a part of a community movement where its role must be recognized as centering on objective research without attempting to twist conclusions to fit established attitudes. The right of privacy must be guarded while the right of access to the public forum is kept unobstructed.

If a librarian truly believes that he must fight censorship that prevents access to intellectual resources, whatever they may be, and yet protect the right of privacy, he must be willing to participate in community affairs to the extent of monitoring events that conflict with these articles of faith. This means aiding librarians who are fighting censorship, either covert or overt in nature, and beyond that entering into the larger areas when any person or group attempts to become the guardians of public morality. The experience is not pleasant; there is much preparation for testifying at an obscenity trial and one must be prepared for the condemnation that is necessarily possible whenever one seems to be protective of "filth," "smut," and "lewd, obscene, and lascivious" material. The results are often not what is expected and one must be prepared both to endure unwarranted enthusiasm when he is successful—because one victory does not end the war, it only achieves a respite before the next attack begins—and to make disappointment only the spur to further effort, not the end of all hope. Failure may be as temporary as success.

This is well demonstrated by what may be called the Strange Case of *Therese and Isabelle* (*141*). As often happens with a *cause célèbre,* the Guild Theatre case began slowly and simply with a review of the film by Win Fanning published in the *Pittsburgh Post-Gazette.* Fanning's use of the word "filthy" excited the late Justice Michael A. Musmanno of the Supreme Court of the Commonwealth of Pennsylvania to insist that District Attorney Robert A. Duggan do something about the floods of pornography in Allegheny County.

The district attorney had been reelected for a second term and confidently thought that the citizens of the county were on his side. Possibly a majority were, as later events seemed to demonstrate, and in any case the local chapter of Citizens for Decent Literature found him receptive to their purpose of enforcing the obscenity laws of the Commonwealth. Mr. Duggan sent a group of twelve persons, a kind of *ad hoc* jury, to see the film. During the showing, which began at eight in the evening of July 19, 1968, a group made up of members of the Knights of Columbus and of Citizens for Decent Literature came to the conclusion that the film was obscene and one of their group telephoned Mr. Duggan. He and his assistants arrived in squad cars and one member of the staff stopped the film. The theater was immediately cleared of some two hundred persons who had paid to see the film.

A week of legal activity ended with a hearing in the court of Judge David Weiss. Judge Vandevoort had refused to hear the case, and Judge Brosky could not do so, because he had issued an injunction against the film before the showing was stopped.

Late in July, Mr. Hubert I Teitelbaum, attorney for the defense, and Mr. Gerald C. Paris, appearing for the district attorney's office, argued the characteristics of the injunction before Judge Weiss, along with Mr. Thomas Kerr, whose *amicus curiae* brief gave the general position of the American Civil Liberties Union. In attendance were members of the Citizens for Decent Literature, The Catholic Daughters of America, and four members, including the author of this article, of the Permanent Association for Intellectual Resources (PAIR). The latter organization had its origin in the case because some members of the School of Library and Information Sciences of The University of Pittsburgh opposed censorship.

Mr. Kerr and Mr. Teitelbaum offered the lengthiest statements. They complained that the statutes were vague and had not mentioned motion pictures specifically, and that the U.S. Supreme Court in its rules made an adversary hearing necessary before an injunction could be obtained. Judge Weiss ruled that the district attorney could enjoin a nuisance and the film could be considered that, if nothing else. The injunction stood.

Mr. Ralph Green and his brother Mr. Millard Green, owners of the theater, had been taken to Sharpsburg on the night the raid took place to appear before a Squire, a method used in the Commonwealth to identify wrongdoers whose cases ought to be heard by the Grand Jury of the County. A week later they were summoned back before the Squire, to conduct their defense. This took place although the Squire had on his desk a manila envelope containing his decision typed in advance of the hearing. He had concluded that the brothers Green had violated the statute and were to appear before the Grand Jury because the film was obscene and they had knowingly shown it.

The attorneys for the defense appealed to the Supreme Court of the Commonwealth for relief from the injunction. Justice Musmanno died on Columbus Day, so that his opinion in the case was wanting, but other justices sharply criticized the district attorney's methods. Their ruling stated that he had used "star chamber procedures" rather than the adversary hearing which law and custom had demanded.

Mr. Duggan stated his position to the press and after announcing various paths that might be taken through the courts to confirm his method, he decided to proceed with an adversary procedure. Motions to have the case thrown out before the jury could hear it were denied by Judge Ralph Smith, Jr., in whose court the hearing would take place. By early December the slow mechanism of the court was ready for the public discussion of *Therese and Isabelle*. The jury had been chosen with care and several potential jurors were dismissed, although the opinion of a jury in this kind of proceeding is advisory only. A very significant case overruling the decision of the U.S. Customs and a federal district court had been reported from the Circuit Court of Appeals for New York, so that the film *I Am Curious (Yellow)* could be shown to American as well as to Danish, Swedish, and other audiences. This case concluded that a judge must decide the law; juries can only decide facts; obscenity is a legal conclusion; hence, the jury may advise but it cannot rule.

Mr. Teitelbaum argued that the case was quite a departure in American law, for the district attorney was suing in a court of equity to enjoin the showing of the film. Heretofore, the plaintiff in such suits had been the theater owner who sought relief from an injunction, but the action of the Supreme Court of the Commonwealth had given Mr. Duggan no other method of procedure, and only a full-scale trial would decide the case. Judge Ralph Smith, Jr., in denying the motion to dismiss, was giving the district attorney his chance. *Therese and Isabelle* had reopened because the Supreme Court of the Commonwealth had ruled the first injunction invalid. The public was interested in the question of obscenity and people were filling the theater in order to make up their own minds. Opinion according to those claiming knowledge ran about fifty-fifty. Of a hundred persons, fifty were disappointed in the film as being neither obscene nor interesting and the remaining fifty found it either obscene or notable for other reasons.

The trial tended to invoke anger and worry. It was a legal wrangle from the outset, exasperating judge, jury, and public alike, who did not appreciate the venom which seemed to attend every difference of opinion and the frequent huddles in front of the judge.

Most of the librarians who had volunteered to testify for the defense were attending a trial for the first time. They found it a grim experience.

Mr. Fanning reiterated his review and after him Miss Marie Torre, who is a television personality in Pittsburgh, gave her views. The film was filthy, they agreed. They could not be drawn into logic-chopping on the theme of community standards: filth is filth, they seemed to say, and this word decribes *Therese and Isabelle*. Another of the plaintiff's witnesses, a professor of literature at the University of Pittsburgh, was subjected to brutal cross-examination by Mr. Teitelbaum, and he floundered badly on his points of social value, the classic values of credibility, universality, and permanence, all three of which *Therese and Isabelle* lacked, he said.

The Citizens for Decent Literature had sent a lawyer to testify on obscenity law from the misbehavior of Charles Sedley in 1688 to the present but objections and argument almost obliterated his efforts. He did not get well started on the eighteenth century before his whole testimony was stopped abruptly, and Mr. Teitelbaum's cross-examination brought on wrangles just as fierce as those during his direct testimony.

The first witness for the defense was to have been Mr. Peter Dana, the chairman of the Pennsylvania Board of Censors during the whole of its brief life, but he had gone home and the defense opened with the author of this article. He found his hours on the witness stand an ordeal. Even the friendly questions of the defense attorney provoked anxiety, and, although he understood the purpose of the attorney for the plaintiff, he felt imperiled. The possibility that he might violate the strict law of the courtroom seemed a vivid threat and the witness is likely to review his testimony endlessly. In his testimony, he disagreed with the contention that the theme of the film was lesbianism and observed that Violette Leduc, who wrote the novel used as a basis for the film (*134*), was an important French writer. He tried to develop a definition of social value as a work which in and of itself is a unique source of information both to the people of our time and to researchers of the future.

A legal argument developed over the manner of the assistant district attorney. When an answer seemed both lengthy and damaging to his case he would interrupt. The crisis came when it was apparent that a description of a stag film was needed, but whether from prudishness or legal acumen, Mr. Paris wanted no such comparison in the record. He wanted the witness to discuss the meaning of such terms as "pornography" and "erotic realism." Judge Smith ruled that if the witness felt he had been interrupted he could ask permission to continue. It happens that the witness, who is the author of this article, had indeed seen a stag film in Bangkok, Thailand, and could give his recollection of it in detail if needed. When interrupted, he got permission to continue, and being asked by the judge to tell what a stag film was, dictated into the record the usual stag film's focus upon genital activity, the lack of setting or of characterization, and the general repetitiveness of the action which at last becomes boring. The witness, asked by Mr. Paris if he had ever read a banned book, stated that he had read *Leaves of Grass* by Walt Whitman. This was widely quoted in the press, and provoked laughter in the courtroom.

Mr. Paris, unable to shake the witness with his brusque and contemptuous manner, changed to the politeness which probably won the case for him. He treated the succeeding witnesses as if they were educated beyond the reach of common sense: Mrs. Mary Dimmick from the Hillman Library at the University of Pittsburgh; Dr. Martin Tweedale from the Department of Philosophy of the university; Mrs. Dellene Tweedale, a librarian with a particular interest in archives; Mrs. Rosemary M. Plesset, the wife of a psychiatrist and herself a social worker; and Mr. George M. Sinkankas, a doctoral candidate in the Library School, University of Pittsburgh.

The one witness who defeated the lawyers and managed to upset Mr. Paris as he tried to maintain a genial air of sobriety and earnestness was Mr. Henry Koerner, the renowned artist. Mr. Koerner saw *Therese and Isabelle*. Others watched, viewed, heard, observed, or noticed the film, but he saw it with the full force of an artist. He saw the symbolism and the meanings of the symbolism. His testimony covered all the use of visual stimulation in the film: the peephole like the eye of a vengeful deity, the shadows like the bars of a prison, the darkness and secrecy used to illustrate the theme of the novel. Mr. Koerner's testimony was so abundant that the court record does not fully reproduce it.

The attorneys summed up their cases and the trial went to the jury a week after it began. Mr. Teitelbaum asked the jury to consider the number and education of the witnesses for the defense, and Mr. Paris asked the jury to consider the state of morality in our time and the harmful effect such films have upon us—causing riots among students and social decay. After deliberating all afternoon, the jury returned not with a verdict but with answers to the questions, the interrogatories, which Judge Smith asked.

Their judgment on *Therese and Isabelle* was that it had no social value of any redeeming sort at all, that it was significantly beyond the limits of candor and shame established by the community, and it appealed predominantly to a prurient interest in sexual matters. Quite clearly, as Judge Smith enjoined the showing of the film, the day in the fight against censorship had been lost. Just as clearly, the adult public of Allegheny County could not be trusted with its moral future. As any politician will tell you as he goes down to defeat, the public can't be trusted with its political future either. For that one night, Allegheny County was protected by the district attorney from a French film which, if it endangered other less sensitive communities, was at least shown everywhere else without so prolonged and insistent a legal battle. No other trial of *Therese and Isabelle* was held.

But the law was to have the final say in the strange affair, for there is a provision in the Commonwealth that a writ of supersedeas must be granted when an appeal is made from the decision of a court of equity to enjoin an action in the public interest. Judge Smith did not grant the writ, but Mr. Justice O'Brien of the Supreme Court, using a conference telephone call to his fellow justices, obtained a ruling and granted the writ which permitted *Therese and Isabelle* to be screened every evening in the Guild Theater so that others in the community could make up their minds as well as the jury. Those twelve good citizens of the jury had seen the film without visible harmful effects, and only adults had ever been permitted into the theater, so that whatever moral deterioration was taking place seemed to be out of sight, and granting human beings the privilege of being human, out of mind as well.

The battle was won in the Supreme Court, where defense of the Constitution of the United States belongs.

Conclusion

It is the belief of the writer that the librarian today, if he is to follow his intellectual peers, cannot take a protective view of his collection while censorship campaigns are mounted within his community. Just as he must be willing to sacrifice his position for his principles, he must extend his principles to the community at large. It is up to him, more than to any other member of the intellectual community, to form anticensorship groups and to counteract the propaganda of those who would limit the freedom of inquiry by making some subjects beyond the pale of honest research. There is no need for him to become the champion of material that is beyond the law, recognized as such by those who sell it, but there is reason for him to insist, just as do the censorship groups, that whatever is permissible according to the standards established by the various courts, from the Supreme Court on down, is not attacked by voluntary groups which claim without basis in fact to represent the community at large. As this lengthy essay has shown, the controversy over censorship has moved to a larger scale than the censors realize, leaving wide areas where the freedom of inquiry may turn for knowledge of man and his society. It is as instruments of social change that the collections used by adults have their greatest importance, and as specialists in the instruments of social change, librarians must be something more than defensive in fighting censorship groups in whatever guise. Dissent is the privilege of those who would remake the laws to be an instrument which preserves law and order, respects above all else the right of privacy, and preserves the freedom to work out in the marketplace of ideas the way society is to progress. The librarian today participates in attempts at censorship, whether directed toward his own collection or toward the resources at large in the community, if he does nothing at all. He can only be its foe by exercising his professional obligation to preserve the record of our society, ugly or beautiful as it may be, and make it freely available to any adult who wants it. All research shows that obscenity has no effect upon adults not inherent in information sources generally.

There is now enough evidence that what made obscene literature interesting to some adults, and perhaps to all at one point or another, was the taboos that surrounded it. The erotic in literature is not in question, whether it is good writing or poor, but whether its treatment is useful to research and valuable as information. What caused the high prices of pornographers and added to the tax burden in the pursuit of them was not what they sold but the laws that assumed that the net effect would be dangerous for society. This may be true, in some remote fashion, but as investigation continues it will surely reaffirm what is known already: that the question is good or bad art, that bad art is self-limiting, that the government of a country, in any case, cannot act either as the chief critic or the arbiter of the state of sexual morality.

REFERENCES

1. "What Shall Libraries Do About Bad Books—Contributed by Various American Librarians," *Lib. J.,* 33, 349–354, 390–393 (1908).
2. J. C. Dana, "Public Libraries as Censors," *The Bookman,* 49(2), 147–152 (1919).
3. C. Bacon, "What Makes a Novel Immoral?" *Minn. Lib. Notes and News,* 3, 4–11 (1910).
4. "Libraries and the Climate of Intellectual Freedom," *Newsletter in Intellectual Freedom,* 7(1), Intellectual Freedom Committee, American Library Association, Chicago, 1958, pp. 1–3.
5. "Kansas City Conference: Growing Pains and Generation Gaps," *ALA Bull.,* 62(7), 827 (1968).

6. A. B. Gerber, *Sex, Pornography, and Justice,* Lyle Stuart, New York, 1965.

7. P. Barrows, *Whores, Queers, and Others,* Traveller's Companion, New York, in association with Olympia Press, 1967.

8. *Jaybird Gallery,* No. 1, May–July 1967.

9. T. Caldwell, *Grandmother and the Priests,* Doubleday, Garden City, N.Y., 1963.

10. "Soviet Criticism of Writers Rises," *The New York Times,* April 1, 1966, p. 13.

11. T. D. Lysenko, *Heredity and Its Variability,* King's Crown Press, New York, 1946.

12. A. Levy, "The Short, Happy Life of Prague's Free Press," *The New York Times Magazine,* Sept. 8, 1968, p. 34.

13. J. Lelyveld, "Mandalay Must Not Become Indianapolis," *The New York Times Magazine,* Jan. 5, 1969, p. 30.

14. J. C. Paul and M. L. Schwartz, *Federal Censorship; Obscenity in the Mail,* Free Press, New York, 1961, pp. 7–8, 31–37, 85–87.

15. F. Pollini, *Night,* Olympia Press, Paris, 1951; F. Pollini, *Night,* Houghton Mifflin, Boston, 1960, Bantam Books, New York.

16. E. Kronhausen and P. Kronhausen, *Pornography and the Law; The Psychology of Erotic Realism and Pornography,* Ballantine Books, New York, 1959.

17. H. Richardson, *The Sexual Life of Robinson Crusoe,* Traveller's Companion, New York, in association with Olympia Press, 1967.

18. M. Girodias, "Introduction," in *The Olympia Reader: Selections from the Traveller's Companion Series* (M. Girodias, ed.), Grove Press, New York, 1965, pp. 11–29.

19. T. a Kempis, *The Imitation of Christ,* 3, 24, Sheed & Ward, New York, 1950, pp. 104–105.

20. U.S. v. 31 Photographs, 156 F. Supp. 350 (S.D.N.Y., 1957).

21. A. Comstock, *Traps for the Young,* Belknap Press of the Harvard Univ. Press, Cambridge Mass., 1967.

22. F. Wertham, *Seduction of the Innocent,* Holt, New York, 1954.

23. H. C. Gardner, *Catholic Viewpoint on Censorship,* rev. ed., Doubleday, Garden City, N.Y., 1969.

24. R. Hauser, *The Homosexual Society,* Bodley Head, London, 1962.

25. P. H. Gebhard et al., *Sex Offenders, An Analysis of Types,* Bantam Books, New York, 1965.

26. J. Purdy, *Eustace Chisholm and the Works,* Bantam Books, New York, 1967.

27. A. C. Kinsey et al., *Sexual Behavior in the Human Male,* Saunders, Philadelphia, 1948.

28. G. Vidal, *The City and the Pillar,* rev. ed., Dutton, New York, 1965.

29. A. Ellis, *Sex and the Single Man,* Lyle Stuart, New York, 1963.

30. W. S. Burroughs, *Naked Lunch,* Olympia Press, Paris, 1959.

31. H. Selby, Jr., *Last Exit to Brooklyn,* Grove Press, New York, 1964.

32. "Obscenity: Test by Jury," *Time,* Dec. 1, 1967, p. 53.

33. G. Vidal, *Myra Breckinridge,* Little, Brown, Boston, 1968.

34. U.S. v. Roth, 237 F. 2d 796 (2d Cir., 1956). This seems a fair interpretation of the Roth decision.

35. R. E. L. Masters, "Introduction," in *Sexual Self-stimulation* (R. E. L. Masters, ed.), Sherbourne Press, Los Angeles, 1967, pp. 11–15.

36. S. A. Tissot, *L'Onanisme, Dissertation sur les Maladies produites par la Masturbation,* 3rd ed., considérablement augm., F. Grasset, Lausanne, Switzerland, 1764.

37. R. E. L. Masters, ed., *Sexual Self-stimulation,* Sherbourne Press, Los Angeles, 1967.

38. W. H. Masters and V. E. Johnson, *Human Sexual Response,* Little, Brown, Boston, 1966.

39. R. von Krafft-Ebbing, *Psychopathia Sexualis,* Physicians and Surgeons Book Co., Brooklyn, N.Y., 1886.

40. J. Copeland, *A Dictionary of Practical Medicine* . . . (C. A. Lee, ed.), Harper & Row, New York, 1846–1860 (3 vols.).

41. E. Lea, "The Monster Hideous in Mien," in *Sexual Self-Stimulation* (R. E. L. Masters, ed.), Sherbourne Press, Los Angeles, 1967, pp. 22–31.

42. B. G. Jefferis and J. L. Nichols, "The Immoral Press," in *Light on Dark Corners,* Grove Press, New York, 1967, pp. 42–44.

43. Jacobellis v. Ohio, 84 Sup. Ct. 1676 (1964).

44. "Suggested Changes in the Statute Relating to Obscene Books," *Mass. Lib. Assoc. Bull.,* **35,** 11–12 (Jan. 1945).

45. PL 90–100. An Act to Create a Commission to Be Known as the National Commission on Obscenity and Pornography (approved Oct. 3, 1967).

46. Z. Chafee, Jr., "Part I. Division A. Protection of Individual Interests Against Untruthful and Unjustifiable Publications," in *Government and Mass Communications,* Vol. I, Univ. of Chicago Press, Chicago, 1947, pp. 77–195.

47. R. Amory, *The Loon Songs Trilogy: Song of the Loon; Song of Aaron; Listen, the Loon Sings;* Greenleaf Classics, San Diego, Calif., 1966, 1967, 1968, resp.

48. W. Churchill, *Homosexual Behavior Among Males,* Hawthorn Books, New York, 1967.

49. O. Wilde, "Preface," in *The Picture of Dorian Gray,* Brentano's, New York, 1913, p. xiii.

50. J. F. Kennedy, "Remarks at Amherst College Upon Receiving an Honorary Degree, Oct. 26, 1963," in *Public Papers of the Presidents of the United States, John F. Kennedy, . . . 1963,* No. 439, Gov. Printing Office, Washington, D.C., 1964, pp. 815–818.

51. H. F. Peyser, "Mendelssohn in Germany; Pfitzner and Strauss Refuse to Replace His Music for 'The Dream,'" *The New York Times,* Dec. 2, 1934, Sec. 10, p. 7.

52. "Juvenile Riles Alabama: White and Black Rabbits Wed," *Publishers' Weekly,* **175**(23), 56 (1959).

53. Kingsley Books, Inc. v. Brown, 354 U.S. 436 (1957).

54. 96 U.S. 727 (1878).

55. Ginzburg v. U.S., 224 F. Supp. 129 (E.D. Pa., 1964).

56. W. S. Burroughs, *Naked Lunch,* Grove Press, New York, 1959, p. xxxiv.

57. C. Rembar, *The End of Obscenity,* Random House, New York, ca. 1968, pp. 74–76.

58. R. L. Hansen, "Da tyskerne de utyske'digtervaerke," *Bogens Verden,* **15,** 101–106 (1933).

59. L. Ash and D. Lorenz, comps., *Subject Collections,* Bowker, New York, 1967, p. 1028.

60. Cf. H. E. Saunders, *The Modern School Library,* Scarecrow Press, Metuchen, N.J., 1968, pp. 101–104.

61. K. R. Popper, *Open Society and Its Enemies,* 4th ed., Routledge & Kegan Paul, London, 1962.

62. B. Berelson, *Content Analysis in Communication Research,* Free Press, New York, 1952.

63. Citizens for Decent Literature, *Procedures Handbook,* Cincinnati, Ohio.

64. P. Kronhausen and E. Kronhausen, *Erotic Art,* Grove Press, New York, 1968.

65. M. Schumach, *The Face on the Cutting Room Floor,* Morrow, New York, 1964, pp. 4–14.

66. N. H. Hunnings, *Film Censors and the Law,* George Allen & Unwin, London, 1967.

67. L. Gorling, *491* (Anselm Hollo, transl.), Grove Press, New York, 1966.

68. A. Adelson, "The Barriers Fall: As Censorship Relaxes, Debate Grows on Impact of New Permissiveness," *Wall Street Journal,* March 10, 1969, pp. 1–12.

69. M. Adams, *Censorship: the Irish Experience,* Univ. of Alabama Press, University, Ala., 1968.

70. Pisanus Fraxi (pseudonym), *Encyclopedia of Erotic Literature,* Vol. II, Documentary Books, New York, 1962, pp. 88–109.

71. J. Randal, "Prague Dismisses Ideological Chief," *The New York Times,* March 6, 1968, pp. 1, 6.

72. L. Ullerstam, *The Erotic Minorities* (Anselm Hollo, transl.), Grove Press, New York, 1966.

73. J. Cleland, *Memoirs of a Woman of Pleasure,* Putnam, New York, 1963.

74. S. Friedman, *Totempole,* Dutton, New York, 1965.

75. J. Baldwin, *Another Country,* Dell, New York, 1963.

76. J. D. Salinger, *The Catcher in the Rye,* Little, Brown, Boston, 1951.

77. Marquis de Sade, [Works], Grove Press, New York, 1965, 1966, 1968 (includes *120 Days of Sodom, Juliette,* and *Justine*).

78. Anonymous, *My Secret Life,* Grove Press, New York, 1966.

79. T. Beer, *The Mauve Decade,* Random House–Knopf, New York, 1926, p. 105.

80. R. H. Rimmer, *The Harrad Experiment,* Bantam Books, New York, 1968.

81. S. de Beauvoir, "Must We Burn Sade?" in Marquis de Sade, *120 Days of Sodom and Other Writings,* pp. 3–63 [in (77) above].

82. Pisanus Fraxi (pseudonym), *Encyclopedia of Erotic Literature,* Vol. I, pp. 189–193; Vol. III, pp. xxi–xxiv; Documentary Books, New York, 1962.

83. J. P. Sartre, *Saint Genet, Actor and Martyr* (Bernard Frechtman, transl.), Braziller, New York, 1963.

84. H. de Balzac, *Droll Stories* (Alec Brown, transl.), Folio Soc., London, 1961.

85. Petronius Arbiter, *The Satyricon of Petronius Arbiter* (W. C. Firebaugh, transl.), Boni and Liveright, New York, 1922.

86. D. Gore, "A Skirmish with the Censors," *ALA Bull.,* 63(2), 193–203 (1969).

87. "Book Reviews," *Sci. Educ.,* 34(5), 341–342 (1950).

88. A. Ellis, *Sex Without Guilt,* 2nd ed., 1966.

89. W. Reich, *The Sexual Revolution,* Noonday Press, New York, 1962.

90. W. Reich, *The Function of Orgasm,* Noonday Press, New York, 1961.

91. N. G. Faber, "Sex for Credit," *Look,* April 1, 1969, pp. 39–40, 45.

92. L. Gardner, *Sex—It Feels Good,* Rapture Books, Los Angeles, 1964.

93. *Peking Rev., passim.*

94. V. Bourke, "Moral Problems Related to Censoring the Media of Mass Communication," in *Problems of Communication in a Pluralistic Society,* Marquette Univ. Press, Milwaukee, Wis., 1956, pp. 113–137.

95. A. Ellis, *The Art and Science of Love,* Dell, New York, 1965, pp. 49–51.

96. A. Richards and R. Irvine, *An Illustrated History of Pornography,* Athena Books, n.p., 1968, pp. 62–63.

97. J. Kavanaugh, *A Modern Priest Looks at His Outdated Church,* Trident Press, New York, 1967.

98. I. and S. Hegeler, *An ABZ of Love,* Medical Press of New York, 1963.

99. G. B. Strunk, *The Anglo Saxon and Sex,* Anchor Pubs., Gardena, Calif., 1965, pp. 150–168.

100. J. R. v. Rosenberg, *The Teen-Age Sexual Revolt,* Brandon House, North Hollywood, Calif., 1968.

101. J. L. Hagerman, *Oral Love,* Medco Books, Los Angeles, 1967, pp. 136–146.

102. G. Vidal, *Williwaw,* Dutton, New York, 1946.

103. J. Baldwin, *Giovanni's Room,* Dial Press, N.Y., 1956.

104. H. C. McIntosh, *This Finer Shadow,* Dial Press, N.Y., 1941.

105. Niall Kent (pseudonym of William Leroy Thomas), *The Divided Path,* Greenberg, N.Y., 1949.

106. P. Roth, *Portnoy's Complaint,* Random House, New York, 1969.

107. A. Gide, *Corydon,* Farrar, Straus, & Giroux, New York, 1950.

108. J. Barr, *Quatrefoil,* Greenberg, New York, 1951.

109. U.S. Army, *Regulations,* Washington, D.C., 1941–1946.

110. L. S. London, *Sexual Deviations in the Male,* Julian Press, New York, 1937, 1957, p. 47.

111. J. Gerassi, *The Boys of Boise,* Macmillan, New York, 1966.

112. L. E. Ohlin and H. S. Ruth, Jr., eds., *Combating Crime,* the complete issue of *Ann. Am. Acad. Political and Social Sci.,* 374 (Nov. 1967).

113. H. S. Ruth, "Why Organized Crime Thrives," *Ann. Am. Acad. Political and Social Sci.,* 374, 113–122 (Nov. 1967).

114. T. Arnold, *Symbols of Government,* cited in S. H. Kadish, "The Crisis of Overcriminalization," *Ann. Am. Acad. Political and Social Sci.,* 074, 160 (Nov. 1967).

115. Model Penal Code Section 207.11, Comments at III, Tentative draft No. 9, 1959 (cited in S. H. Kadish, "The Crisis of Overcriminalization," *Ann. Am. Acad. Political and Social Sci.,* **374,** 160 (Nov. 1967).

116. 370 U.S. 478 (1962).

117. *7 in a Barn,* Guild Press, Washington, D.C., 1969 (Black Knight Classics).

118. *Grecian Guild Pictorial,* Grecian Guild, Washington, D.C., 1960 (bimonthly).

119. "Media Arts, Midsummer Madness Sale" (illustrated brochure), Media Arts Co., New York, 1969.

120. Committee on Adolescence, Group for the Advancement of Psychiatry, *Normal Adolescence,* Charles Scribner's Sons, New York, 1968, pp. 70–72.

121. M. H. Russel, *Male Sexual Anatomy,* Briton Books, New York, 1967, pp. 71–75.

122. *Rugged,* No. 1, 1967, p. 3.

123. Anonymous, "Why Obscenity," in *Rugged,* No. 4, 1967, pp. 9–14.

124. R. M. Lindner, *Rebel Without a Cause,* Grune & Stratton, New York, 1944.

125. J. Rechy, *City of Night,* Grove Press, New York, 1963.

126. J. Rechy, *Numbers,* Grove Press, New York, 1967, pp. 248–249.

127. J. X. Williams, *Born to be Gay,* Corinth Publications, San Diego, Calif., 1966, pp. 158–168.

128. J. Donne, "The Holy Sonnets," I, lines 1–2.

129. Franklin Books Program, *Ann. Rept.,* New York, 1954–.

130. Collector's Editions Advertising Brochure of publications, Collector's Editions, Los Angeles, 1969.

131. E. H. Erikson, *Identity, Youth and Crisis,* W. W. Norton, New York, 1968.

132. L. A. Fiedler, *Love and Death in the American Novel,* rev. ed., Stein & Day, New York, 1966.

133. S. Marcus, *The Other Victorians,* Basic Books, New York, 1964–1966.

134. V. Leduc, *Therese and Isabelle.*

135. S. Freud, "Beyond the Pleasure Principle," in *Complete Psychological Works of Sigmund Freud,* standard ed., V:18, Hogarth Press, London, 1962.

136. C. Corley, *The Black Angel,* Publishers Export Co., San Diego, Calif., 1968.

137. G. Vidal, *Myra Breckinridge,* edition varies, 1968.

138. J. Updike, *Couples,* Random House–Knopf, 1968.

139. J. Harvey, *Pornography for Fun,* EDKA Books, Los Angeles, Calif., 1967.

140. D. Pearson and J. Anderson, *The Case Against Congress,* Simon & Schuster, New York, 1968.

141. *Pittsburgh Post Gazette,* December 1968, *passim.*

JAY E. DAILY

CENTER FOR APPLIED LINGUISTICS

The Center for Applied Linguistics (1717 Massachusetts Avenue, N.W., Washington, D.C. 20036) is an independent, nonprofit institution concerned with language and linguistics. Its principal aims are: (1) to apply the results of linguistic research to practical language problems in the areas of teaching English to speakers of other languages, teaching standard English to speakers of nonstandard varieties, and teaching foreign languages in the United States; (2) to encourage the inclusion of linguistic studies in the school curricula; (3) to collect and disseminate linguistic information through bibliographies, state-of-the-art papers and surveys, and to investigate linguistic documentation; (4) to promote interdisciplinary cooperation and understanding between linguistics and other disciplines interested in language; and (5) to further linguistic studies in general.

The center seeks to achieve these objectives by serving as a clearinghouse for linguistic information; by acting as an informal and impartial coordinating body among government agencies, schools and universities, foundations, professional organizations, and the public; by organizing meetings and conferences both on the national and international level; by conducting surveys and issuing publications; by maintaining a reference library; by preparing educational materials; and by conducting basic research. In its aims and objectives, the center has served as a model for the establishment of similar institutions in Europe, Africa, and South America.

The center is closely associated with various professional organizations concerned with linguistics and language problems. It maintains close ties with the Modern Language Association of America, under whose auspices it was originally established. The center houses the secretariat of the Linguistic Society of America, initiated meeting handbooks for the society, and actively cooperates with the society in certain activities, such as the publication of *University Resources in the United States and Canada for the Study of Linguistics*. It also houses the secretariat of the American Dialect Society and the Committee on Linguistics in Documentation of the Fédération Internationale de Documentation. It maintains liaison with the Association of Teachers of English to Speakers of Other Languages, the American Council on the Teaching of Foreign Languages, and the National Council of Teachers of English. Cooperation with professional groups is achieved by representation on the center's Board of Trustees, by joint sponsorship of meetings and conferences, and by frequent personal contacts.

The center maintains ties with government agencies, foundations, and other institutions. It acts as host and program organizer for foreign scholars visiting the United States under various government and foundation programs, such as those organized by the State Department, the Asia Foundation, and the Institute of International Education. It collaborates in fields of mutual interest with foreign organizations, such as the British Council, the Bureau pour l'Enseignement de la Langue et de la Civilisation Françaises, the Comité International Permanent des Linguistes, the Societas Linguistica Europaea, the Association Internationale de Linguistique Appliquée, the International Committee on Computational Linguistics and other linguistic institutions, academies, and groups, especially in Eastern Europe in connection with a large-scale contrastive language study project. The center also offers consultation services to commercial firms. One of the areas of greatest activity is its information services, responding to thousands of inquiries about language problems from schools, foundations, government agencies, commercial firms, and individuals.

The center was established in 1959 as part of the Modern Language Association of America with the aid of a grant from the Ford Foundation, in response to recommendations of government agencies and professional groups. In 1964 it was incorporated in Washington, D.C., as an independent nonprofit institution. The basic operations of the center have been supported during the first decade by three Ford Foundation grants amounting to $4.7 million. Specific projects have received support from other sources, including the Carnegie Corporation, the U.S. Office of Education, the National Science Foundation, and special grants from the Ford Foundation. The total expenditure of the center during its first eleven years of operation was $10.4 million. The annual operating budget is about $1.6 million; the number of full-time employees is about eighty. Some of the activities of the center are carried out by committees and by scholars specially commissioned to carry out work.

The center operates under a 20-member Board of Trustees, representing the profession and the public at large. It is headed by a Director, who serves as President of the corporation, and is administered by the Office of the Director and the Office of the Controller. The activities of the center fall in the following areas: programs in languages, language pedagogy, linguistic documentation, and general linguistics. These activities are complemented by publications and a library.

Programs in Languages

The center's involvement in language programs includes the field of English for speakers of other languages and foreign languages. In the area of English for speakers of other languages, the center maintains close liaison with a number of national and international institutions, government agencies, and state and city educational systems. It serves as secretariat to the National Advisory Council on the Teaching of English as a Foreign Language, which, as an informal body of recognized leaders in this field, acts in an advisory capacity to government agencies and other interested institutions. In conjunction with the English-Teaching Information Centre of the British Council and the Bureau pour l'Enseignement de la Langue et de la Civilisation Françaises, it sponsors an annual International Conference on Second Language Problems, which is mainly concerned with problems of second language learning, especially English and French, in the developing countries. The center maintains files on educational systems and the position and teaching of English in over 120 foreign countries and on areas of the United States with problems of non-English speaking minorities. It offers free consultation and information and coordination services to schools, institutions, and individuals. It has conducted a broad study on the problems of English language teaching in India and a similar study on the teaching of English to American Indians. It has produced a large-scale, three-volume bibliography, various specialized bibliographies, a variety of reports, and a newsletter for teachers in American Indian schools.

In the area of foreign languages the center is concerned with the teaching of languages not commonly taught in the United States, mainly those of Asia and Africa. It maintains extensive language files with information on the geographic, political, and sociolinguistic background of approximately 400 languages. It conducts surveys of available teaching and reference materials and of institutional and manpower resources. It undertakes course development projects, with related activities in descriptive linguistics and dialectology. A major effort was spent in providing teaching materials for a dozen African languages. Following an earlier center project for contrastive analyses comparing English with the five major languages—French, German, Italian, Russian, and Spanish—the center is currently planning studies contrasting English with certain East European and African languages. The East European language projects aim at contrasting English with a number of languages in that area—Serbo-Croatian, Romanian, Czech, Polish, and Hungarian—and involve a large-scale cooperation between East European and American scholars. The center has participated in the establishment, coordination, and evaluation of language training programs for both the government and private industry. It has administered Ford Foundation grants for the Inter-American Program for Linguistics and Language Teaching and for the Advisory Committee for the Survey of Language Use and Language Teaching in Eastern Africa.

Language Pedagogy

The center is concerned with the exploration of the application of linguistics to problems of American education and the promotion of better communication among scholars, teachers, and the general public. It is interested in both the theoretical and the practical aspects of linguistically oriented methods of language teaching and learning and is actively collaborating with various school systems in the United States. The center has commissioned current awareness projects of relevance to schools, e.g., on reading, and is investigating means to introduce a linguistic component into suitable schools subjects. One major task is the investigation of the use of language in actual classroom situations between teacher and pupils. A significant practical area of concern is the role of language in industrial employment. The center has organized national conferences to clarify pedagogical issues and is involved in the exploration of the world-wide problems of literacy. It served as secretariat for the Interdisciplinary Committee on Reading Problems.

The activities in the area of language pedagogy also involve sociolinguistic research, concerned with the social implications of the use of language, especially of the varieties of English in urban areas. Research is carried out on language variation among social groups, on standard language in relation to nonstandard varieties, and on attitudes toward the use of language by speakers of all social levels. The center is particularly interested in the nonstandard English of the urban disadvantaged and is preparing teaching materials for elementary and secondary schools, as well as participating in teacher training to provide the necessary skills for dealing with nonstandard speech. The teaching materials produced have been tested extensively in the Washington, D.C., school system. The center cosponsors the Clearinghouse Committee on Social Dialect Studies, which deals with the problem of social dialect research on a national level.

The psycholinguistic aspect of the center's activities in the field of language pedagogy aims at relating the findings of experimental and educational psychology to the field of applied linguistics. The center has completed an introductory, totally self-instructional French course. The course represents an attempt to integrate the development of a program and the necessary associated presentation equipment in order to produce a teaching system that is both linguistically and psychologically sophisticated and that could serve as a prototype for the development of programs in other languages. The materials, now being made publicly available, have been evaluated extensively in various universities and other schools.

Linguistic Documentation

In the field of linguistic documentation the center is investigating the long-range problems involved in linguistic information and documentation. The center has collaborated with the Comité International Permanent des Linguistes on the annual *Linguistic Bibliography,* and is also engaged with other organizations in various bibliographical enterprises. It is also conducting research to determine how materials produced by linguists can be made available promptly and extensively. The Educational Resources Information Center (ERIC) Clearinghouse for Linguistics is part of the first nation-wide comprehensive information system designed to serve American education. This clearinghouse collects, abstracts, and reproduces documents on linguistics, the uncommonly taught languages, the teaching of English as a foreign or second language, and the teaching of English to speakers of nonstandard dialects of English. The clearinghouse also commissions state-of-the-art papers representing currently relevant topics, such as the study of nonstandard English, the teaching of sign languages, and bilingual education. The center also maintains a register of linguists as part of the National Register of Scientific and Technical Personnel of the National Science Foundation.

General Linguistics

The program in general linguistics, as a backstop for these three applied areas, covers topics of more theoretical concern. It involves areas that are not traditionally covered in academic curricula, but are important to the understanding of the nature of human language and, therefore, necessary for applied purposes. Such areas are semiotics, language and medicine, language and law, language and poetry, and linguistic maps. The center is also concerned with the collection of a complete set of illustrative and research materials on phonetics, such as films, tapes, and charts, to promote the efficiency of the teaching of speech. It is investigating the optimal format for a world language survey and has organized conferences on dictionary making and on sign languages.

Publications

The center publishes a newsletter, the *Linguistic Reporter,* issued six times a year. The contents of the *Reporter* include news stories, book notices, information on academic programs, and schedules of meetings and conferences. Often a Supplement is issued, making available a document or report which is felt to merit wider distribution at the time. From the beginning, the center has carried out certain publication activities, such as distribution of conference reports and special papers and reprinting materials of access to the neglected languages not generally available to scholars. These activities have expanded to include the publication of documents resulting both from staff research and other activities of the center, such as bibliographical studies, studies in sociolinguistics, and specialized materials related to language instruction and applied linguistics and contrastive studies. The center is publishing a Language Handbook Series in which handbooks for Bengali, Swahili, Arabic, and Mongolian have appeared. The Urban Language Series deals mainly with social dialect variation and related problems in large metropolitan areas. The volumes that have been published in this series are *The Social Stratification of English in New York City,* by William Labov; *Conversations in a Negro American Dialect,* transcribed and edited by Bengt Loman; *Field Techniques in an Urban Language Study,* by Roger W. Shuy, Walter A. Wolfram, and William K. Riley; *Teaching Black Children to Read,* edited by Joan C. Baratz and Roger W. Shuy; *A Sociolinguistic Description of Detroit Negro Speech,* by Walter A. Wolfram; and *Teaching Standard English in the Inner City,* edited by Ralph W. Fasold and Roger W. Shuy. A collection of essays on *Language and Reading* is the first in a planned set of publications on reading problems. Other publications include reference materials, such as *University Resources in the United States and Canada for the Study of Linguistics: 1969–1970; A Provisional Survey of Materials for the Study of Neglected Languages;* and *A Bibliography of American Doctoral Dissertations in Linguistics: 1900–1964.*

An experimental venture in publication is the center's fast dissemination series, where an attempt is made to make results of scholarly research available within a few weeks of its completion in typewriter-composed form. Currently the fields covered are social dialect studies, computational linguistics, contrastive linguistic studies, Uralic studies, and metrics.

Library

The library contains basic works on general linguistics, bibliographical and reference tools in the field of applied linguistics, a unique collection of materials for the teaching of English, and several special collections. It is available for consultation to anyone working in the field.

Secretariats

The center houses the secretariat of the Linguistic Society of America and of the American Dialect Society. It also houses the Committee on Linguistics in Documentation of the Fédération Internationale de Documentation, the only study committee of the FID housed in the United States. The American secretariat of the International Committee on Computational Linguistics is also located at the center. The center performs housekeeping duties for these organizations and assists them in certain publications and other activities, such as the newsletter of the American Dialect Society.

JOHN LOTZ

CENTRAL ASIA, LIBRARIES IN

Central Asia is an imprecise region that includes the western borderlands of the Peoples Republic of China, Nepal, Tibet, Sinkiang-Uigur, Mongolia, and the Russian states of Karakalpakistan, Kazakhstan, Kirgizia, Tajikistan, Turkmenistan, and Uzbekistan (1). The region as a whole is considered strategic. It is also vast, sparsely populated, and has a complex culture (2).

The library movement and the data regarding the libraries in China in general and its western borderlands will be discussed in the article *China, Libraries in the People's Republic of*.

Nepal is a small country with a population of 9 million. In addition to the American Library (in the capitol, Kathmandu) and the British Library (in Kanti Path), there is a National Library in the capitol and a Central Library in Lal Darbar. There are also three other public libraries: Bir Library (15,000 manuscripts), Nepal-Bharat Sanskritik Kendra Pustakalay (13,000 volumes), and Singh Darbar Library (3).

Nepal has one university (Tribhuvan University) in Tripureswor where the English language is mainly the language of instruction. H. M. King Mahendra Bir Vikram Shaha Deva is the Chancellor and it has a student body of 656 (3). There are also fifteen colleges; however, there are no available data about their libraries' holdings.

The six USSR states have a few scattered public libraries, among which are Firdousi State Public Library of the Tadzhik (2,000,000 volumes) and the K. Marx State Public Library at Turkmen which was founded in 1895 (2,500,000 volumes) (4). Some of the Academies of Science Libraries, however, are outstanding, and among them are the library at the Academy of Kazakh (over 3,000,000 volumes), Kirghiz (602,000 volumes), Turkmen (500,000 volumes), and Uzbek (1,500,000 volumes) (5). There is also the Library of the Kazakh Polytechnic Institute (210,000 volumes) and the following university libraries: Fundamental Library of the Kazakh, S. M. Kirov State University (750,000 volumes); Library of the Kirghiz State University (600,000 volumes); the Scientific Library of the Tadzhik, V. I. Lenin State University (300,000 volumes); and the Scientific Library of the Turkmen, A. M. Gorky State University (350,000 volumes) (6).

Except for these scattered data, up-to-date information about the other countries in Central Asia and on the general library movements, trends, and needs in the whole region was not available at the time of publication of this volume.

REFERENCES

1. E. Allworth, "Central Asian Publishing and the Rise of Nationalism," *N.Y. Public Lib. Bull.*, **69**, 493 (1965).
2. *Encyclopedia Americana*, **2**, 443 (1969).
3. *The World of Learning 1969–1970*, 20th ed., Europa, London, 1970, p. 942.
4. *Ibid.*, p. 1267.
5. *Ibid.*, p. 1268.
6. *Ibid.*, pp. 1269–1270.

WILLIAM Z. NASRI

CENTRALIZATION, DECENTRALIZATION, AND SPECIALIZATION*

The information systems developed and used to exploit recorded knowledge may be considered individually and idiosyncratically or globally, depending upon the interests and perceptions of the observer. In other words, the view of the problem of retrieving information depends upon the orientation of the individual.

An example of this phenomenon was given by Dr. Donald F. Hornig, Special Assistant to the President for Science and Technology (1):

> . . . It is only since coming to Washington that I have become aware of the magnitude and importance of the problem of scientific and technical information handling. When I was still an active researcher, I was of the firm opinion that all that was needed was a mixture of common sense with infinite speed of reading and comprehension. I had very little use for formal information retrieval systems—they contributed more paper to the stacks of unread material around me. But still, I was uneasily aware of my inability to keep up with what was going on and of the multiplication of journals and scientific meetings. My common sense solution was to

* Adapted from A. Kent, "Computers and Biomedical Information Storage and Retrieval," *J. Amer. Med. Assoc.*, **196**(11), p. 109.

organize my graduate students and postdoctoral students so that collectively they would see that we didn't miss anything important. They also furnished me with critical evaluations of new work.

I didn't know it, but I had formed an information analysis center.

When I joined the President's Science Advisory Committee in 1960, I learned that my problem was general. . . .

It is perhaps not surprising to discover such changing perceptions of the problem; not too long ago the doctoral student was expected to read essentially all the previously published literature pertaining to a given field and then to continue to read all that was currently published. It was assumed this procedure was necessary to provide assurance that the productivity of the graduate would not be blunted by lack of knowledge of significant developments.

Accordingly, when reference to previously published literature seemed important, the graduate, now professionally active, could rely on memory to specify subjects that could be used to recall relevant material from libraries or personal collections. This type of "information retrieval" tended to be based on a recall mechanism that generally permitted the rapid identification of the desired materials.

A subtle change in the recall mechanism began to take place as the volume of published literature reached the point at which the professional could no longer personally read all the primary material related to his interests. More and more, he was forced to delegate to others—for example, librarians—the task of organizing the new materials that became available for later retrieval. The professional could no longer depend on his own memory to recall subjects he had previously perused. Rather, when information relevant to a current interest or problem was desired, it became necessary to use a memory external to the individual, that is, the "collective" memory of the systems devised by indexers to whom the task of materials organization and storage had been delegated.

There was uncertainty as to how such materials were organized. This uncertainty could have been predicted; the indexers could not be expected to be able to predict every point of view from which information would be requested. Factors such as differences in orientation, background, and experience between indexers and information users inhibited the "perfect" analysis and organization of materials that would allow retrieval of relevant materials to be accomplished in a fail-safe manner.

The reaction of the indexers was to "analyze more deeply," that is, to record more and more subjects that could be used as reference points during literature searches. This reaction, together with the increasing volume of published literature, required increasing commitment of resources, both human and economic, to assure adequate analysis of all the materials that might be of subsequent interest to the professional. Furthermore, the traditional mechanisms for storing the materials and the indexes were strained. The volume of materials, stored in traditional form, required more and more space. The traditional alphabetic indexes, recorded in either printed or card form, grew to become quite unwieldy. Furthermore, although reference to individual subjects recorded in the alphabetic index could still be made effectively, another problem emerged.

As soon as the professional could no longer rely on his recall mechanism, not having read much of the material that was being processed by the indexers, the questions asked of the systems began to change in character. There was an increasing tendency to specify, rather than well-defined subjects, a number of characteristics of the subject of interest, all of which would need to be present in a source material before it was identified as relevant. This meant that when an alphabetic index was used, the entries listed under several characteristics would have to be compared in order to find out whether there were any references in common—a difficult and time-consuming procedure.

An example of such a problem appeared early in the chemical literature. If it were assumed that indexers recorded entries specifying not only a chemical compound but also the individual properties of the compound, a chemist interested in all the compounds (names unknown to him) that exhibited a particular set of properties would be required to consult the index for each of these properties, then compare them to determine common references—a tedious task, considering the number of volumes of indexes of *Chemical Abstracts* that would have to be so manipulated.

But even then the chemist could not be certain, in specifying properties, that he was using the same terminology as the author of the paper in describing the same properties or as an indexer in recording the properties for later retrieval. The traditional library technique has been to use standard terminology for all such index entries. This was appropriate as long as these standards were known by those who used the indexes. When they were not known, cross references were provided from the terms familiar to the user to those used in the index as "standard." The simpler cross references gave way to the more detailed thesaurus as more centralization in services required more users to help amortize the capital costs involved, and each user brought his own perceptions, paradigms, and vocabulary, further complicating the terminology-control problem.

Merely providing a cross reference (or providing a thesaurus type of relationship between words) does not mean the referenced items list relevant information. As a matter of fact, although the provision of more references tends to increase the probability that relevant information is not neglected during a search, there may be a tendency for more irrelevant information to be identified too. Carrying this situation to a ridiculous extreme merely to make the point, it is possible to relate each term to every other in an information-retrieval system, thus identifying all relevant information in a system but carrying with it the entire irrelevant remainder of the system.

Since no quantitative technical solution to this problem has emerged, two alternative approaches have presented themselves—decentralization and specialization.

To insure that proper attention is paid to the problems of individual users on as close to a face-to-face basis as possible, permitting adequate interpretation of a question and adequate review of systems output to screen out irrelevant information before making it available to a user, the large centralized systems have tended to concentrate on input to the system (acquisition of source material, analysis of material, terminology control, recording of results of analysis on a searchable medium, and storage of the full source document in economical and reproducible form). Then copies of the resulting material, such as indexes, abstracts, and microcopies of documents, are made available locally so that exploitation (searching, reviewing of output, and provision of copies of documents) can be handled in many local institutions.

For analysis and terminology control to match specialized user requirements in specific subject fields more closely, the development of specialized information centers has been encouraged. The cost of such specialized activities may be considerably higher than that of wholly centralized operations during input phases, but the efficiency and effectiveness of exploitation is expected to overcome these increased input costs. The approach is not an unmixed blessing, however; users who have interdisciplinary problems may require searches covering the subject matter of several such specialized information centers, cutting down on the effectiveness of the terminology-control mechanisms built into each that are not mutually compatible.

Perhaps, then, a mix of centralized, decentralized, and specialized activities is the answer. The centralized unit could be responsible for wholesale input operations and for stocking the decentralized unit that may wish to exploit the entire system locally. The specialized unit could rely on the centralized unit to identify source materials that could then be reviewed in more detail so that specialized services could be provided as required. Some institutions may then wish to have available the output of one or more of the specialized centers on a decentralized basis for local exploitation.

Allocation of resources among centralized, decentralized, and specialized activities may shift with the emergence of information networks. These networks promise data-, voice-, and image-transmission capabilities, so the need for decentralized activities may disappear if remote inquiry to primary centers (of a specialized or centralized nature) is more convenient and less costly than establishing and maintaining a local decentralized unit.

REFERENCE

1. D. F. Hornig, "Role and Importance of Information Analysis Centers," *Proc. Forum Federally Supported Inform. Analysis Centers,* Committee on Scientific and Technical Information, Federal Council for Science and Technology, PB 177051, Nov. 7–8, 1967.

ALLEN KENT

CENTRALIZED CATALOGING

Centralized cataloging may be defined as the provision of a varying degree of cataloging service to several clients from a central point. This point may be commercial or noncommercial, and it may provide service ranging from simple cataloging to complete book-and-card sets that are completely processed and ready to insert into the client's collection and catalogs. Centralized cataloging units may exist in almost any environment in which the need for cataloging and technical services exists. Centers may supply clusters of tiny public libraries or groups of gigantic research libraries. Examples of centralized cataloging and processing may be found everywhere in the world, and the prospect is for more centralization in the years ahead.

Centralized cataloging may be distinguished from cooperative cataloging in the following manner. Although centralized units aim to provide a complete job at one place and distribute the results to others, cooperative cataloging aims to complete a job by sharing the work involved, and then trading the results from one unit to another. Thus the site and organization of the effort are the distinguishing points. Centralization gathers the work in one site and organizes the work force as a unit; cooperation divides the job among several sites and seeks not to control but to co-ordinate the scattered work force. In spite of such relatively clear theoretical distinctions, in practice the two modes of approach frequently exist side by side in the same system of libraries, and the lines between them are unclear. The reason for this coexistence lies in the attempt to fit the approach to the job. In a system of small public libraries that are scattered widely, some technical services, such as ordering, may be done independently; others, cooperatively; and still others at some central point. All three methods of approach may exist side by side with good results, or simply because the members of the system are unable to gather them into a centralized operation. When possible, the choice of approach should be made according to the nature of the work itself, together with external considerations such as legal authority, communications, and financial restrictions. In cataloging, centralization appears to be the approach of choice.

There are several readily identifiable objectives to be sought when setting up a centralized cataloging unit. These are as follows:

1. Elimination of duplicative work.
2. More effective employment of catalogers in the area.
3. Higher quality of cataloging output.
4. Better service levels for member libraries.
5. Lower per-unit cataloging cost.

The first objective is the most obvious, and has been the subject of a great deal of discussion in the past. The benefits that accrue from the elimination of duplicative work are direct; ten catalogers may process ten books in a given time rather than processing the same book ten times at ten different locations in the same time period. The saving of time is reduced by the need to duplicate the output, distribute it to the client, and alter the output at the destination to fit the client's collection. Obviously, the less alteration and adaptation needed, the greater the savings that accrue from nonduplicative cataloging. If the unit cards can be produced in great numbers, the nonduplicative premise enables cataloging for others to be a commercially viable proposition. Mass production of unit cards is the basis of the activities of several commercial cataloging firms. As the nonduplicative premise is extended beyond the unit card into card sets, circulation records, and book processes, savings are extended in proportion. The extent to which nonduplication is carried comes to depend upon the degree to which the member libraries are willing to standardize their cataloging formats and collection control procedures.

The second objective, more effective use of catalogers, closely follows the first. As books are handled in a nonduplicate manner, so the catalogers handle the books in the same way, freeing them both to process more books and to process books with a greater degree of precision. With the centralization of catalogers come several personnel advantages. The specialist cataloger has more scope for his or her activities, and the central organization may be able to afford more specialist catalogers. In this manner, scarce specialities and competencies may be provided by a system where an individual member is either unable to afford specialists, has too little scope for them, or, regardless of monetary considerations, is simply unable to obtain them. Although independent libraries may have to forego specialist treatment of certain resources, the system can provide that treatment by amalgamating the resources needing it into a mass large enough to justify the services of the specialist. This consideration applies equally to the services of bibliographers and specialist buyers and collections experts. Aside from the more esoteric types of librarian, general line catalogers can be greatly aided by the extensive and efficient use of clerical and technically trained personnel in all the supporting roles that culminate with the finished catalog card. In a large processing center, the searching and verification process can be organized and subdivided, with training of the clericals involved carried to greater lengths because of the ability of the large unit to assign staff exclusively to one phase of an operation. With better training and careful organization, the clerical achieves a competence usually expected only of experienced professional staff. Another consideration of personnel in a large unit is the ability of the unit to cut nonprofessional use of professional personnel to a bare minimum. When the operation is large, assembly-line procedures can be set up, with clericals performing the great bulk of the descriptive cataloging work and professionals providing supervisory talents and subject heading and classification work. In many large centers, subject cataloging may be assigned to technical assistants as well, with the professionals reserved for the specialist cataloging, resolution of cataloging problems, and on-the-line management of large numbers of clericals. Inherent in the more efficient utilization of personnel is the ability of the center to institute careful preparation and orientation of personnel of all types and grades, and to engage in an extensive production of style, procedure, and format manuals for all phases of the work.

Higher quality of output, like greater efficiency of personnel utilization, is not guaranteed by simple size alone. It is a possibility realized only by skillful management and rational planning. Management can ensure quality by assigning personnel where they are most suited to work, carefully training them, providing them with the kind of resources they need to do the job properly such as manuals and relevant reference tools in adequate quantities, and then setting up rational and effective quality-control procedures. Planning is essential because foresight is needed to set up a quality-control system that will do its job without degenerating into a slough of mutual distrust of everybody's work and an exhaustive checking of every detail by several people. Aside from the organizational and management considerations, quality also depends upon the caliber of personnel hired and the ground rules under which they do their cataloging. A larger unit can make itself more attractive to the recent graduate and the excellent experienced professional than can any of the member libraries that it serves. Good quality of work depends as well on cooperation by the members. A standard format must be agreed upon, as each customized feature required adds another chance for error as well as another increment of expenditure. As customizing features multiply into a bewildering array, the chance for error or uncertain workmanship skyrockets, and very careful control is needed to maintain a high-quality output with a low percentage of rejected or repeated work.

Better service for member libraries, the fourth goal, is of central importance to those systems composed of small-town or semirural libraries. To small libraries, a central processing unit can mean a quantum jump in service to their readers, the difference between the minimal and the quietly excellent. For them, the problem of standardization is vastly outweighed by the benefits to be gotten by affiliation with a system. A typical example of the quantum jump is the Seven Rivers Library System, with headquarters in Iowa City, Iowa. Through a scheme of centralized technical services and a rotating collection circulated from the processing center, the resources of the member libraries are increased tremendously, up to ten times the number of books as are purchased with a member's funds in the year. This tenfold increase is achieved by a complete centralization of the technical service function, coupled with a distribution and rotation system for a central collection of books. As of 1967, each member contributed a certain percentage of its budget to the central unit, then depleted this amount by ordering whatever books it chose during the year. A consultant was provided to aid in the choice and in other aspects of the member's operation. The center obtained the ordered books, provided total processing for them, and shipped them to the member. Books thus entering the system would rotate at regular intervals, being joined by a large number of area-wide purchases made with federal funds. In this manner the client of any one of the member libraries would be exposed to a selection four times the size of that available in his library before the system's establishment. The process of centralized cataloging, together with other systemization, has thus extended the scope and quality of library service in America to population groups that ordinarily could never hope to obtain anything resembling good libraries.

Lower cost per capita in cataloging is the sum of the careful planning and supervision that made possible the benefits mentioned above. It should be noted that overall cost may seldom decline, because the central unit is used to extend and improve library service rather than simply to make cheaper that service which already exists, with no thought to improvement. Nevertheless, in a well-planned system, the rising overall cost, when divided by the volumes processed, should not produce figures per capita that are more expensive than those which earlier obtained. This per-capita cost saving can be negated by the same factors that negate other objectives, namely the failure to adequately standardize the job at hand. When custom cataloging is the end result of centralization, the saving will disappear quickly. If, for example, a system contains both the Dewey Decimal and the Library of Congress classifications, books common to several member libraries will be classified twice. If in addition book number systems differ and depth of classification varies, the resultant extra labors will eat up any savings centralization can secure. To achieve true system efficiency and reap maximum per-capita savings, extensive if not total standardization is necessary. Before the system is established planning and study must determine whether the contemplated central unit stands any real chance of success, or will simply be mired down in a welter of divergent detail and unnecessary custom jobs.

In order to achieve the objectives discussed above, planning is needed in a far greater depth than called for in the establishment of a single library. Planning for centralization may include several steps:

1. Identification of system members and their needs.
2. Identification of degree of common resources and objectives.
3. Determination of feasibility of the proposed central unit.
4. Coordination of standardization between members.
5. Planning of the center.

Before any center is actually planned, prospective members should be known and their needs and problems studied, so that the center when set up will address itself to those needs. Identification of commonality between members goes hand in hand with a feasibility study; if the members have little in common and are unwilling to reconcile any divergent features, a center has little hope of achieving its objectives. When commonality has been determined, coordination between members should take place in order to insure that the center will have a standard base upon which to work toward achieving the savings that centralization offers. Along with the setting up of common standards goes the actual planning of the center, with every detail of its activities carefully studied and matched with the practices of all the members. Only when all the previous work has been done can the construction or organization of the center actually proceed.

The outlook for centralized cataloging is bright. The Library of Congress, with its MARC program, is moving rapidly toward the automated provision of cataloging on a real-time basis. Systems of centralized cataloging, through Library of Congress activities, become voluntary subsystems of an emerging national centralized cataloging unit. The layering of systems will increase until the whole nation has access to cataloging of the highest possible quality, of the widest possible variety, in the shortest possible time. Parallel developments are taking place in other countries and regions of the world. Still, the old problem remains not whether centralization is possible, but what use will be made of it. If all libraries are to secure the benefits of national and international centralization they must be willing to give up a bit of individuality—not where it counts, in the collection, but where it is expendable, in cataloging. Centralization and standardization are but sides of the same coin; the library that rejects the one side cannot spend the other.

GEORGE M. SINKANKAS

CENTRE NATIONAL DE LA RECHERCHE SCIENTIFIQUE (CNRS)

Shortly after the creation of the National Center for Scientific Research (CNRS) in 1939, the decision was made to start a Center of Documentation within its organization.

The aim of the Center of Documentation of CNRS is to provide research workers with information. It first dealt mainly with professors and CNRS Laboratories; later it came to deal with greater ranges of activities throughout France and abroad.

From the beginning, the publication of a bibliographical bulletin entitled *Bulletin Analytique* has been the main activity of the Center of Documentation; this bulletin includes 1200 bibliographical references per year.

During World War II, when France had nearly no communications with the whole world, it was still possible to keep publishing the *Bulletin Analytique,* thus giving French research workers their only opportunity to be kept informed on worldly scientific development. Because to this semiclandestine activity, these research workers were able to deal with the postwar problems without any gap in their information.

Together with the *Bulletin Analytique* a service for documentary reproduction was established (microfilms and photographic reproductions). During the year 1940, 1000 pages were microfilmed, and in 1942 the figures reached 182,000 pages (microfilms) and 8000 pages (normal size). From the first day every effort has been made in order to secure the best quality to these reproductions, all of them initially being silver images obtained through the conventional wet process.

By that time, owing to its increasing volume, it became necessary to divide the *Bulletin Analytique* into two sections, one dealing with pure and applied science and the other devoted to biological, medical, and agricultural fields.

Later it became a descriptive bulletin in which abstracts were shortened (limited to 50 words), as it had been found that even an excellent abstract could never be used in place of the genuine document. Thus the only aim of each abstract was to make possible the correct ordering of photostats and microfilms, as microfilms had become current at CNRS. Microfilm readers became available, at that time, at reasonable prices.

Whenever documents have to be carefully read, microfilms do not have the same efficiency as photocopies, but they are a valuable and cheap compromise between the abstract and the full-sized reproduction, which was very seldom ordered at that time.

In 1960 it became necessary to divide the first and the second part of the *Bulletin Signaletique* into seventeen sections, to which were added six others dealing with Human Sciences. It now includes 500,000 references per year.

Afterward came electrostatic reproduction; it resulted in lower costs for reproductions and much quicker work. The number of orders very quickly increased and reached 103,500 articles in 1960 and 202,000 articles in 1964.

This process, however, was not quite satisfactory for reproducing halftones, so two standards were established for users interested or not in perfect reproductions.

Later, and with the help of tapes and computers, the Center was able to print and to store information, thus making possible retrospective bibliographical search.

Since 1964 effort has been directed toward the field of metallurgy. By now a five-years stock is available, recorded on tapes.

The different kinds of users and the different areas of use can be seen from Table 1.

TABLE 1

	France		
	Professors and CNRS Laboratories, per cent	Others (especially private industry), per cent	Foreign countries, per cent
Bulletin Signaletique	25	25	50
Documentary reproduction	55	30	15
Translations	15	85	Unimportant

Aside from the Center of Documentation, CNRS has undertaken to coordinate the activities of the different specialized Centers of Documentation:

1. Normalization of vocabularies and linguistic structurations (in connection with The International French Language Council).

2. Unification (sufficient to realize compatibility) of the designation of various documentary and reprographic equipment (files, sizes, microfilms, etc.) (in connection with France's Association for Normalization, or AFNOR).

3. Research for software, allowing translation from one system to another.

4. For easier exchange with foreign documentation centers, working out of multilingual thesauri (in connection with other specialized documentation centers).

During the years 1967 and 1968 the activities of the CNRS grew rapidly. In particular, the first nine months of 1968 showed a considerable increase over the corresponding period of 1967 (despite the troublesome events in France of May and June).

Several improvements have been undertaken and were in effect in 1969. These improvements consist of:

1. Breaking up into subsections the most voluminous subdivision of the *Bulletin Signaletique* for the purpose of rendering them easier to handle; evolution of the subdivision "Applied Chemistry" and "Technology" into interdisciplinary and technical sections produced with the assistance of investigators from the public and private sectors of the economy.

2. Collection, microfilming, and distribution of literature whose dissemination is

ordinarily very small, namely, doctoral dissertations, reports of the Delegation à la Recherche, and (with the assistance of CEA), "Atomic Reports."

3. Establishment, with the assistance of various professional organizations, of specialized bibliographic services in certain key areas, namely, cardiology (since January 1, 1968) and transplantation of organs (since January 1969).

4. Construction of the monthly subject indexes (in 1969 half of the sections of the *Bulletin Signaletique* were covered by this index).

5. Systematic employment after January 1, 1969, of descriptors in the bulletins of several sections, and keypunching of key terms and corresponding bibliographical indexes. The latter operation began in 1969 and is performed without an increase in funding; this is the consequence of the improvement of CNRS's printing techniques (the assistance of the National Printing Office is gratefully acknowledged). Keypunching operation will permit automatic searching of the bibliography.

6. Construction of French-language thesauri for all disciplines for which lists of descriptors have been established. These thesauri will be published and distributed to the subscribers of all sections of *Bulletin Signaletique*.

7. Investigation of the problem of languages (lexical correspondences), with the goal of establishing intercommunication with great foreign centers of documentation.

In order to resolve the problem of subscription renewal to the numerous periodicals in its collection, CNRS has investigated keypunching of complete records of periodicals (e.g., acronyms, publishers, and frequency of publication). A file of punch cards will enable CNRS to keep its stock of periodicals up-to-date, and a duplicate of the punch card will accompany each periodical during its passage through the editorial route. These "accompanying cards" will replace cards that at present are handwritten.

The main objectives concern, above all, the *Bulletin Signaletique* and bibliographical searches. In the near future—probably 1971—the *Bulletin* will include about forty sections: thirty monthly ones dealing with pure, applied, and biological sciences, and ten quarterly ones dealing with Human Science. Every issue will include subject and author indexes. In addition, annual cumulative indexes (subjects and authors) will be issued. All key words and bibliographical references will be recorded on tapes.

Specialized services by "group profiles" for users working on the same subject will expand very soon. This publication will not be issued as a bulletin but most likely as separate cards (105/150 mm), each of them including a reference and a summary.

Although few bibliographical retrospective searches have been ordered to date, CNRS plans to supply this kind of information service as needs develop.

The help of an encyclopedic center cannot be denied when approaching bibliographical problems and documentary "group profiles," as the same primary material (basic documents and processes) may be used several times, and increasing overlapping would cause highly specialized documentation centers to duplicate their work.

On the other hand, only highly specialized centers are likely to be efficient when specific information is required. Also, these centers will be the only ones in a position to advise users on the most pertinent enquiries to be put into automated systems. Indeed, it is planned to sell duplicates of tapes to specialized centers equipped with computers.

J. H. D'OLIER

CENTRE NATIONAL DE DOCUMENTATION SCIENTIFIQUE ET TECHNIQUE

History, Scope, and Functions

Many Belgian libraries, both public and academic, are doing a great deal to aid the research effort of science and industry. These libraries are not organized for this purpose, however; they have other basic aims to fulfill. Taking into consideration this state of affairs, the Centre National de Documentation Scientifique et Technique (National Center for Scientific and Technical Documentation) was founded in Brussels in 1964 on the initiative of Herman Liebaers and August Cockx, head librarian and librarian, respectively, at the Bibliothèque Royale de Belgique (Royal Library of Belgium).

The Centre National de Documentation Scientifique et Technique (CNDST) is an autonomous body, although from its inception it was fortunate to have a close association with the Royal Library of Belgium, where it is housed in a new and vast functional building, endowed with all the latest in modern techniques. The center also benefits from the exhaustive collections of primary and secondary publications of the Royal Library (3,000,000 books; 20,000 periodicals; and a reference library comprising more than 50,000 titles).

The CNDST is a nonprofit organization; it is financed by state grants. These come from the Ministry of Education and Culture, under whose jurisdiction the Royal Library functions.

A scientific advisory committee, composed of representatives from government, industry, and the academic world, co-determines the policy of the CNDST. The aim of the center is to document scientists in all fields of fundamental and applied sciences and to promote documentation in industry, research, and science. In the interests of good public relations the CNDST answers queries from students, but it restricts the time and effort involved.

The information scientists of the CNDST are responsible for searches in and procurement of information material, for compiling references and abstracts, and for maintaining liaison with individuals and groups that either supply or need these services.

People are encouraged to submit inquiries orally or in writing. A questionnaire form is used for this purpose. The form has ample space for defining the inquiry as well as for the information staff to add a record of how it is answered, so that it can be systematically filed later, and a useful background of material for answering further inquiries built up.

The queries generally fall into five basic classes: exact reproduction (such as a text or a diagram; equal to ± 2000 pages a day); "fill-in-the-blank" (an address, a date, a physical constant); descriptive information (a biography, a definition, a method); "information about" (how something works); and lists of references. According to the 1968 annual report, the CNDST compiled 300 major bibliographies and reference lists that year. These do not include the many hundreds of requests and telephone queries that could be answered immediately from general knowledge.

An inquiry often needs elucidation. Who is the inquirer? What does he want? How far back in time should the search go? How soon is the information needed? Also, duplicate questions are frequently received, particularly when some new development or technique has been given publicity in the press. These recurring queries may often be answered by referring back in the files to previous answers and bringing them up to date where necessary.

One of the most intractable problems of documentation is how to get information to small and medium-sized industrial firms to keep them current on scientific and technological information that may be of importance to their operation. This, in fact, is one of the primary tasks of the CNDST.

When a published printed document cannot be purchased, the CNDST can usually locate a library copy and supply a photocopy or microfilm of the original. The center charges for photocopying and microfilming services, although, since it is a nonprofit operation, all information and services supplied are free.

Activities

Besides the tasks mentioned above, the CNDST has a number of particular activities, some of which are described in the following.

UNION CATALOG

A *Belgian and Luxemburg Union Catalog of Foreign Periodicals Currently Being Published* was established in 1965 (2 vols., 1982 pp.); a supplement is in preparation. This catalog gives an exact listing of the serial and periodical holdings of 400 participating libraries. The cooperation of numerous industrial libraries is particularly valuable here. Coverage of the catalog is also considerably enlarged by the entries of periodicals in the libraries of government offices, making it a kind of documentation center for the ministries and offices of government. An estimated 42,000 periodicals are listed in the first two volumes. The Union Catalog Section also assumes a special responsibility for knowing about new appearances and disappearances among scientific journals.

CALENDAR OF INTERNATIONAL MEETINGS

It is estimated that there are about 3000 international conferences in the fields covered by the center annually. Advance knowledge of these meetings, which is important if appropriate steps are to be taken to acquire the proceedings, can be obtained from a CNDST computerized listing, comprising several indexes. During 1968, the center tested a selective dissemination system. This will be designed to provide all the needed information on scientific meetings to users.

PERMANENT BIBLIOGRAPHY OF BELGIAN SCIENTIFIC PUBLICATIONS

This listing of nonbook material, which is not for sale, is fully mechanized. The source documents are twofold: relevant Belgian journals and articles published abroad by Belgian authors. The procedure is as follows: About ten IBM cards are punched for each article. When 500 articles are assembled, the punched cards are fed into an IBM 360/40 computer, which prints the bibliography and author, subject, organization, and periodicals indexes. The indexes are cumulative.

DIRECTORY OF BELGIAN RESEARCH CENTERS WITH LIBRARIES

To propagate the idea of documentation and to coordinate agencies so engaged throughout the country, the Center compiled its *Inventaire des centres belges de recherches disposant d'une bibliothèque ou d'un service de documentation* (Directory of Belgian Research Centers Having at Their Disposal a Library or Documentation Center). This 330-page directory, which was published in 1967, lists about 1230 of these organizations. It has four parts: the directory itself, listing the organizations by city, and describing them; an index of cited persons; an organizations index; and a bilingual subject index in French and Dutch. The first edition of the directory is out of print. A second edition, which is being revised and augmented, is expected to be published toward the end of 1970.

TRANSLATIONS DEPARTMENT

There is a Centre Belge de Traductions (Belgian Translations Center) that provides copies of available translations and gives information on translations existing elsewhere. It also supplies written and oral translations from Russian into French, and keeps a register of qualified scientific and technical translators.

EDUCATIONAL AND CONSULTING DEPARTMENT

The CNDST's work comprises a vast number of lectures, individual visits and publications on behalf of laboratories, industrial concerns, and others. The center advises on the establishment or organization of special libraries and documentation services. It accepts speaking engagements to describe the work and aims of its services and invokes discussion on ways and means of improving its efficiency.

Although the CNDST does not define professional qualifications or provide extensive training, it does organize short introductory documentation courses for scientists and special librarians. To facilitate the teaching of these courses two syllabuses have been prepared, *Mechanical and Electronic Devices in the Library* (in Dutch, 1968, 122 pp.), and *Information Storage and Retrieval. The Coordinate Indexing Principle. Terminal Digit and Feature Card Systems* (in English, 1968, 49 pp.). The latter monograph comprises a partially annotated bibliography of 300 references. Other monographs are planned.

REFERRAL AND RESEARCH

One of the CNDST's chief functions as a coordinating center for information services is to put an inquirer in touch with the best source of the specific piece of information he happens to be seeking. Very often, this service brings together scientists who are working in the same field. This kind of work necessitates contacts with all sources of information throughout the world. The CNDST works closely with the following organizations: Centre National de la Recherche Scientifique; European Launching Development Organization; European Space Research Association; European Translations Center; Food and Agricultural Organization; International Council of Scientific Unions; International Organization for Standardization; North Atlantic Treaty Organization—Advisory Group for Aeronautical Research and Development; National Lending Library for Science and Technology; Organization for Economic Co-operation and Development; United Nations Educational, Scientific and Cultural Organization; and Vsesoyuznyí Institut Nauchnoí i Tekhnicheskoí Informatsíí Akademíí (All-Union Institute of Scientific and Technical Information, Academy of Sciences U.S.S.R.).

A centralized agency responsible for developing a national information system should conduct research in user needs, including experimentation with new methods for better serving user needs as an important part of its research program. Lack of knowledge about potential audiences and their needs seriously handicaps the efforts at serving the information needs of science, research, and industry.

The first user needs study in the medical field was carried out in 1967. The results were published in *Documentation Scientifique: Les besoins du corps médical belge. Résultats d'une enquête menée au Centre National de Documentation Scientifique et Technique* (1967, 92 pp.). The report is out of print; however, it is still obtainable in microfilm. Mail questionnaires provided most of the data. A second project on scientific information flow, this time in the field of chemistry, is being carried out.

Automation

The CNDST is engaged in research into documentation problems, including automation of its own services, as well as those of the Royal Library. The processes for which mechanization routines are or will be used are the catalog (cards, printed catalogs, shelf lists, alphabetic subject index to the classified catalog, accession lists), periodicals (claims, binding lists), Union lists, circulation, and acquisitions (orders, gifts, and exchanges).

At first, a step-by-step mechanization with retention of manual systems will be carried out. However, the staff of the CNDST believes that ultimately the entire card catalog (several million cards) will be replaced by a mechanized store of vast capacity. Access to this store will be through interrogation consoles that are essentially viewing screens (cathode-ray display tubes) with push-button controls. These will allow for a progressive dialogue between the user and the catalog. The user can modify his index terms in light of the machine response and arrive at the number and relevance of documents needed after seeing a display of title pages or pages of the document on the screen. The system, based on a complete microfilm store, can provide him with a full-size printout of what has been chosen.

To meet the needs of the CNDST alone, about ten such units directly on-line to the computer will be needed. In full operation, such a system will make it possible for information centers all over the country to be part of a telecommunications network, whereby remote consoles could key in to the center for its stored information.

These systems are still in a developmental stage. However, processed computer tapes, obtainable from several abstracting and indexing services, such as *Chemical Abstracts, Chemical Titles, Chemical Biological Activities, Medlars, Excerpta Medica,* and *Engineering Index,* will be used in the near future. This new development will allow the center to implement a series of selective dissemination of information services.

Toward the end of 1968, an improved chemical searching system was installed, based on *Chemical Abstracts* (*C.A.*) in microform. All abstracts published in *C.A.* since 1907 have been placed on 16-mm microfilm. This film is packaged in plastic magazines for use with microfilm reader–printer equipment. Each magazine of microfilm holds approximately 30,000 abstracts. Four magazines contain all the abstracts published in an entire volume (26 issues) of *C.A.* The entire collection of more than 4,000,000 abstracts is contained in 157 magazines.

Use of the microfilmed abstracts begins with consulting the printed volume and collective indexes to *C.A.* to compile a list of abstract references. Abstracts are then read on the viewing screen. Photocopies can be made on demand.

Preliminary experiences indicate that the conversion of a library to electronic data processing usually requires a much longer period than might be expected. A conversion period of 15 to 20 years is not unreasonable.

Publicity and Staff

The members of the CNDST feel that paid advertising of a general nature does little for a documentation service, but is valuable in publicizing special meetings, courses of instruction, and so on. Press releases on the CNDST stir up a flurry of interest, which soon dies down, although the releases probably have some continuing effect. It is felt that direct-mail campaigns, personal contacts, and the word-of-mouth recommendations that follow satisfactory services rendered provide the most successful and lasting publicity.

The CNDST has a staff of 35 including specialists holding academic degrees in the sciences and information specialists. The staff is composed of one director, seventeen subject specialists, four information specialists, seven clerks, and six computer personnel. Technical personnel, including members of the printing department, photoduplication and microfilm department, and so on, is supplied by the parent organization. The professional staff keeps abreast of new developments in chosen fields by reading current literature and attending scientific meetings.

Requests for further information on the CNDST should be addressed to Centre National de Documentation Scientifique et Technique, 4 boulevard de l'Empereur, Brussels 1, Belgium. Telephone (02) 13.61.80, Telex 21157.

HERMAN DE JAEGER

CENTRO DE DOCUMENTACIÓN BIBLIOTECOLOGICA (CDB)

The Centro de Documentación Bibliotecológica (Center of Library Documentation), located in Bahía Blanca, Argentina, was founded November 23, 1962. It is dependent on the National University of the South.

The activities of the center are as follows:

> To establish and maintain a library specializing in library science.
> To investigate, and promote the study of, the problems of library science.
> To diffuse the knowledge and techniques of advanced library science, especially in three ways:
> —Editorial activity (for diffusion on a national level).
> —Teaching activity (for the benefit of librarians, especially in Patagonia and La Pampa).
> —The work of advising (assessing) (for the organization of libraries in the specified zones).

Among the books of CDB are those that formed the private library of Don Alfredo Console, acquired from this librarian. With this contribution, the bibliographical resources of CDB have been considerably enriched, and it incorporates a valuable repertoire of sources for the study of the historical development of the Argentinian bibliographical movement. CDB is the only organization in Argentina (and perhaps in Latin America) that possesses the complete collection of the *Zentralblatt für Bibliothekswesen,* from 1884 to the present. The most relevant reference works it has are the *U.S. Library of Congress Catalog of Printed Cards* (Author List, Supplement, and Book Subjects); the British Museum's *General Catalogue of Printed Books* (Readex compact edition and ten-year supplement, 1956–1960); and the *Subject Index of Modern Books* (1956–1960).

The CDB has edited, publishes, and reedits when necessary the following publications: (1) *Bibliography of Argentinian Library Science*, preliminary edition, 1963; first definitive edition, 1969 (recently published, it includes retrospective bibliography up to 1967 inclusive); second edition, in preparation will contain current Argentinian bibliography on library science). (2) *Who's Who in Argentinian Library Science:* first edition, 1965; second edition, to be published in 1970. This work gives biobibliographical references of 178 Argentinian librarians.

The director of CDB is Professor Nicolas Matijevic; the subdirector, Bachelor Atilio Peralta; the secretary, Mr. Ramon M. Minieri.

Nicolas Matijevic
(*translated by Savina A. Roxas*)

CENTRO DE INVESTIGACIONES BIBLIOTECOLOGICAS DE LA UNIVERSIDAD DE BUENOS AIRES

On July 31, 1967, the Centro de Investigaciones Bibliotecologicas (Center for Library Research of the University of Buenos Aires) was formed. This fulfilled a long-felt need for an organization in Argentina devoted to research in the field of librarianship and documentation. Before the UNESCO General Conference met in 1966, the University of Buenos Aires officials were able to interest Argentina's UNESCO delegation in the possibility of establishing such a center. The proposal was approved by the delegation and included in the program of activities for member states. Although the Bibliographic Department of the Faculty of Philosophy and Letters was responsible for the project, the center operated under the rectorate until March 1969, when it became a part of the Bibliographic Department of the Faculty of Philosophy and Letters in the University of Buenos Aires.

The Center has the following objectives:

1. To do research in the field of librarianship and documentation with the objective of collecting and coordinating resources that will serve as the basis for a national bibliographic information service.

2. To coordinate and study the bibliographic materials in the field of librarianship and documentation on the one hand and pedagogy, sociology, economics, and so on on the other in relation to national library problems.

3. To study the nature, structure, and present state of the country's library and documentation services.

4. To determine the state, organization, utilization, and coordination of bibliographic resources and to make suggestions for utilizing them more efficiently and for facilitating dissemination of information.

5. To contribute, through studies, to the formulation of a national library plan.

6. To use the results of these studies to improve the education and training of librarians and documentalists.

7. To participate in the examination, discussion, and improvement of methods and techniques for teaching bibliographic research.

8. To organize and stimulate research, especially in those areas of librarianship and documentation that directly apply to bibliographic services.

9. To coordinate its own work with that of state and private institutions interested in the same problems and to exchange information with foreign institutions working in the same areas.

The center has completed several of its projected studies on the following topics:

1. Use of a systems approach to the preparation of national library services.

2. Problems encountered in the control of masses of information because of the increased interrelationships of disciplines.

3. Teaching of librarianship in Argentina, Uruguay, Chile, and Peru.

4. Formulation of an emergency training program for assistants to enable them to do library and documentation work until fully trained people are available.

5. Training of recent university graduates to utilize the sources of bibliographic information more effectively.

6. Incorporation of the rudiments for training librarians into the secondary school.

7. Study of existing statistics on libraries and establishment of a plan for their improvement.

8. Comparison of Argentine library legislation with similar legislation in other countries.

9. Study of the possible use of computers for documentation, considering their potential and cost in Argentina.

The research plans grow constantly, incorporating new subjects of interest to Argentina. Those in the center want to accentuate teamwork with specialized groups in other fields of knowledge, so that librarians and documentalists may contribute more, without the usual limits to their work. It is hoped that educators, sociologists, and economists will also interrelate with their programs with those of libraries and documentation services and include the problems of the latter in their work and future planning.

JOSEFA E. SABOR
(*translated by Savina A. Roxas*)

CENTRO NACIONAL DE INFORMACIÓN Y DOCUMENTACIÓN (CENID)

The National Center for Information and Documentation (CENID) was created in 1963 as a permanent program of the Council of Rectors of the Chilean Universities. Following the recommendations made by Dr. Karl Heumann, CENID would act as a "referral center," establishing programs at the national level to make an inventory of the existing collections in the scientific and technical libraries of the country, beginning with the university libraries, and to create a network of services and exchange with the libraries of the country distributing, among the principal ones, microfilm reading equipment, photocopying machines, and card-duplicating machines. In addition, a printing shop (offset) and microfilming camera would be installed at the headquarters of the Council of Rectors.

To finance the acquisition of this equipment, the Council of Rectors decided to set aside $100,000 from the "Smathers Loan" which the government of the United States granted to the Council of Rectors in 1955. This amount was increased in 1966 with a grant of $15,000 from the Rockefeller Foundation. (For more information on the Council of Rectors, the National Chilean Fund for the development of scientific and technical research in the universities of the country, refer to the articles by Mr. César Fighetti in *Ciencia Interamericana* and *Libri,* listed in the Bibliography.)

During 1963–1967 CENID was run by a very small permanent staff, carrying out many of its programs through contracts assigned to librarians and technical personnel from the universities of the country.

Programs

Union List of Serials in the Chilean Libraries. A card catalog is maintained, showing the existence of titles of periodicals available in the libraries with detailed indication of the collections. In addition, this information is printed in a loose-leaf issue, allowing further corrections and additions. One hundred libraries have participated in this program, sixty-nine of which are university libraries, and the catalog covers 12,151 titles, not including humanities, arts, and literature.

Guide to Theses Approved at the Chilean Universities. The main Faculties and University Schools publish lists of the theses approved, but a national publication which included them all was lacking. CENID has published the volumes corresponding to 1962 (science and technology) and 1963 (including humanities); the volume 1964–1965 is now printing. The theses appeared arranged by Universities, Faculties, and Schools, with a short abstract whenever it has been possible to get it. Each volume includes an index of authors and words, based on the main words of the title. It is planned that this system, in which the words are selected according to their contents and manually, will finally become a thesaurus for the mechanical preparation of indexes.

Bio-Bibliographical Guide to the Faculties Personnel, Teaching Staff, and Researchers in the Chilean Universities. Forms were distributed to collect the information necessary to prepare the inventory of human resources (high-level) of the country, and also to compile the present scientific and technical bibliography of Chile. Three volumes have been published, including about 2,000 bits of data (approximately 10% of the total amount, as the number of scientists and technicians working at the universities is estimated as 20,000).

Subject Headings for Engineering Libraries. In its series *Publicaciones Técnicas,* CENID included a work prepared by two Chilean librarians, Mrs. Blanca Matas and Anne Marie Hoffa, as there was a lack of a good list of subject headings in Spanish for engineering.

Bibliography of Natural Resources 1945–1965. By request of the Natural Resources Research Institute, CENID prepared a bibliography, with complementary indexes of geographical places, subject matter titles of periodicals, mining enterprises, authors, etc.

The period 1963–1965 was devoted to strengthening CENID and its relation with the libraries and research centers of the country and abroad. During the period 1965–1968, CENID assumed the responsibility of holding the Presidency and Secretariat of the Latin-American Commission of the International Federation for Documentation (FID/CLA); its President, the Director of CENID, was Mr. Luciano Cabalá, and its Secretary, the Assistant Director of CENID, was Mrs. Betty Johnson deVodanovic. At the Latin-American level CENID is in charge of publishing the following: *Guide to Reprographic Services in Latin America* and *Guide to Special Libraries and Documentation Centres in Latin America.*

According to Dr. Karl Heumann's recommendations, the work of CENID should be evaluated and assessed in 1968 (after five years of work as a pilot project). Last year a Commission of the National Bureau of Planning (ODEPLAN) was created to study the real needs for information requirements in all sectors of the country. The Commission concluded that CENID should be transferred to an organization that could ensure administrative stability and increased financial support to allow for its expansion. Starting on March 1, 1969, CENID will be transferred to the National Commission for Scientific and Technological Research, an organization created by official law in 1967. It should be pointed out that in 1963, the year in which CENID was created, neither the National Bureau of Planning nor the National Commission for Scientific and Technological Research existed in the country. An ample plan for the processing and provision of information is foreseen, which has been unanimously judged as necessary to all interested areas and persons in the country.

BIBLIOGRAPHY

Bentjerodt, Camila, "Catálogos Colectivos Nacionales de publicaciones periódicas," in *Cuartas Jornadas Bibliotecarias Chilenas, la biblioteca y la comunidad,* Antofagasta, August 29 and September 3, 1966, final rept., Asociación de Bibliotecarias de Chile, Santiago, 1966, pp. 24–45.

Cabala Pavesi, Luciano, et al., *Centro Chileno de Bibliografía y Documentación,* Santiago, Chile, Jan. 1961 (10 pp.).

Comision Asesora en Documentación de Odeplan, Informe No. 1, Santiago, Chile, June 1968 (4 pp. and 6 appendices).

Fighetti, S., César, "El Consejo de Rectores de las Universidades Chilenas y el Centro Nacional de Información y Documentación," *Ciencia Interamericana,* 4(6) (1963).

Fighetti, S., Cé́onar, "The Council of Rectors of the Chilean Universities and the National Center of Information and Documentation (CENID)," *Libri,* 11(4), 337–344 (1964).

Heumann, Karl F., *A Scientific and Technical Information Center for Chile.* Santiago, Chile, July 1961 (14 pp.).

Igelsrud, Iver, *Chilean National Center for Information and Documentation.* Santiago, Chile, June 1963 (14 pp.).

Johnson de Vodanović, Betty, "El Centro Nacional de Información y Documentación (CENID) programa del Consejo de Rectores," *Revista Consejo de Rectores Universidades Chilenas,* 2(3), 25–29 (1967).

Johnson de Vodanović, Betty, *Short Report on a New National Network of Documentation and Information in Chile,* International Federation for Documentation, Committee for Developing Countries (FID/DC), Budapest, Hungary, July 1968, Doc. 16/1968/FID/DC (5 pp.).

Pratt, Lorraine, *A Plan for Establishing a Central Technical Library Service in Chile* (SRI Project No. I-2305), Santiago, Chile, June 1958 (38 pp.).

Schleuter, R. A., *Report to CENID,* Santiago, Chile, Jan. 1965 (8 pp.).

Schleuter, R. A., *Documentation and Librarianship in Chile,* TA Rept. No. 229, International Atomic Energy Agency, Nov. 1965 (19 pp.).

BETTY JOHNSON DE VODANOVIĆ

CERTIFICATION OF LIBRARIANS

Certification is an instrument that attests a person is qualified to practice a profession. Certification is distinguished from occupational or professional licensing in that the latter permits only licensed persons to practice under the law, whereas in the case of certification, anyone may practice but theoretically only certified persons are entitled to use the professional title that is regulated by the certification requirements.

The purpose of certification of librarians is to assure the consumer of the services that a standard for the protection of the users of libraries is being preserved. This is premised on the fact that the library user is not able to distinguish between qualified and unqualified persons.

The practice of certification, which permits anyone to function in a library, does have the obligation of informing the library user which of the library staff have fulfilled the requirements of certification and are therefore presumably able to perform their functions and render their services in a manner that reflects the standards adopted by a unit of government, an association or professional body, or both.

Several characteristics of certification may be observed: (1) the requests that go to a governmental or legislative body for certification of personnel do not come from the users of libraries but rather from the practitioners acting in their association; (2) such requests are usually characterized by exemptions (known as grandfather clauses) for those already functioning as librarians; and (3) very frequently the examining boards for those who wish to enter the profession are composed of librarians who are already certified.

Properly administered, certification may be a positive force for educational and professional advancement as well as a protective device. It may be used not only to advance the qualifications of beginning librarians but also to improve the qualifications of librarians in service. It also may be used as a source of information on which a continuous inventory of librarians and their training is based and thus assist in maintaining a balance between supply and demand.

Certification of librarians is perhaps best exemplified by comparing the procedures used in Great Britain and Northern Ireland and in the United States and Canada. In Great Britain, the Library Association, with powers derived from its Royal Charter in 1898, provides for the examination and registration of qualified librarians and maintains a Registry of Chartered Librarians.

In the United States, librarians were also concerned with certification at a period of time that closely parallels the history of the Library Association in Great Britain. The American Library Association was started when the strong New York Library Association was also being started. Both agencies were concerned with library training and the qualifications of the library practitioners, but the American Library Association in 1923 started a serious classification of librarians with subsequent contributions on the duties of librarians, while the New York Library Association and the library associations of the several states promulgated certification requirements for public librarians and for public-school librarians.

While there has never been a national library certification under the American pattern through the American Library Association, there has been a kind of national certification by professional groups, such as the certification requirements of the Medical Library Association. Primarily, the role of certification for public and public-school librarians in the United States has passed to the state governments, frequently in the state departments of education with the professional state associations performing advisory functions.

A second point of divergence between the two systems offered as examples concerns the educational level of the person seeking certification.

The examination system of the Library Association in Great Britain may start with a Qualifying Examination for trainees who enter library work. This is a prerequisite for Part I of the professional examination in addition to the possession of the General Certificate of Education or its equivalent. Graduates of British Universities are exempted from this examination.

Part II of the professional examination is open to those who have passed Part I and is not required for those who hold the University of London Diploma in Librarianship. In addition to examinations in administration and library techniques, this examination offers papers in the specialist and technical fields of librarianship. Librarians who have passed this examination and who have completed three years of successful experience in libraries are eligible for the Associate in the Library Association—the first of the two categories of Chartered Librarians.

The highest category of professional librarian is that of the Fellow (FLA), which requires that a person have served as a Chartered Librarian for at least five years. Fellows are elected upon the acceptance of a thesis or scholarly work.

The American system places the final determinant of the professional qualification of a librarian in the hands of the library schools, even though actual certification of the individual librarian may be through a state agency. The American Library Association through its Committee on Accreditation is the recognized agency for accrediting library schools in the United States and Canada, and hence the course of instruction and the quality of instruction are among the most important concerns of the American Library Association as it functions as a professional group.

The level of instruction is on the postbaccalaureate level as compared with the system in Great Britain (except for the diploma courses), where the highest educational requirement is the General Certificate of Education with a pass in a science or a foreign language. The system of the United States and Canada with its emphasis on academic background is more in accord with world-wide usage of university degrees, where the diversity of qualifications causes no real problems.

In Great Britain, where a person who is not a Chartered Librarian is not regarded as a qualified librarian, a problem exists for the person who comes into the library field with a strong subject background and who is interested in technical or academic library work. There is some evidence that the Library Association is moving more toward the acceptance of academic credentials. Many of the colleges of commerce or technical colleges now offer courses leading to preparation for the Library Association examinations, and the diplomas of the University of London, the University of Sheffield, and Queens University (Belfast) may be utilized in the attainment of the FLA. Possible indications of specialization are also apparent: at the University of London the Diploma in Librarianship may be earned at the School of Oriental and African Studies as well as at the School of Librarianship and Archives; the diploma course at the University of Sheffield (also a one-year postgraduate course) offers special emphasis for those preparing to work in technical libraries; the University of Birmingham offers a one-year course to qualified teachers leading to the Supplemental Certificate in School Librarianship. A person may also fulfill, in part, the requirements of the Institute of Information Specialists by the diploma courses at London and Sheffield or by sitting for the specialist papers in the examinations of the Library Association.

Little difference is found in the certification of school librarians, where the formal requirements of their state or country are essentially those of a teacher with as yet little attention being paid to librarianship or the newer role of media specialist. To illustrate the variety of requirements in the United States (1968), the following library science requirements were in force based upon the basic requirement of certification as a teacher:

   2 states require a library degree.
   5 states require 15 hours in library science.
  10 states require 18 hours in library science.
  12 states require 24 hours in library science.
   7 states require 30 hours in library science.

Requirements of other states range from 6 to 40 hours in library science. Four states have no library science requirements.

It should be noted that the American Library Association has accredited less than fifty library schools in the United States and Canada; many other programs offering library courses, and in some instances library degrees, are to be found in institutions of higher education apart from those recognized by the American Library Association.

In the United States and Canada, the requirements of certification need both refinement and coordination in order to bring more strongly into consideration (1) the mobility of people across state and national lines; (2) simplification of the number and types of certification, especially in the public-school area; (3) a uniform standard of education where certification is based upon the approval of educational programs; (4) more involvement of the library profession and the lay consumer of library services in the formulation of certification requirements; (5) the establishment of competent review boards to evaluate credentials of applicants from other countries and advise certifying agencies on matters of comparability and equivalency.

There is need, especially in the United States, for librarians to examine their certification procedures and evaluate the results of certification. There are indications that there are needs for certification of technicians in the library profession and there are indications, especially in the special and academic libraries, that since certification is not required for those librarians and since the value of library training as opposed to subject specialization may be open to question, the value of certification, and the type of education that lies behind it, may need changing. And last, there is no evidence to show that the various federal programs designed to help libraries of various kinds have had very much, if any, effect on certification, or even upon library personnel.

IRVING A. VERSCHOOR

CEYLON, LIBRARIES IN

The recorded history of Ceylon begins with the coming of a community of peasants from North India who first settled along the North Western coast of Ceylon about the fifth century B.C. These colonists, coming from the Indo-Gangetic plain, were settled agriculturalists and as such the early settlements were riverine in character, being confined to the most important rivers of the island. Anuradhapura, in the dry zone, became the seat of government and the capital city. The population organized itself into village communities largely for the purposes of water supply and tillage and to settle disputes of descent and proprietorship.

During the reign of King Devananpiya-tissa of Anuradhapura (250–210 B.C.), Buddhism was introduced into the island from India by Mahinda, the son of the

Mauriyan emperor Asoka. The coming of Buddhism to Ceylon, its missionary character, its appeal to the intellect, the preaching of sermons, its Code of ethics and conduct of society, and attempts at mass education helped the growth and development of Sinhalese culture and society. Buddhism also contributed substantially to the construction of temples and permanent buildings and to the development of indigenous art and architecture. Perhaps the most notable contribution is seen in the development of language, the writing of the scriptures, and its commentaries and translations which deeply influenced Singhalese literary growth.

Written records in Ceylon have been closely associated with Buddhist temples. Monks and laymen, who often lived in monasteries, devoted themselves to literary pursuits. The first missionaries and their converts lived in Mahavihare (monastery) on the outskirts of the capital city. Besides the Mahavihare, three large monasteries Mirisavati, Abhayagiri, and Jetavana were constructed by the fourth century A.D. These, with their palm-leaf (ola) manuscripts, were well-known repositories of learning. The celebrated Chinese traveller Fa-Hien refers to the flourishing literary activity in Ceylon. Pali, the language of Buddhism, was studied in the monasteries and attempts were made to put down in written form the oral traditions. A major landmark in the history of literature occurred when the Canon was written down for the first time in the first century B.C. The historical traditions of the Mahavihare were collected in Pali verse in the Dipavamsa, which was later replaced by the Mahavamsa and the Culavamsa. By the fifth century A.D. Canonical literature and the commentaries were brought together systematically by the scholars Buddhaghosa and Buddhadatta. The writing of grammar and the composition of prose and poetry were undertaken, and the Singhalese language reached a high standard. After the tenth century, with the spread of Mahayana Buddhism, the language was further influenced by Sanskrit.

Tamil influence on Singhalese literature was considerable after the thirteenth century. The presence of Saiva temples of Tirukketisvaram and Konecar is proof that the Tamils, who are Hindus, occupied the northern part of the island. Literary pursuits in the north became active under the influence of the dynasty of Aryachakravartis, a college of literati called the "Tamil Sangam" was established and the works of this period were preserved in a library called "Sarasvati Mahalayam," which was later destroyed by fire.

Books and Libraries in Ceylon

Libraries have been in existence in Ceylon from very early times and librarianship is somewhat indigenous. The temple libraries were possibly a type of reference library whose resources were carefully preserved and made available to the scholar and to the serious student. These were also the places where writing was actively done. Most of the writing of the early period were done on palm leaves—leaves of Talipat palm (*Corypha umbraculifera*), a native of the wet zone, and the Palmyra palm (*Borassus flabellifera*), a native of the dry zone. These palm leaves, when processed carefully, were found to be especially suitable for writing with the normal steel stylus because of their ability to withstand the combined destructive forces of heat and humidity.

With the arrival of the Portuguese in Ceylon in 1505, considerable interest in Singhalese and Tamil language and literature was seen. The Roman Catholic missionaries began writing religious tracts, grammars, and word books for use by missionaries. The Dutch too, from 1658, when they conquered Ceylon, attempted missionary work and for this purpose consistories were established in Colombo, Galle, and Jaffna. The Dutch clergy in Ceylon stressed the use of the vernacular. The Dutch governor, Gustavus Wilhelmus Baron Imhof, imported a press in 1736 so as to provide Christian literature locally. The first printing in Ceylon was done in 1737, and the first book printed was a Singhalese Prayer Book published in octavo format. This was followed by a Confession of Faith in 1738 and the Four Gospels in one volume in 1739. The New Testament in the Tamil language was printed in 1759. When the British conquered the Maritime Provinces of Ceylon in 1796, they also acquired the printing press from the Dutch. By 1815, the British had completed the conquest of the entire island and the pioneer Methodist missionaries had arrived in Ceylon with a printing press and had set up the Wesleyan Press. This was followed by the Church Missionary Society and the American missionaries who set up presses in Colombo and Jaffna. The Ceylon Government *Gazette,* issued in 1802, was the first periodical and the *Ceylon Observer,* issued in 1834, the first newspaper. Both of these continue to be published at the present time.

The Kings of Ceylon had maintained administrative records from very early times. The Portuguese and the Dutch, as well as the British, followed this practice. These records were in the form of land, parish, and school registers as well as diaries and secretarial papers. The Dutch, knowing the value of these records, took steps to keep them in an excellent state of preservation. But it was during the time of the British that an attempt was made to centralize the widely scattered archival material from the provinces. In 1798 Hugh Cleghorn, the first Chief Secretary of the Ceylon Government, was also appointed Archivist. Legislation was enacted in 1839 and in 1855 for a copy of all papers and books printed in Ceylon to be deposited with the Archivist. In 1947, the Government Archives became a separate and independent department comprising the Historical Manuscripts Commission, Office of Government Record Keeper, Office of the Registrar of Books and Newspapers, and the Office of the National Bibliography administered by a director. Since 1885 the Archivist as Registrar of Books has issued a quarterly accessions list of all books deposited at the Archives which appear as Part V of the Ceylon Government *Gazette.* The main function of the Government Archives is to preserve old documents, to edit and publish documents, and, since November 1962, to publish the *Ceylon National Bibliography.* The Archives today contains one of the most significant collection of documents, diaries, and papers pertaining to Ceylon, and its accessibility is normally limited to research workers.

In response to the growing interest in indigenous literature from local and foreign scholars, the Government Oriental Library was opened in 1870. The library was under the immediate control and supervision of the Colonial Secretary, and Louis de Zoysa was the first librarian. By 1875 the Colombo Museum was established and Richard Van Culenberg appointed as librarian. The library of the Royal Asiatic Society (Ceylon Branch), founded in 1845, was already in existence and this collection, along with the collection of the Government Oriental Library, was transferred to the Museum Library which by June 1877 was open to the public. By 1910 the Museum Library had over 15,000 volumes and the Royal Asiatic Society (Ceylon Branch) had 10,000 volumes. Since 1885 the Museum Library has continued to receive one copy of every book, periodical, and pamphlet published in Ceylon. With the removal of the Society's Library to its own building, the Colombo Museum Library developed on its own, and today it has one of the most important research collections on Ceylon history and culture, oriental languages, anthropology, and zoology. Since 1877 the library has irregularly issued printed catalogs of its books and manuscripts.

The establishment of the first subscription libraries took place in the early nineteenth century. The first of these, the Colombo Library and the Pettah Library, were established as early as 1830 and were subsidized by the Government. The subsidy was, however, withdrawn in 1918 following World War I and this led to the establishment of the Colombo Public Library in 1925 by the amalgamation of the Colombo Library and the Pettah Library (see Figure 1). The control of the

FIGURE 1. *The Colombo Municipal Public Library.*

library is vested in the Colombo Municipality and its general management is entrusted to a committee. Today the library consists of a lending library, a reference library, and five branch libraries within the Colombo Municipality. There is a very severe limitation in space but the foundation for a new library building was laid in October 1965. It is estimated the building will cost approximately 3 million rupees, and it will provide services not available at the present time such as a children's library, music room, lecture room, exhibition hall, and an auditorium.

Most other municipalities and local government agencies have libraries and reading rooms; particularly noteworthy are the libraries at Anuradhapura, Jaffna (see Figure 2), and Kandy. Though the idea of a public library service is not

FIGURE 2. *The Public Library at Jaffna.*

altogether foreign to Ceylon, public library service as such in contemporary Ceylon is somewhat limited and inefficient. If, irrespective of quantity or quality, a mere collection of books can be called a library, then most towns in Ceylon have a library. But the number of towns in which there is a free public library service in the proper sense of the term and where the library is properly housed, adequately supported, and cared for by qualified librarians is very small indeed. There are a number of reasons for this general neglect and inefficiency. The outstanding one is, perhaps, the fact that public library development in Ceylon has been left solely in the hands of local authorities, namely the municipalities, Urban and Town Councils, and Village Committees. There is no legislation, no coordination, no minimum requirements or standards. As a result each local authority functions in isolation providing a service widely differing in nature and usefulness, though often hopelessly inadequate.

There is, however, a very real interest at the present time in public libraries in

Ceylon. The government, UNESCO, the Ceylon Library Association, local authorities, as well as the people of Ceylon have become increasingly aware of the usefulness and purposes of an adequate and efficient public library service, and it is
likely that very substantial achievements will be made in the forseeable future.

Under the Ministry of Education, there were 9550 schools in 1965, providing
primary and secondary education for almost 2.5 million students. In most of these
schools, libraries of some sort are found. In spite of recent improvements in education in the way of increased facilities no parallel improvement in school libraries
has taken place. This is perhaps due to the fact that the importance of the school
library in a system of national education has never been fully appreciated by the
majority of school teachers, educational administrators, or by the Ministry itself.
Further, the funds for the library come out of the general school budget and,
therefore, development and growth depend upon the initiative and imagination of
individual principals and managers. There has therefore been no uniform growth
and while a few good libraries exist, most are poor and inadequate. The money
spent on the library in many cases is far less in proportion to the money spent in
other areas like games and laboratory equipment, with the result that the children
are denied the barest elements of school library service. The average Ceylonese
child is not introduced to books at home, he is rarely encouraged to read widely
in school, and there are not even proper public libraries to go to. Realizing this,
the Ministry of Education has in recent years made special efforts to improve
school libraries. If this emphasis is continued and provision made in the school
curriculum for an effective use of the library, it is possible that school libraries will
begin to play their vital role in education and the school library service will ap-
preciably improve.

The library of the University of Ceylon at Peradeniya, the nucleus of which
dates back to the library of the Ceylon University College founded in 1921, is the
most important academic library in the country (see Figure 3). It has a collection
of over 250,000 volumes and subscribes to about 2000 periodicals. The library
consists of the main library, the faculty libraries of Engineering, Medical, Agriculture, and Veterinary Science, and the departmental libraries of the Science Faculty.
In the Main Library are located the reading rooms, the reference collection, the
Ceylon room, the periodical section, and the stacks. Free access to the stacks is
available to the users and the collection is classified according to Dewey. The public
catalog is easily accessible and is in two parts: class and author. In addition to
serving the needs of its own academic community, facilities for interlibrary loan
with libraries in and outside Ceylon are available. The professional staff is well
qualified and the service provided as a whole is good. The library publishes a
Monthly Accessions List. In 1961 the university conducted a Post-Graduate
Diploma Course in Librarianship although after two years the course was given up.

Three other university libraries must be mentioned. The libraries of the
Vidyodaya University of Ceylon at Gangodavila and the Vidyalankara University
of Ceylon at Kelaniya, both of which were established in 1959. With a holding
of over 25,000 volumes in each, the emphasis is on Buddhism, Buddhist civilization, and Oriental studies. The new University of Colombo was established in

FIGURE 3. *The University Library at Peradeniya.*

1967 and the library has as its nucleus the collections acquired by the University of Ceylon for its Colombo branch. All three libraries have a tremendous responsibility to increase their collections in depth, to provide adequate facilities for research, and to provide for a vastly improved service to their own academic community.

At the Undergraduate level two college libraries are worth mentioning. Aquinas University College, founded in 1954 and located in Colombo, has a library of about 25,000 volumes catering for the special needs of students preparing for the external examinations of the University of Ceylon as well as other professional examinations, while the Peter Pillai Library is devoted to the study of religion and society. The Jaffna College Library located at Vaddukoddai (see Figure 4) has a history dating back to 1823 when the college was founded under the name of Batticota Seminary by the missionaries of the American Board of Commissioners for Foreign Missions. The seminary library formed the nucleus of the Jaffna College Library which in 1963 became the Undergraduate Library. At present the library has over 24,000 books and periodicals and is the only academic library in North Ceylon serving the college community as well as scholars engaged in research. The need to strengthen the collection to provide not only for study and teaching but also for systematic and continued research has been seriously felt, and in spite of limited resources and lack of space, it is hoped that within the next few years a good research collection could be begun.

In Ceylon, special libraries organized by government departments, research institutes, corporations, and commercial firms have provided very useful service. Particularly important are the collections in the libraries of the Senate and the House of Representatives, the Ceylon Institute of Scientific and Industrial Research, the Central Bank of Ceylon, and the Coconut, Rubber and Tea Research Institutes. Unfortunately, however, no bibliographical aids or accession lists are published

FIGURE 4. *The Undergraduate Library at Jaffna College, Vaddukoddai.*

except for the *Fortnightly Review* of the Research library of the Central Bank of Ceylon. Mention must also be made of the libraries of the British Council and the United States Information Service in Ceylon which have done valuable work in providing library services in Colombo and Kandy, two of the major cities.

The first attempt at training for librarianship in Ceylon was made in January 1957 by the Ceylon Institute of Scientific and Industrial Research. Mr. Donald A. Redmond was in charge of the program of training. Six persons were selected for training at the Library of the Institute. The period of training was for one year, with an emphasis on technical librarianship.

Because of an already growing interest in library training, the Ceylon Institute of Scientific and Industrial Research, along with the Ceylon Technical College, also offered two, two-week full time intensive courses, each comprising thirty hours of lectures and thirty hours of practical work. This was particularly designed to meet the immediate needs of untrained persons already in library work. In all, forty-six persons were trained in these two-week courses and of them about half were from school libraries, while most of the others were from government and similar special libraries.

But any attempt at a systematic and continuing program of education for librarianship in Ceylon did not begin until mid-1961 when the Ceylon Library Association and the University of Ceylon at Peradeniya offered training in librarianship at two different levels.

The Ceylon Library Association courses were designed to meet indigenous needs and were primarily for working, untrained librarians. "Librarianship—First Examination," as it was called, was based with some modifications on the syllabus of the First Professional Examination of the Library Association of England. The course was spread over six months initially, the classes meeting in the evenings twice a week for a two-hour lecture. The course first conducted in Colombo became so popular that it was conducted in the provincial towns of Jaffna and Kandy as well. These are being continued at present, and in addition to the First Examination courses, the Intermediate Examination courses are also being offered to selected candidates in Colombo. The staff for these courses are drawn from the professionally qualified librarians in Ceylon.

The University of Ceylon at Peradeniya offered a postgraduate Diploma Course in Librarianship in 1961. The course, based on the University of London School of Librarianship, was spread over one year. Six students were admitted to the course in the first year and the staff consisted of four professionally qualified librarians from the University Library, who in addition to their normal duties did the teaching as well. The course was offered again in 1962, but was not offered again. In a very real sense this was unfortunate as only the university could have given the leadership and the status to such professional studies in Ceylon.

The most recent attempt at providing training for Librarianship has been made in Febrauary 1969. Part xvi of the Higher Education Act No. 20 of 1966 provides for the establishment of Junior University Colleges in Ceylon. These are two-year colleges providing courses with a practical bias designed to meet the manpower requirements of the developing nation. Six Junior University Colleges were established in February 1969 and in two of these—Dehiwala and Palai—librarianship is now being taught. It is perhaps too soon to comment on their program of training. It is certainly good that this program is now available to students and provides opportunities in library training. Yet it is felt that this could at best only provide training at an intermediate level. The teaching of librarianship at its highest level can be done only at the university where the larger purposes of librarianship, its principles, and its problems can be effectively examined and understood.

Ceylon today is an independent country with an estimated population of over 12.5 million. The majority of the population live in villages. The literacy rate is high compared to South Asian standards and increasing educational facilities are being made available. Within such a context libraries are urgently needed to provide for the continuing education of the people as well as for the creation of well informed, tolerant, and sensible men and women who will be able to live their lives intelligently.

Since 1960 there has been an awakening of library consciousness in Ceylon. The formation of the Ceylon Library Association, the publication of its *Journal,* the facilities for education in librarianship afforded by the Association as well as the University of Ceylon, the advice and help received from UNESCO and its library experts, and the constant encouragement and financial support received from the Ministry of Cultural Affairs bear testimony to this new consciousness. This has led to improvement of library personnel, services, and facilities. New libraries have been established and efforts are being made for the creation of an effective public library service and a national library. Since the nation cannot progress with a great majority of its people living a life of cultural and intellectual poverty, it is obvious that libraries of all types have a tremendous role to play. Realizing this, the Ceylon National Library Services Board Act was passed by the Parliament of Ceylon in March 1970. This is an important milestone in the development of library services within Ceylon, for the Act not only provides for the establishment of a National Library but also creates a Central Authority—the National Library Services Board —which will organize, coordinate, and supervise library services at all levels within the country. And although much has been achieved during the past decade, much more remains to be done before the country can have libraries and a service of which it can indeed be proud.

BIBLIOGRAPHY

Adikaram, E. W., *Early History of Buddhism in Ceylon,* D. S. Puswella, Migoda, 1946.

Adikaram, E. W., "Introduction of Buddhism and its influence on learning," in *Education in Ceylon (from the Sixth Century* B.C. *to the Present Day)*, *A Centenary Volume,* Part I, Government Press, Colombo, 1969, pp. 9–16.

Ariyapala, M. B., *Society in mediaeval Ceylon,* K. V. G de Silva, Colombo, 1956.

Blok, S. C., "Current National Bibliography of Ceylon," *J. Ceylon Lib. Association,* 1(2), 32–34 (July–December 1962).

Blok, S. C., "Public Library Service: the formative years," *Ceylon Lib. Rev. (J. Ceylon Lib. Assoc.),* 2(1), 1–6 (July 1967).

Corea, Ishvari (Mrs.), "Public Libraries in Ceylon," *J. Ceylon Lib. Assoc.,* 1(1), 44–46 (January 1962).

Davy, John, *An account of the Interior of Ceylon and of its inhabitants with travels in that Island,* with an introduction by Yasmine Gooneratne, reprinted as volume 16 of *The Ceylon Historical J.,* Tisara Prakasakayo, Dehiwala, 1969.

De Silva, Austin C. M., "Production of books in Ancient Ceylon," in *Education in Ceylon (from the Sixth Century* B.C. *to the Present Day)*, *A Centenary Volume,* Part I, Government Press, Colombo, 1969, pp. 227–233.

De Silva, W. A., *Catalogue of palm leaf manuscripts in the library of the Colombo Museum,* Vol. 1 (Memoirs of the Colombo Museum, Series A, No. 4), Government Press, Colombo, 1938.

Evans, Evelyn J. A., "Library development and the proposed programme for Ceylon," *Ceylon Lib. Rev. (J. Ceylon Lib. Assoc.),* July 1969, pp. 1–4.

Evans, Evelyn J. A., "School libraries in Ceylon," *UNESCO Bull. Lib.,* 23(6), 287–292, 299 (November–December 1969).

Fernando, P. E. E., "Development of the Singhalese Script from the 8th Century A.D. to the 15th Century A.D.," *Univ. Ceylon Rev.,* 8(4), 222–243 (October 1950).

Geiger, Wilhelm (translator and editor), *The Mahavamsa or The Great Chronicle of Ceylon,* Government Information Department, Colombo, 1950.

Geiger, W., and C. M. Rickmers (translator), *The Culavamsa,* 2 vols., published for the Pali Text Society by Oxford University Press, London, 1929–1930.

Geiger, W., *Culture of Ceylon in mediaeval times* (Heinz Bechert, ed.), Otto Harrassowitz, Wiesbaden, 1960.

Godakumbura, C. E., *Singhalese literature,* The Colombo Apothecaries, Colombo, 1955.

Imhoff, Gustaaf Willem (Baron) van, *Memoir to his successor Willem Maurits Bruynink, 1740,* translated by Sophia Pieters, with an introduction and notes by the Government Archivist, Government Press, Colombo, 1911.

Joseph, Gerard Abrahm, "A note on libraries in Ceylon," *Ceylon Rev.,* 3(3), 51–53, 110–112 (1897).

Jurriaanse, M. W., "Gabriel Schade and his invention of the Singhalese type," *J. Dutch Burgher Union of Ceylon,* 32(4), 134–139 (April 1943).

Kanapathi Pillai, K., "Tamil publications in Ceylon," *Univ. Ceylon Rev.,* 16(1 and 2), 6–16 (January–April 1958).

Kanapathi Pillai, K., "Ceylon's contribution to Tamil language and literature," *Univ. Ceylon Rev.,* 6(4), 217–228 (October 1948).

Low, D. A., J. C. Iltis, and M. D. Wainwright, eds., *Government Archives in South Asia: A Guide to National and State Archives in Ceylon, India and Pakistan,* Cambridge Univ. Press, New York, 1969.

Mahalingam, V., "Education for librarianship," *J. Ceylon Lib. Assoc.,* 1(1), 41–43 (January 1962).

McMurtrie, Douglas C., *Memorandum on the first printing in Ceylon: with a bibliography of Ceylonese imprints of 1737–1760,* privately printed, Chicago, 1931.

Malalasekera, G. P., *The Pali literature of Ceylon,* M. D. Gunasena, Colombo, 1958.

Nanayakkara, D. D. P., "The formation of the Ceylon Library Association," *J. Ceylon Lib. Assoc.,* 1(1), 40 (January 1962).

Peiris, Edmund, "Literary Activity in Sinhala and Tamil during the Portuguese and the Dutch Times," in *Education in Ceylon (from the Sixth Century* B.C. *to the Present Day), A Centenary Volume,* Part I, Government Press, Colombo, 1969, pp. 329–335.

Rahula, Walpola, *History of Buddhism in Ceylon: the Anuradhapura Period, 3rd Century* B.C.–*10th Century* A.D., M. D. Gunasena, Colombo, 1956.

Redmond, D. A., "Library training in Ceylon," *UNESCO Bull. Lib.,* 12(10), 230–231 (October 1958).

Rhodes, Dennis E., *The Spread of Printing (Eastern Hemisphere: India, Pakistan, Ceylon, Burma and Thailand),* Routledge and Kegan Paul, London, 1969.

Thani Nayagam, Xavier S., "Tamil culture, its past, its present, and its future with special reference to Ceylon," *Tamil Culture,* 4(4), 341–364 (October 1955).

Wickremaratne, K. D. L., "Palm leaf manuscripts of Ceylon," *Ceylon Today,* 16(1), 16–21 (January 1969).

Wickramasinghe, Martin, *Landmarks of Singhalese literature,* translated by E. R. Saratchandra, M. D. Gunasena, Colombo, 1963.

R. S. THAMBIAH

CHAIN INDEXING

Chain indexing is a method of deriving alphabetical subject index entries in a semiautomatic fashion from the chain of successive subdivision that leads from a general level to the most specific level needed to be indexed. It may be used to provide indexes not only to classification schemes and classified catalogs, but also to all other systematically organized indexes, even when they are arranged alphabetically. The chain is nearly always, but not necessarily, taken from a classification scheme in use, and the method is intended to offer general as well as specific access to all information and thus to avoid the need for arbitrary decisions by the indexer as to how a subject may be approached through the catalog.

Prehistory of Chain Indexing

In general terms the history of chain indexing is a gradual development in response to the demands of more detailed and more complex classification schemes. In particular terms it derives directly from Ranganathan's theories of faceted classification and the consequent theory of a classified catalog (*1*, pp. 114–118 and 164–165; *2*, p. 46).

In any subject access information system the user needs to know two things: the names of the subjects and the relationships between those subjects. In the dictionary catalog this need produces lists of subject headings and references; in the classified catalog it produces a systematic classification and an accompanying alphabetical subject index. The index performs two functions: it translates natural language terms into the unfamiliar notation of the classification scheme, and it brings together under a single term the various aspects of that term that have been scattered among different main classes in the scheme or different parts of the same class. The translating function of the index presents no difficulty; it is needed because the systematic order is not an obvious one and because the notation of the classification scheme is not a natural language, e.g.,

    RADIO   621.384

This sort of entry is entirely satisfactory for specific topics that occur only once in the scheme, but to relate topics scattered in the preferred order of the classification is to introduce composite terms, containing at least the basic term and the name of the general class where each aspect is found, e.g.,

    LIGHTING: electrical engineering
    LIGHTING: illumination engineering
    LIGHTING: photography

Indexing composite terms presents a basic problem: at first glance the topic VIOLIN SONATA might suggest index entries for both VIOLIN SONATA and

SONATA: violin, but the more words there are in the composite term, the more permutation will be needed, involving the indexer in a great deal of work that can be shown to be unnecessary. If the classification scheme divides music first by *instrument* and then by *form* we can expect VIOLIN SONATA to be linked with VIOLIN SUITE and other music for the violin by the systematic arrangement and its associated notation, but we cannot expect it to be related directly to sonatas for other instruments. Since SONATA will be scattered in the systematic arrangement the index must obviously list

        SONATA: flute   Ts3
        SONATA: oboe   Tv3
        SONATA: violin   Tp3

but there will be no need to list

        VIOLIN SONATA   Tp3
        VIOLIN SUITE   Tp4

etc., because these already appear together in the systematic arrangement. If we have an entry under the single word VIOLIN then entry at that point leads to the class VIOLIN in the systematic arrangement, where the different kinds of violin music are listed.

The economy of this kind of indexing led to Melvil Dewey's development of the Relativ Index in the *Decimal Classification*. As Coates points out (*3*, pp. 86–87), a comparison of the indexes of the *Decimal Classification* and Bliss's *Bibliographic Classification* show that the consistent use of this method could reduce the number of entries in a class like chemistry by nearly two thirds; most of the extra entries in the *Bibliographic Classification*'s index simply mirror the listing in the systematic arrangement. In practical terms most of the class numbers for any term in a relative index lie *away* from the main location of that topic; in other words, the relative index provides for what Savage called the *distributed relatives*. As Mills shows (*4*, p. 141), if DYEING is scattered throughout the products dyed, then the index must collect the references together and list the products under the primary index term DYEING. It almost produces an inversion of the systematic arrangement—but not quite, since the secondary terms are listed alphabetically and this may disturb the system, e.g.,

        DYEING, Cotton
               Leather
               Textiles

where LEATHER separates the associated terms COTTON and TEXTILES.

Development of Chain Indexing

It is commonplace that inquiries are often stated too generally, and one of the dangers of the relative index is that if it is restricted to index terms representing documents, it may have to rely for generic searches on the presence of documents at a more general level to ensure the presence in the index of a necessary more general term. It was almost inevitable that relative indexing should abandon reference to the subjects of particular documents and should develop instead the systematic introduction of more generic terms in the same chain of division *whether they represent documents or not;* this method became known as chain indexing. It was first explicitly described by Ranganathan (*1,* pp. 114–118 and 164–165; *2,* p. 46) and was based by him on his own new theories of classification. It is often attributed solely to him, but like his theory of classification, it is really a brilliant restatement and recognition of the undiscovered potential of ideas implicit in the often *ad hoc* developments of predecessors. Indeed Kennedy (*5,* p. 33) suggests that Cutter first expounded the principle in the nineteenth century, but this seems an attribution by hindsight, like Crestadoro's anticipation of the KWIC index. Metcalfe (*6,* p. 249) goes further and says that Ranganathan's ideas are a misunderstanding and even perversion of Cutter's.

The assumed basis of need in chain indexing is that no superordinate term in the chain can be denied as a possible entry term, either because the scope or the terminology of an inquiry may be misunderstood, or because a genuinely more general inquiry may be answered at least partially by specific material. Ranganathan's early ideas encouraged the use of every term in the chain, but he later modified this to exclude terms that were meaningless or were not likely to be sought (*2,* p. 46). Ranganathan has also suggested that a classification scheme whose notation is *expressive* (i.e., where each successive step of division is represented by another digit) responds best to chain procedure. This is true, but provided a logically derived chain of division is discernible in a classification scheme, chain procedure may be used with any kind of notation. Chain indexing received its greatest encouragement and acceptance in the Western world when in 1950 the *British National Bibliography* began to publish its weekly lists as a classified catalog, using the Dewey *Decimal Classification* and an alphabetical subject index based on chain procedure, and for the first time librarians in general had a working demonstration of the method in the context of a whole author and subject catalog.

Method of Constructing a Chain Index for a Classified Catalog

Chain indexing is intended to be a semimechanical process. By relying on the hierarchy of the classification, by using its terminology as a foundation, and by making mostly *negative* decisions (i.e., decisions only to delete or to alter), the indexer's task is made easier. The method that follows is indicative rather than exhaustive; it is intended as a basic guide to the practice.*

List all the steps of division represented in the class number, starting with the first digit and using the terminology of the classification scheme, e.g.,

* Several writers have described methods of constructing chain indexes; among them are Ranganathan (*2,* pp. 287–289 and *passim*), Coates (*3,* Chapter IX), Mills (*4,* pp. 143–148), and Sharp (*7,* pp. 99–100).

```
600  Technology
620     Engineering
624        Civil
```

This is most easily done when the notation is expressive of the steps of division, but even when it is not, the typographical arrangement of the classification schedule will usually indicate the steps, e.g.,

```
QB       Astronomy
QB501    Solar system
QB521      Sun
QB541        Eclipses
```

Sometimes the class number is not *coextensive* with the subject, i.e., it does not fully express the detail necessary. *Verbal extension* is then necessary to indicate the final steps of subordinate division, and these added terms can then be used as index entry terms, e.g.,

```
900     History
940       Europe
942         Great Britain
942.4          West Midlands
942.48           Warwickshire
942.48             Birmingham
942.48               Edgbaston [a suburb of Birmingham]
```

Nonsignificant steps should be deleted. There are several kinds of nonsignificant steps: false, meaningless, and unsought. A well-known example of a false link or step arises from Dewey's subordination of ELECTRICAL ENGINEERING to APPLIED PHYSICS:

```
600     Technology
620       Engineering
621         Applied physics
621.3         Electrical
```

A meaningless step occurs when a symbol of notation is used as an indicator rather than as a substantive element, like the 0 that indicates the form of a document in the *Decimal Classification*. An unsought link or step is usually one whose meaning in natural language is such that few inquirers if any would think of using it, e.g., NONTAXONOMIC BOTANY, or GENERAL LIBRARIES. Subdivisions of time may present a difficulty: periods with recognized names, e.g., RENAISSANCE, can obviously be indexed, but other periods, which are expressed only as a span of years, e.g., 1518–1633, are usually regarded as unsought. Centuries, e.g., NINETEENTH CENTURY, form a borderline case.

Just as some links may be false, so some necessary steps of division may be hidden, usually by the notation, e.g.,

```
970   North America
979     Pacific States
```

conceals the intermediate step

> 973 United States

but such hidden steps are often revealed by the typographical arrangement of the schedules. Any hidden steps should be added, and so should any synonyms that may occur at any level of the chain, although the indexer should remember that if a term is likely to occur frequently, in many classes, a *see* reference from its synonym may save many duplicated entries, e.g.,

> UNITED KINGDOM
> *see* GREAT BRITAIN

It should be noted that common subdivisions of form or subject may be included by the use of general references, e.g.,

> BIBLIOGRAPHIES
> for bibliographies on particular topics *see* the topic

Phase relationships with other subjects (e.g., influence, comparison, etc.) may be included by using nonfiling italic or underlined phrases, e.g.,

> EDUCATION *influence on* PSYCHOLOGY
> PSYCHOLOGY
> SOCIAL SCIENCES

Finally the terminology should be changed if the scheme in use has terms that are unsatisfactory for practical use in the catalog.

The edited series of steps may now be listed as a series of index entry terms, and qualifying or explanatory terms added to them to avoid the ambiguity that might arise if a term is likely to occur as a distributed relative in several places in the systematic arrangement. These qualifying terms (as few as possible, and as many as necessary) are most easily taken in order of increasing generality from the analyzed chain.

The following example demonstrates most of these points.

	582.13097954	FLOWERS OF THE COLUMBIA VALLEY
1	500	Pure science
2	580	Botanical sciences
3	582	Spermatophyta
4	582.1	Special groupings
5	582.13	Flowering plants
6	582.130	[form indicator]
7	582.1309	Geographic distribution
8	582.13097	North America
9	582.130979	Pacific States
10	582.1309795	Oregon
11	582.13097954	Northwestern counties

Step 11 should be extended verbally to provide an entry for

582.13097954   Columbia Valley

Steps 6 and 7 are meaningless and should be deleted, as should the unsought links at steps 4 and 11. The synonym SEEDBEARING PLANTS at Step 3 should have a separate entry. Hidden steps of division occur after Steps 3 and 8: 582–589 appears in the schedule as TAXONOMIC BOTANY; and 582.130973 is the intermediate step UNITED STATES between Steps 8 and 9. Finally the term BOTANICAL SCIENCES at Step 2 might be better rendered by the more popular BOTANY.

To the resulting index entry terms, other qualifying terms may be added in *ascending* order from the chain just analyzed. There is no need to include PACIFIC STATES or UNITED STATES as a qualifier for OREGON, but since the topic is not only OREGON, but its FLOWERING PLANTS, then that term should be included. Further, since FLOWERING PLANTS may occur in either BOTANY or HORTICULTURE, BOTANY should also be used as a qualifier. Note that although all synonyms are used as index entries, only one term should be used constantly as a qualifier.

COLUMBIA VALLEY: Oregon: flowering plants: botany	582.13097954
OREGON: flowering plants: botany	582.1309795
PACIFIC STATES: United States: flowering plants: botany	582.130979
UNITED STATES: flowering plants: botany	582.130973
NORTH AMERICA: flowering plants: botany	582.13097
FLOWERING PLANTS: botany	582.13
SPERMATOPHYTA: botany	582
SEEDBEARING PLANTS: botany	582
TAXONOMIC BOTANY	582–589
BOTANY	580
SCIENCE	500

Although this list may seem long it should be remembered that a very specific topic is being treated, and that no future document on that topic, or on any topic at a superordinate level in the same chain, will need index entries. Further, any specific topic that shares any of this chain, e.g., FLOWERS OF IOWA, will need index entries only for the lower part of the chain; entries for UNITED STATES: flowering plants: botany, and upward, already exist. Finally, it should be noted that although the indexer must still make some decisions (*3*, pp. 106–110), a useful general attitude is to put a doubtful term in rather than leave it out.

Feature Headings in the Systematic Arrangement

Essentially complementary to the chain index entries are feature headings (*2*, pp. 324–326; *8*). Each term of the chain is indexed automatically because the cataloger cannot be certain at what level an inquirer will begin to search. In the absence of certainty the cataloger cannot risk a selection of terms; he must include all levels of the chain from the most specific point to the most general. In order to provide the inquirer with a corresponding framework in the systematic arrangement so that he will always find a reference to the number given him (at any level) by the chain index, a series of feature headings is provided on guide cards, each bearing the relevant class number and the natural language term representing *that step only* in the chain of division. There must obviously be a feature heading corresponding to every chain index entry so that the inquirer may be directed onward (or backward) in the systematic arrangement, whatever his access point. Like the provision of chain index entries, this method may seem to proliferate feature headings, but by natural growth the normal subject file will inevitably fill out until what at first might be a series of feature headings filed one behind another, will become in a card catalog a familiar set of guide cards. It is possible, of course, to omit the feature heading guide card for the ultimate step in a chain, thus grouping a number of entries behind a single guide card at a slightly more general level, but care should be taken to supply the missing feature heading if a future chain proceeds to a more specific level still. The significant feature of this use of guide cards is that rather than simply separating groups of entries, feature headings make dynamic use of the systematic arrangement.

Uses of Chain Indexing

It is often assumed that chain procedure can be applied only to indexes to classified catalogs and to classification schemes. This is not so: any index that refers to terms existing in any hierarchy of general-special relationships can use chain procedure. It is in any case wrong to assume that indexes to classified catalogs and classification schemes are the same. The characteristic feature of a chain index is that it indexes all significant steps in the chain whether those terms occur in the systematic arrangement or not, but by its nature a classification scheme lists *all* terms. The consequent almost infinite number of compounds would be impossible to handle and the chain index to a classification scheme is often modified to show only constituent elements, e.g.,

```
    not SONATA: flute     Ts3
                violin    Tp3
    but SONATA            —3
```

Only Ranganathan's *Colon Classification* (9) of the general schemes of classification uses chain procedure consistently in its index, although the *Universal Decimal Classification* introduces the principle, at least in its recommendations for compiling an index to a classified catalog (*10,* pp. 33–41). The index to the *Colon Classification* is interesting in that it echoes the index to the first edition of the Dewey *Decimal Classification* by giving only the entry term in natural language, and listing all the occurrences in the abbreviated and artificial language of the notation, e.g.,

EGG G[P], K[2P], L[P], 5515. KZ[P], 5, [E], 7, [2P], 5

This means that the number for EGG is G5515 and L5515 in G BIOLOGY and L MEDICINE, respectively, and K5515 in K ZOOLOGY, where the [2P] indicates that it occupies a second level of the personality facet, leaving the first level for the species themselves. In KZ ANIMAL HUSBANDRY the number may be KZ5, KZ:7, or a 5 added to a number in KZ:1/9, depending on the egg's occurrence as an object, a problem, or an agent. This use of the notation saves space in the printed schedule and incidentally compels the librarian to compile his own subject index to the catalog instead of relying on the index to the printed scheme.

The subject reference structure of the dictionary catalog has always had an admitted basis in hierarchical organization, as suggested by Cutter, Pettee and Mann among others, and according to Coates (*3*, Chapter XI; *11, passim*) chain procedure can be used to identify *see* and *see also* references. A set of index entries for the classified catalog for THE PHYSICS OF COLOR,

COLOR: optics: physics   Ngt
OPTICS: physics   Ng
PHYSICS   N
SCIENCE   M/S

may be used for a dictionary catalog simply by referring each term to the next most specific:

COLOR, Optics, Physics (subject heading)
OPTICS, Physics *see also* COLOR, Optics, Physics
PHYSICS *see also* OPTICS, Physics
SCIENCE *see also* PHYSICS

Occasionally an entry term derived in this way will be unsuitable for use in a dictionary catalog. In

INDUSTRY: planning: economics   Gfu4
PLANNING: economics   Gfu
ECONOMICS   Gf
SOCIAL SCIENCES   G/J

the term PLANNING: economics is better replaced by ECONOMIC PLANNING; once this is done the now suppressed term PLANNING is replaced by a *see* reference from the inversion PLANNING, Economics.

INDUSTRY, Economic planning (subject heading)
ECONOMIC PLANNING *see also* INDUSTRY, Economic planning
PLANNING, Economic *see* ECONOMIC PLANNING
ECONOMICS *see also* ECONOMIC PLANNING
SOCIAL SCIENCES *see also* ECONOMICS

The same modification may be applied to any inversion like subject/place or subject/form made necessary by the nature of the dictionary catalog. One advantage of the use of chain procedure in this context is that the use of a classification scheme suggests *see* references for synonyms at all levels and *see also* references to collateral topics. Even without a classification scheme the rigor of a hierarchical foundation has its advantages in alphabetico-specific indexing, as the *British Technology Index* has shown, in spite of the doubts voiced by Ranganathan (*2*, pp. 46 and 330) and Metcalfe (*6*, pp. 251–253).

Another use for chain procedure is in the preparation of book indexes (*12*, pp. 46–48). In many books a topic receives full treatment at one point, while its different aspects are scattered in chapters on other topics. This is directly analogous to a classified arrangement, and it is thus possible to derive book index entries by chain procedure; the detailed analysis of the topics's full treatment need not appear in the index, but can be left (with advantage) to a chapter heading abstract or a detailed contents statement.

Disadvantages of Chain Indexing

There are two main areas of criticism, both arising from chain procedure's dependence on the classification scheme.

Any classification scheme represents a compromise majority decision, as Bliss recognized in his principle of the *relativity of classes,* and it must ignore any other arrangement of topics or any other order of characteristics, of which Sharp (*13*, pp. 69–72), suggests there may be very many. An index that reflects this preferred systematic order must inevitably share any faults of that order. This is the basis of much of Metcalfe's criticisms (*6*, p. 127 and Appendix G, pp. 254–262), in his opposition to the use of chain procedure in dictionary cataloging. Unfortunately much of his further criticism of the chain index to a classified catalog seems to be based on a disappointment that it is not a dictionary catalog, and his condemnation of the index often extends without distinction to the catalog as a whole (*6*, Appendix G, pp. 254–262). Although it is true that a chain index reflects the faults as well as the virtues of the systematic arrangement, it should be remembered that its inversion of the hierarchical order and its use of natural language terms enable it to collect most of the scattered or suppressed collocations of topics.

The omissions that persist in the index give rise to the second criticism: that in citing several terms of a composite subject in the alphabetical index, chain procedure *must* follow the inverted order of the hierarchy. This may have two effects. If the inquirer looks for two terms, the second of which is more general than the first, then they may certainly appear in that order in the index, but if they are accompanied by a third term, more general than the first term but more specific than the second, then the third term will be interposed, and they will not appear where the inquirer expects them to appear in the alphabetical sequence. For example, THE PHYSICS OF COLOR produced index entries

        COLOR: optics: physics
        OPTICS: physics

If the inquirer looked for COLOR: physics he would not find it, and he would have to recognize it some distance away as COLOR: optics: physics. On the other hand, if the inquirer looks for two terms, the second of which is more specific than the first, then he will not find them used in association at all, since the inversion in chain procedure of the order of subordination in the systematic arrangement combines the natural language index terms in an order of increasing generality. So if the inquirer looked for PHYSICS: color, or COLOR: spectrum, he would not find anything apparently relevant at all.

There have been several attempts to find logical systems for indexing classified catalogs that avoid the disadvantages of chain procedure. Of these the two most likely to be successful are selectively permuted indexing and cyclic indexing. Although normal permutation would produce far too many index entries, a rational basis of selection as described by Sharp (*12,* pp. 80–91; *14*) can offer economy without sacrificing too much coverage. Cyclic indexing, particularly if it is used in the classified file, can offer a simpler approach through the specific reference to the elements of the systematic arrangement (*15,16*).

Advantages of Chain Indexing

The customarily acknowledged advantages of chain indexing have been implicit in the discussion of its methods and uses. To summarize, they are: it avoids the haphazard provision of necessary generic index entries by using all significant steps in the chain of division; it offers a nearly mechanical system of indexing that relieves the indexer of much uncertain decision; and it offers a very real economy in the provision of index entries, since many topics share the upper levels of chains of division.

REFERENCES

Full bibliographical details are given only for references not listed in the Bibliography.

1. S. R. Ranganathan, *Theory of Library Catalogue.*
2. S. R. Ranganathan, *Classified Catalogue Code.*
3. E. J. Coates, *Subject Catalogues, Headings and Structure.*
4. J. Mills, "Chain Indexing and the Classified Catalogue."
5. R. F. Kennedy, *Classified Cataloguing: A Practical Guide.*
6. J. Metcalfe, *Subject Classifying and Indexing of Libraries and Literature.*
7. J. R. Sharp, as described in Vickery, B. C., *Classification and Indexing in Science.*
8. D. W. Doughty, "Chain Procedure Subject Indexing and Featuring in the Classified Catalogue."
9. S. R. Ranganathan, *Colon Classification,* 6th ed., Asia Publishing House, London, 1963.
10. British Standards Institution, *Guide to the Universal Decimal Classification (UDC) BS1000C:1963.*

11. E. J. Coates, "The Use of BNB in Dictionary Cataloguing."
12. J. Mills, "Indexing a Classification Scheme,"
13. J. R. Sharp, *Some Fundamentals of Information Retrieval.*
14. J. R. Sharp, "The SLIC Index," *In Looking Forward in Documentation: Proceedings of the Aslib 38th Annual Conference, University of Exeter, 1964,* Aslib, London, 1965, pp. 211–216.
15. D. J. Foskett, "Two Notes on Indexing Techniques," *J. Doc.,* 18(4), 188–192 (Dec. 1962); Also in *London Education Classification,* University of London Institute of Education, London, 1963 (Education Libraries Bulletin, Supplement 6).
16. C. D. Batty, "A Training Model in Documentation," *Amer. Doc.,* 18(3) 125–130 (July 1967).

BIBLIOGRAPHY

British Standards Institution, *Guide to the Universal Decimal Classification (UDC) BS1000C:1963,* British Standards Institution, London, 1963, pp. 33–41.

Coates, E. J., *Subject Catalogues, Headings and Structure,* Library Association, London, 1960 (particularly pp. 89–148).

Coates, E. J., "The Use of BNB in Dictionary Cataloguing," *Lib. Assoc. Record,* 59(6), 197–202 (June 1957).

Doughty, D. W., "Chain Procedure Subject Indexing and Featuring in the Classified Catalogue," *Lib. Assoc. Record,* 57(5), 173–178 (May 1955).

Foskett, D. J., *Classification and Indexing in the Social Sciences,* Butterworths, London, 1963, pp. 163–172.

Jolley, J., *The Principles of Cataloguing,* Crosby, Lockwood, London, 1961, Chapter 4.

Kennedy, R. F., *Classified Cataloguing: A Practical Guide,* Balkema, Cape Town, 1966, pp. 33 *et seq.*

MacCallum, T., "The Subject Approach in the University Library," *Libri,* 6(3) 255–270 (1956).

Mills, J., "Indexing a Classification Scheme," *Indexer* 2(2), 40–48 (Autumn 1960).

Mills, J., *A Modern Outline of Library Classification,* Chapman and Hall, London, 1960, *passim.*

Mills, J., "Chain Indexing and the Classified Catalogue," *Lib. Assoc. Record,* 57(4), 141–148 (April 1955).

Metcalfe, J., *Information Indexing and Subject Cataloguing,* Scarecrow Press, Metuchen, N.J., 1957, pp. 159–166.

Metcalfe, J., *Subject Classifying and Indexing of Libraries and Literature,* Scarecrow Press, Metuchen, N.J., 1959, pp. 127, 160–162, 249–262.

Palmer, B. I., and A. J. Wells, *The Fundamentals of Library Classification,* Allen & Unwin, London, 1951, Chapter XI.

Ram, H. N. A., "Chain Indexing: Its Significance," *Indian Librarian,* 14(12), 131–134 (Dec. 1959).

Ranganathan, S. R., *Classified Catalogue Code,* 5th ed., Asia Publishing House, London, 1964 (particularly Chapters KB, KC, KL, and KZD).

Ranganathan, S. R., *Dictionary Catalogue Code,* Thompson, Madras; Grafton, London, 1945, pp. 169–179.

Ranganathan, S. R., *Theory of Library Catalogue,* Madras Library Association, Madras; Goldston, London, 1938, pp. 114–118, 164–165.

Sharp, J. R., *Some Fundamentals of Information Retrieval,* Deutsch, London, 1960, pp. 43–47, 68–98.

Shera, J. H., and M. E. Egan, *The Classified Catalog,* American Library Association, Chicago, 1956.

Vickery, B. C., *Classification and Indexing in Science,* 2nd ed., Butterworths, London, 1959, pp. 91–111.

Vickery, B. C., *Faceted Classification,* Aslib, London, 1960, pp. 64–67.

C. DAVID BATTY

CHAINED LIBRARIES

The expression chained libraries, familiar in the literature of library history in English, is somewhat misleading. It usually refers to libraries in which chains limited the movement of varying numbers of bound volumes, whether codexes of pre-Gutenberg technology or printed books. The proportion of volumes thus anchored at a given time and place ranged from very small to very large. Some scholars accordingly prefer the German word *Kettenbücher* (chained books) to chained libraries.

The birthdate of chaining cannot be fixed precisely for lack of adequate evidence. There is some direct testimony, however. First, there are the few volumes surviving from that epoch, with either portions of a clip or even chain still attached, or traces on their covers of such attachment in the past. Second, there is the furniture of the same vintage with slanted reading surfaces, having either the rods to which the chains were attached at the anchor end or indications of their probable presence in those days. Enlightening also on occasion, indirectly and not always reliably, are literary data: Library catalogs, other library records, and nonlibrary sources have occasional allusions to items *"cathenati,"* or chained.

Books seem to have been chained initially some time in the twelfth century. For various reasons, collections in many ecclesiastical institutions were divided according to use during that period. The bulk of the codexes, wanted occasionally, were kept as before in cabinets or chests (*"armaria"*) under lock and key; but those in heavy demand for study were brought out and chained to furniture with slanted surfaces. The idea was apparently to relieve the brethren of waiting for the man with the keys. The chained books were thus functionally comparable to the twentieth-century academic library "reserve" collection. Books integral to the conduct of services were often chained at the pulpit or altar, and hymnals to the benches in the choir. (Consider the modern entry, "Liturgy and ritual.") The unchained (locked-up) volumes probably remained the larger category in many libraries for a long time. In fact, at certain institutions like Peterhouse—which boasted the first college library (1284) at England's Cambridge University—the books were never chained.

The next stage, evident at different times in different places, was necessitated by the crowding of the surfaces tenanted by chained "reserve" books. The supporting structure—lectern, *banco, Pult, pupitre*—acquired a flat shelf below the reading surface if it did not already have one; if it did, another flat shelf might be added below. Then shelving began to appear above, although its debut was not always related to provision of space for books. The climax of this trend was the combining of the lectern with the earlier book closet into a prototype—apart from the matter of chains—of what later became known as a "secretary."

Notably in England, this device became a prime feature of the "stall system," believed to have first emerged on the scene in 1480 at Magdalen College, Oxford. Whereas lecterns had been built sometimes for standing readers and sometimes for seated readers, the stall was only for the latter. Back-to-back benches were installed at right angles to a window, and parallel to the benches were open cabinets with at least two, but more often three, shelves of chained books (see Figure 1). The lowest shelf was at about eye height for a seated reader, and between him and that

FIGURE 1. *Seats and desks: Corpus.* [*From B. H. Streeter,* The Chained Library, *Macmillan, London, 1931.*]

FIGURE 2. *Part of a single volume, showing the clasps, the ring for the chain and the mode of attaching it: Hereford.* [*From John Clark,* The Care of Books, *Cambridge Univ. Press, 1901.*]

shelf was a slightly inclined reading surface. One end of each bookcase ("press") was flush against the wall between a pair of windows; in several buildings earlier windows were blocked for that purpose. Usually the arrangement was such that two parallel series of press-bench-press were divided by an aisle. In such libraries, in all likelihood, the chained books decidedly outnumbered the unchained.

FIGURE 3. *Hasps opened to remove chain from rod: Hereford.* [*From B. H. Streeter,* The Chained Library, *Macmillan, London, 1931.*]

FIGURE 4. *Piece of chain, showing the swivel: Hereford.* [*From John Clark,* The Care of Books, *Cambridge Univ. Press, 1901.*]

On the aisle end of each bookcase was a shelf list of the contents. That was not new, similar *tabulae* having often been affixed in like manner to the older lecterns, a vogue that continued in many continental libraries (still on view at the Mediceo-Laurenziana, in Florence).

The nature of chaining seems to have varied in only minor particulars. One end-link of the chain was attached to the book by means of a clip, ordinarily on the back-cover board, for convenience and minimum strain when the book was in use (see Figure 2). The other end-link was looped over a rod which ran parallel to the shelves and long edge of the reading surface. Rods were usually at the fore-edge of the shelf, sometimes just below it. In stall-system furniture, the rod for the books on the lowest shelf was just beneath the shelf edge and the contiguous edge of the inclined reading surface; a narrow aperture allowed ready passage of the chains from the rod to the books slightly above. Adding and removing chain ends from rods was managed by devices permitting the rod to be slipped free of its moorings (see Figure 3); the keys were in the librarian's control. Many, but not all, chains included a swivel at one end, at both ends, or in the middle, which made book handling easier (see Figure 4).

Chains appear to have been made predominantly of iron wire. With a frequency not yet known, they had initially a coating of tin.

The early "wall" system as Thomas Bodley developed it in his last years (1610–1613) had no significant effect on the mode of chaining. Books on the lower shelves, within reach from the open floor, were secured as usual. Those above, on the locked-access galleries, were not chained.

Because of the sharp rise in the number of books from about 1650 onward—tens of thousands—and other factors less easily determined or generalized, chains gradually began to go out of fashion in "public" libraries. By about 1750 they were, by and large, museum pieces. They had never been a familiar feature of private libraries.

SIDNEY L. JACKSON

CHAMBER OF COMMERCE OF THE UNITED STATES OF AMERICA LIBRARY

Since the founding of the Chamber of Commerce of the United States of America Library in 1917, it has basically been interested in dealing with the subjects of business and economics. As the Chamber has grown, so has the library. Community development, finance, foreign commerce, insurance, manufacture-distribution, natural resources, transportation, and education are included in the wide range of subjects.

The library holdings include 10,000 volumes with approximately thirty-five drawers of pamphlets and other vertical file materials. These include maps of leading cities of the United States, information on major associations, annual reports of leading corporations, and magazines published by the larger state and local Chambers of Commerce throughout the United States. The library is supplied with a number of trade and manufacturing directories from various major cities and international countries. The library contains a complete collection of Chamber of Commerce of the United States of America publications and the magazine *Nation's Business,* including the dates 1912 through 1969. Also, the magazine *Fortune* is bound, including the dates 1930 through 1969.

Because the library is not large enough spacewise to collect as much material as is deemed necessary for staff use, the librarians have an active relationship with other libraries through interlibrary loans. Extensive use of the District of Columbia libraries is usually sufficient for needed information. The Chamber of Commerce Library has worked with libraries in foreign countries on an advisory or informational basis as the need arises. Many foreign businessmen consult the Chamber library for industrial information.

The library is located on the first floor of the National Chamber building. It is in what was formally called the Reception Room. Study carrels are available for staff use and for the use of visiting patrons of the Chamber. The library is presently in the process of redecoration, which will be completed in the late summer of 1969. The original ceiling, elaborately decorated by Ezra Winter in an original design after the manner of the Italian Renaissance, will remain in its original state.

The Chamber of Commerce of the United States of America Library is located in 1615 H Street, N.W., Room A, Washington, D.C. While the general public is allowed to use its collections, the main purpose of the library is to aid the staff of the Chamber of Commerce of the United States. It has a staff of three and is open from 8:30 A.M. to 5:00 P.M., Monday through Friday.

B. ROSE WILLIAMS

CHAPBOOKS

Methods of marketing and selling books have varied over the centuries. One outlet which has been common at most times has been the itinerant vendor, akin to the modern door-to-door salesman. From at least as early as the sixteenth century onwards, such a hawker or pedlar was known as a chapman. His name was derived from the same source as "cheap" since both had the connotation of barter. It is in this sense that it remains in place names such as Cheapside.

It is certain that the publications which they sold were cheap in the modern sense of the word also. Nevertheless the term "chapbooks" appears not to have had any currency in the description of these items until the nineteenth century.

In general, the subject matter of these publications was of an extremely popular nature. Popular tales, ballads, and occasionally tracts were the staple diet of the trade. The effectiveness of this type of publication in reaching its public can be judged, to some extent, by the fact that tracts were issued in this form, thereby hoping to turn its proven popularity towards more elevating material. It was in this spirit that Hannah More published her *Repository Tracts* (1795–1798) which led with reasonable directness to the foundation of the Religious Tract Society. The majority of the chapbooks, however, concentrated on the sensational rather than the edifying, although useful, in the sense of commercially successful, morals were frequently drawn from the most unlikely stories. Ballads of popular contemporary events figure largely among the chapbooks with the result that they share a public with the broadsheets, many of which served a similar purpose. It was a kind of publication which was obviously a "natural" for the presentation of material for children, and these chapbooks constitute a vital part of the history of this branch of literature. It is not surprising that F. J. Harvey Darton should have devoted one whole chapter to them in his *Children's Books in England*.

In appearance, they nearly all share certain basic physical attributes. They are small in size, usually made up and stitched into eight pages of somewhat inferior paper. Illustrations were provided by woodcuts which frequently translate into visually effective terms the sensation of the chapbook itself. The result was the cheapest form of "book" publication available during the period of its prime.

Since they are not very strictly definable, it is difficult to be at all confident as to when they appeared on the book selling scene. Nevertheless works which show the main characteristics of chapbooks appear among some of the early pieces of European printing and the New England States provided early evidence of similar popularity across the Atlantic. Their major period of popularity lies between the middle of the seventeenth century and the middle of the nineteenth century. They flourished in the social and economic conditions when cheap reading matter could be easily hawked around and sold directly to the readers. They died out when these conditions no longer obtained; when fairs had died out, when popular newspapers took over the responsibility of disseminating the lurid truths of everyday existence, and when newspaper shops began to provide a new means of distribution.

The term chapbook has some currency today. It is sometimes used to describe a publication that is almost the perfect antithesis of the original. It now often describes the publications of a private society when there is a desire to indulge the latent antiquarianism of its members.

ROY B. STOKES

CHARACTER RECOGNITION

Character recognition is the examination and identification of printed numerals, letters, and symbols and their translation into machine-usable language and is done by reading machines, or, more simply, readers. Readers automatically translate machine-printed and hand-printed characters directly into electric codes.

Modern readers are used as data input devices for scientific and business computers and for message entry in the field of communications. In communications, readers translate printed messages to codes that can be entered directly into the communications systems. More frequently, however, the coded messages are stored temporarily so that they may be entered for transmission into the communications system more conveniently and efficiently. As computer input devices, readers translate printed characters to electric codes that can be entered directly into a computer. However, it is more common to store the codes temporarily so that they may be entered into the computer upon demand, or at least under control of the computer.

Reading machines sometimes translate printed characters into electric codes that are used to form punch paper tapes or punch cards. The cards or tapes are then used in their customary manner for entering data into a computer or for other purposes.

Some reading machines are designed to read stenciled characters, some read embossed characters not unlike Braille, others read characters formed of electrically conductive ink, and still others read magnetic ink characters, but the following deals only with optical character recognition (OCR) and OCR readers. The majority of modern OCR readers can be subdivided into the following components (Figure 1): a transport to move the printed paper through a reading station, an optical scanner that provides video data defining the printed characters on their background areas, a data processor that is a network for processing and interpreting the video data, a decision section that decides the identity of the scanned character, electronic controls for the foregoing, and an encoder to translate the decision to machine language.

Generally speaking, most modern readers operate as follows: An image of each character on the document in the reading station is projected onto the scanner, which provides video signals defining each character and its background. These signals are processed for ease of machine handling and other reasons, and are then

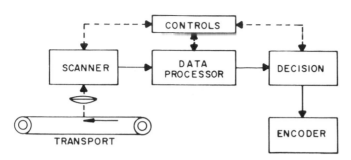

FIGURE 1. *Schematic of a reading machine.*

compared with a set of character standards, usually by electronic signal correlation or by analysis. A decision on the identity of each character is made and is encoded.

The function and the configuration of the machine components vary among commercially available machines. There is also a wide divergence of machine design purpose and performance. For example, some machines read only a single font of characters at low speeds of fewer than 100 characters per second. Other commercial machines read several fonts at speeds of the order of 2000 characters per second, and one company has produced readers that read five fonts at a through-put rate in excess of 14,000 characters per second. Some machines are designed to read one or two lines of print on each document; some read every line on a document of indefinite length, like a journal tape; and still others can be programmed to read the characters on a full page or on any selected portions of the page to the exclusion of other portions.

Historical

The historical background of modern readers can be divided into separate periods following certain discoveries, developments, and market demands. Before 1870 J. Carey of Boston described a picture transmission system using a full-field or total-area scanner made of a mosaic of selenium photocells. In 1884 P. Nipkow invented point-by-point scanning, using a moving scan element. For this purpose Nipkow disclosed a rotating apertured disc. As history shows, point-by-point electronic scanning made modern television possible. The concept of OCR followed Nipkow's disc. An early appreciation of OCR is evidenced by Hyman Goldberg's proposal in 1911 for an OCR reader designed as an on-line message-entry device for telegraphy.

Thereafter, until approximately 1945, there was a growing awareness of the potential of OCR, accompanied by considerable laboratory work. OCR was thought of as a method of transducing printed matter to sound to aid the blind, of entering coded data into such data processors as calculators and tabulators, and of entering messages into many kinds of communications systems. During this period the technology of electronics, as we now know it, came into being.

The largest steps toward modern readers were made after 1945. The advent of the electronic digital computer provided an urgent demand for high-speed data input devices and offered much of the technology necessary to build such devices. For example, modern computer designers and engineers developed a dexterity with available logic circuits (for example, with the Schmidt trigger) and invented many new ones. Computers and readers benefited immeasurably from the transistor and the large family of other solid-state components.

The earliest concepts envisioned OCR as a message-entry medium for communications, but the emphasis shifted to the data input function of business and scientific data-processing systems. At the present time the main demand is for OCR to translate printed characters directly into computer language. However, there is renewed interest in OCR as a message-entry medium for communications.

Source Material

As noted before, OCR as a means of translating printed characters to coded information was conceived of at least as early as 1911. In the years that followed, however, card and paper-tape punches and direct-entry manual keyboards were developed and became the accepted methods to fulfill nearly every data input requirement. These methods are limited to the speed and accuracy of the human operator, who must read the printed data and operate a keyboard in such a way that the punch encoder can translate the data into a set of codes in machine-usable language. For example, a keypunch operator must read numerals or words or both and translate them character by character into coded punched cards by depressing keys. The intermediate record, namely, the card, may then be read by a card reader into a computer, sorting machine, calculator, data transmission system, or other machine. On the other hand, an OCR reader is not limited to the speed and accuracy of a human operator, because it automatically reads printed characters and translates them directly to machine-usable codes.

Although this is an asset, OCR suffers a disadvantage in comparison with its nearest data input competitor, the punch card, card punch, and card reader. OCR uses the originally printed characters as source material. The punch card was designed and standardized for ease of machine reading; alpha-numeric printed characters were not. They were designed for the intellectual reading process of a human being and stylized for eye appeal and ease of human reading. Furthermore, punch-card stock and the punched holes conform to stringent specifications as to thickness, flexibility, size, hole position, and other features. Such ideal conditions do not exist for OCR, for which wide ranges of paper size, shape, weight, and optical reflectance are permitted. The characters may be printed almost anywhere on the paper, and, worse, the characters may be of any font or print quality. For instance, the characters may be formed by a series of dots made by a wire printer, by the ink-spattering impact of typewriter keys, or even by printing done by hand.

Some of these problems were recognized very early. For example, Goldberg's proposal shows a full alpha-numeric font (Figure 2) designed especially to facilitate reading by machine. Today committees of the USA Standards Institute are making

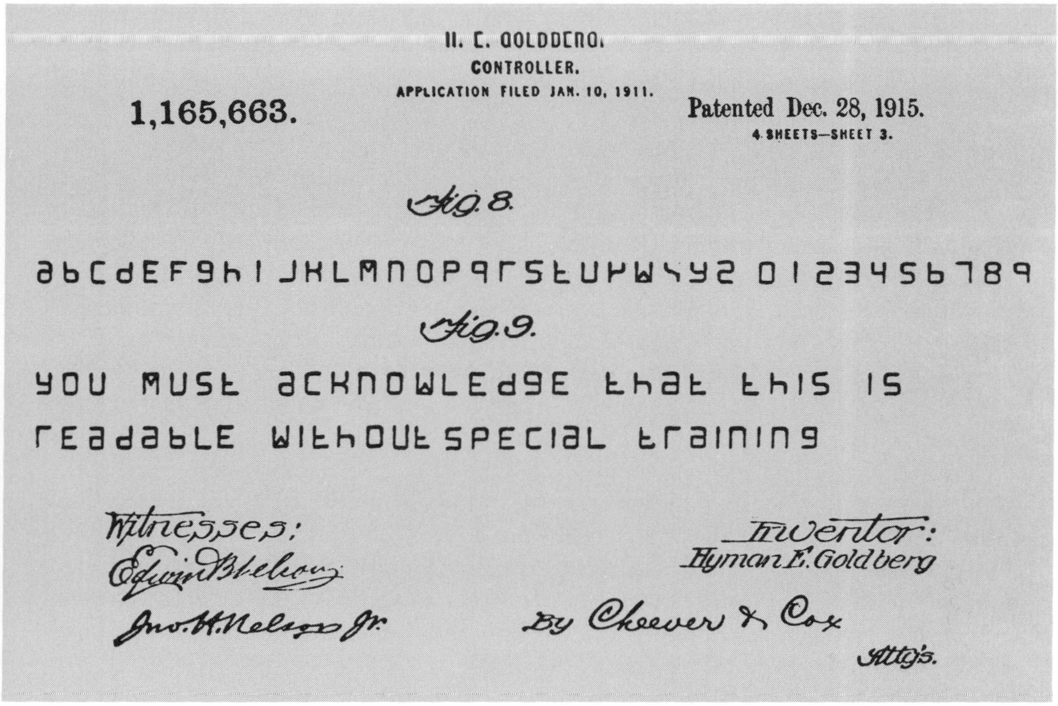

FIGURE 2. *Early font stylized for machine reading.*

an effort to establish acceptable standard fonts for machine reading (Figure 3). These have been offered to industry for its acceptance. Even if such fonts are accepted, a large amount of existing printing equipment will not be changed, and vast quantities of printed matter exist in nonstandard fonts to be read by machine.

Examples of the latter are found in the Library of Congress, where title, author, and other data are printed on a file card for each of its millions of books. If the Library wanted to use OCR to enter all this printed information into a computer system to provide for almost instantaneous recall of works—by subject, for example—the existing file cards would have to be read by machine. This is a small task compared with that faced by the U.S. Post Office, which cannot expect all mailers to use a standard font or even a reasonable number of fonts. The Post Office processed well upward of 70 billion pieces of mail in 1968. Letter mail

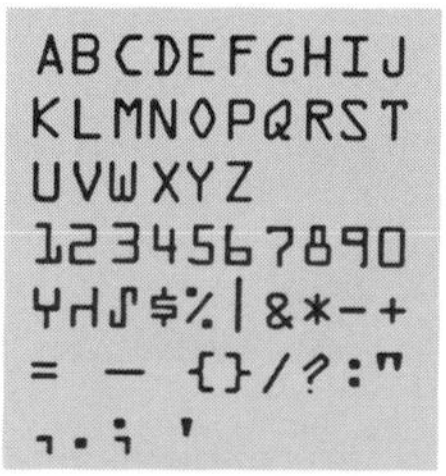

FIGURE 3. *Proposed USA Standards Institute (USASI) font.*

envelopes are of numerous colors, sizes, shapes, and thicknesses. Zip codes alone are machine printed in hundreds of numeric fonts, and no meaningful estimate of the number of hand-printed fonts can be made.

The paper transport for an OCR reader presents more of an engineering problem than a transport for a card punch or a card reader. Cards have sufficient body in their 7-mil thickness to be shaved by a picker knife one by one from a hopper stack, and may be easily transported and stacked. In comparison, present OCR readers must handle paper that is so thin a pneumatic or friction feeder is required, the paper tends to skew and flutter during transport, it is sensitive to static charge accumulation, and it will not stack neatly. With the uniform 7-mil thickness of cards, detection of an occasional double feed (two cards fed at once) requires a simple thickness gauge and brush-back roller. With the wide range of paper thicknesses encountered in OCR, double feeding is more likely and more difficult to detect and correct.

Searching, finding, and registering each printed character or its image are quite difficult in OCR readers. Punches form the columns and the holes in each column with great precision, so card readers do not have a difficult registration problem. On the other hand, printed characters formed by most machines, such as typewriters and high-speed printers, are skewed, rotated, vertically higher or lower than adjacent characters, horizontally spaced different distances from each other, and of differing distances from any edge of the paper.

The very nature of OCR causes the machines to be sensitive to the optical properties of the paper on which the characters are printed. For example, readers function by detecting so-called black characters (100% light absorbing) on a so-called white background (100% light reflecting). These percentages are never encountered, and in a practical case they vary not only from one document to another but also considerably within the same document. In developing video signals (described later) the machine must decide whether a given point on the sheet is to be considered white or black, and the decision becomes difficult with the interplay of the above variables. This decision making can be adjusted manually or dynamically in modern machines, but there is the ever-present risk of the machine deciding that a smudge on the paper is a black part of a character or that a lightly printed character or part of a character is "noise" and should be neglected.

Summarizing, OCR source material, including both the print and the paper, is not, and cannot be expected to be, ideal or near ideal for machine handling and reading. However, highly satisfactory results have been obtained with moderately reasonable care in the selection of paper and in the printing operation, whether by hand or by machine.

Basic OCR Machine Components

As noted earlier, the majority of modern readers are constructed of at least these components: a transport, an optical scanner, a data-processor network, a decision section, and an encoder. They are defined and commented upon below.

DOCUMENT TRANSPORTS

The document transport is a mechanical device for feeding printed matter for machine reading. A printed continuous web, such as pin-fed paper or journal tape, is drawn from a supply and is directed continuously or in steps through an optical reading station. After reading, it is either folded or wound on a take-up reel.

Individual sheets containing one or more lines of print are stored in a hopper stack and are fed one by one, generally by a pneumatic or friction feeder. For single-line reading some machines feed the sheets in a direction parallel to the line of print through a reading station, where they are read on the fly and directed into stackers or into sort bins; other readers have the reading station at the top of the hopper stack, so that the top document can be scanned and, if necessary, easily rescanned and read before transportation to a sort bin; and in some cases each sheet is fed to a reading station, stopped, read, and directed to a sort bin.

Readers for sheets containing a considerable number of lines of print are generally called page readers. The transports use feeders and stackers similar to those already described. However, the sheets are moved by friction or vacuum conveyors in a direction normal to the parallel lines of print through a reading station for reading on the fly. More usually, the sheets are moved to the reading station, deskewed, and stopped under switch or photocell control. They are then stepped through the reading station while each character of the successive lines is scanned, recognized, and encoded.

It is the practice today to request reading machine users to have the lines of printed characters formed perpendicular to one edge of the sheet, which is used as a reference edge for squaring the paper and hence the print in the reading station. Machines may handle only one size and weight of sheets, be adjustable to handle batches of different sizes, or handle intermixed sizes. Almost all machines have some means to detect and correct double-fed documents. They are generally thickness or light-transmissive responsive, although pneumatic logic devices have been used for this purpose.

SCANNERS

The term scanner is often used to designate an entire reading machine, but it is more properly used in its technical sense to designate a component of a reading machine. Although the designs of readers require the scanner to perform many different functions, a scanner basically is a device that photoelectrically examines an area point by point and provides electric signals that correspond to the detected light (or lack of light) at each point. All readers, except optical mask matching machines, which are not now in common use, have scanners.

Mechanical Scanners. The most common mechanical scanner is the disc scanner (Figure 4). It is made of a rotating apertured disc with a photocell located behind it. A moving image of a character is projected onto the face of the disc so that successive holes in the disc traverse the image. Thus, the photocell experiences the

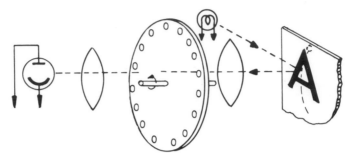

FIGURE 4. *Disc scanner.*

light and dark shades of the image and provides corresponding analog signals. Apertured drums have been used in place of discs to form analogous scanners. Also, there has been a wide variation in aperture shapes, including slots, round holes, character-feature shapes, and others.

Mechanical scanners are limited by the speed of the disc or drum. If design and manufacturing care are exercised, reading rates of approximately 500 characters per second can be achieved with disc scanners. This rate has been more than doubled in the laboratory by one manufacturer, who used a specially designed disc rotating at very high speed in an atmosphere of inert gas.

In reading-machine applications the disc scanner causes successive scanner holes to traverse the character image area by successive scan lines in a manner to form a raster covering the image area. The image area is electrically sampled along each scan line a number of times, usually by gating strobe pulses with the amplified photocell signals. Thus, the entire area is scanned to provide video signals that the reader interprets to recognize the character. The product of sample frequency and the number of scan lines covering the character area defines the scanner resolution, that is, the extent to which the character area is subdivided into a sub-area representing electric signals. The range of resolution in present readers is approximately 30 to 3000 bits.

Column and Row Photocell Scanners. In the mechanical scanner a character image is moved in one direction, usually by a movable mirror or by the motion of the paper, and the mechanical scan device, for example, a disc, is located so that the scan holes travel in a direction coplanar with, and perpendicular to, image movement. The rotational speed of the disc is the reading-rate limiting factor. The column or row photocell scanner used in many present machines scans more quickly. A column scanner consists of a column of photocells or, more usually, an array of fiber optical rods or light pipes, one end of each of which is arranged in a column over which the character image is swept, for instance, by the motion of the paper. The opposite ends of the light pipes are optically coupled with the photocells. Thus, gating the photocell signals with strobe pulses, synchronized with the motion of the paper, results in a column-by-column accumulation of video signals representing the full character area. This type of scanner is limited as to speed by how quickly the paper or the optical device used to sweep the character images over the columnar ends of the light pipes moves. A row scanner is identical to a column scanner, except that one set of ends of the light pipes is arranged in a row instead of a column, with the orientation of the printed character still the frame of reference.

Resolution of the column or row scanner is the product of the number of photocells and the number of strobe signals per character area. In the column scanner, for example, the number of photocells determines the number of samples of the image in each vertical scan line, and the number of scan lines is equal to the number of times the column of photocells is sampled as the character image is moved over the column. As few as five and as many as 512 photocells have been used in commercial machines with this type of scanner.

Photocell Mosaic Scanners. It is believed that the earliest scanner was composed of a mosaic of photocells covering the entire area to be photoelectrically examined. Today two kinds of mosaic scanners are used in OCR, the full-area mosaic and the mosaic with photocells positioned solely at strategic locations in the full area. The latter type of mosaic lends itself well for reading characters by detecting and interpreting only significant points or features of the character image, as described later.

Mosaic scanners function like photocell column scanners, except that the full character area is examined concurrently, rather than column by column, to provide the video signals. Most other scanners develop the video by a point-by-point and line-by-line accumulation of video signals. The mosaic scanner is better suited for analog readers than for the more common digital readers. Analog and digital readers will be considered later.

Flying Spot Scanners. Each of the above scanner types functions by a point-by-point examination of an image of the character area formed on the photosensitive portion of the scanner. The flying spot scanner, on the other hand, functions by sweeping a spot of light over the character itself so as to cover the area by successive adjacent lines, with one or more photocells arranged to respond to the reflected light. Early flying spot scanners were made of a light source and a movable light reflector, such as a mirror or a series of mirrors, to sweep a spot of light over the character area. An appreciable laboratory effort is now being made to perfect use of a laser as the source of light for flying spot scanning. However, the current modern OCR flying spot scanner uses an electron-beam tube to form and sweep a spot of light in controlled paths over selected areas. Many techniques and circuits for this type of scanning have evolved from television technology.

The typical flying spot scanner (Figure 5) includes a flat-face, single-beam cathode-ray tube (CRT), together with x and y deflection and other control circuits to move the scanning spot to ordered positions or in selected paths or patterns. The spot of light is focused by a lens to impinge on the character area.

CRT flying spot scanning is by far the most flexible and versatile scanning method used in OCR at this time. It can be used with any of the several reading techniques that are described later. However, it is especially well suited for curve tracing. In curve tracing the CRT spot follows the outline of the character and the excursions of the beam are interpreted for character recognition.

Whether used for curve tracing, for raster point-by-point scanning, or for other

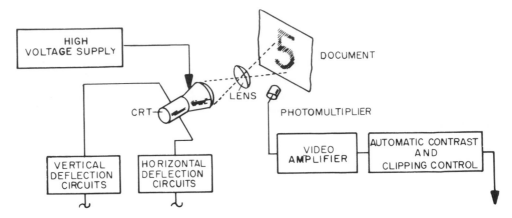

FIGURE 5. *Cathode-ray tube flying spot scanner.*

scanning, the CRT flying spot scanner is used to excellent advantage in other ways. For example, the CRT can be placed in a prescan search mode in which the spot coarsely and quickly examines a large area to locate specific fields or to locate characters on the document. Then the CRT control circuits place the spot in the video extracting scan mode. As a prescan function, the CRT can measure the size of a character, enable light reflectance measurements to be made, or perform other functions.

Although the same relative spot size and resolution can be obtained with CRT scanning as with other types of scanning, CRT scanning suffers certain disadvantages. It is inherently expensive and the excursions of the spot respond nonlinearly with deflection signals. The consequences of all forms of nonlinearity are more serious in OCR than in most other uses of CRT scanning, such as television. Also, flying spot and especially CRT flying spot scanning must take place in a light-tight zone to exclude ambient light. The persistence of the tube phosphor limits speed. Commercial machines using CRT scanning can, however, read more than 1500 characters per second.

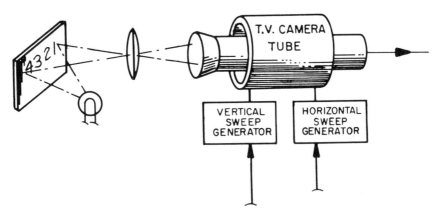

FIGURE 6. *Television camera scanning.*

Television Camera Scanners. Television cameras have been used for OCR scanning (Figure 6). The document is evenly illuminated and placed in the field of view of the camera tube. The raster generated within the tube covers the area of interest, and reflected light is detected by a photo mosaic. Video signals defining the character and its background are derived from the outputs of the camera tube.

This type of scanning is slow because of the persistence of the image in the majority of television camera tubes, for instance, in the Vidicon. In addition, the resolution of the Vidicon is too low for many OCR applications, and the noise level is high. On the other hand, when an image orthicon is used for OCR, the procedure is similar to that with the Vidicon, but the results are considerably better. The major drawbacks of image orthicon scanning are the very high cost of the tube and the high cost and complexity of its necessary precision control circuits.

PRESCANNERS

A prescanner is a photosensitive device located either ahead of or as part of the scanner. It is used to determine one or more conditions of the characters and paper prior to scanning the characters for recognition. A prescanner does not require and does not ordinarily function with as high a resolution as the video extraction scanner. In addition to character size measurements and location of characters on a large area, a prescanner may be used to determine the average light reflectance of the document and the characters, to determine whether characters touch each other, and to determine other conditions for which adjustments can be made automatically by the reader to facilitate the reading function. Sometimes line-tracking circuits are associated with a prescanner. Such circuits predict the probable vertical position of each character in a line by the vertical position of the preceding character.

DATA PROCESSOR

The data processor or processor network is the circuitry that manipulates the video signals from the scanner and prepares them for character identity decision. In machines having a prescanner the pertinent processor functions are controlled by the prescanner signals.

Analog versus Digital. Just as in a television camera, the video signals at the photocell output terminals are analog—that is, neglecting several kinds of non-linearity of the photocell, the signal strength is proportional to the light falling on the photosensitive surface of the photocell. It is more difficult for many types of logic circuits to handle analog signals than it is for such circuits to handle digital data. Accordingly, most commercial readers convert the analog video signals to digital signals early in the data processor network of the machine. In doing this the machine decides that each scanned subarea is either black or white and represents it as a binary digit or bit of information. In other words, the analog video is quantized to black or white digital information. It is not uncommon for machines to quantize the video signals to several levels representing white, shades of gray, and black.

A few commercial machines retain the analog signals throughout to final recognition notwithstanding various design difficulties. The author favors analog machines. One reason is that the source material—namely, the characters as printed on paper—is never perfectly black on a perfectly white background. Both colors vary over wide ranges of light reflectances, and the analog machine more accurately preserves and uses the gradations of gray in the character identification process.

Therefore, except in analog machines, one of the functions of the data processor is to quantize the analog video signals to digital signals representing black and white. The machines that quantize the analog video to digital signals representing black, shades of gray, and white coarsely simulate the original analog values.

In some machines—for example, electronic area correlation types—the data processor includes a shift register that acts as a short-term image register for the video signals. In these machines the data processor moves the video data in the register to cope with the problem of vertically registering the character video with the character standards built into the machine.

In feature analysis machines, the processor directs the video signals so that they will be compared with character feature standards; certain feature analysis machines have the processor network encode the features to facilitate internal handling.

Printed characters that may seem to be well printed can show defects upon magnification for OCR (Figure 7). The data processor of some machines filters isolated dark spots and fills rough edges and holes in the electronic representation of the character by examining points surrounding each subarea and either adding or filtering black video in accordance with sets of logic rules. For example, if a single subarea is black and all the surrounding subareas are white, the black subarea is concluded to be noise and is filtered.

Normalizing is accomplished both in the data processor and, in some machines, ahead of it to reduce the problem associated with reading fonts of different sizes. Normalizing is changing the apparent size of each printed character to a single size or obtaining that effect in the reading machine. Some of the normalizing methods are explained below.

An adjustable lens system interposed between the document and scanner is capable of forming a selected size image of each character on the scanner. Thus, by measuring the size of each printed character—for example, by measuring circuits associated with a prescanner—the lens system can be adjusted by servo signals obtained from the measuring circuits. This is a low-speed system and is subject to mechanical failure because of the millions of mechanical cycles that are rapidly accumulated in normal reading tasks.

Image tubes capable of changing the size of the displayed image have been interposed in the optical path between the printed character and scanner. Such systems are not completely satisfactory because the tubes introduce character distortion and other optical difficulties.

In machines using a shift register for the video signals, normalizing has been

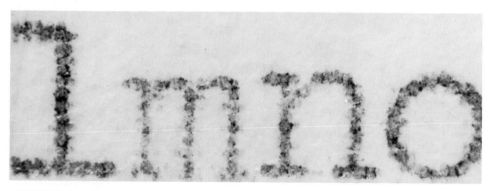

FIGURE 7. *Enlarged characters formed by wire printer (top) and by typewriter (bottom).*

accomplished by enlarging or compressing the temporarily stored video image. Normalizing in this manner is costly and risky because it might discard significant data in compressing the electronic image or add false information in enlarging the electronic image.

Another normalizing process can be practiced with scanners that cover the character area with a number of adjacent parallel scan lines, each of which extracts point-by-point samples of video information. A photocell and disc, a row or column of photocells, and a cathode-ray tube flying spot scanner are examples of these scanners.

Consider the operation with a CRT scanner. The height and width of each character is measured—for example, by measuring circuits operative while the CRT is placed in a search-and-measure mode. Signals representing height and width of the character are stored and used when the CRT is placed in a character scanning mode as follows. The height signal is used to adjust the sample frequency, that is, the spacing of video samples taken point by point in each vertical scan line. The adjustment is such that the character, regardless of its height, is covered by the same number of point-by-point samples. The samples are closer together for a short character than for a tall character. The stored width signal is used to adjust the spacing of the vertical scan lines of point-by-point samples so that characters of all widths are covered with a raster containing the same number of lines and the same number of video samples in each line. The result of using this process is that the varied sizes of the printed characters are each represented as the same by the video signals that are processed by the reader.

Of the normalizing techniques described, this one is considered to be the soundest. However, it is costly, presupposes a prescan, can be used only in high-resolution machines, and introduces a variable in the effective resolution because a very large character is resolved into the same number of bits as a small character.

Although rotational orientation of printed characters, often referred to as character skew, was mentioned elsewhere, it is noted here that the CRT scanner can be controlled so that the raster will be rotated to conform to the orientation of the printed character. Normalizing in the short-term shift register memory mentioned above is accompanied by a deskewing step in certain machines.

Character Standards. Character standards are the devices with which a printed character is compared to identify it. Optical transparencies or stencils configured like the printed characters or their features are the simplest standards.

Many machines have electronic masks usually constructed as resistor adders that are driven by the video signals provided by the scanner. The adders yield character correlation signals that are examined by the decision section of the machine, and the identity of the scanned character is determined from the correlation signals.

Other forms of character standards are counters and logic networks that respond to the video signals and record lengths of features, their positions, curvatures, joining and splitting lines, loops, and other intelligence concerning the character. Standards for features are sometimes designed as resistor adders, usually in hybrid machines, as discussed later.

DECISION SECTION

The decision section of a reader is as often considered a part of the processor as separately. It decides the identity of the scanned character and triggers an encoder to translate the character into machine language.

Machine decision is based upon one of two philosophical approaches. In the first, a character is identified when the video signals indicate that the scanned character has certain parts, pieces, and features and does not have certain other parts, pieces, and features. This is generally accomplished by an electronic logic tree or by a truth-table network of logic elements. A threshold requirement of fulfillment is often a logic rule imposed upon absolute decision.

The second type, originated for OCR by J. Rabinow, is the best-match decision. It identifies the scanned character on the basis of its being more like one particular standard than like any other standard in the machine. A voltage comparator is generally used for this purpose. The best-match decision would seem to be a better choice for reading poorly printed characters because theoretically no threshold is necessary. A scanned character that matches a standard by only 50% correlation, for example, may be the best match, even though that percentage is much lower than a tolerable absolute-decision threshold. In practice, however, this advantage is compromised by the imposition of a threshold for minimum correlation made necessary by subtle machine-reading dynamics and requirements for certain levels of accuracy and reject rates.

CONTROL CIRCUITS

The control circuits of a reading machine actuate and synchronize the operations of all the basic components of the reader. For the most part they are straightforward, and the same is true of the functions performed by them. A few exceptions are mentioned below.

Read Trigger Signals. As each character is scanned, the video signals in analog machines or the processed video signals in digital machines are examined to determine that the scanning of the character is complete. The clear space alongside of or between adjacent characters is sought, and when it is found the decision section of the machine is triggered to decide upon the identity of the character. When adjacent characters touch (Figure 7) or horizontally overlap there is no space between characters and, in simple machines, no read trigger signal is given for the first of the pair of touching characters. Thus the first character of the pair is missed completely, misread, or rejected. Touching characters occur often enough for them to be a formidable problem in OCR. An early solution that was proposed is to scan each line of print first left to right and then right to left, thereby successively recognizing the different trailing characters of the touching pair. The expense in time and equipment is presently considered to be too great for commercial application of this proposal.

Several other solutions are found in commercial readers. One is to note the correlation signals provided by the character standards continually during the scanning of a character. Upon attainment of a threshold correlation signal representing about 65% to 75% correlation, scanning continues for a short time and the read trigger signal is given. In effect this system anticipates where the end of a scanned character should be and provides a trigger signal whether there is a space there or not.

Another solution is to determine the pitch of the printed characters and provide read trigger signals at a frequency corresponding to that pitch. At each existing space between characters the system is resynchronized, making it quite reliable.

Still another solution is found in a system that detects frequency patterns of optimum correlation signals in a line of printed characters. The patterns provide read trigger signals at locations corresponding to positions in a line of print, where character spacing is expected even though no space exists between adjacent characters.

Photocell Automatic Gain Control. Many kinds of photocells have been used as parts of OCR scanners, including a variety of photodiodes, phototransistors, and other solid-state devices. Although small and compact, solid-state photocells are not as widely used as photomultipliers, which have greater gains and other advantages. For example, some solid-state photocells are totally nonresponsive to certain colors or to analine dyes (ballpoint pens) of any color.

Since OCR depends for operability upon optical contrast, servo circuits for the photocells and their amplifiers are desirable or necessary. Otherwise the signal of one photocell of a scanner may represent a point as gray while the signal of another photocell of the same scanner may represent an identical point as white. Fast-acting electrooptical feedback circuits control the photocell circuits so that all the photocells within a scanner respond uniformly. Analogous servo circuits are sometimes used to respond to an area of the paper, generally as a prescan function, and the threshold for quantizing the video signals is adjusted accordingly. This facilitates reading light or bold print on different background shades or colors.

Reading Machines Classified by Reading Technique

OPTICAL MASK MATCHING

Optical mask matching machines recognize characters by projecting an image of a printed character along an optical path toward a photocell. Masks like open stencils or transparencies configured like each character in the machine vocabulary are serially interposed in the optical path to intercept the character image ahead of the photocell. The resulting photocell signals correspond to the correlation between the printed character and each mask, allowing one correlation signal associated with image comparison to one mask to be selected as representing the printed character.

To increase recognition speed, optical mask machines have been constructed that enable the printed character to be compared with all the masks of the machine simultaneously: An optical system simultaneously projects images of the printed character onto all the masks. A photocell behind each mask provides a signal that corresponds to the correlation of the printed character image with its mask, enabling selection and character recognition as above.

Simple optical mask comparison machines cannot distinguish characters that are exact subsets of others. For example, the image of an E will satisfy both an E mask and an F mask perfectly, thereby producing an ambiguity. This problem is overcome in some machines by obtaining the effect of using both negative and positive images and masks for such characters and logically combining the results. This effect is obtained by inverting the signal of the photocell associated with one mask of each pair and logically combining it with the signal of the photocell associated with the other mask of the pair.

A simpler solution to this problem is a logic circuit that functions to identify the printed character as an E in the above example wherever both the E and the F mask photocells provide equal correlation signals. This can be done because an F image will not satisfy the E mask and is unambiguously identified by comparison with the F mask. The same logic is applied to identify other subset pairs of characters, like the O and the Q.

Light attenuation presents a serious problem in multiple-image optical systems. Partially to overcome this and the ambiguity problem, sharing masks that are configured to represent parts or feature groups of closely appearing characters in the machine vocabulary and combining the photocell signals so as to identify the characters has been suggested. However, a more serious problem in optical mask machines is making the image of a printed character register precisely with each optical mask, even at low reading rates. The subject of character registration has been mentioned before and will be discussed later.

Simple forms of direct-comparison optical mask machines rely on the measurement of light resulting from comparing a character image with the masks of a set. In an optical sense total light extinction is deemed to signify a perfect match. The difference in shape and area between some characters, for example, O and Q, is so small as to impair reading reliability. To overcome this difficulty some mask machines have a scanner in the optical system to scan the image-to-mask comparison, causing the photocell to experience comparatively large mismatch (nonextinction) signals. Such signals are stored in one of numerous ways, for example, in peak detector circuits, and the character identity is determined on the basis of the stored signals.

The use of a scanner in an optical mask type of machine suggests the possibility of using holography in OCR. Typically, an image match in a hologram appears as a bright spot that can be detected by scanning the hologram. Holographic techniques are not used in OCR outside the laboratory; the other types of optical mask machines described so far have been built and used, but not extensively.

In addition to simple mask readers, optical mask machines of considerable sophistication have been constructed. For example, one alpha-numeric machine uses a CRT scanner in combination with a dual-beam kinescope, providing a display of negative and positive images of the scanned character. An optical tunnel and lens system projects a multiplicity of vertically displaced reproductions of the negative and positive kinescope images onto a set of comparison masks. The set contains adjacent groups of vertically displaced positive and negative transparencies. Photocells optically aligned with the masks have their signals logically processed to yield the correct character identity signal.

CURVE TRACING

Optical mask machines recognize characters by comparing character images to optical masks and measuring the correlation. When a scanner is used in such machines it produces a raster covering the image-to-mask comparisons to detect subareas of mismatch, namely, subareas where there is incomplete light extinction. Curve-tracing machines, on the other hand, recognize characters by tracking the outline of a character, noting the shapes, slopes, lengths, relative positions, junctures, and divergences of portions of the line trace that forms the character, and analyzing them for a character identity decision. Analysis is ordinarily accomplished by a logic tree or by comparison with a logic truth table of characteristic features of each possible character.

The scanning in a curve-tracing machine is ordinarily more complex than the simple scanning in other machines. In one curve-tracing machine a cathode-ray tube flying spot scanner produces a high-speed circular scan of small diameter that is propagated in a way so as to straddle the character outline. In another the circular scan follows the outside edge of the printed character. Tracking is accomplished by servo circuits that change the direction of propagation of the circular scan so that it continually touches, and hence follows, the character outline. Such characteristics as line slopes, arcs and their directions, loops, line junctures, and splits are detected by noting the excursions of the circular scan as it tracks the character. Thus, in this form of machine, the scanner does not provide video signals in the usual sense of the term.

In another curve-tracing machine the scan pattern is in the form of a raster of adjacent scan lines covering the character area. The first position of engagement of each scan line with the character is noted and from groupings of adjacent engagements with the character, the shapes, slopes, junctures, and so on, of one edge, say the left edge, of the character are noted. Then the scan pattern is rotated 90° and the features of the top edge of the character are found. Another 90° rotation of the scan pattern yields similar information about the right side of the character, and another 90° rotation gives us the bottom edge of the character. The character is identified by analysis of the noted characteristics. For example, a set consisting of two left arcs facing two right arcs, plus facing top and bottom arcs, will be analyzed as representing an 8.

Since curve-tracing machines extract information concerning the shape of the character by tracking the character outline, tracking must ordinarily progress in any direction to follow the character outline. CRT scanning is well suited for tracking by applying servo control signals to the deflection circuit signals, but other scanning methods can and have been used. For example, a line scanner producing a raster over the character image area has been used. Upon detection of a part of the character by a scan line a first tracking circuit is energized. All subsequent scan line crossings of the character that are close in scan time or in space to the preceding crossing maintain the energized condition of the tracking circuit. If two or more crossings of the character occur in one scan line, two or more additional tracking circuits are energized and independently propagated, as above. On completion of the scan raster covering the character area, the tracking circuits will have specific excursion characteristics on which to base the character identity decision. This machine tracks the character image in only one direction— for instance, from left to right. In that respect it differs from other curve-tracing machines, and can almost as easily be classified as a feature analysis machine.

FEATURE ANALYSIS

One of the earliest truly modern OCR readers was an analysis machine developed by D. Shepard. Feature analysis machines, like most curve-tracing machines, recognize characters by noting characteristic shapes, curves, loops, line feature lengths, directions, position, and any other geometric aspect of a character the designer selects. By interpreting the noted features a character identity decision is reached. The difference between curve-tracing and feature analysis machines may seem superficial, but it leads to significant differences in capability. At present, suffice it to say that curve-tracing machines have an inherent capacity to read characters of many sizes and shapes—for example, hand-printed numerals. The reason is that a closed loop above another is always an 8, no matter how large or small either or both of the loops are, and, very importantly, the tracing scan spot follows the loops regardless of their sizes. Feature analysis machines, on the other hand, extract features from a character by means other than tracking the outline of the character and are more sensitive to size and shape variations.

Typically, feature analysis machines have a scanner and feature recognition devices whose outputs are in logic tree (Figure 8), truth-table, or another recognition configuration. As an example, four recognition devices may be used to recognize an E. One notes the vertical feature and the other three note the vertically spaced horizontal features. Figure 8 shows a more comprehensive recognition system that relies upon area shapes as well as character lines in the analysis. Many feature analysis machines have been built, with a great deal of variety in their designs.

An early analysis machine was very similar in concept to the more advanced optical mask machines. It had all the features formed as stencils in a rotating disc. An image of a printed character was projected onto the disc and interrogated for features by a photocell located behind the stencils. Not only were the features detected but their positions—left, right, top, and bottom—were noted by the feature recognition devices. These each consisted of one of the stencils and a relay or flip-flop operating in response to photocell signals. Upon completion of the examination of the character image, the feature recognition device relays were analyzed to identify the character.

Later analysis machines omit the stenciled disc and have electronic feature recognition devices, such as counters arranged to record successions of scanner extracted dark video signals and other signal patterns that represent features of the scanned character. Positional information is very important in feature machines.

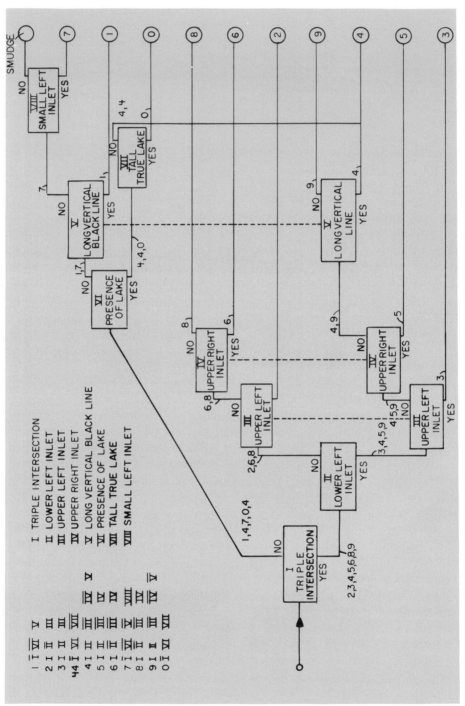

FIGURE 8. *Logic tree for character recognition by feature analysis or by curve tracing.*

For example, a printed comma and apostrophe are identical but distinguishable by their respective low and high positions with respect to the nearest character. The same is true of dimensional information. A comma and a period are so nearly alike and so small that the logic used is that if a dot is low in the line of print and has considerable height relative to width, it is a comma. If it is low and approximately symmetrical, it is a period.

INTERCEPT DETECTION

Intercept detecting machines are not unlike feature analysis machines. Intercept detection is practiced in a variety of ways. The machines read both machine-printed and hand-printed numeric characters. They recognize characters by observing the presence or absence of character line fragments at specific locations (which are "intercepted" by scan lines). In the simplest case a single vertical reference line and two vertically spaced horizontal reference lines cross the vertical line to form seven reference positions along the reference line sections. Assume that an image of the character 3 is projected onto these crossed reference lines. Note the number and relative locations of the intercepts where the reference line sections are crossed by the 3. They are at the top, upper right, lower right, and bottom positions, with a logical OR condition at the center (there may, but need not be, an intercept at the center). There is an absence of intercepts at the upper and lower left positions. By such logical analysis the machine determines the identity of the 3. A wide range of sizes and shapes of numeric characters can be recognized in this way. However, reading a full alpha-numeric set is not possible, nor can symbols be identified.

The intercept principle has been used for reading conductive ink characters by having each section of the three crossed reference lines made as an electric contact and pressing the printed character thereon. The same kind of equipment is used to recognize characters while they are being hand printed by placing the paper over the contacts and having them closed by the pencil or pen moving over the paper in forming the characters. However, such machines are outside the scope of OCR.

An early simple intercept machine used a scanning disc having slots representing the two horizontal reference lines and other slots representing the vertical reference line described before. In operation, two images of a character, one rotated 90° with respect to the other, are simultaneously projected onto the disc. As the disc rotates, two photocells provide signals on the occurrence of character intercepts and on the lack of intercepts at the seven reference positions. From these data the identity of the character is determined.

In machines having a shift register for temporary storage of the video representation of the scanned character, intercept reading has been done by interrogating the seven reference positions in the shift register for character intercepts and for lack of character intercepts. Intercept reading has also been done with dilating scans and with spiral scans combined with radial scans originating from the center of the character and/or originating from two vertically spaced centers.

In one machine a spiral scan is used to determine the width and height of the character image and hence the vertical centers for the radial scans. Intercepts of the radial scan lines are detected and analyzed. More reading capability is inherent in this machine because the number of possible intercept locations is increased from seven to a larger number. CRT scanning seems to be the only practical scanning method for the last few examples of intercept reading.

Curve tracing is inherently suited for recognizing hand-printed characters, but so is intercept detection, when the task is limited to numerals, because it tolerates a great many size and shape variations in the printed characters.

ELECTRONIC AREA CORRELATION

In principle only, electronic area correlation machines are akin to mask matching machines. Both compare an a real representation of a printed character with a set of character standards and determine character identity on the basis of correlation. In the mask machine the character image is compared with an optical mask. In the electronic correlation machine the printed character is scanned in such a way that an electronic representation will be stored in a short-term memory for comparison with character standards that are often referred to as electronic masks. The similarity ends here.

In an electronic area correlation machine, the image of a printed character is scanned by any kind of scanner that covers the area with a raster of adjacent scan lines to provide video signals. These are stored in the short-term memory, for example, a shift register, so that operations can be performed on them, the primary operation being to determine correlation with character standards. In many machines the register is composed of flip-flop stages, each of which has complemental, that is, negative and positive, outputs that invert depending on whether the stage is storing black or white video.

The character standards are usually resistor adders connected to the black output terminals of the register stages wherever the character representation is expected and, for the NOT terms, to the white output terminals of the stages of the register wherever the character is not allowed to appear. Often the important details of each character are stressed, for instance, the tail of the Q to distinguish it from the O, by weighting accomplished by selecting values for the adder resistors corresponding to these character details.

After the register is loaded and the adders energized, a comparator determines which adder's signal correlates best with the stored video, that is, which adder provides the best correlation signal. Thus, the scanned character is recognized and is encoded for translation to machine language.

SELF-LEARNING AND ADAPTIVE

Although one or perhaps a few adaptive and self-learning machines have been constructed to special order, they are not available as commercial products. Much theoretical study, computer simulation, and experimental breadboarding has been and is being accomplished. Generally speaking, other types of readers function by comparing a printed character with fixed standards, such as optical or electronic masks, or by feature analysis, which relates to fixed standards by detection and interpretation of the character parts and pieces. Thus, the masks and interpreters must be designed for the particular font or few fonts that the machine is expected to recognize, granting that curve tracing and, to a lesser extent, intercept detection and feature analysis machines tolerate some latitude in character configuration.

The underlying thought of the adaptive machine is to compare characters with nonrigid or random masks and enable the machine to learn in a random fashion. As described later, one of the pressing needs in OCR today is a technique that will enable a machine to read characters of any machine-printed (Figure 9) or hand-printed font. Hand-printed numerals by different persons or even by the same person represent an uncalculable number of fonts; two hand-printed characters are seldom identical to each other. Self-learning and adaptive machines are said to satisfy this pressing need. Several have been suggested.

One proposed typical operation has a set of characters and their identities presented to the machine. A great many different kinds of alterable information concerning each character are stored in the machine. Then initial "training" and "learning" are begun. A large number of characters are presented to the machine for recognition. Each correct recognition reinforces the stored information. Rejection or incorrect identification of a character causes the stored information to be penalized by being altered to identify the character correctly. Thus, the machine is conditioned to read many variations of the characters of the original set.

The machine keeps a qualitative and quantitative record of each reinforcement and penalty of the alterable stored information, which is used to modify the nature and/or extent of subsequent reinforcements and penalties, and to initiate the process of adding a new character to the set that forms the machine vocabulary. Accordingly, as the machine performs reading tasks the stored alterable information continually adapts to the characters being read in the sense that there is dynamic reference adjustment responsive to the variations in characters being read.

Obviously, the rules and procedures for altering the stored information vary greatly in the independent work being done in connection with this class of machine. Also, while the unsolved problems are formidable, the objective, an all-font reader, will be a major accomplishment if it is realized. As a reference for comparison, a large hybrid machine using electronic area correlation, feature analysis, and other techniques was designed for numerals only. Nearly 100 fonts (1000 different shapes of the numerals 0 to 9) are read by that machine. Yet this machine can read only a fraction of the machine-printed numerals on envelopes handled by the Post Office, and none of the hand-printed numerals, except by chance. The problem of reading alphabetic characters was not entertained in the design of that machine. The point is that reading techniques like optical or electronic masks that require a set of fixed standards, or feature analysis and curve tracing, that require partially fixed standards, seemingly cannot hope to meet the design goal of an all-font machine. If one considers a change in character shape and/or size to be a change in font, there are entirely too many fonts. Indeed, the most powerful commercially available machines are capable of reading only a few full alpha-numeric

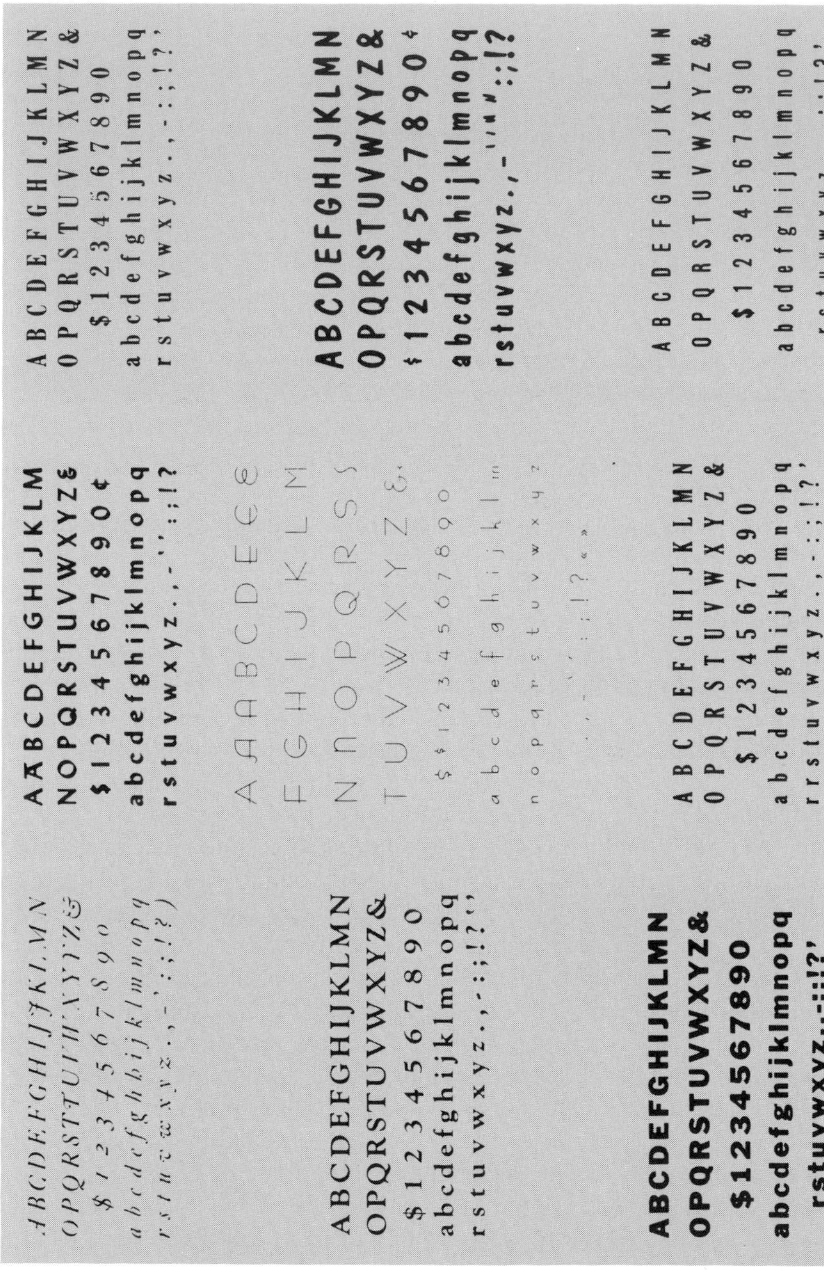

FIGURE 9. *Examples of selected fonts.*

fonts, and certain of these machines have such restrictions as reading only one font at a time.

One of the criticisms of the self-learning machine is that of early saturation to character convergence. For example, as numerous fonts of Os are presented to the machine and/or as the machine must identify the same O in numerous slightly displaced positions, the O recognition capacity becomes so enlarged that separation between O and Q becomes impossible. Although this same criticism has not been applied to other classes of multifont readers, it seems just as applicable. In other words, self-learning and adaptive machines should not be any more sensitive to such a limitation than the brute-force approach to multifont reading, where each possible character shape is represented by a separate standard, or where a comparatively low-order combining of features forms the standards.

HYBRID

Early machines and present simple machines use only one of the above classified techniques. The majority of readers built to special order or offered as commercial products are hybrid machines. They combine the more favorable aspects of several reading techniques. A common combination is an electronic area correlation machine that has elements of feature analysis and intercept detection to assist in the recognition of certain characters. Another common hybrid is a feature analysis machine with area correlation and intercept detection capabilities.

Word Recognition

There has been some effort to recognize words, particularly where the reading task can be satisfied with a moderately limited vocabulary. Reading the names of the fifty states and a limited number of cities in postal addresses is an example. The earlier proposed reading systems for word reading are variations of intercept detection combined with curve tracing, where the entire word is treated as a character. Thus, the character standards are designed to represent the cities and states, with the cities and states treated as characters.

Another proposed reader would use word recognition in several interesting ways. The machine is a character reader with a buffer at its output to store the recognized characters of a word. The buffer is unloaded after the last character of each word is recognized so long as no character in the word is rejected for failure to read it. When the reader rejects one or more characters of a word they are represented in the buffer with search symbols. Upon completion of such a word the buffer content is compared with a memory that forms a dictionary containing all possible words that will be cities and states in the above postal mail example. Comparison is made by substituting trial characters for the search symbols and searching the dictionary for a match after each substitution. The machine reads all the recognizable characters of a word and uses trial and error or guesswork to identify the remaining characters. It can be used not only to read words but also to verify and correct spelling, for instance, in proofreading documents by the reading machine.

Context as a Reading Aid

The above word reading technique can be considered to be character reading that draws upon context to assist reading. This is not uncommon, particularly when computer assistance is available in the total reading system. The extreme-case examples noted below exemplify the difficulties and show the extent to which context helps overcome them.

Many typewriters use the lower-case letter L to print the numeral 1. In most fonts the letter O and the zero are identical. Obviously the characters of each pair cannot be distinguished by their configuration. The problem is handled in several ways, one of which is to program the reader to read all characters in a given field on the document as numerals or as letters, for example, by disabling the numeric or alphabetic reading part of the machine when reading in the given field. It is not always known beforehand that certain fields contain only letters or only numbers. In most cases the characters are not so nicely separated in fields. Therefore, designers have programmed readers to identify a character as a number or a letter depending on whether the adjacent characters are recognized as numbers or letters. In some reading tasks this is acceptable, but in others, it is not. Other logical procedures can be programmed into a reader or, more usually, into a small computer that controls the reader, but it is considered impossible for a reader to distinguish the characters 10 as one-zero or L-zero or L-oh or one-oh by an alpha-numeric reader when nothing more is known about the characters, context, or field position.

Large research-oriented companies have probed the question of machine reading of cursive script. Within the framework of present technology it seems that some form of context assistance will be required if there is to be any hope of commercially acceptable machine reading of cursive script.

Remote Scanning

Computer systems often include more than one reading machine, and sometimes the readers are at diverse locations. Alternative reading-machine systems or services are now being offered. The paper transport and scanner of one reader has been packaged as a small unit to form a remote-terminal data collector. These units can be installed at locations that satisfy customer needs. As one of many possible examples, such data collectors can be located throughout a department store or a chain of stores, on one city or interstate. The units scan the source documents and provide video signals that are transmitted over communication lines to the video input portion of a central reader for translation to computer-acceptable codes. One of the advantages of this type of reading system is that even though the volume of data originating at each remote terminal is small, the number of input terminals economically justifies a very powerful central reader.

Existing OCR Problems

Some of the more urgent or difficult problems in OCR today include hand-printed character reading, multifont reading, vertical registration, and document transport.

HAND-PRINTED CHARACTER READING

Although it is possible to read hand-printed characters by most of the techniques described, some are more suitable than others. For example, it is obvious that a simple optical mask machine would be a failure because the source printing cannot be controlled sufficiently. Hand-printed characters vary in size, shape, angle, line thickness, and style, and readers are sensitive to each of these variables. Efforts to provide printing constraints for the writer have been resisted, and, furthermore, constraints only partially solve the problem.

One of the earliest constraints suggested consists of two vertically spaced dots around which the writer is asked to write numerals. This constrains size and rotational orientation of the numerals, and it was proposed for reading by the intercept detection method. Later, numerous variations of the two dots, such as six dots, guidelines, and others were field tested. Preprinted boxes formed by lines or contrasting color areas were also tried. Machine design either took advantage of the preprinted marks to assist vertical registration or ignored the marks by preprinting them in a drop-out color. For example, scanners using solar photocells are insensitive to red, so the marks were printed in red. Blue is the drop-out color for the more commonly used photomultiplier. However, at this time the market demand is still for a machine that will read unconstrained hand-printed characters.

Excluding adaptive machines, which are not commercially available, curve-tracing machines are least sensitive to character size and style and permit large rotation variations. In practice, however, they operate only reasonably satisfactorily, and then only with carefully formed, well-spaced, hand-printed characters. To a lesser extent hybrid curve-tracing feature analysis machines and pure feature analysis machines will tolerate character size, style, and rotation variations, but they read hand-printed characters only reasonably well. Intercept detection machines do not extract sufficient information from the printed characters to be as reliable as desired, and they are at least as sensitive to the above variables as curve-tracing and feature analysis machines.

MULTIFONT READING

Although hand-printed characters are formed in innumerable fonts, when used in connection with OCR the expression multifont connotes plural machine-printed character styles and/or sizes. The need for a multifont reading capability stems from the existence and use of untold numbers of typewriters, printers, imprinters, and other devices that print a variety of fonts. Only a limited number of potential users of OCR machines can or are willing to restrict their printing to a single font to accommodate the reading machine.

A number of multifont machines have been built to special order. However, they are expensive and usually quite slow, and their multifont capability is generally limited to a few fonts or is not truly multifont at all. Certain so-called multifont machines are more properly called selected font readers, since the machines must be programmed automatically or manually to disable all font capabilities except for the font actually being read. The reader mentioned before that reads approximately 100 intermixed fonts reads only numbers, and there is a vast difference between reading ten digits and trying to read the full alpha-numeric set together with the customary symbols.

Most multifont readers being offered commercially are selected font machines. For the most part they are feature analysis machines, electronic area correlation machines, or hybrids of the two. Curve tracing has not as yet been very successful for this task for several reasons. The tracking logic requires that the characters be free of breaks in the print and that they be well separated as printed. Also, the CRT tracking type of scanning is comparatively difficult and expensive.

Area correlation and feature analysis to a lesser extent read by comparing a scanned character with a set of physical standards representing both the shape and the size of possible characters. Thus, when there is disparity in either or both, the different sizes and/or shapes must be treated by the machine logic as separate characters. A single alpha-numeric font with both capital and lower-case letters, numbers, and symbols contains more than sixty-two characters, the exact figure depending on the number of symbols used. As fonts are added, machine complexity increases exponentially, accuracy is reduced, and speed is diminished. Fonts that differ only in character size are not as troublesome as fonts that differ in shape, because of the normalizing techniques some machines employ.

In conclusion, a high-speed, accurate, general-purpose reader for more than five or six alpha-numeric intermixed fonts printed with only average care will require technological advances to remain within the cost parameter established by economic justification.

VERTICAL REGISTRATION

The vertical registration problem has a profound effect on machine design, cost, and speed, and it is not unrelated to other machine design problems. At the outset, it is manifest that a character cannot be recognized with certainty unless it comes into the field of view of the scanner. If it comes only partially into view, it will be rejected as unreadable or, worse, erroneously read. The obvious solution is to scan a tall area.

This is done in some machines, but there are limits. For example, there is the risk of scanning fragments of characters above and below the desired character. These fragments can be excluded from the video, but only at the expense of the logic circuitry and the uncertainty introduced by any data-exclusion logic. Expense is an important consideration, particularly in area correlation machines that use a column of photocells in the scanner. The number of photocells needed to scan a tall area can become prohibitive when the cost of the photocells, amplifiers, and servo circuits is considered. Also, the shift register memory would have to be enlarged to accept all the video provided by the column of photocells. It becomes harder to make the video image in the register coincide with the character standards that are connected to the register at a fixed location. Also, it takes more time for the data processor to complete its assigned functions.

Suffice it to note that compromises are reached in machine design with respect to the size of area scanned for each character. In addition, it is not uncommon for the transport of a machine to adjust the position of the document to register the character vertically with the scanner. This is a slow process.

In optical mask machines, one of the methods used to obtain vertical registration with the scanner and with the character standards is to oscillate or otherwise move the character image vertically at a high rate while it moves horizontally at a slower speed. Oscillating mirrors, rotating multisided mirrors, rotating prisms, and the like have been used for this purpose. During such compound motions of the image there is a short period of time when the image coincides with the optical masks.

Cathode-ray tube spot scanning machines can move the scanning spot to the character location so that the scan raster covers the character area. Such machines are least troubled by vertical registration problems. However, keystone, barrel, and other distortions, as well as spot position inaccuracy, are troublesome.

Some machines have servo signal-controlled mirrors in the optical path of the scanner to adjust the vertical position of the character images on the scanner. The process is slow and presupposes a prescanner or plural scans of the same line of printed characters.

One commercial machine uses an oscillating mirror that oscillates the character image vertically at high speed over a horizontal row of photocells while the image is moved horizontally at a lower speed. The video passes upward and downward through the shift register in synchronization with the mirror oscillations. An area approximately twice the character height is covered, yet the register is small, corresponding with the tallest character. As the video shifts up and down in the register it must coincide with the character standards wired into the register. As in most machines of this general class, the highest correlation signals from the standards are stored in capacitors or other devices, and the character identity decision is based on the stored signals. The reading rate of this machine is limited to approximately 400 characters per second by the speed of the oscillating mirror whose purpose is to overcome vertical registration difficulties.

Many area correlation machines scan a character area much taller than the character and store the full video image or feature codes in a drum or shift register. The video image data or codes are then made to shift to a reference location or to pass through all possible positions in the register to require them to coincide with the character standards. This method overcomes the vertical registration problem at the expense of equipment and reading speed.

It is not uncommon to scan a tall area and by logical gating to compress the video in such a manner as to exclude all white areas above and below the vertical extremities of the character. However, all these systems are costly and time consuming, and introduce risks of error in reading.

To provide vertical registration tolerance without penalizing speed, parallel sets of character standards, each set vertically displaced from the other, have been connected to the shift register. In analog mosaic scanner machines that have no shift register, parallel sets of standards are overlapped but slightly vertically displaced in their connections with the photocells of the mosaic. Although speed is increased this way, the cost in equipment is still high.

DOCUMENT TRANSPORT

The subject of paper handling has been mentioned before and is summarized here. Transports for readers handling sheet material are expected to feed, convey, align precisely, stop, start, and stack numerous weights, thicknesses, kinds, and shapes of paper, one at a time, at speeds of as much as thirty pieces per second. At this time no known paper handler completely fulfills these expectations. Experimental work continues in many laboratories to improve and/or develop new paper handling mechanisms and techniques.

JOSEPH A. GENOVESE
CONTROL DATA CORPORATION

CHARGING SYSTEMS

See also *Automatic Data Processing, Library and Information Center Applications; Computers and Computing; Batch Processing*

The perfect charging system has been an elusive goal in libraries for almost a century. In 1880 the prescription for such a system included: (1) the location of every book absent from the shelf, how often every book has been issued, and the character of each day's loans; (2) the number of books taken out by each reader, with dates of loan and return; (3) the number of books issued each day, and the books overdue each day so that notices can be sent promptly; and (4) the borrower should be provided with the dates his books are due, and with receipts for their return. This prescription still covers the requirements for charging systems.

Concern with charging systems has been recurring about once each thirty years. Until the establishment of the *Library Journal* in 1876 there was no forum for exchange of ideas in library administration, so that it is impossible to ascertain earlier interest in the subject. But for the next quarter century there was continuing groping for systems that would combine the ideals of perfection and the practicalities of economy.

Systems in existence in 1876 frequently consisted of recording loans in consecutive order in a bound volume, comparable to the journal or day book used in accounting. In some libraries these journal entries were transferred into two ledgers: one a record of books by borrower, the other a record of borrowers of each book. As accounting practices moved to the use of separate ledger sheets, the practice was applied also to the library circulation registers. Although providing the data prescribed for the perfect system, two disadvantages emerged: patrons had to wait while the records were made, and the system was too expensive.

Transition from ledger sheets to cards for loan records was quite natural. An ingenious system involving use of a book card and a borrower envelope (or pocket) was described by Nina Browne in 1895. Each borrower was issued envelopes bearing his name and address equal to the number of books that he might have on loan at one time. Upon receipt of a book the borrower surrendered an envelope. The book card was removed from the book, inserted in the envelope, and then filed by call number behind a date guide. The date due was stamped in the book. Upon return, the record was removed from the file, the envelope returned to the borrower, and the card to the book.

Other experiments before 1900 included what were called indicator systems. One used in Leeds (England) provided for assignment of a small pigeon hole, approximately $\frac{1}{3}$ in. high $\times$ $2\frac{3}{4}$ in. wide to each book. The front of the bank of pigeon holes was covered with a glass door. When a borrower was issued a book, he relinquished his borrower card which was inserted into the proper compartment. Thus at a glance both patrons and librarians could know when a book was on loan.

By the turn of the century these and other experimental systems had been almost uniformly replaced by one of two book card systems: the Newark system for public libraries, a two-card system for academic libraries.

The Newark system involved the insertion of a card usually 3×5 in. in a pocket in each book. At the top of the card were typed call number, author, title, and perhaps accession number. Below these items were lines on which successive loans were recorded (see Figure 1).

The borrower upon registration was issued a card, also usually 3×5 in., similar in design to the book card, except that the lines were divided into two columns headed "due" and "returned." At the top of the card appeared the borrower's name, address, and registration number.

A loan transaction was executed by the library attendant's writing the borrower registration number on the first blank line of the book card, then stamping the date due on the book card, on a date due slip in the book, and in the "due" column of the first blank line on the borrower's card. The book and borrower card were given to the borrower, and the book card subsequently was filed by call number behind a date due guide. When returning a book the borrower was required to present his card, upon which the date was stamped in the "returned" column opposite the date due. The removal of the book card from the file and its return to the card pocket in the book would be performed later.

This system sacrificed the ready availability of the answer to the question, "Where is this book?", since the answer was available only by consulting daily files successively until the record was found.

The system also eliminated a borrower status file, by having the borrower him-

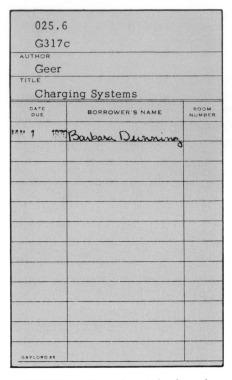

FIGURE 1. *Newark type book card.*

self carry his own record. But it did give the borrower a record of the number of books charged to him, and the dates they were due. For most public libraries these solutions appeared entirely satisfactory for at least a quarter of a century.

Almost simultaneously with the adoption of the Newark charging system in public libraries a two-card adaptation was being widely adopted in college and university libraries. At the time, book stacks were closed to students in most libraries, so that a call slip or card filled out by the patron was given to an attendant who went to the stacks to fetch the book. This call slip was retained as one part of the double record of the book on loan.

In this typical two-card system, a book card similar to that used in the Newark system was placed in a pocket in each volume. At the time of loan, the attendant removed the card, wrote the borrower's name or number on the next blank line, stamped the date due on the book card, the date due slip in the book, and the call slip. In this system the book cards were interfiled by call number with those already on loan, the call slips by call number behind a guide for the date due.

Thus, the question "Where is this book?" could be answered readily, and follow up on overdue loans could be made from the call slip file. The system did not provide for limitation of the number of loans to an individual, nor did it provide for answering the question "What books does John Smith have checked out?" The system also required double work in filing and discharging from two files.

In some libraries with open stacks the call slip was replaced by a second book card, usually of a different color, with the borrower signing his name on the next blank line.

The stability in charging systems which had existed for twenty-five years began to be upset in 1927 with the introduction of the Dickman Book Charging Machine in the Washington, D.C. Public Library. The machine used an embossed borrower card to imprint the borrower's number on the book card. This operation was supposed to increase both the speed and accuracy of the previous manual transcription of the Newark system. Otherwise there was no change in the traditional methods. The Dickman machine was followed shortly by the Gaylord Charging Machine, which performed the same operations, but also automatically positioned the book card to the next blank line. Both found considerable favor in public libraries. Some college libraries began using the machines, but the traditional double files and the necessity of additional operations after books were delivered from the book stack reduced the attractiveness of the machines in many colleges and universities.

Instead of adoption of embossing machines, college and university libraries began experimenting with single card record systems which abandoned the book card. The first such installation was at the University of Texas in January 1936, using tabulating machine cards as call slips. Borrowers filled out call slips on IBM card forms to show call number, author, title, borrower name and address. To complete the transaction, the date due was stamped on the date due slip in the book. This system utilized a duplicating key punch and a sorter with a multiple column selection device. At a later time the date due was punched into the call slips using the automatic duplicating capability of the key punch (see Figure 2).

The accumulated call slips were from time to time manually arranged by call number and filed into the circulation file, which was in call number sequence. At regular intervals, daily or somewhat less frequently, the entire circulation file was run through the sorting machine to select overdue loans. At this time special classes of loans, e.g., those to faculty, were identified and punched to prevent their being selected as overdue every time and to permit special runs to select the particular type of loan when required.

This system had the advantage of requiring only one file, but the necessity of special machines, costing some $40 per month rental, often proved to be a deterrent. A large number of variants requiring simpler mechanical devices emerged. The first and perhaps most widely adopted utilizing edge notched (Keysort) cards was first used at the Widener Library at Harvard in 1938. Other call card systems included preparation of call slips in different colors and with tabs in various positions to represent the date of the loan; another modification involved attaching a plastic tab to the regular call slip at the time of the loan (see Figure 3).

In time another development was the creation of a duplicate call slip for use with either tabulating or edge notched cards, with the copy inserted in the pocket of the book at the time of issue. This made possible expediting the reshelving of books by removal of the duplicate call slip from the volume at the time of return and using it to match against the copy in the file at some later time.

Public libraries showed little interest in the machine-oriented call slip systems.

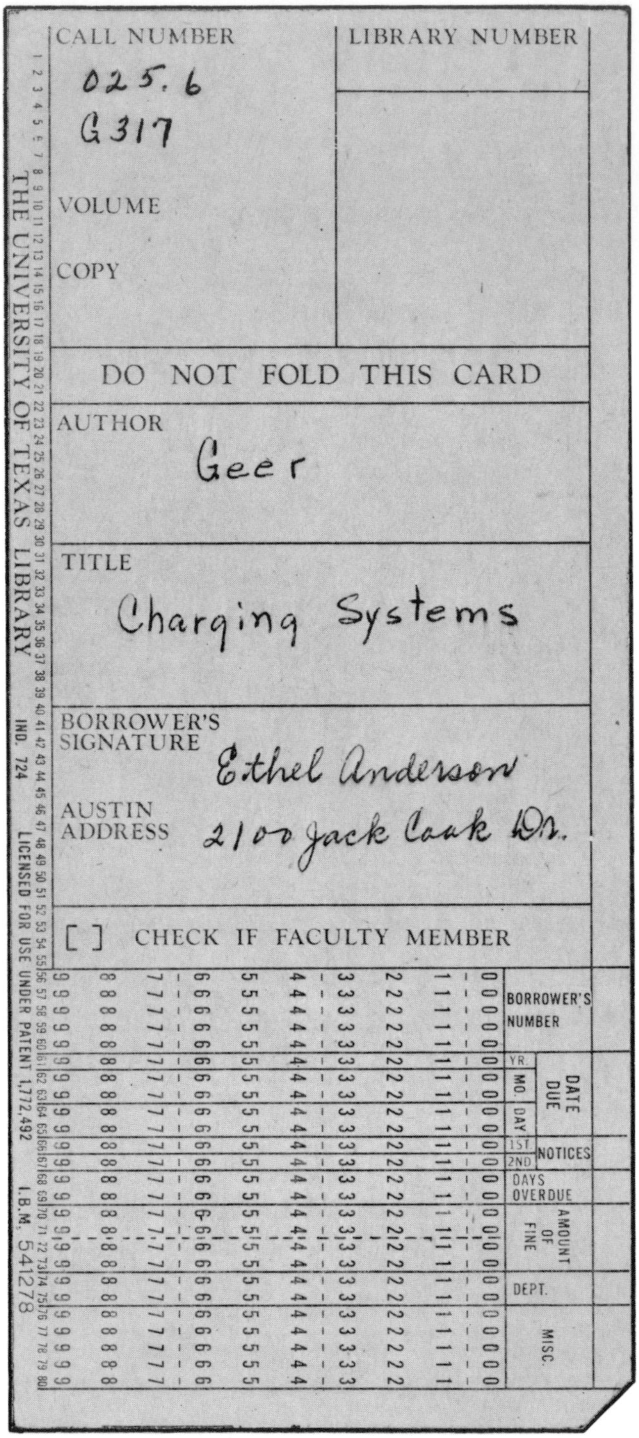

FIGURE 2. *IBM type call card.*

FIGURE 3. *Keysort call card with carbon copy.*

But there soon developed interest in another type of file which also abandoned the traditional book card. There are several versions of these systems which collectively may be termed Transaction Control systems.

In each version, the loan record consists of a transaction number, the identification of the book, and the identification of the borrower (see Figure 4). The file of these records is in transaction number, i.e., chronological, sequence. A transaction card bearing the number is inserted in a card pocket in the book. This card often serves also as a date due card. The first version was the Photo-charge system instituted at Gary Public Library in 1940. It was followed by an audio-charge modification, and by systems using written loan records.

In the Photo-charge version, the record is made by photographing, usually on microfilm, the transaction card, some record of the book (it could be the title page, for example, or the call number on the inside cover), and the borrower's identification card. In the audio-charge the transaction number, the book identification,

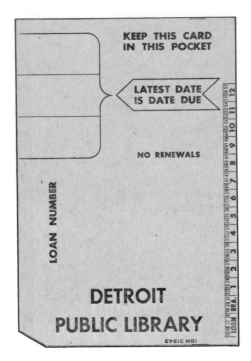

FIGURE 4. *Transaction control card.*

and the borrower identification are dictated into an office dictation machine or tape recorder.

When a book is returned, the transaction card is removed from the pocket, and from time to time these cards are arranged by transaction number. As of any date the missing numbers represent books not yet returned. At appropriate intervals the file is checked for overdue books by looking up transactions for which there is no record of return. The file search may be by running the microfilm file through a reader or the magnetic tape through a player. In some large systems the transaction control cards are punched tabulating cards, so that the identification of missing numbers, and hence of active records, is expedited.

Transaction control systems are perhaps the most economical of all those in use, but they yield the least information. It is practically impossible to locate any specific book in the file, and statistical by-products are minimal.

The tabulating call card system was a natural precursor to more sophisticated systems utilizing electronic data processing equipment. An experimental system installed in the Montclair (New Jersey) Public Library in 1941 contained all the elements of systems that became popular after 1960, but the library profession was not ready for it at the time. The elements of the system were a machine-readable book card (see Figure 5), a machine-readable borrower card, and a set of machines that would create a machine-readable card recording the transaction. A reading device at the circulation desk into which were inserted the book card and the borrower card, and an attached keyboard into which were entered variable

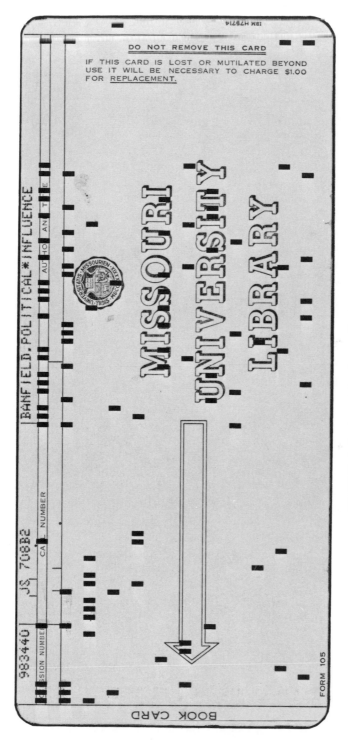

FIGURE 5. Book card for data collection system.

data such as loan period, were connected by cable to a punching device in a machine room. A punched card record of the transaction record was made for each loan and for each return. The punched transaction records were sorted, filed, and extracted from the file by other automatic machines.

The resultant file was capable of being consulted in locating a book, overdue books could be controlled by mechanical selection, and borrower records could be monitored by the same means. All manual filing and discharging were eliminated. For various reasons, including the intervention of World War II, the equipment was never put on the market.

It was not until the late 1950s that data collection equipment became commercially available, and not until 1963 was it utilized in a library. In the first library systems using data collection equipment, the record of the transaction was a punched card similar to that created by the Montclair system. But instead of filing the cards, the accumulated transactions were read into a computer and the electronic images of the cards were arranged by it into call number sequence, merged with earlier transactions, and recorded on magnetic tape. Simultaneously with this process, records of books which had been returned were purged. Such updating, combined with creation of overdue notices, and preparation of a list of all books on loan usually occurred daily (see Figure 6).

This type of charging system has found its users chiefly in university libraries, and in most cases the computer operations are performed by a central computer facility (see Figure 7).

The next step in sophistication of the charging system involves recording the transaction directly on computer disk or tape, eliminating the intermediate punched card transaction record. Such an operation is said to be on-line. The first on-line circulation system was at the Illinois State Library. In this system, a record of each borrower and of each book for which there is a reservation or "hold" is on-line. When a loan is to be made, the computer checks the borrower number for status and the "hold" list before recording the loan. If the record is made, a small printer at the circulation desk types out the date due, the name of the borrower and other pertinent information; if the record is not made the message indicates the reason.

The loan, or the return, is recorded on a magnetic disk file in consecutive order. At the close of the day this file is sorted and merged with the main circulation file in a manner similar to the magnetic tape systems described above.

The next step in sophistication is the establishment of a real-time system. The Illinois system is on-line, but the processing of the file is delayed and performed in the batch mode. In a real-time system, the circulation file is also on-line and each transaction is processed until the file is completely updated. It thus becomes possible to inquire of the computer, at any time, the location of any book. Access to the file does not depend upon a printed list.

There are at present very few real-time charging systems. The chief reasons are costs involved and the complexity of programming real-time operation in time sharing mode. For the operation to be economically feasible, it must be possible for the computer to perform other tasks when not updating the circulation file. Operating systems must be developed for interrupting some other operation when

```
                    PAGE        74

        CALL NUMBER                    BOOK  BORROWER NO.TRANS.DATE


        DT0471.D33               C72087  428303469-3  3  69-11-19
        DT0471.H5                A88956  428303469-3  3  69-11-19
        DT0471.J3;1961           B05780  428303469-3  3  69-11-19
        DT0471.O35;1967          D60214  428303469-3  3  69-11-19
        DT0471.Z6                D54419   146439-0  3  69-11-13
        DT0500.B6;1964           B60188   072397-1  3  69-10-20
        DT0502.C7                B32096  498444852-3  3  69-11-03
        DT0511.W28;1958          B80308   152631-0  3  69-11-11
        DT0511.W3;1957           F07825   152631-0  3  69-11-11
        DT0512.A64               E78389   152631-0  3  69-11-11
        DT0515.A182              958348   159667-1  3  69-10-27
        DT0515.G4;1965           C23465   159667-1  3  69-10-27
        DT0515.N516;1967         D74350   141479-0  3  69-11-26
        DT0515.P45               A70165   159667-1  3  69-11-1
        DT0515.42.S3             C02289   141479-0  3  69-
        DT0515.5.C68             B33227   003597-5  3
        DT0515.6.B4A3            A96701   000002-8        11-05
        DT0515.6.G6F55           986419   15 966          69-11-04
        DT0515.7.A48             C91384                4  69-11-04
        DT0515.7.K6              C86652          95-0  3  69-11-10
        DT0515.7.R65             94157         154095-0  3  69-11-10
        DT0515.8.S3                           154095-0  3  69-11-10
        DT0515.8.S55                          154095-0  3  69-11-10
        DT0549.5.C7                 43       154095-0  3  69-11-11
        DT0551.8.F6              994849       003597-5  3  69-11-11
        DT0624.A62               A48664       003597-5  3  69-11-11
        DT0624.M                 976737       003597-5  3  69-11-11
        DT063                    B77559  MG;000000-9  &  68-12-01
        DT0       8.G6           B14447  MG;000000-9  &  68-12-01
             0658.L4             B15898  MG;000000-9  &  68-12-01
        DT0658.Y6                B84939  MG;000000-9  &  68-12-01
        DT0671.F4M3              C57823   003984-5  4  69-11-10
        DT0703.C3;1916           D95211  BD;000000-0  1  69-11-14
        DT0733.N5                B93282  495407791-3  3  67-06-01
        DT0763.M3;1963           D08759   151310-1  3  69-11-13
        DT0768.B33               B40619   155835-0  3  69-11-11
        DT0775.H6                F16714  BD;000000-0  1  69-10-21
                                 E14344   135887-0  3  69-11-10
```

FIGURE 6. *Computer printout of circulation file.*

there is need to handle a loan transaction and for returning to it when ready. Only in large third generation computers is this usually feasible, and there are few installations capable of performing the task.

Even when efficient utilization of a large computer is possible, there are many additional costs involved in communicating with the computer including telephone

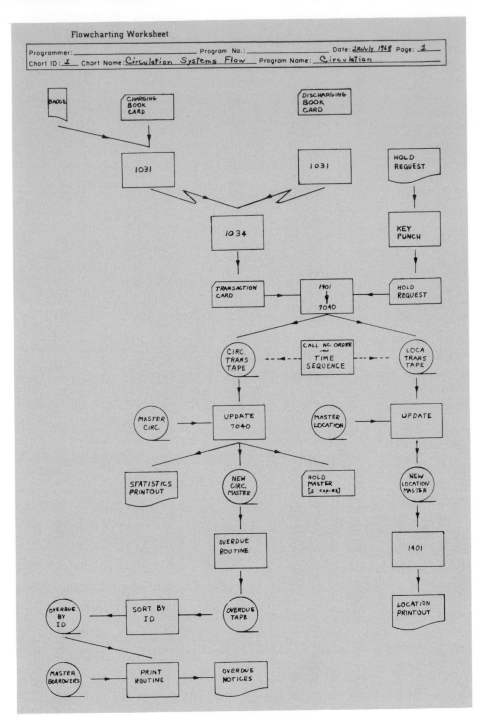

FIGURE 7. *Flowchart of a computer charging system.*

line charges and equipment for interfacing with the computer. The additional value of the real-time system may in many cases not offset the increased cost.

The real-time computer charging system approaches the perfect system as conceived by nineteenth century librarians. It is possible to locate any book on loan immediately, even a few seconds after the loan; reader records, including limitation of number of books, policing overdue books, or uncollected fines, are instantly available, and statistical data is automatically gathered; circulation statistics, overdue notices, etc., are created automatically; and it is possible at any time with little delay to answer a borrower's query as to the books he has on loan and the dates they are due.

Yet there remains the question of how much these benefits are worth. The off-line tape oriented system will provide all these answers with no more than twenty-four hours of delay.

BIBLIOGRAPHY

DeJarnett, Larry R., "Library Circulation" in *Proceedings, Ninth College and University Machine Records Conference,* Texas A & M University, College Station, Texas, 1964.

Geer, Helen, *Charging Systems,* American Library Association, Chicago, 1955.

Kennedy, R. A., "Bell Laboratories' Library Real-Time Loan System (BELL REL)," *J. Lib. Automation,* 1, 128–146 (June 1968).

Kilgour, Frederick G., "New Punched Card for Circulation Records," *Lib. J.,* 64, 553 (July 1938).

Parker, Ralph H., "Punched Card Method in Circulation Work," *Lib. J.,* 61, 903–905 (December 1936).

Shaw, Ralph R., "Reducing the Cost of the Lending Process," *ALA Bull.,* 35, 504–510 (October 1941).

RALPH H. PARKER

CHEMICAL ABSTRACTS SERVICE

Chemical Abstracts Service (CAS) is the world's largest secondary information service in chemistry and chemical engineering. Since its founding in 1907, its mission has been to make chemical and chemical engineering information available and usable by extracting and providing improved routes of access to what is of chemical interest in the published literature of science and technology. Today, CAS abstracts and indexes over a quarter of a million papers, patents, and reports and publishes more than 120,000 pages of digested and indexed information annually. To accomplish this, CAS employs some 3000 part-time scientist-abstractors around the world, 100 part-time section editors, and a full-time staff of about 1000 at its facilities in Columbus, Ohio.

CAS produces *Chemical Abstracts,* a weekly, omnibus abstracting and indexing journal in chemistry and chemical engineering, and some 20 other publications and computer-based information services, including *Chemical Titles, Chemical Abstracts* Section Groupings, *Chemical-Biological Activities, Polymer Science & Technology, CA* Condensates, and the *Ring Index.* CAS is also currently implementing an advanced, computer-based system for processing, storing, searching, and disseminating scientific and technical information.

As a division of the American Chemical Society, CAS is governed by the society's elected board of directors through the executive director of the society. Since 1956, however, CAS has been financially independent of the society's other programs and dependent entirely upon subscription revenues to meet its operating expenses.

History

The present-day CAS owes its existence to the efforts of some prominent American chemists of the late nineteenth and early twentieth centuries. In 1895, Professor Arthur A. Noyes of the Massachusetts Institute of Technology, convinced that the world was neglecting to credit American chemists for work accomplished, organized and brought into being the *Review of American Chemical Research.* This publication, which can be regarded as a predecessor of *Chemical Abstracts,* appeared first as part of MIT's *Technology Quarterly* and later as part of the *Journal of the American Chemical Society.* It published abstracts of American chemical papers only.

In the early 1900s pressure grew for the publication of an American abstracting journal that would cover "the whole field of chemistry, the world over," and in 1906 *Chemical Abstracts* was authorized by the Council of the American Chemical Society. It began publication in 1907 under the editorship of W. A. Noyes, Sr.

The first editorial offices were at the National Bureau of Standards in Washington, where the editor was chief chemist. Late in 1907 the offices moved with the editor to the University of Illinois. In 1909 Austin M. Patterson became editor, and the offices moved to the Ohio State University campus in Columbus, where they remained until 1965. Dr. Patterson was succeeded as editor by J. J. Miller in 1914. In 1915 the editorship was assumed by E. J. Crane, who remained at the helm for the next 43 years.

In recognition of its growing mission, the *Chemical Abstracts* editorial organization in 1956 was renamed Chemical Abstracts Service and made a division of the American Chemical Society with Crane as its first director. Crane was succeeded as director by Dale B. Baker in November 1958. In 1965 CAS moved from its quarters on the Ohio State campus to its own $7-million facilities on 50 acres just north of the campus in Columbus (see Figure 1).

Although it began as a service for American chemists, CAS today is truly international in scope. Its volunteer abstractors reside in 70 different nations, including

FIGURE 1. *Chemical Abstracts Service headquarters in Columbus, Ohio.*

the Iron Curtain nations, and *Chemical Abstracts,* with 60% of its circulation out-side of the United States, has become the principal source of digested and indexed chemical information for scientists throughout the world.

Chemical Abstracts

Today, the great majority of effort at CAS still is devoted to the production of *Chemical Abstracts (CA).* Most of the other CAS publications and services are by-products of the processing of information for this omnibus record of chemical progress.

The scope of *CA* is best summarized by a statement that has appeared on the publication's masthead since the 1930s: "It is the careful endeavor of *Chemical Abstracts* to publish adequate and accurate abstracts of all scientific and technical papers containing new information of chemical interest and to report new chemical information revealed in the patent literature." This "careful endeavor" now ex-tends to the regular monitoring of more than 12,000 scientific and technical periodicals published in 106 different nations, patents issued by 26 nations, and important books, reports, and conference proceedings from all over the world and to the preparation of more than a quarter of a million abstracts annually.

Because the mission of *CA* has always been accurate, complete, and timely coverage of the world's chemical literature, its growth has paralleled the exponen-tial growth of chemical science and technology in the twentieth century. In 1907 *CA* published just under 8000 abstracts. With the exception of war years, when the international flow of information was restricted, the annual total has increased nearly every year (see Figure 2). The cumulative total of abstracts recorded in the pages of *CA* has doubled approximately every 12 years and passed the 4 million mark in mid-1968.

In recent years science and technology have become, essentially, one vast inter-

Thousands of Papers, Patents and Reports
Abstracted in Chemical Abstracts

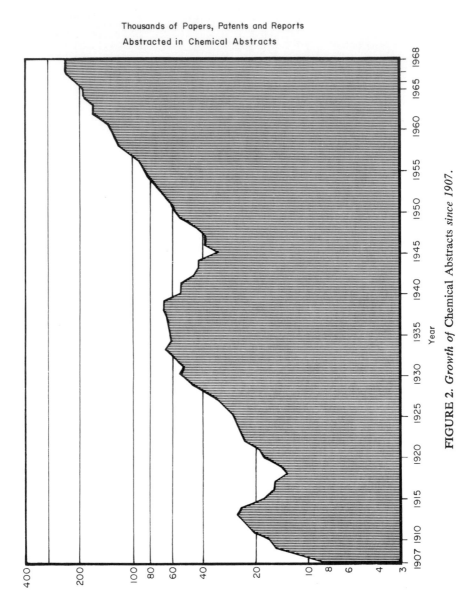

FIGURE 2. *Growth of Chemical Abstracts since 1907.*

disciplinary network. Although most scientific journals restrict their content to one specialty or discipline, nearly every article published contributes to the information store of several disciplines. Thus, to assure complete coverage of all important information bearing on chemistry or chemical engineering, CAS extends its journal coverage well beyond the purely chemical journals.

Of the 12,000 journals monitored for *CA* only about 240 are entirely devoted to chemistry or chemical engineering. These 240 yield more than half of the total papers covered in *CA*. Over-all, just over 2000 journals yield 90% of all *CA* abstracts of articles. But another 10,000 journals, mostly outside the field of chemistry, are monitored to assure complete coverage, and each of these 10,000 yields at least one article for abstracting in *CA* over a five-year period.

To select the material for abstracting in *CA*, the CAS staff now reviews some 1.5 million papers, patents, and reports annually. Of the material abstracted, 70% originates outside the United States (see Figure 3). Although 54% of the world's chemical literature is now published in English, CAS abstracts information from 55 other languages to complete its coverage (see Figure 4).

Most journal articles are abstracted from advance page proofs airmailed to CAS by the publishers. Much of the abstracting for *CA* is now done by full-time staff members in Columbus, who either prepare complete abstracts or revise author abstracts to conform to CAS standards, but CAS still depends on its worldwide corps of 3000 part-time volunteers for the majority of the abstracting effort. On the median, an abstract of a journal article appears in *CA* within 110 days of the publication date of the source journal. Patent abstracts appear, on the median,

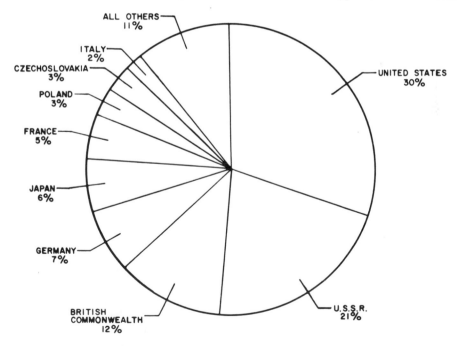

FIGURE 3. *National origin of the world's chemical literature (1968).*

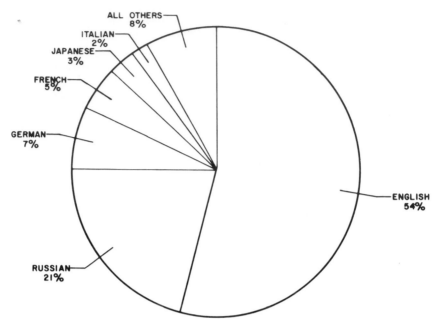

FIGURE 4. *Language of publication of the world's chemical literature (1968)*.

within 150 days of the issue date of the patent. For U.S. patents, the lag is less than 100 days.

CA, for the most part, publishes informative abstracts that summarize the information of chemical interest in a paper, report, or patent in sufficient detail to enable a reader to determine if it is necessary to consult the complete document. It also publishes a number of brief indicative abstracts to call attention to books, comprehensive chemical reviews, articles on chemical education and the history of chemistry, and biographies of well-known chemists. A *CA* abstract may range in length from a few lines describing a review to several hundred words with chemical equations and structural formulas for a paper on the synthesis of a new chemical compound. The heading of each abstract contains the complete bibliographic citation for the article, patent, or report, including the authors' or assignees' addresses and the language in which the original document was published.

For convenience in locating information on any specific subject, abstracts in *CA* issues are organized into 80 specialized subject sections, and each weekly issue is indexed by author, patent number, and a computer-organized alphabetical listing of keywords selected from the abstracts. Although *CA* has been issued weekly since 1967, the subject coverage is on a biweekly cycle. Sections 1 through 34 (covering the fields of biochemistry and organic chemistry) appear one week, Sections 35 through 80 (macromolecular chemistry, applied chemistry and chemical engineering, and physical and analytical chemistry) the next. Each weekly issue also includes a Patent Concordance that lists, by country of issue, new patents corresponding to a patent previously abstracted and references the pertinent abstract.

Because of its size and cost, the whole *CA* has become primarily a tool for retrospective searching of the chemical literature. To make current abstracts more conveniently available to the individual chemist and chemical engineer, CAS since 1963 has also published *CA* abstracts in five separate groupings, covering applied chemistry and chemical engineering, biochemistry, macromolecular chemistry, organic chemistry, and physical and analytical chemistry. Since 1966 *CA* has also been available in a microfilm edition that compresses the more than 4.25 million abstracts published since 1907 into 173 four-inch-square cartridges of 16-mm film, coded to provide rapid access to any specific abstract through modern microfilm reader-printer equipment.

CA Indexes

Scientific research and development start with what is known about a subject or phenomenon and build upon this knowledge. Thus, the scientist or engineer not only needs to be kept aware of the latest developments in his specialized field, he must also have a means of access to all of the previously published data in that field.

The accumulated volumes of *CA* contain, in highly digested form, essentially the entire record of the world's chemical research since 1907. To assure full retrospective access to this information, each abstract in *CA* is carefully and completely indexed. In addition to the issue indexes mentioned above, each volume (26 weekly issues) of *CA* is indexed cumulatively by author, molecular formula of all chemical compounds referenced, patent number, and subject. Every five years (every ten years prior to 1957), CAS compiles and organizes these Volume Indexes into a Collective Index that provides a detailed key to the period's chemical and chemical engineering literature. The Patent Concordance is also cumulated at six-month and five-year intervals. Through the accumulated indexes of *CA,* one can be led to essentially all of the information published on any specific aspect of chemistry or chemical engineering since 1907.

As the chemical literature has grown, the indexing of *CA* has become an immense undertaking that now occupies half of CAS's full-time professional staff and consumes 60% of the *CA* budget. The indexes for *CA*'s seventh collective period (1961–1966), for example, occupy some 40,000 pages in 24 volumes.

The most thorough and most extensively used of *CA*'s indexes are the Subject Indexes. Set in finer type than the abstracts, the Subject Indexes for any volume of *CA* fill almost half as many pages as the abstracts themselves. The Subject Indexes are complete and self-contained, offering the user numerous cross-references, synonyms, and scope notes to guide in the effective location of indexed information. Subjects, not words, are indexed, and the words used as subject entries are not necessarily to be found in the abstracts. In deciding on the subject entries, the indexer takes into account the author's purpose, his point of view, and the new data, compounds, theories, or uses reported, working in many instances from the original article or patent specification as well as from the abstract.

The great majority of entries in the Subject Indexes concern specific chemical compounds, and the problems of chemical nomenclature often vex both the compiler and user of the indexes. Chemistry has grown up with a variety of unrelated schemes for naming compounds. In an alphabetically arranged subject index, however, the naming of compounds must be based on consistent and systematic rules. The chemical nomenclature used in the *CA* indexes is based on the official rules of the International Union of Pure and Applied Chemistry (IUPAC), although some nonsystematic names are also included because of their wide usage among chemists. A basic knowledge of IUPAC nomenclature and *CA* indexing policy for compounds (which is described in the Introduction to the index) is needed to use the Subject Indexes effectively for locating references to specific compounds.

For those not versed in indexing nomenclature, the *CA* Formula Indexes provide a more convenient route to data on individual chemical compounds. Entries under the molecular formula of a compound in this index (see Figure 5) give the preferred indexing name through which that compound can be located in the Subject Indexes as well as references to all abstracts that contain information on the compound. With the indexing names found in the Formula Index, it is possible to search further in the Subject Index for derivatives of the compound and related information.

Molecular formulas in the Formula Indexes are ordered according to the Hill system which, for all carbon-containing compounds, lists carbon atoms first, followed immediately by hydrogen atoms, then the remaining atom symbols in alphabetical order. For compounds that do not contain carbon, the arrangement of element symbols is strictly alphabetical. Then within the index the formulas are arranged alphabetically by element symbol, with the number of atoms of the in-

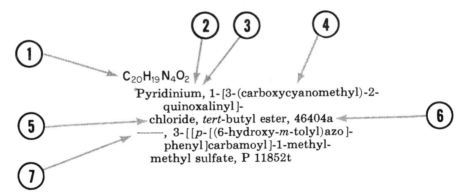

FIGURE 5. *Entries in the* CA *Formula Index are arranged by molecular formula (1) ordered according to the Hill system. The entries under each formula give the* CA *systematic name for each indexed compound corresponding to that formula and the number (6) of the abstract that contains a reference to the compound. The indexing name consists of the name of the parent compound (2) and the index compound (3) (in this example, the parent compound, pyridine, with the suffix -ium) followed by a prefix (4) made up of the names of the substituents arranged in alphabetical order and a modification (5) which completes the name of the specific compound referenced. In subsequent entries under the same formula, a long dash (7) replaces the name of the index compound.*

dividual elements used to break ties between formulas appearing in the same alphabetical order. Thus, all formulas containing one carbon atom are ordered before any of those that contain two, etc.

This arrangement of the Formula Indexes makes it somewhat difficult to locate formulas of carbon-based compounds containing specific hetero (noncarbon, nonhydrogen) atoms. To alleviate this situation CAS, beginning with the indexes for Volume 66 of *CA* (January–June 1967), added a Hetero-Atom-In-Context (HAIC) Index. This computer-produced formula listing orders the molecular formulas according to the hetero elements they contain and highlights the symbols of these elements within the context of the formula. It contains no direct references to abstracts, but is designed as an aid in locating specific hetero-atom compounds in the Hill order Formula Index.

Still another aid in locating references to specific compounds is the Index to Ring Systems included in the *CA* Volume and Collective Indexes. This index is based on the skeletal structure of cyclic chemical compounds, arranged according to the number, size, and elemental composition of the component rings. It provides the systematic indexing names for these compounds, which can then be used to gain entry to data on them through the Subject Indexes.

Not all the *CA* indexes extend back to 1907. Subject and Author Indexes are complete since 1907. The Molecular Formula Index was first included in the Volume Indexes in 1920 and in the Collective Indexes in 1947, but a special 27-year Collective Formula Index to *CA,* covering the years 1920–1946, is available. Numerical Patent Indexes are available only for 1935 and later years. Nevertheless, the various indexes to *CA* now contain some 40 million entries, each of which will lead the information seeker to within one-sixteenth of a page in the more than 350,000 pages of abstracts published in *CA* since 1907.

CAS Computer-Based Information System

The proliferation of new chemical knowledge is rapidly outpacing the capabilities of traditional information-handling and publishing techniques, and CAS is now turning to computer-based methods to help speed and channel the flow of information. Financial support for the development of the emerging computer-based information system at CAS has come in approximately equal proportions from CAS subscription revenues and from federal funding provided principally through the National Science Foundation.

The approach taken by CAS is not the computerization of its manual publishing system, but rather the development of an integrated information system designed to take full advantage of the computer's speed, accuracy, and flexibility. The CAS system, which has been under development since 1959, is designed primarily to eliminate the redundant human effort and paper handling required in producing abstracted and indexed scientific information. The CAS goal is to process all incoming documents through a single human analysis, followed by a single recording of each element of data derived from this analysis in machine language and a single human verification of the accuracy of the recorded data. Subsequent manipulation and organization of the data and composition of publications for printing are then performed by a computer system.

This approach to information handling not only promises substantial savings in manpower, time, and money, it also greatly enhances the usefulness and accessibility of the information processed. The information is being recorded permanently in a form that can be manipulated by machine for a variety of subsequent uses. Since any portion of the machine-language data store can be selected automatically and reprocessed through the computer publication system with a minimum of human intervention, it becomes economically feasible to produce any number of specialized alerting publications, bibliographies, abstract collections, or indexes covering any selected part of the total data collection. Moreover, the data appearing in printed abstracts and indexes are also available in a form that can be rapidly and efficiently searched by computer to locate references on any specific topic.

In the system as it is now emerging, document acquisition, selection, subject classification, and abstracting and indexing are performed, for the most part, in the traditional manner, but the results of this human processing are recorded in a unified computer-manipulable data base through magnetic-tape-generating data recorders. Input to this data base occurs by several routes during the initial data processing. Heading data—titles, authors, names, and bibliographic references—are put into the system at the time of selection of an article for abstracting. Structural formulas and compound names enter via the Chemical Registry System (see below) as part of the indexing process. Abstracts and subject indexing terms follow yet another route.

Once all the necessary data for a given issue of a particular publication are in the unified computer store, the processing system, through programmed instructions, selects those headings and abstracts that are appropriate for the particular issue in question, organizes and formats them in the proper form for publication, and composes pages for offset reproduction through a computer-directed typesetting process. In a parallel step, issue index entries are selected from the data base, ordered, and composed. Printing, binding, and distribution of the publication are then handled in the traditional manner.

At the same time, the selected and organized data can be copied on magnetic tape to be searched on a subscriber's computer. When the necessary capability is developed, it will also be possible to load this material into direct-access computer files for remote searching and to produce microfilm directly from the computer composition step.

The abstracts and index data are also permanently recorded in computer-manipulable archives from which appropriate portions can be retrieved and reprocessed through the same system, with some additional editing and checking, to produce Volume and Collective Indexes or specialized bibliographies and compilations of abstracts. The system thus extracts a multiplicity of uses from a single human analysis and handling of information and eliminates the redundant processing and checking of data that appear in more than one publication or service.

The processing of chemical information through a computer system has required the development of techniques and technology well beyond the existing state-of-the-art of computer data processing. For example, because of the complexities of chemical nomenclature, some 1500 different symbols are needed to print *CA* issues. To process *CA* abstracts and indexes through the computer system, it was necessary to develop techniques for recording these 1500 symbols through the 88 keys of a typewriter keyboard. This has been accomplished through flagging conventions and codes to indicate case, font, superscripts, subscripts, and special characters and through special keyboarding shortcuts, such as computer programs that expand keyboarded abbreviations or automatically provide capitalized and italicized characters in chemical names. CAS is also working on techniques for displaying and printing chemical structural formulas from computer records, direct computer translation from systematic chemical nomenclature to machine-language representations of chemical structure, and automatic computer editing and checking of nomenclature.

Computer-directed typesetting also posed a problem. Most existing computer-operated composing devices offered a very limited selection of characters and typeface variations. CAS worked with the International Business Machines Corporation to develop a modification of the IBM 2280 film recorder unit capable of functioning as a computer-operated photocomposing device. The modified 2280 can generate a virtually unlimited range of type characters and compose columns with text and line illustrations intermixed. The quality obtained through this process is excellent, and composition proceeds at a rate of 1000 characters per second or more, depending upon the character range used and the printing quality desired.

Although parts of the CAS computer system are still under development, as of late 1970 there was no part that was not operating in at least a minimal fashion. Heading data for all abstracts processed by CAS were being input to the computer data base, as was the full text of about 25% of the abstracts processed, and the Formula, Author, HAIC, and Subject Indexes of *CA* were being produced through the system.

The Chemical Registry System

Any information system that would effectively serve the community of chemists and chemical engineers must necessarily include a mechanism for storing and manipulating data on chemical compounds and related substances. Most information generated in chemical research concerns the nature and properties of compounds. There are now several million known chemical compounds, and about 100,000 new ones are reported in the world's chemical literature each year. The processes of identifying a specific compound and providing access to the available data on it through a manual information system is complicated by the complexities and inconsistencies of chemical compound nomenclature.

Since the early 1960s CAS, with financial assistance from the National Science Foundation and other federal agencies, has been developing the computer-based Chemical Registry System. The Registry, which will eventually bring together in machine-searchable form information on the structure, names, and bibliographic references for virtually every known chemical substance, provides both a means for identifying each compound or substance and a mechanism for interlinking all available information on any specific compound or family of compounds.

The basis for identifying compounds in the Registry is the one relatively constant and universally understood language among chemists, the structural formula. To translate these two-dimensional structural diagrams into a form that can be stored and manipulated by computer, CAS uses a coded description, in table form, of the atoms and bonds in the structure and the manner in which they are interconnected. The computer itself generates the table from a representation of the structure input to its memory and converts it to a unique and unambiguous form. Once the unique identification of the compound has been established through this structural representation, the compound is assigned a Registry Number, which serves as a permanent, unique identification tag for that compound throughout the CAS information system. This number is then used as the basis for organizing related collections of data on the compound, including the various names by which it is known and references to the literature that describe its characteristics, properties and uses. Thus it is possible to locate the available data on any compound through its structure, its Registry Number, or any of its recorded names.

Moreover, the presence in the computer store of a detailed representation of the structure adds an entirely new dimension to the searching capability. It is possible, through an associated substructure search system, to search by computer for compounds that contain particular arrangements of atoms and bonds within their structures.

CAS began large-scale input of data to the Registry in 1965. As of late 1970, the system contained more than 1.5 million unique structural representations, 1.9 million associated names, and more than 3 million bibliographic references.

The Registry is currently operating as an integral part of the CAS information system, assisting in the exact identification and naming of compounds in the indexing of *CA* and other CAS publications and services. The first publication to be derived entirely from the Registry—a computer-generated index of the names, Registry Numbers, molecular formulas, and principal sources of published data for some 33,000 substances of importance in foods, drugs, pesticides, cosmetics, and related products—was issued through the Clearinghouse for Federal Scientific and Technical Information in December 1968.

The Chemical Registry System has obvious value as an alerting and information-retrieval tool for chemists. CAS intends to make Registry data as widely accessible as possible by providing Registry Numbers for publication in chemical journals and handbooks, by supplying duplicate tapes of the collection for use in corporate or institutional information centers, and by deriving from the system a variety of printed indexes, handbooks, and card files of compound data.

Computer-Based Publications and Services

As the development of the CAS computer-based information system has proceeded, CAS has gradually introduced a series of new information services derived from the system. Some have been the natural by-product of a completed step in the conversion of *CA* information to computer processing. Others have been intentionally designed as pilot services to evaluate various methods of disseminating data from the system or to provide the CAS staff with experience in handling smaller quantities of data through the computer system before undertaking the volume of processing required to produce *CA*. Descriptions of those CAS computer-based services currently available follow.

CHEMICAL TITLES

The first service to grow out of CAS's research on computer-based information-handling methods was *Chemical Titles* (*CT*), a low-cost, biweekly alert to the titles of new papers appearing in 650 journals of pure and applied chemistry and chemical engineering. Introduced in 1961, *CT* was the world's first computer-produced periodical. Each issue of *CT* contains a bibliographic listing of new titles in the form of tables of contents of the journals, an author index, and a keyword-in-context index in which each significant word of every title printed in the issue is arranged in alphabetical sequence down the center of a column with the context of the title on either side. The entire publication is organized by computer and composed for printing through a standard 48-character computer print chain with boldface headings added manually. Throughout the processing of data for *CT,* the emphasis is on speed, and the listing of a title in *CT* will often appear before the publication date of the journal that contains it. Since 1962 *CT* has been issued simultaneously in printed form and in a magnetic tape edition for computer searching.

CHEMICAL-BIOLOGICAL ACTIVITIES

Chemical-Biological Activities (*CBAC*), introduced in 1965, is a biweekly, computer-produced abstracting and indexing service in biochemistry. Oriented primarily toward the pharmaceutical industry, it covers in depth some 15,000 articles per year dealing with (1) the effect of exogenous organic compounds on biological systems, (2) the metabolism of organic compounds in biological systems, and (3) *in vitro* reactions between compounds of biological interest. Pertinent articles from approximately 585 journals are covered.

The highly concise abstracts (called digests) in *CBAC* include descriptions of the substances studied, pertinent structural formulas, conditions under which observations were made, and results obtained. The digests are arranged to simplify scanning (see Figure 6): individual sentences are identified numerically to help in locating indexed concepts, and words considered significant are printed in capital letters. CAS Registry Numbers are included for each structurable organic compound mentioned.

Each biweekly *CBAC* issue includes a molecular formula index, an author index, and a keyword-in-context index in which each sentence of each digest is rotated around each significant word to produce an average of 36 index entries per digest. These indexes are cumulated semiannually. A Registry Number index is also included in the cumulated indexes.

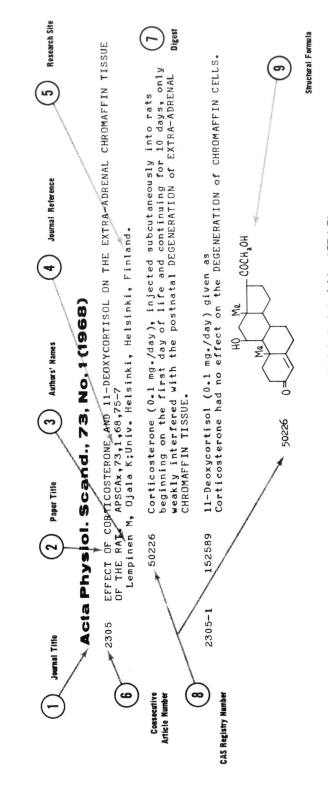

① Journal Title

② Paper Title

③ Authors' Names

④ Journal Reference

⑤ Research Site

⑥ Consecutive Article Number

⑦ Digest

⑧ CAS Registry Number

⑨ Structural Formula

Acta Physiol. Scand., 73, No.1 (1968)

2305

EFFECT OF CORTICOSTERONE AND 11-DEOXYCORTISOL ON THE EXTRA-ADRENAL CHROMAFFIN TISSUE OF THE RAT. APSCAx,73,1,68,75-7
Lempinen M, Ojala K;Univ. Helsinki, Helsinki, Finland.

50226   Corticosterone (0.1 mg./day), injected subcutaneously into rats beginning on the first day of life and continuing for 10 days, only weakly interfered with the postnatal DEGENERATION of EXTRA-ADRENAL CHROMAFFIN TISSUE.

152589   11-Deoxycortisol (0.1 mg./day) given as Corticosterone had no effect on the DEGENERATION of CHROMAFFIN CELLS.

2305-1

50226

FIGURE 6. *Typical digest in Chemical-Biological Activities (CBAC)*.

CBAC is organized and composed for printing by computer. Since 1966 CBAC has also been issued in a magnetic tape edition for computer searching.

POLYMER SCIENCE & TECHNOLOGY

Introduced in late 1967, *Polymer Science & Technology* (*POST*) is a weekly computer-based guide to the current journal, report, and patent literature on the chemistry, chemical engineering, and technology of polymers. Subject areas covered include: (1) the preparation, properties, technology, and uses of synthetic and natural organic polymers, synthetic inorganic polymers, monomers (as starting materials), catalysts, and adjunct materials; (2) processes and equipment used directly in the manufacture of monomers and polymers; (3) determination of the properties of monomers, polymers, and adjunct materials; (4) fabrication of polymers into end products; and (5) information on new tests, standards, and health and safety procedures in the polymer industry. Some 450 journals and patents issued by 26 nations are regularly covered.

POST is published in two separate units—*POST-J,* covering the journal and report literature, and *POST-P,* covering patents; they are issued on alternate Mondays. Either section may be subscribed to separately. Both are issued simultaneously in printed form and on magnetic tape for computer searching.

Digests published in *POST* are highly concise summaries organized to convey at a glance the polymer-related information from the paper, report, or patent. Names of monomers, polymers, and adjunct materials are printed in capital letters for rapid scanning. Registry Numbers are published for all structurable organic compounds, and structural formulas are provided to alert the reader to new or uncommon compounds. Each issue includes a keyword subject index, a molecular formula index, and an author index. *POST-P* sections also include a patent index and patent concordance. All indexes are cumulated semiannually.

The keyword subject index used in *POST* is controlled by an open-ended, computer-based vocabulary system. Keywords to be indexed are flagged by the chemist preparing a digest. The computer then matches the flagged terms against a thesaurus with one or more of the following results: (1) the flagged term itself is allowed as an index entry, (2) a preferred term is substituted, or (3) additional entries or cross-references are generated. Flagged terms not included in the thesaurus are printed in a discrepancy list so that appropriate indexing decisions can be made by an editor and the thesaurus can be updated if necessary. The discrepancy lists provide a system of vocabulary control that signals advances in the subject field and allows updating of the thesaurus accordingly. The thesaurus is also available in printed form for use as a search guide in framing questions for computer searching of *POST* or manual searching of the indexes.

CA CONDENSATES

Introduced in 1968, *CA Condensates* was the first service to extend computer searching to the full range of the world's current chemical and chemical engineering literature. *Condensates* consists of weekly computer-searchable tapes containing the complete abstract headings and *CA* issue keyword index terms for every journal article, report, and patent covered in the corresponding weekly issue of *CA*. These data comprise essentially a computer-searchable condensed abstract that includes the following information: the title of the paper, patent, or report; names of authors or assignees; complete bibliographic citation (including both the abbreviated title and ASTM Coden for the journal); the *CA* abstract number; and an average of four indexing terms from the *CA* issue keyword indexes. With the *Condensates* tapes and search programs it is possible to scan by machine the pertinent content of more than 5000 new articles and patents each week to identify those of immediate interest.

Condensates grew primarily out of procedures instituted at CAS in 1968 for unified computer processing of abstract heading data for *CA, CBAC,* and *POST*. Data from the unified heading system are automatically merged with data processed for the computer-composed *CA* issue keyword indexes to form *Condensates*. The *Condensates* tapes are issued weekly and are available a week or more in advance of the corresponding printed issue of *CA*.

BASIC JOURNAL ABSTRACTS

Basic Journal Abstracts (*BJA*) consists of biweekly machine-language tapes containing the complete *CA* abstracts for all articles appearing in 35 chemical journals. The headings and full text of these abstracts can be searched by computer to derive a bibliography of those articles whose titles or abstracts contain terms of interest to the searcher. Printed copies of the abstracts are provided with the tapes.

BJA is an outgrowth of an experiment in selective dissemination of information conducted in 1967 by CAS and 24 cooperating organizations. It was introduced as a subscription service in 1968 to allow wider evaluation of the usefulness of whole-text searching of *CA* abstracts, which permits computer searching of information content in greater depth than does searching of titles and index terms, but is considerably more costly in computer time.

COMPUTER TEXT SEARCHING

As noted, all of these CAS computer-based services are issued on magnetic tape in a form that permits computer searching of the titles, abstracts, or index terms contained in each issue. Although computer searching of data in machine language does not always lend itself to exact answers, it does make it possible to scan large stores of data without the limitations of a hierarchically arranged index. As a result, the number of possible access points to the information is increased greatly, and retrieval is not limited to those elements of data at the highest index hierarchy level.

For searching the textual data in the record, the computer is programmed to match terms selected by the searcher with terms appearing in the recorded information and print out bibliographic references for all titles or abstracts containing the specified terms. These search terms may be words, phrases, authors' names, molecular formulas, coded journal titles, or CAS Registry Numbers. Through a term-truncation feature, the search term may also be a word fragment that may be common to several forms of the word. For example, the truncated term, *polymer*, would retrieve references containing the terms polymer, polymers, polymerize, polymerized, prepolymer, and the like. The terms may also be assigned numerical weights to indicate their relative importance in the search.

By applying Boolean logic operators, the searcher can construct correlative search questions requiring that several parameters be present (or absent) in a specified combination. AND logic makes the search more restrictive. A question consisting of terms A and B with AND logic would retrieve only references that contain both of the terms. OR logic expands the basic search terms to include synonyms and related terms. The question A OR B would retrieve references to all documents that contain either term A or term B in the text. NOT logic specifies that a particular term must not be present in the retrieved reference. Thus, the search strategy may be highly specific or very general at the user's option.

COMPUTER INFORMATION CENTERS

In addition to producing printed copies and supplying duplicate tapes of its services for use on subscribers' computer equipment, CAS is now experimenting with a third method of disseminating information from its computer data base—the provision of search services and other assistance to individual users by independent computer information centers. As of late 1970, seven centers in the United States were providing such services, as were centers in Belgium, Canada, Denmark, The Netherlands, Sweden, the United Kingdom, and West Germany. Many were offering searches of data bases supplied by other scientific and technical information processors as well as searches of CAS data. Some also were offering educational programs in the effective use of computer information services.

Links with the Source Literature

The function of any abstracting and indexing service is to make the user aware of the presence of certain information in the source literature of a discipline and to guide the user to the documents that contain the information he needs. The usefulness of any abstracting and indexing service thus depends upon the ability of the library community to supply the necessary source documents.

The very large volume of literature that is pertinent to chemistry and chemical engineering is scattered throughout the literature of science and technology. No single library could be expected to maintain current subscriptions and complete back files of all the journals, patents, reports, monographs, books, and the like covered by *CA*. To help guide users to the available source documents, CAS since 1922 has published a quinquennial *List of Periodicals Abstracted by Chem-*

ical Abstracts with data on library holdings of the listed periodicals. Data for these listings have been generously contributed by a wide range of academic, public, private, governmental, and industrial libraries throughout the world. The last complete edition of the *List* was published in 1961, and annual supplements were issued through June 1967.

The CAS *List of Periodicals* has now been augmented and expanded into a new CAS *Source Index,* which provides a comprehensive and continuing key to the source literature of chemistry and chemical engineering. Listings in the *Source Index* are not limited to periodicals currently abstracted by *CA,* as were previous editions of the CAS *List,* but provide a sixty-year cumulation of titles previously abstracted, including discontinued titles and nineteenth- and early twentieth-century journals covered by *Beilstein's handbuch der organischen Chemie* and *Chemisches Zentralblatt.* In all, some 21,000 entries for journals and monographs appear in the first edition of the *Source Index,* representing essentially all important publications in chemistry and chemical engineering since 1830.

The listing for each publication in the *Source Index* includes the full title in the original language of publication and its English translation, the title abbreviated according to American National Standard* Z39.5, Periodical Title Abbreviations, the American Society for Testing and Materials CODEN for the journal title, the language of publication, the publication history with references to any former titles, the current frequency of publication and volume number data, price, publisher's address, the title cataloged according to library cataloging rules, and a key to library holdings of the publication. Some 400 of the world's leading resource libraries have contributed information on their holdings for inclusion in this compilation.

The first edition of the CAS *Source Index* was published in September 1969. Supplements covering new titles and changes are being issued quarterly as a subscription service. The fourth quarterly supplement each year cumulates the data in the previous three. Both the complete edition and supplements are also available to subscribers on magnetic tape for computer searching and updating.

Other CAS Publications

In addition to its periodical publications and services, CAS publishes several reference works derived primarily from information processed for *CA.* The most widely used of these is the *Ring Index,* which enables one to determine if a particular organic ring system has ever been reported in the chemical literature and how specific ring systems are numbered and named. The Second Edition of the *Ring Index* and its three supplements contain data on 14,265 ring systems reported in the world's chemical literature through 1963. For each such system, the *Index* gives a structural formula showing the standard International Union of Pure and Applied Chemistry procedure for numbering members of the ring for

---

* Published by the American National Standards Institute, formerly the USA Standards Institute.

identification and other numbering orders that have been used in the literature, a serial number that identifies the system, its preferred name and other names given in the literature, and a reference to the primary document in which the system was first reported. Entries are arranged according to the size of the ring structures, proceeding from the simplest to the most complex, and a name index is included in each volume.

CAS also currently publishes the SOCMA *Handbook of Commercial Organic Chemical Names,* a glossary of some 20,000 known names for 63 widely used commercial organic compounds compiled jointly by CAS and the Synthetic Organic Chemical Manufacturers Association of the United States. For each listed compound this *Handbook* provides the CAS indexing name and Registry Number, the molecular formula and structural diagram, the various chemical and trade names by which the compound is known, and the names of derivatives and salts.

Toward a Scientific Information Network

The laborious and expensive translation and transcription required to transfer information from one processor or service to another in a manual publishing environment have always hindered productive cooperation and exchange of information among publishers with overlapping subject interests. However, as CAS and other information processors convert to computer-based systems, with their inherent ability to translate the form and format of information reliably and economically, the potential for efficient interchange of information between processors is greatly increased. To exploit this potential, CAS is engaged in experiments with a number of scientific information processors on the large-scale mechanized exchange of information.

One highly useful form of interchange is the direct transfer of bibliographic data and abstracts between the primary and secondary publishing systems. Publishers of primary journals are currently setting in type all of the necessary information for complete bibliographic citations, and, in many instances, are publishing author abstracts of a caliber that can be used directly in the secondary services. Even so, with manual publishing techniques this information must, as a minimum, be edited and reset in type by the secondary services. However, if the primary and secondary services are both publishing through compatible computer-based systems, the bibliographic data and abstracts keyboarded for publication in primary journals can be fed directly into the computer system of the secondary processor.

The vastly greater flexibility of access to information through a computer system can also permit effective interlinking of the secondary information systems serving the various scientific and technical disciplines and various nations. An example of this capability is the experimental link established over the past several years between CAS and the National Library of Medicine's Medical Literature Analysis and Retrieval System (MEDLARS). This experiment has linked the different forms of nomenclature used to index chemical substances in MEDLARS and *Chemical Abstracts* through the computer-based chemical structure recognition system of the CAS Chemical Registry. Hence, the user searching for information on a chemical substance in either system has a means of identifying the corresponding index access points in the other. Similarly, CAS and Germany's Internationale Dokumentationsgesellschaft für Chemie (IDC) are standardizing methods of handling chemical structure representations in the CAS Registry and IDC's developing computer-based chemical information system to permit direct exchange of data between the two systems.

In April 1969 the American Chemical Society and The Chemical Society (London), acting on behalf of a consortium of ten scientific and professional societies in the United Kingdom, forged the first formal link in an international network for handling secondary chemical information. The British society is now marketing CAS publications and services in the United Kingdom and has begun to develop a system for processing data from the British journal and patent literature into the CAS computer system in Columbus. In September 1969, ACS and West Germany's Gesellschaft Deutscher Chemiker entered into a similar agreement, and the Chemisches Zentralblatt staff in Berlin has begun supplying data from the German chemical literature to CAS. The Chemical Society and Gesellschaft Deutscher Chemiker are two of five or six overseas input centers envisioned for such an international network. Each will supply computer-readable information to a central processing system in Columbus and share in output—both in the form of printed publications and machine-searchable tapes—from this central system.

Ultimately, the application of computer and electronic data transmission technology throughout the scientific information-handling community can make possible the interlinking of the many specialized information services into an effective information network, with each processing a share of the data and each able to refer a query it is not equipped to handle to the appropriate one of the others. If this can be accomplished, much of the current overlap and duplication of effort between primary and secondary information processors and between the various national, international, discipline-oriented, and mission-oriented secondary services can be eliminated. CAS intends to work actively in this direction.

BIBLIOGRAPHY

HISTORY

Browne, C. A., and M. E. Weeks, *A History of the American Chemical Society,* American Chemical Society, Washington, D.C., 1952.

CHEMICAL ABSTRACTS

Baker, D. B., "The Chemical Literature Expands," *Chem. Eng. News,* 44(23), 84 (1966).

Bernays, P. M., K. L. Coe, and J. L. Wood, "A Computer-Based Source Inventory of *Chemical Abstracts,*" *J. Chem. Doc.,* 5, 242 (1965).

CAS Today, 60th Anniversary Ed., Chemical Abstracts Service, Columbus, Ohio, 1967.

Platau, G. O., "Documentation of The Chemical Patent Literature," *J. Chem. Doc.,* 7, 250 (1967).

Rowlett, R. J., Jr., "Key to the World's Chemical Knowledge," *Chemistry,* 41, 12 (1968).

CA INDEXES

Combined Introductions, Subject, Formula, Ring System, and HAIC Indexes to Volume 66 (*of Chemical Abstracts*), Chemical Abstracts Service, Columbus, Ohio, 1968.

CAS COMPUTER-BASED INFORMATION SYSTEM

Davenport, W. C., "CAS Computer-Based Information Services," *Datamation,* 14(3), 33 (1968).

Davenport, W. C., and J. T. Dickman, "Computer-Based Composition at Chemical Abstracts Service," *J. Chem. Doc.,* 6, 221 (1966).

Hefner, R. G., P. M. Keesecker, and D. F. Rule, "Keyboarding Chemical Information," *J. Chem. Doc.,* 7, 232 (1967).

Tate, F. A., "Progress Toward a Computer-Based Chemical Information System," *Chem. Eng. News,* 45(4), 78 (1967).

Vander Stouw, G. G., I. Naznitsky, and James E. Rush, "Procedures for Converting Systematic Names of Organic Compounds into Atom-Bond Connection Tables," *J. Chem. Doc.,* 7, 165 (1967).

Whittingham, D. J., F. R. Wetsel, and H. L. Morgan, "The Computer-Based Subject Index Support System at Chemical Abstracts Service," *J. Chem. Doc.,* 6, 230 (1966).

THE CHEMICAL REGISTRY SYSTEM

Leiter, D. P., Jr., H. L. Morgan, and R. E. Stobaugh, "Installation and Operation of a Registry for Chemical Compounds," *J. Chem. Doc.,* 5, 238 (1965).

Morgan, H. L., "The Generation of a Unique Machine Description for Chemical Structures," *J. Chem. Doc.,* 5, 107 (1965).

Tate, F. A., "A Mechanized Registry for Chemical Compounds," *Chemistry,* 41(7), 18 (1968).

Tate, F. A., "Handling Chemical Compounds in Information Systems," in *Annual Review of Information Science and Technology,* Vol. 2 (Carlos A. Cuadra, ed.), Wiley (Interscience), New York, 1967, pp. 285–309.

COMPUTER-BASED PUBLICATIONS AND SERVICES

Ish, C. J., and S. W. Terrant, Jr., "Chemical-Biological Activities: A Specialized Information Service in Biochemistry," *Amer. J. Pharm. Educ.,* 32, 201 (1968).

Siegel, H., D. C. Veal, and D. A. McMullen, "Polymer Science and Technology: A Computer-Based Information Service," *J. Polym. Sci., Part C,* 25 191 (1968).

LINKS WITH THE SOURCE LITERATURE

Tate, F. A., and J. L. Wood, "Libraries and Abstracting and Indexing Services—A Study in Interdependency," *Lib. Trends,* 16, 353 (1968).

Wood, J. L., "A Comprehensive List of Periodicals for Chemistry and Chemical Engineering," *Lib. Trends,* 16, 398 (1968).

DALE B. BAKER

CHEMICAL INFORMATION CENTERS

A new type of service institution providing computer-based information service to chemists has begun to develop during the last five years. This article will attempt to describe the status of these institutions as of January 1970, realizing full well that by publication time the rapid changes in this field will have rendered some portions of it obsolete. Although there are many organizations providing different types of information services to chemical users, relatively few of them make routine computer searches of large data bases for large numbers (50 or more) of outside users. This discussion is restricted to those information centers providing such services to general customers because we believe that librarians and information officers who will read it are primarily concerned with sources of such information for their own clientele rather than those private companies providing mainly in-house service. Although we will focus primarily on the large publicly available chemical information centers, our coverage and tabulation is by no means comprehensive. The reader is referred to the Bibliography at the end of this article for a more comprehensive listing of such sources.

The Need and Opportunity

Probably no other field of human endeavor is so ideally suited to exploitation through computer techniques for manipulating large files as is Chemistry. During the last 120 years, approximately 4 million different chemical compounds, each with a known unambiguous molecular structure, have been isolated and identified. Their preparation and properties, both chemical and physical, are described in detail in the chemical literature. Although any given compound may have a number of unambiguous names assigned to it through various nomenclature systems, each has a unique structure which describes the way its atoms are joined in three-dimensional space. It was realized during the late 1800s that further progress of chemistry was greatly dependent on the development of international conventions for reporting chemical information and of reliable indexes and catalogs for accessing it. Thanks to the efforts of the American Chemical Society, The Chemical Society (London), and The Gesellschaft Deutscher Chemiker (formerly The Deutschen Chemischen Gesellschaft), such comprehensive and updated works as *Chemical Abstracts* and *Chemisches Zentralblatt* make it possible for any chemist with a good library at his disposal to make a remarkably complete survey of the literature with little or no training in how to use these indexes. Using the more recent *Science Citation Index,* he may also update his search by finding who has recently cited the important articles which he has identified in his retrospective search.

Chemistry is a central field in physical science penetrating into many other disciplines such as medicine, biology, physics, and pharmacology. Consequently, information of interest to chemists has always been broadly diffused through many scholarly journals. Chemical Abstracts Service (CAS) was founded in order to provide an abstracting service so that readers could evaluate the potential value of articles discovered in the index before expending the effort and expense of locating full articles which might be widely scattered through the primary literature. Since CAS was established in 1907, the total chemical literature has doubled in size every eleven to twelve years with an accumulated total of over 4 million abstracts. Although the unlimited exponential growth of any activity is impossible, it is clear that the storehouse of chemical information is already very large, very well-organized, and expanding at an alarming rate. Also, in view of the central importance of chemistry to many sectors of the scientific and technological economy, there is great pressure and financial incentive for exploiting the capabilities of digital computers for organizing and manipulating vast quantities of this stored information. It should be clear from this brief history that because chemistry is perhaps the largest and best organized of any discipline and is also the first to make extensive use of computer-based searching, the lessons learned from chemical information centers, data banks, and networks of such centers may have profound implications in the development of other fields as they begin to take advantage of these techniques.

Development of Chemical Information Centers—Past, Present, and Future

Because of the special problems that chemists face in handling information, they were quick to take advantage of machine sorting and indexing using Hollerith cards, edge sorted punched cards, and the like. However, it was soon obvious that massive, high-speed, computer facilities would be needed to do the job properly, and during the 1950s CAS, with the support of the American Chemical Society and the National Science Foundation, began a massive program which produced several publications available in printed form and on magnetic tape. Included in these were *Chemical Titles* (1962), *Chemical Biological-Activities* (*CBAC,* 1965), *Polymer Science and Technology* (*POST-P&J,* 1967), *Basic Journal Abstracts* (*BJA,* 1967), and *CA Condensates* (1968). These can be used as a basis for computer-based SDI systems in chemistry using keywords in titles and digests, author's names, journal coden, molecular formulas, and registry numbers; searchable terms are dependent on the particular data base. In 1965, the Institute for Scientific Information in Philadelphia began an SDI alerting service (ASCA) based on citations of about 2000 journals, of which 600 were chemical journals. Numerous other tape services are also available, but no attempt has been made to list them here.

Although CAS has provided custom searches of their own tapes for several years, it was at the University of Nottingham in England that the first major experiment on introducing computer-based chemical information to a large group of users was begun in 1967. Since then, a number of other major centers in the United States

TABLE 1
Some Information Centers Currently Offering Chemical Information Services[a]

Center	Address	Chemical data bases[b]	Other data bases	Number of users Chemical	Number of users Non-chemical	Output forms	Interactions with users
Dow Chemical Company	Midland, Michigan 48640	Chemical Titles, CA Condensates	Biological Abstracts, Compendex[c]	400	30	Cards	Workshops, Personal interviews, Feedback questionnaires
IIT Research Institute, Computer Search Center	10 West 35th Street, Chicago, Illinois 60616	CA Condensates	BioResearch Index, Biological Abstracts	165	100	Paper listings, Cards	Workshops, Personal interviews, Feedback questionnaires and cards
Institute of Scientific Information (ISI)	325 Chestnut Street, Philadelphia, Pennsylvania 19106	ISI Citation and Source Tapes-ASCA (R-1961), Index Chemicus Registry Service (R-1960)	All major scientific disciplines are covered in the ISI data base	Confidential		Paper listings, Magnetic tape	Workshops, Personal and telephone interviews, Feedback questionnaires and cards
Pittsburgh Chemical Information Center	Knowledge Availability Systems Center, University of Pittsburgh, Pittsburgh, Pennsylvania 15213	Chemical Titles, CA Condensates		300	—	Paper listings, Cards	Workshops, Personal interviews, Feedback questionnaires and cards
University of Georgia, Information Science	Computer Science, University of Georgia, Athens, Georgia 30601	Chemical Titles (R-1962), CA Condensates (R-1968), Chemical Biological Activities (R-1965), Nuclear Science Abstracts (R-1966)	BioResearch Index, Biological Abstracts, Compendex[c]	420	350	Paper listings, Cards, Magnetic tape	Workshops, Seminars, Special purpose feedback questionnaires
3i Company/Information Interscience Incorporated	2240 Walnut Street, Philadelphia, Pennsylvania 19103	Basic Journal Abstracts, Chemical Titles, Chemical Biological Activities (R-1965), CA Condensates (R-1968), Polymer Science and Technology J.	Compendex[c], Excerpta Medica, Other specialized data bases	Confidential		Paper listings, Cards	Personal and telephone interviews, Return cards

Center	Data bases		Number	Number	Output	Services
National Science Library / National Research Council of Canada, Ottawa, Ontario, Canada	*Chemical Titles* / *CA Condensates* / *ISI (ASCA IV)*	Inspec	400	200	Paper listings / Cards	Workshops / Feedback questionnaires and cards
United Kingdom Chemical Information Service / University Park, Nottingham NG7 2RD, England	*Chemical Titles* / *Chemical Biological Activities* / *CA Condensates* / *Polymer Science and Technology-P & J*		600	—	Paper listings / Cards	Workshops / Personal interviews / Feedback questionnaires and cards
Danmarks Tekniske Bibliotek / Oster Voldgade 10, 1350 Copenhagen K, Denmark	*Chemical Titles* / *CA Condensates*	*Engineering Index*	200	5	Paper listings	Workshops / Personal interviews / Feedback questionnaires and cards
Netherlands Organization for Chemical Information / 1 Burnierstraat, The Hague, The Netherlands	*Chemical Titles* / *CA Condensates*		50		Paper listings	Personal interviews
Biomedical Documentation Center / Karolinska Institutet, Fack, 10401 Stockholm 60, Sweden	*Chemical Titles* / *Chemical Biological Activities* / *CA Condensates*	*Biological Abstracts Previews* / *Medlars*	300	500	Paper listings / Cards	Workshops / Seminars / Personal interviews
Royal Institute of Technology / S-100 44 Stockholm, Sweden	*Polymer Science and Technology*	ISI Tapes / Inspec / *Metal Abstracts* / Own engineering data base	100	500	Paper listings	Workshops / Feedback questionnaires and cards
IDC—International Dokumentationsgesellschaft für Chemie m.b.H. / 6 Frankfurt am Main, Hamberger Allee 26-28, Germany	Own data base for patent and journal literature in organic chemistry		13 firms employing 6500 chemists		Paper listings and copies of abstracts	Introductory course / Personal interviews
Chemie Information and Dokumentation / 1 Berlin 30, Geisbergstr. 39, Germany	CAS Tapes / *Chemischer Informationsdienst (Chem Inform)*, own data base					Personal interviews

a This is not intended as a comprehensive list of all centers that offer some type of chemical information service, but rather as a representative selection of such centers with information on services as of January 1970. Brochures giving further information on specific services and their costs are available from each concern.

b All centers supply regular current awareness services. If retrospective searches are also presently offered this is indicated by an "R" and the earliest year for which that service is available.

c In 1970.

and Western Europe have been established at nonprofit institutions. Several commercial houses are also supplying computer services to increasingly large groups of users. The services offered chemists by several information centers are shown in Table 1.

In order that the needs of the chemical information centers may be strongly represented, a number of them joined forces to form two organizations: in North America, Association of Scientific Information Dissemination Centers (ASIDIC), and in Europe, Group of Operators of Chemical Information Systems (USIDIC, formerly CHEOPS). Their memberships as of January 1, 1970, are shown in Table 2.

The next several years should see a rapid expansion and acceptance of SDI alerting services from these centers and the possible development of networks through which the centers can cooperate in providing a variety of services to different users. One may expect through development of satellite communication and remote facsimile reproduction that even those countries and areas which are inaccessible to large technical libraries will have rapid access to the latest chemical information. The development of a computer-based chemical information center at this time requires a critical mass of facilities in terms of personnel, equipment, and users. This fact has prompted a number of observers in the field to conclude that future developments will center in a rather small number (perhaps ten or fifteen) of major installations around the world providing to the world's scientific community the various types of services described below.

Types of Services and Searches

Chemists, like any other researchers, are faced with two fundamental types of literature problems. A *retrospective search* through the past literature is required whenever a chemist begins work in a field that is new to him. If the field itself is relatively new, such as some of the more exotic areas of spectroscopy or chemical physics, his search may take him back over only the last five or ten years. However, in many areas of preparative chemistry, such as organic and inorganic chemistry, a complete coverage of the literature may take him back into the 1870s or 1880s through a host of different journals written in different languages in various decades of the past. Once the scientist is satisfied that he has covered the earlier literature, he is faced with the second major problem; that of keeping up in the field if he decides to stay in it. It is this latter activity of providing up-to-date *current awareness* service that has been reduced to a successful, practical, and economical level during the past few years.

As of this writing, broad-scale computer-based retrospective searching of the chemical literature even over the past five to ten years has not proved economically feasible and it seems most unlikely that computer searches of the entire chemical literature will be feasible during the coming twenty years—if indeed it is ever done. In addition to the problems of supplying the enormous computer memory that would be required for storage and of developing the software and techniques to search the data base economically, there seems little likelihood that money and

TABLE 2
Associations of Information Centers

A. ASIDIC[a]

Eastman Kodak Company	Research Labs
	343 State Street
	Rochester, New York 14650
IIT Research Institute	10 West 35th Street
	Chicago, Illinois 60616
University of Georgia	Computer Center
	Athens, Georgia 30601
University of Pittsburgh	Knowledge Availability Systems Center
	Pittsburgh, Pennsylvania 15213
National Science Library	National Research Council of Canada
	Ottawa 7, Ontario, Canada
The Dow Chemical Company	Midland, Michigan 48640
IBM Technical Information Retrieval Center	Old Orchard Road
	Armonk, New York 10504
E. I. du Pont Company	Information Science Division
	3211 Centre Road Building
	Wilmington, Delaware 19898
General Telephone and Electronics	Technical Information Program
	208–20 Willets Pt. Boulevard
	Bayside, New York 11360
Aerospace Research Applications Center	Indiana University Foundation
	Indiana Memorial Union
	Bloomington, Indiana 47401
Lawrence Radiation Laboratory	University of California
	Berkeley, California 94720
3i Company	2204 Walnut Street
	Philadelphia, Pennsylvania 19103
Clearing House for Federal and Scientific Information	Springfield, Virginia 22151

B. USIDIC

United Kingdom Chemical Information System (UKCIS)	University of Nottingham
	Nottingham, United Kingdom
Karolinska Institutet	Biomedical Documentation Centre
	Fack 10401
	Stockholm, Sweden
The Royal Institute of Technology	Industrigarden 2
	Stockholm 70, Sweden
Danmarks Tekniske Bibliotek	Øster Voldgade 10
	1350 Kobenhavn K., Denmark
The German Chemical Society	Chemischer Informationsdienst
	Geisbergstrasse 39
	1 Berlin 30, Germany
IDC—Internationale Dokumentations-gesellschaft für Chemie m.b.H.	Liebigstrasse 19
	6 Frankfurt/Main, Germany
The Royal Netherlands Chemical Society	The Netherlands Organisation for Chemical Information
	Burnierstraat 1
	The Hague, The Netherlands
Centre National de Documentation Scientifique et Technique	Biblioteque Royale
	4 Boulevard de l'Empereur
	Bruxelles 1, Belgium

(continued)

TABLE 2 (*Continued*)

State Institute for Technical Research	Zonrotink 37
	Helsinki 18, Finland
Institute for Industrial Research and	Ballymun Road
Standards	Dublin 9, Ireland
Societé Nationale des Pétroles	Tour Aquitaine
d'Aquitaine (SNPA)	92 Courbevoie, France
S.N.A.M. Progetti, S.p.A.–L.R.S.R.	20097 S. Donato Milanese
	Milan, Italy
Shell Research Ltd.	Woodstock Agricultural Research Centre
	Sittingbourne, Kent, United Kingdom
Shell Central Offices	Information Division
	Bataafse Internationale Petroleum
	Maatschappij N.V.
	P. O. Box 162
	The Hague, The Netherlands

a Full members of the organization are listed; there are approximately another thirty associate members.

manpower will be available for indexing and coding the past chemical literature in searchable form.

Although a great majority of the chemical literature is related to molecular-structural information, there is no means at this time for making general searches of literature through chemical structures. Suitable strategies using word stems can be applied within the nomenclature rules for many classes of compounds. However, although each systematic name must, by requirement, apply unambiguously to a single molecular structure, many compounds have a wide variety of equally correct chemical names, so that word stems are not very reliable as an alerting method for many classes of compounds.

An approach towards giving alerting service on chemical substructures is presently being provided through the Index-Chemicus registry system by the Institute for Scientific Information using Wiswesser line notations. This will alert the user whenever a new compound containing the desired substructure is reported. However, no provision is made for alerting him to new uses for old compounds.

The CAS registry system aims towards providing a unique registry number for each of the 4 million compounds presently known. In principle, it should be possible eventually to provide substructure searches through an atom by atom search of each structure and thus be taken back to literature citations in *Chemical Abstracts*. However, at the present time, this search capability is restricted to less than 100,000 compounds included in the *Common Data Base* and the *CBAC* file, and the linkage between the registry numbers for hits which the computer makes and the original literature is a difficult and tenuous one. Structure searching is undoubtedly the most basic and powerful tool for computer-based chemical information and permits many means of penetrating the literature which would be impossible through manual searches. However, at the present time, it is in its experimental infancy and is not only impractical for most chemical users, but also very expensive. In some specialized areas of pharmacology where chemical and biological activity correlations are important, it does have immediate promise. Readers are referred to the groups at the University of Georgia and the Food and Drug Administration for further details.

In view of the fact that most of the presently available computer-based information services simply involve weekly or biweekly SDI searches, most of these are run in the batch mode. Although there has been considerable speculation and enthusiasm for real-time interactive searching, there are few, if any, chemical data bases other than spectroscopy files where real-time accessing is presently useful. In those cases where it is feasible, there seems little justification for providing the users with such rapid service when the cost involved is usually many times greater than that for batch service.

The Relationship of Computer-Based Services to Chemical Users and to Conventional Services

It is easy to forget that computer-based information services have only one ultimate function—to save time and give satisfaction to the user who requested the service. Now that three or four years of experience have been gained in providing alerting services to chemical users, several generalizations can be made.

1. Not all kinds of scientists are apt to benefit from these services. Direct observation and careful behavioral study support the common notion that scientists vary enormously in their personalities and styles of doing research, and this affects their literature needs and the ways they respond to service. Obviously, well-organized, literature-conscious researchers who have had long experience working in a clearly defined field with a diffuse literature have much to gain by using a computer alerting service. Experience shows a relatively low drop-out rate of those scientists who have taken the initiative to subscribe to computer-based alerting services. Granted that they are a self-selected sample, it follows that most of them have selected well. At the other extreme, neither the theoretician who depends primarily on the "grapevine" or the face-to-face contacts within the "invisible college," nor the "hit and run investigator" who moves rapidly from one problem to the next, has much to gain from such systems.

2. Another generalization is that considerable effort must often be spent by the individual and an experienced information officer in developing a good *interest profile*. This is a list of terms which describe his area of interest. The types of search terms that are used include word terms which are matched against titles, digests, or descriptors; authors; journal coden; registry numbers; and molecular formulas. Citations, such as would normally appear in the footnotes of scientific articles, are searched at the Institute for Scientific Information through the service known as Automatic Science Citation Alert (ASCA). The user may specify single terms, a group of alternative terms, or specific term combinations which must be matched in the data base to cause retrieval of a citation. Most systems permit the use of "and," "or," "not" combinations and some allow the use of weighted terms.

The following sample search strategies illustrate briefly how a question may be handled. Precise details of strategy formulation are dependent upon the specific data base and the search program used by the particular information center.

Example 1: *Statement of interest.* Information on curium. This is a very simple strategy; the single term CURIUM should be adequate.

Example 2: *Statement of interest.* Information on sodium and potassium halides. The search strategy might be:

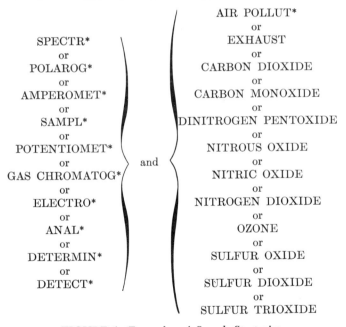

Example 3: *Statement of interest.* Electrochemical analysis of air pollution. This question requires more terms to cover the broad area: (Note: Most search programs permit term truncation so that one word stem will retrieve several words. In the following listing, an asterisk indicates that any word starting with the given root will trigger the retrieval of a citation. Thus, SPECTR* will match "spectra," "spectral," "spectrum," "spectroscopy," "spectrophotometry," etc.)

FIGURE 1. *Examples of Search Strategies.*

In searching free-text material such as titles, keywords, and digests, the user must try to anticipate the various ways in which a given concept might be expressed by different authors. Examples of simple strategies are shown in Figure 1. Obviously a certain amount of speculation is involved, and for this reason search strategies should be reviewed and refined after examination of the output received from the first few searches. An information specialist who is familiar with the data base can be of tremendous help to a user in the development of an efficient interest profile. The acceptance and success of computer services is greatly enhanced by good communication between the users and the information center staff.

3. Although librarians are primarily concerned with providing the best possible service to their users, the real limit to the value of computer-based information centers is often the ability of the user to assimilate the information which is brought to him; he may feel harassed and bothered if faced with a deluge of new paperwork. Any productive scientist would prefer to devote his precious hours with the literature to studying primary information rather than managing a host of secondary publications and printouts.

4. It is important for the librarian to maintain perspective in offering expensive new services to his users, especially if they jeopardize the budget for the conventional collection.

5. It is our experience, reinforced by discussions with a number of other information centers, that computer-based alerting services are best used to support and backup the user's routine scanning and browsing of a small number of his favorite journals. A good profile of keywords, citations, and authors will give him almost complete recall of the general literature leaving him free to study his favorite journals at comparative leisure. Simple search strategies using and/or/not combinations are least expensive and are usually entirely adequate.

In summary, we conclude that computer-based chemical alerting service is now a valuable information source for many scientists. While retrospective searches are widely demanded, they are not economically feasible at present; this problem may be surmounted in the near future. Although interactive searching and a number of other "blue-sky" applications of computer to chemical literature needs are now technically feasible, we believe that the trend will be towards simple, practical, inexpensive services which will have to meet the crucial test of user acceptance in the market place.

The authors acknowledge financial support in the development of the Pittsburgh Chemical Information Center from National Science Foundation Grant GN-738 and a grant from the Commonwealth of Pennsylvania P-SEF 60.

BIBLIOGRAPHY

American Library Association, *A Guide to a Selection of Computer-Based Science and Technology Reference Services in the U.S.A.*, Reference Services Division, Chicago, 1969.

Housman, Edward M., *Survey of Current Systems for Selective Dissemination of Information (SDI)*, Report No. SIG/SDI-1, American Society for Information Science, Washington, D.C., 1969.

National Science Foundation, *Nonconventional Scientific and Technical Information Systems in Current Use*, No. 4, Washington, D.C., 1966.

Science Associates/International, Inc., *Directory of Computerized Information in Science and Technology,* New York, **1968.**

Troutman, Joan C., *Inventory of Available Data Bases,* Institute of Library Research, University of California, Los Angeles, 1967 (CFSTI PB 178441).

EDWARD M. ARNETT AND MARY JANE PUGH

CHEMICAL NOTATIONS

The term "chemical notation" was first proposed in 1871 (*82*) to describe a method for representing chemical structures wherein symbols were used to represent atoms and structural fragments. The history and further developments of this technique for a line-formula notation have been briefly summarized by Wiswesser (*150*) and are discussed in the *Survey of Chemical Notation Systems* (*104–106*). Although earlier introduced by Richards (*116*), the present use of this term was reintroduced by Dyson, in 1946, when he proposed a "cipher" or "cipher notation" to represent chemical structures in a unique and unambiguous manner (*31,32*). Chemical structures were to be divided into structural components, e.g., rings, chains, and functional groups, organized in a hierarchial manner, and written in a linear form.

The development of the Dyson Cipher can be followed in the literature (*9,24–27,33–46,80,81,111,112,139*). The pioneering work by Dyson stimulated others to report different approaches for ciphering chemical compounds: Gordon-Kendall-Davison (*29,30,57*), Gruber (*64,65*), Silk (*118–121*), Cockburn (*18*), Wiswesser (*1–5,8–10,12–15,17,24,28,48,53–56,58–63,66,74,75,77–79,83,84,98,101a-n, 103,107,113–115,117,123–127,130,132,138,140,142–152,159*), Hayward (*67–71,87,122,129,136,137*), Eisman (*47*), Bouman (*11*), Skolnik (*122,122a*), McDonnell (*100*), Welch (*141*), Lederberg (*85,86,133*), Lefkovitz (*88–93*), and Hiz (*73*). A review of the earlier methods (up to 1951) was prepared for the International Union of Pure and Applied Chemistry (IUPAC) Commission on Codification, Ciphering, and Punched Card Techniques (*6*). A summary of this report was published (*7*).

Chemical notations can be unique or nonunique and ambiguous or unambiguous. A detailed discussion of the combinations and their implications is presented in the *Survey of Chemical Notation Systems* (*104*).

Chemical Nomenclature

Chemical nomenclature has been the traditional linear notation for uniquely representing chemicals. However, nomenclature has evolved from common names, trivial names, author-derived names, and the multiplicity of standards established by the Geneva Conventions, IUPAC, and Chemical Abstracts Service (*76*). Therefore, nomenclature can be either ambiguous or unambiguous. The prime function of nomenclature has been to index chemicals for locating specific compounds in the literature and has been supplemented with molecular formula indexes. Consequently, analog, homolog, substructure, and related compound searching, using nomenclatural methods, has proved to be a difficult task (128). Rules of nomenclature usually lag behind the discovery of new structural types, and uniqueness does not occur until officiating experts establish new standards.

Conversely, notations of the type proposed by Dyson, Silk, Wiswesser, Hayward, and Skolnik have been constructed so that most newly determined structural characteristics can be uniquely and unambiguously described in a concise manner. These notations, by-and-large, are reduced to about 30% of the space requirements (on punched cards or printed) for a standardized chemical name (145).

IUPAC-Dyson Cipher

In 1947, IUPAC established a Commission on Codification, Ciphering, and Punched Card Techniques (19). This Commission was directed to examine and report on the emerging notational systems. In 1949, the Commission submitted the following desiderata for an internationally acceptable chemical notation (20):

1. Simplicity of use.
2. Ease of printing and typewriting.
3. Conciseness.
4. Recognizability.
5. Ability to generate a unique chemical nomenclature.
6. Compatibility with the accepted practices of inorganic nomenclature.
7. Uniqueness.
8. Generation of an unambiguous and useful enumeration pattern.
9. Ease of manipulation by machine methods, for example, by punched cards.
10. Exhibition of associations (descriptiveness).
11. Ability to deal with partial indeterminants.

The Commission noted that these desiderata were not listed in order of relative importance. In 1951, the Commission recommended the adoption of a provisional notation for organic compounds based on the proposals of the Dyson Cipher (21). The proposed revision of this cipher was tentatively drafted in 1958 (80), and the final version published as the Approved IUPAC Notation in 1961 (81). Dyson, serving as Director of Research at Chemical Abstracts Service, attempted to utilize the IUPAC-Dyson Cipher as the machine-record for the Chemical Abstracts Compound Registry System (38–42). However, the cipher was "shelved" in favor of a connection table approach (134,135). Development of this cipher has continued in England (43–46) by Dyson and his colleagues.

Shell Research, Ltd., at the Woodstock Agricultural Research Center, in 1962 adopted the IUPAC Cipher as the means to store and retrieve chemical structure information. Computer programs have been written to search the cipher and automatically generate fragments. A checking routine for determining duplicates has been developed (*25–27,111*).

A modified IUPAC Cipher was studied by the Swedish Patent Office to determine the possibility of mechanizing patent examiners' searches (*106*). The results of this study have not been published.

Wiswesser Line-Formula Notation (WLN)

The interest initiated by the efforts of Dyson and the review of the available notation systems by the IUPAC Commission encouraged the respondents to continue the development of their respective systems.

The first application of the use of punched cards with a notation was by Wiswesser in 1951. He demonstrated notation listings before the IUPAC Commission (*6*). These were prepared from mechanical equipment.

In 1953, Benson presented an application of a chemical notation using punched cards (*5*) before a meeting of the American Chemical Society. Modified Wiswesser Notations were machine organized with standard Remington Rand card sorting equipment.

This method interested Bonnett, who was responsible for organizing and maintaining the chemical file for a pharmaceutical organization. This file, predominantly steroids, did not lend itself to fragmentation schemes, such as those developed by Wiselogle (*16*) and Frear (*49–52*), because of stereoisomeric differences and positional substitutions. Nomenclature of steroids was not sufficiently developed to provide management of the file. The possibility of uniqueness and unambiguity, plus machinable organization, enticed Bonnet to try this novel approach.

Smith, via a colleague at the University of Hawaii, became aware of the Wiswesser Notation. He had studied the Dyson Cipher but was unable to utilize it to his satisfaction with IBM card sorting equipment. Smith was intrigued with the ideas of machine organizing chemical structures so that all similar compounds could be arranged by a common parameter, e.g., melting points, in ascending order, within a class of compounds. He encoded into the WLN several thousand compounds from Lange's *Handbook* and the *Merck Index*. He later encoded some 50,000 of the compounds cited in Heilbron's *Dictionary of Organic Compounds* (*72*).

Bonnett and Smith corresponded with each other, and with Wiswesser, to offer recommendations for modifications in the notation rules. This encouraged Wiswesser to continue to develop details which had been inferred in a manual (*145*) but were not well defined for the application that Bonnett and Smith were undertaking. Wiswesser had originally conceived of the notation based on a "least effort principle" (*153*). The notation was developed for a typewriter keyboard, taking advantage of the upper and lower case letters, which doubled the symbol set. However, punched cards restricted letters to one character set, so Wiswesser redesigned the symbols for the Teletype by adding a blank space. In the notation it functioned as a shift key operator so that a letter following a blank would represent a position of substitution; a number following a blank would mean that the number was a multiplier. In this manner, the symbol set was again doubled, and visual clarity was improved because the blank spaces set off chemical information units like separate words. Symbol count studies have established the blank space as the symbol with the highest frequency of use.

In 1959, Gelberg was assigned the responsibility for organizing a file of some 8000 chemical structures in the Industry Liaison Office (ILO), for the U.S. Army Chemical Research and Development Laboratories, Edgewood Arsenal, Maryland. This file was growing at a rate of 400–500 structures per month (ultimately to level at 1200 per month). The system to be installed had to be designed so that it could provide rapid answers for specific compounds, as well as analogs, homologs, and related structures. The file was to be initially managed by only one chemist, and it had to be inexpensive to operate. A review of the available systems, essentially fragmentation codes, indicated that the system in operation at the G. D. Searle and Co., directed by Bonnett, should be the method of choice. The earlier three-way correspondence evolved into a four-way flow. Bonnett, Smith, and Wiswesser were interested in having a novice learn the notation, and to feedback ideas and problem areas. The ILO file was unique in that it encompassed the entire spectrum of chemicals, whereas the Heilbron compendia tended to favor simple compounds, and the Searle file was overweighted with steroids. As the ILO program and file grew, additional help was required. The Wiswesser Notations fulfilled the need for registry and inventory requirements, but the location of structural fragments necessitated the development of an auxiliary code. Smith had published a fragment code based on Wiswesser symbols (*123*) but it proved to be limited. Bonnett had modified the BATCH (*4,144,146*) classification code (*8*) to index his notation file, but this did not provide fragment search capability. The ILO code (*53*) proved to be time-consuming and inconsistent in the fragment assignments. Two weeks before being separated from the U.S. Army (having been assigned to the ILO), Sorter proposed that the Wiswesser Notations be machine organized in the key-word-in-context manner (*97*), as the Chemical Abstracts publication *Chemical Titles,* the difference being that each symbol (with certain constraints) would be treated as a "key-word." This idea was developed by Sorter at Hoffmann-LaRoche, Inc., and by Granito and Gelberg at the ILO (*54,55,58,59,62,75,101f,101h*). The "key-word-in-context" or "permuted" approach eliminated the need for the fragmentation code.

Interest in the WLN expanded to a number of organizations. A partial list of those organizations that have announced their interest, as evidenced by publication, includes:

> J. T. Baker and Co. (*3,4,101a,151*)
> Chemical Abstracts Service (*17*)
> Diamond-Shamrock (Alkali) Co. (*54,55,62*)
> Dow Chemical Co. (*12–15,84,101b*)
> Food and Drug Administration (*1*)
> General Aniline and Film Corp. (*132*)
> Goodyear Tire and Rubber Co. (*28*)

Hebrew University (Israel) (*74*)
Hoffmann-LaRoche, Inc. (*101l,130*)
Imperial Chemicals Industries, Ltd. (*77,78,101i,117,138*)
Institute for Scientific Information (*79,113,154*)
Eli Lilly and Co. (*114*)
Mills College (*2,123,124*)
Ministry of Defence (Israel) (*107*)
National Bureau of Standards (*48,101h*)
National Library of Medicine (*1,115*)
Olin (*66*)
G. D. Searle and Co. (*8–10,101b*)
Stanford Research Institute (*75,101h*)
University of Pennsylvania (*83,101j,101m,103,140*)
University of Sheffield (England) (*98*)
U.S. Army Chemical Information and Data Systems (CIDS) (*101*)
U.S. Army, Fort Detrick (*101n,152,159*)
U.S. Army, ILO (*53,56,58–60,101g,101k,130*)

By the end of 1969, over twenty organizations had adopted the WLN for the management of chemical structure files (*127,152*).

Chemical Notation Association

The rapid growth of the number of chemical information scientists and organizations that became interested in the WLN established a need for uniform control of the rules. A tentative revised manual had been prepared by Wiswesser, Smith, and Bonnett in 1962 (*148*). The needs of many users of this notation brought about the development of an "invisible college," and led to the formation of the Chemical Notation Association in 1965. As stated in the Association Constitution, Article 2:

> The purposes of this Association are (1) to promote and conduct research in the field of chemical notation systems and to advance the development and application of these systems; (2) to educate chemists in the uses and advantages of these systems; and (3) to act as an official adjudicating body to determine and control the standard rules of any chemical notation system entrusted to this Association for this purpose by its authors, inventors, and developers.

In early 1970, the Chemical Notation Association had over 70 members representing industry, government, and academia, in the United States, the United Kingdom, and France.

Public Availability of WLN Files

The WLN was selected by the Institute for Scientific Information for the chemical structures cited in *Index Chemicus* (*79,113,154*). A new service for subscribers, *Index Chemicus Registry System,* was provided. Alphabetically ordered listings and a computer tape of the monthly WLNs were made available. In 1968, over 150,000 notations were provided, and in 1969, an estimated 180,000 notations were made available. Each of the notations was linked to the *Index Chemicus* digests.

The Excerpta Medica Foundation in The Netherlands adopted the WLN for organizing drug information by chemical structure for their computer-based information service (*127*). These tapes are available by subscription.

A cooperative program between the Chemical Abstracts Service, the Dow Chemical Co., and Prof. Smith provided the Wiswesser Line Notations of the structures in *The Ring Index* (*110*). This listing is available from the U.S. Department of Commerce Clearinghouse for Federal Scientific and Technical Information (*17*).

In the United States, the National Library of Medicine adopted the WLN for organizing the chemicals occurring in the literature for the Toxicological Information Project (*1,115*).

J. T. Baker Co. organized their chemical catalog of commercially available compounds utilizing the BATCH classification code and the WLN (*3,4,101a,151*).

Aldrich Chemical Co. provided, for subscribers, the WLNs on punch cards for the organic chemical compounds in their chemical catalog.

The Food and Drug Administration and the National Library of Medicine jointly sponsored the preparation of the WLNs for the chemicals in the Common Data Base, a file of chemical compounds that are commonplace or have been reported to exhibit biological activity (*108*). These notations, on magnetic tape, were released to the Clearinghouse for public distribution in 1970.

Permuted listings of the WLNs for the compounds cited in Frear's *Pesticide Index* were distributed privately by Gelberg in 1965–1967.

Horner privately distributed the WLN permuted listings for the chemical structures in the first four *Collected Volumes of Organic Synthesis*.

A WLN listing of screened insecticides from the files of the U.S. Department of Agriculture, with accompanying biological data, was offered for sale by Horner in 1969.

Learning the Wiswesser Line Notation

Considerable effort has been expended in training chemists to encode and decode Wiswesser Line Notations. The National Science Foundation supported a study in 1961 to determine the ease of decoding the WLN (*149*). About 700 chemists (students, teachers, and practicing chemists) were provided with programmed learning sets of notation reading tests, with simple decoding rules. Over 90% accuracy in drawing chemical structures from the notations was achieved.

In 1966, the U.S. Army Chemical Information and Data Systems (CIDS) invited the Chemical Notation Association to present a state-of-the-art of the WLN at a two-day meeting at Edgewood Arsenal, Maryland (*101*).

At a National Meeting of the American Chemical Society held in San Francisco (April 1968), the Division of Chemical Literature and the Chemical Notation

Association jointly sponsored an open tutorial for chemists to learn the fundamentals of the WLN. Prof. Smith gave a full-day lecture (*125*). The success of this lecture (over 60 attendees) prompted the Chemical Notation Association to offer another tutorial on the East Coast, after the September 1969 American Chemical Society New York Meeting. This session was attended by over 80 chemists. A third public presentation had been planned for the September 1970 meeting in Chicago.

In 1968, Smith was invited by Imperial Chemicals Industries, Ltd., in the United Kingdom, to present a tutorial before the company staff. He was invited to the United Kingdom again, in 1969, to give a three-day tutorial before the Wellcome Foundation. Representatives from other British organizations also attended Smith's lectures: Fisons, Boots Pure Drug, Unilever, Beecham Research Laboratories, International Computers Ltd., and the Oxford Group of the British Government's Office of Scientific and Technical Information (OSTI).

Horner established a consulting and service organization to prepare Wiswesser Notations for organizations, to train their personnel in the use of the WLN, to prepare computer software, and to provide a systems design service. During 1969, Horner built the WLN files of in-house compounds for three industrial organizations.

Searching the WLN

The following methods for searching a Wiswesser Line Notation file of chemical structures have been individually developed.

> Fragmentation: Smith (*123*), Gelberg (*53*), Bowman (*14*), Rice (*114*), and Thomson (*138*).
> Classification codes: Bonnett (*8*), Barnard (*3,4*), and Bowman (*14*).
> Permutation: Sorter (*130*), Granito (*58,59*), Gelberg (*54*), Horner (*75*), Starke (*132*), and Bowman (*14*).
> Key-word-out-of-context: Rice (*114*).
> Word or string match: Ofer (*107*), and ISI (*63,79*).
> Connection table: Hyde (*77*), Thomson (*138*), and Bowman (*14*).

WLN File Maintenance and Editing Routines

The Dow Group developed a CHECKER program to convert WLN symbols to a molecular formula for comparison with a hand-calculated formula (*12*). Horner has expanded the capabilities of the CHECKER by adding a number of editing routines and checks which are required for establishing uniqueness in the WLN. This latter program is available for lease.

Complicated ring systems require extensive topographical analysis in order to establish uniqueness of the notation. A computer program, termed PATHFINDER, was prepared by the Dow Group to determine the correct ring notation from any trial input of ring-closing connections and to generate the unique notation (*13*).

Imperial Chemicals Industries, Ltd., assembled a package of programs called CROSSBOW (*C*hemical *R*etrieval of *O*rganic Structure*S* *B*ased *O*n *W*iswesser) (*117*). This package contains routines for a CHECKER, duplicate-matching, generation of a connection table, fragment generation, and a computer-printer graphic display. It is available for lease.

Duplicate checking and auto-registration was developed at the ILO (*60,101k*).

Machine-generation of modified Wiswesser Notations, by means of a cathode ray tube and manually drawing chemical structures on the tube face with a light-pen, has been announced by the Goodyear Group (*28*).

Wiswesser has explored the use of high-speed printers for preparing structural diagrams and notations with a program called DOT-PLOT (*101n*).

Tracing synthesis pathway through the chemical intermediaries (reactants and products) in a permuted WLN listing has been demonstrated by Gelberg (*54*).

Statistical analysis of WLN fragments from permuted indexes, generated by chemicals screened in a pesticide program for a structure-activity relationship, was discussed by Granito (*62*). Listings of the most active "groups" and the least active "groups" within a specific screen provided guidance for further synthesis and research sample acquisition. The "groups" are isolated strings of WLN symbols.

The Hayward Notation

In 1961, the inadequacies of the earlier cited notations prompted Hayward to develop a notational method for organizing the chemical structures on file with the U.S. Patent Office (*67*). The Patent Office problem is unique in that it is not only concerned with specific compounds (compositions of matter), but also has to provide access to chemical materials covered by a generic Markush type structural representation which encompasses many classes of chemicals (*129*). A collaborative study was undertaken with the National Bureau of Standards as part of the HAYSTAQ project (*69,99*), resulting in a search program based on symbol string matching. Graph theory and topological analysis indicated that Markush structures could be reduced to five distinct structural forms which, in turn, could be converted to the Hayward Notation for file checking (*137*). Path-tracing through the Hayward Notation by means of a program entitled TOPKAT has been described (*87*). The algorithms for the topographic analysis, coupled with TOPKAT, have been thoroughly developed. However, at the end of 1969, the actual computer programming was awaiting preparation (*71*).

The Skolnik Notation

Toward the end of 1969, another unique and unambiguous notation was announced (*122a*). The Skolnik Notation was designed to have a one-to-one correspondence with the chemical structures represented by the notations. The symbols used are compatible with computer input and output characters and denote carbon in terms of bonds and attached hydrogen(s). The primary objectives in the design were to retain accepted numbering schemes, to have the notations conform to accepted chemical structures, and to invoke relatively few rules.

Machine-Generated Notations

A registry system for chemical compounds, developed at Chemical Abstracts Service (*108,134,135,155*) converts a redundant connection table to a unique string of symbols (*22,23,94–96,102,109*). This notation is an unnested connection table which completely describes each atom, its degree of connectivity, the bond type with which each atom is associated, and other features of each atom, e.g., ionic charge, isotopic labeling, and free radical.

An application of the search capabilities of the connection tables and fragment file generated from the connection tables was presented by Vasta (*158*).

The Chemical Abstracts system is based on an early version of the DuPont Chemical Structure Storage and Search System developed by Gluck (*156*). Modifications and extended versions of this system have been described by Hoffman (*157*). The capabilities of the system were expanded to include coordination compounds, complexes, and polymers.

Utilizing the feature of uniqueness established by the Chemical Abstracts Service connection tables, Lefkovitz converted these, by machine, into the Mechanical Chemical Code (*93*). From this notational form an open-ended analytical fragment file was generated. The fragments are searched either from a keyword-out-of-context listing, or on-line via a remote terminal linked to an inverted file disk.

Hyde and Thomson have transformed, by machine, unique Wiswesser Notations into a machine notation to expand the concise WLN and to define the heuristics that are inherent in the WLN (*77,78,101i,117,138*). The connection tables then are generated from the machine-generated notation. The basis for this approach was established by Wiswesser's DOT-PLOT (*101n*).

Polish Notations

A Polish Notation is a mathematical manner for describing the nodes and circuitry of a graph. It describes chain structures very much like standardized line formulas. It is unambiguous, but lacks uniqueness because the chain can start at any point and trace the path back to the starting position. This principle has been applied to chemical structures.

Linearization of "tree-structures" has been described by Eisman (*47*); conversion of a two-dimensional graph to a linear form has been reported by Hiz (*73*); and utility of these strings as an internal machine symbolic language, for substructure searching, has been presented by Welch (*141*).

The Polish Notation contains exactly as many letters of a kind as there are atoms of a given element in the molecule. The chemical compound, *glycine*, is structurally represented as:

$$O$$
$$\|$$
$$H_2NCH_2COH$$

Graphically, this structure can be represented in the following forms:

The Polish Notations that can be prepared for this structure, or these graphs, are:

C	C	O	H	2O	N	H	H	H	H	(a)
C	C	O	H	2O	H	N	H	H	H	(b)
H	O	C	2O	C	H	H	N	H	H	(c)
H	C	H	C	O	H	2O	N	H	H	(d)
H	N	C	C	O	H	2O	H	H	H	(e)
O	2C	C	H	N	H	H	H	O	H	(f)

Each of these notations, a–f, are synonymous, and match the molecular formula for *glycine* ($C_2H_5NO_2$). In a condensed form, notation (a) can be written as: C(((C(O(H)2O)N(HH))HH), wherein the parentheses serve to separate the connecting units.

Skolnik applied this principle, i.e., rotating the functional group symbols, to index notations of pesticides (*122*).

Differences among the Unique and Unambiguous Notation Systems

By the end of 1969, no official studies had been undertaken to compare the relative merits of the various notation schemes. As evidenced by the publication records, the Wiswesser Notation had had the highest degree of exposure and use. The Hayward Notation was insufficiently developed to assemble a group of users. The IUPAC-Dyson Cipher did not lend itself to simple punched card application, and appeared to be limited to computers or modified punched card equipment because of the use of subscripts, lower-case letters, underlinings, brackets, the colon, and the semicolon. The Skolnik Notation is relatively too new to be evaluated. Like the Wiswesser Notation, it has limited its symbol set to those characters that are available on the typewriter and keypunch.

Examples of these notations are:

Androsta-1,4-diene-3-one

Hayward: 6L:LLVL:YLLYY5L3YMLLYYM
IUPAC: A6₃513b7C38EQ13
Wiswesser: L E5 B666 O̅V AHTTT&J A E
Skolnik: B2KBRT☐C2J2☐C2TJ☐C3.A2

Pyridine, hydrochloride

Hayward: [6nH:LL:LLL];[K]
IUPAC: [B6ZN⁺][Ch⁻]
Wiswesser: T6NJ &GH
Skolnik: B5Z*.LH

Benzenesulfonic acid, p-(4-tolyloxy)

Hayward: 6R(O@6RRR(SWQ)RR)RRRMRR
IUPAC: B6C:4Q/4B6SO₂Q
Wiswesser: WSQR DOR D
Skolnik: B2DB2D.SQ3H.Q(DB2DB2.A)

The Hayward Notation describes each atom in the molecule, and in a sense is a unique form of a Polish Notation. It resembles a topological code more than a pictorial description of the chemical.

The IUPAC Cipher is essentially based on IUPAC nomenclature rules in that the longest chain is cited and substituents are attached accordingly. Ring systems are given hierarchial preference.

The Wiswesser Notation places indexing emphasis on functional group symbols and ring systems.

The Skolnik Notation follows the *Ring Index* numbering pattern, and depicts each atom in the molecule. Bond types are implied from the symbol set. This notation is undergoing minor revision, and will undergo a number of changes in the early 1970s.

To some extent, there is a common agreement on the use of certain symbols by Dyson, Hayward, Wiswesser, Lefkovitz, and Skolnik. The "Q" is used by all to represent an oxygen atom, but Hayward, Wiswesser, and Lefkovitz restrict it to the Hydroxyl group, an oxygen with a hydrogen atom attached. The trisubstituted nitrogen atom is an "n" in the Hayward system, but an "N" is used by IUPAC, Wiswesser, and Skolnik. The latter differentiates between a trisubstituted >N— and a =N—, the latter being a "Z" symbol. The relative merits of the symbols used by each notational system are subjective.

Insofar as meeting the requirements of the IUPAC Commission's desiderata, none of the notations fully meet them:

1. *Simplicity of use.* Each notation requires an extensive training period to learn encoding.

2. *Ease of printing and typewriting.* The Wiswesser and Skolnik notations are the easiest. The IUPAC Cipher requires shifting to upper and lower case, moving the platen for sub- and superscripts, and hand drawing brackets. The Hayward Notation requires hand drawn brackets and shifting to upper and lower case.

3. *Conciseness.* The Hayward Notation cites every atom in the molecule, and therefore is the longest. The Skolnik Notation cites every different atom and condenses those that are identical. The Wiswesser and IUPAC condense ring sizes and chain lengths.

4. *Recognizability.* The Hayward Notation is more of a topographical map, and to a lesser extent, so is the Skolnik Notation. However, the notations are acceptable to the respective users of each system.

5. *Ability to generate a unique chemical nomenclature.* The Hayward, IUPAC, Wiswesser, and Skolnik Notations each meet this requirement.

6. *Compatibility with the accepted practices of inorganic nomenclature.* The Hayward and Wiswesser Notations are further developed than IUPAC. In late 1969, the Skolnik Notation apparently had not addressed itself to this item.

7. *Uniqueness.* All four notation systems produce unique notations.

8. *Generation of an unambiguous and unique enumeration pattern.* Each of the four notations intrinsically meets this requirement.

9. *Ease of manipulation by machine methods, for example, by punched cards.* The Wiswesser Notation has distinct advantages for simple punched card apparatus, particularly the sorter, because no more than 2-hole (Hollerith/IBM punch pattern) symbols are used. The Hayward, IUPAC, and Skolnik systems require computer tape sorting and file organization. The IUPAC Cipher has a distinct disadvantage in printing with standard equipment.

10. *Exhibition of associations (descriptiveness).* Each of the four notation systems meets this requirement.

11. *Ability to deal with partial indeterminants.* Each of the notations can handle partial indeterminants. The Hayward system is particularly strong in this area because of its ability to reduce Markush generic structures by algorithm to Hayward Notations. Tentative rules for the Wiswesser Notation have been established, but have not been thoroughly resolved.

REFERENCES

1. Anon., "FDA, Medicine Library to Test Wiswesser Line Notation," *Chem. Eng. News,* 46, 21–22 (1968).

2. Anon., "Mills College Offers Course in Wiswesser Notation," *Vortex,* 448 (November 1968).

3. A. J. Barnard, Jr., C. T. Kleppinger, and W. J. Wiswesser, "Retrieval of Organic Structures from Small-to-Medium Sized Collections," *J. Chem. Doc.,* 6, 41–48 (1966).

4. A. J. Barnard, Jr., and W. J. Wiswesser, "Computer-Serviced Management of Chemical Structure Information," *Lab Management,* 5(10), 34–44 (October 1967).

5. F. R. Benson, "Recording and Recovering Chemical Information with Standard Tabulating Equipment," Paper presented at the 124th National Meeting, American Chemical Society, Chicago, Illinois, September 1953.

6. M. M. Berry and J. W. Perry, "A review of notational systems for designating organic structural formulas," Submitted to the IUPAC Commission on Codification, Ciphering, and Punched Card Techniques, Massachusetts Institute of Technology, Cambridge, Massachusetts, 1951, 431 pages.

7. M. M. Berry and J. W. Perry, "Notational Systems for Structural Formulas," *Chem. Eng. News,* 30, 407–410 (1952).

8. H. T. Bonnett and D. W. Calhoun, "Applications of a Line-Formula Notation in an Index of Chemical Structures," *J. Chem. Doc.,* 2, 2 (1962).

9. H. T. Bonnett, "Chemical Notations—A Brief Review," *J. Chem. Doc.,* 3, 235 (1963).

10. H. T. Bonnett, "The Current Status of Mechanical Manipulation of Chemical Structural Information," Paper presented at the 151st National Meeting, American Chemical Society, Chicago, Illinois, September 1964.

11. H. Bouman, "Computer Program for the LINCO System," *J. Chem. Doc.,* 5(1), 14–24 (1965).

12. C. M. Bowman, F. A. Landee, and M. H. Reslock, "A Chemically Oriented Information Storage and Retrieval System (I): Storage and Verification of Structural Information," *J. Chem. Doc.,* 7, 43–47 (1967).

13. C. M. Bowman, F. A. Landee, N. W. Lee, and M. H. Reslock, "A Chemically Oriented Information Storage and Retrieval System (II): Computer Generation of the Wiswesser Notations of Complex Polycyclic Structures," *J. Chem. Doc.,* 8(3), 133–138 (1968).

14. C. M. Bowman, F. A. Landee, N. W. Lee, M. H. Reslock, and B. P. Smith, "A Chemically Oriented Information Storage and Retrieval System (III): Searching a Wiswesser Line Notation File," Paper presented at the 157th National Meeting, American Chemical Society, Minneapolis, Minnesota, April 1969.

15. W. C. Brasie and D. W. Liou, "Structure Notation for Computer Calculation of Critical Constants," *Chem. Eng. Progr.,* 61(5), 102–108 (1965).

16. E. L. Buhle, E. D. Hartnell, A. M. Moore, L. R. Wiselogle, and F. Y. Wiselogle, "A New System for the Classification of Compounds," *J. Chem. Educ.,* 23, 375–391 (1946).

17. Chemical Abstracts Service, "Wiswesser Line Notations Corresponding to Ring Index Structures," a report to the National Science Foundation under Contract NSF-C521, American Chemical Society (1968); available from the U.S. Department of Commerce Clearinghouse for Federal Scientific and Technical Information (PB 180 901).

18. J. G. Cockburn, "The Newcastle System of Representation of the Formulae of Organic Compounds," Private communication to the IUPAC Commission on Codification, Ciphering, and Punched Card Techniques, 1951.

19. *Comptes rendus de la 14me Conference,* International Union of Pure and Applied Chemistry, 64 (1947).

20. *Comptes rendus de la 15me Conference,* International Union of Pure and Applied Chemistry, 64 (1949).

21. *Comptes rendus de la 16me Conference,* International Union of Pure and Applied Chemistry, 104 (1951).

22. W. E. Cossum, M. L. Krakiwsky, and M. F. Lynch, "Advances in Automatic Chemical Substructure Searching Techniques," *J. Chem. Doc.,* 5(1), 33–35 (1965).

23. W. E. Cossum, M. E. Hardenbrook, and R. N. Wolff, "Computer Generation of Atom-Bond Connection Tables from Hand-Drawn Chemical Structures," *Proc. 27th Ann. Mtg., ADI,* 1, 269–275 (1964).

24. E. M. Crane and M. M. Berry, *Chem. Eng. News,* 33, 2842 (1955).

25. H. F. Dammers, "Computer Handling of Literature Information and Research Data in an Industrial Research Establishment," Paper presented at the 36th International Congress on Industrial Chemistry, Brussels, 1966.

26. H. F. Dammers, "Computer-Based Chemical Information System," *New Sci.,* 31, 325–327 (1966).

27. H. F. Dammers and D. J. Polton, "Use of the IUPAC Notation in Computer Processing of Information on Chemical Structures," *J. Chem. Doc.,* 8(3), 150–160 (1968).

28. J. E. Davis and L. E. Straka, "Automated Coding Via a Cathode Ray Tube," Paper presented at the 158th National Meeting, American Chemical Society, New York, September 1969.

29. W. H. T. Davison and M. Gordon, "Sorting Chemical Groups Using Gordon-Kendall-Davison Ciphers," *Am. Doc.,* 8, 202–210 (1957).

30. W. H. T. Davison, "Programs and Equipment for Sorting Gordon-Kendall-Davison

Punched Cards for any Structurally Defined Group," Paper presented at the 120th National Meeting, American Chemical Society, New York, September 1951.

31. G. M. Dyson, "A Notation for Organic Compounds," *Nature*, **154**, 7 (1944).

32. G. M. Dyson, "A New Notation for Organic Chemistry," Royal Institute of Chemistry Lecture, published jointly with the Chemical Society and the Society of Chemical Industry, London, 1946.

33. G. M. Dyson, *A New Notation and Enumeration System for Organic Compounds,* Longmans, London, 1947; 2nd ed., 1949, 138 pp.

34. G. M. Dyson, "Some Applications of Mechanical Methods to Library Problems in Organic Chemistry," *Aslib. Rep. Proc. 22nd Conf.,* 23–36 (1947).

35. G. M. Dyson, "A New Notation for Organic Chemistry," *Research* (London), **2**, 104–114 (1949).

36. G. M. Dyson, "Codification of Organic Structures," *Research* (London), **2**, 576 (1949).

37. G. M. Dyson, *Bul. Soc. Chim. France,* **19**, 29 (1952).

38. G. M. Dyson and E. F. Riley, "Mechanical Storage and Retrieval of Organic Chemical Data. Identification of Structural Features," *Chem. Eng. News,* **39**, 74–80 (November 20, 1961).

39. G. M. Dyson et al., *The Detection and Orientation of Substructures in Organic Compounds,* 1st Report on NSF-programs 10339 and 16849, February 1962, 179 pp.

40. G. M. Dyson, "Chemical Ciphers or Notations: Their Nature and Use," *ICSU Rev.,* **4**, 73 (1962).

41. G. M. Dyson et al., "Mechanical Manipulation of Chemical Structure: Molform Computation and Substructure Searching of Organic Structures by Use of the Cipher-Directed, Extended, and Random Matrices," *Inform. Stor. Retr.,* **1**, 66–69 (1963).

42. G. M. Dyson, "A Cluster of Algorithms Relating the Nomenclature of Organic Compounds to their Structure Matrices and Ciphers," *Inform. Stor. Retr.,* **2**, 159–199 (1964).

43. G. M. Dyson, "Generic (or Markush) Groups in Notation and Search Programs, with Particular Reference to Patents," *Inform. Stor. Retr.,* **2**(2), 59–71 (1964).

44. G. M. Dyson, "Computer Input and the Semantic Organization of Scientific Terms (I)," *Inform. Stor. Retr.,* **3**, 35–115 (1967).

45. G. M. Dyson, M. F. Lynch, and H. L. Morgan, *Inform. Stor. Retr.,* **4**, 27 (1968).

46. G. M. Dyson, "Modifications and Abbreviations Recommended for Computer and Visual Handling of the IUPAC Notation," Paper presented at the 155th National Meeting, American Chemical Society, San Francisco, California, April 1968.

47. S. H. Eisman, "A Polish-Type Notation for Chemical Structures," *J. Chem. Doc.,* **4**, 186–190 (1964).

48. G. F. Fraction, J. C. Walker, and S. J. Tauber, "Connection Tables from Wiswesser Structure Notations—A Partial Algorithm," *NBS Tech. Note* 432, National Bureau of Standards, Washington, D.C., 1968.

49. D. E. H. Frear, "Punch Cards in Correlation Studies," *Chem. Eng. News,* **23**, 2077 (1945).

50. D. E. H. Frear, E. J. Seiferle, and H. L. King, "A New Classification System for Chemical Compounds," *Science,* **104**, 177–178 (1946).

51. D. E. H. Frear and E. J. Seiferle, "Chemical Structure and Insecticidal Efficiency," *J. Econ. Entomol.,* **40**, 736–741 (1947).

52. D. E. H. Frear, "A Catalog of Insecticides and Fungicides," Vols. I and II, Chronica Botanica, Waltham, Massachusetts, 1947.

53. A. Gelberg, W. Nelson, G. S. Yee, and E. A. Metcalf, "A Program for Retrieval of Organic Structure Information," *J. Chem. Doc.,* **2**, 7 (1962).

54. A. Gelberg, "Rapid Structure Searches via Permuted Chemical Line-Notations, IV: A Reactant Index," *J. Chem. Doc.,* **6**, 60 (1966).

55. A. Gelberg, "Information Centers in Management and Planning," *Trans. 11th Ann. Mtg., Am. Assoc. Cost Eng.,* Cleveland, Ohio, 1967.

56. G. W. Gibson, C. E. Granito, D. E. Renard, and E. A. Metcalf, "The Wiswesser Line-

Notation: An Introduction," *Tech. Memo.* 7-3, CRDL, Edgewood Arsenal, Maryland, 1965. 29 pp. Available from the U.S. Department of Commerce Clearinghouse for Federal Scientific and Technical Information (AD 624 525).

57. M. Gordon, C. E. Kendall, and W. H. T. Davison, "A New Systematisation of Chemical Species," *Proc. 11th Int. Cong. Pure Appl. Chem.* (London), **2**(3), 115–132 (July 1947); Royal Inst. of Chem. Monograph, Reprint (1948).

58. C. E. Granito, A. Gelberg, J. E. Schultz, G. W. Gibson, and E. A. Metcalf, "Rapid Structure Searches via Permuted Chemical Line-Notations, II: A Key-Punch Procedure for the Generation of an Index for a Small File," *J. Chem. Doc.*, **5**, 52–55 (1965).

59. C. E. Granito, J. E. Schultz, G. W. Gibson, A. Gelberg, R. J. Williams, and E. A. Metcalf, "Rapid Structure Searches via Permuted Chemical Line-Notations, III: A Computer-Produced Index," *J. Chem. Doc.*, **5**, 229–233 (1965).

60. C. E. Granito, D. E. Renard, and L. A. Holly, "Use of the Wiswesser Line-Notation for Determining Duplicate Chemical Structures," *J. Chem. Doc.*, **6**, 252–253 (1966).

61. C. E. Granito and A. Gelberg, "Symposium on Notation Systems, Introductory Remarks," *J. Chem. Doc.*, **8**, 127 (1968).

62. C. E. Granito, "A Method of Analyzing Structural Fragments Using the Wiswesser Chemical Line-Notation," Paper presented at the 155th National Meeting, American Chemical Society, San Francisco, California, April 1968.

63. C. E. Granito and W. J. Wiswesser, Paper presented at the 5th Middle Atlantic Regional Meeting, American Chemical Society, Newark, Delaware, April 1970.

64. W. Gruber, "The Geneva Nomenclature in Code and its Extension to Ring Compounds," *Angew. Chem.* **61**, 429–431 (1949).

65. W. Gruber, "Die Genfer Nomenklatur in Chiffren," *Beihefte Angew. Chem. und Chem.- Ingenier-Technik, Nr.* **58**, 1950, 72 pp.

66. J. B. Haglind, H. J. Ackermann, R. E. Maizell, T. N. Manning, and B. S. Schlessinger, "Storage and Retrieval of Agricultural Screening Data," Paper presented at the 156th National Meeting, American Chemical Society, Atlantic City, New Jersey, September 1968.

67. H. W. Hayward, "A New Sequential Enumeration and Line Formula Notation System for Organic Compounds," *U.S. Patent Office R&D Rept., No.* **21**, Washington, D.C., 1961.

68. H. W. Hayward, "A Second Look at Chemical Notation Systems in View of Projected Machine Interconversion of Cipher Forms," *Automation and Scientific Communication,* 26th Annual Meeting, American Documentation Institute, Chicago, Illinois, 1963, pp. 59–60.

69. H. W. Hayward, H. M. S. Sneed, J. H. Turnipsneed, and S. J. Tauber, "Some Experience with the Hayward Line Notation System," *J. Chem. Doc.*, **5**, 183–189 (1965).

70. H. W. Hayward, "Molecular Structure, Connected Sets, Topological Linguistics, and Chemical Notation," Paper presented at the 155th National Meeting, American Chemical Society, San Francisco, California, April 1968.

71. H. W. Hayward, Lecture presented at American University, Washington, D.C., Workshop in Chemical Information Systems, November 1969.

72. I. Heilbron and H. M. Bunbury, *Dictionary of Organic Compounds,* 2nd ed., Eyre and Spottiswoede, London, 1943.

73. H. Hiz, "A Linearization of Chemical Graphs," *J. Chem. Doc.*, **4**, 173 (1964).

74. E. Hoffmann, "Use of a Modified Wiswesser Notation for Encoding of Proteins," *J. Chem. Doc.*, **9**, 137 (1969).

75. J. K. Horner, "Low-Cost Storage and Retrieval of Organic Structures by Permuted Line Notations: Small Collections," *J. Chem. Doc.*, **7**(2), 85–88 (1967).

76. E. H. Huntress, "Influence of Nomenclatural Evolution upon Comprehensive Literature Searches," in *Searching the Chemical Literature* (Adv. in Chem. Series, No. 4), American Chemical Society, Washington, D.C., 1951, pp. 10–18.

77. E. Hyde, F. W. Matthews, L. H. Thomson, and W. J. Wiswesser, "Conversion of

Wiswesser Notation to a Connectivity Matrix for Organic Compounds," *J. Chem. Doc.,* **7**, 200–204 (1967).

78. E. Hyde and L. H. Thomson, "Structure Display," *J. Chem. Doc.,* **8**(3), 146 (1968).

79. Institute for Scientific Information, *The Index Chemistry Registry System,* Philadelphia, Pennsylvania, 1968, 16 pp.

80. International Union of Pure and Applied Chemistry, *A Proposed International Chemical Notation. Tentative Version,* Issued by the Commission on Codification, Ciphering, and Punched Card Techniques of the IUPAC, Longmans, Green, London, 1958.

81. International Union of Pure and Applied Chemistry, *Rules for I.U.P.A.C. Notation for Organic Compounds,* Issued by the Commission on Codification, Ciphering, and Punched Card Techniques, Wiley, New York, 1961, 96 pp.

82. S. W. Johnson, *Chemical Notation and Nomenclature,* New York, 1871.

83. S. Kulpinski et al., *A Study and Implementation of Mechanical Translation from Wiswesser Line Notation to Connection Table,* Vols. I and II, University of Pennsylvania Annual Report, Contract NSF-C467, (PB 177 292), Philadelphia, Pennsylvania, 1967, 74 pp.

84. F. A. Landee, "Computer Programs for Handling Chemical Structures Expressed in the Wiswesser Notation," Paper presented at the 147th National Meeting, American Chemical Society, Philadelphia, Pennsylvania, April 1964.

85. J. Lederberg, *DENDRAL-64, A System for Computer Construction, Enumeration and Notation of Organic Molecules as Tree Structures and Cyclic Graphs. Part I: Notational Algorithms for Tree Structures,* Interim report to NASA (CR-5729), 1964.

86. J. Lederberg, "Topological Mapping of Organic Molecules," *Proc. Nat. Acad. Sci., U.S.,* **53**(1), 134–139 (1965).

87. R. W. H. Lee et al., *TOPKAT (Topological Kind of Attack); a Computer Based Substructure Search on Generic Structures,* National Bureau of Standards Report, Contract NSF-AG-69, Washington, D.C., 1968, 39 pp.

88. D. Lefkovitz and C. T. VanMeter, "An Experimental Real Time Chemical Information System," *J. Chem. Doc.,* **6**(3), 173–183 (1966).

89. D. Lefkovitz, "The Impact of Third Generation ADP Equipment on Alternative Chemical Structure Information Systems," Paper presented at the 153rd National Meeting, American Chemical Society, Miami Beach, Florida, 1967.

90. D. Lefkovitz, "Use of a Nonunique Notation in a Large-Scale Chemical Information System," *J. Chem. Doc.,* **7**, 192 (1967).

91. D. Lefkovitz, "A Chemical Notation and Code for Computer Manipulation," *J. Chem. Doc.,* **7**, 186 (1967).

92. D. Lefkovitz and R. V. Powers, "A List-Structured Chemical Information Retrieval System," in *Information Retrieval: A Critical Review,* Thompson, Washington, D.C., 1967.

93. D. Lefkovitz, "Substructure Search in the MCC System," *J. Chem. Doc.,* **8**(3), 166–173 (1968).

94. D. P. Leiter, H. L. Morgan, and R. E. Stobaugh, "Installation and Operation of a Registry for Chemical Compounds," *J. Chem. Doc.,* **5**(4), 238–242 (1965).

95. D. P. Leiter and H. L. Morgan, "Quality Control and Auditing Procedure in the Chemical Abstracts Service Compound Registry," *J. Chem. Doc.,* **6**(4), 226–229 (1966).

96. D. P. Leiter and L. H. Leighner, "A Statistical Analysis of the Structure Registry at Chemical Abstracts Service," Paper presented at the 154th National Meeting, American Chemical Society, Chicago, Illinois, 1967.

97. H. P. Luhn, *Am. Doc.,* **11**, 288 (1960).

98. M. F. Lynch, "Conversion of Connection Table Descriptions of Chemical Compounds in to a Form of Wiswesser Notation," *J. Chem. Doc.,* **8**, 130–133 (1968).

99. B. A. Marron, G. R. Bolotsky, and S. J. Tauber, "Chemical Substructure Searching with Linear Notations," *J. Chem. Doc.,* **6**(2), 92–95 (1966).

100. P. M. McDonnell and R. F. Pasternack, "A Line-Formula Notation System for Co-ordination Compounds," *J. Chem. Doc.,* **5**(1), 56–60, (1965).

101. J. P. Mitchell, ed., *Proceedings of the Wiswesser Line Notation Meeting of the Army CIDS Program,* EASP 400–408, Edgewood Arsenal, Maryland, 1968; available from the U.S. Department of Commerce Clearinghouse for Federal Scientific and Technical Information (AD 665 397). It includes the following: (*a*) A. J. Barnard, Jr., W. C. Broad, C. T. Kleppinger, and W. J. Wiswesser, "Some Techniques for the Machine Management of Small Chemical Data Systems," pp. 85–101. (*b*) H. T. Bonnett, "Use of the Wiswesser Line Notation at the Searle Laboratories: Motivation and Status," pp. 15–23. (*c*) C. M. Bowman, F. A. Landee, B. P. Smith, and M. H. Reslock, "Automatic Generation of Structural Fragment Codes from the Wiswesser Line Notation for Rapid Structure Searches," pp. 49–56. (*d*) G. F. Fraction, J. C. Walker, and S. J. Tauber, "Connection Table from Wiswesser Line Notation: a Partial Algorithm," pp. 139–195. (*e*) A. Gelberg, "Quick Scan and Symbols," pp. 43–48. (*f*) A. Gelberg, "Permutations and Classification Numbers," pp. 80–84. (*g*) C. E. Granito, "Use of the Wiswesser Line Notation for Registering Compounds," pp. 35–37. (*h*) J. K. Horner, "Low-Cost Storage and Retrieval of Organic Structures by Permuted Line Notations: Small Collections," pp. 25–33. (*i*) E. Hyde, "Computer Generated Open Ended Fragment Code," pp. 57–67. (*j*) J. Munz, "The Formal Analysis of Notation Systems," pp. 197–202. (*k*) D. E. Renard, "Updating Program for the Industry Liaison Office," pp. 117–119. (*l*) P. F. Sorter, "File Maintenance and Updating Procedure," pp. 39–42. (*m*) C. T. Van Meter, "Utilization of the Wiswesser Notation in CIDS," pp. 121–137. (*n*) W. J. Wiswesser, "The Dot-Plot Computer Program," pp. 103–116.

102. H. L. Morgan, "The Generation of a Unique Machine Description for Chemical Structures—A Technique Developed at Chemical Abstracts Service," *J. Chem. Doc.* 5, 107–113 (1965).

103. J. Munz, The Formal Evaluation of a Simple Chemical Cipher System," Univ. of Pa., Analysis of Chemical Notations Project, paper No. 3, 1968, 42 pp.

104. National Academy of Sciences–National Research Council, *Survey of Chemical Notation Systems,* Publ. 1150, Washington, D.C., 1964, 467 pp.

105. National Academy of Sciences–National Research Council, *Survey of European Non-Conventional Chemical Notation Systems,* Publ. 1278, Washington, D.C., 1965, 78 pp.

106. National Academy of Sciences–National Research Council, *Chemical Structure Information Handling. A Review of the Literature, 1962–1968,* Prepared by the Committee on Chemical Information, Publ. 1733, Washington, D.C. 1969, 133 pp.

107. K. D. Ofer, "A Computer Program to Index or Search Linear Notations," *J. Chem. Doc.,* 8(3), 128–129 (1968).

108. P. D. Olejar, "The Interagency Chemical Information Program," Paper presented at the Meeting of the Office of Science and Technology (OST), Washington, D.C., March 24, 1966.

109. M. K. Park, R. E. Stobaugh, and R. J. Zalac, "The Use of a Computer-Generated Notation for Handling Compounds in a Mechanized System," Paper presented at the 155th National Meeting, American Chemical Society, San Francisco, California, April 1968.

110. A. M. Patterson, L. T. Capell, and D. F. Walker, *The Ring Index,* 2nd ed., American Chemical Society, 1960; *Supplement I,* 1963; *Supplement II,* 1964; *Supplement III,* 1965, Chemical Abstracts Service, American Chemical Society, Washington, D.C.

111. D. J. Polton, "The IUPAC Cipher: Optimising Its Internal Representation for Computer Processing," *Inform. Stor. Retr.,* 5, 7–25 (1969).

112. A. D. Pratt and J. W. Perry, *Chemical Notation Study: Dyson-Wiswesser Notation Systems Encoding Operations; Phase Report,* rev., Center for Documentation and Communication Research, Western Reserve Univ., Cleveland, Ohio, August 1960, ASTIA Doc. No. AD 245 936.

113. G. S. Revesz and A. Warner, "Index Chemicus, an Important Tool for Chemical Information Processing and Retrieval," Paper presented at the 156th National Meeting, American Chemical Society, Atlantic City, New Jersey, September 1968.

114. C. N. Rice, K. D. Ofer, and R. B. Bourne, "A Pilot-Study for the Input to a Chemical-Structure Retrieval System," Paper presented at the 151st National Meeting, American Chemical Society, Chicago, Illinois, September 1966.

115. C. N. Rice, "Toward a National Systems Resource in Toxicology," *J. Chem. Doc.,* 9, 181–183 (1969).

116. A. R. Richards, "A System of Notation for Petroleum Hydrocarbons," *Nature,* 153, 7 (1944).

117. M. A. T. Rogers, "CROSSBOW," Paper presented at the 158th National Meeting, American Chemical Society, New York, September 1969.

118. J. A. Silk, "A New System of Organic Notation," Unpublished, Privately distributed monograph, 1950.

119. J. A. Silk, "An Improved System for the Enumeration and Description of Ring Systems," *J. Chem. Doc.,* 1, 58–62 (1961).

120. J. A. Silk, "A Linear Notation for Organic Compounds," *J. Chem. Doc.,* 3, 189–195 (1963).

121. J. A. Silk, "A Notation-Based Fragment Code for Chemical Patents," *J. Chem. Doc.,* 8(3), 161–165 (1968).

122. H. Skolnik and A. Clow, "A Notation System for Indexing Pesticides," *J. Chem. Doc.,* 4, 222–227 (1964). (*a*) H. Skolnik, "A New Linear Notation System Based on Combinations of Carbon and Hydrogen," *J. Heterocycl. Chem.,* 6, 689 (1969).

123. E. G. Smith, "Machine Searching for Chemical Structures," *Science,* 131, 142–146 (1960).

124. E. G. Smith, *The Wiswesser Line-Formula Chemical Notation,* McGraw-Hill, New York, 1968, 309 pp.

125. E. G. Smith, "Wiswesser Notation Tutorial," Paper presented at the 155th National Meeting, American Chemical Society, San Francisco, California, April 1968.

126. E. G. Smith, "Wiswesser Notation Tutorial, Revised," Presented at the Chemical Notation Association Tutorial Session, New York, September 1968.

127. E. G. Smith, "The Wiswesser Notation: State of the Art in 1969," A report to the Chemical Notation Association, September 1969.

128. J. F. Smith, "Indexes, Happy and Unhappy Hunting Grounds," in *Searching the Chemical Literature* (Adv. in Chem. Series, No. 4), American Chemical Society, Washington, D.C., 1951, pp. 19–23.

129. H. M. S. Sneed, J. H. Turnipsneed, and R. A. Turpin, "A Line-Formula Notation System for Markush Structures," *J. Chem. Doc.,* 8(3), 173–178 (1968).

130. P. F. Sorter, C. E. Granito, J. C. Gilmer, A. Gelberg, and E. A. Metcalf, "Rapid Structure Searches via Permuted Chemical Line-Notations," *J. Chem. Doc.,* 4, 56–60 (1964).

132. A. C. Starke, F. R. Whaley, E. C. Carson, and W. B. Thompson, "The GAF Document Storage and Retrieval System," *Am. Doc.,* 19, 173–180 (1968).

133. G. Sutherland, *Dendral—A Computer Program for Generating and Filtering Chemical Structures,* Stanford Univ., Artificial Intelligence Project, Memo 49, Stanford, Calif., 1967, 24 pp.

134. F. A. Tate, H. L. Morgan, D. P. Leiter, and R. E. Stobaugh, "A Mechanized Registry of Chemical Compounds," Paper presented at the Congress of the International Federation for Documentation, Washington, D.C., 1965.

135. F. A. Tate, "Progress Toward a Computer-Based Chemical Information System," *Chem. Eng. News,* 45(4), 78–90 (1967).

136. S. J. Tauber, G. R. Bolotsky, G. F. Fraction, C. L. Kirby, and G. R. Reed, "Algorithms for Utilizing Hayward Chemical Structure Notations," ICEREPAT, 351–378 (1965), Chapter 27.

137. S. J. Tauber, G. F. Fraction, and H. W. Hayward, "Chemical Structures as Information Representations, Transformations, and Calculations," in *Colloquium on Technical Preconditions for Retrieval Center Operations* (B. F. Cheydleur, ed.), Spartan Books, Washington, D.C., 1965.

138. L. H. Thomson, E. Hyde, and F. W. Matthews, "Organic Search and Display Using a Connectivity Matrix Derived from Wiswesser Notation," *J. Chem. Doc.*, 7, 204–209 (1967).

139. P. E. Verkade, "The IUPAC Ciphering System for Organic Compounds," *Chem. Weekbl.*, 58, 137–143 (1962).

140. G. A. Weaver, *A Mathematical Model for Chemical Cipher Systems,* Univ. of Pennsylvania, Analysis of Chemical Notations Project, paper No. 2, 1968, 31 pp.

141. J. T. Welch, "Substructure Searching of Chemical Compounds Using Polish-Type Notation," *J. Chem. Doc.*, 5(4), 225–229 (1965).

142. W. J. Wiswesser, *Simplified Chemical Coding for Automatic Sorting and Printing Machinery,* Willson Products, Inc., Reading, Pennsylvania, 1951.

143. W. J. Wiswesser, "The Wiswesser Line Formula Notation," *Chem. Eng. News,* 30, 3523–3526 (1952).

144. W. J. Wiswesser, "A Systematic Line-Formula Chemical Notation," *Aslib Proc.,* 5, 137–147 (1953).

145. W. J. Wiswesser, *A Line-Formula Chemical Notation,* Crowell, New York, 1954, 149 pp.

146. W. J. Wiswesser, "Literature Sources of Mammalian Toxicity Data with Special Emphasis on Tabulating Machine Applications," in *Advances in Chemistry Series,* No. 16, American Chemical Society, Washington, D.C., 1956, pp. 64–82.

147. W. J. Wiswesser, "A New Tool for Teaching Structural Chemistry," Paper presented at the 139th National Meeting, American Chemical Society, St. Louis, Missouri, March 1961.

148. W. J. Wiswesser, E. G. Smith, and H. T. Bonnett, *A Line-Formula Chemical Notation,* Mimeographed revision, March 1962.

149. W. J. Wiswesser, *A Decoding Study of the Line-Formula Chemical Notation,* NSF Final Report, 1965. Available from the U.S. Department of Commerce Clearinghouse for Federal Scientific and Technical Information (PB 169 364).

150. W. J. Wiswesser, "107 Years of Line-Formula Notations (1861–1968)," *J. Chem. Doc.,* 8, 146–150 (1968).

151. W. J. Wiswesser and A. J. Barnard, Jr., "The Retrieval of Chemical Structure Information," *Brit. Soc. Rheol. Bull., No.* 2, (1968), 15 pp.

152. W. J. Wiswesser, "Computer Applications of the 'WLN' (Wiswesser Line-Notation), Tech. Manuscript 490, Ft. Detrick, Frederick, Maryland, January 1969, 29 pp.

153. G. K. Zipf, *Human Behavior and the Principle of Least Effort,* Hafner, New York, 1949, 573 pp.

154. A. W. Elias, G. S. Revesz, and G. H. Foeman, "Effects of Mechanization on a Chemical Information Service," *J. Chem. Doc.,* 8, 74 (1968).

155. M. L. Krakiwsky, R. W. White, and W. C. Davenport, "Searching for Subsets in Machine Records of Chemical Structures at the Chemical Abstracts Service," Paper presented at the Congress of the International Federation for Documentation, Washington, D.C., 1965.

156. D. J. Gluck, "A Chemical Structure Storage and Search System Developed at DuPont," *J. Chem. Doc.,* 5, 43 (1965).

157. W. S. Hoffman, "An Integrated Chemical Structure Storage and Search System Operating at DuPont," *J. Chem. Doc.,* 8, 3 (1968).

158. B. M. Vasta, M. L. Spann, and G. T. Guthrie, "Experience with the CAS Substructure Search System," Paper presented at the 4th Middle Atlantic Regional Meeting, American Chemical Society, Washington, D.C., April 1969.

159. W. J. Wiswesser, "Computer-generated Correlations Among the Organo-phosphorous Pesticides," Paper presented at the 153rd National Meeting, American Chemical Society, Miami Beach, Florida, 1967.

ALAN GELBERG

CHEMICAL SOCIETY RESEARCH UNIT IN INFORMATION DISSEMINATION AND RETRIEVAL

In August 1966, The Chemical Society of London established a Research Unit in Information Dissemination and Retrieval at the University of Nottingham, England under the direction of Dr. A. K. Kent.

For some years prior to the establishment of this Unit, the Chemical Society had become increasingly aware of the need for a United Kingdom involvement in the rapidly developing field of computer-based chemical information systems. The close association between the Chemical Society and the American Chemical Society suggested the possibility of a program of evaluation, in the United Kingdom, of the computer-based information services of Chemical Abstracts Service which is a division of the American Chemical Society and pre-eminent in the field of chemical information dissemination. The objectives of the Research Unit in Information Dissemination and Retrieval were to assess the possibility of introducing computer-based chemical information services into the United Kingdom and to develop a body of expert knowledge capable of exploiting the anticipated future developments in this area, both at Chemical Abstracts Service and elsewhere. Financial support for the establishment and development of the Research Unit came both from the Chemical Society and the Office for Scientific and Technical Information of the Department of Education and Science and indirectly, by provision of data base tapes and technical assistance of various kinds, from Chemical Abstracts Service.

The first steps in achieving the Unit's objectives involved the preparation of search programs for use on an English Electric KDF9 computer and the introduction in January 1963 of an experimental current-awareness SDI service based on *Chemical Titles* and *Chemical-Biological Activities* to a population of some 250 industrial, academic, and government-employed research chemists. This experiment highlighted the major problems of providing such services on a routine basis.

Further experiments on other Chemical Abstracts Service data bases involved different populations of users and concentrated on improving some of the most evident deficiencies of the first experiment. In particular, attention was concentrated on improving search software so as to give more economic operation and permit more sophisticated search strategies, and on the development of tactics for improving the user-system interface. In this latter area the Research Unit produced a series of Search Manuals which analyze the problems of preparing search profiles (and which have formed the basis of similar guides produced by groups which followed the Unit into this field), developed a novel Key-Letter-In-Context (KLIC) Index to aid in the choice of appropriate word fragments as search terms in such profiles, and pioneered the concept of user workshops or "teach-ins" as a tool in user education.

By 1968 the Research Unit was in a position to explore, through its Cost-Recovery Experiment, the introduction of commercially viable services and in January 1969 introduced a full range of current-awareness SDI services, based on Chemical Abstracts Service data bases, for payment.

The activities of the Research Unit have had significant influence on the development of an international network of chemical information dissemination centers. During 1967 and 1968 Chemical Abstracts Service significantly modified its overall policy so as to limit its activities to data base production. In order to serve the needs of users for retrieval and dissemination of information from these data bases, they stimulated the establishment of a number of regional and national dissemination centers modeled on the Nottingham Unit. Such centers are now active in several parts of the U.S.A. (University of Pittsburgh, University of Georgia, Illinois Institute of Technology Research Institute, and others) and in Europe (Sweden, Denmark, Holland).

In parallel with this, the American Chemical Society developed the concept of an international collaboration on input to the Chemical Abstracts Service system. During 1969 an agreement covering both marketing of existing Chemical Abstracts Service products (both conventional and computer-based) in the United Kingdom and the development of a United Kingdom input capability was signed between the Chemical Society and the American Chemical Society.

To support this extension of activity and because the primary objectives of the Research Unit had been achieved, the Chemical Society Research Unit in Information Dissemination and Retrieval was incorporated as the Research and Development arm of the United Kingdom Chemical Information Service (UKCIS) which came into existence in August 1969.

ANTHONY K. KENT

CHICAGO PUBLIC LIBRARY

The roots of the Chicago Public Library can be traced to the Chicago Lyceum, the first subscription library to be organized in the city. It was established in 1834, only one year after the founding of Chicago. The life span of the Lyceum was rather short, however, since it was absorbed by a more permanent organization in 1841 called the Young Men's Association. This association not only conducted a reading room and library but also sponsored lectures which at a later period attracted such eminent speakers as Ralph Waldo Emerson, Oliver Wendell Holmes, James Russell Lowell, Charles Sumner, and Henry Ward Beecher. As the Young Men's Association grew and prospered, the library was expanded until it became eventually an institution of magnitude and importance. Throughout its existence, the association enjoyed the support of the leading citizens of the city, among whom were William B. Ogden, John Wentworth, Marshall Field, Joseph Medill, Potter Palmer, Cyrus McCormick, Thomas Hoyne, Walter Newberry, John Crerar, and a host of other giants. It is interesting to observe that both Walter Newberry and John Crerar were later to bequeath large sums of money to establish two distinguished research libraries in Chicago that bear their names.

In 1868, the Young Men's Association changed its name to the Chicago Library Association, an indication that the operation of the library had become the paramount interest of this organization. By 1870, the Chicago Library Association had a book collection of 30,000 volumes, issued printed catalogs to its members, and boasted an annual circulation of 20,000 volumes.

In the following year, on October 9, 1871, the cataclysmic Chicago Fire occurred which consumed the entire book collection of the Chicago Library Association in its flames as well as those of the Chicago Historical Society and other institutions.

It was out of the ashes of this tragic catastrophe that the Chicago Public Library was born. The world was shocked by the overwhelming disaster and contributions of every description began to pour in from all quarters of the globe. England exhibited unusual generosity, and cargoes of food and clothing were shipped from Liverpool. But there were also those in England who realized the urgent need to replace the books that had been destroyed. An Englishman by the name of A. H. Burgess, who to this day has not been identified, proposed in a letter published in the *London Daily News* "that England should present a new Free Library to Chicago, to remain there as a mark of sympathy . . . and a token of true brotherly kindness forever."

This proposal came to the attention of Thomas Hughes, a member of Parliament and author of the celebrated book *Tom Brown's School Days,* who organized a general committee for this purpose. A circular appealing to British authors, booksellers, publishers, and learned societies was issued inviting donations of books for the stricken city located on the shores of Lake Michigan. The response to the appeal was electric. Almost every living author made a contribution of his works. Among the more illustrious names were Alfred Tennyson, Thomas Carlyle, Matthew Arnold, William Gladstone, Benjamin Disraeli, Herbert Spencer, Robert Browning, Lewis Carroll, Charles Kingsley, Charles Darwin, and Thomas Huxley. Her Majesty Queen Victoria was greatly moved and lent the prestige of the Royal Crown to this project. In all more than 8,000 volumes were collected and shipped to Chicago.

While these events were transpiring in London, some important moves were being taken in Chicago. On January 8, 1872, exactly three months after the conflagration, a public meeting was called by Mayor Joseph Medill to consider the establishment of a free tax-supported public library. The meeting was "large and enthusiastic" as reported in the press and was attended by the leading citizens of the city. There was general agreement that Chicago needed a tax-supported public library. A committee was, therefore, appointed headed by Thomas Hoyne, a distinguished member of the Chicago Bar, to draft a bill to be introduced in the Legislature authorizing municipalities to establish and levy taxes for the support of public libraries. The committee worked with dispatch and on January 24 a bill was ready to be sent to Springfield. When members of the committee appeared in

Springfield, they found that another bill had already been introduced by the representative from Peoria which contained similar provisions. Peoria had been considering the formation of a free tax-supported public library, and had caused a bill to be introduced. The Chicago committee accepted this bill and after attaching some necessary amendments to fit its needs, it was adopted on March 7, 1872, and became the first Free Public Library Act of Illinois.

Since an emergency clause was appended to the bill, the law went into effect immediately upon passage. On April 3, 1872, the City Council of Chicago enacted an ordinance establishing a public library and a few days later Mayor Medill appointed the board of directors.

One of the first official acts of the board was to adopt and transmit a resolution of thanks to Thomas Hughes and the government of England for the beneficent gift contributed by its people. The next step was to discover suitable quarters to house this large collection of books. In a city that had suffered such devastation only six months previously, it was no small task to find proper accommodations. The city had hastily constructed a two-story building to serve as a city hall on the southeast corner of LaSalle and Adams Streets which was promptly dubbed, for some unknown reason, "the Rookery." Behind the Rookery stood a circular iron water tank, 58 feet in diameter and 21 feet in height, mounted on a solid stone foundation, which had survived the Fire. The tank was no longer used as a water supply reservoir, and because it was fireproof, the board of directors considered it to be eminently suited for storing the gift books. Book shelving was installed inside the tank and an additional story was added to the Rookery to serve as a library reading room. It was here that the Chicago Public Library opened its doors for service on New Year's Day, 1873.

The first librarian to be appointed was William Frederick Poole, one of the ablest practitioners of his day, who had just completed the organization of the Cincinnati Public Library. Poole was a graduate of Yale University, and while still an undergraduate, he was chosen assistant librarian of a college society library where his zeal for making information accessible to others led him into the publication of a comprehensive guide to periodicals which came to be known as *Poole's Index to Periodical Literature*. He served as librarian of the Boston Mercantile Library and the Boston Athenaeum before assuming the librarianship of the Cincinnati Public Library.

When Poole arrived in Chicago on January 2, 1874, to enter upon his new duties, the library was still housed in the "tank." One of his first recommendations was to move the library to more suitable quarters. Within a few months convenient space was leased on the corner of Wabash Avenue and Madison Street at an annual rental of $5000. The library occupied the second floor as a reading room, while half of the third and fourth floors were secured for storage and expansion. Circulation of books was made available for the first time on May 1, 1874. Pending the printing of a catalog, finding lists were issued, copies of which were sold at twenty cents each.

Having obtained adequate quarters for the library, Poole turned his attention and applied his great fund of knowledge to the task of building up a collection suited to the needs and tastes of a growing constituency. At the end of the first year of his administration, the number of borrowers increased to 24,000, the number of books to 40,000, and the circulation to 399,156 volumes, surpassing any other single library in the country save Boston.

The financial condition of the library was not satisfactory and for a period the purchase of new books was suspended. With a view to economy, the Library again moved in May, 1875, to a building located on the corner of Lake and Dearborn Streets. Further curtailments forced the Library to close evenings.

One of Poole's innovations was close cooperation with the public schools. After conferring with the Superintendent of Schools, a plan was developed for high school teachers to bring their classes to the library on Saturday mornings for instruction in the use of the library. An agreement was reached between the Library Board and the Board of Education by which principals were allowed to borrow books for class use, a privilege which was later extended to teachers.

On June 9, 1884, the library opened two delivery stations for the delivery and exchange of books as a substitute for branch libraries. In a short period of time four additional delivery stations were opened.

Because of lack of space and the danger of fire, the library was compelled to move again. On May 24, 1886, the library was transferred to the City Hall, where it remained for eleven years before taking up its permanent quarters on Michigan Avenue.

Dr. Poole resigned his position on July 23, 1887, to accept the post of librarian of the newly organized Newberry Library. During his tenure of office, the Chicago Public Library ranked as one of the leading bibliographical institutions of this country.

Frederick H. Hild, a native of Chicago, was selected to succeed Dr. Poole. He had been a member of the library staff since 1874 and he was familiar with its problems. Early in Hild's administration several important bequests were made to the library. In 1889 at the Paris Exposition, the library was awarded a gold medal for its exhibit, which consisted of the annual reports, finding lists, and a volume showing in detail the administrative procedures and techniques of the Library.

In the late 1880s it appeared that the time was ripe for a permanent library building. Chicago's population in 1890 reached 1,099,850 and the city was expanding rapidly. The location that was deemed most desirable was a tract of land referred to as Dearborn Park fronting on Michigan Avenue between Washington and Randolph Streets. It was part of the original old Fort Dearborn built by the federal government in administering the Northwest Territory. This piece of property was rectangular in shape and comprised 62,500 square feet. It was in the heart of the city and considered a choice location.

The campaign to acquire this land for library purposes cannot be related here. Suffice it to say that the legal battle which ensued was long and complicated, and was fought on many fronts including the halls of Congress, the legislative chambers in Springfield, and the meeting room of the City Council of Chicago. Victory came when the City Council enacted an ordinance on May 19, 1890, authorizing the library to take possession of Dearborn Park for the erection of a building. The final obstacle was removed when the Library Board concluded an agreement with a Civil War veterans' organization in which the latter conveyed to the library a one-quarter interest in the land on which the building was to be erected.

Having acquired a site for the proposed library building, the board prevailed upon the Legislature to amend the Library Act permitting the city of Chicago to levy a two-mill tax for five years in order to finance this building project. Thirteen designs were submitted in an open competition of architects and on February 13, 1892, the board adopted the design of Shepley, Rutan and Coolidge.

Architecturally, the library building, which is still standing, presents a combination of Renaissance, Neo-Greek, and Roman forms, and is famous for the magnificent scheme of marble and mosaic decoration to which the attention of visitors is immediately invited. The exterior is of Bedford limestone with a granite base. In treatment the lower part of the exterior is in the Neo-Greek style with wide arched windows, and the upper part in Grecian style with pillars and columns separated by windows. The entablature is of pronounced Roman character, with heavy garlands and lions' heads sculptured on the frieze.

The third floor of the interior is especially noteworthy because of the lavish use of mosaic fashioned of colored stone, mother-of-pearl, and Favrile glass in intricate patterns and frescoes and graceful borders. The separate pieces are often set irregularly and at slight angles in order to catch the light and thus enhance their jewel-like luster. The dome of stained glass is supported by arches richly adorned with scrolls and rosettes bearing the symbols of famous printers of earlier times. In the wings, inlaid in green marble panels, are inscriptions in ten languages, beginning with ancient Egyptian and Hebrew, in praise of books and reading. Inscriptions and decorative patterns are also applied to the frieze and beams over the staircase, and flanking the elaborately coffered ceiling. This scheme of decorations was designed and executed by the famous New York house of Tiffany and constitutes the largest and finest system of mosaics in the modern world. It should be added that this type of decoration was adopted for very practical reasons. Because of the smoke-filled air of central Chicago, any painted mural decorations would soon have been submerged or scoured off. Mosaic and marble, enduring forever, and made brighter and more lustrous by frequent polishing, were therefore chosen —for wear as well as beauty. The woodwork in this room is primavera or white mahogany of massive and dignified design, with graceful hand carving.

The scheme of decoration on the fourth floor is much less elaborate than on the floor below. That of the Reference Department is everywhere purely Grecian, the molding and forms being copied from the best existing examples. The wainscoting is of beautifully mottled Sienna marble. The furniture is of hand-carved oak in natural color. There are three great double doorways in this room, treated very like the principal entrance of the Erechtheum at Athens, except that the frieze is here decorated by upright and reversed honeysuckle ornaments.

The Social Sciences and Business Department, which adjoins the Reference Department, is one of the most imposing rooms in the building. The wainscoting is of verd antique marble. The pilasters are paneled with Renaissance designs with a frieze above, ornamented by garlands and masks in high relief. The ceiling is deeply coffered and boldly decorated by reliefs and moldings. With the exception of the doorways, which are copied from the doors of the Palazzo Vecchio in Florence, the general form and color treatment of this room are based on those of an assembly hall in the Doge's palace in Venice.

Directly below, on the second floor, is the Grand Army Memorial Hall, in which the deep green of the verd antique marble is combined with rich reds and greens, producing an effect of great beauty. Plaster reliefs of ancient accouterments of war are introduced in the frieze. The handsome lobby leading into the hall is lighted by a dome similar to that at the south end of the building. Heavily veined Tennessee marble is used in the north staircase, and in all the subsidiary corridors and rooms.

On October 9, 1897, the anniversary of the Chicago Fire, the new building was dedicated with appropriate ceremonies and on October 11 it was opened for public service.

Some of the highlights of the Hild administration were the following: Provision was made for book service to the blind in 1893. In 1895, all employees were placed under civil service. Delivery stations were extended with stations being organized in business and manufacturing establishments for the use of their employees. Some of the more prominent companies to take advantage of this service were Marshall Field, Sears Roebuck, International Harvester, and R. R. Donnelley. The first branch reading room was opened in 1890 with three others established soon thereafter. These reading rooms were housed in rented quarters on commercial streets and served as small branch agencies. In 1901, the Library received a gift from Mrs. T. B. Blackstone offering to construct a branch library building, which was opened for service in 1904. Through the efforts of the Library Board, a bill was introduced into the Legislature and enacted into law authorizing the creation of a pension fund for the employees of the library. A young people's room was opened in 1907 at the Central Library, named the Thomas Hughes Reading Room for Young People, and in the following year a regular Saturday "story hour" program was initiated. In 1909, the American Library Association accepted an invitation from the Chicago Public Library to move its headquarters into the Central Library building, where it remained for many years.

In 1895, the Chicago Public Library entered into an informal agreement with the Newberry Library and the John Crerar Library shortly after their establishment. The effect of this agreement was that the two privately endowed institutions undertook to concentrate their financial resources on collecting rare and scholarly materials in their respective subject fields of specialization, and the Chicago Public Library assumed the responsibility of supplying the more general book needs of the community. As a result of this historical turn of events, the Newberry and the Crerar became oriented toward the scholar and the specialist, whereas the Chicago Public Library directed its revenues and energies in serving the diverse reading and informational requirements of the general public.

After 22 years of service, Frederick H. Hild ended his career as librarian on April 30, 1909. Under his administration, the library progressed steadily and systematically under the lines established by the founders. Under him, also, the long cherished aim of a permanent home was accomplished.

Hild's successor was Henry E. Legler, Secretary of the Wisconsin Free Library Commission, whose achievements in organizing statewide library extension programs in the Badger state drew national attention. Legler's major contribution to the Chicago Public Library was in the field of branch development.

In *A Library Plan for the Whole City* designed by Legler in 1916, he proposed the establishment of 5 regional branches, 70 local branches, 60 deposit stations, 100 industrial and commercial branches, 22 high school branches, 3000 classroom libraries, and 100 special deposits. This was an ambitious undertaking and aimed to achieve the goal of bringing library service within walking distance of home for every person in the city. The most unique feature of the plan was the proposal of creating five regional branches that would not only serve readers directly but would also provide auxiliary services for the local branches within the region. This concept of a regional branch proposed by Legler was an original idea in librarianship, for which he is to be credited. In a period of eight years Legler was successful in establishing 30 branches in the city, most of which were in rented quarters.

Legler was a dynamic and creative individual, and moved in many directions. Some of the more significant accomplishments were the following: He began the installation of branch libraries as well as classroom collections housed in public schools. He initiated an "Open Shelf" collection in the Central Library. He organized a training class in the library for the purpose of recruiting and training a force of competent and experienced assistants. He was responsible for the first scientific classification and pay plan for the library staff. He began a free monthly publication called the *Book Bulletin* which has been continued to the present day. In 1912, he opened a Civics Room devoted to the social sciences but laying great stress on government with a comprehensive collection of public documents. In 1914–1915, a Music Room was established containing a collection of opera scores, chamber music, and sheet music, both instrumental and vocal. A Foreign Language Room was equipped to provide reading matter for the large foreign population of the city. He also started a Rental Collection in order to make it possible to meet more adequately the heavy demand for new books.

Legler developed a scheme of "package libraries" which were provided by the library in cooperation with a movement of the Chicago Association of Commerce for the study of civics in the high schools and the upper elementary school grades. These libraries consisted chiefly of pamphlet material, magazine separates, public documents, and other ephemeral material. Each package dealt with one subject or a principal division of a large topic. The libraries were subject to call from school principals and social service students and workers for varying periods according to need.

In the midst of all this activity, Henry E. Legler died suddenly in 1917 at the early age of 56. During his short tenure of office, the library made great progress and his influence has continued to the present day.

The man selected to succeed Legler was Carl B. Roden. Entering the Chicago Public Library in 1886 as a page, he was elevated through successive stages to the position of librarian, in which capacity he presided over the destiny of this institution with distinction for 30 years. In 1927 he served as President of the American Library Association.

One of his major accomplishments was the planning and construction of three regional branches designed to improve library service in the three principal sectors of the city. Legler Regional Branch located on the west side was built in 1920; Hild Regional Branch located on the north side was erected in 1931; and Woodlawn Regional Branch located on the south side was opened in 1939.

In 1923 Roden was successful in concluding an agreement whereby the high school libraries were to be jointly administered by the board of education and the Chicago Public Library. The former was responsible for paying the salaries of the school librarians, purchasing the permanent book collections, and providing physical quarters. The library was responsible for the selection and supervision of personnel, processing the books, and binding. This arrangement remained in force until 1948 when the board of education assumed full responsibility for the total operation of high school libraries.

In September, 1923, a new service was inaugurated through the establishment of a Readers' Bureau. The service provided for a systematic course of study tailored to individual needs and conducted under the personal supervision of a member of the library staff. Those enrolling in these courses were provided with bibliographies, and the necessary reading materials were made available to them. In the same year a Teachers' Room was installed combining in one convenient location all of the resources of the library devoted to the teaching profession and all phases of educational development.

While the library experienced several periods of financial crisis, none was as severe as that during the Depression which struck in 1929. The whole framework of library service was affected, and the effects were sustained for more than a decade. Despite the lack of funds and payless days, the library circulated nearly 16,000,000 volumes in 1931, the largest figure to be reported at any time by an American public library.

In 1936, Roden proposed that a survey of the library be made under the direction of the Graduate Library School of the University of Chicago. After conferring with representatives of the School, he requested the Carnegie Corporation of New York to make available a grant for this purpose. The Corporation approved the request and granted the sum of $10,000 for the survey. Professors Carleton B. Joeckel and Leon Carnovsky were designated by the School as Director and Associate Director of the project. Work began in January, 1938, and on May 10, 1939, the report of the survey was published under the title *A Metropolitan Library in Action*. Insofar as funds permitted, Roden attempted to implement many of the recommendations and findings of the survey.

In 1950, Carl B. Roden retired after 64 years of dedicated service to the library. He was succeeded by Gertrude E. Gscheidle, who had been connected with the library in various capacities since 1924. Miss Gscheidle continued to carry out many of the ideas proposed in the survey. She was responsible for establishing eight subject departments at the Central Library. She also initiated a photographic charging circulation system. During her administration, eight branch buildings were constructed. In July, 1967, Miss Gscheidle retired and Alex Ladenson was appointed acting librarian.

Over the years, the Chicago Public Library has produced a number of important members of the profession. Pearl I. Field, Librarian of Legler Regional Branch, and Jessie E. Reed, Librarian of Hild Regional Branch, helped to develop the regional branch system. John R. Patterson was a leader in the field of book preservation. Adah F. Whitcomb was a pioneer in the establishment of high school libraries as branches of the Public Library. Alice M. Farquhar won national recognition in the field of Adult Education by establishing a Readers' Bureau. Nathan R. Levin made contributions in the area of library personnel and civil service. Agatha L. Shea promoted library service to children.

As the Chicago Public Library approaches its centennial, the scope of its responsibilities appears to be broadening. With the two endowed research libraries of the city (Newberry and John Crerar) limiting the use of their facilities to a rather highly restricted core of scholars, the Chicago Public Library finds itself in a position where it must serve a larger clientele than ever before in its history. Although the John Crerar Library had originally preempted the aim of collecting specialized materials in the field of the Social Sciences, in recent years it has been compelled to abandon this objective. Consequently there is no public library today in Chicago that is making the Social Sciences its peculiar province of specialization. It has been proposed that the Chicago Public Library assume the task of developing an exhaustive research collection in this broad area, thus filling a bibliographical gap so vital to the scholarly needs of the city.

Moreover, as the major public library in the metropolitan area, the Chicago Public Library serves a multitude of persons not residing within the central city. By tradition the Chicago Public Library has always given free library service to the residents of five counties. It also serves as one of the four Research and Reference Centers established under the Illinois Library Development Act. The total number of people with direct access to the Chicago Public Library constitutes a majority of the people of the state.

During 1968 the Chicago Public Library has been concentrating on programs designed to serve the residents of the black communities of the city. In attacking this problem it has become clear that the traditional patterns of library service are ineffectual, and that new methods and techniques need to be explored and devised to reach the people in the slum-ridden ghettos of the city. The library has undertaken a number of projects utilizing a variety of approaches in this critical area of service.

In 1968 a full-scale Survey of the Library was undertaken under the direction of Dr. Lowell A. Martin. The scope of this study contemplates a three-pronged approach:

1. A comprehensive study and appraisal of the service programs, activities, book collections, and physical plant including the Central Building and the branch system, with recommendations for their expansion, improvement, and revitalization.

2. A critical examination of the role and relationship of the Library to the

rapidly changing character of the urban environment to include the inner city and the outer ring of neighborhoods.

3. A management study for an effective organizational and administrative structure for the Library, including the efficient use of personnel and the introduction of computerized techniques not only for fiscal and record-keeping purposes but for the storage and retrieval of information.

The major findings and recommendations of the survey team are broad. Dr. Martin proposed that the present 62 branches of the Chicago Public Library be progressively shifted into a system of 10 large regional library centers and 100 relatively small local neighborhood branches to be housed in rented quarters. He also recommended that the extension of library service to the disadvantaged areas of the city be given top priority. Martin proposed a new building for the Central Library with greater emphasis on the research function. Proposed also was the establishment of a central information center to be directly tied to all branches in a citywide information network. It was also suggested that the card catalog be abandoned and replaced by a catalog produced in book form employing an electronic automated system. The formation of a Metropolitan Library Council was advocated to plan for a library network to serve the greater Chicago area. Finally, the survey proposed a substantial increase in the library tax levy to defray the cost of the total program.

Concluding this brief account of the library, it is fitting to recall the words of Carl Sandburg, who at the fiftieth anniversary of this institution declared:

> I think it is safe to say here today that there are thousands of people who feel strong strands of their lives interwoven with the Chicago Public Library located here in a city that is in a sense a center of the nation—not politically the capital of the nation, but often spoken of by people in different parts of this country and often spoken of by European travelers as the capital of this country.

BIBLIOGRAPHY

Joeckel, Carleton Bruns, and Leon Carnovsky, *A Metropolitan Library in Action: A Survey of the Chicago Public Library,* University of Chicago Press, Chicago, 1940.

Chicago Public Library, Board of Directors, *Proceedings,* 1872 to date.

Chicago Public Library, Board of Directors, *Annual Reports,* 1873 to date.

The Chicago Public Library 1873–1923. Proceedings at the Celebration of the Fiftieth Anniversary of the Opening of the Library, Board of Directors of the Chicago Public Library, Chicago, 1923.

Prichard, Louise Gilman, "History of the Chicago Public Library," unpublished Master's Thesis, Library School, University of Illinois, Urbana, Ill., 1928.

Spencer, Gwladys, *The Chicago Public Library: Origins and Backgrounds,* University of Chicago Press, Chicago, 1943.

ALEX LADENSON

CHICAGO. UNIVERSITY OF CHICAGO, GRADUATE LIBRARY SCHOOL

The Graduate Library School of the University of Chicago, officially established in 1926 and open to students in 1928, was an outgrowth of two important studies: Charles C. Williamson's *Training for Library Service* and W. S. Learned's *The American Public Library and the Diffusion of Knowledge*. Williamson emphasized the need for a library school that would truly be on a graduate level, and would devote itself to investigation and research. Learned's report led to a reformulation of the library-aid program of the Carnegie Corporation, and one feature of this program was a million-dollar allotment for a possible graduate library school. The geographic position of the University of Chicago, the presence of numerous and diverse libraries in the city, the importance and prestige of the university, and the fact that its president, Ernest DeWitt Burton, had been director of the university libraries, all contributed to the choice of the University of Chicago for the establishment of such a school.

Originally, and until 1946, the school made no provision for traditional preparation for library operations and services. As an early statement published in *Library Quarterly* [1, 27 (1931)] made clear: "The School allows other library schools to assume the responsibility for passing on to their students a body of principles and practices that have been found useful in the conduct of libraries. Such training is not a function of this School, but is an essential prerequisite for admission." During its first 2 years (1928 to 1930) investigations were under way in adult reading, cataloging and classification, children's reading, bibliographic history, school and college libraries, and education for librarians.

The first dean and organizer of the Graduate Library School was George A. Works, an authority in educational organization and administration. Although he remained only 2 years he assembled the first faculty and set the course the school was to follow. Upon his departure and after a 3-year interim, Louis Round Wilson was brought from the University of North Carolina. He remained as dean from 1932 until his retirement in 1945.

The period of Wilson's administration saw the school advance in a number of directions, with research by faculty and students in such areas as the sociology and geography of reading, public library government and administration, and printing and library history. The faculty conducted public and academic library surveys, and the school initiated its series of annual conferences on topics relevant to contemporary library interest. Among the publications issued by the faculty during Wilson's deanship were *Investigating Library Problems* (Waples), *What People Want to Read About* (Waples and Tyler), *The Government of the American Public Library* (Joeckel), *The Geography of Reading* (Wilson), *The University Library* (Wilson and Tauber), *The College Library* (Randall), *The Medieval Library* (Thompson), *The Origin of Printing in Europe* (Butler), *An Introduction to*

Library Science (Butler), and *A Metropolitan Library in Action* (Joeckel and Carnovsky).

Wilson was succeeded as dean by Carleton B. Joeckel. Under Joeckel the school extended its program to embrace the preparatory phase of library training. This was done to enable experimentation in the basic program of library education and to provide a pool from which promising research students might be drawn. Joeckel in turn was followed by others (Ralph Beals, Clarence Faust, Bernard Berelson, Lester Asheim) who solidified and extended the training and research programs. The appointment, in 1963, of Don R. Swanson added a new dimension, with emphasis on computerization, library systems planning, and related research in information science.

The Graduate Library School today provides an opportunity for basic and advanced professional study and research in library science. Its courses of study lead to the degrees of Master of Arts and Doctor of Philosophy.

The purposes of the Graduate Library School are to prepare students for professional practice in librarianship with emphasis upon basic principles and with attention to the implications of future technology on the handling of information in libraries and special centers; to prepare students for responsible roles in the planning of future libraries and information systems; to advance the state of the art of communicating recorded knowledge through theoretical, historical, and experimental research; and to provide a philosophy for education in librarianship.

Areas of specialization at the Graduate Library School include school libraries, children's literature, public libraries, processes of social communication, academic research libraries, cataloging, history of books and libraries, libraries in special subject fields (business, theology, law, medicine, Far Eastern materials, music, art and so on), and research on problems of intellectual access to information.

A central goal of the academic program is to study the planning of future libraries and information services. Since computer and microform technology are significant in library planning, attention is given to the study of their capabilities and limitations. The planning of future systems involves, in addition to technological aspects, an understanding of the purposes and objectives of libraries, how and by whom they are used, their role in society, and their history and achievement. It also involves a comprehension of the techniques of intellectual access to information—including indexing, cataloging, classification, and bibliography.

The educational and research activities of the school in all specialties center, accordingly, around the problems of bibliography; the organization of books and other materials in libraries; book selection; problems of library administration; systems planning in libraries; automation in libraries; problems of communication and reading; theoretical studies of indexing, cataloging, subject analysis, and classification; and studies of the library in its interaction with its users.

Accordingly the school has established a core program of courses designed to reflect those elements of general librarianship and of library science common to all types of specialized libraries. This work in the basic principles of librarianship is designed for the student who enters the school in possession of a well-rounded general education.

In addition to formal course work the students have considerable opportunity for individual supervised research projects and reading courses. Research is regarded as an important component in the students' educational experience at the M.A. level, where a thesis is required, as well as at the Ph.D. level.

The program of study in the Graduate Library School should usually be supplemented by a number of subjects taught in other schools and divisions of the university. This supplementary work is particularly necessary for advanced research in the field of information science. This latter specialty involves a considerable number of mathematics courses, among others, and is particularly designed (though not exclusively so) for the student who enters the school with good undergraduate preparation in engineering, science, or mathematics. Nearly all students, however, are encouraged to take some of their elective courses in other schools and divisions of the university. The Graduate School of Business, the Graduate School of Education, the Medical School, the Department of Statistics, the Committee on Information Sciences, the Computation Center, and the divisions of Humanities and Social Sciences exemplify some of the areas of the university that are of relevance to the program in librarianship.

The school publishes three journals: the *Library Quarterly,* a pre-eminent scholarly journal in the field of librarianship; the *Bulletin of the Center for Children's Books,* a critical reviewing medium in the field of books for children and young people; and *Mechanical Translation and Computational Linguistics.* Another important continuing publication of the school is a notable monograph series based on the proceedings of its annual conferences, each of which develops some special aspect of librarianship.

The Graduate Library School is located in the university's Harper Memorial Library, one of the great libraries of America, and is scheduled to move, in 1970, to the new Joseph Regenstein Library. Students have access to many special collections and libraries of the university, including that of the Center for Children's Books. Outside the university, the city of Chicago offers many outstanding libraries, notably the Newberry, the John Crerar, the Chicago Public, and the libraries of the Art Institute.

LEON CARNOVSKY AND DON R. SWANSON

CHICAGO. UNIVERSITY OF CHICAGO LIBRARY

Summary

The University of Chicago Library, holding 3,000,000 volumes early in 1970, was at that time the ninth largest United States academic library. It serves the teaching and research programs of a relatively small private university (9500 students), which has been ranked among the nation's leading universities in excellence. The library system includes strong departmental libraries in addition to the major new Joseph Regenstein Library, but by policy the book collection is segmented rather than fragmented, so that in general each departmental unit holds essentially all the University's books in a given subject. The Regenstein Library's holdings, too, are primarily related to specific classes of the Library of Congress classification scheme. This policy minimizes duplication and has produced a research collection which in terms of the number of different titles available has greater scope and depth than the volume count alone might suggest and affords a scholarly resource of unusual richness and distinction. In recent years the library has added over 150,000 volumes annually, and it receives over 34,000 current serial and journal titles. Its yearly recorded circulation of nearly 1,000,000 items represents what may be the highest per capita use of library materials among American university libraries. Library expenditures in 1968–1969 totaled $3,610,322, of which $1,226,293 or 34% was spent for books and binding, and $1,994,793 or 55% was spent for salaries. The staff of the library in early 1970 had 567 persons filling 349 positions in full-time equivalent, of which 83 were professional, with the balance divided between nonprofessional and student positions. Like its parent institution, the University of Chicago Library has been innovative, pioneering in such fields as the use and development of microphotography, library applications of Xerography, and contributing major work on the computerization of library services and operations. Its huge new social sciences and humanities research library facility, the 577,000-square-foot Joseph Regenstein Library, opened for use in the 1970–1971 academic year. The history of the University of Chicago Library reveals interesting responses to some of the basic problems of university libraries, including centralization versus decentralization, responsibility and control, and the development of book selection practice and policy. The remainder of this article amplifies the above comments in detail, describing the plant, the administration and staffing of the library, and the collections, and offering enough history to place the contribution of this library in context.

The University

The University of Chicago is a private, nondenominational, coeducational, primarily graduate institution of higher learning and research. Conceived of as a college, it was chartered in September 1890 and its first president and guiding genius, William Rainey Harper, assumed office on July 1, 1891. Only fourteen months later, on October 1, 1892, it opened its doors, more a university than a college, with a junior college, a senior college, a graduate school, and one professional school. The initial student body of 594 included only 166 graduate students, but since the first few years the graduate students have far outnumbered the undergraduates; in 1970, for example, there were 2500 degree students in the undergraduate college and 7000 in the graduate divisions and professional schools. The distinguished initial faculty of 120 included eight former college presidents, lured to teaching and research careers at Chicago—partly by high salaries, but also and perhaps primarily by President Harper's vision of a true university and by his promise of ample time for "investigation." By 1970 the university had 1160 faculty members, and an additional 800 research associates, lecturers, field workers, and consultants. The work of the university is conducted for undergraduates by the college, and for graduate students by four divisions (Biological Sciences, Physical Sciences, Social Sciences, and Humanities), and seven professional schools (Business, Divinity, Education, Law, Library, Medicine, and Social Service Administration). A further unit, University Extension, conducts adult education programs for both degree and nondegree students. The university has been innovative from its inception, pioneering, among other advances, the four-quarter system, extension programs and courses in the liberal arts, a full-time medical school teaching faculty, and general undergraduate education.

The Library's Physical Plant

BACKGROUND

By the time the new university opened its doors in 1892 it had already acquired at least 120,000 volumes, including manuscripts, incunabula, and early imprints, which gave it one of the three or four largest academic libraries in the United States. The initial absence of adequate space for a central library collection resulted in locating most of the book collections with the appropriate academic departments. Although a central collection did exist from January 1893, in quarters shared with the University Press and the gymnasium, the library "system" for twenty years consisted primarily of a group of small faculty-managed departmental libraries surrounding a rather poor central collection. The departmental libraries, where they were cataloged at all, were cataloged and classified under one of some fifteen or twenty different locally-designed systems.

A strong move toward central processing and central administrative control began in 1910 when Professor Ernest DeWitt Burton became Director and brought J. C. M. Hanson from the Library of Congress to become Associate Director and operating head of the library. The move was reinforced in 1912 when the building of a true "main library," the William Rainey Harper Memorial Library, attracted some of the by-then-overcrowded departmental collections. But, although administrative control and the processing operations gradually became centralized, the initial dispersion of books set an early pattern for a high degree of departmentation. From 1912 to 1970 the University of Chicago Library consisted of Harper Library, containing the administrative, technical, and general service departments and the book collections in the general social sciences and humanities, and fifteen or more different lecture hall and laboratory buildings housing among them some twenty or more departmental libraries servicing the other half of the library's collections in units ranging up to 280,000 volumes in size. In 1970–1971, the books in Harper, together with those in almost all of the departmental libraries in the social sciences and humanities, moved into the

Regenstein Library where they were merged into a single collection. Pending further new construction, the library consists physically of the new and central Joseph Regenstein Library, an Undergraduate Library established on the third floor of the Harper complex, and nine departmental and professional school libraries located outside the main library.

THE JOSEPH REGENSTEIN* LIBRARY

The Regenstein Library is designed primarily as a graduate research library for the social sciences and the humanities (see Figure 1). It also houses the University Library's administrative offices, its central acquisitions and processing departments, its Photoduplication Department, space for a computer, and the Depart-

FIGURE 1. *The Joseph Regenstein Library at the University of Chicago.*

ment of Special Collections, including the university's rare book collections. The first floor in the southeast wing is occupied by the offices and classrooms of the Graduate Library School.

In the planning of the Regenstein Library critical attention was given by the library staff and by a faculty planning committee to the fundamental problem of creating the optimum relationships between the book collection, reading facilities, reference and bibliographical resources, and reference and service staff for the particular needs of the University of Chicago. With a prospective ultimate collection within the building of over three million volumes, an extremely high per

* The Regenstein Library honors the memory of Joseph Regenstein (1889–1957), an industrialist, a fourth-generation Chicagoan, and a life-long resident of the city. Interested in research, and himself responsible for many innovations in the paper, plastic, and chemical fields, Mr. Regenstein maintained an intense interest in the development of the city and its institutions. To honor him, the Joseph and Helen Regenstein Foundation, on November 9, 1965, gave $10,000,000 toward a new graduate research library. Said Joseph Regenstein, Jr.: "My father understood the importance of the University of Chicago. We agree with President Beadle that a new library building is vital to the continued pre-eminence of this institution. We feel privileged to help make this library a reality."

capita use, a constituency composed primarily of a large number of graduate students and faculty, and teaching and research programs typified by individual interests requiring access to an unusually wide range of subject materials, it was felt that neither the traditional stack with carrels surrounding it, nor the more recent system of interspersed books and readers, nor the subject-divisional type of reading rooms in combination with a bookstack, would be sufficiently responsive to the intellectual, operational, environmental, and economic factors inherent in this complex set of relationships and in a library of such large size.

Rather, local research interests and use patterns suggested the need for a single, unified book collection, all parts of which somehow would be arranged so that the portions of the collection most frequently used by a discipline or area program would be as close as possible to the specialized reference and service facilities provided for that discipline.

Thus, the Regenstein Library draws under one roof all the university's book collections in the social sciences and humanities, with the exception of Law, Art, Social Service Administration, and Theology, and merges them into a single collection in a single bookstack deployed vertically over seven service floors. On each floor the resources for several related disciplines are associated by bringing together the books in appropriate, broad sections of the Library of Congress Classification. In this way the resources on one floor—which can number up to 500,000 volumes—can respond to the needs of the student or scholar working intensively in a concentrated subject field, or in a group of closely-related fields. The scholar whose sources are drawn from several widely-different subject areas may, of course, find his materials on several different floors—frequently, however, adjacent to one another.

On each service floor, and with direct access to the book collections assembled on that floor, is a large reading area that provides the major specialized reference tools, indices, abstracts, and bibliographies for the disciplines or fields to be serviced on the floor; the runs of key journals in each such field; and the current issues of all related serials. These materials are located on open shelves in useful proximity to a variety of carrel and other seating and study accommodations; to seminar and typing rooms; to the offices for the library's specialized bibliographers and reference personnel in the relevant subject fields; to a circulation, control, and information desk for the floor; and to a number of faculty studies. Thus, for each group of related disciplines or fields, the major study facilities are immediately adjacent to, but not actually within, the corresponding bookstack area, and much of the intellectual apparatus for the effective use of the resources on a particular floor is immediately at hand for all readers.

Although materials for regional and area programs are classified and located primarily by subject, the reference and service needs of scholars in such programs are met as are the needs of those in subject disciplines—by bringing together in a designated area on the most appropriate service floor, the reference tools, current journals, vertical files, the specialized personnel, and in some cases a regional catalog, necessary to facilitate work in such programs. The exception to this policy is the 240,000-volume Far Eastern Library which, because it does not use the Library of Congress Classification, because it has its own acquisitions and processing staff, and because both language differences and the format of its materials pose service problems, has been assigned separate stack, work, and reading quarters on the fifth floor.

The variety of seating arrangements provided in the reading areas offers different degrees of privacy. Some carrel desks are rather fully enclosed, and others are only partially enclosed. Conventional open study tables are available in one-man, two-man, or four-man sizes. Each graduate student may have a locking shelf or two in which to keep his personal books, the library books charged to him, and his notes, papers, and related materials. Banks of such shelves are located adjacent to study tables and carrels, but not within the carrels, and it is anticipated that the carrels themselves will only rarely be assigned to individuals.

All reading areas are carpeted and are designed to provide a comfortable acoustic environment and a sustained light level of 70 to 75 foot candles. It is permissable to smoke in designated portions of the reading areas on each floor.

The decision to provide for some separation between the reading areas and the bookstack areas evolved as the product of many considerations, of which the most important was the desire to provide an exceptionally attractive and intellectually efficient reading environment. Others were to provide some control of the unrecorded internal migration of books, and reasonable economy in the interior treatment required for the largest percentage of space in the structure—the bookstack. A reader may enter the bookstack from any reading room, move at will throughout the stacks, and exit from the stacks to the reading area on any other floor—pausing, as he leaves the stacks, to charge any books he may have selected from the shelves. Or a reader may proceed from one reading room to another without entering the stacks. Even with this degree of accessibility, it is believed that optimum control over the current location of materials taken from the bookstacks and the reading areas can be achieved without sacrificing either accessibility or an attractive and functional reading and service environment.

This separation of the very large areas required for books from reading facilities also means that a somewhat lower volume of air is required for the bookstack areas, compared with the air volume that would be needed for a system of interspersed study tables and stack shelving; it is possible to keep the temperature of the bookstacks somewhat below that of the reading areas in order to help mitigate the effects of heat upon the deterioration rate of paper; the acoustic treatment of the stack area is minimal with the lighting and floor surfaces designed for the optimum accommodation of books rather than readers. A substantial number of consultation tables has been located in the stack areas.

The space necessary to accommodate 3,000,000 volumes requires by far the largest percentage of the building's floor area. Nevertheless, all the service floors are built upon a modular plan so that the stacks can be extended into reading areas if necessary, or an entire floor may be shifted to an open interspersed plan, if desired. Conversely, new or specialized reading areas can be established within what are now stack areas. This potential for maximum long-term flexibility appears also in the central core of circulation and staff work areas, which has been positioned and designed so that the charging records can either be centralized on the main floor, or decentralized to each of the pertinent service floors, and so that some flexibility in the location and operation of other control and service functions is possible. Communication between all service desks is provided by a mechanized book conveyor and a pneumatic tube system.

The Serial Records Department has been located on the second floor, within the Social Science reading area, rather than in the Preparations Division. Here it is adjacent to the largest concentration of current journals and to the central microform and documents collections. The serials staff thus has public service as well as technical functions, and responds to holdings queries from all parts of the library during all the hours the Regenstein Library is open.

The library provides space for the installation of a computer and has an extensive system of in-the-floor ducts and conduits to facilitate the installation of computer terminal or other display and communication devices at almost any point in the building.

The detailed description of the reading, stack, and service facilities given above applies to six of the seven service floors—those serving specific groups of subject disciplines or area programs. The main floor is arranged on a similar principle, but serves a general reference and circulation function, maintains the central bibliography collections and the complete dictionary catalog of all holdings of the University Library system, and is related to the general reference and bibliography collections rather than a stack collection. The relatively small bookstack area (40,000 volumes) on the first floor serves to link the larger stack areas above and below into a single, continuous bookstack. It houses library science books and other portions of the "Z" classification.

The location of the major elements of the Regenstein Library is as follows: The main entrance to the building is on the south, in line with the north-south axis of the main quadrangles. There is a secondary entrance from the east, but both entrances bring the reader to the building's single entrance-exit control point. The first floor contains the public catalog listing all books in the University Library, the general reference and circulation departments, the library's general administrative offices, the Preparations Division, the Department of Special Collections, and a large Reserve Book Reading Room for the required readings in all courses in departments served by the Regenstein Library. In ascending order from the main floor are the following services: *Second Floor:* the social sciences, documents, central microfilm collection, Serial Records Department, and current journals for both social sciences and humanities; *Third Floor:* the humanities (with the reading area on this floor joined to the social sciences floor by an open internal stairway); *Fourth Floor:* education and psychology; *Fifth Floor:* nonwestern and ancient history and literature, including the Far Eastern Library, and the general and reference collections for classics, the ancient Near East, the ancient, medieval, and modern Middle East, and Southern Asia. In descending order from the main floor are: *"A" Level:* business, economics, and geography; *"B" Level:* the Map Library, the Photoduplication Department, the library systems staff, and (located temporarily in future expansion space) the Biology Library.

The building contains 577,045 gross square feet. There are seven service floors of which the first and second floors each contain over 85,000 square feet. An eighth floor and parts of a subbasement house air-handling equipment which provides the building with an elaborate air conditioning, filtering, and treatment system. The structure is of reinforced concrete with the exterior walls consisting of large slabs of Indiana limestone, heavily scored vertically. The building's module size is 27 feet square.

There are, in the southeast wing of the building, 253 faculty studies averaging about 60 square feet in size, each with individual temperature controls. The studies are available to the occupants twenty-four hours a day—with entrance through the library reading areas during service hours, and through a special, keyed entrance for the study wing at other times. The building is designed for a capacity of 3,150,000 volumes. It has 2926 seats, including 1048 at carrel seating, and, in addition, about 160 lounge seats and 270 stack consultation tables. The Chicago office of Skidmore, Owings and Merrill, with Walter Netsch heading the design team, were the architects.

OTHER LIBRARIES

The nine departments outside Regenstein are listed in Table 1. The largest of the remaining, physically separated units, the 290,000-volume Law Library, occupies a combination library and faculty-office building which is the central structure in a handsome Law School complex designed by Eero Saarinen and completed in October 1959. Swift Library, in the Divinity School's office and classroom building, houses the university's 100,000-volume collection in theology and the history of religion. The Library of the School for Social Service Administration has impressive quarters in a Mies van der Rohe building designed for the school and occupied in November 1964. It operates as a reference, reserve-book, vertical file collection to meet most of the day-to-day needs of the school's students and staff. As of 1970, the Art Library has its books and services in Goodspeed Hall. All four science libraries located outside Regenstein offer excellent book collections, and only two require special comment.

TABLE 1
University of Chicago Departmental Libraries

Library	Building	Subjects	Volumes, June 1970
Law	Law	Law	290,000
Swift	Swift Hall	Theology	100,000
Art	Goodspeed/Classics	Art	45,000
Social Service Administration	Social Service Administration	Welfare; administration of social work	7,000
Billings	Billings Hospital	Clinical medicine of last ten years	30,000
Chemistry	G. H. Jones	Chemistry	21,000
Eckhart	Eckhart	Mathematics/physics	64,000
Yerkes	Yerkes Observatory	Astronomy	25,000
Harper	Harper/Wieboldt/Business East	Undergraduate library	35,000

The Yerkes Observatory Library is located 100 miles from the campus at Williams Bay, Wisconsin, with its acquisitions carefully coordinated with purchases for the lesser astronomy collection on campus, and ordered through and processed in the Regenstein Library. Billings Library is one of the two units forming the Bio-Medical Libraries.

A part of the Harper complex will be remodeled as an undergraduate library, to be called "Harper Library." It is planned to use the three, great, connecting third floor reading rooms which until 1970 were the Business and Economics, Social Sciences, and Modern Languages reading rooms. The remodeled quarters will provide seats for 500 students, a carefully-selected collection of 60,000 to 80,000 volumes, several hundred periodicals with five or ten year backfiles, and representative scholarly journals from the major disciplines. It also will contain scholarly and critical monographs, landmark and standard titles, and the *avant-garde* literature of the day. The collection thus can also serve as a carefully-selected general collection for the "nonspecialist" reader in all parts of the university, but the primary purposes of the undergraduate library will be to meet most undergraduate library needs for the first two or three years of the four-year program; to be one of the centers of undergraduate intellectual life; to support a respectable level of preliminary work on student papers; and to make the student familiar with the apparatus of scholarship and with the way in which recorded knowledge is organized, disseminated, and retrieved—to the end that the student will in time not only be led to the greater scope and depth of the graduate research libraries, but will also be qualified to use them.

FUTURE BUILDING PLANS

Plans for the future look toward the construction of a fine arts center (north of Regenstein) which will have library facilities for Art, and a unified science library (south and west of Regenstein). If the science library is built, it is expected to house all science collections except those in Mathematics. Completion of all these units would give the University Library plant a total book capacity of 5,000,000 to 6,000,000 volumes—3,150,000 in Regenstein, 800,000 in the science libraries, 500,000 in other departmental libraries, and 1,000,000 in compact storage.

Control, Support, and Administration

CONTROL

The University of Chicago Library is responsible under the University's statutes and by-laws ". . . for the selection, custody, maintenance, and service of the various collections of books. journals, manuscripts, microfilms, maps and other related materials for the teaching, research, and scholarly activities of the faculty and students of the University." The Director of the Library is responsible to the Provost of the University, and is subject to the general policy guidance of the

Board of the Library. That body is composed of the President (*ex officio*), the Provost of the University and Dean of Faculties (*ex officio*), the Director of the Library (*ex officio*), and from six to fourteen members of the faculty. Faculty representatives are appointed for one-year terms by the Board of Trustees upon nomination of the President. They may not serve for more than four consecutive years, and, by custom, the board has consisted of one faculty representative from each of the divisions and schools. The primary functions of the board are to recommend or to approve major library policies, to advise the Director of the Library, and to provide a formal mechanism to facilitate communication between the library and the faculties. Meetings of the library staff, of department heads, and of *ad hoc* groups and committees of the staff are relied upon heavily in developing library policy. Student advisory committees are also available.

SUPPORT

The university provides for a single, consolidated budget insofar as unrestricted funds are concerned, for all parts of the University Library to cover acquisitions, binding, staff, equipment, and all other needs. A system of regular reporting, supplemented by meetings with individuals and department heads, has been effective in maintaining the flow of information required to construct such a consolidated budget and to help formulate library acquisition and other policies. In addition to its allocation from the university's general funds, the library derives support from two other sources: gifts and the income from endowed funds, and grants made by government or private foundations, either directly to the library for specific projects, or to academic departments of the university which then transfer or allocate a portion of the grant funds to the library for books and, in some cases, library services.

The distribution of the library's actual expenditures for the eleven years from 1958–1959 to 1968–1969 is given in Table 2.

ADMINISTRATION

The library is organized and administered on a functional basis. The Director is assisted by several Associate Directors, each of whom has operating responsibility for a division of the library (e.g., Preparations, the Regenstein Library services, the departmental and professional school libraries), but each of whom also is assigned responsibility for some planning and nonoperating activities. One Associate Director acts as Deputy Director and has over-all responsibility for the coordination of the day-to-day operations of all divisions and support units. Also reporting to the Office of the Director are the Law Librarian, the Bibliographers for the Social Sciences, for Slavic Studies, and for certain other areas, as well as staff officers responsible for budget analysis and control, for personnel, for physical planning, and for systems planning and automation. The librarians in charge of the departmental and professional school libraries located outside the Regenstein Library supervise the work of their units and, in addition, have primary responsibility for the development of the book collections in their areas. Within Regenstein,

TABLE 2

University of Chicago Library: Distribution of Expenditures 1958–1959 through 1968–1969

Year	Books and binding	Salaries	Other, including fringe benefits	Total
1958–1959	$290,991	$657,795	$45,228	$994,014
1959–1960	348,035	749,594	78,201	1,175,830
1960–1961	366,832	867,006	81,220	1,315,058
1961–1962	457,213	963,010	111,727	1,531,950
1962–1963	517,775	1,071,245	141,826	1,730,846
1963–1964	570,488	1,150,921	170,653	1,892,062
1964–1965	692,648	1,230,173	187,765	2,110,586
1965–1966	904,012	1,377,797	265,615	2,547,424
1966–1967	1,045,007	1,558,321	330,042	2,933,370
1967–1968	1,239,112	1,862,755	445,760	3,547,627
1968–1969	1,226,293	1,994,793	389,236	3,610,322

both book selection and advanced reference service are assigned to the librarians who, as subject specialists, have their offices, catalogs, reference tools, and supporting staff on the service floor which also houses and services the book collections falling in their major fields of responsibility. Book ordering is handled centrally through the Regenstein Library for all departments except the Far Eastern Library. Cataloging and classification are performed centrally except for the Far Eastern and the Law Libraries.

STAFFING

By university statute, professional librarians hold academic appointments which, after a probationary period, are normally "without limit of time." Members of the professional staff of the Library are eligible for benefits substantially identical to those of the faculty, including participation in T.I.A.A. contributory retiring allowance plan, major medical insurance, group life insurance, cumulative sick leave, and various forms of tuition reduction for children.

USE

Annual recorded circulation in recent years has ranged from 900,000 to 1,200,000 volumes. With a total Quadrangle enrollment of around 9000 students and 1160 faculty members, the average per capita use is extremely high. Unrecorded use adds very substantially to these totals. The heavy use reflects, of course, the great preponderance of graduate students in the university and a faculty that is heavily research oriented.

LIBRARY DATA PROCESSING

Well before 1966, the University of Chicago Library undertook a systematic effort to analyze the nature of its basic bibliographic and other data processing requirements, to examine many of its other operational procedures, and to relate these operations to the needs of readers. These analyses indicated that an integrated system to handle bibliographical, processing, and other operational data by means of a third generation computer with suitable peripheral equipment might be expected, over a reasonable period of time, to help improve such aspects of library operations as reader access to relevant materials, library response times, the general quality and evolutionary capability of library services, the generation of library performance data, and the flexibility of library processing, operational, or bibliographic data bases, and ultimately, moreover, should assist in stabilizing or improving certain cost/benefit ratios. In 1966, with the help of a grant from the National Science Foundation, the library began to build such a system, using its own systems staff as well as assistance from the University's Computation Center. Initially, the program shared an IBM 360/30 computer with two other users. During the first three years, work was largely concentrated upon the development of a capability for the handling of bibliographical and monographic processing data. While most of the design for handling such data preceded the development by the Library of Congress of the MARC II data system, the two systems are sufficiently similar to be highly compatible. The Chicago system provides for the machine input, tagging, storage, and variable output of major items of bibliographical and processing information. Stored data can be completely or partially extended, corrected, or deleted at any time by simply-coded input messages.

By 1969, the system was operating on a 360/50 shared-time university computer, and in early 1970 it was transferred to a 360/65 computer. A teleprocessing system provides for remote input to the Computation Center from the library by means of perforated paper tape. Some 100 integrated software programs have been developed for the day-by-day output on a high-speed printer of detailed proof, status, and related work sheets; input error messages; all book purchase orders; all catalog cards in Roman characters; book pocket labels; circulation book cards; a portion of the required book fund accounting; and certain other kinds of outputs. The system also provides for the automatic matching and input conversion of wanted, current, MARC II records from the Library of Congress. Catalog cards are printed in alphabetical order for a particular catalog or shelf list with all headings added, and purchase orders are grouped by dealer in printing. Both cards and orders are generated with a special print train providing upper and lower case and virtually all diacritical marks required for languages that use the Roman alphabet.

It is planned to extend the capabilities of the system into multikey file access, a fast-response circulation system with certain other characteristics, and programs for the generation of more fiscal, operating, and performance data as rapidly as funding for developmental purposes can be provided. The library staff has worked closely with a number of other libraries, especially Stanford and Columbia, in the planning and analysis of library system requirements.

The library's experience in the development of this system suggests that the intellectual, technical, and economic problems of creating broadly-responsive, computer-based, reliable, and evolutionary bibliographical and operating data-processing systems are greater than many experts believed would be the case in the later 1950s and early 1960s. Despite these problems, the library staff sees no logical alternatives to the development of such a complex apparatus if long-range, significant improvements in the responsiveness and evolutionary capability of large library and other information systems are to be achieved.

CONTRIBUTIONS TO LIBRARIANSHIP

The University of Chicago Library has contributed significantly to the analysis of a variety of fundamental problems of research libraries, and frequently has been among the innovators in the development of new approaches or methodologies for improving library services. It was among the first university libraries to adopt the Library of Congress Classification System (1910–1911). A faculty-trustee committee undertook one of the earliest objective analyses of the effects of centralization versus decentralization of library services and resources in a large university library (1923). The University Library was an early experimenter with special libraries for undergraduates (1931), and for the general, nonspecialist reader within a large university (1942). It was among the first university libraries to establish positions for senior, subject-trained bibliographers with primary responsibility for selection and coordination in the development of the University Library's book collections. The library was a pioneer (1936) in the large-scale production and utilization of microfilm, including the development of suitable equipment for the continuous processing and continuous printing of nonperforate 35 mm and 16 mm microfilm. It was also a very early developer (1947) of processes for the fast and economical production of catalog cards from Library of Congress proof slips by means of Xerox copying and offset printing—now a common procedure. Members of the library staff, sometimes in association with students in the Graduate Library School, have undertaken some of the more basic studies of the use of library resources for research purposes. Members of the staff also were early participants in the conception of and planning for the Center for Research Libraries. Finally, the library has been a pioneer in the development and application of computer-based systems for the handling of bibliographical and library processing data.

LIBRARIANS OR DIRECTORS

Zella Allen Dixon	Assistant Librarian, and later Associate Librarian	1891–1910
Ernest D. Burton	Director	1910–1925
James C. M. Hanson	Acting Director (Associate Director, 1910–1928)	1926–1928
M. Llewellyn Raney	Director	1927–1942
Ralph A. Beals	Director	1942–1946
Allen T. Hazen	Director	1946–1948
Herman H. Fussler	Director	1948–

The Book Collections

DEVELOPMENT AND GROWTH OF THE COLLECTIONS

Over the years book selection for the University Library has utilized the services of librarians, faculty members, and other specialists in a variety of combinations and differing degrees of emphasis. In recent years book selection has been almost entirely the responsibility of the library's departmental librarians or of bibliographers on the library staff with the advice and assistance of interested members of the faculty. Book funds are allocated by the Director to the subject bibliographers and departmental librarians on the basis of current need. The allocation is based on the level of expenditure previously found adequate, modified by changing or special needs, and changing or special market conditions as reported by the bibliographer for the subject field. Such reports include descriptions of the ways in which book funds are being expended, analyses of the materials purchased during the previous year, and an annual statement of unrestricted book fund needs justifying any change in terms of serious lacunae, new faculty interests, new frontiers in research, and the impending publication of major reprints or reference sets. Expenditures for books for each of the eleven years between 1958–1959 and 1968–1969 have been given above in Table 2.

Yearly growth of the book collections for the twenty-one years between 1948–1949 and 1968–1969 is shown in Table 3.

The three-million-volume book collection of the University of Chicago Library was built by steady, thoughtful, day-by-day selection and acquisition of materials related to the work of the university—and by the occasional, usually fortuitous and often dramatic acquisition of entire collections of books or manuscripts, or of individual titles of great rarity and value. The following section describes some of the strengths of the general collections, while a later section describes some of the special separate collections which add to the depth and richness of the library as a whole.

THE COLLECTIONS IN GENERAL

With the exception of Art, Law, Social Service Administration, and Theology, all the collections in the humanities and the social sciences are housed in the Regenstein Library, representing a very strong concentration of resources. Virtually all sections are exceptionally well-developed, but special mention should be made of unusual strength in the publications of major learned societies and academies, in bibliographical works, in collected statistics, and in the state, federal, and international documents necessary to support research—particularly in the social sciences. The social science collections themselves are outstanding, particularly in sociology, economics, international relations, and constitutional history. The 290,000 volumes in law include substantially all the reported decisions of the courts of the

TABLE 3
Annual Growth of the Book Collections, 1948–1949 through 1968–1969

Year	Gross volumes added	Volumes in library,[a] June 30
1948–1949	61,361	1,763,012
1949–1950	57,029	1,797,953
1950–1951	53,971	1,862,071
1951–1952	51,763	1,885,602
1952–1953	49,560	1,883,621
1953–1954	45,896	1,901,232
1954–1955	47,282	1,912,206
1955–1956	43,038	1,926,849
1956–1957	46,917	1,953,469
1957–1958	49,829	1,988,700
1958–1959	54,741	2,044,335
1959–1960	60,040	2,094,824
1960–1961	55,263	2,142,223
1961–1962	87,323	2,210,662
1962–1963	90,609	2,271,450
1963–1964	103,595	2,333,913
1964–1965	109,390	2,406,142
1965–1966	122,560	2,504,250
1966–1967	128,080	2,607,998
1967–1968	177,715	2,730,260
1968–1969	152,778	2,853,671

[a] During the twenty-one year period covered by Table 3, 145,507 volumes were withdrawn and sent to the Center for Research Libraries. These volumes no longer are counted in the University's collections.

United States and the British Commonwealth, together with the statutes and session laws, periodicals, digests, and classified and annotated reports of those jurisdictions; an extensive collection of the original briefs and records of cases in the United States Supreme Court; and a representative collection of the reports and opinions of the various state and federal administrative agencies. In recent years, concentration upon the field of International Law is developing an outstanding collection in that area. The cataloged books in the social sciences are supplemented by other materials such as extensive files of corporation reports, in print and microfilm, for the economist; and the massive Human Relations Area Files for the anthropologist and sociologist. The 120,000 volumes in Education are enriched by a collection of current school and college curricula normally running to over 2,000 items, by one of the most comprehensive collections of standardized tests and testing materials in the country, by a collection of continuously changed, recent textbooks numbering 9400 volumes, and by a constantly-updated collection of selected children's books published in the most recent ten-year period—a matter of about 9500 volumes.

In the Humanities, the collections are strong in American and English literature and in the modern European languages and literatures, especially German, French, and Italian. Materials for the drama in all these literatures are exceptionally well developed. Although the library had acquired some Russian material beginning early in the century, a major program to acquire materials in Slavic literature, history, and political science was begun in 1960, was greatly intensified in 1962, and by 1970 has made the library one of the major centers for Slavic resources with over 120,000 carefully-selected and painstakingly sought-out volumes. Brought to unquestionable distinction at an earlier period, but still being enriched with both current and retrospective publications, is an outstanding collection of about 80,000 volumes in Greek and Roman History, classical archaeology, philology, and literature, and classical religion and mythology. Collections serving area programs include: the Far Eastern collection, with 167,000 volumes in Chinese and 50,000 volumes in Japanese; a widely-known research collection of over 48,000 volumes on the history, philology, art, and literature of the civilizations of the ancient Near East; a rapidly-growing collection on the ancient, medieval, and contemporary Middle East; and a notable scholarly apparatus for research related to Southern Asia in the form of catalogs, tools, and staff designed to guide the reader to over 100,000 monographic volumes, 3700 serials, and 90 newspapers concerned with that region. The Art and Music collections have been developed with other major Chicago libraries in mind (the Library of the Chicago Art Institute and the music collections of the Newberry Library), and both, therefore, are more limited in early works than are the university's collections in most fields. Nevertheless, each collection has rarities and strengths that cannot be overlooked, and each now has about 45,000 carefully-selected volumes providing a solid foundation for the teaching and research programs in those subjects.

The book collections in the sciences reflect the university's focus on pure science and basic research rather than on the applications of scientific knowledge. Moreover, except in a few areas relating to the nation's space programs and nuclear technology, the collections in technology are sketchily developed—as can be expected in a university having no departments of architecture or engineering. The science libraries' holdings are of sufficient scope and depth to support the very advanced scientific research and teaching programs of the university. As in other areas, careful attention has been paid to the acquisition of the publications of learned societies and all major scientific serials. The library is also rich in the history of science.

THE SPECIAL COLLECTIONS

Enriching and extending the library's general collections are a large number of special collections, both of manuscripts and of printed works.

The collection of Medieval and Renaissance manuscripts, with some 15,000 or so letters, documents, and manuscript volumes from these two periods, includes some notable and useful materials. The largest single group of early examples are the approximately 5000 court rolls, manor rolls, muniments, inventories, letters, and other documents relating to the English lands held by Nicholas Bacon and his family. The papers run in time from the thirteenth to the seventeenth century, and have been and continue to be a rich source for research in political, social, economic, linguistic, and literary history. Of other Medieval and Renaissance manuscripts, there are four of works of Boccaccio, one of the eighty known manuscripts of the *Canterbury Tales,* manuscripts of works by Saint Jerome and by Saint Augustine, a collection of grammatical and rhetorical treatises, and an early and significant manuscript of Alberti's *De re Aedificatoria.* There are devotional books, legal works, and family records and archives. Of manuscripts of the Bible, the library holds, in its Edgar J. Goodspeed Collection, seventy Greek, Syriac, and Armenian manuscripts of the New Testament, of which the most noted is the Rockefeller-McCormick New Testament (A.D. 1265).

The nearly 3,500,000 modern manuscripts in the library represent a range and variety of interests that make the collections difficult to describe. They are strongest, perhaps, in American History, with the Reuben T. Durrett Collection (Kentucky and the Ohio River Valley); the William H. English Collection (Indiana history); the 15,000 letters in the Stephen A. Douglas Collection; and the papers of Governor Frank O. Lowden of Illinois as examples. For literary studies, the major manuscript collection consists of the office files of *Poetry* magazine from its founding in 1912 through 1956. The 70,000 items include the manuscripts and letters of almost every major poet writing in the last decades of the nineteenth century and the first half of the twentieth century. The library also has the papers of the American novelist, Robert Herrick, and is the repository for the papers of such distinguished modern authors as Saul Bellow, James T. Farrell, and John Gunther. There are two major manuscript collections relating to European history and international affairs: the Samuel N. Harper papers (over 30,000 pieces dealing with Russia in the first four decades of the twentieth century), and the Salmon O. Levinson papers (40,000 documents and letters concerned with international peace movements and particularly with events leading to the Kellogg-Briand Pact). In scientific fields, the single outstanding collection relates to nuclear fission. Here, on shelves only sixty yards from the site where man achieved the first controlled, self-sustaining nuclear chain reaction, is the largest nongovernment-held collection of manuscripts and archival materials concerning that event and its social and political aftermath. The collection includes the professional and scientific papers of Enrico Fermi and Samuel K. Allison, among others, and it houses the extensive files of the Federation of American Scientists and of several other organizations of scientists that gave their attention to major public policy issues following World War II.

The library also has a variety of important special book collections. *The Helen and Ruth Regenstein Collection of Rare Books* has brought and continues to bring to the library fine copies of the first editions of the most significant works in English and American literature. These volumes both ornament and lend research depth to resources that already are rich through possession of the *William Vaughn Moody Collection of American Authors,* and the *Harriet Monroe Collection* whose 13,000 volumes, together with an outstanding collection of "little magazines," include all poetry of significance published since 1900. The drama—English and American and to a lesser extent that of the European continent—has been a major collecting interest. The *Celia and Delia Austrian Collection* covers eighteenth century drama with particular richness. The great strength in American drama rests in large part on the *Atkinson Collection,* supported by the specialized resources of three unusual collections—the *Morton Collection,* largely unpublished prompt copies from the popular stage; the *Beyer Collection,* acting editions of the nineteenth century productions; and the *Briggs Collection,* reviews of American stage productions from 1895 to the 1930s.

Bible manuscripts have already been described, but the holdings of printed Bibles are preeminent among American university libraries. Early printed Bibles from the continent are found in the *Hengstenberg* and *American Bible Union* collections, while practically all the great English Bibles in many of their major editions are available to scholars in the *Grant Collection.*

American History has reached eminence over the years with the aid of the *Benjamin E. Gallup Memorial Fund,* supplemented by such distinguished additions as the *William E. Barton Collection* which has virtually every printed source for the study of Abraham Lincoln and his times, and the *Carter H. Harrison Collection* on early voyages and the American frontier. Collections in German language and literature are notable, particularly for the classical period from 1740 to 1832. Here, the library has the works of major and minor authors in the distinguished *Hirsch-Bernays Collection* and in the extensive *Kossman Collection* of taschenbucher, while the 15,000 nineteenth-century novels in the *Lincke Collection,* exemplifying the subliterary productions of the period, add yet another dimension to the library's resources.

Named collections also provide the chief strength of the library's resources in the history of science and medicine. The library has first and other early editions of Copernicus, Galileo, Brahe, Vesalius, and Newton, along with many other titles which, although of lesser stature, are necessary to an understanding of the history of scientific discovery. Many such works are found in the *Morris Fishbein Collection,* and among the gifts of Louis H. Silver. Special emphasis on the history of anatomy and physiology is provided by the *Mortimer Frank Collection,* and the fields of gynecology and obstetrics find major support in the *Fehling, Ahlfeld* and *Adair* collections.

STANLEY E. GWYNN

CHILDREN'S LIBRARIES AND LIBRARIANSHIP

Library service to children is the selection for and presentation of library materials to children through a community or institutional library. The community library is a tax-supported public library serving children from pre-school usually through eighth grade or at least through elementary school. The institutional library may be in an elementary school, public or private, in a hospital, orphanage, correctional institution, or social service center with its materials and services designed to serve only the special needs of its clientele.

From humble beginnings, children's services had expanded by 1950 to the point that Robert Leigh in *The Public Library in the United States* was moved to call it the "classic success in the public library movement." The basic goals of library service to children have changed little since the pioneering days of such able figures as Caroline M. Hewins, Frances Jenkins Olcott, Mary E. Dousman, Clara Whitehill Hunt, Elva S. Smith, Anne Carroll Moore, and Effie Louise Power. In her *Library Service for Children* first published in 1929 as part of a Library Curriculum Studies Series, toward the culmination of her long distinguished career, Miss Power defined the immediate purpose of the children's library to be "to provide children with good books supplemented by an inviting library environment and intelligent and sympathetic service and by these means to inspire and cultivate in children love of reading, discriminating taste in literature, and judgment and skill in the use of books as tools." We find echoes of these purposes in Harriet Long's *Rich in Treasure* where she sets forth the tenets that have become the credo of present day children's librarians: "To make a wide and varied collection of books easily and temptingly available; to give guidance to children in their choice of books and materials; to share, extend and cultivate the enjoyment of reading as a voluntary, individual pursuit; to encourage lifelong education through the use of public library resources; to help the child develop to the full his personal ability and his social understanding and to serve as a social force in the community together with other agencies concerned with the child's welfare."

While accounts of ancient libraries and, later, monastic and museum libraries of Europe have little to tell us of library service to children, we can assume that children received at least peripheral service wherever and whenever they were allowed in the company of their elders. We do know that after the Public Libraries Act in England in 1861 some public libraries had children's books which they kept behind locked doors and circulated only to children over twelve years of age. Later a new act remedied this situation by lifting the tax limitation on the amount that local authorities could spend for library service and books.

In the United States at least in some cities reading rooms were open to children almost from the beginning of the library movement. In the very early 1800s some few had circulating collections for children. We find evidence in the treasured stories of Boston bookseller and publisher Caleb Bingham who, in 1803, presented 150 titles to the town of Salisbury, Connecticut, to be used for a library for youths between the ages of nine and sixteen under the supervision of a self-perpetuating board; of the Reverend Abiel Abbott, a Unitarian minister who organized a children's library in Petersborough, New Hampshire, in 1827; and of the $100.00 bequeathed by Dr. Ebenezer Learned to West Cambridge, Massachusetts. The latter collection according to Alice Jordan's account "traveled to its first home in a wheelbarrow. Uncle Dexter (the librarian) would make hats during the week and on Saturdays open the library to children." Early Sunday School, Subscription and Fee Libraries no doubt served as a stimulus toward establishing tax-supported library service for children, but it was between 1890 and 1900 that children's libraries really got under way.

Contributing to the growth and strength of children's libraries have been the librarians themselves. Even before there were training schools for children's librarians there were a few great innovators in the library profession such as Caroline M. Hewins who saw service to children as part of the mainstream and a very important part of librarianship. For fifty years librarian of the Hartford Public Library and its forerunner the Hartford's Young Men's Institute, Miss Hewins with no guidelines to follow except her firm convictions and unerring taste, built up collections of children's books, issued quarterly lists of suggested good reading, and urged schools to become subscribers to the Young Men's Institute. When the Institute became the Public Library, Miss Hewins continued to emphasize children's books and service for children. Opening a small branch in a settlement house, she moved in and lived there for twelve years. We can imagine the enrichment the lives of the boys and girls received through reading aloud, story-telling, dramatics, and nature clubs and walks, all typical of the activities she initiated in the children's room she managed to open in 1904 in a house next door to the Hartford Public Library.

Another person of great influence in library work with children, though not a children's librarian, was Mary Wright Plummer who started the second library school in the country at Pratt Institute, Brooklyn. She was its director as well as librarian of the Pratt Institute Free Library. With a very special interest in children, she opened a children's room and appointed Anne Carroll Moore as children's librarian.

Anne Carroll Moore went from Pratt Institute in 1906 to the New York Public Library to become the superintendent of the newly formed Department of Work with Children and there she remained for thirty-five years, her name almost legend at home and abroad. As an unparalleled critic, writer, and lecturer, her influence embraced children, librarians, authors, and illustrators. Her great gift for "festival" set a pattern for "Bringing children and books *happily* together."

A Canadian librarian whose influence has not only reached children's librarians of the United States but throughout the English-speaking world is Lillian Smith, formerly librarian of Boys and Girls House, Toronto Public Library. Her book the *Unreluctant Years* is a source of inspiration and a guide in book selection. In 1949 Edgar Osborne, librarian of Derbyshire County, England, gave the Osborne Collection of Early Children's Books to the Toronto Boys and Girls House as a memorial to his wife Mabel, a successful producer of children's plays and in recognition of its outstanding work with children and young people, another tribute to Miss Smith.

Although elementary school libraries had their beginnings earlier in religious schools, one room rural schools, or in classroom collections, they have, until recently, developed toward their potential more slowly than children's services in public libraries. The same general philosophy, however, is shared in all children's libraries: the recognition of the child as an individual human being with the right to read and use all types of materials according to his interests and needs. The growth of all children's libraries has been influenced by the development of a vast body of children's literature, changing attitudes toward children, changing emphases in education and, in recent years, the development of social consciousness.

Both school and public library children's departments operate within the philosophy of their parent institutions. The public library concerns itself with the individual child as a voluntary borrower who is motivated to use books and other library materials for whatsoever reason.

Library services for children are organized in a variety of ways in public libraries depending for the most part on the size of the system. Large cities may have a central children's room, extensive collections and children's departments in regional branches, children's divisions in branch libraries, and bookmobile service. County and multicounty or systems libraries may be similarly organized. In such an organizational pattern the chief responsibility for children's services is centered in a coordinator who may serve as a line officer in relation to the central children's room and as staff in relation to branch and other agencies. In cities served by a single library there is usually a children's room or division with a children's librarian in charge and additional staff according to need. In the small community library, more often than not, the librarian serves both children and adults. More and more small community libraries joining systems enjoy the benefit of a coordinator or consultant from the headquarters library.

The children's librarian is first of all a librarian and part of the administrative staff of the library. He must have the same basic education in library principles, and understanding of and interest in the whole profession of librarianship. The specialist in library work with children must have a background in child psychology and an understanding of educational programs, a wide knowledge of children's books and other library materials, as well as a sincere and unsentimental interest in the child as an individual. Since the children's librarian also works with adults who are concerned with children, it is also necessary that he have facility in speaking to groups and in working with individual adults from many child-centered agencies. The knowledge and skills for children's librarianship are acquired through specialized professional training and strengthened by experience.

The first library to departmentalize children's services was the Carnegie Library in Pittsburgh. As an outgrowth of an in-service training class for the library's own children's staff a Training School for Children's Librarians was opened in 1900, the first in the world. Today nearly all of the fifty accredited graduate library schools offer courses in library work with children. In addition many colleges and universities give undergraduate courses and although these courses are usually structured for school librarians, in some public libraries one finds children's librarians who received their training in these undergraduate programs. Strong contributions have been made to children's librarianship by such well known instructors as Frances Henne, Anne Carroll Moore, Elizabeth Nesbitt, Harriet Long, Elizabeth Gross Kilpatrick, Frances Clarke Sayers, Dorothy M. Broderick, Marie Hostetter, Alice Lohrer, Margaret Hodges, and others not only in the number of students they have inspired but also through their lecturing and writing for a wide audience in the library profession.

Children's librarians have long been defining their task as "bringing books and children together." A myriad of techniques and skills are needed for the accomplishment of this service. Next in importance to the staff in a children's library, headed by a professional children's librarian, is the collection of books selected by that staff. The selection starts with a book selection policy adopted by the board of trustees as part of the over-all policy of the library. The policy states the standards of book selection but the children's librarian must bring to bear all her knowledge of children, their interests, and their needs with special thought for the educational program of the community and availability of books from other sources. Other library materials are considered in the same light. Decisions must be made qualitatively and quantitatively. If the children's department staff does not catalog its own books, the children's librarian often makes decisions on classifications and subject headings.

An "inviting library atmosphere" is considered even more important today than when Miss Power stated it as a goal in 1929. Newer children's libraries are bright with color, well lighted, carpeted, and comfortably arranged. Attractive exhibits draw attention to books, records, and events.

Reading guidance through contact with the individual child is considered the most important work of the children's librarian. The librarian introduces the new borrower to the library; locates reference material for his needs; helps further his hobbies; considers his maturing interests; answers the question "Would I like this book?" or "Do you know a book I would like?" He is intuitively alert to the child who does not ask for help but who he knows would welcome such an offer.

Libraries have a variety of group programs for children (see Figures 1 and 2). Children's librarians visit the schools, give auditorium programs, or give book talks in individual classrooms. School classes visit the library where they are

FIGURE 1. *A family story hour in Sioux City, Iowa, is culminated with live media. (Courtesy McCarty, Sioux City Journal.)*

FIGURE 2. *Baltimore County Library takes advantage of foreign visitors for an international program.* (*Photo by Robert L. Galinsky.*)

given orientation in the location and use of materials and are introduced to books through talks or story-telling. Ongoing story hours for all ages are held in many libraries. Pre-school story hours have become increasingly popular in recent years. Some libraries hold book discussion clubs for several age groups. Many have special interest clubs for such subjects as Science, Poetry, Puppetry, or Creative Dramatics. Television and radio are utilized for book discussions and story-telling programs.

Book lists are prepared and used not only to attract readers to the library but also as a supplement to individual reading guidance in order to further the child's independence in exploration and choice of reading.

Since the public library is responsible to the citizens of all ages, naturally service to children is community related and children's librarians perform an effective liaison function. Parents can rightly expect help in building their home libraries for children and advice on the best approach in choosing encyclopedias and other reference books for home use. Book stores and children's libraries cooperate to their mutual benefit. Boy Scout, Girl Scout, Campfire Girl, and 4-H Club leaders welcome the children's librarian's contribution to their planning and training programs. The children's librarian needs to know the goals and programs of all organizations related to children, from Sunday School to the Mayor's Committee on Juvenile Delinquency. There are meetings to attend, talks to be given, and bibliographies of helpful books to be prepared for both the leaders and the children involved.

In cities where the most satisfying and complete library service is available to children, the school and public library departments cooperate in defining responsibilities, sometimes having joint book selection meetings, supplementing each others' programs and keeping in close communication on all matters pertaining to materials, service, and trends. While the federal funds and development of school library standards have catapulted school libraries to the foreground in recent years, there are still many places without professionl elementary librarians and little or no service within the school. In spite of a firm conviction that the role of the public library is that of serving the individual borrower, public libraries are continuing in many instances to supplement educational programs with pertinent materials. However, with the present-day broader concept of education stimulating independent study, the public library is well situated and within its scope to carry out this function with the individual.

The organizational pattern of the Children's Services Division of ALA, growing with the times, has had committee studies in all areas related to children and has provided new patterns of service for children. The most notable recent example is the involvement of children's libraries with the disadvantaged. Many cities have assigned special "Inner-City" or "Community" librarians who have developed dramatic programs to bring children and books together.

The Children's Book Council provides a chance for publishers, editors, and children's librarians to work together not only in providing good books for children but in publicizing them as well. Book fairs, a calendar of book news, and posters for Book Week available to libriaries are provided by the Children's Book Council.

The growth of reviewing media and other professional literature has served to strengthen children's services. *The Library Journal* with its midmonthly issue now embracing a special section for children's and school librarians, and the *Horn Book Magazine* solely devoted to children's books and reading are a source of book reviews, inspiration, and information on many aspects of children's services. The American Library Association's *Booklist and Subscription Books Bulletin* and the Chicago University's *Bulletin of the Center for Children's Books* are other sources of book reviewing on which children's librarians depend.

The children's materials in the Library of Congress have been made more accessible and useful by the appointment of Virginia Haviland, an experienced librarian as Head of the Children's Book Section. Similarly, children's services have benefited by the appointment of Anne Pellowski as Director of the United States Committee for UNICEF Children's Cultural Information Center. Miss Pellowski is keeping children's librarians in close touch with materials from and about United Nations countries. Her monumental book *The World of Children's Literature* carried out under grants from the Fulbright Commission and the Council of Library Resources is a bibliography, world-wide in scope, of works relating to the whole field of children's literature and public and school library service for children around the world.

Libraries built especially for children have benefited from the interest of influential individuals in many parts of the world. Well known examples are L'Heure Joyeuse in Paris, opened in 1924, and the striking and well designed Children's Library in its own building close to the main library of the Ghana Library Board in Accra.

Frederic G. Melcher, beginning in 1918 when he became editor of the *Publishers'*

Weekly, comes readily to mind with gratitude in connection with library service to children. Devoted to the cause of children and books, Mr. Melcher attended meetings with librarians, spoke eloquently and enthusiastically about children's books, co-founded Children's Book Week, and instituted and donated the annual awards known as the John Newbery and Randolph Caldecott medals. The Children's Services Division of the American Library Association made him a life member and established a library school scholarship honoring his name.

Awards such as the John Newbery and the Randolph Caldecott medals have added respect for children's books as well as providing criteria for judging their values. The Laura Ingalls Wilder award established in 1954 gives an opportunity to honor an author for his entire contribution to children's literature. An award to the best translation of a foreign children's book has recently been established and named for Mildred L. Batchelder, distinguished children's librarian who served many years as executive secretary for the Children's Services Division.

The International Board on Books for Young People, which awards the Hans Christian Andersen prize, publishes *Bookbird,* and concerns itself with bringing international understanding through children's books, is furthering the communication between children's libraries around the world.

International ties are also strengthened by the Children's Division of the International Federation of Libraries which meets in yearly conference.

Opinion is divided on the future of library services for children in the public library. There are those who feel that children's librarians will continue to be attracted to school library service and that school libraries can give all needed service to children. It seems more likely that good school libraries will stimulate an interest in children and create a need for more sources of material which they will seek on their own. The children will expect the newer media, e.g., films, filmstrips, and recordings which they have become expert in using in school, to be available in public libraries for their individual personal use. The public library is by nature the only agency equipped to reach all the children during pre-school years. With better school libraries, strong in reference and curriculum-related materials, the public library children's services can devote more time to the preschool child, to the handicapped, to the retarded, and to the disadvantaged. They can develop ways of reaching adults who need to be made aware of the importance of children's reading.

If children's libraries continue to improve to more nearly meet the standards set by the profession, if children's librarians continue to revaluate these standards, if they recognize the challenge of today's world with its expanding knowledge and automation, we can be assured that the public library children's room will continue to be the place "to cultivate the enjoyment of reading as an individual and voluntary pursuit."

FLORENCE W. BUTLER

CHILDREN'S LITERATURE

Literature for children is a dynamic field of challenging and creative materials, constantly changing in emphasis and growing in volume. Since the mid-eighteenth century there has been a continuous effort to provide a literature written especially for the enjoyment and pleasure of children. With the passing years a few of these books capture the imagination and are in demand by each successive generation, while some titles not quite so universal in appeal are enjoyed for a span of time and then forgotten.

The period from 1925 to 1940 has been referred to by Dora Smith (*1*) as the "golden age" of children's literature. Ruth Hill Viguers (*2*) added fifteen years to make it 1920 to 1950. If those were the golden years, then 1950 to 1970 was surely the "diamond age," a period when many new authors and illustrators entered the field and they, along with the established ones, created more outstanding books of beauty and varied themes than at any other period in history. Yet when viewing the over-all output, one conclusion is inescapable: the percentage of worthwhile books produced each year falls far below the halfway mark. In each period there is an inevitable flow of series of books with formula plots that offer children nothing but hair-raising adventure, as well as books that talk down to them or that explain everything, leaving nothing to the imagination.

A sure-fire remedy to the inconsequential must be those people—authors, artists, publishers, editors—who make a sincere effort to produce quality literature. Then, there must be parents, teachers, and librarians who insist that the best in literature is accessible to children. The library profession has been reminded that by its purchases it is responsible for what is published. Books stay in print because of demand.

In the late nineteenth century Caroline Hewins made an appeal to all librarians to give youth the best in literature; she compiled book lists and encouraged parents to read everything they gave to their children. Since that time many librarians, teachers, and laymen have taken giant strides to provide quality literature for children.

Books of excellence are available for children. Only those with simplicity and truth; wonder and imagination; excellence of style; variety in subject matter; books with illustrations that enhance the story; books that speak to all ages; books that leave one richer for having read them are worthy of childhood.

History of Children's Literature

Literature written especially for children had an early beginning but limited success as far as the child was concerned, for most of the books were didactically written to teach the morals, manners, and religion that adults wanted them to know. Most of the stories or tales enjoyed by children which have come down through the centuries were those sung by minstrels and bards in the castles or those told orally by grandmothers in the peasants' cottages.

Scribes, monks, and learned men wrote and copied manuscripts for children; however, the invention of printing made possible more books, for example, *Babees' Boke, or, A Lytle Reporte of how Young People should behave* (1475). This book, done in prose and poetry, dealt with such subjects as manners at home and at church, courtship and marriage, and was generally for young people rather than the child. Several of the chapters in this book were titles of earlier manuscripts, including *Aristotle's ABC* (1430) and *The Boke of Curtasye* (1430–1440).

William Caxton, the first English printer, contributed to children's literature very early in his career by publishing *A Book of Curtesye* (1477) and *The Knight of the Tower* (1484). He also translated and published adult books that have remained children's favorites, such as Sir Thomas Malory's *Morte D'Arthur* (1485), *Aesop's Fables* (1484), and *Reynard the Fox* (1481).

About the middle of the fifteenth century the hornbook had its origin in England (see Figure 1). Even though sizes varied, the true hornbook was generally

FIGURE 1. *The hornbook, an early textbook for children, originated during the fifteenth century. Facsimile by Horn Book, Inc.*

a 2¾ × 5 in. paddle-shaped board with a printed page of vellum or parchment, covered by a clear sheet of transparent horn. This "instructive book" contained the alphabet, a combination of vowels and consonants, "In the Name of the Father and of the Son, and of the Holy Ghost, Amen," and the Lord's Prayer. It was available in wood that could be afforded by most children, but more luxurious copies could be purchased in leather, ivory, or silver filigree inlaid with satin. The content of the hornbook did not vary until it reached America, at which time the cross of Christ was omitted and the metal rim was left open at the top so a new lesson could be inserted. After the hornbook came other teaching devices such as primers, rhymed alphabets, and battledores. *The Royal Primer* in England and *The New England Primer* in America were important textbooks during the seventeenth and eighteenth centuries. They contained a rhyming alphabet with representative woodcuts, words with a variety of syllables, prayers, hymns, and catechisms. Millions of copies were sold of each. One of the favorite writers among adults who believed in ruling the child with a firm hand was James Janeway. His *A Token for Children, an exact account of the Conversion, Holy and Exemplary Lives and Joyful Deaths of Several Young Children* (London, 1671– 1672) was first published in America in 1700; it appeared later, according to A. S. W. Rosenbach, with Cotton Mather's *A Token for Children of New England. Or, Some Examples of Children, in whom the Fear of God was remarkably Budding before they died, in several Parts of New England. Preserved and published for the Encouragement of Piety in other Children* appended to it. The lengthy title and its implications were characteristic of the period.

Published in 1678 was John Bunyan's *Pilgrim's Progress,* an allegory on the development of the human soul. A very special edition for today's children is a retelling by Mary Godolphin in 1884 which Robert Lawson skillfully illustrated in 1939. Two other books written for adults that deserve mention as children's classics are Daniel Defoe's *Robinson Crusoe,* published in 1719, and *Gulliver's Travels* by Jonathan Swift which appeared in 1726.

One of the most beloved books to come out of the late seventeenth century was a French publication, *Les Contes de ma Mère l'Oye* (Tales of Mother Goose), which appeared in 1697 and was translated into English by Robert Samber in 1729. This collection of eight fairy tales contained some of the favorites of all times. Opinions differ as to whether it was Charles Perrault or his son Pierre who recorded "Cinderella," "Sleeping Beauty in the Woods," "Little Red Riding Hood," and "Puss in Boots" told at the Court of Louis XIV. Marcia Brown chose the Perrault version for her beautifully illustrated *Cinderella* and *Puss in Boots.*

The Arabian Nights, or a Thousand and One Nights, Scheherazade's tales of Arabia and the East, was translated into French by Antoine Galland from a Syrian manuscript in 1704 and by 1712 it had appeared in English. Originally for adults, it contained such children's favorites as "Aladdin and the Wonderful Lamp," "Ali Baba and the Forty Thieves," "Sindbad the Sailor," and "The Flying Carpet."

Isaac Watts' *Divine and Moral Songs for Children* was published in 1715. In it were familiar songs and rhymes that showed a love for children and a desire to introduce them to a God who loved them.

A most memorable person in the history of children's literature was John Newbery. Not only did he advocate books that would bring joy to children, but he wrote, published, and sold them with great enthusiasm. His first book was *A Little Pretty Pocket-Book* (1744), an attractive blue and gold book, 3¾ × 2½ in. in size (see Figure 2). In it Newbery evidenced his desire to please children by including letters to Little Master Tommy and Pretty Miss Polly, ostensibly written by Jack the Giant Killer praising them for their good behavior at home, school,

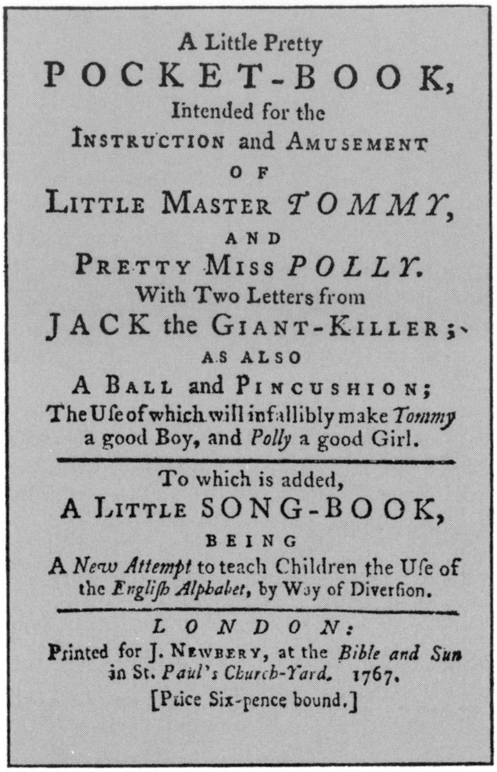

A Little Pretty
POCKET-BOOK,
Intended for the
INSTRUCTION and AMUSEMENT
OF
LITTLE MASTER *TOMMY*,
AND
PRETTY MISS *POLLY*.
With Two Letters from
JACK the GIANT-KILLER;
AS ALSO
A BALL and PINCUSHION;
The Ufe of which will infallibly make *Tommy*
a good Boy, and *Polly* a good Girl.

To which is added,
A LITTLE SONG-BOOK,
BEING
A *New Attempt* to teach Children the Ufe of
the *Englifh Alphabet*, by Way of Diverfion.

LONDON:
Printed for J. NEWBERY, at the *Bible and Sun*
in St. *Paul's Church-Yard*. 1767.
[Price Six-pence bound.]

FIGURE 2. *The very descriptive title page was typical for books of the period. From* A Little Pretty Pocket–Book, *printed for J. Newbery, at the Bible and Sun in St. Paul's Church-Yard, 1767. First published in 1744. From the facsimile by Harcourt, Brace & World, 1967.*

and play. It contained rhymed games, then carefully explained the moral or rule of life as it applied for each game. Another book for the amusement of children was *The Lilliputian Magazine,* issued as a volume in 1752, bound in Dutch-paper boards, published at Mr. Newbery's shop. Newbery constantly encouraged his friends to write for children. An example was Oliver Goldsmith, to whom many authorities attribute *The Renowned History of Little Goody Two Shoes, Otherwise called Mrs. Margery Two Shoes,* perhaps the first book of fiction done solely for children, published in 1765. This small paperback book, originally 4 × 2¾ in., had a fast-moving plot but was dominated by contemporary social conditions of rural England. While no copy is extant, John Newbery is said to have collected and published *Mother Goose's Melody, or Sonnets for the Cradle, 1760–65,* considered by many authorities as the first English collection of nursery rhymes for children. One can almost hear this man who wanted to bring joy into the lives of children repeating "Sing a Song of Sixpence." The American Library Association chose to honor the Newbery name with the children's book award, given annually since

1922 to the author of the most distinguished book for children published during
the preceding year.

During the seventeenth and eighteenth centuries the very popular chapbooks,
or "penny histories," were published and peddled for a sixpence on the streets by
chapmen. These poorly constructed, adventurous ballads, folk tales, and hero
stories were from sixteen to sixty-four folded pages. Many of the *Arabian Nights'*
tales were published in this form.

Another type of book with an enviable sales record was the three-leaved cardboard battledore first produced in 1746 by Benjamin Collins, a Salisbury bookseller
and associate of Newbery (see Figure 3). It contained the alphabet, short
moralistic stories, and numerous woodcuts.

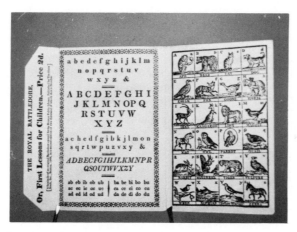

FIGURE 3. *The three-leaved cardboard battledore contained the alphabet, short moralistic
stories, and numerous woodcuts. Facsimile by Horn Book, Inc.*

In 1762 Jean-Jacques Rousseau expressed a shockingly new philosophy in his
Émile. He believed that children should be permitted to live vigorously out-of-
doors, learn from experiences and activities "free of all books except *Robinson
Crusoe*," carefully guided by a patient adult. Rousseau's philosophy for over a
century exerted an influence on many authors, including Thomas Day, Anna
Laetitia Barbauld, Sarah Trimmer, and Maria Edgeworth. They chose subjects
with child appeal, but often developed them in a painfully didactic manner, although admittedly Maria Edgeworth was a more creative author than the other
three.

Many nineteenth century authors successfully produced creative works for
children by consciously trying to bring joy into their lives. Charles and Mary Lamb
produced *Tales from Shakespeare* in 1807, the first children's version of Shakespeare's plays. The following year their *Adventures of Ulysses* was issued. Johann
R. Wyss, noted Swiss author, is remembered for *Swiss Family Robinson* (1813)
which was translated into English in 1814. Originally written for his children in

And the Squirrel well pleas'd such Diversions to see,
Mounted high over head, and look'd down from a Tree.
Then out came the Spider, with Finger so fine,
To shew his Dexterity on the tight line.

FIGURE 4. *This fascinating illustration for a nursery rhyme from* The Butterfly's Ball, *1807, by William Roscoe is only one of the many found in* Pages and Pictures from Forgotten Children's Books, *by Andrew W. Tuer. Published by Charles Scribner's Sons, 1899.*

1822, Clement C. Moore's *A Visit from St. Nicholas* first appeared anonymously in the Troy (New York) *Sentinel,* December 23, 1823. Outstanding illustrators such as Arthur Rackham, Jessie Wilcox Smith, Leonard Weisgard, and Brian Wildsmith have added zest to this favorite Christmas poem with their illustrations. *Popular Stories* by Wilhelm and Jacob Grimm was translated into English and illustrated by George Cruikshank in 1823. The brothers Grimm were philologists who sought to preserve the language of the peasants from whom they collected these folk tales. The *Fairy Tales* of Hans Christian Andersen was translated and published in England in 1846 (see Figure 5). This shy Danish writer gained worldwide fame for his 168 fairy tales. Edward Lear's *Book of Nonsense* also made its appearance in 1846. The inventive language of these limericks excites children as much today as it did a century ago. An Edward Lear *ABC* holograph illustrated manuscript was unearthed and published in 1965. One of the notable books of 1968 was Edward Lear's *The Scroobious Pip* completed by Ogden Nash and beautifully illustrated by Nancy E. Burkert. Other well-known English authors, who, though noted primarily for their adult books, also wrote titles enjoyed by children include Charles Dickens (*Christmas Carol* and *Magic Fishbone*), William Makepeace Thackeray (*The Rose and the Ring*), and Sir Walter Scott (*Tales of a Grandfather*).

Finally, in 1827 appeared the first book written and published in America for American children, *The Tales of Peter Parley About America,* part of a long series by Samuel Goodrich, written under the pseudonym of Peter Parley. Jacob Abbott, a New England author, started his prolific writing career in 1834 with a

FIGURE 5. *Maurice Sendak revitalized this familiar tale of "The Steadfast Tin Soldier." From the book,* Seven Tales *by Hans Christian Andersen, translated from the Danish by Eva Le Gallienne, illustrated by Maurice Sendak. Picture copyright* © *1959 by Maurice Sendak. Reprinted with permission of Harper & Row, Publishers.*

series about Rollo. Though both authors were pedantic, their travel books played a role, though minor, in American literature. On the other hand some American writers who made a lasting contribution to children's literature were Washington Irving ("The Legend of Sleepy Hollow" and "Rip Van Winkle" in *The Sketch Book,* 1819 and 1820), Nathaniel Hawthorne (*The Wonder Book,* 1852, and *Tanglewood Tales,* 1853), and Henry W. Longfellow (*The Song of Hiawatha,* 1855, and *Paul Revere's Ride,* 1860).

In the mid-century, the sea stories *Peter Simple, Mr. Midshipman Easy,* and *Masterman Ready* by Captain Frederick Marryat (1792–1848); the adventure tales *Young Fur Traders* and *Gorilla Hunters* by Robert Michael Ballantyne (1825–1894); and the school stories *Tom Brown's School Days* and *Tom Brown at Oxford* by Thomas Hughes (1822–1896) were widely read.

Three English authors whose writings for children began in the nineteenth century and were very successful in the United States in the early twentieth century were Juliana H. (Gatty) Ewing (1841–1885), Mary Louisa (Stewart) Molesworth (1839–1921), and Charlotte Mary Yonge (1823–1901). Mrs. Ewing, a prolific writer, was very popular for her Queen's treasures series, among which were *Jackanapes* (1884) and *Brownies and Other Stories* (1870). Mrs. Molesworth, popular for both fairy tales and realistic stories, wrote *The Cuckoo Clock* (1877), and *The Tapestry Room* (1879) and *Carrots, Just a Little Boy* (1876). Miss Yonge, editor of the *Monthly Packet,* a British children's magazine, had many books published in this country, some of which later were illustrated by Marguerite De Angeli, namely, *Dove in the Eagle's Nest, Prince and the Page,* and *Little Duke.*

In 1865, *Alice's Adventures in Wonderland,* by Lewis Carroll, pseudonym for Charles Lutwidge Dodgson, was published. It was followed by *Through the Looking Glass* in 1871. This new dimension in writing proved that children's books did not have to be moralistic. It was truly the beginning of a new era in writing for children. Also in 1865, *Hans Brinker, or the Silver Skates,* by Mary Mapes Dodge was published, followed by Louisa May Alcott's *Little Women* in 1868. Popular American writers for girls in the latter part of the nineteenth century were Susan Warner (1819–1885), who wrote *The Wide, Wide World* and *Queechy* under the pen name of Elizabeth Wetherell; Martha Finley (1828–1909), also known as "Martha Farquharson" (the Gaelic for Finley), who did *Elsie Dinsmore* and twenty-five sequels, and Sarah Chauncey Woolsey (1835–1905), pseudonym "Susan Coolidge," who wrote *What Katy Did* and its sequels. Harriet Lothrop (1844–1924), pen name "Margaret Sidney," wrote *Five Little Peppers and How They Grew* series, which began in 1880. Boys at this time were devouring the adventure stories of William Taylor Adams (1822–1897), pseudonym "Oliver Optic," Charles Austin Fosdick (1842–1915), pseudonym "Harry Castlemon," and Horatio Alger (1834–1899). The historical adventure tales *Under Drake's Flag* and *With Clive in India* by the English author George Alfred Henty (1832–1902) were widely read on both sides of the Atlantic Ocean. Far more lasting contributions now considered "classic" are exemplified by the following list:

1871	*At the Back of the North Wind,* George MacDonald
1872	*Sing-Song,* Christina Rossetti
1876	*The Adventures of Tom Sawyer,* Mark Twain (Samuel Clemens)
1877	*Black Beauty,* Anna Sewell
1879	*Under the Window,* Kate Greenaway
1880	*The Peterkin Papers,* Lucretia Hale
1880	*Boy's King Arthur,* Sidney Lanier
1883	*Treasure Island,* Robert Louis Stevenson
1883	*Nights with Uncle Remus,* Joel Chandler Harris
1883	*The Merry Adventures of Robin Hood,* Howard Pyle
1884	*Heidi,* Johanna Spyri (first English translation)
1885	*The Adventures of Huckleberry Finn,* Mark Twain
1886	*Little Lord Fauntleroy,* Frances H. Burnett
1888	*Otto of the Silver Hand,* Howard Pyle
1892	*The Adventures of Pinocchio,* Carlo Lorenzini (first English translation)
1894	*The Jungle Book,* Rudyard Kipling
1899	*The Treasure Seekers,* Edith Nesbit Bland

History of Illustrations

The history of illustrated books for children parallels the history of children's literature. Even the chapbooks, battledores, and primers had small drawings frequently done in woodcuts. The first picture book conceived for children was *Orbis Sensualium Pictus* (The Visible World in Pictures) in 1657 (see Figure 6). In this John Amos Comenius attempted to present the whole realm of knowledge to children as he meticulously named and represented each object in the contemporary world of children. Thomas Bewick (1753–1828), the renowned English engraver, is noted for his intricate work in children's books. William Blake (1757–

FIGURE 6. *Comenius carefully numbered each item in his attempt to give children a view of the outside world. From the* Orbis Sensualium Pictus *of John Amos Comenius (1657).*

1827) worked with copperplate engravings and water colors, and in some instances engraved both text and illustrations. *Songs of Innocence,* which he wrote, illustrated, and bound especially for children, was an example of his many talents. However, these were isolated instances. In the nineteenth century many English illustrators made an effective contribution to children's books. George Cruikshank (1792–1878) illustrated many folk tales for children, making his fairies, elves, and gnomes come alive. His illustrations for the Grimms' *Popular Stories* may be considered the first modern picture book for children. Sir John Tenniel (1820–1914) had attained some recognition in illustrating *Aesop's Fables* and *The Arabian Nights,* but he achieved fame for his art work in *Alice's Adventures in Wonderland* and *Through the Looking Glass.* Arthur Hughes (1832–1915) throughout his long and fruitful career did many beautiful black and white pictures for children's books, but he is best remembered for illustrating George MacDonald's *At the Back of the North Wind* and *The Princess and the Goblin.* Randolph Caldecott (1846–1886), Walter Crane (1845–1915), and Kate Greenaway (1846–1901) were known for their color as well as black and white picture books for children.

Caldecott was able to communicate with children through his imaginative illustrations that have an endless appeal. There is an evident sense of humor in his drawings of both animals and people, but none are more charming than those for "Hey Diddle Diddle" (see Figure 7). This man is honored in America by the annual Caldecott medal which is awarded to the artist who has illustrated the most distinguished American picture book for children during the preceding year. Walter Crane who used flat, primitive colors and a very decorative style, illustrated many books, including well-known folk tales, shilling toy books, and a picture book series. Kate Greenaway, famed for her English gardens with clipped hedges and ivy-grown walls, has her prim childen, attired in hats and bonnets, as the center of attention. She is particularly remembered for her books of poetry, alphabet books, and *Mother Goose, or the Old Nursery Rhymes*. Edmund Evans, English printer, pioneered in color illustrations, particularly for children's books. He recognized the ability of these illustrators and produced many of their works. Frederick Warne Company also published the books of Caldecott, Crane, and Greenaway, many of which are still available with the original illustrations.

At the turn of the century two very successful English illustrators were Leslie Brooke (1862–1940) and Arthur Rackham (1867–1939). Brooke is best known in America for charming illustrations of old nursery classics such as the "Three Bears" and the "Three Little Pigs" in *Golden Goose Book,* the nursery rhymes in *Ring O' Roses* and his own "Johnny Crow" books. Rackham, a very prolific and talented illustrator, used water color as well as black silhouettes in his grotesque and dramatic compositions. He illustrated such books as *Wind in the Willows, English Fairy Tales,* Poe's *Tales of Mystery and Imagination,* Lamb's *Tales from Shakespeare, Mother Goose,* and Dickens' *Christmas Carol.* Among other early twentieth century English illustrators were Beatrix Potter (1866–1943), who

FIGURE 7. *Caldecott's illustrations come alive in his "A Frog He Would A-Wooing Go."* From The Hey Diddle Diddle Picture Book, *by Randolph Caldecott. Reproduced by permission of the publisher, Frederick Warne & Co., n.d.*

beautifully pictured in water color her small animals, and Ernest Shepard (1879–), who illustrated A. A. Milne's *Winnie-the-Pooh, The House at Pooh Corner, When We Were Very Young* and *Now We Are Six,* as well as Kenneth Grahame's *Wind in the Willows* and *The Reluctant Dragon.*

Howard Pyle (1853–1911), American author and illustrator, set a new and universally lauded standard with his accurate detailing in costume and historical setting (see Figure 8). He is particularly noted for his heroic black and white pictures in *Robin Hood, King Arthur,* and *Otto of the Silver Hand.* However, *Book of Pirates* has fascinating colored illustrations from his works originally published in *Harper's Magazine.* Among Pyle's students were Jessie Wilcox Smith (1863–1935), Newell C. Wyeth (1882–1945), and Maxfield Parrish (1870–1966). Mrs. Smith is remembered for illustrations of *Little Mother Goose,* Samuel Crothers' *Children of Dickens,* and Stevenson's *A Child's Garden of Verses.* Wyeth, who eventually rivaled his teacher, is known for his three-dimensional, heroic pictures of the many Scribner's classics such as *King Arthur, Robinson Crusoe,* and *Rip Van Winkle.* Maxfield Parrish's rich, luminous colors, especially blue, had great charm for children of the period. He is best remembered for his illustrations of *The Arabian Nights* and Eugene Field's *Poems of Childhood.*

FIGURE 8. *"The poor man welcomes Saint Christopher to his house." From* The Wonder Clock, *by Howard Pyle. Published by Harper and Brothers, 1915.*

Special and Rare Collections

There are many special collections of early and rare books for children which have enabled researchers to study first hand the development of children's literature. These collections may include all the works of an author or illustrator on a particular subject or type of literature, or be limited to certain volumes within a period. One of the most outstanding collections of early American children's books was assembled by A. S. W. Rosenbach. The approximately 4000 volumes are a part of the Rare Book Department of the Free Library of Philadelphia. In *Early American Children's Books, 1682–1836* (*3*), Dr. Rosenbach traces the bibliographical history of 816 items in his collection. Now housed with the Rosenbach books are early hornbooks, many first editions, including those of Kate Greenaway, Beatrix Potter, and Arthur Rackham and publications of the American Sunday School Union.

Edgar Osborne, English bibliophile and librarian, in 1949 presented his collection of early children's books to the Toronto Public Library. *The Osborne Collection of Early Children's Books 1566–1910* (*4*), catalogs approximately 3000 volumes gleaned from the many titles in the collection to describe and trace the history of children's books. Osborne and his wife started the collection as a hobby to preserve books they fondly remembered as children.

Subject Collections, compiled by Lee Ash and Denis Lorenz (*5*), and *Subject Collections in Children's Literature,* edited by Carolyn W. Field (*6*), provide directory information to a variety of specialized children's book collections, the latter including private collections.

Twentieth Century

Literature for children has reached a new dimension in the twentieth century; however, the first fifty years, marked by two wars and an economic depression, were less productive in children's books than the last two decades. The fifties and sixties, particularly, witnessed the production of a wide variety of books which resulted from a prosperous economy, technical developments in printing processes making possible the manufacture of more beautiful books, the translation of much worthy foreign literature for children, and an increasing awareness of the child's needs and interests.

Although several thousand juvenile books are published annually in the United States, only a small segment can be regarded as noteworthy. Those who work with children and books are aware of the fine publications offered boys and girls of today, the well-written, beautifully illustrated books that go far toward establishing worthy lifetime reading habits.

The twentieth century opened with the appearance of Helen Bannerman's beloved *Little Black Sambo* (1900), followed in succession by a remarkable parade: Rudyard Kipling's *Just So Stories* (1902), Beatrix Potter's *Peter Rabbit*

(1903), Leslie Brooke's *Johnny Crow's Garden* (1903), Kenneth Grahame's *Wind In the Willows* (1908), Sir James Barrie's *Peter Pan and Wendy* (1911), and A. A. Milne's *When We Were Very Young* (1924), *Winnie-the-Pooh* (1926), and *Now We Are Six* (1927). These are all British writers, yet the books are so completely a part of the American child's literature that one never stops to consider where the books were first published. This detail, however, is not the complete picture. To survey children's literature in America today is to observe that authors and illustrators from all parts of the world have lent their diverse talents and experiences to enrich the field. Hendrik Willem Van Loon came from Holland to the United States in 1903 where he made a tremendous contribution with his factual books of history, geography, and biography. His first children's book was *History with a Match* (1917), followed by *The Story of Mankind* (1921), winner of the first Newbery award. Padraic Colum, Irish author, arrived in New York in 1914, where he immediately began writing for a children's page in the *New York Tribune*. Willy Pogány, Hungarian-born artist, became acquainted with Colum and a collaboration resulted in *The King of Ireland's Son* (1916). Kate Douglas Wiggin's career began in 1888 with *The Birds' Christmas Carol;* her popular *Rebecca of Sunnybrook Farm,* one of America's bestsellers, was published in 1903. *Little Lord Fauntleroy* was Frances Hodgson Burnett's first success appearing in 1886; her very popular *Secret Garden* was published in 1909.

Ernest Thompson Seton, Canadian-born author, achieved immediate success at the age of 37 with the publication of *Wild Animals I Have Known* (1898), followed by *Biography of a Grizzly* (1900). Jack London's dog story, the popular and endearing *Call of the Wild,* was published in 1903.

Elmer Boyd Smith wrote the very American *Pocahontas and Captain John Smith* in 1906, though he is better known for his picture books *The Farm* and *Chicken World,* both published in 1910. John Bennett's *Master Skylark* (1897) and *Barnaby Lee* (1902) are excellent British historical fiction, while Joseph Altsheler's *The Horseman of the Plains* (1910) and *The Guns of Bull Run* (1914) were popular historical adventures of America. Cornelia Meigs' *Kingdom of the Winding Road* (1915) launched her long and successful career. She is best known for her historical novels, two of which were runners-up for the Newbery awards, and *Invincible Louisa,* the life of Louisa May Alcott, which did win the coveted award in 1934.

Storyteller and author, Ruth Sawyer's career in writing for children started with *This Way to Christmas* (1916). The following year Dorthea Canfield Fisher's *Understood Betsy* appeared and in 1920 Stephen Meader's *Black Buccaneer* was published.

Hugh Lofting's "Doctor Dolittle" series originated in 1920. In 1923 his *Voyages of Doctor Dolittle* was chosen as the Newbery winner. Charles B. Hawes wrote *Mutineers* (1920), *Great Quest* (1921), and *Dark Frigate* (1923), the Newbery winner of 1924.

Margery Clark's *Poppy Seed Cakes,* illustrated by Maud and Miska Petersham, was published in 1924. The following year Margery Bianco's *Little Wooden Doll* appeared, followed by *Velveteen Rabbit* (1926). Several books by Rachel Field were published in 1926, among which was *Taxis and Toadstools,* a book of poetry; in 1929 *Hitty* (Newbery, 1930) was published followed by *Calico Bush* in 1931.

Berta and Elmer Hader's *Picture Book of Travel* (1928) launched a long and successful career for this couple, *The Big Snow* being acclaimed the Caldecott award winner of 1949. Another husband and wife team, Maud and Miska Petersham, after earlier success as illustrators, initiated their writing career for children in 1929 with *Miki.* Books concerning transportation, houses, clothing, and foods followed, and in 1946 *The Rooster Crows,* American nursery rhymes and jingles, won the Caldecott medal for them. Eric Kelly's success with the *Trumpeter of Krakow* (Newbery, 1928) prompted additional books about Poland.

Many of today's successful authors and author-illustrators began their writing careers in the 1930s. Marjorie Flack's picture-stories of the dog Angus began in 1930 with *Angus and the Ducks;* Alice Dalgliesh's *The Blue Teapot* (1931); Ingri and Edgar d'Aulaire's *Magic Rug* (1931); Eleanor Frances Lattimore's *Little Pear* (1931); Alice Gall's and Fleming Crew's *Wagtail* (1932); Carol Brink's *Anything Can Happen on the River* (1934); Frances Clark Sayers' *Bluebonnets for Lucinda* (1934); Elizabeth Enright's *Kintu* (1935); Kate Seredy's *Good Master* (1935); and Louise Andrews Kent's *He Went with Marco Polo* (1935).

Thus the early decades of the twentieth century provided the background essential to the creation of a more mature form of literature, to which, as noted earlier, technological developments added their influence in the fifties and sixties. A survey of types of literature follows with emphasis on productions since 1935.

Picture-Story Books

The young child has a wealth of picture books from which to choose. Some are books with pictures only, while the majority have a story designed to meet the interests of young listeners. In both types the pictures tell the story for the child who cannot read for himself. Not only do the illustrations accurately portray the subject, but also because of the variety of media, techniques, and styles used by the artists, the child may savor rich aesthetic experiences. Through these books, furthermore, the child finds enjoyment, and may also develop reading readiness and increase his vocabulary. They may help him relate to other children, expand his knowledge, broaden his interests, extend his depth perception, and provide a rapport with the person who shares the book with him.

Millions of Cats, by Wanda Gág published in 1928, is considered by many as the first American picture book. The rhythmic quality in both story and illustrations has given this charming folk tale wide appeal. Since its publication numerous picture books have been produced both in America and in other countries. They have dealt with every conceivable subject of interest to the young child and represent the works of many outstanding authors and illustrators.

Robert McCloskey's *Blueberries for Sal, One Morning in Maine,* and *Time of Wonder* (see Figure 9) are realistic stories about his own family, *Make Way for*

FIGURE 9. *Form, space relationship, and design are evident in* One Morning in Maine, *by Robert McCloskey. Published by Viking Press, 1952.*

Ducklings relates the life of a duck family, while *Burt Dow, Deep-Water Man* is a humorous sea yarn.

Maurice Sendak evidences obsession with childhood as he carefully and successfully captures his young audience with his illustrations for *The Nutshell Library,* the "Little Bear" books by Else Minarik, and his own *Where the Wild Things Are.* The latter has given children an abundance of security as they *identify* with Max who is in command of the "wild things" at all times. The climax comes when Max leaves the imaginary world and finds himself in his own room where his mother has brought his warm supper.

Virginia Lee Burton displayed her talents as artist, author, and dancer in her books about machines. *Mike Mulligan and His Steam Shovel* and *The Little House,* the latter noted for its nocturnal scenes and passing of time, have rhythmic flowing lines that dance off the pages into the hearts of all children. Also noted

for personified machinery, Hardie Gramatky uses cartoon sketches for *Little Toot,*
Loopy, and *Hercules.* Ezra Jack Keats contributes richly to children's literature.
His stories and collages in *The Snowy Day, Whistle for Willie, Peter's Chair,* and
Goggles are realistic portrayals of the young Negro child. Among other books for
young children that have the Negro child as the main character are *Evan's Corner*
by Elizabeth Starr Hill, illustrated by Nancy Grossman; *Stevie* by John Steptoe,
and *Sam* by Ann Herbert Scott with beautiful illustrations by Symeon Shimin
(see Figure 10).

An appreciation of earthy things, of the spiritual life, and a love for people are

FIGURE 10. *"Sam picked up a book and turned the pages to find a picture." From the*
book Sam, *by Ann Herbert Scott, illustrated by Symeon Shimin. Copyright © 1967 by Ann*
Herbert Scott and Symeon Shimin. Used with permission of McGraw-Hill Book Company.

characteristics of the books by Leo Politi (see Figure 11). His Mexican, Italian, Chinese, and Japanese protagonists introduce children to their festivities, songs, and customs. The illustrations marked by muted tones, aerial views, and heart-shaped faces are very effective.

Leo Lionni provides an aesthetic experience for every child who discovers the clever inchworm in *Inch by Inch,* the poetic mouse, *Frederick,* or the sensitive bird in *Tico and the Golden Wings.* Ludwig Bemelmans in his five books about Madeline capably alternated childlike drawings in black, yellow, and white with colorfully illustrated scenes of Paris.

FIGURE 11. *Mexican children are the subject of this illustration from* Rosa, *by Leo Politi* (*copyright* © *1963 Leo Politi*). *Reproduced with the permission of Charles Scribner's Sons.*

Evaline Ness' range and versatility as an artist are evident in such books as *Sam, Bangs & Moonshine,* occurring near a large harbor with a lighthouse and amidst wonders of the sea, and *A Pocketful of Cricket,* by Rebecca Caudill, set in the country with its lush red apples.

Roger Duvoisin also contributed in a variety of ways with his very colorful, realistic illustrations for "The Happy Lion" books by his wife, Louise Fatio, the season and weather books by Alvin Tresselt, and his own books about *Petunia,* the silly goose, and *Veronica,* the conspicuous hippopotamus. Lois Lenski satisfies the curiosity of very young children with her informative books about Mr. Small as he becomes a cowboy, a pilot, a policeman, and a farmer. For the two- and three-year olds she has done the "Little Davy" books and those about "Debby."

Leonard Weisgard, the very prolific children's artist, illustrates books for numerous authors and in so doing has dealt with a variety of types of literature,

FIGURE 12. *Title-page illustration from* A Book About God, *by Florence Mary Fitch, illustrated by Leonard Weisgard. Copyright © 1953 Lothrop, Lee and Shepard Company, and reproduced by permission.*

including simple picture books, poetry, classics, modern and historical fiction, art, and religious books (see Figure 12). Noteworthy are his illustrations for Margaret Wise Brown's picture-story "Noisy Book" series in which he makes use of shapes to express sound and movement; *The Little Island,* the 1947 Caldecott award winner that portrays the wonders of nature, and *The Golden Egg Book,* which projects a rich feeling of belonging.

Among the many other contributors in this field who should be recognized are H. A. Rey, Garth Williams, Marie Hall Ets, Don Freeman, Russell and Lillian Hoban, Janice Udry, Tomi Ungerer, Gene Zion, Charlotte Zolotow, Theodor Geisel (Dr. Seuss), and Brian Wildsmith (see Figure 13).

Alphabet and Counting Books

Many artists have successfully communicated a wide variety of subjects to young children by means of alphabet and counting books. One of the earliest modern American alphabet books was the *ABC Book* (1923) by Charles Falls,

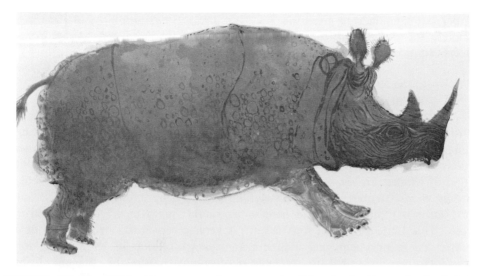

FIGURE 13. *Mr. Wildsmith captures the nature of wild animals. From the book* Brian Wildsmith's Wild Animals, *copyright 1967 by Brian Wildsmith, and published by Franklin Watts.*

wherein animals and birds are portrayed in colorful woodcuts. Wanda Gág in her rhythmic book, *The ABC Bunny,* cleverly has a rabbit weave in and out of the pages without allowing it to dominate the scene, while Clare Newberry is justifiably famed for her portraits of all kinds of cats in her *Kitten's ABC.* Feodor Rojankovsky uses brown tones to picture *Animals in the Zoo,* each animal being captioned in both large and small letters. *John Burningham's ABC* is similar, but with very colorful illustrations. *Celestino Piatti's Animal ABC* has animals in action with a four line rhyme about each. Bruno Munari's *ABC* employs not only beautiful, clearly depicted animals, but also objects and foods to represent each letter of the alphabet. Brian Wildsmith's *ABC* is one of the most exquisite of all picture books. His bright, lush colors provide an aesthetic experience for all ages. *I Love My Anteater with An A,* by Dahlov Ipcar, based on an old game, has many words beginning with the same letter of the alphabet in each rhyme. It should intrigue the precocious child who loves to experiment with sounds of words. Marcia Brown's *Peter Piper's Alphabet,* H. A. Rey's *Curious George Learns the Alphabet,* and Edward Lear's *ABC* add even more variety to the vast array of alphabet titles.

Authors tend to treat counting books in unique ways. Fritz Eichenberg's *Dancing in the Moon,* for example, shows animals doing ridiculous things, and Françoise, the French author-illustrator, tells a story as *Jeanne Marie Counts Her Sheep.* Tasha Tudor's *1 is One* is a rhythmic counting book of delicate, old-fashioned paintings, while James Krüss' *3 × 3 Three by Three,* embellished with bold, humorous illustrations that show action, is designed for all children who can count to three. In Dahlov Ipcar's *Brown Cow Farm,* animals are added and multiplied in pictures full of variety and interest.

Margery and Leonard Everett Fisher's *One and One,* deliberately shows how numbers are combined to give other numbers. *Brian Wildsmith's 1, 2, 3's* is a work of beauty for all children; the gifted child, on the other hand, may derive from it concepts for geometrical shapes, figures, and forms.

Mother Goose

For most children their first experience with literature is listening to mother sing a nursery rhyme. Among the child's first books is one containing many of these familiar verses in a Kate Greenaway, Arthur Rackham, or Jessie Wilcox Smith edition of Mother Goose. Another early favorite is *Ring O' Roses* (1922), which has only twenty rhymes but is profusely illustrated by the inimitable Leslie Brooke (see Figure 14). Only he could have a pig riding "piggy-back" as shown in the rhyme "This Little Pig Went to Market." A version which has been passed down through generations achieving a fiftieth anniversary edition in 1965 is the *Real Mother Goose,* illustrated in quaintly old-fashioned attire by Blanche Fisher Wright. *Mother Goose Panorama* published by Platt and Munk Company is a folded ten foot long colorful book especially for two- and three-year old children. Feodor Rojankovsky's *The Tall Book of Mother Goose* is brilliantly and humorously illustrated. In 1954 Kathleen Lines' *Lavender's Blue,* illustrated by

FIGURE 14. *Leslie Brooke is noted for his illustrations of animals. From* Ring O' Roses, A Nursery Rhyme Picture Book, *illustrated by L. Leslie Brooke. Reproduced by permission of the publisher, Frederick Warne & Co., n.d.*

Harold Jones, was published in England and Marguerite De Angeli's *Book of Nursery and Mother Goose Rhymes* was published in America. Both have a beautiful quaintness about them that reaches out to all age levels. More recent versions are *Mother Goose and Nursery Rhymes* with wood engravings by Philip Reed; *Brian Wildsmith's Mother Goose* with brilliant, vibrant colors; Raymond Briggs' *The Mother Goose Treasury,* and *Chinese Mother Goose Rhymes* by Robert Wyndham, illustrated by Ed Young. To add to the variety of Mother Goose books are Barbara Cooney's *Mother Goose in French,* with a very authentic French background, and the multivolume *The Mother Goose Library,* illustrated by Peter Spier. These are a mere sampling of the numerous renderings of Mother Goose.

Books for the Middle Years and Older

The seven to nine year olds enjoy reading for themselves many of the same books that earlier have been read aloud to them. In addition to some of the authors already mentioned whose books have more story and can be read by this age group are Alice Goudey, Jerrold Beim, Clyde Robert Bulla, Ann Nolan Clark, Carolyn Haywood, Elizabeth Coatsworth, Ruth and Latrobe Carroll, Beverly Cleary, Alice Dalgliesh, Meindert De Jong, Astrid Lindgren, and James and Marion Renick.

The range of subject areas available for children nine to twelve years old and older is as numerous as their interests, and the approach to these subjects is unlimited. They include traditional literature, fantasy, animal stories, science fiction, realistic stories, and historical fiction.

Traditional Literature

In the beginning the legacy of social customs, beliefs, history, and traditions was communicated orally from generation to generation. The fables, myths, folk tales, epics, and nursery rhymes resulting constitute a category perennially the most popular children's literature. New versions appear regularly and are a favorite vehicle for the talented illustrator. In recent years, particularly, there has been a steady stream of lavishly illustrated folklore for children. Since 1955, fifty per cent of the Caldecott winners have been folklore.

The fable as a type of traditional literature is usually attributed to the Greek slave Aesop (620 B.C.–560 B.C.), who perhaps told his simple tales for political purposes. The first English edition of *Aesop's Fables* was translated and published by William Caxton in 1484. Among the notable Aesop collections for children are those by Joseph Jacobs, Boris Artzybasheff, James Reeves, and Anne Terry White. From India came two ancient collections of fables, the *Jatakas* and *Panchatantra.* The Jataka tales relate to the incarnations of the Buddha in the form of different animals as he appeared briefly to teach his followers wise conduct. The *Panchatantra,* composed of long, involved stories and verses, is about both human beings and animals. Thirty-four of these stories are in the collection *The Tortoise and the Geese and Other Fables of Bidpai.* Among other collections of fables from India are *Jataka Tales* and *More Jataka Tales* retold by Ellen C. Babbitt, *Eastern Stories and Legends* by Marie Shedlock, and *The Fables of India* by Joseph Gaer.

Mythology personifies the forces of nature, explains the existence of the universe, and relates the development of religion as we know it today. However, many of the tales are pure entertainment to be relished as a literature. The Greek, Roman, and Norse myths are an important part of literature for children, exemplified by Sally Benson's *Stories of Gods and Heroes;* Thomas Bulfinch's *A Book of Myths,* illustrated by Helen Sewell; Olivia E. Coolidge's *Greek Myths;* Ingri and Edgar d'Aulaire's *Book of Greek Myths;* Robert Graves' *Greek Gods and Heroes;* Charles Kingsley's *The Heroes,* illustrated by Joan Kiddell-Monroe; Olivia E. Coolidge's *Legends of the North;* Padraic Colum's *The Children of Odin,* illustrated by Willy Pogány; Ingri and Edgar d'Aulaire's *Norse Gods and Giants,* and Dorothy Hosford's *Thunder of the Gods.*

The epic portrays the ideals and moral standards of a nation in a long narrative heroic poem. *The Iliad* and *The Odyssey* attributed to Homer, ninth century B.C., set the pattern for the epic. These tales relate to the Trojan War and the journeys of Odysseus. Among the fine retellings are those by Barbara Picard, Padraic Colum, Alfred J. Church, and Roger L. Green. *Beowulf,* the oldest Anglo-Saxon epic, has been skillfully retold by Ian Serraillier, Rosemary Sutcliff, Dorothy Hosford, and Robert Nye. Also from England are the perennial favorite heroes King Arthur, who became famous about the sixth century, and Robin Hood, who appeared about the thirteenth or fourteenth century. Howard Pyle wrote and illustrated important editions of both of these legendary heroes. Other books about King Arthur have been written by Sidney Lanier, Mary MacLeod, and Barbara Picard. J. W. McSpadden, Anne Malcolmson (see Figure 15), and Ian Serraillier have written about Robin Hood.

Children may be introduced to other important legendary characters such as: Roland, the hero of France; Cuchulain, hero of Ireland; Sigurd, the Norseman; Siegfried, the German, and Väinämöinen, the Finn. Among the recommended titles are E. M. Almedingen's *The Treasure of Siegfried;* James Baldwin's *The Story of Roland* and *The Story of Siegfried;* Eleanor Clark's *The Song of Roland;* Babette Deutsch's *Heroes of the Kalevala;* Dorothy Hosford's *Sons of the Volsungs;* Rosemary Sutcliff's *The Hound of Ulster;* and Jay Williams' *The Tournament of the Lions.*

The folk tale, the most popular of all folklore, has been collected from all parts of the world and makes up a rich segment of literature from every nation. Among the well-known collectors are Jacob Grimm (1785–1863) and his brother Wilhelm (1786–1859) who traveled about the countryside of Germany writing down the tales the people told and carefully preserving the original quality. Peter C. Asbjörnsen (1812–1885) and Jörgen E. Moe (1813–1882) were scholars who preserved the Norwegian narratives in *Popular Tales from the Norse,* translated into English in 1858 by Sir George Dasent. Collections of these tales frequently are given the title of one of the stories "East O' the Sun and West O' the Moon." Joseph Jacobs (1854–1916) collected the English folk tales from both

FIGURE 15. *"Robin Hood Rescuing Three Squires." From* The Song of Robin Hood, *edited by Anne Malcolmson, illustrated by Virginia Lee Burton. Published by Houghton Mifflin Company, 1947.*

oral and printed sources while the prolific Andrew Lang (1844–1912) selected and retold tales he found in other collections. Charles Perrault (1628–1703) is noted for his French collection, *Les Contes de ma Mère l'Oye.*

The United States is rich in folklore, also. Joel Chandler Harris (1848–1908) collected the tales of the plantation Negro in Georgia and through the character of Uncle Remus, he tells in colorful dialect the charming stories of Brer Rabbit, Brer Fox, Tar Baby, and many others. The North American Indian tales have been collected from different tribes and recorded by many good storytellers; for example, Robert Ayre's *Sketco, the Raven,* Corydon Bell's *John Rattling-Gourd of Big Cove,* Anne Fisher's *Stories California Indians Told,* Christie Harris' *Once upon a*

Totem, and Frances G. Martin's *Nine Tales of Coyote.* Richard Chase has collected folk tales of the Southern mountain folk and recorded them in *Grandfather Tales* and *Jack Tales.* The United States also has variants from other countries, such as the "Gingerbread Boy" which closely resembles the English "Johnny Cake." However, a product of its own is the tall tale, which evolved as men sat around camp fires. Well-known American tall tale characters are Pecos Bill, Paul Bunyan, Tony Beaver, John Henry, Mike Fink, Kemp Morgan, Old Stormalong, and Casey Jones. Collections by Walter Blair, James C. Bowman, Harold Felton, Moritz A. Jagendorf, Anne Malcolmson, Glen Rounds, and Irwin Shapiro are a sampling.

Many of the nursery rhymes, folk tales, fables, epics, and myths have been lifted from a collection and attractively illustrated and issued separately. Among the illustrators who have made this type of contribution are Paul Galdone (*Old Mother Hubbard and Her Dog, The Golden Touch, The Three Wishes*), Hans Fischer (*Traveling Musicians, Puss in Boots*), Felix Hoffmann (*Rapunzel, The Seven Ravens*), Adrienne Adams (*The Shoemaker and the Elves, Snow White and Rose Red*), Brian Wildsmith (*The Lion and the Rat, North Wind and The Sun*), Marcia Brown (*The Three Billy Goats Gruff, Stone Soup*), Ezra Jack Keats (*John Henry and His Hammer*), Beni Montresor (*Cinderella*), Feodor Rojankovsky (*Frog Went A-courtin',* retold by John Langstaff), Evaline Ness (*Tom Tit Tot*), and Margot Zemach (*The Fisherman and His Wife*).

Fantasy

Fantasy, the imaginative story involving some realm of the impossible, often has a theme of love versus hate or the conflict of good and evil. Lewis Carroll's *Alice's Adventures in Wonderland* (1865) and *Through the Looking Glass* (1871), apparently left a legacy of talent to English writers, for they have continued to produce the most enchanting literature in this field. Kenneth Grahame's *Wind in the Willows,* A. A. Milne's *Winnie-the-Pooh,* Pamela Travers' *Mary Poppins,* C. S. Lewis' chronicles of Narnia, Mary Norton's *The Borrowers,* J. R. R. Tolkien's *The Hobbit, or, There and Back Again,* Lucy Boston's *The Children of Green Knowe,* and Rumer Godden's doll fantasies are examples. However, it should be remembered that Italy produced *The Adventures of Pinocchio* by Carlo Lorenzini and Sweden, *Pippi Longstocking* by Astrid Lindgren. The United States can claim E. B. White's *Charlotte's Web,* Robert Lawson's *Rabbit Hill,* Lloyd Alexander's fantasies in the imaginary land of Prydain, Edward Ormondroyd's *Time at the Top,* Carolyn Bailey's *Miss Hickory,* and Elizabeth Orton Jones' *Twig.*

Animal Stories

Animal stories have been a favorite of many children and again the variety is enormous, ranging from the excellent fantasies mentioned above to the very realistic stories like Joseph Lippincott's *Wilderness Champion* and Sheila Burnford's *Incredible Journey*. The latter has been made into a motion picture as have Eric Knight's *Lassie Come-Home,* Walt Morey's *Gentle Ben,* Felix Salten's *Bambi,* Marjorie Rawlings' *The Yearling,* and Mary O'Hara's *My Friend Flicka.* Marguerite Henry is noted for her skillful stories about different breeds of horses, set in various countries and in different periods of history. Among her many titles are *King of the Wind, Brighty of the Grand Canyon* (see Figure 16), *Misty of Chinco-*

FIGURE 16. *From* **Brighty of the Grand Canyon,** *by Marguerite Henry, illustrated by Wesley Dennis. Copyright 1953 by Rand McNally & Company.*

teague, and *Gaudenzia, Pride of the Palio.* James Kjelgaard has written fine dog stories (*Big Red, Snow Dog, Desert Dog*) in which the tame animal frequently must survive in the wilderness, while Glen Rounds (*Blind Colt, Stolen Pony*) and Will James (*Smoky*) present the ranch horse in a similar situation. No author has written with more empathy for animals than Meindert De Jong as evidenced in his *Along Came a Dog, Hurry Home, Candy,* and *The Last Little Cat.* John and Jean George (*Vulpes, the Red Fox, Masked Prowler: The Story of a Raccoon*), Rutherford Montgomery (*Kildee House*), and Michel-Aimé Baudouy (*Old One-Toe*) have presented insight into the characteristics of wild animals of the forests while Theodore Waldeck has portrayed jungle animals in *The White Panther* and *On Safari.*

Science Fiction

Science fiction deals with any scientific possibility which at the time of writing is an unproven theory or known only to scientists, and varies extremely in its treatment and subject matter. It has experienced great waves of popularity since Jules Verne's *Twenty Thousand Leagues Under the Sea* (1870). William Pène DuBois' *Twenty-One Balloons* is a fabulous tale of a balloon trip; Eleanor Cameron's books are about space flights to the planet Basidium; Ellen MacGregor has sent Miss Pickerell to Mars; while Louis Slobodkin brings an outer space character to invade the planet Earth in *Space Ship Under the Apple Tree*. Madeleine L'Engle's *Wrinkle In Time,* a story of love overshadowing evil powers, is an adventure to other dimensions by the means of a tesseract, or a wrinkle in time. John Christopher's trilogy (*The White Mountains, City of Gold and Lead, Pool of Fire*) projects to a future time when the twentieth century civilization has been destroyed and its people are referred to as the Ancients. Lester Del Rey, Robert Heinlein, André Norton, Alan Edward Nourse, and Robert Silverberg, well-known science fiction writers for the young adult, have written books that can be read and enjoyed by the twelve-year-olds, resulting in an excellent transition to stories for the adolescent.

Realism—Family Stories

Many realistic stories concern family life in all its circumstances. They cover all periods of history and all parts of the world, and range from the classics to books dealing with the most current situations. Among the many authors noted for some special contribution to family life in the twentieth century are Carolyn Haywood and Beverly Cleary, both of whom portray the typical child in a humorous predicament; Eleanor Estes and Elizabeth Enright, who each won a Newbery award for books that focus on family life, but perhaps are better known for their series— Miss Estes for her Moffat family, a trilogy of four fatherless children, and Miss Enright for the Melendy family, four motherless children. Sydney Taylor's *All-of-a-Kind Family* is a trilogy of a Jewish family in New York in the World War I period. Lois Lenski has written many regional books set in remote environments, witness the 1946 Newbery award winner *Strawberry Girl,* a story of the Florida Crackers; *Cotton in My Sack,* set in Arkansas; and *Shoo-fly Girl,* an Amish family in Pennsylvania. Doris Gates and Zilpha K. Snyder both vividly portray the migrant workers and minority groups. Marguerite De Angeli writes about the Amish and the Mennonites. Joseph Krumgold presents very diverse settings for family life in his books about boys growing up, one on a sheep ranch in New Mexico (*And Now Miguel*), another in a small town in New Jersey (*Onion John*), and still another in a suburb of New York City (*Henry 3*). Ann Nolan Clark's *Little Navajo Bluebird* and *Medicine Man's Daughter* portray the struggles of the North American Indians as they seek to preserve their own customs and at the same time accept the white man's ways. For the setting of their books Emily Neville and Elaine Konigsburg chose New York as have many other current writers. Miss Neville's books (*Berries Goodman* and *It's Like This, Cat*) deal with serious situations while Mrs. Konigsburg's (*From the Mixed-Up Files of Mrs. Basil E. Frankweiler; Jennifer, Hecate, Macbeth, William McKinley, and Me,*

Elizabeth, and *About the B'nai Bagels*) are in a more humorous vein. Meindert De Jong bases some of his family stories of the Netherlands (*Shadrach, Far Out the Long Canal,* and *Journey from Peppermint Street*) on his own childhood as does Kate Seredy for some of her books about Hungary (*Good Master* and *Singing Tree*). Margot Benary-Isbert (*The Ark* and *Rowan Farm*) presents a postwar German family in their struggle to rebuild their lives while Elizabeth Janet Gray (*Cheerful Heart*) writes about a Japanese family in Tokyo after World War II. Shirley Arora (*What Then Raman?*), Jean Bothwell (*Little Flute Player*), and Aimée Sommerfelt (*Road To Agra* and *White Bungalow*) give insight into family life in different regions of India while Reba Mirsky (*Thirty-One Brothers and Sisters, Seven Grandmothers* and *Nomusa and the New Magic*), and Louise Stinetorf (*Musa, the Shoemaker*) introduce different areas of Africa.

Realism—Humor

Humorous stories are important in the child's total reading program. Robert McCloskey's *Homer Price* and *Centerburg Tales,* Florence and Richard Atwater's *Mr. Popper's Penguins,* Oliver Butterworth's *Enormous Egg,* Astrid Lindgren's *Pippi Longstocking,* Keith Robertson's *Henry Reed, Inc.,* and William Pène Du Bois' *Porko Von Popbutton* are but a few on the menu of thoroughly enjoyable fare.

Realism—Adjustment to Situations

There is a wealth of material to enrich the lives of children; books written so realistically, developed so logically with a theme so personal that children can live vicariously the experiences of the book characters. Many books help children understand how others feel in certain situations. On the other hand children gain insight into personal dilemmas as they identify with book characters who face problems similar to their own. Books may deal with emotional problems, physical handicaps, and mental retardation; the main characters may have divorced or alcoholic parents, or they may experience the death of a loved one, racial prejudice, a search for moral values, or group acceptance. These books invariably have successful endings; for example, the characters may have adjusted to their problems, overcome them, or accepted them in a constructive manner. It is the main characters who usually change and adjust to the situation rather than society changing for their convenience.

Jean Little is one of the more versatile among the many authors who are known for their contribution in this field. She has effectively handled sudden death of a twin child in the family and the care of two foster children in *Home from Far;* the physical handicap of cerebral palsy in *Mine for Keeps;* a terrible liar in *One To Grow On;* and mental retardation in *Take Wing. Don't Take Teddy* by Babbis Friis-Baastad also treats the subject of mentally retarded children as do *Cathy's*

Secret Kingdom by Nancy Faber, *a Racecourse for Andy* by Patricia Wrightson, and *A Different Kind of Sister* by Pamela Reynolds.

There are many well-developed themes of physical handicaps; *Windows for Rosemary* by Marguerite Vance; *Door in the Wall* by Marguerite De Angeli; *Kristy's Courage* by Babbis Friis-Baastad; *David in Silence* by Veronica Robinson; and *Let the Balloon Go* by Ivan Southall. These titles concern children who are blind, lame, injured, mute, and spastic, respectively.

Robert Burch, who depicts rural Georgia in Depression days, presents a variety of problems in his books. In *Queenie Peavy,* resentful Queenie has an imprisoned father; *Skinny* experiences the death of his alcoholic father; and D. J., who is growing up, does everything wrong in *D. J.'s Worst Enemy.*

Ester Wier's three books *The Loner, The Barrel,* and *Easy Does It* evidence her versatility in handling the themes of loneliness, fear, and courage. The latter title deals with racial prejudice. There have been many other well-written books that have effectively delved into experiences of racial or religious prejudice. Among these are Emily Neville's *Berries Goodman,* Natalie Carlson's *The Empty School-house,* Jesse Jackson's *Call Me Charley,* and Bella Rodman's *Lions in the Way.*

Many of the books concerning problems show resourcefulness in children as in *Tomás Takes Charge* by Charlene Talbot. Tomás, a Puerto Rican boy in New York, must provide for himself and his psychopathic sister when their father fails to return home. *My Side of the Mountain* by Jean George tells of a boy who spends the winter alone in the Catskill Mountains, and *Trouble in the Jungle* by John Rowe Townsend presents a fight for survival in the Jungle, a ghetto in northern England, as four children are abandoned by their uncle.

A variety of situations involving divorced parents or broken homes is encountered in books. Titles include *A Girl Called Al* by Constance Greene, *The Egypt Game* by Zilpha Snyder, *Ellen Grae* and *Lady Ellen Grae* by Vera and Bill Cleaver, and *Lisa and Lottie* by Erich Kästner.

Historical Fiction

Some of the most successful children's books are in the area of historical fiction. Many authors depict a period in history so vividly that one feels he is experiencing the same problems, events, and situations that the book characters encounter. While the period may be far in the past, it is often possible for present day children to identify with the characters in the areas of human relations and personal development. A child reading *Across Five Aprils* by Irene Hunt gets a vivid picture of the Civil War period, and he also experiences the heartaches of a loving family which finds itself divided in attitude toward the war. In *Johnny Texas* by Carol Hoff a German immigrant family lives through Texas' fight for independence. In very brief, but personal episodes, Miss Hoff gives the reader an insight into what democracy meant to Johnny's father and then to Johnny. *Carolina's Courage* by Elizabeth Yates enables young children to mature as they journey with Carolina and her family through some fearful days including Carolina's giving up her most prized possession to enable her family and other pioneers to cross Indian territory. *I, Juan de Pareja* by Elizabeth B. de Treviño, a picture of seventeenth century Spain as reflected through the lives of Juan and his master Diago Velázquez, is a story of courage, life and death, slavery and freedom, history, and art.

A book of historical fiction that has been widely read and loved is *Johnny Tremain* by Esther Forbes. As found in other successful historical fiction, this book offers more than facts of a period in history. This is a book of adjustment to both physical and emotional handicaps, of acceptance of one's self, and of growing up.

Historical fiction has been effectively written for all ages; however, the books for the older group cover more places and periods in history.

The prehistoric period has included such books as *One Small Bead* by Byrd Baylor Schweitzer, beautifully and dramatically illustrated by Symeon Shimin, *And the Waters Prevailed* by D. Moreau Barringer, and *The Faraway Lurs* by Harry Behn. Effectively portraying the ancient period are such authors as Elizabeth Speare, Eloise McGraw, and Hans Baumann.

FIGURE 17. *Garth Williams vividly portrays the pioneer Ingalls family. From* Little House in the Big Woods, *by Laura Ingalls Wilder. Illustrations copyright 1953 by Garth Williams; text copyright 1932. Reprinted with permission of Harper & Row, Publishers.*

Every period in United States history has been treated but none more dramatically than the colonial, Civil War, and the Westward Movement. Among the many fine authors who have written of the eras of United States history are Laura Ingalls Wilder (see Figure 17), Elizabeth Coatsworth, Alice Dalgliesh, Wilma Pitchford Hays, Elizabeth Speare, Walter D. Edmonds, Clyde Bulla, Rachel Field, William O. Steele, and Leonard Wibberley.

Special writers of European historical fiction include Clyde Bulla, Rosemary Sutcliff, Barbara Picard, Elizabeth Janet Gray, Marchette Chute, Mary and Conrad Buff, and Barbara Willard.

Biography

Living, breathing heroes and just plain folks step off the printed page in books about people and no literature is more widely read by children than biography: factual, fictional, or collective. Biographies range from accounts of well-known figures who played a vital role in world history to those on the current scene. There are accounts of statesmen, explorers, inventors, men and women of medicine, musicians, and artists portrayed for all age levels. For the younger group there are Alice Dalgliesh's *The Columbus Story,* Aliki Brandenberg's *A Weed Is a Flower: The Life of George Washington Carver,* Clyde Bulla's *Squanto: Friend of the White Man,* and Ingri and Edgar d'Aulaire's colorfully illustrated biographies of early contributors to the founding and development of America. For the older group there are many outstanding biographers including James Daugherty, Jeanette Eaton, Genevieve Foster, Clara Judson, Ronald Syme, Katherine Shippen, Shannon Garst, and May McNeer (see Figure 18).

Not to be overlooked are biographies of the more obscure personalities whose lives add variety and depth to the collection. Jean Lee Latham's *Carry on, Mr. Bowditch* and *Young Man in a Hurry: The Story of Cyrus W. Field,* Elizabeth Yates' *Amos Fortune: Free Man* and *Prudence Crandall: Woman of Courage,* and Esther Hautzig's *The Endless Steppe* are representative.

The biographical fiction such as Robert Lawson's *Ben and Me, Mr. Revere and I,* and *Captain Kidd's Cat* are not only good reading, but are also excellent spring boards to the factual biographies.

Poetry

From the time mothers begin to sing lullabies, nursery rhymes, and jingles, children are delighted with poetry. No other category has more charm or variety. Poetry for the young is often characterized by humor, rhythm, and repetition; poetry for the older child may have these same qualities but may also embody more serious elements. Children may select the work of an individual poet, or one of the many excellent anthologies, or even a profusely illustrated volume of only one poem. Favorite poets of the nineteenth century and their works include Edward Lear's *Nonsense Book,* Robert Louis Stevenson's *A Child's Garden of*

FIGURE 18. *Lynd Ward realistically illustrates both in color and black and white. From* America's Mark Twain, *by May McNeer, illustrations by Lynd Ward. Published by Houghton Mifflin Company, 1962.*

Verses, Henry Wadsworth Longfellow's *Children's Own Longfellow,* Clement C. Moore's *A Visit from St. Nicholas,* Christina Rossetti's *Sing-Song,* and Eugene Field's *Poems of Childhood.*

Some notable early twentieth century works are A. A. Milne's *When We Were Very Young* and *Now We Are Six,* Rachel Field's *Taxis and Toadstools,* Rose Fyleman's *Fairies and Chimneys,* Walter de la Mare's *Peacock Pie,* Langston Hughes' *The Dream Keeper and Other Poems,* and Laura Richards' *Tirra Lirra: Rhymes Old and New.* Favorites of more recent years are John Ciardi's *I Met a Man,* Siddie Joe Johnson's *Feather in My Hand,* Myra Cohn Livingston's *Wide Awake* and *Whispers,* Mary O'Neill's *Hailstones and Halibut Bones,* Polly Cameron's*"I Can't,"Said the Ant,* Aileen Fisher's *Listen, Rabbit* and *Skip Around the Year,* Robert Frost's *You Come Too,* Eleanor Farjeon's *The Children's Bells: A Selection of Poems,* and Harry Behn's *The Golden Hive.*

Non-Fiction Books

Factual or informational books have been written about every subject of interest to children and on a wide range of reading levels. They deal with areas of the school curriculum, hobbies, and world events. In science they vary from space discoveries and atomic elements to prehistoric animals and microscopic organisms, while in travel they range from Australia to Iceland. Many of these factual books are part of a publisher's series. These books have photographs, diagrams, charts, bibliographies, glossaries, and indexes. While science, social sciences, geography, and history have the greatest amount of material available, other areas have not been neglected, particularly art and music.

Awards in the Field of Children's Literature

Numerous awards at the international, national, regional, and state level have been established to recognize and to honor individuals who have contributed significantly to the field of children's literature, and to encourage better quality in children's books. These are the more widely recognized awards:

Hans Christian Andersen Award—An international award given biennially since 1956 by the International Board on Books for Young People to a living author and an illustrator for their contribution to good literature for children and young people.

John Newbery Medal—Presented annually since 1922 by the American Library Association to the author of the most distinguished book for children published in the United States during the preceding year.

Randolph Caldecott Medal—Given annually since 1938 by ALA to the illustrator of the most distinguished American picture book for children published in the United States in the preceding year.

Carnegie Medal—Awarded annually since 1936 by the [British] Library Association for the outstanding children's book written in Great Britain by a British author and published during the preceding year.

Greenaway Medal—Awarded annually since 1956 by the [British] Library Association to an artist for the most distinguished picture book for children published in Great Britain during the preceding year.

Book of the Year for Children—Presented annually by the Canadian Library Association for two outstanding children's books, one in English, the other in French, written by Canadian citizens during the preceding year.

Laura Ingalls Wilder Award—Awarded every five years by the ALA in recognition of an author or an illustrator whose works published in the United States have made a lasting and substantial contribution to literature for children.

Mildred L. Batchelder Award—Given annually since 1968 by the ALA to an American publisher for the most outstanding children's book originally published in a foreign language, in a foreign country, and subsequently published in the United States.

Regina Medal—Awarded annually since 1959 by the Catholic Library Association "to an individual whose lifetime dedication to the highest standards of literature for children has made him an exemplar of the words of Walter de la Mare 'only the rarest kind of best in anything is good enough for the young'.

National Book Award—Awarded annually since 1950 by the National Book Committee, and expanded in 1969 to include children's literature. A prize of $1,000 is given to one of the five nominees for creative excellence in children's literature.

Children's Spring Book Festival—Awarded annually since 1937 for books published during the first half of the year to encourage spring publication of children's books. Presented by *Book World* (formerly presented by *New York Herald Tribune*).

Jane Addams Children's Book Award—Presented annually since 1953 by the Women's International League for Peace and Freedom for a book of literary quality that conveys the idea of friendship, cooperation, and world mindedness.

Children's Book Award—Presented annually since 1943 by the Child Study Association for the best book of the preceding year written for children or young people which presents realistically problems in their contemporary world.

Boys' Clubs of America Junior Book Award—An annual award chosen from the books given the best reviews by members of the Boys' Clubs of America. An adult committee selects the five books for gold medals and the five books for certificates.

Contributors

Caroline M. Hewins was among the first of a long line of librarians, authors, illustrators, children's book editors, publishers, and interested laymen to play an important role in the development of a literature designed especially for children and in the endeavor to get these books into their hands. She wrote extensively and effectively on behalf of good books for children, but she was also an advocate of direct action. "What are you doing to encourage a love of good reading in boys and girls?" she wrote inquiring and prodding twenty-five leading libraries. In her honor Frederic G. Melcher established in 1946 the Caroline Hewins Lecture series, devoted to the subject of children's literature. The first of these lectures, "From Rollo to Tom Sawyer; the Development of Children's Books from 1870–1880," was read in 1947 by Alice M. Jordan, a pioneer herself, who was the head of the Children's Department at the Boston, Massachusetts Public Library from 1902 to 1940.

Anne Carroll Moore, supervisor of the Children's Department, New York Public Library from 1906 to 1941, contributed richly to the field. Like Caroline Hewins she picked up the pen to propagandize for the spread of worthwhile children's books. She regularly contributed articles to periodicals and wrote books about children's literature. She became the first person to do serious reviewing of children's books when in 1918 she began her monthly essays in *Bookman*. The sign of "The Three Owls" became her trademark for the department in the *New York Herald Tribune Books* in 1925, and later for *The Horn Book Magazine*. Miss Moore was noted for sponsoring the art of storytelling and for the organization of the section of ALA for Library Work with Children. The New York Public Library honored Anne Carroll Moore immediately following her death in 1961 when they named their annual spring lecture series the Anne Carroll Moore Lectures.

Bertha Mahony Miller in 1916 established the Bookshop for Boys and Girls in Boston, Massachusetts, under the auspices of the Women's Educational and Industrial Union. From this time forward she, too, devoted her career to promoting the best in books for children. Perhaps her crowning achievement was in founding and editing *The Horn Book Magazine* (1924). Elinor Whitney Field joined Mrs. Miller in 1919 at the Bookshop and collaborated in compiling surveys on children's books with annotated lists and in the editing of such books as *Newbery Medal Books: 1922–1955* and *Caldecott Medal Books: 1938–1957*. Mrs. Miller compiled *Illustrators of Children's Books 1744–1945*.

The Macmillan Company in 1919 recognized the need for more attention to children's books with the appointment of Louise Seaman Bechtel as editor of the first children's department in a publishing house. In 1922 both Doubleday, Doran and Company and Frederick Stokes and Company reported the appointment of children's editors, May Massee for the former, and Helen Dean Fish for the latter. Alice Dalgliesh became children's editor of Charles Scribner's Sons in 1934. In 1943 the Association of Children's Book Editors was established with Miss Dalgliesh as the first president. A year later the Association established the Children's Book Council. By 1946 membership of the Association had risen to forty children's editors representing forty publishing houses.

Children's book editors should rightfully be recognized for their contribution to the book field. They have demanded high standards, discovered and encouraged authors and illustrators, and have played an important role in the final production of books.

No name is higher on the roster of contributors to the field of children's literature than that of Frederic G. Melcher, who has been rightly called the god-father of children's literature. He spent a lifetime encouraging and supporting children's editors, writers, and librarians. Mr. Melcher was instrumental in the development of Children's Book Week, he suggested the awarding of both the Newbery and Caldecott awards, and was the donor of both medals. In his honor the Frederic G. Melcher Scholarship was established in 1955 by the Children's Services Division of the American Library Association to be given to a candidate interested in preparing for a career in children's librarianship.

Children's Book Week

World War I forestalled the initial efforts of Franklin K. Mathiews, the chief librarian of the Boy Scouts of America, who traveled across the country promoting the idea of a week devoted to the recognition of good books for children. But in 1919, Frederic G. Melcher, then Secretary to the American Booksellers Association, persuaded Mr. Mathiews to present his plan to the Association. A resolution to organize Children's Book Week was adopted and the American Library Association's official approval followed quickly. There have been many slogans with posters by leading illustrators of children's books since the first "More Books in the Home" was aptly illustrated by Jessie Wilcox Smith.

Book Week is a time for parents, teachers, librarians, book publishers, and bookstores to rededicate themselves to the mission of providing the best books for children.

Children's Services Division

The Children's Services Division of the American Library Association is dedicated to the improvement of literature for children. Towards this end committees are responsible for the annual publication of notable children's books of the preceding year; lists of books of permanent value; bibliographies of foreign children's books available and recommended for purchase. Also, committees are responsible for the awarding of the Newbery, Caldecott, Mildred L. Batchelder, and Laura Ingalls Wilder awards. Advisory committees aid organizations such as Boy Scouts of America, the African-American Institute, and the U.S. Jaycees in their publications for children. Other committee projects are publicizing children's books on radio and television, selecting titles for the Hans Christian Andersen Award, and recommending American books for translation and distribution through International Board on Books for Young People; United Nations Educational, Scientific and Cultural Organization; and United States Information Agency.

Children's Book Council

The Children's Book Council was established by the Association of Children's Book Editors in 1944 for the purpose of assuming responsibility for the activities related to Book Week as well as working with schools, libraries, bookstores, and child welfare agencies for the promotion and distribution of good books for all children in this country. The Council has expanded its services throughout the years to provide many special types of material including the Summer Reading Programs.

The Council's quarterly publication, *The Calendar,* notes special dates to observe, lists materials and publications available, publicizes Children's Book awards and prizes, and runs features about children's trade books. In January of 1970, *The Calendar* was enlarged to include four columns of special articles in each issue.

Children's Book Section

After many years of persuasion and promotion by individuals and organizations, the Children's Book Section was established at the Library of Congress in March of 1963. Its primary purpose is to provide reference, research, and bibliographic services to those who serve children. The collection is composed of catalogs, bibliographies, indexes, histories, and critical works related to children's literature in both English and foreign languages. In addition to this special collection the Library of Congress has over 100,000 children's books published in America and received through the copyright deposit. Numerous books published in other countries are received through exchange, gift, or purchase. The Rare Book Section also houses some 14,000 old and rare children's books. The Children's Book Section headed by Virginia Haviland is one more contribution to the field of children's literature.

International Organizations

There has always been an international element in children's literature, particularly in the translation of books from one language to another and in the retelling of folk literature. The International Bureau of Education in Geneva was the first agency to undertake a formal study of children's literature around the world. Its first report of that study appeared in 1930 with subsequent reports in 1932 and 1933. After World War II there was a revived interest in promoting literature for children around the world and in the 1960s there was much international cooperation through International Federation of Library Associations (IFLA); United Nations Educational, Scientific and Cultural Organization (UNESCO); International Youth Library (IYL); and International Board on Books for Young People (IBBY) to promote literature for children around the world. Mrs. Jella Lepman, who believed in the value of children's literature in the moral reconstruction of Germany, was instrumental in many of these developments. This very determined woman promoted the first international event in Germany after World War II by encouraging nations to send their representative children's books to be enjoyed by German children and to promote better world understanding. Through her efforts and the sponsorship of the American Military Government, the International Exhibitions of Children's Books were held in Germany in 1946–1947. The first exhibition opened in Munich on July 3, 1946, followed in the next six months by exhibitions in Würtemberg, Frankfurt, and Berlin. One of the most fascinating incidents in connection with the exhibition occurred during the Berlin exhibit which opened December 6, 1946. Mrs. Lepman conceived the idea of translating and publishing on newsprint 30,000 copies of Munro Leaf's *Ferdinand the Bull* (*Ferdinand der Stier*), illustrated by Robert Lawson, to be distributed to the children as Christmas presents. What should have been an ample number of copies was quickly exhausted and Mrs. Lepman related that blackmarket price was paid to retrieve copies for their permanent files (7).

Erich Kästner, Munich newsman and author of *Emil and the Detectives,* lauded the International Exhibitions of Children's Books, stating that the shows not only afforded a wide view of the differences and similarities in the children's literature of various nations; but also vividly showed "the mutual influences they depend on" (*8*).

The successful exhibitions in Germany, coupled with Mrs. Lepman's enthusiasm, encouraged ALA to apply to the Rockefeller Foundation of New York for a grant to establish the International Youth Library. The grant was awarded with the stipulation that local support be available for its formation and operation. The library opened in Munich on September 14, 1949, with the purpose of providing the best in children's books from all countries and in all languages and promoting international understanding. Mrs. Lepman, the director, was assisted by a Friends of the IYL group. Twenty years later it is supported by the government of the Federal Republic of Germany and consists of over 140,000 volumes representing children's literature from all parts of the world.

In 1953 the IYL became affiliated with UNESCO which commissioned the preparation of an exhibition of 150 *Children's and Youth Books from the Western World,* which was sent to many countries in all parts of the world. Its success encouraged the formation of other traveling exhibits dealing with various subjects. The affiliation with UNESCO brought reward of another kind when the children's book collection of the International Bureau of Education in Geneva was given to the IYL. The collection of more than 25,000 books, mainly titles from the 1920s and 1930s, but also containing valuable eighteenth and nineteenth century books, enhances the reference and documentation services of IYL.

As authors, illustrators, publishers, booksellers, librarians, and educators visited the IYL, Mrs. Lepman recognized the need for a conference that would bring together these people with a common interest in children's books. As a result on November 18, 1951, the International Board on Books for Young People was established with Zurich, Switzerland designated as the permanent center of the International Board. This group has been responsible for important developments for further promoting world interest in children's books. One was the establishment in 1956 of the first international award for a children's book. The Hans Christian Andersen Award is given every two years by an international jury to a contemporary author. Originally it was given for an outstanding book; however, in 1962 the award was expanded to incorporate the complete works of an author. In 1966 it was again extended to include an additional award to a living illustrator as well as a living author. This same year all member nations of IBBY were asked to send a list annually of representative books from their country, which should give impetus to the exchange or translation of books around the world. Authors who have received the Hans Christian Andersen Award are Eleanor Farjeon of England, Astrid Lindgren of Sweden, Erich Kästner of Germany, Meindert De Jong of the United States, René Guillot of France, Tove Jansson of Finland, James Krüss of Germany, and Gianni Rodari of Italy. The illustrators honored with this award are Alois Carigiet of Switzerland, Jiri Tranka of Czechoslovakia, and Maurice Sendak of the United States.

The second activity of the Board is the sponsoring of International Children's Book Day on April 2, the birthday of Hans Christian Andersen. The 1969 theme "Friends Across the Frontiers" exemplified the purpose of the observance to "develop international understanding among the young by increasing their knowledge of other cultures through literature and thus serve the cause of peace."

IBBY has been responsible for many publications, notably *Bookbird,* a quarterly which began in 1957. Currently it is a joint effort with the International Institute for Children's, Juvenile and Popular Literature (Vienna, Austria). *Bookbird's* particular appeal is the worldwide view of its contributors and the regular reviewing of books recommended for translations.

At the Twentieth Session of IFLA, held in Zagreb, Yugoslavia, in 1954, a Sub-Committee on Library Work with Children was organized within the Public Libraries Section; and in 1961 the Sub-Committee became a Sub-Section. Primary objectives of the group are to improve standards for children's books, further the development of children's libraries throughout the world, and prepare lists, reports, and reviews for publication.

More recently the Biennale of Illustrations Bratislava (BIB) was established in Czechoslovakia in 1967. It is an international exhibition of original art from children's books designed to recognize the artists of the participating countries and to promote the best of illustrations in children's books.

The Information Center on Children's Cultures, a service of the United States Committee for UNICEF, New York, is an organization responsible for the publishing of important educational and cultural materials about children in countries where UNICEF has projects which include Africa, Asia, Near East, and Latin America.

Doubtless, the "International Course on Children's Literature Today," held annually in Loughborough, England, and tours for the study of Children's Literature Abroad will have an impact on the literature for children in the future.

Translations

The universal appeal of children's literature is enormously enhanced by the many translations from all continents. In the seventeenth century *Orbis Sensualium Pictus* by Comenius was translated into English shortly after its publication in Latin and Charles Perrault's *Les Contes de ma Mère l'Oye* was translated from the French into English in 1729. The English translation of the Grimm brothers' *Popular Stories* from the German appeared in 1823, Hans Christian Andersen's *Fairy Tales* from the Danish in 1846, and Carlo Collodi's *The Adventures of Pinocchio* from the Italian in 1892. Other well-known nineteenth century translations are Johann Wyss' *Swiss Family Robinson,* Johanna Spyri's *Heidi,* Heinrich Hoffman's *Slovenly Peter,* and Jules Verne's *20,000 Leagues Under the Sea.* The volume and quality of translations into English continued in the early twentieth century: Elsa Beskow's *Ollie's Ski Trip* (1928), *Aunt Green, Aunt Brown, and Aunt Lavender* (1928), *Pelle's New Suit* (1929), and Selma Lägerlof's *Wonderful Adventures of Nils* (1907) and *Further Adventures of Nils* (1911). A contem-

FIGURE 19. *The dramatic illustrations by Celestino Piatti are enjoyed by children in many countries. From* The Happy Owls, *by Celestino Piatti. Copyright © 1963 by Artemis Verlag, Zurich, Switzerland. First U.S.A. edition 1964 by Atheneum. Used by permission of Atheneum Publishers.*

porary trend is the simultaneous publishing in two or more countries (see Figure 19), particularly of picture books. Among the many authors whose works have been successfully translated from the original into English are:

French

Paul Berna	*The Mule on the Expressway*
	The Knights of King Midas
	The Horse Without a Head
	The Clue of the Black Cat
	Flood Warning
René Guillot	*African Folk Tales*
	The Fantastic Brother
Marcel Aymé	*The Wonderful Farm*
Michel-Aimé Baudouy	*Old One-Toe*
Paul Jacques Bonzon	*The Orphans of Simitra*
Andrée Clair	*Bemba, an African Adventure*

German

Erich Kästner	*Little Man*
	Emil and the Detectives
Hans Baumann	*Sons of the Steppe*
	The Barque of the Brothers
	The Caves of the Great Hunters
	I Marched with Hannibal

Bettina Hürlimann	*William Tell and His Son* (illustrated by Paul Nussbaumer)
	Barry; the Story of a Brave St. Bernard (illustrated by Paul Nussbaumer)
Hans P. Schaad	*Gunpowder Tower*
	The Rhine Pirates
Ursula Schaeffler	*The Thief and the Blue Rose*
Heidrun Petrides	*Hans and Peter* (see Figure 20)
Margot Benary-Isbert	*The Ark*
	Rowan Farm
Henry Winterfeld	*Trouble at Timpetill*
James Krüss	*My Great-Grandfather and I*
	The Talking Machine
Thomas and Wanda Zacharias	*But Where Is the Green Parrot?*

Danish

Anne Holm	*North to Freedom*
	Peter

Swedish

Astrid Bergman Sucksdorff	*Chendru: The Boy and the Tiger*
Astrid Lindgren	*Pippi Longstocking*
	The Children of Noisy Village
Gunnel Linde	*The White Stone*
Karin Anckarsvärd	*The Mysterious Schoolmaster*
	Doctor's Boy
	Robber Ghost

Norwegian

Berit Braenne	*Trina Finds a Brother*
Babbis Friis-Baastad	*Don't Take Teddy*
	Kristy's Courage
Aimée Sommerfelt	*Miriam*
	The Road to Agra
	The White Bungalow

Russian

Anton Chekhov	*Kashtanka*
Mikhail Sholokhov	*Fierce and Gentle Warriors*

Greek

Alki Zei	*Wildcat Under Glass*

Hebrew

Yehoash Biber	*The Treasure of the Turkish Pasha*

While good books first published in another language and country have inevitably found their way to American publishers, the establishment of the Mildred

FIGURE 20. *From* Hans and Peter, *written and illustrated by Heidrun Petrides,* © *1962 by Atlantis Verlag, Zurich, Switzerland. Reprinted by permission of Harcourt Brace Jovanovich, Inc. One of the many books translated and published in the United States.*

L. Batchelder Award in 1966 by ALA Council should advance the cause of eminent foreign literature for children in the United States.

Numerous American books have been translated and published abroad with great success. Laura Ingalls Wilder's "Little House" series, for example, has been translated into twenty-six languages. Among authors whose works have been published in foreign countries are Hendrik Willem Van Loon, Meindert De Jong, Joseph Krumgold, Marguerite Henry, Maurice Sendak, Elaine Konigsburg, and Elizabeth Janet Gray.

Nonprint Media

Literature comes alive for children in many ways: the story-hour, dramatization, group discussions, and reading aloud. The many kinds of media now available add even more variety and enrichment. Portfolios of prints of illustrations may be purchased and framed to charm many children in their homes as well as in classrooms and libraries. Early twentieth century favorites are Margaret Tarrant's fairies and animals and Ernest Shepard's water colors from *The World of Pooh* and *The World of Christopher Robin.* Notable contemporary portfolios are Leonard Weisgard's and Brian Wildsmith's pictures from their "Mother Goose" books.

In some instances realia have been available for children. Christopher Robin's stuffed animals that inspired A. A. Milne's "Pooh" stories have been displayed in museums and libraries in the United States and in England. The original toys were acquired by E. P. Dutton and Company, New York City, after Mr. Milne's death in 1956. Ceramics of Beatrix Potter's animal characters are displayed in many libraries (see Figure 21).

FIGURE 21. *Beatrix Potter's animals that appear in her books are available in ceramic models. Made in Beswick, England, and copyrighted by F. Warne & Co.*

Recordings have long been a source of enrichment; the variety and volume continues unabated. Mrs. Gudrun Thorne-Thomsen, storyteller from Norway, lectured in America on the art of storytelling and also recorded Norse myths and legends. Padraic Colum recorded Irish folk tales while Harold Courlander did African tales from his many folk tale collections. Well-known storytellers Ruth Sawyer, Frances Clark Sayers, and Augusta Baker have recorded folk tales and Christmas stories. Poetry has been effectively recorded by May Hill Arbuthnot, Frederic G. Melcher, and Judith Anderson. Langston Hughes, Robert Frost, John Ciardi, Harry Behn, and Aileen Fisher have recorded their own poems. Recorded dramatizations of Newbery Award winning titles have been made available in recent years.

Sound filmstrips of favorite children's books are quite successful. A sampling of these for the younger group are James Daugherty's *Andy and the Lion,* Edward Ardizzone's *Little Tim and the Brave Sea Captain,* Taro Yashima's *Crow Boy,* Claire Bishop's *Five Chinese Brothers,* illustrated by Kurt Wiese, and Edward Lear's *The Owl and the Pussycat,* illustrated by Barbara Cooney. For the older group the librarian may choose from epics, legends, myths, and many other classics.

Very artfully and skillfully produced 16 mm films for the older group include *Paddle to the Sea*, based on the book by Holling C. Holling; *And Now Miguel*, a documentary film on which Joseph Krumgold based his Newbery Award winning book by the same title; *The Loon's Necklace*, an Indian legend; *Johnny Tremain*, based on the book by Esther Forbes; *Hailstones and Halibut Bones*, by Mary O'Neill; and *The Red Balloon*, a fantasy photographed in France by Albert Lamorisse. Titles for the younger group are Ludwig Bemelmans' *Madeline*, Ezra Jack Keat's *The Snowy Day*, and *Puss in Boots* from the Charles Perrault version.

The super-8 mm sound cartridges are available of children's books, such as Jack Tworkov's *The Camel Who Took a Walk*, "The Doughnuts" from Robert McCloskey's *Homer Price*, and Marjorie Flack's *Story About Ping*.

Many tapes, both cassettes and reel-to-reel, have been produced of favorite books, interviews with authors, and dramatizations of classics and modern literature. These types of media will undoubtedly be utilized in many effective ways in the future.

Trends

The number of titles published in the United States in the last two decades mushroomed to an unprecedented figure; so much so that more children's books were produced in the 1950s and 1960s than had been published in the preceding fifty years.

The sixties were, furthermore, a period of educational and technological development that left its impact on the young child perhaps more than on any age level. Large amounts of federal monies, particularly Title II of the Elementary and Secondary Education Act, were available for the purchase of books and other types of materials. The act enabled some elementary schools to procure trade books for the first time; many jobbers employed professional librarians to compile catalogs of recommended titles. The change in the school curriculum, placing emphasis on the individual child, resulted in the extensive use of trade books in the classroom. Perhaps this, as well as the fact that it is a profitable business, is an explanation of the constant proliferation of publisher's series. These factual books of uniform size, shape, paging, illustrations, and price touch every phase of the curriculum. They have been written by established and well-known authors of both adult and children's books and also by new authors inspired by the potential field. The present enormous production of controlled vocabulary books for independent reading by young children began in 1956 when Theodor Geisel (Dr. Seuss) accepted the proposal of some educators to write a book with a controlled vocabulary for first grade children. The highly successful *The Cat in the Hat* opened the floodgate and since that time the market has been virtually inundated with similar picture-stories, factual sciences, and biographies. Some of these books are good literature while others are very limited in value. It should be recognized that exemplary controlled vocabulary books like *The Cat in the Hat* and *The Cat in the Hat*

Comes Back by Dr. Seuss and *Little Bear* and *Little Bear's Visit* by Else Minarik, illustrated by Maurice Sendak, have distinctive qualities that stir the child's imagination, develop awareness of rhythmic sounds, and read well aloud.

Books for children about contemporary social and moral problems follow the pattern of adult publication; frankness on every conceivable subject is evident. The books are concerned with lying and stealing; divorced, alcoholic, or imprisoned parents; homosexuality and reproduction; and, to place them where the action is, have settings in large cities and suburbs. Each year the problem books seem tc be geared to an even younger group than the preceding one. Many are poorly written with contrived situations, some appear to be talking to the parents rather than the children, while others are masterpieces of literary quality.

There is a veritable avalanche of books that reflect society's changing attitude toward ethnic groups, particularly the Afro-American. Some titles concern integration, but more recently there is a setting wherein the Negro, Mexican, Puerto Rican, Italian, Hebrew, Anglo-American, and other races and nationalities work and study in a heterogeneous situation.

There is a trend to illustrate profusely and dramatically a poem, folk tale, song, myth, or nursery rhyme lifted from a collection and issued separately. In fact, some illustrators are known particularly for this type of contribution. Other trends include reissuing classics and, more recently, reprinting books of value for new and expanding collections. Unfortunately, some out-dated books that have long since been weeded from the shelves of libraries are among the reprints.

The Future of Children's Literature

To project into the future always places one in a precarious situation; however, in the 1970s, certain trends seem inevitable in the future of children's literature. The national goal announced by the United States Commissioner of Education to assure that by 1980 "no one shall be leaving our schools without the skill and the desire to read to the full limits of his capability" will doubtless have a heavy impact on book production. The desire to read is stimulated by enjoyment of what one reads and by a love for books instilled at an early age. It will be imperative, then, to all interested in this commitment to provide that literature which is best for each child.

Fine literature that has previously appeared in hardback will be more readily available in paperback for the three to twelve year olds. The paperback will, in fact, move boldly to supply the demand. Outstanding hardback titles already in paperback are *The Snowy Day, Madeline, Curious George, What Do You Say, Dear?, Charlotte's Web, Across Five Aprils, All-of-a-Kind Family, The High King, Where the Wild Things Are,* and *Brian Wildsmith's Mother Goose.* Since children read what is available and parents purchase what is accessible, educators, librarians, and interested laymen should make an effort to get worthwhile, inexpensive books into the supermarkets, newsstands, and department stores to replace the many books of poor quality customarily found there. A concomitant to this move would be a worthwhile goal for the 1970s: the education of parents on what to purchase. This would, in addition, affect children's book club selections, forcing clubs to observe the need for good format, creative illustrations, and worthy varied content. Articles with recommended lists of children's books will appear more regularly in newspapers and popular magazines. If the success of December 1969 telecasts of *Hans Brinker; or, The Silver Skates, J. T.,* and *Little Drummer Boy* is indicative, then perhaps good literature will not only become a regular feature of national television programs, but also of regional and local stations.

While international cooperation in book production is in its infancy, there are some discernible signs likely to become stronger, namely, exchange programs, simultaneous publishing in two or more countries, and the rise of international bookseller-publisher organizations.

The movement to educate all children will accelerate and could result in a larger number of commissioned books written for a particular group—the mentally retarded, the bilingual, the average and the gifted child. Experience, however, indicates that the mentally retarded child reads with joy a book written for the average child, while the average child stretches his level upward when interested in a subject. Focused books might, therefore, have a deleterious effect on purely creative writing. This should be kept in mind as schools eschew the mass assignment in favor of allowing the student to pursue interests of his own. Books may lead to a new period of discovery, to solving and thinking through problems; for books, unlike television, permit the reader time to accept or disagree with the characters, to ponder what he would do in a similar situation, to be an individual. Books dealing with social and moral problems probably will continue to appear but will be more objective and less contrived.

The achievements in book production and illustrations in recent years would lead one to expect an equal quality of excellence in the future. However, caution must be taken so that the visual does not overshadow the text. There will be more experimenting with size of type, color of paper, binding materials, printing processes, textures, and page design. Studies will continue to determine if length of words and sentences play as important a role in reading as believed in the past, or if the page design is a more relevant factor.

The new media will continue to develop at a rapid pace and many additional ways of presenting good literature to children will be exploited: sound filmstrips, films, talking books, tapes, 8 mm film loops. Reading aloud to children, dramatization, storytelling, discussion groups, and dial-a-book will add impetus to the total program of children's literature. Let those who influence the neophyte reader remember the words of Walter de la Mare, "only the rarest kind of best in anything is good enough for the young."

REFERENCES

1. Dora V. Smith, *Fifty Years of Children's Books, 1910–1960: Trends, Backgrounds, Influences,* The National Council of Teachers of English, Champaign, Illinois, 1963, p. 32.

2. Ruth Hill Viguers, "The Golden Age," in *A Critical History of Children's Literature* (Cornelia Meigs, ed.), Macmillan, New York, 1953, pp. 427–603.

3. A. S. W. Rosenbach, *Early American Children's Books,* Kraus Reprint, New York, 1966.

4. Judith St. John, comp., *The Osborne Collection of Early Books 1566–1910: A Catalogue,* Toronto Public Library, Toronto, Canada, 1958.

5. Lee Ash, Denis Lorenz, et al., *Subject Collections,* 3rd ed. rev. and enl., Bowker, New York, 1967.

6. Carolyn W. Field, ed., *Subject Collections in Children's Literature,* Bowker, New York, 1969.

7. Jella Lepman, *Bridges of Children's Books,* tr. by Edith McCormick, American Library Association, Chicago, 1969, p. 66.

8. *Ibid.,* p. 54.

SELECTED BIBLIOGRAPHY

Books

Adams, Bess Porter, *About Books and Children: Historical Survey of Children's Literature,* Holt, New York, 1953.

Arbuthnot, May Hill, *Children and Books,* 3rd ed., Scott, Foresman, Chicago, 1964.

Arbuthnot, May Hill, *Children's Reading in the Home,* Scott, Foresman, Glenview, Illinois, 1969.

Avery, Gillian, *Nineteenth Century Children, Heroes and Heroines in English Children's Stories 1780–1900,* Hodder and Stoughton, London, 1965.

Becker, May (Lamberton), *First Adventures in Reading; Introducing Children to Books,* Stokes, New York, 1936.

Cameron, Eleanor, *The Green and Burning Tree,* Atlantic-Little, Brown, Boston, 1969.

Colby, Jean Poindexter, *Writing, Illustrating and Editing Children's Books,* Hastings, New York, 1967.

Dalgliesh, Alice, *First Experiences with Literature,* Scribner's, New York, 1932.

Darling, Richard L., *The Rise of Children's Book Reviewing in America, 1865–1881,* Bowker, New York, 1968.

Darton, F. J. Harvey, *Children's Books in England: Five Centuries of Social Life,* 2nd ed., Cambridge Univ. Press, Cambridge, England, 1958.

Duff, Annis, *Bequest of Wings: A Family's Pleasures with Books,* rev. ed., Viking, New York, 1944.

Duff, Annis, *Longer Flight; A Family Grows Up with Books,* Viking, New York, 1955.

Eaton, Anne T., *Reading with Children,* Viking, New York, 1940.

Ellis, Alec, *A History of Children's Reading,* Pergamon, New York, 1968.

Ellis, Alec, *How To Find Out About Children's Literature,* 2nd ed., Pergamon, New York, 1968.

Fenner, Phyllis, *The Proof of the Pudding: What Children Read,* Day, New York, 1957.

Fenner, Phyllis, *Something Shared: Children and Books,* Day, New York, 1959.

Fenwick, Sara, ed., *A Critical Approach to Children's Literature; (The Thirty-First Annual Conference of the Graduate Library School, August 1–3, 1966),* Univ. Chicago Press, Chicago, 1967.

Field, Elinor Whitney, ed., *Horn Book Reflections: On Children's Books and Reading, Selected from Eighteen Years of "The Horn Book Magazine" 1949–1966*, Horn Book, Boston, 1969.

Fisher, Margery, *Intent Upon Reading*, Brockhampton Press, Leicester, England, 1961.

Frank, Josette, *Your Child's Reading Today*, new and rev. ed., Doubleday, New York, 1969.

Freeman, Ruth (Sunderlin), *Children's Picture Books: Yesterday and Today*, Century House, Watkins Glen, New York, 1967.

Fryatt, Norma R., ed., *A Horn Book Sampler on Children's Books and Reading*, Horn Book, Boston, 1959.

Green, Roger L., *Tellers of Tales, British Authors of Children's Books from 1800 to 1964*, Watts, New York, 1965.

Haviland, Virginia, ed., *Books in Search of Children: Essays & Speeches* by Louise Seaman Bechtel, Macmillan, New York, 1969.

Haviland, Virginia, ed., *Children's Literature, A Guide to Reference Sources*, Library of Congress, Washington, 1966.

Hazard, Paul, *Books, Children and Men*, Horn Book, Boston, 1960.

Huck, Charlotte S. and Doris Young Kuhn, *Children's Literature in the Elementary School*, 2nd ed., Holt, Rinehart, and Winston, New York, 1968.

Hürlimann, Bettina, *Three Centuries of Children's Books in Europe*, World, Cleveland, 1968.

Jordan, Alice M., *From Rollo to Tom Sawyer*, Horn Book, Boston, 1948.

Karl, Jean, *From Childhood to Childhood: Children's Books and Their Creators*, Day, New York, 1970.

Kiefer, Monica, *American Children Through Their Books 1700–1835*, Univ. Pennsylvania Press, Philadelphia, 1948.

Kingman, Lee, ed., *Newbery and Caldecott Medal Books: 1956–1965*, Horn Book, Boston, 1965.

Klemin, Diana, *The Art of Art for Children's Books*, Potter, New York, 1966.

Larrick, Nancy, *A Parent's Guide to Children's Reading*, 3rd ed., Doubleday, Garden City, New York, 1969.

Larrick, Nancy, *A Teacher's Guide to Children's Books*, Merrill, Columbus, Ohio, 1960.

Library Association, *Chosen for Children*, Library Association, London, 1967.

Mahony, Bertha E., Louise Latimer, and Beulah Folmsbee, *Illustrators of Children's Books 1744–1945*, Horn Book, Boston, 1947.

Mahony, Bertha E., Louise Latimer, and Beulah Folmsbee, *Illustrators of Children's Books 1946–1956*, Horn Book, Boston, 1958.

Meigs, Cornelia Lynde, et al., *A Critical History of Children's Literature*, rev. ed., Macmillan, New York, 1969.

Miller, Bertha Mahony and Elinor Whitney Field, eds., *Caldecott Medal Books: 1938–1957*, Horn Book Papers, Volume II, Horn Book, Boston, 1957.

Miller, Bertha Mahony and Elinor Whitney Field, eds., *Newbery Medal Books: 1922–1955*, Horn Book Papers, Volume I, Horn Book, Boston, 1955.

Moore, Anne Carroll, *My Roads to Childhood, Views and Reviews of Children's Books*, Horn Book, Boston, 1961.

Muir, Percy, *English Children's Books 1600 to 1900*, Batsford, London, 1954.

Pellowski, Anne, *The World of Children's Literature,* Bowker, New York, 1968.

Pitz, Henry C., *Illustrating Children's Books,* Watson-Guptill, New York, 1963.

Robinson, Evelyn Rose, ed., *Readings About Children's Literature,* McKay, New York, 1966.

Sayers, Frances Clarke, *Summoned by Books,* Viking, New York, 1965.

Sloane, William, *Children's Books in England and America in the Seventeenth Century,* Kings Crown, New York, 1955.

Smith, Dora V., *Fifty Years of Children's Books 1910–1960: Trends, Backgrounds, Influences,* National Council of Teachers of English, Champaign, Illinois, 1963.

Smith, Elva S., *The History of Children's Literature,* American Library Association, Chicago, 1937.

Smith, James Steel, *A Critical Approach to Children's Literature,* McGraw-Hill, New York, 1967.

Smith, Irene, *A History of the Newbery and Caldecott Medals,* Viking, New York, 1957.

Smith, Lillian, *The Unreluctant Years: A Critical Approach to Children's Literature,* American Library Association, Chicago, 1953.

Spain, Frances Landers, *Reading Without Boundaries,* New York Public Library, New York, 1956.

Spain, Frances Landers, *The Contents of the Basket, and Other Papers on Children's Books and Reading,* New York Public Library, New York, 1960.

Targ, William, ed., *Bibliophile in the Nursery,* World, Cleveland, 1957.

Thwaite, Mary F., *From Primer to Pleasure: An Introduction to the History of Children's Books in England, from the Invention of Printing to 1900,* Library Association, London, 1963.

Townsend, John Rowe, *Written for Children: An Outline of English Children's Literature,* Lothrop, Lee and Shepard, New York, 1967.

Viguers, Ruth Hill, *Margin for Surprise, about Books, Children, and Libraries,* Little, Brown, Boston, 1964.

Walsh, Frances, *That Eager Zest: First Discoveries in the Magic World of Books,* Lippincott, Philadelphia, 1961.

Periodicals

Bookbird, International Board on Books for Young People and the International Institute for Children's, Juvenile and Popular Literature, Vienna, Austria.

The Calendar, Children's Book Council, New York, New York.

Childhood Education, Association for Childhood Education International, Washington, D.C.

Elementary English, National Council of Teachers of English, Champaign, Illinois.

Elementary School Journal, University of Chicago Press, Chicago, Illinois.

The Grade Teacher, Teachers Publishing Corporation, Darien, Connecticut.

The Horn Book Magazine, Horn Book, Boston, Massachusetts.

The Instructor, The Instructor Publication, Dansville, New York.

Library Journal, R. R. Bowker and Company, New York, New York.

Publishers Weekly, (special issues), R. R. Bowker and Company, New York, New York.

Saturday Review, (special issues), Saturday Review, New York, New York.

School Libraries, American Association of School Librarians, American Library Association, Chicago, Illinois.

School Library Journal, published separately as well as being included in the *Library Journal* (15th of the month issue).

Top of the News, Children's Services Division and Young Adult Services Division, American Library Association, Chicago, Illinois.

Wilson Library Bulletin (special issues), The H. W. Wilson Company, Bronx, New York.

FRANCES DECORDOVA

CHILE, LIBRARIES IN

During the first years of conquest by the Spaniards the only concern of Chile was war. There were neither books nor schools, and there was such a shortage of paper that the poet Ercilla had to write many stanzas of the *Araucana* on strips of leather. With the establishment of religious communities, however, came the beginnings of culture and education, and during the seventeenth century there was a concern for reading.

Censorship, which was common in Europe at the time for religious, political, and moral reasons, was extended to works printed in Mexico and Peru, where printing has been done since the sixteenth century.

Nevertheless, besides religious and educational works, a goodly number of scientific and literary books were introduced into Chile, and these became part of private and ecclesiastical libraries. Among the private libraries, we know of one with more than 500 volumes.

The ethnic transformation produced by the constant introduction of Spanish blood into Chile for three centuries; the cultural work of the Jesuits; the "learned despotism" of the Bourbons who after Charles III were determined to encourage cultural education in the colonies; and the contacts with Europe of young creoles who traveled to study were the causes for the marked intellectual progress observed during the last century of colonization. Along with this progress came the development of libraries and the selling of books.

The most important libraries were, as in earlier years, those of the religious communities. On the date of their expulsion from the country in 1767, the Jesuits had in their possession 20,000 volumes distributed among their establishments in Chile. The majority of them were not, as one would believe, exclusively ecclesiastical books, but rather there were a great many dealing with science, philosophy, law, history, and literature. Some of them later went to the University of St. Philip, the first Chilean university, founded in 1738.

In this same century the laity begin to show interest in books and reading. In spite of their high prices, books were ordered from Spain or Lima by many cultured men.

The largest private library in Chile, that of Don Francisco Ruiz Berecedo, a lawyer, General Defender of the Indians, Attorney General of the Court of Lima, and Mayor of Santiago, dates from the beginning of the eighteenth century. This library consisted of 2058 books, mainly law, but there were also works of literature, science, and history. The library, inherited by his nephew, Bishop Manuel Alday, later passed on to the Cathedral of Santiago, where it has been preserved to this day.

During the last part of the seventeenth century the Magistrate, Francisco Larrenaga, a distinguished mathematician, lived in Mendoza. His library was small but notable because of the type of works it included.

The struggle for independence in the nineteenth century caused a temporary decline in the dissemination of books. The few colonial libraries had lost the spirit of renewal after the exile of the Jesuits, and were now abandoned, closed, or became disorganized. The importation of Spanish books ceased completely and that from other places had not yet begun.

Although the rest of the country continued to lag culturally, Santiago recuperated quickly after 1817. The rupture with Spain left the country free to receive the seeds of other cultures from other sources. French, English, and German books, translated into Spanish, began to arrive from Buenos Aires and Europe, and many of them contributed to Chilean thought during the remainder of the nineteenth century and the beginning of the twentieth.

Among the new libraries, in first place and much ahead of the others was that of Mariano Egaña, a statesman, diplomat, and eminent lawyer. This library consisted of 5000 volumes, carefully selected by Bello, and later it grew to over 10,000 volumes.

The library of General Francisco Antonio Pinto was also outstanding containing a comprehensive collection of the authors of Greco-Roman antiquity, the Spanish classics, and the major masterpieces of English, French, Italian, and Portuguese literature. It also contained books on military tactics, the works of the philosophers of the seventeenth, and eighteenth, and early nineteenth centuries and numerous scientific treatises. This library, after suffering some losses, was given by the descendents of the general to the historian Don Francisco Encina.

In the eighteenth century bibliographies were few in number but their names are important and well known in the history of Chilean literature as, for example, the Abbot Juan Ignacio Molina, an expelled Jesuit who published the *Catalog of the Writers about the Matters of Chile* in Europe. Among the chroniclers we find José Peréz Garciá, a native Spaniard, and the Chilean Vicente Carvallo Goyenche.

In the nineteenth century the historians were the ones who dedicated themselves with fervor to the study of bibliography. By strictly following scientific methods they became true bibliographers. Miguel Luis and Gregorio Victor Amunátegui contributed much valuable bibliographical information through their books. Benjamín Vicuña Mackenna is remembered for the catalog of his American Library and of the Baeche Library. Diego Barros Arana, especially in his *General History of Chile,* stands out because of his talent for dealing with national bibliography.

The first professional Chilean bibliographer was Ramón Briseno who, by applying his own techniques and methods, compiled Chilean bibliography from 1812 to 1859 and from 1860 to 1876.

From that point on there is an increase in the number of writers who make up the Chilean bibliographical tradition. The greatest was José Toribio Medina (1852–1930) who, besides being an eminent historian and critic, produced bibliographical work of extraordinary proportions both because of the quantity of his effort and its excellent quality. Most of his works, which add up to 392 titles, are long bibliographical studies on the effects of the printing press on the Spanish colonial empire in America and Oceania and on the works about these continents.

Contemporaries of Medina were the historical bibliographers, Domingo Amunátegui Solar, Alejandro Fuenzalida Grandon, Thomas Thayer Ojeda, Nicolás Anrique, Enrique Blanchard Chessi, Aníbal Echeverría, Victor Maria Chippa, José Manuel Frontaura, Ramón A. Laval, Luis Montt, Juan Enrique O'Ryan, Manuel Antonio Ponce, Rómulo Ahumada, Carlos E. Porter, Justo Abel Rosales, Enrique Sanfuentes, Ricardo Latcham, Julio Saavedra, Juan Brüggen, Rodolfo Shüller, and Luis Ignacio Silva. To these names should be added that of the literary critic Omer Emeth, who made bibliography a profession.

More recently, Guillermo Feliú Cruz, Raúl Silva Castro, Ricardo Donoso, R. P. Alfonso Escudero, Walter Hanish, Eugenio Pereira, Carl H. Schaeble, Arturo Torres Rioseco, and José Zamudio have made of bibliography an important part of their intellectual activity.

The National Library of Chile was founded in 1813 by an act of the Independent Government of the Republic, but when the Chilean revolution surrendered to the Spanish forces it was closed and did not reopen its doors until national independence was definitely established in 1818. Don Manuel de Salas, one of the most learned men of his times, reopened the library and was its director until 1823. Brother Camilo Henríquez, the journalist of the revolution, succeeded him, and among the later directors of the library we find the names of Ramón Briseno, the first Chilean bibliographer; Francisco Garciá Huidobro, who in 1846 obtained for the library the right of legal trust and the control of the law of intellectual property; Alejandro Vicuñā, priest and writer; the historian Ricardo Donoso; the writers Eduardo Barrios and Augusto Iglesias; Guillermo Feluí Cruz, a bibliographer and historian; and Roque Esteban Scarpa, professor and writer.

The National Library had as its nucleus the ancient colonial library of the Jesuits which was preserved in the University of San Felipe. To this were added the private collections of Don Mariano Egaña, Don Ignacio Victor Eyzaguirre, the eminent historian Benjamín Vicuña Mackenna, and the very valuable collections of the historian Barros Arana and José Toribio Medina.

The present collection has 1,500,000 volumes, housed since 1925 in a building constructed for this purpose.

At the present the library is made up of the following sections:

    Administration
    Offices
    Chilean section
    Chilean journals, newspapers, and magazines

The American section
Section on general editorials
Cataloging and bibliographical reference section
General exchange
Information and catalogs
American libraries: José Toribio Medina and Diego Barros Arana
Enrique Matta Vial Seminar
Map section
Audiovisual section
Cultural extension: Mapocho Magazine, Musical extension. Archives on words.
    Archive on authors. Discussion films. Critical references. Literary workshop.

There is a general reading room and reading rooms for the special collections of José Toribio Medina and Diego Barros Arano as well as one for the Enrique Matta Vial Seminar for the consultation of rare, old books.

The National Library publishes the *Year Book of the Chilean Press* which compiles all Chilean bibliography from 1877 up to the present. The *Year Book of Periodical Chilean Publications* records the titles of all periodicals published in Chile since 1930.

The development of libraries in Chile has not followed a comprehensive plan which is concerned with every aspect of the Chilean system, but rather has limited itself to the simple solution of furnishing the most needed services. In spite of the lack of a governmental library policy, the authorities in higher education, conscious of the importance of the library as an active factor in education and research, have sought to furnish good library services in the universities. They exerted the most effort for organizing and developing libraries by initiating the systematic training of professionals at all levels through the creation of the School of Librarians. (See *Chile. University of Chile, School of Library Science.*)

The beginnings of an organized library system thus started with the universities where libraries evolved along with the educational system. This did not happen with primary and middle education, which progressed while libraries and librarians lagged far behind.

Public libraries, in their strict modern concept, barely exist. Isolated moves by collectors who, in philanthropic gestures, donated their books to the municipal government or to an institution, were the basis of what are presently called public libraries. Among them are municipal, school, and special libraries.

The National Library tried to fill all the gaps and was, until recently, the habitual recourse for all kinds of students, professionals and scholars, investigators, and readers of newspapers and magazines.

The specialized libraries, in particular the libraries of Institutes of Research, have become prominent because of their interest in perfecting their organizations, and they have succeeded in attracting trained librarians through adequate renumeration.

On a national scale the highest level of organization is found in the university and special libraries, followed by the public libraries, and last, the school libraries.

The university libraries, about 174 in number, are spread throughout the country in the nine universities:

1. University of Chile	92
University Center of the Northern Zone	1
2. Catholic University of Santiago	17
3. University of Conception	30
4. Austral University	13
5. State Technical University	12
6. University of the North	1
7. Catholic University of Valparaiso	6
8. Technical University of Federico Santa Mariá	1
9. University of the North (Sede Arica)	1

Their organization is modern in a great majority of cases, and many more are now modernizing their organization.

In spite of this tendency toward centralized organization, there exist a great number of university libraries in which the absence of centralization causes serious technical, economic, and administrative problems. Examples are the centralization of technical processes in the central libraries of universities, combined with the decentralization of services to the reader (the libraries of the Catholic University of Santiago, for example), and the total or partial centralization of technical procedures in the central libraries of schools, maintaining the separation of services and collections (the Schools of Medicine, Philosophy, and Education at the University of Chile).

During the last few years other changes have been observed: a predominance of the system of free access to books, which allows the reader to directly choose what he needs; a great increase in the collections of reference books, which are located in the reading room; and the creation of the services of information and reference, which allows direct guidance of the reader by the librarian, especially with the use of the collection of books, the mechanics of preparing a bibliography for professors, and the search for materials in different libraries in the country.

Some university libraries were enlarged through the incorporation of important private or institutional collections.

To the present Central Library of the University of Chile, founded in 1936 with books from the Reading Room which had been started at the same time as the university, was incorporated the valuable collection of the National Institute, a library which contained the collection of documentary books and especially pamphlets, unique in America, which had belonged to Don Pedro Montt and Don José Antonio Rojas, an outstanding personage in the Enlightenment. Afterward is was enlarged with the libraries of the bibliographer and historian Alejandro Fuenzalida, the educator Amanda Labarca, and the poet Pablo Neruda. In this last collection of 9000 volumes, mainly bibliographical treasures, there are manuscripts, unpublished works, and first editions of literary, geographical, and scientific works.

The Central Library of the Catholic University, founded in 1896 and moved to its present site in 1921, was formed through valuable private collections, outstanding among which are those of the statistician and public servant, Don Manuel José Irarrazabal, 1835–1896; of Archbishop Joaquin Larraín Gandarillas, 1829–

1897; of Don Uldaricio Prado, a famous engineer and mathematician; and of the priest Don Rafael Fernández Concha, lawyer and writer.

The contributions of institutions, foundations, and foreign governments have been important in the formation and development of the departmental libraries in the universities. Among the most important are the Rockefeller, Ford, and Kellog Foundations, CARE, and the governments of the United States, France, Germany, and Spain.

The financial resources of university libraries are generally insufficient. None receives as much as 5% of the university's budget. Nevertheless, they constitute, along with the National Library, the most important collection in the country of bibliographical material used for investigation. The total number of works in the universities is 1,167,411 books, 205,706 pamphlets, and 21,465 collections of periodicals.

Within the Ministry of Education there is a Department of Libraries, Archives, and Museums, but the libraries of educational institutions do not depend on it but rather on the administrative departments of the ministry. This indicates that up to now the concept of a school library has been merely a collection of books, regardless of its location, barely serving the school program. The role of librarian, almost always without professional training, is limited to taking care of the shelving and the lending of this material.

In recent years, however, there has been an awareness of this situation and a National Commission of Libraries in the Ministry of Education has been formed by well-known librarians and presided over by the Director of Libraries, Archives, and Museums. This commission has analyzed the present situation, formulated specific recommendations, and organized activities to make clear the function of the libraries at different levels.

Among the public libraries there are eleven that depend on the Department of Libraries, Archives, and Museums, sixty-six municipal libraries, and eighty-two that are school or institutional libraries that lend their services to the public. Until a few years ago the National Library and the Severin Library of Valparaíso were the only public libraries in the country.

Generally the services of the public libraries are limited to giving a minimum amount of information and lending reading material in the reading room and at home. In some libraries the latter is not even done. The majority of the public libraries do not lend the services they should.

The resources of the municipal libraries are used almost exclusively by students, due to a lack of knowledge of their existence on the part of the community. As an example, in 1963 one municipal library served 2335 adults and 11,305 students, mostly in grammar school and high school.

The municipal governments have to set aside 1% of their income and 5% of the mayor's budget for the foundation, aid, or support of cultural activities, among which are included the libraries. This explains why the libraries of these institutions are the ones which show the most dynamism. However, there is no coordination or cooperation among institutional libraries except for their common entry in the register which the Department of Libraries, Archives, and Museums keeps and the delivery of books to the registered libraries, of which there are a total of 624, both school and public.

Among specialized libraries are included those with a fiscal, semifiscal, private, international, or binational organization. This type of library has received the greatest amount of attention on the part of the authorities of the organizations it serves, thus leading, together with the university libraries, in organization and quality of services. In 1964 there were fifty specialized libraries registered with CENID (National Center of Information and Documentation).

The use made of the collections in these libraries is a good indication of the usefulness of their services. Twenty-eight of them annually lend about 250,000 items (books, pamphlets, magazines, etc.). The total number of books in these libraries amounts to 400,000 volumes. In addition they contain important collections of periodicals.

The Library of the National Congress deserves to be mentioned for its special character and its rich collection. In 1883 the Library of the House of Representatives was founded through the initiative of Representative Don Pedro Montt, and later in 1885 it started to serve both legislative bodies. Among its first directors was Don Arturo Alessandri Palma, twice the President of Chile.

This library has the right of legal trusteeship and has the trusteeship of material of the United Nations, of the DEA, and the OIT. It has a collection of 400,000 bibliographical works on law, economy, sociology, statistics, etc. Besides a collection of Chilean laws, it possesses a repertoire of laws of many countries and keeps extensive collections of journals or bulletins of sessions of many foreign parliaments. It also maintains an archive on the press (clippings from newspapers and some Chilean magazines), classified by subject. At the present it owns the following catalogs which make extensive material accessible:

1. Catalog of printed (published) works.
2. Catalog of articles from Chilean, and also many foreign, newspapers. These include over 1,000,000 cards.
3. Catalog on the Chilean press. It files the main content of the newspapers of Santiago according to subject.
4. Catalog on foreign legislation. The collection of foreign laws the library has is on about 1,000,000 cards.
5. Catalog on Chilean legislation. It is made up of all the national legal texts from the beginning of the Republic to the present.
6. Catalog on the Memoirs of the Foreign Relations of Chile. It analytically catalogs the content of the publication.
7. Catalog of parliamentary labor. Alphabetical catalog of all parliamentarians, from the beginning of this legislative body up to the present, with a record of all their interventions, speeches, motions, etc. Around 1,000,000 cards.
8. History and index of laws. Index with references to the Bulletins of the Sessions for all the procedures the shaping of laws require.

Since 1947 the Library of Congress, along with the School of Juridical and Social Sciences of the University of Chile, has mantained the Juridical Editorial of Chile. Both the university and the specialized libraries collaborate through interlibrary loans. The work of CENID (see *Centro Nacional de Información y Documentación*) contributed to making this collaboration possible, especially by putting together the Collective Catalog.

The Association of Librarians, created in 1953, is made up of most of the professional librarians of Chile. Its principal objectives are to cooperate in the creation and patronization of libraries in the country; to study, propose, and support initiatives toward the scientific and technical betterment of the national libraries; to contribute to the fulfillment of the international library treaties agreed to by Chile; to favor professional advancement; and to maintain an information publication and print technical works.

The association has accomplished the work of bringing its members closer together, has studied library problems on a national scale, has promoted the creation of libraries, and has patronized interlibrary cooperation by issuing the *Code of Inter-Library Lending*.

Its investigations, done every two years, have studied the following: the exchange of publications; the basics for planning libraries; the analysis of the present state of Chilean libraries, and of libraries and the community. It publishes *Bulletin of the Association* and *Bibliotheka*.

BIBLIOGRAPHY

Asociación de Bibliotecarios de Chile, *Código de Préstamo Interbibliotecario de la Asociación de Bibliotecarios de Chile, 1966.*

Asociación de Bibliotecarios de Chile, "Problemas de los Servicios Bibliotecarios en Chile," *Terceras Jornadas Bibliotecarias Chilenas. Santiago 16–20 Noviembre, 1964. Informe final.*

"Enfoque a la realidad bibliotecaria nacional," *Documentos sobre planeamiento integral de la educación chilena,* Publicaciones de la Comisión de Planeamiento de la Educación Chilena, No. 4.

Feliú Cruz, Guillermo, *Historia de las fuentes de la bibliografía chilena, Ensayo crítico,* Biblioteca Nacional, Santiago, 1968.

Montt, Luis, *Notice historique sur la Bibliothèque Nationale de Santiago du Chili. Extrait des procès-verbaux et mémoires du Congrés International des Bibliothècaires,* H. Welter, Paris, 1901.

Sales Viú, Vicente, "Significado y valor histórico de la Biblioteca Central de la Universidad," *Bol. Univ. Chile.,* No. 5, 57–60 (August 1959).

Thayer Ojeda, Tomás, "Las bibliotecas coloniales de Chile," *Rev. Bibliog. Chilena Extranjera,* 1(2, 3, 5, 6, 7, 9, 10, 11) (February–March, April, May, June, July, August, September, November 1913).

Unión Panamericana, *Planeamiento nacional de servicios bibliotecarios. Volumen II: por países, parte 1, Chile y México,* Washington, 1966.

Vaïsse, Emilio, "Las bibliotecas coloniales de Chile," *Revista de Bibliografía Chilena y Extranjera.* 1(8), 73–76 (August 1913).

MARÍA TERESA SANZ B-M.
(*translated by Savina A. Roxas*)

CHILE. UNIVERSITY OF CHILE, SCHOOL OF LIBRARY SCIENCE

Chile is a country with nine million inhabitants and eight universities: two of them are state schools (the University of Chile and the State Technical University) and six are private schools (Catholic University of Chile, University of Concepcion, Catholic University of Valparaiso, The University of Federico Santa Maria, University of Austral, and University of the North).

There is only one School of Library Science; that of the University of Chile, dependent on the School of Philosophy and Education. This school is the historical product of a series of partial and isolated innovations that go back to 1913, with the National Library offering the first library science courses.

In 1922 the first two scholarships for the study of library science were granted: one to the teacher and poet Lucile Godoy, also known as Gabriele Mistral, who won the Nobel Prize for Poetry in 1945; and the other to Benjamin Cohen, who in his position of diplomat represented the republic during several decades and became a high official in international organizations.

In the period between 1923 and 1940, August Eyquen, Margaret Mieres, and Hector Fruenzalida-Villegas studied library science in the United States. Due to Mr. Fruenzalida-Villegas' efforts on his return, the Central Library of the University of Chile was begun.

The Central Library, in conjunction with the Rockefeller Foundation, brought the well-known North American library expert Prof. Edward Heiliger for a visit to Chile in 1945–1946 to teach basic courses in library science to the "Librarians in Service." He taught these courses again in 1946–1947 and in 1947–1948. The course offerings by Mr. Heiliger gave impetus to the formation of the "Librarians of Universities" in Chile.

Parallel to this, the lawyer Alberto Villalon-Galdames obtained his B.A., M.A., and Ph.D. degrees at the University of Michigan between 1947–1951. Professores Luisa Arce-Rovedy and Mary Bustamante-Sanchez not only studied with Mr. Heiliger, but also obtained their M.A. degrees at the University of Denver.

In 1949 the Central Library of the University of Chile founded the first school for training professional librarians, the School of Library Economy.

After one decade, in March 1959, Prof. Alberto Villalon-Galdames, the then head of the school, and also the Director of the School of the Faculty of Philosophy and Education, was officially named the Director. The School was created officially by the University of Chile in August 1959, and officially recognized by the Government in January 1960. In 1966 the name of the school was changed to the School of Library Science.

In October 1967, a very serious reform movement, which is still not completed, was initiated in the University of Chile. The University's structure will be revised and new groups will participate in the study of important university problems.

One consequence of the reform that directly affects the School of Library Science is the addition of Documentation to its area of concern.

The School of Library Science is one of the Professional Schools of the Faculty of Philosophy and Education. As a result of reform, the actual schools will disappear now that the new structure is based on departments. The Commission for Reform of the Faculty has recommended that the present School of Library Science be changed to the Department of Library Science and Documentation. This will give the department the responsibility for education, research, and expansion in these related disciplines.

The Faculty of Philosophy and Education is the largest university within the University of Chile. It has registered the highest number of students, 7200, plus 2000 students of the "Licero Manuel de Salas," a secondary school dependent on it. The matriculation of some departments or schools is higher than the total matriculation of the thirteen other Faculties of the University.

The faculty includes a Department of Education, in which there are the most students. It works in cooperation with the departments of the different specialities: Spanish, German, French, English, Italian, Classical Languages, Philosophy, History, Mathematics, Physics, Chemistry, Biology, etc. Among Professional Schools besides Library Science are Elementary Education, Geography, Journalism, Psychology, and Sociology. In all, it prepares professionals in twenty-nine specialities and it relies upon a central library and more than thirty branch libraries.

The School of Library Science's goal is to prepare professionals for their highest potential level. It gives its students complete preparation in the basic disciplines that constitute the science of library work; its teachings are provided with an historical focus; it offers criticism of present-day society; it analyzes the current trend of thought in library science; and above all, it gives its graduates an insight into the problems that affect the country and an ability to analyze foreign developments in library science and documentation in relation to the needs of Chile within the Latin-American context. The school believes that the theoretical and practical knowledge of national problems in librarianship must be instilled in its graduates so that they can contribute to the solution of the socio-economic problems of the country.

Admission to the school requires a secondary education and a passing grade on an academic aptitude test. This has replaced the old Bachelor's degree and is a test similar to the one used for matriculation in any university in Chile.

The number of matriculated students has ranged from 20 in 1946 to 177 in 1969. As of July 31, 1969, 512 librarians in Chile were graduated from the school.

Two types of study plans exist: the common and the special. The common plan, in experimental form, consists of a total of four years of studies plus three months of professional practice in large libraries under the supervision of the school. The special plan is organized for professionals, graduates, and advanced university students in other areas who also want a library science degree. The difference between plans of studies is that students of the common plan must pursue studies of general culture as well as courses in the professional areas. Students in the special plan may study only the professional subjects without doing the three months practice work.

The professional university degree for library science granted by the University of Chile is a legislative prerequisite for working in state libraries. On July 10, 1969, legislation legally ratified this and approved Law 17.161 that created the College of Librarians of Chile.

The school has matriculated both European and Latin-American students without discrimination.

The courses offered between 1946–1948, as well as those of the first ten years of the school, had a one-year academic plan of study. The class of 1959–1960 had a two-year academic plan of study. This was augmented to five semesters for the class of 1960–1962. From 1961–1967 university students were distributed among the three central departments in the faculty to follow a two-year general studies program.

Students who were interested in librarianship, however, were required to take their two-year general studies program in the Central Department of Philosophy and Letters. After completing the two-year studies program, students were awarded a Certificate of General Studies. After this, the certificate holders from the Central Department of Philosophy and Letters were eligible for a further year of study in the School of Library Science. During this time (1961–1967) the entire training period for librarians was three years.

Upon the disappearance of the central departments of the faculty at the end of the academic year of 1968, students entered directly into the School of Library Science. The curriculum was maintained for the last time as a three-year plan for the class that began their training in 1968.

The Assembly of the School consisted of an academic group made up of three types of people: professors and assistants who had 65% of the decision making power; students who had 25% of the decision making power; and a nonacademic group composed of professionals, technicians, administrators, and service officials who collectively had 10% of the decision making power. This assembly was firmly of the belief that the three-year program was insufficient academic preparation for professional librarians.

At the end of the 1969 academic year, therefore, a four-year plan of experimental studies was initiated. This removed the need for a possible postgraduate supplementary study program.

In the course of 1969, the Interdepartmental Commission of Careers began and, as such, appointed a Commission of Library Sciences to study the new four-year Plan. The faculty is responsible for the administration of the program. The final responsibility for inaugurating the change will rest officially with the University Organization Council.

The new plan of study consists of 44 credits (1 credit represents 3 semester hours of work), grouped in three well-defined areas: 12 of General Culture, 24 of Professional Formation, and 8 of Specialization. The subjects of General Culture and Specialization are offered by three different departments, the Professional courses are offered by the School of Library Science only.

Twelve credits of General Culture are Literature, Language A, Language B, Introduction to Philosophy, and Culture of Chile. Eight credits of elective subjects permit the student to choose an area of specialization. Twenty-four credits of

Professional Formation offered by the School of Library Science are Fundamentals; Methods of Investigation; Documentation and Scientific Development; History of the Book, the Publisher and the Library; Administration and Planning; Cataloguing and Classification; Bibliographical Resources; Documentation; Seminar of Specialized Libraries; Seminar of Thesis; Seminar of Practice; and University Libraries, Scholastics, and Publishing.

In the professional sequence the theoretical introduction is combined with practical work, materials are displayed and discussed, and students work actively with professors. The students are instructed in the handling of bio-bibliographical sources and in the practice of specialized techniques to familiarize them with bibliographical tools. The students are assigned individual research and also work as teams under supervision. They participate in seminars and symposia organized by the school; they attend lectures on library science given by national professors, specialists, and occasionally by a foreign speaker. The students visit different types of libraries, publishing companies, bookstores, and scientific and technical institutions. They attend obligatory and optional lectures; they make bibliographies, resumes, bulletins of bibliographical information; they work on projects of library planning; and they submit reports. They participate critically in the political and educational progress of the various schools with regard to library and cultural expansion, and develop programs of diverse groups in the community under the supervision of their teachers.

An old aspiration of the school—the annual evaluation of the work of each professor—has been finally accepted by the faculty. This idea was developed in March 1959 by the director and was finally approved at the end of 1967 within the movement for reform. Therefore, 1968 was the first academic year in which students evaluated the work of the professor. For this evaluation *ad hoc* committees will be used that have been approved by the Assembly of Professors and Students.

Some major accomplishments should be noted. For example, from 1960 to 1968 the school organized annual five to six week sessions for graduates. These courses had as their objectives research into the development in library science on a worldwide basis; instructing professionals in the most modern techniques used in libraries; scientific research; and documentation. National and international experts have offered lectures in these sessions.

Relations between the school and the Association of Libraries is excellent. The school has participated in the organization and preparation of material for, and development of, the various Chilean Library Association Journals. The President of the Association attends the sessions of the Assembly of the School. This is the only example in Chile of such collaboration between the university and its alumni. Moreover, the school has collaborated with the Supreme Government and the Council of Rectors in innovations, studies for library planning, and information services in the country. The school has assisted the community in establishing pilot libraries in secondary schools, and eventually this work will be extended to primary schools and industry, with short courses offered to the personnel in various types of libraries.

The School has an annual publication, *Annual Bibliography of the Faculty of Philosophy and Education* (4 volumes). A single volume covers the years 1960–1964. This publication reports the works of the professors and researchers of the faculty. There is interest in extending this publication of bibliographical information to all university organizations.

The school aspires to put into effect, as soon as possible, a year of postgraduate studies leading to Ph.D.'s in Library Science, Documentation, Archivology, and Musicology. Later, after creating a fifth year of studies, it aspires to offering the Ph.D. of Library Science in a six or seven year study program.

The school also plans to offer a correspondence training program on a technical level for people already working in libraries who lack any specialized training. This will be offered to anyone in the Latin-American countries requesting it.

In the service planned for the community, the School of Library Science will try to establish an extension of its specialized activities through bookmobiles. Specifically, the action of joining the forces of the University of Chile and the Municipality of Nunoa for bringing a bookmobile service to Nunoa is well under way.

The School of Library Science, taking advantage of the capacity of its professors and the quality of its researchers, aspires to initiate a progressive publication of original Chilean works, national bibliographies, bio-bibliographical works, resumes of articles, and texts of study.

With the participation of representative institutions of other Latin-American countries, it intends to make the publication of a *Latin-American Library Science Journal* a reality as soon as possible.

Finally, it is the aspiration of the School of Library Science to become in itself, a true Regional School of Library Science.

ALBERTO VILLALÓN-GALDAMES AND ABRAHAM PIMSTEIN-LAMAS
(*Translated by Savina A. Roxas*)

CHINA, LIBRARIES IN THE PEOPLE'S REPUBLIC OF

Historical Introduction

Libraries in China, as in Greece, were first organized as official archives, followed by the establishment of centralized libraries by the government and private collections. The earliest known Chinese documents surviving today are those written or incised on animal bones and tortoise shells, which formed part of the royal archives in the latter part of the Shang dynasty (1765?–1123? B.C.). Although inscriptions were made on bronze, stone, and pottery, the direct ancestry of the Chinese book is traced to bamboo or wooden slips and silk rolls. The use of these materials lasted until the third or fourth century A.D., by which time paper was extensively used for writing and for books.

During the Chou dynasty (1122?–256 B.C.) the use of documents in various branches of the government for interstate communication led to the establishment of archives in the royal court and feudal states. The ministers in charge of rites and education were entrusted with the custody of official records on military campaigns, appointments, conferment of honors, royal proclamations, and diplomatic documents. The archives were under the care of officials called *shih* or historiographers, whose duty was to record important events of the court, utterances of the king or the princes, and activities of the government. Members of a technical profession by inheritance, they served as recorders, writers, or custodians of documents in the archives of the royal court and feudal states.

With the gradual disintegration of feudalism, the lower classes began to acquire education and enter the service of the government. Plebeian writers of various schools of thought and of science and literature flourished. This was the beginning of writings by individual authors and of private collections.

The feudal period in Chinese history ended in 221 B.C., when a unified empire was formed under the first emperor of Ch'in. In order to insure unification, a series of precautionary measures, including the standardization of writing and censorship of literature, was instituted. In 213 B.C. the emperor decreed that, with the exception of certain technical works and state documents, all books be burned. Those which were concealed and which survived were destroyed in 206 B.C. when the imperial palaces were sacked and burned by the insurgents.

After the Ch'in empire was overthrown and succeeded by the Han dynasty (206 B.C.–A.D. 220), systematic recovery of works of antiquity was ordered. Official agents were dispatched to search for cached books and books kept by private families, and these were transferred to the imperial library. For the first time in Chinese history, a centralized imperial library was established and used by scholars. The collection was catalogued and described by Liu Hsiang (80–8 B.C.) under the title *Pieh lu* (Separate Records) and later arranged by his son Liu Hsin (d. 23 A.D.) into seven categories called *Ch'i lueh* (Seven Epitomes). This scheme was composed of seven main classes: generalalia; classics; philosophy; poetry; military works; science and occultism; and divination, medicine, and trades, with 38 subdivisions. This is the earliest known annotated catalog, and the first classification scheme used in China.

Paper was invented around A.D. 100 and gradually displaced wood, bamboo, and silk as writing material. It gave great impetus to the production of books and the development of libraries.

The four centuries which span the period from the fall of the Han dynasty in A.D. 220 to the establishment of the T'ang dynasty are generally referred to as the "Dark Ages," and were marked by incessant political upheavals and incursions by barbarian hordes. However, distinct advances in library development were made during this period. All books were for the first time transcribed on paper. A standard classification system known as *ssu pu* (Four Divisions) was devised by

Hsun Hsu (A.D. 231–289), a curator of the imperial library of the Chin dynasty, and this has been used with some modification and subdivisions as a standard system for book classification for well-nigh fifteen centuries. This period also witnessed a prodigious production of Buddhist literature, especially under the Sui dynasty (590–618), when the empire was again unified. More than 130,000 rolls of Buddhist works were transcribed and several comprehensive bibliographies compiled. Imperial collections were stored in palaces at the eastern capital, Loyang. Unfortunately all these were consumed by a conflagration which swept the palaces at the fall of the Sui dynasty. It is possible that some 8,000 rolls were salvaged, for these were passed on to the T'ang dynasty.

The T'ang dynasty (618–907), which overthrew the Sui and unified the whole nation, is regarded as one of the most brilliant in Chinese history. Many of its emperors were ardent patrons of literature and libraries. Block printing originated in the seventh century with the reproduction of Buddhist icons and Taoist charms. It was employed on a relatively small scale in the eighth and ninth centuries for the printing of Buddhist sutras which were still in the form of rolls, and hand copying remained the principal method of duplication until the following dynasty. In the middle of the eighth century a rebellion broke out and both the eastern and western capitals, Loyang and Changan, were invested and sacked. The country was again thrown into turmoil and books in the various depositories were dispersed and destroyed. After the rebellion was completely suppressed, efforts were again directed toward the restoration of the libraries. Although the T'ang dynasty continued to exist for another century and a half, it soon deteriorated and was unable to regain its former grandeur. Toward the end of the ninth century the country was confronted with a series of civil wars and the dynasty eventually collapsed.

The interregnum of half a century following the fall of the T'ang dynasty was a period of incessant warfare and turbulence. The country was divided and subjected to the mixed rule of native and alien rulers. Relatively little progress was made in the development of libraries; yet ironically block printing was popularized and employed on a large scale at this time through the efforts of Feng Tao (882–954) who devoted twenty-one years between 932 and 953 to supervise the editing and printing of the Confucian classics and their commentaries. From this time onward the supply of books became more plentiful and easily accessible to scholars and libraries.

The Sung dynasty (960–1279) was established after five decades of chaos. It was important militarily and was constantly harassed by nomadic hordes from the north and northeast. Yet it made considerable progress in philosophy, art, and literature. It was an era of great encyclopedias and catalogs, destined to play a major role in Chinese libraries. With the increased demand for printed books, Sung artisans brought the art to a high standard of excellence.

After the Nuchen Tartars took the Sung capital at Kaifeng and founded the Chin dynasty, the Sung court was forced to take refuge at Linan (modern Hangchow) and established the Southern Sung empire (1127–1279) there. Comparative peace and prosperity prevailed and the emperors spared no effort in building up the imperial depositories. Both imperial and private libraries flourished at this time. One of the greatest contributions by Sung scholars and collectors was the compilation of voluminous annotated catalogs, many of which survive today.

The Mongols vanquished both the Chin Tartars in the north and the Southern Sung in the south, and established the Yuan dynasty (1260–1368). It in turn was overthrown by Chu Yuan-chang (1328–1398) who founded the Ming dynasty (1368–1644). The most memorable literary achievement of the Ming period was the compilation of the great thesaurus *Yung-lo ta tien*. It contains reproductions in part or in whole of existing literature preserved at that time. Completed in 1408, it comprised 11,095 handwritten folio volumes. This compilation has been instrumental in the preservation of many ancient and rare works which would otherwise be irretrievably lost to the world. According to the latest census, less than 400 volumes are extant today, scattered all over the world.

The Wen yuan ko and the Huang shih ch'eng were two of the important buildings housing imperial libraries in the Ming dynasty. Private libraries, including those of the princes, also proliferated. The T'ien i ko, a private library belonging to the Fan family in Ningpo, was an outstanding one and is preserved to this day.

The Ming dynasty was overthrown by the Manchus who founded the Ch'ing dynasty (1644–1912). Although an alien people, the Manchus were admirers of Chinese culture. An outstanding achievement in this period was the compilation of the *Ssu k'u ch'üan shu* (the Four Treasure Library, covering the four categories of Chinese literature). It was completed in 1782 after nearly ten years of unremitting labor. It consists of some 3500 titles in 36,000 handwritten volumes, selected from books which were in existence at that time. The first set was stored at the Wen yuan ko in the imperial compound in Peking. Subsequently six additional manuscript sets were made and stored in specially built libraries, three in the north and three in the south. Of the seven sets, only four survive today. One is in the custody of the National Palace Museum in Taiwan and three are preserved in mainland China.

In 1909 toward the end of the Ch'ing dynasty a national library in the modern sense (first known as The Capital Library and later as The National Library) was founded with books formerly preserved in the Hall of Classics and the Library of the Imperial Cabinet as its nucleus. Subsequently the holdings of a few private libraries as well as 8500 Buddhist manuscripts of the T'ang dynasty discovered in 1907 were added. With the establishment of the Republic in 1912 the library was reorganized and many notable collections, including the Jehol copy of the *Ssu k'u ch'üan shu* (known as the Wen Ching ko set) and 60 stray volumes of the *Yung-lo ta tien,* were transferred to the library. In 1929 the Metropolitan Library and the National Library, supported respectively by the China Foundation and the Ministry of Education, amalgamated to form the National Library of Peiping. A modern building with several connected units was erected and completed in 1931.

Another national library known as the National Central Library was established in Nanking and was opened to the public in 1933. About 50,000 volumes belonging to the Ministry of Education were transferred to serve as its nucleus; subsequently many other substantial collections were added.

Library Development in Communist China

Since the Chinese Communists took over the mainland in 1949 they have made all-out efforts toward the development of libraries and extension of library facilities. They recognize that the library is a viable and effective instrument for guiding and controlling the masses toward the construction of a Communist society. Library service is geared to the Communist Party's cultural policy "to serve the politics of the proletariat, to serve production, and to serve the workers, peasants and soldiers."

In the Common Program adopted by the Chinese People's Political Consultative Conference, the cultural and educational objectives of the party are "to elevate the cultural standard of the people, train personnel for national reconstruction, eradicate all feudal, compradore and Fascist thinking, and foster thoughts of service to the people."

In recounting library development in Communist China during the two decades of its existence, we may conveniently divide the review into two periods. The first decade saw the proliferation of libraries and library activities; the entire nation was library conscious and phenomenal progress was made. The First Five-Year Plan (1953–1957) was introduced and libraries played an important role in the reconstruction of the nation. The objective of library service in this decade, in common with other economic and cultural endeavors, was "to readjust and consolidate, concentrate on essentials, raise both quality and quantity, and aim for steady progress."

In 1956 the Communist Party raised the cry "March toward the Sciences." College and research libraries concentrated their efforts on building up their scientific and technical resources to support reference and research work. In the same year was launched the short-lived "Let the hundred flowers bloom" movement, when citizens were encouraged to voice any criticism they might have of the regime, but it came to an abrupt end in the following year, resulting in the repression of free expression among the intellectuals. In 1958 was launched the campaign called the "Great Leap Forward," designed to catapult China into an advanced state of industrialization and to demonstrate that the will of the masses could overcome seemingly insurmountable obstacles. The results of this unrealistic approach proved far from satisfactory. The ensuing burgeoning of the communes resulted in a heavy demand for popular reading materials.

During the first decade Soviet influence on Chinese libraries, in common with other areas of Chinese life, was predominant. Translations from Russian works on library science were popular and Russian librarians were invited to visit China to give lectures and advice. All these developments had important repercussions on libraries, which kept pace with and reflected the aspirations and needs of the times.

An excellent summary on library service during the first decade of the Communist regime appeared in the 1959, No. 4, issue of the *Peking University Journal*. It was written by two faculty members and seven students of the Department of

Library Science of the University. It relates the progress that had been made in this period.

The second decade (1959–1969) was marked by a number of momentous events which adversely affected library activities. The Second Five-Year Plan (1958–1962) was set in operation, but it seemed to have overreached itself and the national economy suffered a great reverse. In 1960 relations between China and Soviet Russia began to deteriorate, followed by acrimonious polemics between the erstwhile friends. Soviet influence and assistance began to wane and eventually ceased.

The year 1964 witnessed the first nuclear explosion, followed two years later by the commencement of the Third Five-Year Plan. These developments provided some impetus to the expansion of library facilities, but all hopes were shattered by the cataclysmic Great Proletarian Cultural Revolution which was launched in early 1966. It shook, and in many instances upset, the cultural, political, social, and economic structure of the nation. Library development has been curtailed and in some cases disrupted because of the rampage of the hordes of fanatic Red Guards all over the country. Except for the tremendous volume of works of Mao Tse-tung and propaganda materials, very little has been published in recent years. Since the early 1960s it has become increasingly difficult to obtain printed materials from Communist China. Information on Chinese libraries in the later half of the second period has been especially meager.

In April 1969 the Ninth National Congress of the Communist Party was convened, and since then order has to a large extent been restored. In the wake of the turbulence the Communist leaders are striving against tremendous odds to achieve stabilization, moderation, and unity. The Congress reaffirmed observance of the basic philosophy of Marxism-Leninism and Mao Tse-tung thought. To carry out the revolutionary movements of class struggle, the struggle for production and scientific experiment, the library as a source of enlightenment will no doubt play an important role in the future as Communist China enters a new decade.

The legal basis for the development of library service in Communist China is the National Book Coordination Act promulgated in 1957. In order to achieve a better coordinated and controlled library system in the country to facilitate scientific research, a Library Section was created under the Science and Technology Committee of the State Council. The act specified two immediate objectives: (1) the establishment of national and regional library network centers; (2) the compilation of union catalogs covering the holdings of the entire nation.

The responsibilities of the library network centers are: (1) to serve scientific research; (2) to collect publications in a greater variety and of a higher quality; (3) to compile union catalogs and checklists of new publications; (4) the international exchange of publications (to be conducted by certain library network centers); (5) the development of photoduplication services (to be conducted by certain library network centers); and (6) the training of basic personnel.

As the result of this act, two national library network centers were organized, one in Peking and the other in Shanghai, composed of several leading libraries in each area. The Peking Library serves as the core of the network in the capital as well as the center of guidance for activities of all libraries in the nation. Nine regional library network centers were set up in Tientsin, Liaoning, Heilungkiang, Shensi, Kansu, Szechwan, Hupeh, Kwangtung, and Kiangsu. Other library network centers were set up voluntarily in Kirin and Chekiang. The regional library network centers are composed of libraries designated by authorities of the provinces or municipalities in which they are located. Additional library network centers are to be established when necessary.

The national library network center in Peking is composed of the following units: the Peking Library, the Chinese Academy of Sciences Library, libraries of the Peking Union Medical College and the Chinese Academy of Medical Sciences, the National Geological Library, libraries of the Chinese Academy of Agricultural Sciences, the Agricultural University, the Chinese People's University, Peking University, Tsing-hua University, and Peking Normal University.

The national library network center in Shanghai is made up of the following components: the Shanghai Library, the Shanghai Science and Technology Library, the Library of Historical Literature, the Shanghai Branch of the Chinese Academy of Sciences, the libraries of Futan University, the First Medical College of Shanghai, the Shanghai University of Military Medicine, and Chiao-tung University.

The national library network centers are open to scientists from all over the country. Libraries of institutions of higher learning, in addition to satisfying the needs of their faculties and students, are expected to make available their special collections to scientists in order to supplement the public libraries. For example, the library of the Normal University in Peking makes its holdings available to students of education.

To promote standardization and to strengthen coordination, committees are to be set up in each library network center. Their primary responsibilities are: (1) to assist in the over-all planning of library development; (2) to study and plan the allocation of responsibilities among member libraries within the network such as acquisition, distribution, exchange, and interlibrary loan; (3) to study and plan the compilation of union catalogs and checklists of new publications; and (4)`to study problems relating to the betterment of quality of work among library personnel.

The second major objective of the National Book Coordination Act deals with the compilation of union catalogs. Under the national library network center an office is to be established in Peking Library. Its functions are: (1) to make a study and survey of the holdings of the country and the status of their cataloging; (2) to make plans for the compilation of union catalogs; (3) to draft rules for their compilation; (4) to coordinate, plan, and supervise the compilation work; and (5) to combine holding reports of various libraries, to edit, collate, and publish the catalogs. Target dates are set for the completion of a number of union catalogs in various categories. Among them are Western language works in certain fields, Western language periodicals, Chinese periodicals, local histories, collectanea, the history of Chinese revolution, and works on Chinese agriculture.

In 1955, before the enactment of the National Book Coordination Act, the Ministry of Culture issued a directive requiring all publishers in China to submit a copy of each of their publications to various agencies within three days of publication. These are to be distributed as follows: two copies to the Library of the Bureau of Publications Control of the Ministry of Culture, one copy each to the Central Department of Propaganda of the Chinese Communist Party, the Library of the Academy of Sciences, the Peking Library, and the local Office of Culture at the place of publication.

Supervision and control of the various types of libraries are as follows: public libraries (including national, provincial, municipal, county, and cultural center libraries) are to be supervised by and under the control of the Ministry of Culture; college and university libraries, under the Ministry of Higher Eduation; elementary and secondary school libraries, under the Ministry of Education; trade union libraries, under the National Trade Union; and special libraries, under appropriate government agencies. In its attempt to achieve a better coordinated and controlled library system, the government has vigorously pushed its "mass-line" policy stipulating that all library activities be oriented toward the welfare and needs of the masses.

To demonstrate their support, representatives of public libraries in forty-seven provinces, municipalities, and autonomous regions in the country offered eight suggestions on the tenth anniversary of the establishment of the People's Republic of China.

1. To expand the study clubs for the masses under the unified guidance of the party and in cooperation with related units, in order to further advance Communist education, to serve production, and to serve the cultural and technological revolution.
2. To increase book circulation and reading efficiency; strengthen readers' guidance service.
3. To extend positive assistance to counties, clubs and factories in the establishment of libraries and reading rooms.
4. To extend guidance service.
5. To participate in farm work and production brigades.
6. To improve the quality of library work by revolutionizing library techniques and procedures.
7. To promote cooperation between libraries and between libraries and related agencies.
8. To develop a library service oriented toward socialism.

These suggestions are applicable not only to the public libraries but are applicable, by and large, also to other types of libraries. The general trends of library development in the country are discernible as we review the highlights of a few of them below.

The Peking Library (known as the National Library of Peiping before 1949) is the largest in China and one of the largest in the world (see Figure 1). In 1965 its collections were reported to be in the neighborhood of 7,000,000 volumes, including more than 220,000 rare books and manuscripts. It holds portions of imperial libraries: the Chi hsi tien of the Southern Sung dynasty (thirteenth century) and the Wen yuan ko of the Ming dynasty (fifteenth century). It possesses a com-

FIGURE 1. *The Peking Library.*

FIGURE 2. *Tsing-hua University, Peking.*

FIGURE 3. *Tientsin People's Library.*

FIGURE 4. *Szechuan University Library.*

plete set of the *Ssu k'u ch'üan shu* in 36,300 manuscript volumes formerly housed in a palace in Jehol (known as Wen ching ko), 215 volumes of the manuscript encyclopedia *Yung-lo ta tien,* and over 8000 rolls of the Tun-huang Buddhist manuscripts made in the T'ang dynasty.

Since 1949 the Peking Library has been greatly enriched by numerous transfers and donations. Major transfers include about seventy volumes of the *Yung-lo ta tien* from foreign as well as domestic sources; 4500 rolls of Buddhist *Tripitaka* printed in Chao-ch'eng, Shansi, between 1118 and 1173; and more than 300 titles in Emperor Ch'ien-lung's library known as "T'ien lu lin lang," which was formerly in the custody of the Palace Museum. It is stated that many public-spirited collectors also have contributed their private libraries to the state. The library of nearly 100,000 volumes of the late Cheng Chen-to, Vice Minister of the Ministry of Culture and an outstanding bibliophile, was added to Peking Library's collections.

The Peking Library is a depository of all books published in the country; it is also entrusted with international exchange of publications with about 100 countries. A reference as well as a free public library, the Peking Library is the center of all types of library activities in the country. Training classes for different segments of library work are given. Of interest is one established in 1961 for the training of technicians in the repair of books in the traditional format.

Under the auspices of the First National Library Network Center, the Peking Library compiled and published in 1961 an exceedingly useful work, entitled *Ch'üan kuo Chung wen ch'i k'an lien ho mu lu,* which is a union list of serials published during the years 1833–1949. It records the issues of 19,115 titles held by fifty libraries throughout mainland China.

The main library of the Chinese Academy of Sciences in Peking was founded in 1951, with the 330,000 volumes inherited from the Institute of History and Philology of the Academia Sinica. Branch libraries were subsequently established in Shanghai, Nanking, Lanchow, Wuhan, Canton, and many other cities. Up to the end of 1958 there were 113 branch libraries and reading rooms in the various research institutes of the Academy. At the end of 1960 the main library of the Academy had a collection of 4,480,926 pieces (including 2,359,461 issues of periodicals), 1,836,465 patent reports of twenty-two countries, and 285,000 reels of microfilm. The microfilms comprised 19,000 reports of the U.S. Atomic Energy Commission, 130,000 pieces of U.S. government publications, the Stein collection of 2,000 Tunhuang scrolls in the British Museum, proceedings of more than 2000 meetings of international learned societies, and more than 100 Chinese local histories held by Japanese libraries.

The Chinese Academy of Sciences Library is also one of the depositories of new publications in the country and is responsible for the exchange of scientific and technical works with nearly 100 foreign countries. In addition to a union list of serials in Western languages, it has compiled and published a number of bibliographies of various subjects. It publishes a monthly newsletter with the title *Reference Materials for Library Work.* It has held training classes for the personnel of its many branches.

FIGURE 5. *Shanghai Library and Shanghai Museum.*

Shanghai, where the second national library network center is located, boasts one of the largest libraries in the country (see Figures 5 and 6). The Shanghai Library was formed in 1958 as a result of the amalgamation of the following libraries in the city: the Shanghai Library, the People's Library of Shanghai, the Science and Technology Library of Shanghai, the Historical Literature Library, and the Newspaper and Periodical Library. The total number of volumes was in the neighborhood of 5,000,000 in 1958. The Shanghai Library directs the compilation of a number of useful bibliographical tools. The *Chung-kuo ts'ung shu tsung lu,* an important index to Chinese books, was published by the Shanghai Library in 1959–1961. In three massive volumes, it includes 38,891 individual titles found in 2797 collectanea held by forty-one different libraries. The Shanghai Library is also responsible for organizing a network of community or street libraries in the city. In 1958 it was reported that there were 3400 such libraries or book stations.

FIGURE 6. *Shanghai Library reading room.*

The Nanking Library is the successor to the National Central Library. When the latter was removed to Taiwan in 1949, it was able to evacuate only its rare books, and left the bulk of its collections of about 1,000,000 volumes in the mainland. By the end of 1957 the Nanking Library had a collection of 3,000,000 volumes with a number of special reading rooms. It is especially rich in local materials pertaining to the province of Kiangsu.

Institutions of higher learning also play a prominent part in library development in Communist China. In June 1958 there were 229 college and university libraries. In 1965 eight of them had a collection of 1,000,000 volumes each; eighteen had over 500,000 volumes each, and no fewer than fifty had over 300,000 volumes each. The more important of the university libraries are those of Peking University, the Chinese People's University, Tsing-hua University in Peking; and Nankai University in Tientsin; Futan University and Chiao-tung University in Shanghai; Nanking University; Wuhan University; and Chungshan University in Canton.

Peking University, the cradle of the May 4, 1919, student movement, has one of the largest university libraries in the country. The library was established in 1902 with a basic collection of 78,000 volumes transferred from more than six provincial bookstores and books acquired at that time. Before the Communist takeover in 1949 it had a collection of 724,894 volumes. In 1950 it took over the Yenching University library's holdings of 403,221 volumes, making a total of 1,128,115 volumes. Many private libraries were also acquired so that at the end of 1961 it had a collection of 2,379,848 volumes. It subscribes to nearly 3000 Chinese and foreign language magazines. The Peking University Library is one of the first to conduct various types of surveys to help develop its acquisitions, loan, and development policies.

Many different types of popular libraries catering to the masses have been established during the last two decades. Foremost among them are the rural libraries which take an active role in adult education. Since the organization of the people's communes for the 500 million farm population, rural libraries and reading facilities have literally sprung up like mushrooms in the countryside.

The smaller of these libraries hold several hundred volumes and the larger ones hold several thousand. They consist mostly of popular pamphlets on current events, general and scientific information, and picture storybooks. As a basic component in the structure of public libraries, they are regarded as a tool to combat illiteracy and to disseminate knowledge on socialism and farming techniques.

Housed mostly in makeshift quarters, the libraries are supported by funds set aside by the communes for welfare and recreation purposes. Members are encouraged to donate books or money, and to volunteer their services in staffing the libraries. Various devices are introduced to encourage the use of books and make known the resources to potential borrowers such as story hours, posters, exhibits, lantern slides, blackboard notices, cartoons, reading and discussion groups, poetry recitation, and plays.

In many communes mess halls are used as reading stations. Mobile circulating units deliver reading material to production brigades in workshops and farmlands and to village cultural centers scattered in rural communities. The popular slogan is "to deliver books to the readers." Commune libraries are regarded as a gigantic force "to elevate the consciousness of the peasants, to popularize cultural and technical knowledge, to incite enthusiasm in production, and to stimulate production." Municipal libraries also deliver books to the communes through the mobile service units and library workers are dispatched to train local personnel for library service.

In 1958 about ninety students and faculty members of the Department of Library Science of the Wuhan University went to Hsi-shui in Hupeh province with the dual purpose of participating in farm work and of guiding the development of commune libraries in rural communities. After a period of three months they went back to Wuhan and wrote five brochures on all aspects of commune libraries based on their experiences in the countryside.

There are also so-called "street libraries," initiated and supported by neighborhood residents to satisfy the cultural demands of the citizens and to familiarize them with party policy and programs. Each family is urged to donate a book to the community library. The popular slogan is, "by donating one book you are enabled to read 100."

To enlighten people of the minority groups and border regions, public libraries have been established. Many of the minority languages, hitherto in only spoken form, are now transcribed in written form with books printed and circulated. Libraries have been established for the Ning-hsia Moslem Autonomous Region, the Inner Mongolian Autonomous Region, the Yenpien Korean Autonomous Chou, and Sinkiang-Uighur Autonomous Region. Municipal libraries were also set up in

Urumchi, Sinkiang, and Lhasa, Tibet. A library of National Minorities Cultural Palace was established in Peking to serve as a liaison center.

Youth and children's libraries have been established in major cities; elsewhere reading rooms have been set aside in public libraries and cultural centers for their use. In Shanghai alone there were in 1958 more than sixty youth and children's libraries outside of schools. The main library, established in 1952, had a collection of more than 200,000 volumes in 1959. There is also the "Red Neckerchief Library Network," established, operated, and used by the youth and children themselves, with advice and assistance from the city library.

Libraries and reading rooms are set up in factories, mines, and commercial establishments for use of members of labor and trade unions. In 1955 the All-China Federation of Trade Unions called a conference in Peking to clarify the policy, tasks, and scope of these libraries. Although they are small in size, averaging 1000 volumes each, they aim to meet the cultural, scientific, and technical needs of the laboring masses. Up to the end of 1958, there were more than 35,000 such libraries throughout the country, with a total collection of 34 million volumes. A training class for the library personnel was conducted in that year by the Federation.

In their attempt to improve library service, librarians in mainland China have revamped some old procedures, discarded outdated practices, and introduced more streamlined operations. One of the most significant developments was the publication in August 1951 of a new national bibliography, the *Ch'üan kuo hsin shu mu*. This lists 10,406 titles published between October 1949 and December 1950. Until November 1954 it was edited and published by the National Bureau of Publications in Peking; subsequently it was published by the Accessions Library of the Bureau of Publications of the Ministry of Culture. Entries in the bibliography are arranged according to the Classification Scheme for Medium and Small Libraries. The frequency of publication has varied from time to time; it was first issued as a quarterly and in 1966 it appeared as a semimonthly. The status of the bibliography since the Cultural Revolution is not known. The *Ch'üan kuo tsung shu mu* is a cumulative national bibliography compiled by the Library of the Bureau of Publications of the Ministry of Culture. It is more selective and has a title index not found in the above title. The first volume covering the years 1949–1954 contains 21,809 titles; the volume covering 1958 contains 28,090 titles.

The *Ch'üan kuo chu yao pao k'an tzu liao so yin,* an index to materials in the principal newspapers and periodicals of the country, is a monthly first issued in 1955 by the Shanghai Municipal Library of Newspapers and Periodicals. Beginning in 1959 the index was divided into two separate series: Philosophy and Social Sciences and Natural Science and Technology.

In order to make research resources and holdings of various libraries known and in order to assist in the systematic development of their collections, numerous catalogs, union catalogs, and indexes have been compiled, including those on special subjects such as library science, local histories, periodicals, collectanea, agriculture, Chinese traditional medicine, and scientific and technical subjects. A national union catalog editorial section under the Science Planning Commission of the State Council is responsible for the planning and organization of such a compilation.

A few important union catalogs may be mentioned in passing. In 1957 the Chinese Academy of Sciences published a catalog of 1060 Russian language journals in its sixty-four affiliated institutes. In 1958 a bimonthly union catalog of Western publications on natural sciences acquired by more than 230 important libraries in the country was issued. The Peking Library sponsored in 1959 the publication of a union catalog of Western language journals held by 168 libraries. In two volumes, it contained 20,270 titles. It also published in 1961 a union catalog of works on Chinese traditional medicine representing the holdings of fifty-nine collections. The Ministry of Education also participated in the compilation in 1958 of a union list entitled *Foreign Language Periodicals in 47 College and University Libraries of China,* listing 12,044 titles.

Several newly devised classification schemes are in use in the Chinese mainland. The *Chung-kuo t'u shu fen lei fa* (Classification Scheme for Chinese Books), a decimal system devised by Liu Kuo-chun, was first pubished in 1929 and was revised and enlarged in 1957. Although it is widely used, it has been denounced as capitalist-inspired and reactionary in nature, incompatible with the Marxist-Leninist-Maoist concept of socialism.

The *Chung hsiao hsing t'u shu kuan t'u shu fen lei piao* (Classification Table for Medium and Small Libraries) was devised by the Peking Library. There are 26 main classes and a mixed notation of Roman letters and Arabic numerals is employed.

The *Chung-kuo jen min ta hsueh t'u shu kuan t'u shu fen lei fa* (Chinese People's University Library Classification System) was first published in 1953; its fourth enlarged edition appeared in 1962. There are twenty-five main classes with ten tables for subdivisions and four appendices. For notation, Arabic numerals are employed. A subject index is arranged by the number of strokes of key words. This system is widely used, since it was adopted by the national bibliography as the newspaper and periodical index.

The *Chung-kuo k'o hsueh yuan t'u shu kuan t'u shu fen lei fa* (Classification Scheme of the Library of the Chinese Academy of Sciences), published in 1959, contains twenty-five classes. There is a separate index volume arranged according to the new Latin spelling of the key words.

The *Wu-han ta hsueh t'u shu fen lei fa* (The Wuhan University Library Classification System) was first published in 1958. It has five main divisions with twenty-six headings: A. Marxism, Leninism, and Mao Tse-tung thought; B. Philosophy (including religion); C–L. Social sciences; M–V. Natural sciences; Z. General. Mixed notation of Roman letters and Arabic numerals is used.

One common characteristic of the various systems is that "Marxism, Leninism, and Mao Tse-tung thought" forms a separate class at the beginning of every scheme.

In August 1958 the Peking Library, in cooperation with the Chinese People's University Library and the Chinese People's University Press, commenced the printing and distribution of catalog cards. Using title as the main entry, the card contains all relevant bibliographical data. Added entries are overprinted on the unit cards. All entries are given also in the romanized form, called *Han yü p'in yin* (Chinese phonetic alphabet) at the top of the cards. Presumably romanization is added for the purpose of filing. In addition to the unit cards, there is for each title a card containing a brief descriptive note of the work.

At the bottom of each unit card, classification numbers for four different systems are given: 1. The Chinese People's University Library system; 2. The system for medium and small libraries; 3. Liu Kuo-chun's system; 4. The Chinese Academy of Sciences system. Unlike the Library of Congress catalog cards, no subject headings are given; these are not used in China. Subscribers who wish to order the cards by subjects may make their selection under seventy broad headings. In 1958 it was estimated that about 2500 titles were published every month and cards were available for 2000 titles.

Cards for Western books are also printed and distributed. Participating in this project are the Peking Library, and the libraries of the Chinese Academy of Sciences and Tsing-hua University. The Peking University and the International Bookstore are responsible for the cataloging of Western books.

It is reported that a considerable amount has been done in international exchange of publications. The Peking Library is the principal body of exchange with foreign libraries, maintaining exchange relations with leading libraries all over the world. Between 1950 and 1957 it sent out some 380,000 volumes, mostly books published by the Foreign Languages Press, in return for 200,000 it received, including books and periodicals in more than fifty languages. Of the publications it received from foreign exchange the library keeps three copies of each for its own use and distributes the rest to larger public libraries, universities and colleges, and to government agencies, factories, and mines.

The Chinese Academy of Sciences Library is another important source of exchange of publications, mostly of a scientific and technical nature, with foreign libraries. Some universities also carry on international exchange with their counterparts abroad. Domestic exchange also has been practiced extensively; and interlibrary loan is reported to be widely used. The large and more affluent libraries are reported to transfer their surplus materials and loan their books to small libraries in the country.

In order to meet the increasing demand for adequate personnel to man the increasing number of libraries at all levels, many training classes and workshops are conducted from time to time. For advanced training there are two important centers, one at Peking University in the north and the other at Wuhan University in the south. The departments of library science in both universities have been instrumental in training the bulk of professional librarians in the country, and some senior members of the faculties have been trained in the United States. Courses offered are oriented toward the Communist Party's cultural policy. Students and faculty members spend part of each academic year in the countryside to participate in farm work and to give advice to rural and commune libraries. The Peking University initiated in 1956 a correspondence school of library science. Special training classes have been sponsored by both the Ministry of Education and the Min-

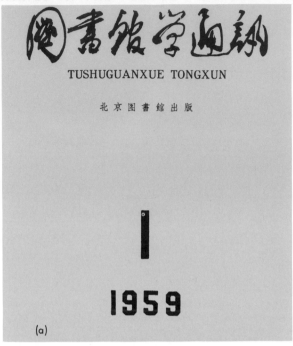

FIGURE 7. *Three library journals.* (*a*) T'u shu kuan hsüeh t'ung hsün (Library Science Bulletin). (*b*) T'u shu kuan kung tso (Library Work). (*c*) T'u shu kuan (chi k'an) (The Libraries, a quarterly).

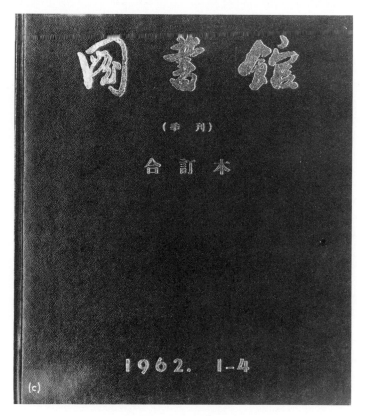

FIGURE 7 (*continued*).

istry of Culture. Library courses are also offered in other universities throughout the country.

Several professional journals have been published by the Peking Library (see Figure 7). The *T'u shu kuan kung tso* (Library Work), intended for those who work for school libraries and libraries in rural areas, is a monthly journal which first appeared in 1955. The *T'u shu kuan hsueh t'ung hsun* (Library Science Bulletin), a bimonthly which commenced publication also in 1955, contains more scholarly articles. Beginning in January 1959 it became a monthly journal. Both of these journals ceased publication in 1960 and were superseded by the more scholarly *T'u shu kuan* (The Libraries), a quarterly journal.

The *Tu shu* (Book Reading), a semimonthly journal which commenced publication in 1958, is a bibliographical journal for the general public. It contains book reviews, short articles, and publication news. Similar in nature is the *Ch'u pan hsiao hsi* (Publishing News), a weekly journal first issued in 1958. Published by the New China Bookstore in Peking and distributed by the Post Office, it contains lists of new publications in the country, excerpts from book reviews, brief notes pertaining to the publishing world, and other pertinent items.

Very little is known of library automation activities in mainland China. For many years scientists and engineers there have been actively engaged in research on machine translation as well as the manufacture and use of computers. It is possible that automated techniques have been introduced and implemented in some leading institutions such as the Institute of Scientific and Technical Information, the Chinese Academy of Sciences, and the Peking Library. The present status of automation in Chinese libraries, however, is unknown.

The director of the Peking Library since 1955 has been Ting Hsi-lin, a British-educated physicist. A versatile scholar, Ting is also a playwright, a Chinese language reform advocate, and an educator active in the political arena. Although not a professional librarian, he has exerted a tremendous influence on the development of library facilities in mainland China. Some leading librarians have been educated and trained in the United States, Soviet Russia, and other countries; but the majority are trained in Peking, Wuhan, Nanking, and other centers. The roster includes Liu Kuo-chun, Li Hsiao-yuan, Wang Chung-min, Wang Ch'ang-ping, Ku Chia-chieh, Ch'en Hung-hsun, Hsu Chia-lin, Chu Shih-chia, Tu Ting-yu, Chang Chao, Ch'eng Te-ch'ing, Ch'ien Ya-hsin, and Chang Hsiu-min.

BIBLIOGRAPHY

Cheng, Chi, "Libraries in China Today," *Libri,* 9, 105–110 (1959).

Chi, Yen-lang, "National Library of Peking: A Working Encyclopaedia," *New Zealand Lib.,* 24, 205–207 (1961).

"Chinese Communist Library Service in the Past Decade," *Union Res. Service,* 19(8 and 10) (April and May 1960). Translated from the *Peking University Journal: Humanistic Science,* 1959(4), 93–107.

Hsia, Tao-tai and Kathryn Haun, "Communist Chinese Legislation on Publications and Libraries," *Quart. J. Lib. Congress,* 27, 20–37 (1970).

Huang, Nancy Lai-shen, "Library Development in Communist China, 1949–1962," M.A. Thesis, University of Chicago, 1964.

Kuo, Leslie T. C., "Communist China, Restoration and Expansion," *Lib. J.,* 87, 4133–4136 (1962).

Nunn, G. Raymond, "Libraries and Publishing in Mainland China," *Lib. J.,* 91, 3327–3332 (1966).

Rafikov, A., "In Chinese Libraries," *Spec. Lib.,* 51, 527–532 (1960).

Wang, Chi, *Mainland China Organizations of Higher Learning in Science and Technology and Their Publications,* Library of Congress, Washington, D.C., 1961.

Wang, Julia, *A Study of the Criteria for Book Selection in Communist China's Public Libraries, 1949–1964,* Union Research Institute, Kowloon, Hong Kong, 1968.

K. T. WU

CHINA, LIBRARIES IN THE REPUBLIC OF

In China, early in the Chou Dynasty (about 500 B.C.), an office was established in the imperial court for the preservation of official records and documents. Subsequent dynasties each contributed material, including books, to this imperial collection. A list of such material was included in the official dynastic histories under the part of I-wen-chih or Ching-chi-chih, which may be regarded as national bibliographies of the period. During the Ming (1368–1644) and Ch'ing (1644–1912) Dynasties two comprehensive collectanea, Yung-lo-ta-tien and Szu-k'u-ch'uan-shu, were compiled. In the meantime, private collections proliferated. However, as was then the practice, most of these book collections were not open to the public.

In the latter part of the Ch'ing Dynasty, modern concepts and practices of library service began to be introduced into China. Book depository pavilions were established in provinces such as Hunan, Hupei, and Chekiang. In 1910, on the campus of Wen-hua University, a small public library named Wen Hua Public Book Collection, with the assistance of Miss Mary Elizabeth Wood, an American librarian, became the first modern library in China. In 1920 she organized the first library school at the Boone University in Wuchang. Graduates from this school introduced American library practice to most libraries in China.

Traditionally, Chinese books were classified according to the fourfold scheme, i.e., classics, history, philosophy, and belles-lettres. However, as new publications proliferated, new classification schemes had to be adopted to accommodate both the old Chinese books and new publications of the emerging disciplines. In so doing, the Dewey Decimal Classification system became the most influential one. Most of the classification schemes used in China today, such as Liu Kuo-chun's *System of Book Classification for Chinese Libraries,* and Y. W. Wong's *System for the Uniform Classification of Chinese and Foreign Books,* were adapted from Dewey's system. In order to meet the special needs of Chinese characters, many kinds of author tables have been devised for the arrangement of books within each subject. There were also various kinds of codes and manuals prepared for Chinese book cataloging. Among them, the National Central Library's *Cataloging Code and Rules for Chinese Books* has been widely adopted and serves as a standard in Taiwan.

In 1929 the Capital Library in Peking was merged with the Peiping Metropolitan Library to form the National Peiping Library. With a collection of more than 300,000 volumes, it was the first and largest modern national library in China. In the following years prior to the Sino-Japanese War (1937–1945), most Chinese libraries made great progress in technical service as well as in bibliographical compilations. The National Library of Peiping followed the example of the United States Library of Congress by issuing and distributing printed cards for Chinese books. Later the National Central Library was established in Nanking in 1933. At the end of 1937, when the Sino-Japanese War broke out, there were a total of 1502 public libraries, 990 public reading rooms, 162 school and college libraries, and 2542 libraries affiliated with research institutes in China. However, most of these were destroyed during the war.

Shortly after the war, the Chinese Communists intensified their rebellious activities and eventually overran the mainland. Only a few select collections were removed to the island of Taiwan. When the seat of the National Government was moved to Taiwan in 1949, there were only 17 public libraries, 6 college libraries, and a handful of special libraries in operation.

In spite of great difficulties in rebuilding and developing the library service in Taiwan, the government and the library profession have spared no efforts in improving library service.

As of 1967 there were a total of 695 libraries including 1 national library, 2 provincial libraries, 18 city or county libraries, 4 private libraries, 67 university and college libraries, and 87 special libraries. A brief account of these libraries follows.

The National Central Library

The National Central Library was founded in Nanking in 1928 and opened to the public in 1933 (Figure 1). It was reinstated in Taiwan in 1954, with its magnificent buildings located in the Botanical Gardens in Taipei, with a staff of around 150 members.

The library maintains a number of reading rooms for general books, periodicals,

FIGURE 1. *National Central Library, Taipei.*

newspapers, government publications, rare books, arts and music, and special reference rooms for the humanities, social, natural and applied sciences, with a total seating capacity of 600.

Through purchase, exchanges, gifts, and copyright deposit, the library has amassed a collection of over 500,000 volumes, including 143,974 volumes of Chinese rare books, the largest collection in the world. There are 300 titles of the Sung imprint, 360 of the Yuan, and 8239 of the Ming, and 133 rolls of ancient manuscripts. The library also owns 747 fragments of Shang-Ying Dynasty's "oracle bones," 30 pieces of Han Dynasty's wooden tablets, 5645 sets of rubbings of bronze and stone inscriptions, and 261 scrolls of maps.

On behalf of the Republic of China, the library has established exchange relationship with 527 institutions in 58 countries and 3 territories. The library also keeps in touch, and exchanges information, with about 200 sinologists all over the world, and often sends books to participate in international book exhibitions.

In order to better serve the scholarly world, the library has set up a microfilm center to produce photocopies and microfilms of its rare books collection upon request.

The library renders reference and other services for foreign libraries, research institutions, and individual scholars. Occasionally, it also prepares bibliography on special subjects on request.

Based on available materials, the library has published a number of bibliographies and catalogs, they include:

> *Monthly List of Chinese Books,* Vols. 1–8 (1960–1969).
>
> *Chinese Bibliography,* Vol. 1, No. 1, January 1970.
>
> *National Bibliography of Chinese Publications,* 1949–1963, 2 Vols.
>
> *Catalogue of Periodicals in the National Central Library.*
>
> *Catalogue of Rare Chinese Books,* rev. ed., 1968, 4 Vols.
>
> *Catalogue of Sung Editions in National Central Library Collections.*
>
> *Union Catalog of Local Histories in the Public Collections in Taiwan,* 1969.
>
> *Bibliography of Biographical Materials of the Ming Dynasty.*
>
> *Cataloging Code and Rules for Chinese Books.*
>
> *Directory of Cultural Organizations of the Republic of China,* rev. ed., 1970.
>
> *Handbook of Current Research Projects in the Republic of China,* 1964.
>
> *A Selected and Annotated Bibliography of the Republic of China,* 1958–1959, 1959–1960, 2 Vols.
>
> *Bulletin of the National Central Library,* new issue, Vol. 1, No. 1, July 1967.
>
> *Catalogue of Children's Books Published in Taiwan,* 1969.
>
> *Index to Chinese Periodicals,* Vol. 1, No. 1, January 1970.
>
> *Newsletter,* Vol. 1, No. 1, April 1969.
>
> *Catalogue of Sinological Books in Western Languages,* 1970.
>
> *Union Catalogue of Chinese Rare Books in Taiwan,* 1970.

Union Catalogue of Regular Stitched Books in the Public Collections in Taiwan, 1970.

Union Catalogue of Government Publications and Periodicals on Humanities and Social Science in Public Collections in Taiwan, 1970.

Supplement to the National Bibliography of Chinese Publications, 1970.

Public Libraries

PROVINCIAL LIBRARIES

The provincial libraries are tax supported and under the direct supervision of the provincial government's Department of Education. There are two provincial libraries in Taiwan.

The *Provincial Taipei Library* (Figure 2) was founded in August 1915 during

FIGURE 2. *Taiwan Provincial Taipei Library, Taipei.*

the Japanese occupation as the Governor-General Office Library and adopted its present name in 1948. Its new four-story building has two reading rooms with a seating capacity of 1500. Among its total holdings of about 327,000 volumes is a comprehensive collection on Taiwan and Southeast Asia, some of which are manuscripts dating as early as 1675, and written in Chinese, English, French, German, and many other languages.

The library has three branches located in Musha, Peitou, and Hsintien. In addition to a mobile unit, the library also maintains a number of "boxes of books" to convey books to small towns and villages. Some audio-visual services have also been initiated.

Its publications are:

A Bibliography on Taiwan, 1958.

A Bibliography of Western Languages Books on Southeast Asia.

A Union Catalogue of Bibliographies Available in Taiwan Libraries.

Topographies Published in Taiwan Since 1946: An Exhibition List.

Books Monthly, 1946–1948, 2 Vols. 12 issues; 1966–1967.

Bulletin of the Provincial Taipei Library, July 1964, Sept. 1965, 2 issues.

The *Provincial Taichung Library* has a collection of more than 70,000 volumes including about 40,000 volumes of Chinese, 30,000 volumes of foreign languages, 200 titles of magazines, and thirty-five titles of newspapers. There are four reading rooms with a total of 200 seats.

COUNTY AND CITY LIBRARIES

There are fourteen county and four city libraries in Taiwan. The Taipei Municipal Library is the largest with a collection of more than 90,000 volumes divided among the main library and three branches. The other libraries have collections ranging from a few thousand to 50,000 volumes. All of them contain mainly recent and popular books. In addition, various Social Education Centers and Public Service Stations also provide library service for the public.

University and School Libraries

According to a survey in 1967, there were sixty-four college and university libraries in Taiwan. They have a combined holding of 3,281,069 volumes, serving 85,346 students. Collections of more than 100,000 volumes include the following:

The *National Taiwan University Library* (Figure 3) has two physically separate branches—the Law Library and the Medical Library—and thirty-three divisional and departmental libraries, with a total collection of 860,000 volumes. Among them 32% are in Chinese, 28% in Japanese, and 40% in Western languages. Its collection of the "Li-tai Pao-an" (documents of Sino-Riukiu relations kept in the court of Riukiu Islands) is the only nearly complete one in the world. The bound periodicals total more than 440,000 volumes, including seven incunabula. Recently a graduate school library has been completed, increasing the total seating capacity to 3200. The library publishes:

Classified Index to Chinese Periodicals, 1960–1967.

Public Lectures and Symposia in Commemoration of the 10th Anniversary of the Founding of National Taiwan University, 1965.

Catalogue of the National Taiwan University Publications, 1962.

Bibliotheca; Bulletin of the Library Science Society, National Taiwan University, published irregularly beginning April 1967.

FIGURE 3. *National Taiwan University, Graduate Library.*

National Chengchi University Library has a respectable collection on social sciences, totaling 121,512 volumes.

National Taiwan Normal University Library (Figure 4) has sponsored the compilation of the *Index to Chinese Educational Periodicals* since 1962. Its book collection amounts to 190,000 volumes.

Taiwan Provincial Cheng Kung University Library has 115,390 volumes of books and most of them are in the field of engineering.

FIGURE 4. *National Taiwan Normal University Library, Taipei.*

FIGURE 5. *Tunghai University Library, Taichung.*

Taiwan Provincial Chung Hsing University Library has a collection of 143,500 volumes.

Christian Tunghai University Library (Figure 5) has a collection of some 102,800 volumes. It has published many books on library science in Chinese as well as a *Journal of Library Science.*

Library of the College of Chinese Culture has a book collection of 105,000 volumes.

Most middle school libraries have collections of 10,000 to 20,000 volumes, but the Library of the Taiwan Provincial First Girls' High School in Taipei has more than 30,000 Chinese and Western books. Some elementary schools have libraries.

Special Libraries and Documentation Centers

There are many governmental and other special libraries. A detailed guide can be found in the *INSPEL,** Vol. 1, No. 2; Vol. 2, Nos. 1 and 3, under the title "Representative Special Libraries in Taiwan, Republic of China" by Chien-chang Lan. The important collections are as follows:

Fu Ssu-nien Library, Institute of History and Philology, Academia Sinica (Figure 6): It has a collection of 210,800 volumes of Chinese and Western books, 687 titles of periodicals, 30,000 pieces of ink rubbings, and 310,000 pieces of Ming and Ch'ing state archives. Based upon its archives collection the Institute has compiled eighty volumes of *Historical Data of Ming and Ch'ing Dynasties.*"

* Published by Special Libraries Association, 31 East 10th Street, New York, New York (quarterly).

FIGURE 6. *Fu Ssu-nein Library, Institute of History Philology, Academia Sinica, Nankang, Taipei.*

Library of the Institute of Modern History, Academia Sinica, has 27,000 volumes of books, 134 titles of periodicals, 12,000 volumes of diplomatic archives from 1850 to 1945, and 1000 volumes of current affairs clippings. As its name implies, its collection is centered on modern Chinese history.

National War College Library (Figure 7) has a collection of 170,000 volumes.

FIGURE 7. *Shih-chien Library, National War College, Taipei.*

Most of them are Chinese rare books including some manuscripts. It publishes an *Index to Chinese Periodical Literature* monthly.

Library of the Chinese Engineers Society was founded in 1951. Its collection numbers 9000 volumes in the engineering field.

The book collection of the *National Palace Museum* exceeds 150,000 volumes. More than half of them are rare books, especially the Ssu-k'u-ch'uan-shu and Ssu-k'u-ch'uan-shu-hui-yao.

The collection of the *National Educational Materials Center* amounts to 10,000 volumes. Aside from the compilation of an educational series, it publishes a *Monthly Education Digest*.

Library Schools and In-Service Training

The Taiwan Normal University first established a library training program in 1956 as an undergraduate library science section in the department of Social Education. The degree of B.E. is conferred upon students who complete a four-year program. There has been a total of 126 graduates up to July 1968.

The National Taiwan University established its Library Science Department in 1961. The department offers a balanced program in liberal arts with an individual subject emphasis and a basic professional curriculum. After four academic years a B.A. degree is conferred. There has been a total of 152 graduates up to the present.

In 1964 the private World College of Journalism set up a Department of Library Science offering three-year (for graduates from senior high school) and five-year (for graduates from junior high school) technical training.

Since July 1956 the Library Association of China has sponsored twelve Summer Library Workshops offering in-service training to library employees in various libraries. In addition to books on library science and standards for libraries, the association has published a Bulletin annually since 1954.

The Future of Chinese Libraries

For a population of 13 million, with increasing number of students enrolled in the universities, colleges, and schools, the present facilities for library service are far from adequate both in terms of quantity and quality. To improve the situation, efforts should be made to establish more new libraries as well as improving the service of the present libraries. The National Central Library and the Library Association of China are taking a vigorous lead in this direction.

IGNATIUS T. P. PAO

CHINA, LIBRARY ASSOCIATION OF

The Library Association of China was founded in 1925 in Peiping. Through the promotion of a Committee on Library Education and Development, organized in 1922 under the Chinese National Association for the Advancement of Education, a number of provincial and local library associations had been established before the inauguration of the national association. During its existence, the association advanced the study of library science, the compilation of reference tools, the development of services for academic and public libraries, and encouraged library cooperation on both national and international levels.

The Association had an Executive Committee of fifteen members and a Supervisory Committee of nine, elected directly by members of the association. About a dozen special committees, including those on library cataloging, classification, indexing, filing, professional education, library buildings, library budget and revenues, printing blocks, Dewey Decimal subdivisions on China, endowment funds, and editorial work, operated under the Executive Committee. Membership composition of the Association included: (1) individual members, (2) institutional members, (3) life members, (4) sustaining members, and (5) honorary members. According to the reports and rosters of the association, the number of its enrollment was as follows:

Year	Institutional members	Individual members[a]	Total membership
1926	129	202	331
1930	186	334	520
1935	288	562	850
1939	84	191	275
1947	—	714	—

[a] Including all types of membership other than institutional.

The drop in membership in 1939 was caused by the Chinese-Japanese war, which resulted in the transfer of the association to Kunming in 1938, to Chengtu in 1940, to Chungking in 1942, and to Nanking in 1945, when the war ended.

The Association held its first membership meeting in Nanking in 1929, its second in Peiping in 1933, its third in Tsingtao in 1936, and its fourth in Chungking in 1938. Both policy and technical problems were discussed at such conventions. The association was also active among many international library organizations and conferences. It sponsored and participated in the First World Library and Bibliographical Congress in 1929 in Rome–Venice with a well prepared exhibit of Chinese books, printing, and library development. A collection of articles in English, entitled *Libraries in China,* was issued for this occasion. A second edition with different articles under the same title was published on the occasion of the tenth anniversary of the association in 1935. The most important contribution of the association was the publication of a series of reference works and two periodicals in Chinese. The monographs included a dozen or more reports, survey of Chinese libraries, bibliographics, Indexes to periodical literature, and works on reference and cataloging. The periodicals included the *Bulletin of the Library Association of China* (*Chung-hua t'u-shu-kuan hsieh-hui hui-pao*), Vol. 1, No. 1–Vol. 21, No. 4 (1925–1948), published bimonthly in Peiping and later in Kunming, Chengtu, Chungking, and Nanking; and the *Library Science Quarterly* (*T'u-shu-kuan hsüeh chi-k'an*), Vol. 1, No. 1–Vol. 11, No. 2 (1926–1937); index, 1–10 (1937), published in Peiping and suspended because of the war.

During World War II, the association cooperated closely with the library associations of the allied countries. In answer to an appeal by the association, the American Library Association launched a Book-for-China campaign in 1938–1939 and sent over 20,000 volumes of publications on science, technology, medicine, literature, and reference works to China. Similar donations were also made by Great Britain. The books and periodicals were distributed to various universities and research institutions in need of such materials. In return, the Chinese association acquired many Chinese publications for Far Eastern collections in American libraries.

Activities of the association have been suspended in the mainland since 1949. It was, however, reorganized in Taiwan in 1953 under a new name in Chinese, *Chung-kuo t'u-shu-kuan hsüeh-hui* (formerly *Chung-hua t'u-shu-kuan hsieh-hui*), and a new constitution was adopted. The present association has a Board of twenty-one directors and a committee of seven supervisors. Five directors and one supervisor were elected to an Executive Committee. Membership meetings have been held in Taipei annually since 1953 and a summer workshop for participation by local librarians since 1956. The association had a total of 547 individual members in 1968. It has been active in the preparation of Chinese library standards, sponsoring book exhibits and public lectures, awarding scholarships to library science students, and publishing the *Bulletin of the Library Association of China* (*Chung-kuo t'u-shu-kuan hsüeh-hui hui-pao*) in Chinese as a new series annually since 1953. The main office is now located in the National Central Library, 43 Nan-hai Road, Taipei, Taiwan, China.

BIBLIOGRAPHY

ALA Bulletin, **32,** 403–404, 710, 1046 (1938); **33,** 352 (1939); **36,** 660–661 (1942).

Library Association of China, *Libraries in China,* LAC, Peiping, 1929, 1935.

Library Journal, **63,** 714 (1938); **64,** 386 (1939); **69,** 235–238 (1944).

National Taiwan University, "Some Notes on the Library Association of China," *NTU Library Science Circular No.* **9,** (December 1968).

TSUEN-HSUIN TSIEN

CHOICE

This monthly book selection tool, published by the Association of College and Research Libraries, began in March 1964 to meet the acquisitional needs of United States college libraries. Since the beginning of World War II, college libraries lacked a general, authoritative measure such as that which was provided by Charles B. Shaw's *A List of Books for College Libraries* (1937) and its supplement (1940). In 1953, Philip J. McNiff's *Catalogue of the Lamont Library, Harvard College* appeared and was valuable as a comparative checklist although it reflected the milieu of one college.

Between the end of World War II and 1959, college librarians debated the need and method of a "New Shaw." In 1959 through the initiative of Verner Clapp, President of the Council on Library Resources, and his staff member, Robert Jordan, an effort was begun to evaluate points-of-view. After surveying the library profession (on an individual basis and by an in-depth conference) it was decided that two elements were necessary to handle the rapid growth of college libraries under the increased budgets expected in the 1960s. First, a periodical was mandatory if there was to be any selection sense to be made out of the rapidly expanding U.S. book publishing (which had more than doubled since 1959—14,000 titles to over 30,000). Second, after the periodical was established, a "New Shaw" list would be developed from it.

The Council on Library Resources granted the American Library Association $150,000 in 1961 to underwrite the first three years of the new reviewing journal. ALA had accepted responsibility for the magazine. The Association of College and Research Libraries Division agreed to publish the magazine and formed an editorial board. Two years later, Richard K. Gardner was appointed editor. Gardner's job was formidable: publishers had to be convinced about this unknown quantity; reviewers had to be recruited from the faculties of universities, colleges, and junior colleges; offices had to be found; and a name had to be given. This last problem was solved by a contest among original subscribers in which a majority selected *CHOICE: Books for College Libraries* (the subtitle was dropped in 1966). The search for a home ended with the selection of Olin Library at Wesleyan University in Middletown, Connecticut. A prerequisite of *CHOICE*'s beginning was that it should be housed in or near an excellent college library.

At this writing, every U.S. publisher or distributor (as well as some Canadian houses) send review books to *CHOICE*. The reviewer corps now numbers over 2,800 individuals recommended by librarians and faculty members. Over 80% have the Ph.D. and all have a subject mastery or a strong equivalency.

With *CHOICE* established as a kind of continuing "New Shaw," 1965 saw increased efforts to publish a bibliographic list. Since the *CHOICE* staff was not sufficiently equipped to undertake such a mammoth task, the California "New University Campuses" project, directed by Joseph Treyz, was contacted to see if their list could be adapted. Supported by the Council on Library Resources, the

NUC list was examined by 37 *CHOICE* reviewers (subject specialists suggested by the editorial staff) under the guidance of Treyz. NUC was reduced to 53,400 titles from some 75,000 and published by ALA in 1967 as *Books for College Libraries*. The 1970s will see a new basic list developed by *CHOICE plus* supplements.

CHOICE has modified and expanded since 1964. Peter M. Doiron, Assistant Editor, succeeded to Editor in February 1966. Although its basic frame of critical reference remains the undergraduate liberal arts library, *CHOICE* subscribers range from high school libraries to special ones like the Atomic Energy Commission. Current reviewing in all fields (save cookbooks, murder mysteries, etc.) has been extended to paperbacks and reprints. In Volume I, 3434 titles were reviewed; Volume VI commented on 6560. To assist this increase in service *CHOICE* publishes a "Reviews-on-Cards" service and compiles the annual "Outstanding Academic Books." Bibliographic articles (e.g., "No One Over 30: Books Toward an Understanding of Student Protest") and extensive reviews of major reference books are additional features.

Great pains are taken in assigning books to reviewers, i.e., the right book to the most qualified consultant. Since the reviews are necessarily brief, the technique of comparative reviewing is heavily used (a value placing of the title in its subject bibliography—past and present). The reviewers are unpaid and therefore review at their own pace; most of the 2800 review 5–6 books a year. The combination of an uneven reviewer spread over subject areas and the fact that no reviewing is done from galleys, inhibits promptness by the average reviewer.

With the current staff as a firm basis, *CHOICE* plans to expand into government documents (federal, state, U.N.), foreign language publications, and other media. Editor Doiron has stated that these new endeavors may mean additional publications; e.g., *CHOICE—EUROPE*.

BIBLIOGRAPHY

"The Council on Library Resources and CHOICE: An Appreciation," *College Res. Lib. News,* **28,** 221 ff. (October 1967).

Doiron, Peter M., "CHOICE and Book Selection," *Florida Lib.,* **18,** 33–37 (March 1967).

"An Evaluation of CHOICE," *Missouri Lib. Assoc. Quart.* **28,** 3–38 (March 1968).

Gardner, Richard K., "CHOICE: Books for College Libraries; Its Origin, Development, and Future Plans," *Southeastern Librarian,* **15,** 69–75 (Summer 1965).

Lehmann, James O., "CHOICE as a Selection Tool," *Wilson Lib. Bull.,* (May 1970).

PETER M. DOIRON

CHRONICLES

A chronicle is a historical register of events arranged in chronological order of their occurrence. Ordinarily, it is more than a bare chronology, but it is less consciously interpretive than a general history. Of course, any account of history is interpretive, at least implicitly, because of the necessity to select events to record. Thus chronicles may be identified by nationality, religion, and other factors that affect the way the chronicler observes and reports the passing scene. Closely related to chronicles are *annals*, a form of writing that strictly deals with court appointments and other events organized on the basis of the calendar year. Since authors, editors, and publishers do not observe precise distinctions in titles, a list of chronicles may contain some that are entitled chronologies, annals, histories, or even memoirs.

Chronicles are characteristically uncritical in their reporting of events. Ancient and medieval chronicles mixed eyewitness reports with information drawn from traditional lore and other written accounts. The eyewitness reports are often the only extant records of important events. The chronicler's use of secondary sources also has value for reconstructing the past, because it reveals the state of knowledge and belief of the times. *The Chronicles of England, Scotland, and Ireland* by Raphael Holinshed, for example, are chiefly drawn from secondary sources. Published first in 1577, they were known to Shakespeare and are clearly reflected in Shakespeare's historical plays. Thus they provide a good insight into Shakespeare's historical consciousness. Furthermore, when Shakespeare's preeminence as a writer is considered, the study of his plays, the multifarious reprintings of them, scenes from them, allusions to them, and commentaries on them have made the chronicles of Holinshed an important influence on the historical consciousness of our own time.

Chronicles are an ancient form of historical writing. Assyrians, Babylonians, and Egyptians made chronicles of their own and earlier times. Historians had no direct access to them for over 1500 years, however, because they could not read the ancient scripts. The decipherment of the cuneiform and Egyptian scripts in the nineteenth century restored the chronicles to use. The biblical Books of Kings written about the eighth century B.C. and the works of the biblical chronicler written perhaps as late as the third century B.C. cover the same ground and were not lost. At the Alexandrian library during the third century B.C., Manetho, an Egyptian priest, composed an Egyptian Chronicle in Greek, a task repeated by Eratosthenes, the librarian. Eusebius, the early Christian chronicler (ca. 260–340) whose *Chronographia* attempted a chronology of all known peoples, had access to the Greek versions. Very ancient with a continuous textual and reading history are the Chinese *Spring and Autumn Annals,* brief records of current events from 722–481 B.C., attributed to Confucius (ca. 551–479 B.C.).

Medieval chronicles are numerous and exist for every European country. Some will be mentioned here. The *Anglo-Saxon Chronicle* is the chief source for Anglo-

Saxon history. Probably brought together during the reign of Alfred the Great, it drew from several local annals for earlier periods and continued recording current events until after the Norman Conquest, with different versions being maintained in different monasteries. It is a monument of Anglo-Saxon prose.

The *Historia Regum Britanniae,* a twelfth-century chronicle by Geoffrey of Monmouth, presents the legendary genealogy of British kings from Brutus the Trojan to Cadwallader of Wessex. This is a major source for the legends of King Arthur and the Knights of the Round Table.

Jean Froissart, born in France in 1337, devoted his life to compiling the *Chroniques de France, d'Angleterre, d'Ecosse et d'Espagne,* for the years from 1326 to 1399. Dependent on courtly patronage, he found patrons alternately in England, Burgundy, and France, and his account of the wars in France during that period varied in their bias according both to the sources of his sustenance and the sources of his information.

A medieval manuscript to win recent notoriety is a copy of the *Tartar Relation,* copied in the fifteenth century from a chronicle composed by Friar John of Plano Carpini of his mission to the Mongols from 1245 to 1247. Although the chronicle records facts about the Mongols not found in other sources, the manuscript is more famous for a map of Vinland, the Viking settlements in North America, bound with it and discovered by ingenious detective work to have been originally bound with a copy of the *Speculum Historiale,* a thirteenth-century encyclopedia composed by Vincent of Beauvais. In a waggish mood, the Yale University Press published the map and manuscript on October 12, Columbus Day, in 1965—to the great consternation of Italian-American societies.

Early printers published chronicles. A noteworthy example is the *Nuremberg Chronicle* published at Nuremberg by Anton Koberger in 1493. It included 1809 illustrations printed from 645 wood blocks, using twenty-two cuts of countries and cities to represent sixty-nine different places and ninety-six cuts of emperors, kings, and popes to represent 598 different people. Though not a carefully crafted book, the *Nuremberg Chronicle* because of its early date and profuse use of a limited number of cuts is a memorable example of early printed book illustration.

Among printed chronicles with great historical impact, the *Acts and Monuments of the Martyrs* by John Foxe must be included. This is a chronological rendering of instances of Christian martyrdom illustrating the bitterly partisan theme of a struggle between the papacy and true believers, emphasizing events in sixteenth-century England. Published first in a large folio in 1563, though a relatively expensive volume, it was reprinted six times before 1640. Even in 1968 it was in print in several American editions—some scholarly and some popular.

Although printed chronicles of the sixteenth century were influential, the revolution in scholarship that followed the invention of printing detracted from the value of chronicles as unique records of general cultural import. Printed statutes, proclamations, relations, and broadsides in abundance recorded actions taken. Learned treatises, polemical tracts and pamphlets, and the blossoming national literatures issued in printed editions better documented the thought, aspirations, and knowledge of the time than any chronicler or succession of chroniclers could.

The expanding book trade made it possible for a scholar to collect as many books in his own study as he could have consulted in a lifetime of searching for manuscripts before printing was invented. The multitude of sources resulting from this development were beyond the power of a single chronicler to impose a medieval unity. New labors were needed for this, and in a sense the chronicler was succeeded by the bibliographer.

During the nineteenth century, affected partly by the growing nationalism of the time, governments, scholarly societies, universities, and individuals made a concerted attempt to collect, often to translate to modern vernacular, to edit, and to publish the ancient and medieval chronicles. From 1857 to 1896, the Master of the Rolls in Great Britain supervised the publication of *The Chronicles and Memorials of Great Britain and Ireland During the Middle Ages.* Commonly known as the Rolls Series, it includes ninety-nine separate works in 251 volumes, of which a large number are chronicles. During the same period, the Camden Society, the Caxton Society, the English Historical Society, and other societies and individuals published many chronicles. In Germany, university scholars collected and published the original texts of medieval chronicles and in addition between 1849 and 1892 published *Die Geschichtschreiber der deutschen Vorzeit in deutsche Bearbeitung,* a series then consisting of over ninety volumes of German medieval chronicles in German translation. Resumed later, the series has gone over 100 volumes. Similar labors of collecting, editing, and translating were carried on in other countries. The examples of Great Britain and Germany give an idea of the extensiveness of the writing—imposing enough when gathered together on modern library shelves but not so impressive in volume when the long period of time covered and large geographical expanse embraced are considered. Bibliographical access to these publications is provided by the standard guides to historical literature.

HOWARD W. WINGER

CHURCH LIBRARIES

See also *Church and Synagogue Library Association*

There are estimated to be about 40,000 church libraries in the United States. Several questionnaire surveys* show that most church library collections contain less than 500 volumes, although a sizable number contain about 2000 volumes (2).

Church libraries are staffed almost exclusively by volunteers, most of whom are nonprofessional. A large number of these volunteers, however, are married women with library science degrees, and many others are retired professional librarians.

* See items marked with an asterisk in the References and Bibliography.

In most cases, one of the organizations within the local church is the church library committee. This group constitutes the staff of the library. Although many church libraries are spearheaded at the beginning by one enthusiastic person, it is common for a committee ranging from three to twenty-five persons to operate the library.

All church libraries are open and staffed on Sunday, before, during, or after services. In addition, some of them are open with staff during the week on occasions when other groups meet at the church. Others are open on a self-service basis all the time, and are thereby available at any time the church building is open (7).

The church library is a special collection of informational materials gathered to serve the needs of the individual church and its members. It provides resources for the study of church teachings, by making available those items not generally found in the local public library. These small religious libraries are special libraries in the sense that they are set up primarily to serve the institution in which they are housed.

Although the modern concept of church libraries did not develop until the middle of the present century, the idea of churches with libraries antedates Colonial times. Naude (12) reports in 1627, for example, that the library of the Augustinian Friars in Rome was open to any who would enter and read. In the New World, too, missionary libraries were established early in the seventeenth century by Jesuits in Montreal and Franciscans in Saint Augustine, Florida (14). Probably the most noted, and the first collection to be designated a "parochial library," was the "Biblioteca Bostonian" started by an Anglican clergyman, the Reverend Thomas Bray. His goal was a library in every parish, and he is reported to have accepted a new appointment to Maryland in 1689 with the condition that parochial libraries be supported by the Bishop of London. In cooperation with the Society for Promoting Christian Knowledge, founded in 1698, 34,000 volumes were sent from England to 39 different libraries in the Colonies under his jurisdiction (19). The Reverend John Wesley, too, was actively interested in encouraging education and reading in Methodist churches, and is sometimes called "the father of the church library idea" (8).

Most of these seventeenth- and eighteenth-century libraries, however, were maintained for the benefit of the clergy for use in their study and teaching, although the literate layman was also encouraged to use them. Since virtually all pre-Revolutionary education was sponsored through churches of all denominations, it is almost impossible to separate schools, churches, and libraries during this period. The Revolution, however, left in its wake deserted and neglected collections of books, many of which were destroyed completely.

During the first half of the nineteenth century, various denominations established academies and special schools for the education of young people. However, inasmuch as universal schooling was not an established concept, and child labor was common, the Sunday school movement made rapid strides in America as the only instruction available to most of the children. Only six years after the American Sunday School Union was formed in 1824, it reported a membership of over 6000 Sunday schools (13).

The Sunday School Union published a great variety of curriculum materials for use in these schools. In addition, various denominations began to produce publications of their own. The Presbyterian Board of Publications, for example, was established in 1839, "to produce Sabbath-School books." By 1870, 600 titles were listed in its catalog (*1*). Thus began a new influx of printed materials aimed solely at the denominational Sunday school. The Sunday school library met the need for housing and organizing this mass of religious resource material.

During this same period, the public library movement also gained great momentum. By the time the American Library Association was formed in 1876, the public library had become a major institution in American communities. These libraries were careful, however, to maintain a nonsectarian atmosphere, and indeed, in some sections of the country, omitted almost completely the collecting of works in the religious field.

Meanwhile the denominational presses were expanding their output to include works in the religious field. Among these were histories of their denominations, books of theology and worship, and instructional materials for the Sunday schools. Therefore, interest in church libraries began to germinate in many parts of the country simultaneously in order to organize existing materials, to provide an outlet for new books from the denominational presses, and to counteract the dearth of information in the religious field.

The organization of church library centers falls into four basic groupings. A review of fourteen denominations shows that most church library activity and publications are included in, or are a subdivision of, the denominational board of Christian education. Another large number of denominations places the sponsorship of church library activity under the denominational publisher. The third type consists of denominational groupings separate from the official denominational headquarters. The fourth group is nondenominational.

The first and most active denomination to pioneer this field was the Southern Baptist Convention. Arthur Flake, head of the Convention's Department of the Sunday School Board, initiated the Church Library Service in 1927. This was a mail service, designed as a correspondence course to the churches. It consisted of booklets and booklists describing how to start and arrange a library. Local congregations were required to meet specific conditions in order to be eligible for the service. These consisted of the appointment of a church librarian; a specific location for the library within the church building; and a commitment of funds, however small, from the budget of the church. At the same time, the Baptist bookstores cooperated in the promotion of Baptist libraries through help with publicity and book selection. In some cases special offers of books were made as an incentive to start a collection.

An example of such local activity is the Union Association Church Library Council organized in Houston, Texas, in 1949. This group of about twenty churches is sponsored by the Baptist bookstore in Houston. It meets quarterly to provide training in library techniques and to inform its members of services available through the Baptist Church Library Service headquarters in Nashville, Tennessee (*10*).

The Church Library Service headquarters has employed a full-time librarian since 1931. The first workshop conference specifically organized for church librarians was conducted at Dallas, Texas, in 1945. The first School of Church Librarians was held on the Southern Baptist Conference Grounds at Ridgecrest, North Carolina, in 1947. Church library workshops are also offered annually at Glorietta, New Mexico.

In 1968, the Southern Baptist Church Library Service reported a membership of 16,000 church libraries. It publishes a quarterly periodical, *The Church Library Magazine* (9).

The Cokesbury Church Library Service of the Methodist church was the second to be established. Inaugurated in 1948, it was designed to work closely with the Methodist Board of Education. Since the beginning, the Service has provided leadership classes and workshops for church librarians on jurisdictional, conference, and district levels. Annually, since 1956, summer jurisdictional workshops have been provided at Mount Sequoyah, Fayetteville, Arkansas; and Lake Junaluska in North Carolina. Schools and workshops during the year are scheduled by the Board of Managers for each district or conference. These average about eight per year.

The Cokesbury Church Library Service publishes a manual for church librarians entitled *Your Church Library,* and *The Church Library Newsletter,* issued quarterly. In 1968, it reported a membership of 13,000, including 2000 from non-Methodist churches (17).

The American Baptist Church Library Plan, the Seabury Church Library Plan, and the Westminster Church Library Plan are also sponsored by their respective denominational publishing houses. Each of these plans offers its members a certain discount on books purchased for the church library, as well as reviews or notices of new titles. The oldest of the plans is the Westminster one, established in 1944. Designed for United Presbyterian churches, it produces a booklet sent to all subscribers entitled *The Church Library.* In 1968, the plan reported a membership of 3500 libraries (14).

The Lutheran Church Library Association is a somewhat different organization for the encouragement and development of church libraries. This group was formed in 1958 in Minneapolis, Minnesota, as a fellowship of church librarians from Lutheran churches in the area. It is not an official Lutheran organization, and from the beginning was open for membership to church librarians from any denomination. In 1968, the Association reported a membership of about 2000. It has published a quarterly periodical, *Lutheran Libraries,* since 1958, and encourages church library workshops across the country.

The first workshop was held in 1959 on the campus of Gustavus Adolphus College, Minneapolis. During its first ten years, local chapters of the association sponsored conferences or workshops for church librarians in such varied locations as Jamesville, Wisconsin; Denver, Colorado; Sidney, Montana; Hartford, Connecticut; Stouchberg, Pennsylvania; Fargo, North Dakota; Decorah, Iowa; and Springfield, Illinois, as well as many in St. Paul and Minneapolis, Minnesota. (See the periodical *Lutheran Libraries,* 1958–1968.)

Still another form of church library organization is the Parish Libraries Section of the Catholic Library Association. This section was formed in 1957 to encourage the development of libraries for adults in parishes as distinct from the parochial school library. Parish libraries are aimed almost entirely at the adult layman, and with a few exceptions do not encourage a mixture of children's and adult books. A booklet entitled *The Parish and Catholic Lending Library Manual,* and the *Parish Library News,* issued quarterly, are available from the Catholic Library Association headquarters in Haverford, Pennsylvania. There are estimated to be about 1000 parish libraries organized nationally into forty-four units. The Section reported a membership of 200 persons in 1968 *(14)*.

The Church Library Council in the Greater Washington area began in 1959 at an informal meeting of seven people representing Baptist and Methodist church libraries. The mutual exchange of ideas led to a formally organized interdenominational fellowship. Member churches and chapters are now established in the District of Columbia, northern Virginia, and Prince George's and Montgomery Counties in Maryland. Associated groups have also formed in Baltimore, Maryland, and Detroit, Michigan.

The first workshop in the area was planned by the Silver Spring Leadership Training School for the benefit of these local church librarians in 1959. Two years later, the group had developed sufficiently to sponsor a church library workshop in conjunction with the Council of Churches of Greater Washington, at their Seminar for Leadership Training in the spring of 1961. This Workshop and those in 1962 and 1963 were planned for one evening a week for six weeks. Since 1964, the annual workshop has been a one-day session, sponsored independently by the Church Library Council.

On invitation, the Council meets quarterly at participating member churches. This meeting includes a business session and a special program of interest to church librarians. The one big project of the Council is the annual Church Library Workshop. In addition to the Workshop, the Council also publishes several booklets on various aspects of church libraries and issues a quarterly publication to its members entitled *Church Library Council News.*

In 1968, the Council reported seventy members representing twelve denominations *(11)*.

The Pacific Northwest Association of Church Librarians began ecumenically in 1960 at an informal gathering of several persons with a common interest in church libraries. From 1961 to 1967, it sponsored annual workshops at Pacific Lutheran University. Other annual workshops were scheduled at Seattle Pacific College; Whitworth College, Spokane, Washington; and Williamette University, Salem, Oregon.

In addition to these annual two-day programs, the Association sponsors seminars at a public library during National Library Week, and roundtables at frequent intervals in local churches.

Since 1965, it has cooperated with the Council of Churches of Greater Washington in presenting classes in library techniques at its Fall School of Christian Service.

The group was formally organized in 1967 and reported a membership of 150 persons in 1968. The first number of their official publication, *The Lamplighter,* was issued in June 1968 (*5*).

The Church Librarians' Fellowship was formally organized within the Division of Christian Education of the Maryland Council of Churches in September 1968. Membership in the Fellowship is open to all church librarians in the city of Baltimore, and the four surrounding counties of Harford, Carroll, Howard, and Anne Arundel. The formal organization is an outgrowth of an informal fellowship group which began in 1965. The group provides encouragement and exchange of ideas among church librarians, produces printed aids of various kinds, and sponsors an annual workshop for church librarians. The Fellowship is also affiliated informally with the Church Library Council of Washington, D.C., and the Church and Synagogue Library Association. (See *Guidelines for Church Librarians' Fellowship,* Sept. 1968, mimeographed, 1 p.)

The District of Columbia Library Association, a local chapter of the American Library Association, established in Interfaith Library Committee as a special interest group in 1966. The members are full-time professional librarians in a variety of libraries with a common interest or experience in church or synagogue libraries. The intent is that they will be available as consultants to nonprofessional people working in church or synagogue libraries. In 1967 and 1968 the group sponsored tours of religious libraries in the Washington, D.C. area (*14*).

The Library Administration Division of the American Library Association published a mimeographed *Bibliographic Guide to Church Libraries* in 1965 (*6*).

The initial exploratory session for the Church and Synagogue Library Association was held at the American Library Association Conference in New York in 1966. (For further discussion of this subject, see *Church and Synagogue Library Association.*)

A few large public libraries have shown interest and support in the church library movement. An outstanding program and probably the pioneer in this area is one conducted by the East Orange Public Library in New Jersey. This is in the nature of an extension service to the churches. A librarian of religious education was appointed to the public library staff in 1954. Through this liaison person, training sessions for church librarians are planned frequently at the public library. Books loaned to church libraries for one month are in turn circulated to church members on a weekly basis. Library aid is provided for volunteer church librarians in the way of oral book reviews and book lists of seasonal interest (*15,16*).

The Oklahoma County Libraries, Oklahoma City, Oklahoma, sponsored a one-day workshop for church librarians of the county in 1967. Over 100 persons attended and it is thought to be the first such conference sponsored solely by a public library (*18*).

In a similar kind of program, the Seattle Public Library has cooperated with the Pacific Lutheran University in producing several workshops and seminars for church librarians since 1958. These have been held in conjunction with the Pacific Northwest Association of Church Librarians (*5*).

The public library in Madison, Wisconsin, and the University of Wisconsin have also done some work in this area.

In April 1963, the Graduate School of Library Science at Drexel Institute of Technology in Philadelphia, Pennsylvania, sponsored a workshop for church librarians with the support of the Philadelphia Council of Churches. This experiment, to the knowledge of the steering committee, was unprecedented in the country. For the first two years, these annual workshops were directed primarily to librarians from local Protestant churches. By 1965, however, the Conference had drawn participants from far outside the Philadelphia area; and by 1966, it had become ecumenical. About 200 persons attended the first year, and it is thought to be the first church library conference sponsored by a professional library school (3,4). The conference was held annually from 1961 to 1967, when it was superseded by the annual conference of the Church and Synagogue Library Association.

A direct outgrowth of the Conference at Drexel Institute was one held in 1968 in Providence, Rhode Island, for New England church librarians. This Conference was sponsored by the Graduate Library School of the University of Rhode Island together with the Rhode Island Council of Churches, the Parish Libraries Section of the Catholic Library Association, and the Jewish Library Association. It drew about 200 persons and is the first interfaith workshop to be sponsored by a professional library school.

In the spring semester of the same year, another "first" was added to the church library field. A course entitled "The Administration of Church Libraries" was offered by the Department of Library Science at Baylor University in Texas. This is the first course in church librarianship to be listed in the catalog of a professional library school (10).

During the two decades from 1950 to 1970, less than twenty theses had been written in the library schools of the country on the subject of church libraries (see listing below). In April 1970, the *Drexel Library Quarterly* published a compendium of materials that surveyed the contemporary state of church librarianship in the United States. This issue synthesized the research previously done in the history, development, characteristics, and problems of church libraries. It was designed to relate this group of libraries to the American library profession as a whole (14).

Meanwhile, The Special Libraries Association had begun to recognize the embryonic state of this new group of special libraries. Accordingly, they published a comprehensive resume of the activities leading up to the establishment of the Church and Synagogue Library Association in an article entitled "An Ecumenical Concern for Quality Service in Religious Libraries" (9).

The church library concept in its present form is still very new. Almost all the literature about church libraries has been written during the past fifteen years, and the associations of church librarians have been formed during the past ten years. The growing interest in the field, together with its potential size, seems to indicate that future developments could result in more church librarians than all school, university, and public librarians combined.

CHURCH LIBRARY SERVICES AND ASSOCIATIONS

These are as follows:

American Baptist Church Library Plan
American Baptist Headquarters
Valley Forge, Pennsylvania 19481

Church and Synagogue Library Association
Bryn Mawr, Pennsylvania 19010
Attention: Miss Joyce L. White
          University of Pennsylvania
          School of Education Library
          Philadelphia, Pennsylvania 19104

Church Librarians' Fellowship
Maryland Council of Churches
Baltimore, Maryland 21200
Attention: Mrs. William J. Hyde

Church Library Council
Washington, D.C. 20014
Attention: Mrs. Ruth Smith
          Bethesda Methodist Church
          Bethesda, Maryland, 20014

Church Library Department
Christian Herald
27 East 39th Street
New York, New York 10016

Church Library Plan
Westminster Press
Philadelphia, Pennsylvania 19104

Church Library Service
Board of Christian Education
Presbyterian Church in the U.S.
Richmond, Virginia 23209

Church Library Service
Sunday School Board
Southern Baptist Convention
Nashville, Tennessee 37203

Cokesbury Church Library Service
Methodist Publishing House
Nashville, Tennessee 37203

Lutheran Church Library Association
112 West Franklin Avenue
Minneapolis, Minnesota 55400
Executive Secretary: Mrs. Wilma Jensen

Lutheran Library Service
Board of Publications
2900 Queen Lane
Philadelphia, Pennsylvania 19129

Pacific Northwest Association of Church
  Librarians
Seattle, Washington 98155
Attention: Mrs. Elmer White
          University Lutheran Church
          Seattle, Washington 98155

Parish Libraries Section
Catholic Library Association
461 West Lancaster Avenue
Haverford, Pennsylvania 19041
Attention: Miss Jane Hindman

Seabury Church Library Plan
Seabury Press
815 Second Avenue
New York, New York, 10017

CHURCH LIBRARY PERIODICALS

Catholic Library World, published by the Catholic Library Association, carried many articles on parish libraries from 1928 to 1956.

Church and Synagogue Libraries (6 issues per year), Vol. 2– (1969–), Church and Synagogue Library Association, P.O. Box 530, Bryn Mawr, Pa. (Superseded the *News Bulletin.*)

Church Library Bulletin, Vols. 1–14 (1944–1958), Sunday School Board of the Southern Baptist Convention, Nashville, Tenn.

Church Library Council News (quarterly), Vols. 1– (1960–), Church Library Council, Washington, D.C.

Church Library Magazine (quarterly), Vols. 1– (1959–), Sunday School Board of the Southern Baptist Convention, Nashville, Tenn.

Church Library News and Views (quarterly), Vols. 1– (1968–), (circulated by the Presbyterian Bookstores of Atlanta, Dallas, Charlotte, Richmond), Presbyterian Church in the United States, Richmond, Va.

Church Library Newsletter (quarterly), Vols. 1– (1963–), Cokesbury Press, Nashville, Tenn.

Lutheran Libraries (quarterly), Vols. 1– (1958–), Lutheran Church Library Association, Minneapolis, Minn.

News Bulletin (quarterly), Vol. 1 (1968), Church and Synagogue Library Association, P.O. Box 530, Bryn Mawr, Pa.

Parish Library News (quarterly), Vols. 1– (1957–), Catholic Library Association, Haverford, Pa.

Sunday School Builder, published by the Sunday School Board of the Southern Baptist Convention, carried articles in nearly every issue from 1929 to 1943 concerning church libraries.

CHURCH LIBRARY MANUALS

Althoff, Leona L., *The Church Library Manual,* Sunday School Board of the Southern Baptist Convention, Nashville, Tenn., 1937 (137 pp.).

Buder, Christine, *How to Build a Church Library,* Bethany Press, St. Louis, 1955 (60 pp.).

Carter, W. T., "How to Organize the Small Library in the Home or in the Church," Oklahoma Christian College, Oklahoma City, 1962 (17 pp.).

Cedarbaum, Sophia N., "Manual for Jewish Community Center, School and Congregation Libraries," Jewish Book Council of America, New York, 1962 (49 pp).

Celnik, Max, "Synagogue Library: Organization, Administration, United Synagogue Book & Art Service, New York, 1959 (16 pp.).

Central Council for the Care of Churches, *Parochial Libraries of the Church of England,* Faith Press, London, 1959 (125 pp.).

Church Library Resource Guide; Books and Audiovisual Materials Recommended for Church Libraries, Southern Baptist Convention Sunday School Board, Nashville, Tenn., 1960 (285 pp.).

The Church Library: How to Organize and Maintain It with Help Through the Westminster Church Library Plan, Westminster Press, Philadelphia, n.d. (16 pp.).

Criswell, W. A., *The Church Library Reinforcing the Work of the Denomination,* Southern Baptist Convention Sunday School Board, Nashville, Tenn., 1945.

Deseret Sunday School Union, *Filing in Latter-day Saint Church Libraries,* Salt Lake City, 1966 (61 pp.).

Deseret Sunday School Union, *Organization of Books in the Ward Library,* Salt Lake City, n.d. (47 pp.).

Dunning, A. E., *The Sunday School Library,* Congregational Sunday School and Publishing Society, Boston, 1883.

Elliot, R. L., *Library Handbook for Church and Sunday School,* Gospel Light Press, Glendale, Calif., 1946.

Foote, E. L., *The Church Library, a Manual,* Abingdon Press, New York, 1931.

Hill, C. F., *An Improved System for the Management of Public Libraries Arranged Especially for the Use of Sunday Schools,* William Mann, Philadelphia, 1877.

John, Erwin E., *Key to a Successful Church Library,* rev. ed., Augsburg Publishing House, Minneapolis, 1967 (47 pp.).

Johnson, Marion J., *Planning and Furnishing the Church Library,* Augsburg Publishing House, Minneapolis, 1966 (48 pp.).

Lavender, Leona, *The Church Library, Its Organization and Operation,* The Sunday School Board of the Southern Baptist Convention, Nashville, 1932 (112 pp.).

Lutheran Church in America, *Church Library Manual,* Board of Publications, L.C.A., Philadelphia, n.d. (24 pp.).

National Council of Churches of Christ in the United States of America, *Your Church Library,* National Council, New York, n.d.

Meinke, Darrel M., *From Box to Bookshelf: a "How" Manual for School Librarians and Church Librarians,* Concordia Publishing House, St. Louis, 1962 (55 pp.).

Moyer, Elgin S., *Building a Minister's Library,* Moody Press, Chicago, 1944.

Newton, Charlotte, *Church Library Manual,* University of Georgia, Athens, Georgia, 1964 (21 pp.).

Newton, LaVose, *Church Library Manual,* Zondervan Press, Grand Rapids, Mich., n.d.

Presbyterian Church in the U.S., *A Manual for the Church Library,* Board of Christian Education, Richmond, 1963.

Protestant Episcopal Church, *When a Parish Starts a Library,* National Council, New York, n.d.

Rogers, William L. and Paul H. Vieth, *Visual Aids in the Church,* Christian Education Press, Philadelphia, 1946 (214 pp.).

Schneider, Vincent P., *The Parish and Catholic Lending Library Manual,* 2nd ed., Catholic Library Association, Parish Libraries Section, Haverford, Pa., 1965 (64 pp.).

Smith, Jay, *A Minister's Library Handbook,* W. A. Wilde, Natick, Mass., 1958 (148 pp.).

Smith, Ruth S., *Outline for Building Vitality in Your Church Library,* rev. ed., Church Library Council, Washington, D.C., 1967 (44 pp.).

Smith, Ruth S., *Publicity for a Church Library,* Zondervan Publishing House, Grand Rapids, Mich., 1966 (48 pp.).

Southern Baptist Convention, Sunday School Board, *Church Library Development Plan,* Nashville, Tenn., n.d. (12 pamphlets).

Stark, Barbara R., *How to Start Your Church Library,* Congregational Christian Churches, Board of Home Missions, Division of Christian Education, Boston, 1957 (16 pp.).

Stranghan, Alice, *How to Organize Your Church Library,* Zondervan Publishing House, Grand Rapids, Mich., n.d.

Thatcher, Floyd W., *How to Have an Effective Church Library,* Revell Press, Westwork, N.J., 1962 (62 pp.).

Thomas More Association, *How to Organize and Run a Parish Library,* 2nd rev. ed., Chicago, 1952.

Wages, Orland J., *A Handbook for Church Librarians,* Texas: the Author, Commerce, Texas, 1961 (113 pp.).

Waite, Florida, *The Church Library,* Southern Baptist Convention, Sunday School Board, Church Library Service, Nashville, Tenn., n.d.

Willging, Eugene P., *The Apostolate of the Printed Word,* National Catholic Welfare Conference, Washington, D.C., 1951 (23 pp.).

Your Church Library, a Manual of Instruction, Cokesbury Press, Nashville, Tenn., 1960 (81 pp.).

UNPUBLISHED STUDIES ABOUT CHURCH LIBRARIES

* Coogan, Helen M., "A Survey of Parish Libraries in the Archdiocese of Los Angeles," M.A. in Library Science thesis, Immaculate Heart College, 1961 (a questionnaire survey of 68 parish libraries in the Archdiocese of Los Angeles, Calif.; 89 pp.).

* Durrance, Joan C., *A Survey of Church Libraries,* M.S. in Library Science thesis, Univ. of North Carolina, 1964 (a questionnaire survey of 30 libraries in the West Palm Beach–Lake Worth, Florida area representing ten denominations; 103 pp.).

Gordon, Norma S., "Thomas Bray: A study in Early 18th Century Librarianship," M.S. in Library Science thesis, Catholic Univ. of America.

* Gray, Nancy J., "Needs Met by Methodist Church Libraries in the South East," M.A. thesis, Emory University, 1951 (a questionnaire survey of 133 Methodist church libraries in Virginia, North Carolina, South Carolina, Kentucky, Tennessee, Georgia, Florida, Alabama, Mississippi, Louisiana, and Arkansas; 56 pp.).

* Hall, James H., "Criteria for the Administration of Library Services in Christian Education in the Independent Autonomous Church at the Local Level," Ph.D. thesis, Washington Univ., Saint Louis, Mo., 1950 (268 pp.).

* Hartos, Marsha A., "Provision of Libraries in Protestant Churches in the USA with Examples of Current Practice Drawn from Libraries in Houston, Texas," M.S. in Library Science thesis, Univ. of Texas, 1966 (an extensive discussion of the church library field in addition to case studies of six church libraries in Houston, Texas; 120 pp.).

Kaegi, Merrill A., "The Church Library Council; an Example of Church Library Cooperation," M.S. in Library Science thesis, Catholic Univ. of America, 1967 (not denominationally oriented; a historical development of church libraries discussed from the library profession point of view; 100 pp.).

Meder, Stephen A., "Library Resources and Services for Adult Catholic Readers in the City of Cincinnati, Ohio." Catholic University of America, 1953.

Meirose, Leo H., "St. Elizabeth's Parish Library; a History and a Survey," M.S. in Library Science thesis, Western Reserve Univ., 1951 (a discussion of the development of a single parish library in existence since 1934, now containing over 6000 volumes; 21 pp.).

Mollahan, Molly A., "Library Resources and Services for Adult Catholic Readers in the City of Washington, D.C.," Catholic University of America, 1953.

Murdock, J. Larry, "Church Libraries: A Bibliography on Sources of Information from 1876 Through 1966," University of Washington Libraries, Seattle, Washington (mimeographed; 9 pp.).

* Nolan, John G., "The Parish Library: A Study of Its Place in Parish Life, Its Functions and Services," M.S. in Library Science thesis, Catholic Univ. of America, 1954 (a survey of 15 parish libraries in the Greater Washington, D.C. area; 100 pp.).

* Smith, Dora M., "The church library with special emphasis on church libraries in Texas," M.S. thesis in Library Science, Texas State College for Women, 1951 (a questionnaire survey received from 15 Baptist and 8 Methodist churches in Texas; 56 pp.).

* Smith, Ruth, "Survey of Church Libraries in the Washington, D.C. Area, 1966," Church Library Council, Washington, D.C. (mimeographed; 8 pp.).

Swarthout, Arthur W., "The Church Library Movement in Historical Perspective," 1967 (21 pp.).

* Whitehurst, Lillonteen, "Survey of the Purposes and Trends of Church Libraries in the Southern Baptist Convention of North Carolina," M.S. thesis in Library Science, Univ. of North Carolina, 1964 (a questionnaire study of 32 libraries; 48 pp.).

REFERENCES

1. F. Allen Briggs, "The Sunday-School Library in the Nineteenth Century," *Lib. Quart.,* **21**(2), 166–177 (April 1961).
* *2.* Ruth Smith, "Survey of Church Libraries in the Washington, D.C. Area," Church Library Council, Washington, D.C. (mimeographed; 8 pp.).
3. Joyce L. White, ed., *Church Library Guide,* Drexel Institute of Technology, Graduate School of Library Science, Philadelphia, 1965 (52 pp.) (Proceedings from the Third Annual Conference).
4. Joyce L. White, ed., *Proceedings of the Second Church Library Conference,* Drexel Institute of Technology, Graduate School of Library Science, Philadelphia, 1964 (75 pp.).
5. "Church Libraries," Prepared . . . by The Pacific Northwest Association of Church Libraries, (3-fold brochure).
6. "Church Libraries: a Guide to Their Administration and Organization." American Library Association, Library Administration Division, Chicago, 1965 (mimeographed, 7 pp.).
7. Dorothy Rodda and John Harvey, eds., *Directory of Church Libraries,* Drexel Press, Philadelphia, 1967 (87 pp.).
8. Calvin T. Ryan, "The Methodists of Yesterday Read," *Zions Herald,* **124**(1), 81 January 23, 1946).
9. Claudia Hannaford, "An Ecumenical Concern for Quality Service in Religious Libraries: Church and Synagogue Library Association," *Spec. Lib.,* **61**(1), 9–14 (January 1970).
10. Zula Z. MacDonald, Letter of July 20, 1968, from Dept. of Library Science, Baylor Univ., Waco, Texas.
11. "History of the Church Library Council," in *Church Library Council,* n.p., n.d. (4 pp.).
12. Gabriel Naude, *Advice on Establishing a Library,* University of California Press, Berkeley, Calif., 1950, p. 75.
13. *The New Schaff-Herzog Encyclopedia of Religious Knowledge,* Funk and Wagnall, New York, 1911, "Sunday Schools," Vol. 11, p. 158.
14. Church and Synagogue Library Association, "Church and Synagogue Libraries," *Drexel Lib. Quart.,* **6**(2), (April 1970).
15. Jessie D. Crawford, "The Church Library," *Lib. J.,* **80**(15), 1761–1762 (Sept. 1, 1955).
16. Jessie D. Crawford, "A City Library serves the churches," *Internat. J. Religious Educ.,* **35**(7), 16–17 (March 1969).
17. Mildred Eagen, A letter of July 22, 1968, from Cokesbury Church Library Service, Nashville, Tenn.
18. Josephine Howard, A letter of June 17, 1968, from Oklahoma County Libraries, Oklahoma City, Okla.
19. John F. Hurst, (Bishop), Parochial Libraries in the Colonial period, *American Society of Church History, Papers,* Vol. 2, Putnam's Sons, New York, 1890, pp. 37–50.

JOYCE L. WHITE

CHURCH AND SYNAGOGUE LIBRARY ASSOCIATION
See also *Church Libraries*

Background

As an increasing number of churches and synagogues were setting up libraries to serve the congregation, regional as well as denominational church and synagogue library groups emerged. Workshops, conferences, seminars, and training classes for library volunteers were sponsored by denominations, public libraries, councils of churches, and schools. The church library movement grew and expanded at rather a rapid rate, especially during the 1960s.

DREXEL'S ROLE

During these years the Graduate School of Library Science at the Drexel Institute of Technology in Philadelphia evidenced a strong interest in guiding the direction of church and synagogue librarianship. They held a Seminar in Synagogue Librarianship in 1961, followed by the first of several Church Library Conferences which involved sponsorship by both Protestant and Catholic church groups and drew participants from all over the country.

Locally, Drexel encouraged the formation of a Church Librarians' Exchange, a fellowship of church library workers in the greater Philadelphia area. They also published the *Proceedings of the Second Annual Church Library Conference* (*1*), a *Church Library Guide* (*2*), and a national *Directory of Church Libraries* (*3*). As a further service to the profession, it was natural that they were instrumental in drawing together the forces that established the Church and Synagogue Library Association.

Founding of the Association

DEAN HARVEY'S EXPLORATORY MEETING

John F. Harvey, dean of the Graduate School of Library Science, Drexel Institute of Technology in Philadelphia, sent out an invitation on June 15, 1966, to forty leading church and synagogue librarians, representatives of denominational groups, councils of churches, and publishers of religious literature to meet in conjunction with the 1966 American Library Association Conference in New York City to discuss the possibilities of an interfaith library association that would be national or international in scope. His letter outlined opportunities for service for such a group and read in part as follows:

The church library movement is gaining momentum. Already several denominations have one or more staff members at their headquarters or their publishing offices whose primary duties deal with church libraries. The movement is ecumenical with growing numbers of libraries in Catholic, Jewish, and Protestant churches and synagogues. As the educational role of the church increases this movement promises to help the layman deepen and clarify understanding of his religion. Increasingly the superior church, parish, or synagogue library will have the same vital relationship to the church school, faculty, and curriculum that the modern public school library or curriculum materials center has to its school, faculty, and curriculum.

This letter is a call for a meeting to consider formation of a national Church Library Association. We would like for you to attend an initial discussion meeting to be held in New York next month in connection with the American Library Association conference. . . .

At this meeting the idea of forming a national Church Library Association will be explored. No formal commitment will be required of attendees, however they will be expected to participate in the discussion, consider the opportunities and problems presented, consider in unbiased fashion the best interests of church and synagogue libraries throughout the entire religious world, and where appropriate, carry back to their parent organizations the relevant information where a decision can be reached regarding participation. . . .

A Church Library Association would have many opportunities for service. Some of them can be listed here:

(1) A national conference of church librarians with high level programming would enable us to bring in as speakers outstanding national church and library figures and to attract as exhibitors representatives from the religious publishing, library supply, and equipment manufacturing worlds. Superior local church libraries in the conference city could be visited also. Such a conference could be held in conjunction with the national meeting of a denominational group of church librarians, a group of religious publishers, or a national library association.

(2) Close affiliation could be achieved with accredited library schools through (a) cooperation in conference programming, (b) offering formal and correspondence courses and workshops in church and synagogue librarianship, (c) by applying the latest concepts of leading library scientists to church librarianship, and (d) design and execution of research projects and compilation of data on church libraries, their nature and problems.

(3) Close cooperation and committee activity is needed with religious publishers to reflect book librarians' book and audio-visual needs and interests and also to aid publishers with editorial and sales problems.

(4) A national church library periodical or newsletter could stimulate and focus publication of significant contributions for the entire spectrum of practitioners and in turn could represent that group to the wider church and library worlds.

(5) Closer affiliation could be achieved than ever before with national church organizations such as the National Council of Churches and with national library groups such as the American Library Association (with which formal affiliations might be achieved and a seat on the Council), the Catholic Library Association, the Association of Jewish Libraries, the American Theological Library Association, and the many specialized associations of school, public, college and special librarians.

(6) This association would be the natural sponsor and publisher of national and inter-denomination projects such as the Directory of Library Periodicals, the Church Library Guides and Manuals, and other bibliography and booklist projects.

(7) A better understanding is needed of the new church library movement by ministers, priests and rabbis, by christian education directors, and their national and regional groups. Representation is overdue on their national and regional conference programs and committees. But it is also necessary to keep church librarians well informed about church curricular and procedural changes.

(8) At the present time denominational and regional workshops exist for certain church librarians but not all denominations or all regions are covered. A back-up role is needed in filling in these gaps to provide more widespread orientation and education where other agencies are unable to do so.

(9) Fostering cooperation and coordination for their mutual benefit among the various denominations through inter-denominational committees and sections, conferences and institutes. For instance the Southern Baptist group has much to teach other church library groups.

Since there are now at least 25,000 church libraries, more than all the public, college, and special libraries combined, this group may have reached a point where a national association is needed to achieve proper recognition of their importance and significance and to obtain proper influence for them. Drexel's interest in calling this meeting is a natural outgrowth of its concern for the orderly development of church and synagogue librarianship into a significant branch of the profession and also of its recent inter-faith conference, seminar, research, data compilation and publication activities to promote this growth. We hope to see you in New York on July 10th.

Twenty-eight people representing the three major faiths—Catholic, Protestant, and Jewish—reacted favorably and Dean Harvey was asked to appoint a steering committee which could explore the possibilities in depth and report back to the group at a future meeting.

FIRST EXECUTIVE BOARD MEETING

The first meeting of the executive board was held in July 11, 1967, at the Bellevue Stratford Hotel in Philadelphia. The first officers were installed and committee chairmen appointed.

Bylaws incorporating the aims and purposes expressed in Dean Harvey's letter were presented for adoption. Included in the bylaws, however, was an article that provided for the establishment of denominational sections, which became a controversial issue as some people believed this to be an attempt to absorb existing denominational library associations.

The executive board, however, decided to accept the bylaws as they were written and live with them until possible revisions or amendments could be proposed and presented to the membership for vote. In 1969, when the bylaws were revised, the article on denominational sections was dropped and emphasis was placed on the interfaith ecumenical concept of the association.

Purpose of the Association

According to its constitution, adopted in 1969,

> This Association is formed for the following purposes:
>
> a. To provide an ecumenical association for those interested in the work of church and synagogue libraries.
>
> b. To investigate, discuss, and promote every phase of church and synagogue librarianship.
>
> c. To issue regular and occasional publications relating to the interests of church and synagogue librarians.
>
> d. To provide through its membership such counseling and guidance services as are incident to its program.
>
> e. To conduct such conferences, seminars, workshops, or meetings as will serve the needs of its members.
>
> f. To foster adherence to educational and religious standards and criteria in the development of church and synagogue libraries.
>
> g. To pursue these objectives without contemplation of pecuniary gain or profit, incidental or otherwise.

Membership in the Association

Membership is open to all persons, with no discrimination by race, color, or creed, and with citizens of all nations eligible to join. The six categories of membership include Individual, Church or Synagogue, Affiliated (open to any local denominational, interdenominational, or nondenominational association, group, or council whose membership is organized because of a concern for effective libraries), Institutional (open to any business or industry; also open to any international, national, or regional library association, educational or religious association, or institution concerned with the interests of church and synagogue libraries), Contributing, and Honorary.

Membership count by the end of the first year totaled 244, of which 3 were in the Institutional category, 65 in the Church or Synagogue category, and 176 in the Individual category. These represented 35 states (including Alaska), the District of Columbia, and the World Council of Churches in Switzerland.

Committees

Standing committees established by the bylaws and special committees appointed at the discretion of the president or the executive board work on short-term projects and long-range assignments; these committees include the following:

> *Awards Committee,* responsible for establishing association awards and selecting their winners each year.

Bylaws Committee, responsible for recommending changes in the bylaws.

Church Relations Committee, responsible for developing the association's influence with groups of ministers and rabbis, directors of Christian education, and heads of church and synagogue schools.

Conference Arrangements Committee, responsible for local meetings, rooms, meals, housing, and other annual conference arrangements.

Conference Site and Exhibits Committee, responsible for establishing conference location and exhibit policies, soliciting invitations from conference sites and recommending choices, and soliciting conference exhibits and making arrangements for them.

Membership Committee, responsible for carrying out an annual membership drive for new and renewal memberships.

Education Committee, responsible for improving the library education level of all members.

Nominations and Elections Committee, responsible for selecting a slate of new association officers each year, conducting the election, tallying votes, and announcing winners to the president.

Projects Committee, responsible for recommending, planning, and supervising the completion of special projects.

Publications Committee, responsible for all aspects of the association book and serial publication program.

Public Relations Committee, responsible for directing the association's public relations program and for recommending appropriate public relations activities including participation in National Library Week, Catholic Book Week, Jewish Book Month, etc.

Publishers' Liaison Committee, responsible for working closely with book and periodical publishers on cooperative programs.

Research Committee, responsible for developing a research program on church and synagogue librarianship and related topics and locating funds for it.

Standards Committee, responsible for establishing and promoting library standards in this field.

Publications

NEWS BULLETIN

The first publication to be issued by the association was the *News Bulletin,* Vol. 1, No. 1, Winter 1967, under the editorship of Sidney August, librarian, Pedagogical Library, Philadelphia Board of Education, Philadelphia. The second issue appeared as Vol. 1, No. 2, Fall 1968. These two issues contained news of the annual conference, a message from the president, a brief history of the founding of the association, a list of the officers and executive board, and articles of general interest, such as "Let's Take a Tour" by Margaret Korty and "Organize a Library for Your Church" by Sue Lau.

CHURCH AND SYNAGOGUE LIBRARIES

In November 1968 the *News Bulletin* was superseded by *Church and Synagogue Libraries,* the first issue of which was designated Vol. 2, No. 1. The editor was the Reverend Arthur W. Swarthout, librarian, Department of Library Science, West Virginia Wesleyan College, Buckhannon, West Virginia.

This was designated "the official bulletin of the Church and Synagogue Library Association" and carried news of activities of the association and related groups, articles of help to librarians of local congregations, such as "Book Notes," "Tips and Trends," and "Magazines in the Church Library Field." Also included were items reflecting the ecumenical spirit embodied in the origin of the association, such as "Learning Each from Each," the story of an unusual reading list developed by an interfaith committee in the Free Library of Philadelphia.

OTHER PUBLICATIONS

Occasional publications, including guidebooks, directories, etc., are published to further the purposes of the association. Publication efforts are coordinated with existing regional, religious, and other groups to provide access to the best information and resources for church and synagogue libraries.

Conferences

An annual conference to further the work and purposes of the association is held and all members and other interested persons are invited to attend. An annual meeting of the membership is held in connection with this conference.

Additional self-supporting conferences, seminars, workshops, lectures, and institutes are held on a national, regional, state, or local basis to further the aims of the association.

The First Annual Conference, held May 27–29, 1968 at the Bellevue Stratford Hotel in Philadelphia, was on "The Challenge of Books in Today's World." Featured speakers were the Reverend Donald Clifford, S.J., professor, Saint Joseph's College, Philadelphia; Miss Anne F. Sturtevant, head of the Education, Philosophy and Religion Department, Free Library of Philadelphia; and Dr. James C. Logan, associate professor of systematic theology, Wesley Theological Seminary, Washington, D.C.

The program included small group simultaneous conferences on aspects of setting up or operating a library, exhibits of sixteen publishers, library supply houses and the public library, and a bus tour of the Temple Beth Sholem Library, Elkins Park, Pennsylvania; the Dominican Retreat House, Elkins Park, Pennsylvania; and the Carmel Presbyterian Church Library, Glenside, Pennsylvania.

One hundred fifty-four people, representing fourteen denominations and faiths, attended the Conference. Sixty-five of these came from states other than Pennsylvania, including Tennessee, Texas, and Washington. Approximately two-thirds of those attending were members of the association.

The Second Annual Conference was held July 13–15, 1969, at the Shoreham Hotel in Washington. Future conferences are scheduled to be held in Minneapolis, Baltimore, and Detroit.

AWARDS

Association awards are presented each year at the annual conference when recommended by the Awards Committee. The first award presented by the association was an Honorary Membership for life. This award was presented at the First Annual Conference, May 1968, to Mrs. Josephine H. Kyles, director, Division of Services, Metropolitan Detroit Council of Churches, Detroit, as an outstanding Christian educator who "used her creative imagination and unique abilities to make an impact on the growth of church libraries, by training present and prospective church librarians in two large metropolitan areas, an impact that has carried with it an eloquent witness of interfaith and interracial fellowship." Mrs. Kyles, during the years she was director, Department of Christian Education, Council of Churches of Greater Washington, was instrumental in cosponsoring annual church library workshops in the District of Columbia–Maryland–Virginia area and thus

FIGURE 1. *Official emblem of the Church and Synagogue Library Association.*

in broadening the influence of the Church Library Council, and interfaith association of church librarians.

The Official Emblem

The design for an official seal or emblem was prepared by the Reverend Fr. Henry Syvinski, Villanova University, Villanova, Pennsylvania, and was adopted by the association in 1968. The emblem (see Figure 1) consists of an open book (learning, study, and knowledge) superimposed by the Star of David (Judaism) and the Cross (Christianity) all within a circle inscribing the name of the association.

Father Syvinski's original design included a lamp of knowledge, which he said he was sorry to eliminate because it is only through knowledge of each other that the association will achieve its purpose. The lamp was eliminated for simplicity of design in the official emblem.

REFERENCES

1. *Proceedings of the Second Annual Church Library Conference* (Joyce L. White and E. J. Humeston, Jr., eds.), Drexel Press, Philadelphia, 1964. (Sponsored by the Philadelphia Council of Churches and the Graduate School of Library Science, Drexel Institute of Technology.)
2. *Church Library Guide* (Joyce L. White and Mary Y. Parr, eds.), Drexel Press, Philadelphia, 1965. (From the Third Church Library Conference, sponsored by the Philadelphia Council of Churches, the New Jersey Council of Churches, and the Graduate School of Library Science, Drexel Institute of Technology.)
3. *Directory of Church Libraries* (Dorothy Rodda and John Harvey, comps.), Drexel Library School Series No. 22, Drexel Press, Philadelphia, 1967.

RUTH S. SMITH